# 1992 YEARBOOK
## EVENTS OF 1991

*Boris Yeltsin, president of the Russian republic, with the tricolor Russian flag.*

# 1992
# FUNK &
# WAGNALLS
# NEW
# ENCYCLOPEDIA
# YEARBOOK

LEON L. BRAM
Vice-President and
Editorial Director

NORMA H. DICKEY
Editor in Chief

**Funk & Wagnalls Corporation**

Publishers since 1876

---

ISBN 0-8343-0093-1

# CONTENTS

# MEMBERS OF THE STAFF

# FOREWORD: THE EVENTS OF 1991

On August 19, 1991, the world was shaken by the news that Soviet President Mikhail Gorbachev had been ousted from power. The August coup quickly collapsed, but by year's end the Soviet Union itself had fallen apart. Drawing upon historic photos, paintings, and posters, one of our three Yearbook feature articles traces key developments in the decades of Soviet Communist rule, from the Russian Revolution to the dramatic events of 1991 that appeared to reverse the tide of history and signal a new era.

Earlier in this remarkable year, U.S.-led forces waged a devastating air and ground campaign that not only drove Iraqi troops from the tiny oil-rich kingdom of Kuwait, which they had invaded in 1990, but also helped restore confidence in the U.S. leadership role in the world. Nevertheless, Saddam Hussein remained in power in Iraq, and brutally put down internal rebellions. The Gulf War and some of its far-reaching consequences are described in another of our feature articles.

Some of the most exciting advances in computer technology were occurring in the area of artificial reality—the subject of a third feature article.

In other dramatic developments, Israel and its Arab neighbors, despite fiery rhetoric, sat down together at an international conference, taking what many hoped could be the first steps toward peace. The release of Western hostages held in Lebanon was another promising development. On the other hand, Yugoslavia was plunged into civil war, India was shaken by the assassination of Rajiv Gandhi, and Haiti's democratically elected government was ousted in a military coup.

The world events occupying center stage gave U.S. President George Bush an opportunity to shine. Democrats, off to a slow start in the 1992 presidential campaign, accused Bush of neglecting domestic concerns, particularly an economy that was declining or stagnant for much of the year. Bush's nomination of Judge Clarence Thomas to the Supreme Court was almost derailed, as law professor Anita Hill accused Thomas of sexual harassment. After three days of nationally televised hearings on the allegations, Thomas narrowly won Senate confirmation, but the episode raise more questions than it answered and put the spotlight on the issue of sexual harassment. Another startling event was the disclosure by basketball superstar Magic Johnson that he was retiring from the sport because he had the AIDS virus; he assumed a new role as the nation's most prominent spokesman for safe sex.

In baseball, the Minnesota Twins edged out the Atlanta Braves in one of the most exciting World Series in memory. The Chicago Bulls topped the Los Angeles Lakers to take their first National Basketball Association title. Arnold Schwarzenegger was—once again—a box office smash, in the film *Terminator 2*. In concert halls and opera houses, it was the year of Mozart, as the music world marked the 200th anniversary of the composer's death.                                    THE EDITORS

# WAR IN THE GULF

## by THOMAS M. DeFRANK

At 2:20 A.M. in the desert darkness of January 17, 1991, a task force of 12 U.S. Air Force MH-53J Pave Low night-sighted helicopters and Army AH-64 Apache attack helicopters crossed the border of Saudi Arabia and slipped undetected into Iraq. Their assignment was to punch a hole in Iraqi early-warning air defenses by destroying two ground radar stations 30 miles inside the border. Flying low to avoid radar detection, the choppers arrived at their targets precisely on schedule

*Thomas M. DeFrank is a deputy bureau chief and White House correspondent for* Newsweek.

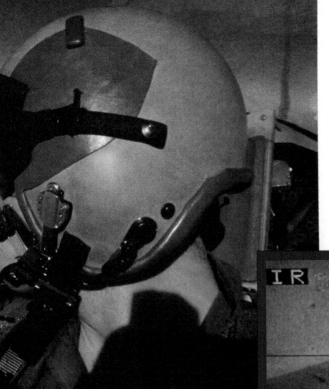

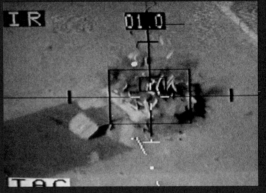

The Gulf War began with a powerful and devastatingly effective allied air offensive against Iraq and occupied Kuwait. Left, an American pilot makes a bombing run in an F-16 over the Kuwaiti desert. Below, a view from a French pilot's infrared camera of bomber-launched missiles destroying an enemy ammunitions dump.

at 2:38 A.M. Laser-guided Hellfire missiles from the lead Pave Low obliterated one ground station; five seconds later, Apaches demolished the second. Within minutes, hundreds of allied warplanes streamed through a 40-mile gap in Iraqi air defenses and reached Baghdad unnoticed. As a result, not a single aircraft was lost to enemy fire in the first raids of Operation Desert Storm—an auspicious beginning to what was the most riveting military campaign since World War II.

While it may have served more far-reaching geopolitical purposes, the immediate goal of Desert Storm was to expel the shock troops of Iraqi leader Saddam Hussein from Kuwait, which they had invaded five months before. The operation, carried out by a multinational coalition led by the United States and using primarily American forces, took only 43 days to dispatch a military machine said to number a million troops. A relentless aerial bombardment so pulverized Iraqi defenses that the ground war that followed was over in a mere 100 hours.

The war stilled whispers that U.S. dominance as a world power was on the wane, and the U.S. military, scarred by Vietnam, redeemed its reputation with a stunning performance that made national heroes of its leaders—particularly General H. Norman Schwarzkopf, Jr., the field commander. The logistical achievement alone seemed miraculous—541,000 American servicemen and servicewomen and their equipment shipped halfway around the world and readied for war in a handful of months—and casualty figures were a fraction of prewar estimates.

### Prewar Maneuvering

Iraq's sudden seizure of oil-rich Kuwait in early August 1990 had shocked the world. Saudi Arabia, with oil reserves far exceeding Kuwait's, seemed threatened. In the following months, the U.S. government pursued a two-track approach: while steadily increasing the size of American military forces in the Persian Gulf region in case war became necessary, the United States led efforts at the United Nations to isolate Iraq economically in hopes of ending the crisis without bloodshed. The UN Security Council imposed an embargo on all trade with Iraq except for humanitarian purposes, and an international naval blockade was organized to enforce it.

As Saddam Hussein remained defiant, President George Bush, in November, 1990, announced a massive new deployment of U.S. combat forces, more than doubling the 230,000 troops already in place.

Meanwhile, the United States, hoping the specter of overwhelming military superiority would bring Saddam to his senses, mobilized an international coalition of well over two dozen nations, which provided more than 200,000 troops. By mid-January 1991 the largest contingents of non-U.S. ground combat troops based in Saudi Arabia were from Saudi Arabia, Egypt, Great Britain, Syria, and France. Some nations that declined to contribute troops, warships, or planes to the coalition pledged aid in cash or goods (as did some allies that lent military support), with the largest amount—over $50 billion—going to the United States.

It was all to no avail; Saddam Hussein apparently concluded that the United States lacked the will to fight and that Bush was bluffing.

As prospects for a negotiated settlement waned, the Bush administration quietly expanded its objectives. Beyond expelling the invaders from Kuwait, Bush and his aides hoped to annihilate Saddam Hussein's military machine so he would no longer possess an offensive capability with which to threaten his neighbors, notably Saudi Arabia, Egypt, and Israel. The destruction of his chemical, biological, and nuclear weapons industries also became a priority. Finally, it was hoped that the Iraqi defeat would be so crushing as to lead to his overthrow within a few weeks or months.

On November 29, 1990, the UN endorsed the use of force if Iraqi forces remained in Kuwait by midnight on January 15. As the deadline approached, diplomatic activity intensified. But six hours of talks in Geneva, Switzerland, between U.S. Secretary of State James Baker III and Iraqi Foreign Minister Tariq Aziz ended in failure on January 9. Three days before the deadline, the U.S. Congress passed a resolution authorizing Bush to go to war against Iraq. Desert Shield—the defense of Saudi Arabia—was about to become Desert Storm.

*Iraqi President Saddam Hussein (sitting third from right) visits with Iraqi soldiers in Kuwait, shortly before the outbreak of hostilities.*

### Air Offensive

In the early hours of January 17, Tomahawk cruise missiles launched from U.S. warships and Air Force F-15E strike aircraft began hitting targets deep inside Iraq. Initial targets included air defense installations, command and control centers, airfields, chemical and nuclear weapons production facilities, troop concentrations, and missile complexes. Aircraft from Saudi Arabia, Great Britain, France, and Italy, as well as from the Kuwaiti Air Force, joined U.S. warplanes in the first wave of attacks, which were expanded to include oil fields and critical civilian targets such as electric power stations.

Venerable B-52 bombers from the Indian Ocean island of Diego García blasted installations of the Iraqi elite Republican Guard on both sides of the Kuwait-Iraq border, while 16-inch guns on the battleships *Missouri* and *Wisconsin* pounded reinforced targets. U.S. special forces troops were inserted behind enemy lines to search out and destroy mobile Scud missile launchers in western Iraq. In the first 24 hours of combat, coalition aircraft flew more than 1,000 combat sorties from bases in Saudi Arabia, Turkey, Bahrain, Oman, and the United Arab Emirates. They were joined by Navy and Marine attack jets from six U.S. aircraft carriers in the Persian Gulf and Red Sea.

Within days U.S. commanders proclaimed total air superiority. It became quickly apparent that the Iraqi Air Force was no match for the American-led air armada; after dozens of Iraqi jets were shot down in aerial combat, Iraqi pilots repeatedly refused to intercept enemy fighters or broke off contact beyond the lethal range of allied weapons. Numerous instances were also reported of Iraqi air-defense batteries blindly firing their missiles without activating directional radars because of the lethal accuracy of U.S. air-to-ground missiles, some of which could home in on radar signals.

The air campaign had a devastating impact on military and civilian targets. Within days, Iraq's air defenses had been obliterated, and its fighters driven from the skies. U.S. briefers reported that a majority of Iraqi airfields had been rendered unusable and that many of Saddam's chemical, nuclear, and biological weapons complexes had been destroyed. (However, reports by United Nations inspection teams later in the year indicated that some important nuclear facilities escaped significant damage.) The damage to the country's power, telecommunications, and transportation facilities was massive; bomb damage assessments conducted after the war concluded that it would take years to rebuild Iraq's infrastructure.

The coalition forces flew more than 100,000 sorties, but their air losses were surprisingly light—75 aircraft,

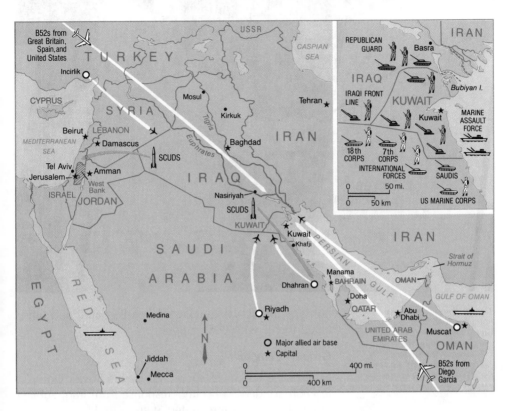

Map labels:

B52s from Great Britain, Spain, and United States
USSR
CASPIAN SEA
IRAN
REPUBLICAN GUARD
Basra
TURKEY
Incirlik
IRAQ
IRAQI FRONT LINE
KUWAIT
Bubiyan I.
CYPRUS
Mosul
Tehran
Kuwait
MARINE ASSAULT FORCE
SYRIA
Kirkuk
Beirut LEBANON
Damascus
Baghdad
IRAN
18th CORPS
7th CORPS
MEDITERRANEAN SEA
SCUDS
INTERNATIONAL FORCES
SAUDIS
Tel Aviv
Amman
IRAQ
0    50 mi.
Jerusalem
West Bank
0    50 km
US MARINE CORPS
ISRAEL JORDAN
Nasiriyah
SCUDS
KUWAIT
IRAN
SAUDI
Kuwait
Khafji
ARABIA
PERSIAN GULF
Strait of Hormuz
Manama
Dhahran
BAHRAIN
OMAN
EGYPT
RED SEA
Doha
GULF OF OMAN
Medina
Riyadh
QATAR
Abu Dhabi
Muscat
UNITED ARAB EMIRATES
OMAN
N
Jiddah
O  Major allied air base
★  Capital
Mecca
0          400 mi.
B52s from Diego Garcia
0          400 km

compared to 123 Iraqi planes destroyed. (An additional 147 Iraqi aircraft fled to Iran and were not returned.) Proportionately speaking, the heaviest allied air losses were suffered by the British, as Iraqi antiaircraft defenses shot down several Tornadoes, low-flying fighter-bombers given the risky mission of attacking runways.

The stunning success of the air campaign led to speculation that the war would be over quickly, possibly even without the necessity of ground combat. U.S. Secretary of Defense Dick Cheney and General Colin Powell, chairman of the U.S. Joint Chiefs of Staff, returning from an inspection tour of Saudi Arabia in early February, told Bush that a ground campaign would indeed be necessary but should be delayed for two to three weeks so that air operations could concentrate on "softening up" enemy ground forces in Kuwait and southern Iraq, thereby reducing casualties to allied ground forces.

At the end of January, in an attack meant as a diversion, or perhaps to draw the allies into a ground war, Iraqi troops had seized the nearly deserted Saudi town of Khafji, a few miles south of the Kuwaiti

*In the arena of combat, the U.S.-led coalition controlled the sea and the air, flying sorties from carriers in the Persian Gulf and from land bases north and south of Iraq and beyond. Iraqi thrusts outside Kuwait and Iraq were limited primarily to the launching of Scud missiles at Saudi Arabia and Israel. In the concluding phase of the war allied ground forces encircled the Iraqis by sweeping around their western flank.*

13

*The allied ground offensive took just a hundred hours to rout the enemy forces in southern Iraq and Kuwait. Here, the chief U.S. commander, General H. Norman Schwarzkopf, explains the allied ground tactics for the press.*

border. Khafji was quickly retaken by Saudi and other allied forces with U.S. support.

### Ground Campaign

New peace initiatives sponsored by the Soviet Union in February drew a positive response from Iraq, subject to conditions that the United States found unacceptable. On February 22, Bush issued an ultimatum: Iraq must begin withdrawing from Kuwait by noon New York time on February 23 or face a ground assault. The ultimatum was again ignored, and at 4 A.M. Gulf time on February 24 the biggest ground offensive since World War II roared into combat as over 200,000 allied troops in five massive columns invaded Kuwait and Iraq across a 300-mile front.

The crux of the plan was a gigantic "left hook"—a huge flanking maneuver from the west deep inside Iraq to cut off escape routes from Kuwait and trap Republican Guard divisions in southern Iraq. With its Air Force obliterated, Iraq did not realize that Schwarzkopf had secretly moved two corps to the west of Kuwait. By massing naval forces and rehearsing amphibious landings, as well as through disinformation, the coalition had tricked the Iraqis into expecting an amphibious assault from the east. To further confuse the Iraqis, at H hour a Marine and Army task force attacked Iraqi defenses in southern Kuwait while a Saudi-Kuwaiti force pushed north near the coast. Meanwhile, to the west, the true main assault went forward—with stunning success. The

U.S. 7th Corps attacked southern Iraq, then quickly turned east to encircle the Republican Guards. In the extreme west, the U.S. 18th Airborne Corps leapfrogged by helicopter and armored columns into Iraq. The 101st Airborne Division, the "Screaming Eagles," deployed air-assault helicopters to establish an enormous forward operations and supply base, code named Cobra Zone, deep inside Iraq. British and French armored units joined the U.S. forces as they sliced into Iraq, meeting occasionally fierce but largely token resistance. The chief road between Baghdad and Kuwait was cut near Nasiriyah on the Euphrates River. Within hours after the offensive began, demoralized Iraqi troops began surrendering by the thousands. What Saddam Hussein had vowed would be "the mother of all battles" had become the mother of all mismatches.

To draw attention to the Arab contribution to the allied cause, Schwarzkopf had the liberation of Kuwait City led by Saudi and Kuwaiti troops.

Bush ordered that offensive operations be suspended at 8 A.M. Gulf time on February 28. At that time Iraqi forces were in frenzied retreat from Kuwait, and coalition forces occupied all of Iraq south of the Euphrates River. Between 25,000 and 50,000 Iraqi soldiers had been killed in action, and an estimated 80,000 taken prisoner. In a nationally televised address Bush declared: "Kuwait is liberated. Iraq's army is defeated. Our military objectives are met."

### Aftermath

On April 6, Iraq accepted the terms of a permanent cease-fire approved a few days before by the United Nations Security Council. Among other things, Iraq was required to provide information on its stocks of chemical and biological weapons, to permit on-site

*Allied troops head for Kuwait City, led by Saudi and Kuwaiti units.*

inspection of the destruction of its "weapons of mass destruction," to return Kuwaiti property it had seized, and to pay war reparations.

The first contingent of U.S. troops moved back across the border into Saudi Arabia on April 8. Within two weeks, nearly half of Desert Storm's U.S. troops had been redeployed to the United States or Germany. The last unit to see combat left Kuwait in June, and by September, only 40,000 troops still remained in Saudi Arabia, Kuwait, or offshore.

The triumphal withdrawal of American fighting forces was slightly tarnished, however, by an Iraqi-caused environmental catastrophe in Kuwait, where the Iraqis had torched hundreds of oil wells, shrouding much of the region in darkness at midday.

Furthermore, Saddam Hussein, still in power, proceeded to brutally repress uprisings by Kurds, a non-Arab ethnic group, in northern Iraq and by Shiite Muslims in the south. (The Iraqi leadership belongs to the Sunni branch of Islam.)

Responding to criticism he wasn't doing anything to help the many hundreds of thousands of Kurdish refugees who were fleeing into Turkey and Iran, Bush announced in April that the allies would build and operate refugee camps in northern Iraq and maintain several thousand combat troops to protect refugees from further attacks. Threats to shoot down any Iraqi aircraft venturing into the allied "safe zone" stabilized the situation, and in July the last allied forces withdrew from northern Iraq. About 3,000 combat troops were stationed at military camps in southern Turkey as a rapid deployment force to deter further attacks against the Kurds.

The survival of Saddam Hussein and several divisions of the Republican Guard led some analysts to question Bush's decision to halt the ground war when

*Civilian casualties were an inevitable result of the air offensive. In one incident of "collateral damage," on February 13, the U.S. bombing of an air raid shelter (below) in the Baghdad suburb of Amiriya killed over 300 Iraqis. A U.S. spokesman asserted that the bunker had been used as an Iraqi "command and control facility."*

*This view of a Kuwaiti road to Iraq, dubbed the Highway of Death, shows the remains of a retreating Iraqi column that had been pounded by allied war planes.*

he did. Schwarzkopf himself told television personality David Frost in an interview that he had recommended continuing ground operations in order to complete "a battle of annihilation." After White House officials disputed this account, Schwarzkopf apologized to Bush for his remark. But several major field commanders sided with Schwarzkopf, anonymously confiding to reporters and colleagues that Bush had blundered by prematurely stopping the war. Only a few more days of fighting, they claimed, would have completely destroyed Saddam Hussein's war machine and strengthened prospects for his overthrow.

Bush's timing in ending the war may have been motivated not only by a desire to avoid unnecessary allied casualties—the objective of liberating Kuwait had already been achieved—but also, at this point, by fear of the power vacuum and political chaos in the region that might follow Saddam Hussein's sudden overthrow. Nevertheless, his decision was unpopular. A Washington *Post*-ABC News poll, reported in early April, found that while the majority of Americans strongly backed Bush's handling of the war, 55 percent believed he should not have concluded it with Saddam still in power.

### Casualties and Losses

Defying sobering prewar estimates by outside experts and Pentagon planners alike, allied casualties during Desert Storm were surprisingly modest. Official Pentagon statistics listed 146 U.S. soldiers killed in action and 467 wounded in action. There were also 159 nonbattle deaths during and after the war, mostly the result of accidents. Twenty-three soldiers were taken prisoner by the Iraqis and later repatriated.

*When the Iraqis pulled out of Kuwait, they left behind a legacy of environmental disaster, with damaged and burning oil wells releasing huge pools of oil and darkening the sky with smoke.*

Combat deaths among other allied forces were estimated at about 75.

Even the most optimistic war planners had privately predicted thousands of dead and wounded in what was expected to be a protracted war. In late 1990, for example, the Pentagon had placed an order for several thousand "body bags" in anticipation of significant casualties. It appeared that all sides underestimated the proficiency of the U.S.-led forces and their sophisticated weaponry and overestimated the professionalism and will to fight of Iraqi troops still recovering from a brutal eight-year war with Iran. Casualty estimates had also been predicated on the expectation that the Iraqis would use chemical weapons in significant quantities, but these fears never materialized.

By contrast, Iraqi war deaths were stratospheric. The Pentagon refused to make an official estimate of enemy casualties, in part reflecting a lingering controversy over the "body counts" reported by U.S. forces during the Vietnam War, which critics claimed were falsified to inflate claims of military success. But credible government officials privately estimated that between 100,000 and 200,000 Iraqi soldiers had died during the war, with at least 300,000 wounded. Approximately 71,000 Iraqis were taken prisoner.

Also, according to U.S. intelligence estimates, about 3,700 out of 4,280 Iraqi tanks in southern Iraq and Kuwait were destroyed or captured, 2,400 of 2,870 armored personnel carriers were lost, and only 510 of 3,110 artillery pieces escaped destruction or capture. Coalition losses of such matériel totaled several dozen.

Despite the ferocity of allied air operations, officials maintained that the use of technologically sophisticated weaponry had reduced the number of noncombatant casualties in Iraq and Kuwait. Still, as in all wars, Desert Storm produced instances of what military jargon describes as "collateral damage." In the most serious documented incident, on February 13, hundreds of Iraqi civilians, including many children, died when a U.S. Air Force F-117A Stealth fighter-bomber bombed an air raid shelter in the suburbs of Baghdad. U.S. officials asserted that the facility was in fact a reinforced bunker used as a military command center for senior Iraqi government and military officials. The tragedy prompted allied commanders to reexamine targeting plans, and no further such incidents were reported.

Another somber note was the unusually high percentage of allied combat deaths from accidental attacks by allied troops. At first the Pentagon insisted that such incidents were minimal, but officials later conceded that nearly a quarter of the U.S. military personnel killed in action in Desert Storm (35 soldiers) died as a result of "friendly fire"—the highest proportion in American military history. Seventy-two soldiers were wounded by friendly fire, and three-quarters of all U.S. combat vehicles seriously damaged were struck by American weapons.

Military officials cited the frenzied pace of the ground battle, inclement weather, and the use of sophisticated technology enabling military units to engage at far greater ranges than in previous conflicts. The very success of the allied ground attack also was a factor; on several occasions American units that had captured Iraqi positions were fired upon by other U.S. forces attacking predetermined enemy positions.

### High-tech Weaponry

Desert Storm provided a dramatic test bed for a host of sophisticated new weapons never before exposed to combat, and for the most part they performed remarkably well. The U.S. Army's M1A1 Abrams tank, for instance, consistently bested the Iraqis' Soviet-made T-72. Advanced computer technology and a greater range frequently enabled the M1A1 to destroy enemy armor without even being seen. The new machines also proved effective when put to unsophisticated uses. The Army's new Armored Combat Earthmover, along with plow-equipped Abrams tanks, was used in the February 24 offensive to simply bury Iraqi troops in their front line trenches.

Allied air power was used to devastating effect; the Pentagon released videotapes of laser-guided "smart"

*The performance of the sleek high-tech F-117 Stealth fighter (above) won praise from U.S. Air Force officials, though the star of the war may really have been the less glamorous A-10 Thunderbolt, nicknamed Warthog.*

bombs being delivered through hangar doors and ventilator shafts. (The overwhelming majority of the U.S. bombs, however, were of the old-fashioned "dumb" type—not precision guided—and often missed their target.) The U.S. Navy's Tomahawk cruise missile proved its worth, destroying with great accuracy scores of hardened sites like command bunkers. The F-117 Stealth fighter was praised by Air Force officials, although some critics later claimed that the plane, which was designed to elude detection by enemy radar, had been tracked by friendly radar on several occasions.

Ironically, the star performer of the war may have been a low-tech airplane scorned by the U.S. Air Force for its lack of sophistication. The A-10 Thunderbolt, a close air-support jet nicknamed

Warthog for its ungainly appearance and low airspeed, was credited with more than two-thirds of the Air Force's Iraqi armor kills.

The performance of the U.S. Army's Patriot air-defense missile system, however, was the subject of considerable controversy. Patriot batteries were rushed to Israel in the first days of the war after several Iraqi Scud missiles were fired against Israeli population centers, and the U.S. missile was hailed as a technological marvel after destroying a number of Scuds subsequently launched against Israel and Saudi Arabia. The seeming success of the Patriots was widely considered a decisive factor in Israel's decision not to retaliate against the Iraqis. (The United States had opposed retaliation by Israel, which could have pushed the Arab allies into withdrawing from the coalition.)

The Patriot, however, was a stopgap weapon. It had been designed for the defense of military installations rather than populated areas. In Israel, target areas were on some occasions hit by falling debris from both Patriots and Scuds.

The worst single loss of American lives in the war was the result of a Patriot failure. Twenty-eight U.S. soldiers were killed, and 98 wounded, on February 25 when a Scud hit a military barracks near Dhahran in Saudi Arabia. An investigation determined that a computer failure had prevented the launch of a Patriot to intercept the incoming Scud.

### Reserves and Women

The war provided the first combat test of the readiness of Reserve and National Guard units since the all-volunteer U.S. military was created in 1973. More than 228,000 "weekend warriors" were called to active duty, and 106,000 served in the Persian Gulf. These troops provided the bulk of combat service support for Desert Storm, in such areas as transportation, maintenance, airlift, security, and water purification. Their critical role was underscored by the necessity to maintain thousands of these troops on active duty for months after the war ended to manage the redeployment of equipment and personnel.

However, the record of reserve combat units was mixed. Air Force Reserve and National Guard jets flew thousands of combat sorties and were credited with destroying hundreds of Iraqi armored vehicles. But officials expressed disappointment with the

*Once the ground offensive began, thousands of Iraqis soldiers, like those shown on the facing page, surrendered to allied troops. At right, a female member of the U.S. 101st Airborne Division escorts an Iraqi POW.*

readiness of the Army National Guard. Three "round-out" Guard brigades designed to augment regular Army units never made it to the Gulf, because senior commanders decided they were not battle-ready.

The participation of female American soldiers in the war intensified the continuing debate over whether the Pentagon's ban on women in combat should be modified. By law, the 32,000 women soldiers who served with the U.S. forces in Desert Storm were barred from combat jobs. Yet 11 of the 15 women who lost their lives in the war were listed as having been killed in action. Two women were taken prisoner, and many served with valor in combat support units that saw action in Kuwait and Iraq during the ground campaign.

## Press Restrictions

Long-standing tensions between the military and the news media resurfaced during Desert Storm. The Pentagon imposed restrictive news coverage policies, which it defended as necessary to protect operational security, especially in an era of sophisticated technology that permitted U.S. military briefings to be viewed live by enemy commanders in Baghdad on the Cable News Network. But many reporters assigned to the combat zone alleged that military commanders deliberately limited journalists' access to military personnel and operations in a calculated attempt to sanitize coverage and minimize critical reporting of the war.

Coverage of combat operations was restricted to a small number of heavily escorted "pools" of reporters, and all pool dispatches had to be reviewed by military censors before being distributed. Before the war began, there were several incidents in which reporters who had filed dispatches judged to be unflattering were barred from visiting additional combat units. In one celebrated incident in the first days of the war, a military censor changed a reporter's description of pilots returning from air strikes from "giddy" to "proud." The Pentagon's hard-line approach to coverage was emboldened by the public's general disenchantment with the press; several public opinion polls reported minimimal support for the media in their running feud with the military.

23

*Ubiquitous yellow ribbons greeted American soldiers returning home from the Gulf War in victory. Above, an infantry division deplanes at Fort Stewart, Ga., in March.*

### War Heroes

The war, in fact, rekindled patriotic fervor in the United States; public support remained steadfast throughout, and as troops returned from harm's way, they were welcomed by a frenzy of homecomings ranging from a huge ticker-tape parade in New York City and a flyby over the Washington Monument to small-town picnics in hundreds of communities. Yellow ribbons were seen everywhere, symbolizing for many Americans their hope for their soldiers' safe return. "You helped us revive the America of our old hopes and dreams," an emotional President Bush exulted at a welcome-home party in Sumter, S.C. "When you left, it was still fashionable to question America's decency, America's courage, America's resolve, and no one—no one in the whole world—doubts us anymore."

The stunning success of Desert Storm made celebrities of its architects in a country always hungry for heroes. Secretary of Defense Cheney's calm, understated style conveyed a confident air of credibility and authority. General Powell's cool yet blunt professionalism was also highly praised. The hero's mantle settled most surely of all, however, on Schwarzkopf, commander in chief of the U.S. Central Command (the unified military command watching over U.S. interests in the region from East Africa to Pakistan) and the tactical architect of Desert Storm. He proved himself not only a successful battlefield commander but also a brilliant showman in his briefings from Riyadh, Saudi Arabia, beamed live throughout the world to millions of viewers.

### Glitches and Lessons

As in every conflict, things went wrong with Desert Storm, but postwar euphoria made it easier for the Pentagon to acknowledge the inevitable glitches. Schwarzkopf complained about the performance of U.S. intelligence agencies, telling Congress in June that intelligence analyses were excessively hedged and watered-down and often outdated. A preliminary Pentagon assessment released in mid-July praised the overall performance of the war effort but listed several deficiencies, including a lack of sealift and airlift capability, which slowed the deployment of troops and equipment; a slow response from U.S. industry for emergency procurement of critical equipment; shortcomings in readiness for an enemy biological warfare attack; and vulnerability of military communications systems to jamming. Inevitably, reports of interservice rivalries surfaced after the fighting; Marine commanders were angry when plans for an amphibious assault on Kuwait were scrapped as too risky.

In retrospect, however, the most important lessons of Desert Storm were learned by the U.S. military before a hostile shot was ever fired. In the two decades since Vietnam, the Pentagon had overhauled its standards as well as its tactics. The all-volunteer U.S. force was more professional, more highly motivated, and better trained than its predecessors. The doctrine of superior force and attrition that failed in Vietnam had been scrapped for a new doctrine, called AirLand Battle, which emphasizes joint air and ground operations featuring mobility, speed, and deception. Another important difference in the Gulf War was the absence of micromanagement: civilian leaders from Bush down confined themselves to the key political decisions and allowed their commanders wide latitude in prosecuting the battle. As a result the United States carried out its most impressive military expedition in a half-century.

# A New Reality Through Computers

by RICHARD SANTALESA

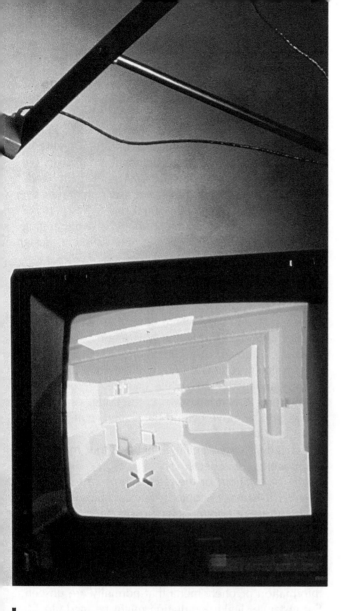

A new computer-based technology called virtual reality creates highly realistic illusions users can interact with in ways never before possible. In the architectural application at left, the user can check the design for a project before it is built, viewing a representation of each room through EyePhone goggles and employing the DataGlove (an image of which can be seen on the video screen) to move furniture around and open doors into other rooms.

Imagine hovering 20 miles above the surface of the earth, enjoying the view below as the globe slowly turns on its axis. Over your right shoulder you can see the brilliant pinpoint of a satellite scudding toward the horizon. At your left hand your young daughter points to a small mass of glowing lights below and asks, "What is that?" You answer, "New York City," and grab her hand to zoom down for a closer look. You feel your bodies drop closer to the surface as you whiz down through clouds.

In your ear a buzzer goes off. It's time for dinner. You remove the neural cap that feeds signals directly to the parts of your brain involved with the senses and step from your home's virtual-reality room into the dining room. Perhaps before bed you will send your daughter on a virtual trip to a tree's roots to help her answer a homework question on how nitrogen-fixing bacteria are vital to a forest's survival.

Farfetched? Not if the concept of virtual reality lives up to its vast and wondrous potential. If it does, we will be able to go beyond the bounds of reality and tinker with perception, time, and space in ways never before possible. Although virtual reality has many critics, there is little argument about its wide-ranging future implications for business, entertainment, design, medicine, education, and science.

### What Is Virtual Reality?

Virtual reality, also called "artificial reality," is the illusion of being somewhere other than where you physically are. Regardless of how engrossing a TV program, a movie, or a computer game may be, you are physically removed from what is going on. The action happens "there" while you are "here." Virtual reality, or VR as it is known in the trade, essentially allows you to move behind the screen, putting you into the "there."

Basically, "virtual reality" involves four main components, or aspects:

*Reality simulation*, or the re-creation of a reality, whether it is macroscopic or microscopic, in the past or the future, a commonplace experience or something inaccessible. Through simulation we will be able to travel to such places as the electron rings of a molecule or the interior of a volcano.

*Signal conversion*, which puts into visible form information or phenomena that normally are unseen. For instance, leaking radiation might be made to appear as a red cloud, or high stress levels along a geologic fault could be outlined by coded contours.

*Remote manipulation and telepresence*, which allow one to manipulate virtual items that represent real items elsewhere, while feeling as if one is in the same surroundings as the real item. For example, a person on the ocean surface could control a robot on the

---

*Richard Santalesa is the technical editor at* Computer Shopper *magazine and a member of the Society of Environmental Journalists.*

Two pioneers of virtual reality: Jaron Lanier (left) heads VPL Research, a company that produces such devices as the EyePhone goggles visible atop the video monitor and the sensor-equipped DataGlove in front of it. Myron Krueger (below), who coined the term "artificial reality," foresees applications for virtual reality in art, science, and business. Behind him is the screen of his Videoplace system, which can create images from body contours.

bottom while experiencing the conditions on the ocean floor.

*Annotation*, or the ability to highlight or label reality. A typical example would involve medical students observing an operation while wearing virtual glasses. As the operation proceeds, a highlight effect appears superimposed on various areas.

Admittedly, it is impossible, using current technology, to completely fool someone into believing he or she is within another world; the quality of the reality that can be generated by a virtual-reality system remains too limited. Furthermore, the computing technology needed to create even a somewhat realistic virtual reality can easily wear a price tag, today, of several hundred thousand dollars. Yet, despite being in its early infancy, virtual reality, and related products, was a $120 million market in 1990. California-based VPL Research Inc., a pioneer in the field, claims to have already signed up 500 customers, ranging from NASA to Pacific Bell, with an eclectic mix of companies in fields such as aircraft and auto design and medicine.

### Fooling the Senses

Simple forms of virtual reality are possible with today's technology because the mind can be tricked by the

29

*Mattel's Power Glove brought a simple form of virtual reality to the video game mass market. The hand on the screen duplicates the player's movements.*

senses. Feed the right mix of light, sound, touch, and smell to the senses, and we suddenly seem to be in a different world. Add powerful computer graphics and computations, and it is possible to create a virtual reality where we can interact with the elements of a created environment as though they were real.

In the most widely known form of virtual reality, a user dons a helmet, goggles, and gloves to enter another world. This is sometimes called cyberspace, a term popularized in the science fiction novel *Neuromancer*, by William Gibson. In the book people connect to a global computer-generated reality through neural links. In short, they plug their minds directly into the other world.

Today, virtual reality is nowhere near the stage envisioned by Gibson. The present three-dimensional virtual worlds are created largely by exploiting the fact that our eyes produce depth perception through viewing a scene from slightly different angles.

Computers can display two slightly different perspectives on liquid crystal screens (like the ones in pocket TVs), one for each eye, inside goggles (such as VPL's Eye Phone) or a helmet. The brain's visual processing power then re-creates the view, bestowing three dimensions to it in a manner reminiscent of, though vastly superior to, those ill-fitting glasses handed out to watch 3-D movies.

Other visual virtual technology includes head-mounted units called laser microscanners. Rather than generating an optical image in front of the eyes, laser microscanners project an image directly on the retina. While still experimental, laser microscanning holds large potential for superior high-resolution images at low cost.

Speakers within the helmet or headset add sound to the virtual world. A variety of sensors record head position and movement and transmit changes to a computer or group of computers, which process changes in viewing position and update the scenes shown within the goggles to reflect any movement.

### Sensors for the Hand

In order to fully interact with this brave new world, the ability to touch, hold, and move objects is necessary. To make this possible, researchers from VPL and various universities, such as the University of North Carolina at Chapel Hill, have developed "data gloves." (VPL calls its version the DataGlove.) A typical data glove is made of Lycra and features fiber optics and sensors that register finger and hand movement. Like the data registered by head position sensors, this information is routed to a computer. Combining the information relayed by the gloves with the model of the virtual world and the display on the goggles' screen, it is possible to reach out and touch, move, and pick up items in a world that exists only within the computer.

### Reality's Price

VPL Research's high-end virtual-reality equipment is still too expensive for everyday applications. Virtual-reality Audiosphere headsets, providing both the sights and sounds of the virtual world, cost a stiff $10,000 to $49,000, depending on the desired capabilities. The fiber-optically wired DataGloves are tagged at $8,800 apiece. A system like VPL's Reality Built for 2, which comes with various tool kits to define a virtual world, includes two headsets and two pairs of DataGloves. The software runs on Macintosh computers, and modules can link the Macs to more powerful Silicon Graphics and Digital Equipment workstations, which can easily cost up to $200,000.

More affordable equipment from VPL Research includes a $200 data glove for users of personal computers. When combined with special processing chips and a $1,300 pair of stereo glasses, basic entry into the worlds of virtual reality is possible.

The first low-cost commercial application of data glove technology is in video games. Since 1989, Mattel has sold a $50 virtual-reality "Power Glove" using technology licensed from VPL Research. The glove acts as a replacement for a joystick, but provides elements of virtual reality when mated to a game recognizing and utilizing its capabilities. Linked to a video game like Nintendo's Super Glove Ball, the Power Glove lets its wearer play virtual handball on the screen against a virtual opponent.

### Feeling the Force

Beyond data gloves that only track movement, the next step is the addition of "feel." One development on the road to a virtual world with texture and feel is known as force feedback. With roots in research done as part of Project GROPE by computer scientist Frederick P. Brooks, Jr., at Chapel Hill in the early 1970s, force feedback is still fairly rudimentary. It does not mean you can pick up a virtual rose and be pricked by a virtual thorn. But it does offer a physical response to events occurring in a virtual world.

For example, force feedback enables chemists designing new molecules in a 3-D virtual world to "feel" how the new molecules fit at various binding sites. Operating a servomechanism that works like a joystick—gloves cannot yet duplicate the effect—the chemists place virtual molecules together. As they do this, the servo pulls and twists to simulate the torque, repulsion, and attraction produced by the atomic interactions of the molecules the chemists are manipulating. Allowing chemists to feel the size and the direction of forces translates into greater efficiency.

Researchers at the Massachusetts Institute of Technology's Media Laboratory are working on Sandpaper, a force-feedback system that simulates the roughness of objects through a joystick. When traveling over a rough virtual object, the system

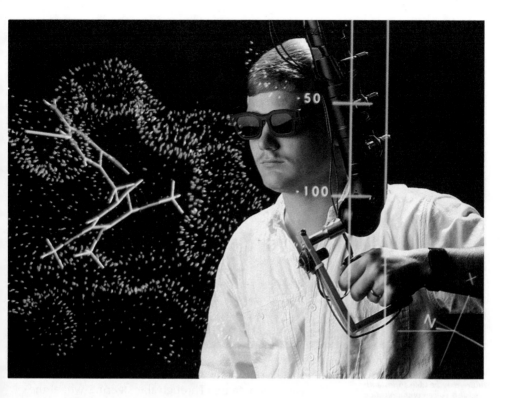

computes the forces involved in moving up and down the peaks and valleys of the object's bumps and re-creates these by moving the joystick. The MIT researchers hope to travel beyond mere roughness to the eventual re-creation of the feel of soft, sticky, and slippery items.

Meanwhile, projects at other research facilities will determine whether tactile gloves, which apply pressure directly to parts of the hand, are feasible. Such a glove would be a major breakthrough in endowing a virtual world with realistic touch and feel. Using this kind of glove, an engineer could travel inside a turbine to feel how parts are weathering, in addition to visually checking otherwise inaccessible components.

The ability to feel forces and patterns of flow is one of the most promising areas of virtual research. For example, combining virtual reality with force feedback could allow an electric utility worker to view and "feel" the patterns of power flow through the grid, leading to more efficient routing. Humans are incredibly adept at understanding complex patterns presented physically and visually. Virtual reality is made to order for these purposes.

One of the most successful examples of force

*Some forms of virtual reality simulate the texture of objects or the strength of physical forces. Here, a scientist uses a pistol-grip device to "feel" the atomic forces of attraction and repulsion as he fits models of two molecules binding with each other.*

*Air traffic controllers in the future may be able to instantly establish voice communication with a pilot by "grabbing" the image of a plane, as illustrated in the experimental system shown above.*

feedback, outside of flight simulators, is Atari's Hard Drivin' video game. Through the steering wheel the arcade game conveys bumps that occur whenever the car drifts off the road. The mass market of sophisticated video games is where the leading edge of servodevices conveying feel and touch may well make its first appearance.

### Crash at Will

Many of today's most realistic and cutting-edge applications of virtual reality can be found in the field of aeronautics. Designing and testing planes are expensive processes. Mistakes and labor are costly, and crashing a multimillion-dollar prototype can easily lead to death. Virtual-reality techniques offer ways to cut design time and eliminate problems, ultimately achieving the goal of safely and fully testing a plane before it has been built.

Boeing is one aircraft manufacturer where virtual reality is taken seriously. In a computer lab at the company's Seattle headquarters, engineers can don virtual headsets and goggles paired to data gloves and enter a virtual world where they can realistically walk around, fly, explore, and scrutinize planes that exist only within a computer. Boeing hopes that this will help it develop better planes at lower cost.

Construction and maintenance work can benefit as well. For example, using see-through goggles upon which 3-D images are superimposed, a person assembling a wing structure could compare how the finished structure, projected on top of a bare beam, should look.

Virtual reality can also ease the burden on commercial and fighter pilots overloaded by information. A typical fighter cockpit contains up to 73 warning indicators, 10 throttle switches, 19 controls on the HUD (head-up display), 675 acronyms, 3 cathode-ray tubes, and a wide assortment of other instruments all vying for attention in a machine traveling faster than the speed of sound. Since 1978 the U.S. Air Force at the Wright-Patterson Base in Dayton, Ohio, has researched how virtual reality can help pilots process the avalanche of information that threatens to bury them.

A prototype helmet, dubbed the Bug That Ate Dayton and looking right at home in a 1950s insect horror movie, is only one of many research projects the Air Force has under way. The goal is to present as much information as possible on the helmet's display in an easy-to-understand, visual fashion. More advanced helmets will depict the pilot's environment in an arcade-gamelike fashion while showing the plane's

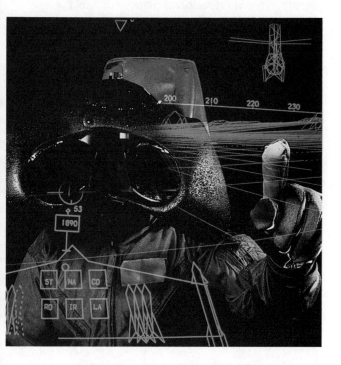

*An Air Force pilot points to a target on a virtual control panel that he sees inside his helmet; the buglike prototype helmet is one of various devices under development to help pilots process the avalanche of information from today's high-tech cockpit instrument panels.*

flight path and potential routes in response to enemy actions, as well as weather, terrain, and aircraft status.

Virtual reality has an important application in flight-training simulators. The Federal Aviation Administration's newest training facility in Oklahoma City, dubbed TOTS, for Tower Operator Training System, combines computer voice recognition, graphics, and visual projection to lend a realism to air traffic controller training previously impossible without the use of real planes and real lives. The trainees conduct business much as they would in a real tower, but instead of placing at risk 400 lives aboard a plane traveling at 300 miles per hour, they are dealing with a mass of computer technology.

At NASA's Langley Research Center at Hampton, Va., scientists are diligently working on the next generation of graphics and video technologies, which will probably grace the cockpits of supersonic commercial planes. One experimental hypersonic design does away with the forward-looking cockpit; the pilot sees a virtual-reality re-creation of what is in front of the plane.

Even if virtual reality does not make it into the cockpit anytime soon, the fact that nearly all airplanes are controlled by computers has nearly eliminated the difference between flying a simulator and an actual airplane. Newly developed planes such as the Northrop F-20 Tiger Shark use the same software to control both the simulator and physical plane—which guarantees that the experience and mechanics of flying the plane and the simulator are almost identical.

### Virtually All Business

Given that business rarely spends money on new technology until its value is clearly proven, or until a competitor has picked it up, virtual reality may not make its way to the office until long after every arcade and theater has had it for several years. When it does arrive en masse, the business world may never be the same.

Most likely the tide of virtual reality will first reach the design and creative fields, simply because these areas are fundamentally visual and have already eagerly embraced computer technology. Further, they can garner immediate benefits without radical change in work patterns. Architects already use computer programs to create highly realistic views and models.

Widespread use of virtual reality promises to change

*Using virtual reality technology, a man on a steerable treadmill takes a walk "in" a church planned for construction, viewed on a large screen.*

design the way the spreadsheet revamped number crunching. For example, Autodesk Inc. is currently working on, and hopes to soon release, a product prosaically named Cyberspace. The Cyberspace tool kit includes the familiar DataGlove and a head-mounted EyePhone display composed of a team of wide-angle lenses matched to two small liquid crystal screens to create a 3-D effect. With this equipment in place, an engineer or engineering designer interacting with a special version of Autodesk's popular design program AutoCAD can design in three dimensions and easily learn if a knob on a control panel or dashboard is located in an awkward position or obscured by the arm of a chair or by the steering wheel.

With a virtual-reality design tool, an architect who is designing a day-care center could "step" into a virtualized representation of the center and view it from the perspective of a small child in order to learn the best positioning for water fountains, shelves, and doorknobs.

Another area where virtual reality is likely to be met with open arms is in businesses that deal with dangerous or inaccessible locations. A virtually controlled robot could be piloted within a damaged nuclear reactor or toxic chemical spill without ever placing the operator in danger. The operator, safe and sound, would see a virtual re-creation of the location.

The essence of business is selling, and virtual reality is already being used in this area. Matsushita Electronic Works opened a virtual kitchen "showroom" in Tokyo in April 1990 that uses headsets and data gloves from VPL Research to help sell custom-built kitchens. A person interested in a new kitchen simply provides the existing kitchen's dimensions along with choices from a list of various cabinets and appliances. After donning a virtual-reality helmet and data gloves, the potential buyer enters a virtual kitchen where doors open, chairs can be arranged, and faucets turn on. Consumers can try different combinations of colors, appliances, and cabinets in order not only to "see" how their kitchen will look but also to try it on for size before opening their wallets.

Since virtual reality allows information to be viewed in completely new ways, it also has many potential uses in research. For instance, medical researchers could spot trends in disease patterns much earlier if such information could be superimposed over a 3-D virtual map along with historical and environmental

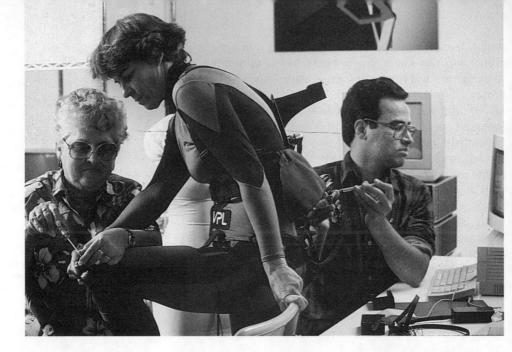

*The DataSuit, made by VPL Research, does for the entire body what the DataGlove does for the hand. By detecting body movements, it immerses the body into a virtual world. The version shown here is equipped with 50 sensors and uses 300 feet of fiber-optic cable.*

data, such as past locations of heavy industry and landfills. A researcher could reverse virtual time to see how past disease patterns fit into current patterns or could zoom out to see how a locality fits into a statewide pattern.

Even something as fundamental as going to work could change. By combining virtual reality and telecommuting (working at home with a computer connected to the office), an "office" in Tokyo could actually exist in a basement in Toledo. A "virtual conference" would not only eliminate travel time and expense; it could also prove more efficient for covering large territories. A manager wishing to check on progress at factories in the Far East, Pacific Northwest, and Germany could conceivably inspect all three in an extended day, rather than taking a week.

### Coming Soon to a Theater Near You?

Why simply watch characters on a movie screen when you can be a character within the movie? Besides enabling you to actually enter a movie's virtual reality, where you could, for example, be flying a fighter in *Star Wars*, there is the potential for virtual characters. The use of such characters, completely created by computer, could conceivably put W. C. Fields in a modern movie next to Marilyn Monroe.

Meanwhile, in the fall of 1991, television's first computer-generated cohost was to appear in the documentary *Computer Visions*; this "host," Ray Tracy, is a completely 3-D computer-generated character created by Digital Vision Entertainment. (The digital-looking talking head Max Headroom who made his debut on cable and broadcast television a few years ago was actually an actor whose appearance was altered by a makeup artist and computer enhancement.)

While virtual movies are a promise waiting to happen, virtual arcades have already opened in both the United States and Europe. At the 4,000-square-foot BattleTech Center in Chicago, game players battle opponents in 100 square miles of futuristic virtual landscape while being physically located in closet-sized rooms connected to the virtual world and each other through a computer network. The virtual world is created by four custom-built computers that use techniques found in military flight simulators.

### The Downside and the Future

Critics continue to point to the constraints imposed by present-day technology—such as computers not powerful enough to generate detailed, rapidly changing color images, or display screens whose limited resolution results in fuzzy pictures. Devices like data gloves and goggles are probably too cumbersome for everyday use by business.

There are other concerns as well. Thomas Zimmerman, who developed the DataGlove, has mixed feelings about the "artificial-reality bandwagon." He thinks that "this technology could make us more machinelike, more inhuman." Some speak in an alarmist tone about the addictive possibilities of virtual-reality entertainment. Virtual-reality researcher Thomas Furness warns of the danger of creating "socially immature people. Virtual realities will do what people want them to do, and that's not the way the real world works." A related fear is that virtual reality could work to isolate users from their neighbors and their community. But any new technology brings risks as well as rewards.

Predictions about the future are notoriously inaccurate, but it is fairly realistic to expect that virtual reality will play an important role once the technology improves and drops in price. While it will be years before virtual reality is a mainstream mass-market phenomenon with noticeable social impact, we clearly have not seen the last of this exciting new technology.

# THE RISE AND FALL OF SOVIET COMMUNISM

*In 1905 the "Bloody Sunday" massacre of peacefully demonstrating workers outside the Winter Palace in St. Petersburg (below) touched off a revolution that shook but did not topple the tsarist regime. Another revolution, in March 1917, brought down the tsar and paved the way for Vladimir Lenin (right) to lead the Communist Party to power eight months later.*

The Union of Soviet Socialist Republics came to a startling end in 1991.  The Communist Party had built a powerful state out of the former Russian Empire, which collapsed in 1917 in the face of widespread unrest stemming from economic failings and the strains wrought by World War I.  The Soviet Union weathered World War II heroically and became a postwar superpower militarily rivaling the United States—but eventually sank into economic paralysis and political disarray.  Through a selection of historic photographs, paintings, and posters, this article traces the history of the Soviet Communist state.

A bloody civil war followed the Communist seizure of power— the 1920 Red Army poster at right asks, "Have you volunteered?" The war, which the Communists won, brought privation and famine (left) to the populace. Lenin died in 1924, and Joseph Stalin, already general secretary of the Communist Party, maneuvered his way to supreme power. He pushed the country into rapid industrialization. Below, a hydroelectric plant is erected in the Caucasus.

Stalin (right) subjected agriculture to "collectivization," eliminating individual farms. In the bottom photo, the banner calls on everyone to join the collective farm. Those resisting were forced to join or deported to labor camps. Life in the countryside was often grim, and millions of peasants died in a famine in the early 1930s. Later in the decade Stalin unleashed a campaign to destroy potential or imagined opposition through the arrest and liquidation of millions of people. Andrei Vyshinsky (below, second from left), chief state prosecutor from 1935 to 1938, played a key role in show trials that resulted in the execution of prominent party and military leaders.

In World War II the Soviet Union suffered horrendous destruction and loss of life—at least 20 million people perished. The German Army penetrated deep into the country; Kiev was captured, and Leningrad was besieged for 900 days, during which as many as a million people may have died. "Avenge," says the patriotic poster at left. The Soviet forces regrouped and finally stood fast against the German advance in a ferocious battle at Stalingrad; after fierce house-to-house fighting, the Soviets freed the city in early 1943 (above), turning the tide in the war in Europe. The Soviet counteroffensive eventually reached Berlin (below).

After Stalin's death in 1953 the repressiveness of the Soviet system was slightly moderated by Nikita Khrushchev (above, applauding), who shook a 1956 party congress with a denunciation of Stalinist crimes. Leonid Brezhnev (below) presided over the period following Khrushchev's 1964 ouster, which was later branded a time of stagnation. One major postwar achievement of the Communist regime was its space program, inaugurated in 1957 with the launching of the first artificial earth satellite, Sputnik. The poster at right says, "We conquer space and time."

Мы покоряем пространство и время

In the 1980s, with the Soviet economy stifled by central planning and political barriers to creative initiative, a new leader, Mikhail Gorbachev, sought to rejuvenate the country through glasnost (openness) and perestroika, or economic and political restructuring. Religion was accorded new freedom. Above, Patriarch Aleksi, holding an icon, stands outside St. Basil's Cathedral near the Kremlin on the occasion, in 1990, of the first Orthodox service in the cathedral in over 70 years. Despite reforms, the economy continued to falter; consumers faced long lines and widespread food shortages (below).

The traditional power structure was gradually losing its authority, and in August 1991 a group of high government officials staged a coup. They held Gorbachev at his vacation home in the Crimea and ordered tanks into the streets of Moscow (left). The coup failed as a result of its leaders' hesitancy, their failure to ensure the support of key segments of the Soviet power structure, and an effective popular resistance rallied by Boris Yeltsin, the president of the Russian republic. Below, shortly after the coup, Yeltsin waves to a crowd at the Russian Parliament building, the nerve center of the resistance.

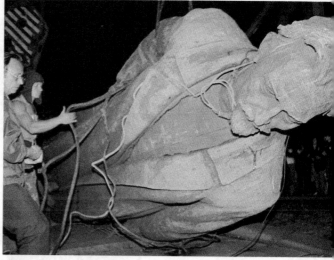

Gorbachev returned to Moscow (left) after the coup (in the background, his wife and granddaughter). But the Communist Party was discredited, and in the absence of a strong central authority separatist movements in the individual republics gained strength. Statues of Communist greats were toppled—in Moscow (above), Feliks Dzerzhinski, the founder of the KGB security police, falls. Below, Ukrainians—with a symbolically paint-smeared image of Lenin—demonstrate in front of the Communist headquarters in Kiev.

The party was virtually disbanded by the end of August. Gorbachev fought to save the union, but the Soviet power structure continued to disintegrate, with Yeltsin, as head of the Russian republic, increasingly taking the initiative. In early December, Ukrainians voted for independence by a wide margin. A few days later, Russia, Ukraine, and Byelorussia (renamed Belarus) formed a Commonwealth of Independent States, soon joined by eight other republics. On December 25, Gorbachev resigned as president of the Soviet Union. The next day, the Supreme Soviet, the Soviet Parliament, voted itself out of existence; few delegates bothered to show up (right). The Soviet hammer-and-sickle flag, which had flown over the Kremlin for seven decades, was lowered and replaced by the Russian flag (above).

# CHRONOLOGY FOR 1991

## January

**12** • The U.S. Congress approves the use of military force to reverse Iraq's occupation of Kuwait.

**13** • A crackdown by Soviet troops on pro-independence forces in the Soviet republic of Lithuania leaves over a dozen dead.

**17** • The Persian Gulf War begins, as U.S.-led forces bomb targets in Iraq and Kuwait.

**18** • In the first of several such attacks, Iraq hits Israel with Scud-type missiles.

## February

**4** • U.S. President George Bush proposes a $1.45 trillion federal budget for fiscal 1992.

**7** • The Irish Republican Army mounts a mortar attack on the offices of British Prime Minister John Major, hitting an adjacent yard.

**9** • In a nonbinding plebiscite, Lithuanians overwhelmingly endorse the republic's 1990 declaration of independence.

**13** • As the air war against Iraq continues, U.S. bombs hit an Iraqi shelter, killing hundreds; U.S. officials say the building was a disguised military communications center.

• Liberia's three warring factions sign a formal cease-fire accord.

**24** • After five weeks of intensive aerial bombardment, U.S. and allied forces launch a ground offensive in the Persian Gulf War.

**25** • An Iraqi Scud missile kills 28 soldiers in a U.S. barracks in Dhahran, Saudi Arabia.

**26** • Rebel forces seize Somalia's capital, ousting President Muhammed Siad Barre.

**27** • With Iraqi forces routed and Kuwait retaken by allied troops, Bush calls a halt to the al-

**FEBRUARY 25**

lied military offensive in the Persian Gulf War.

## March

3 • In nonbinding plebiscites, citizens of the Soviet republics of Latvia and Estonia vote overwhelmingly for independence.

• Members of the Los Angeles Police Department are videotaped brutally beating a black motorist.

5 • Growing numbers of clashes are reported between troops loyal to Iraqi President Saddam Hussein and Shiite rebels in the south, Kurdish rebels in the north.

14 • The emir of Kuwait returns home after 7½ months in exile.

15 • The United States and Albania resume full diplomatic relations after 52 years of nonrecognition.

19 • Khaleda Zia, whose Bangladesh Nationalist Party won a plurality in parliamentary elections, is sworn in as the country's first woman prime minister.

21 • The British government announces that the unpopular poll tax will be abandoned.

26 • Iraqi troops loyal to Saddam Hussein are reported to have suppressed the Shiite rebellion in the south.

## April

1 • Kurdish leaders confirm that hundreds of thousands of Kurds are seeking refuge in Turkey and Iran following suppression of their uprising against Saddam Hussein.

6 • Iraq accepts terms of a permanent cease-fire in the Persian Gulf War.

15 • The European Community lifts its economic sanctions against South Africa.

16 • The United States announces plans to build

and operate camps in northern Iraq for Kurdish refugees who had fled to or across the border with Turkey.

25 • The U.S. economic downturn is officially declared to have been a recession since July 1990.

30 • A cyclone batters Bangladesh, killing over 125,000 people and displacing 10 million others.

## May

6 • President Bush leaves the hospital after treatment for an irregular heartbeat.

21 • Shortly before scheduled national elections, former Indian Prime Minister Rajiv Gandhi is assassinated in a bombing during a campaign stop.

23 • The U.S. Supreme Court upholds a ban on abortion counseling at family planning clinics receiving federal funds.

28 • In Ethiopia, rebels take full control of the capital, a week after President Mengistu Haile Mariam resigned his office and fled.

31 • The government of Angola signs a peace accord with the rebel faction Unita to end 16 years of civil war.

## June

5 • The South African Parliament votes to repeal the laws used to justify racial discrimination in property ownership and where people may live.

• Algeria declares a state of emergency after violent protests by Islamic fundamentalists.

12 • Albania's Parliament approves a nonCommunist cabinet.

• Boris Yeltsin is elected president of the Russian republic.

17 • South Africa's Parliament repeals the law

51

## JUNE 20

that laid the legal foundation of apartheid by classifying citizens by race.

**20** • India's Congress Party selects P. V. Narasimha Rao as the leader of a new coalition government.

• The last Soviet troops leave Hungary.

**25** • The parliaments of the Yugoslav republics of Slovenia and Croatia overwhelmingly pass declarations of independence.

• The last Soviet troops withdraw from Czechoslovakia.

**27** • Fighting erupts between the Yugoslav Army and Slovenian forces.

• U.S. Supreme Court Justice Thurgood Marshall announces his resignation.

### July

**1** • The Warsaw Pact disbands.

**5** • Assets of the Bank of Credit and Commerce International are seized by financial regulators in seven countries.

**10** • The United States lifts economic sanctions against South Africa.

• Slovenia ratifies a peace agreement, suspending its independence declaration.

**11** • The longest solar eclipse until the 22nd century takes place.

**22** • Croatia rejects a peace agreement meant to end clashes between Croatian units and Serbs backed by the Yugoslav Army.

**31** • The United States and the Soviet Union sign a strategic arms treaty mandating reductions in long-range nuclear weapons.

### August

**19** • Soviet President Mikhail Gorbachev is reported to have been ousted by a group of hard-line Communists.

**21** • The coup in the Soviet Union collapses, after angry crowds rally behind Yeltsin.

**24** • Gorbachev resigns as head of the Communist Party and disbands its leadership. The Ukraine declares independence.

## September

**2** • A cease-fire in Yugoslavia negotiated by the European Community is shattered hours after the agreement is signed.

**6** • The Soviet Union recognizes the independence of Lithuania, Latvia, and Estonia.

**25** • The president of El Salvador and five guerrilla commanders endorse a broad peace agreement.

• Pro-democracy protesters and government supporters clash violently in the Soviet republic of Georgia.

**26** • Romanian Prime Minister Petre Roman resigns, after antigovernment riots by miners.

**27** • President Bush announces U.S. plans to remove short-range nuclear missiles from Europe, Asia, and all U.S. Navy vessels.

**28** • Iraq releases 44 UN inspectors detained after they discovered secret Iraqi plans for making nuclear weapons.

**29** • Zaire's President Mobutu Sese Seko agrees to share power with a coalition government led by the opposition.

**30** • Haiti's President Jean-Bertrand Aristide is ousted in a violent coup by the country's military.

## JULY 1

## October

**4** • Twenty-four countries agree to ban mineral and oil exploration in Antarctica for a period of 50 years.

**15** • The U.S. Senate narrowly approves Clarence Thomas's appointment to the Supreme Court, after subcommittee hearings that considered allegations against him of sexual harassment.

**22** • The European Community and the European Free Trade Association agree to form a new 19-nation free-trade area, the European Economic Area.

**23** • Cambodia's warring factions sign peace accords providing for a transition to democratic rule.

**27** • Kiichi Miyazawa is elected president of Japan's governing Liberal Democratic Party, positioning him to become prime minister.

**30** • The Middle East peace conference opens in Madrid, Spain.

**31** • Zambian voters soundly defeat longtime President Kenneth Kaunda.

## November

**7** • Basketball star Magic Johnson announces his retirement, saying he is infected with the AIDS virus.

**16** • Former Governor Edwin Edwards easily defeats David Duke, a former Ku Klux Klan leader, in the Louisiana gubernatorial runoff election.

**20** • The U.S. Senate Ethics Committee reprimands Senator Alan Cranston (D, Calif.) for interceding with savings-and-loan regulators in exchange for receiving campaign contributions.

**21** • Boutros Ghali, an Egyptian, is unanimously recommended by the UN Security Council to become the next secretary-general.

## DECEMBER 13

### *December*

**1** • Voters in Ukraine overwhelmingly endorse independence and elect ex-Communist Leonid Kravchuk president.

**3** • Embattled White House Chief of Staff John H. Sununu resigns.

**4** • The last and longest-held American hostage in Lebanon, Terry Anderson, is freed by his captors, after nearly seven years.

**11** • Concluding a meeting in Maastricht, the Netherlands, European Community leaders agree to work for closer political and economic union.

**13** • North and South Korea sign a reconciliation and trade treaty.

**16** • The UN General Assembly repeals its 1975 resolution equating Zionism with racism.

• The Canadian government announces an accord granting native Inuit control over one-fifth of the country's area.

**19** • Bob Hawke is ousted as Australia's prime minister, replaced by former Treasurer Paul Keating.

**21** • Eleven former Soviet republics formally constitute themselves as the Commonwealth of Independent States.

**25** • Gorbachev resigns as Soviet president.

**26** • A militant Muslim fundamentalist party triumphs in the first round of Algeria's parliamentary elections.

• The Soviet Union's Parliament votes itself out of existence.

**30** • A car bomb kills 20 in Beirut.

**31** • A UN special envoy wins agreement from Serbian and Yugoslav officials to a peace plan to end fighting with Croatia.

• In Australia, President Bush begins a trip promoting free trade and American exports that will also take him to Singapore, South Korea, and Japan.

**ACCIDENTS AND DISASTERS.** Some of the major disasters that occurred in 1991 are briefly described below.

Jan. 13, South Africa: Forty people were killed in a crush after fighting broke out in the stands at a soccer game between two popular teams from Soweto.

Feb. 1, Afghanistan and Pakistan: An earthquake whose epicenter was in the Hindu Kush mountains killed more than 1,000 people. Most victims were in remote villages made inaccessible by snow.

Feb. 1, California: A USAir jetliner landing at the Los Angeles International Airport collided on the runway with a small commuter plane, which it destroyed, then slammed into a nearby building; 34 people lost their lives.

Feb. 13, Mexico: More than 40 people were suffocated or trampled to death in a narrow alleyway while participating in a pilgrimage in Chalma, Mexico.

Mar. 3, Colorado: A Boeing 737 jet plunged sharply to the ground, crashing into a park in Colorado Springs. All 25 on board died.

Mar. 5, Venezuela: A CD-9 airliner strayed off course and crashed in a mountainous region in western Venezuela. All 43 on board were killed.

Mar. 16, California: Seven members of country singer Reba McEntire's band, her road manager, and two crew members died when

*A collision with an oil tanker in April caused a fire on an Italian ferry, the Moby Prince, and all but one of the 143 aboard were listed as dead or missing.*

*A jungle in Thailand became a scene of horror when an Austrian airliner on its way from Bangkok to Vienna crashed in May.*

their private plane crashed shortly after take-off near San Diego.

Mar. 21, Pacific Ocean: A midair collision between two P-3 Orion antisubmarine planes off the coast of southern California resulted in the deaths of 27 Navy servicemen.

Mar. 21, Saudi Arabia: Ninety-two Senegalese troops sent to the Persian Gulf region as part of the multinational force there were killed, along with six Saudi crewmen, when their C-130 transport plane crashed at a Saudi air base.

Apr. 4, Pennsylvania: Senator John Heinz (R, Pa.) and six others died in a collision between his chartered plane and a helicopter making a midair inspection of the plane's landing gear. Two of those killed were children hit by burning wreckage in a schoolyard.

Apr. 4, Peru: An earthquake that measured 7 on the Richter scale left at least 100 people dead. The jungle city of Moyobamba, home to about 50,000, was leveled, and 20 people died in Nereva Cajamarca, near the quake's epicenter.

Apr. 5, Georgia: Former U.S. Senator John Tower and 22 others were killed when their commuter flight from Atlanta crashed into the woods just 2 miles from its intended destination in Brunswick, Ga.

Apr. 10, Italy: An Italian ferry collided with an oil tanker, triggering a fire. While all of the tanker's 28-man crew survived, 142 aboard the ferry lost their lives.

Apr. 26, United States: At least 26 people were killed as approximately 70 tornadoes ripped through a seven-state area centered in eastern Kansas; at least 17 died amid the destruction of a trailer park in Andover, Kan.

Apr. 29, Soviet Union: An earthquake struck Soviet Georgia, killing more than 100 and leaving 100,000 homeless, mostly in remote mountain villages.

Apr. 30, Bangladesh: More than 125,000 people lost their lives when a cyclone tore through densely populated regions of southeastern Bangladesh, flattening huts and villages and sweeping away crops. As many as 10 million were left homeless.

May 26, Thailand: All 223 people aboard lost

their lives when an Austrian-owned Lauda Air Boeing 767-300 crashed about 100 miles from Bangkok. According to Austrian officials, a computer malfunction had switched one of the jet's engines into reverse.

Late May, China: Severe flooding devastated large areas of southeast China, leaving 1,700 dead and millions homeless.

June 3, Japan: On the southern island of Kyushu, 43 journalists, scientists, emergency workers, and others died in the eruption of Mount Unzen, as superheated ash and toxic gases spewed from the volcano.

June 5, Ethiopia: More than 100 people were reportedly killed by an explosion at a munitions depot in a slum area of Addis Ababa.

June 8, Pakistan: A crowded passenger train slammed into a standing freight train at a rural station in Ghothi, in Sindh province, killing 100 people.

June 10, Philippines: Over 320 people died soon after the Mount Pinatubo volcano began to spew gas, ash, and rock; about 85,000 people were evacuated from the surrounding area, which included the Clark Air Base complex. In the ensuing months, hundreds more died as a result of flooding, mudslides, and disease.

June 18, Chile: More than 115 people died as a massive mudslide brought on by unusual torrential rains swept down a hillside in the desert city of Antofagasta.

July 11, Saudi Arabia: A DC-8 airliner crashed in the desert near Jiddah, Saudi Arabia; all 261 on board, mostly Nigerian Muslims returning from a pilgrimage, lost their lives.

July 28, Romania: A wall of water 12 feet high swept through northeastern Romania after a dam burst following heavy rains. About 100 people were reported dead or missing.

July 30, India: A river overflowed into the village of Mohad, killing as many as 500 people and destroying 2,000 homes.

July 31, South Carolina: An Amtrak passenger train traveling from Miami to New York derailed near Camden, killing seven.

Aug. 3, Zimbabwe: At least 80 schoolchildren and 7 adults died when a crowded, speeding bus crashed southeast of Harare.

Aug. 16, India: An Indian Airlines Boeing 737-200 flying from Calcutta to Impahl crashed

in a remote jungle after catching fire in flight. All 69 on board were killed.

Aug. 28, New York: A subway train running down Manhattan's east side derailed while switching tracks shortly after midnight, killing 5 people and injuring about 170 others.

Sept. 3, North Carolina: A fire that started near a deep fat fryer spread quickly through a chicken processing plant in Hamlet, N.C., killing 25 people. Blocked fire exits and other safety violations were cited as factors in the deaths.

Sept. 5, Congo: A passenger train and a freight train on the same track collided head-on near Dolisie; more than 100 people were killed.

Sept. 11, Texas: A Continental Express commuter plane flying through clear, calm skies from Laredo to Houston caught fire and crashed in a cornfield, killing all 14 on board.

Sept. 28, Japan: The country's worst typhoon in 30 years ripped through the southwestern island of Kyushu and the northernmost island of Hokkaido, leaving a total of 43 dead and thousands of buildings and houses severely damaged.

Oct. 5, Indonesia: A military transport plane crashed after takeoff from Jakarta, demolishing a government building; 137 people were killed.

Oct. 17, France: A head-on collision at Melun between a passenger train and a freight train resulted in 16 deaths.

Oct. 20, California: At least 25 lives were lost as fire engulfed an affluent area of Oakland. The blaze, ranked as the worst in California's history, grew from a small brushfire. More than 5,000 people were displaced; damage was estimated at $5 billion.

Oct. 20, India: More than 2,000 people were killed when an earthquake struck the foothills of the Himalayas in the vicinity of Almora, destroying or damaging hundreds of remote villages.

Oct. 30, Canada: A Canadian C-130 military supply plane crashed on the frozen tundra near the outpost of Alert, located on the tip of Ellesmere Island. Five crewmen froze to death during the 30 hours it took rescuers to arrive.

Oct. 30, North Korea: As many as 80 people died in an explosion near a railway station close to the South Korean border.

Nov. 5, Philippines: More than 7,000 people died and thousands were left homeless after a tropical storm hit Samar Island and the island of Leyte.

Nov. 19, Haiti: A boat carrying Haitian refugees bound for the United States was wrecked off the coast of Cuba, killing an estimated 135 people.

Nov. 19, Mexico: A freight train derailed near the city of Tehuacan and crashed into a line of traffic. At least 30 people died.

Nov. 20, Soviet Union: A helicopter returning from a peace mission flew into a mountain in heavy fog in the Nagorno-Karabakh region, killing 22 people.

Nov. 29, California: During a swirling dust storm near Coalinga, 17 people died and 150 were injured in a series of violent wrecks over a 1½-mile stretch of highway.

Dec. 15, Egypt: More than 460 passengers and crew were killed when a ferry sank in the Red Sea after being tossed into a coral reef by 10-foot waves.

Dec. 22, Germany: A World War II-vintage DC-3 crashed into a hillside while on a charter flight near Heidelberg, killing 28 people.

Dec. 28, New York: Nine people were crushed to death in a crowded stairwell at City College at a charity basketball game.

**ADVERTISING.** War and the sluggish economy dampened the growth of U.S. advertising revenues in 1991. As a result of the small number of commercials run during coverage of the Persian Gulf conflict, networks lost millions of dollars in advertising revenues. The recession also severely affected ad revenues. The ad agency McCann-Erickson projected in December that ad spending volume for 1991 would drop for the first time in 31 years, by an estimated 1.5 percent. The problem was felt especially by the traditional print media—magazines and newspapers. Even upscale magazines, usually untouched by recession, lost pages due to cutbacks by makers of luxury goods. Many leading retailers cut their advertising spending in newspapers, and while some of that money was shifted to direct mail catalogs, some was eliminated completely.

**Campaigns.** Taster's Choice coffee, a Nestle brand, ran a series of TV commercials revolving around two neighbors named Sharon and Tony, who first meet when Sharon borrows some coffee from Tony. A hint of romantic flirtation had viewers waiting to see what happens next. The campaign was based on a series of ads originally developed for another Nestle brand in London, where Sharon and Tony's relationship was more fully developed.

Jimmy Connors, the 39-year-old tennis star, began appearing in print and television ads for Nuprin. Connors shared stories with young tennis player Michael Chang and football quarterback Joe Montana about the benefits of the pain reliever after too much sports activity. Older athletes have particular appeal as product endorsers because of the aging of baby boom consumers.

The American Marketing Association's New York chapter had an unusual winner for its Grand Effie. The award, made on the basis of campaign effectiveness rather than creativity alone, honored the 1990 campaign designed to elect Minnesotan Paul D. Wellstone, who was the only U.S. Senate candidate to defeat an incumbent. His campaign effectively used humor instead of the negative advertising strategy that has characterized many recent political campaigns.

In September, Pepsi-Cola unveiled a new logo, intended to make Pepsi look younger and trendier than archrival Coca-Cola. The new logo was the eighth to appear in Pepsi's 97-year history.

**Regulation.** The Federal Trade Commission charged Scali, McCabe, Sloves and its client Volvo with deceptive advertising. They were alleged to have faked a demonstration of the car's strength by reinforcing the roof of the vehicle. The Volvo was then put into a line of cars that were driven over by a large-tire pickup truck, with only the Volvo withstanding the test. The incident was first investigated by the Texas attorney general late in 1990. As a consequence, Scali, McCabe, Sloves resigned the Volvo account. The FTC investigation resulted in $150,000 fines for both the client and the agency. This appeared to be the first time an agency ever paid a fine as part of a consent agreement with the FTC.

In November the U.S. surgeon general, Dr. Antonia Novello, called on beer and wine companies to stop directing advertising at children. Company spokespersons denied their ads were aimed at, or were meant to encourage, teenagers, but both houses of Congress were considering bills mandating warning statements on beer and wine ads.     B.B.R.

**AFGHANISTAN.**  As Afghanistan entered its 14th year of civil war in 1991, combat intensified between the Kabul government and the scattered forces of the Islamic resistance. Late in the year, however, the United States and the Soviet Union agreed to end military aid to the warring sides, giving rise to hopes for peace.

**The Civil War.**  In April the Mujahedeen resistance captured Khost, a major military base in southeastern Afghanistan.  In the northeast, Commander Ahmad Shah Mausood's Supervisory Council strengthened its hold over Takhar and Badakshan provinces; Mausood gained virtual control over the crucial highway between Kabul and the Soviet border and consolidated his own supply routes from Pakistan. Combat escalated in western Afghanistan, where Commander Ismael Khan regained the initiative from government and allied militia forces.  In the south, Kandahar remained under siege.  Fighting around Kabul was constant but indecisive.

Despite rebel successes, the Kabul government was able to hold its own through technical superiority.  Its air force prevented the Mujahedeen from holding any large cities. Government armored and infantry units displayed improved morale and fighting ability in the assault which cleared the Kabul-Gardez highway in May, but many militia units, short of manpower, were unable to continue fighting for the government.

**The Government and the Resistance.** President Najibullah continued to strengthen his political position.  Senior members of the hard-line Khalq wing of Najibullah's People's Democratic Party, however, resented his abandonment of Marxism.  He also faced a challenge within his own Parcham wing of the party with the return from the Soviet Union in July of his prominent rival, Babrak Karmal.

Disarray within the resistance leadership was even more serious.  Rivalries and the col-

1898

1940

1987

1991

*For yet another time in its long history, Pepsi-Cola redesigned the company logo. Seen here are three of the previous versions, going back as far as 1898, plus the latest model—intended to give Pepsi a trendier look than its archrival, Coca-Cola.*

lapse of outside funding destroyed its interim government, which was unable to achieve effective control over commanders in the field. Disputes were further aggravated by the politics of the Persian Gulf War. The moderate Afghan parties sided with the anti-Iraq forces, supplying some 300 Mujahedeen to fight for the liberation of Kuwait, but the most militant resistance leaders, Gulbuddin Hekmatyar and Rasul Sayyaf, backed Saddam Hussein.

Hekmatyar remained the most formidable resistance leader, with his party enjoying close relations with Pakistan's military leadership. During the summer his heavily-armed, well-disciplined forces seized control of most of Kunar province from rival militants.

**International Developments.** Within three weeks of the failed Soviet coup in August, the new Soviet government and the United States agreed to stop supplying weapons to the Afghan civil war. Soviet officials and a rebel delegation meeting in November urged the formation of an undefined "Islamic interim government" in Afghanistan. The Kabul regime responded that such a government must include Najibullah and called for wide-ranging peace talks to end the conflict.

On May 21, Javier Pérez de Cuéllar, the United Nations secretary-general, had announced a peace plan calling for free elections and the installation of a "broad-based" government. In a tripartite meeting sponsored by Iran and Pakistan in late July, however, the resistance groups declared their opposition to the Kabul government's participation.

*See* STATISTICS OF THE WORLD. N.N.

*The capture of Khost, a major military base in southeastern Afghanistan, by rebel forces in April was a clear demonstration that the antigovernment Mujahedeen, though politically divided, had the ability to escalate the level of conflict in the long-running civil war.*

# Africa

**The year 1991 saw the apparent end of long-burning conflicts in Angola, Western Sahara, Ethiopia, and Eritrea. New civilian governments took office in several African countries.**

The economic crisis remained desperate for most of the continent, while famine threatened as many as 30 million people. South Africa's white minority regime abolished many apartheid laws and began negotiations aimed at creating a nonracial democratic constitution. In Algeria's first multiparty elections, Islamic fundamentalists scored a landslide victory.

**Regional Developments.** At the Organization of African Unity (OAU) summit in Abuja, Nigeria, in June, African leaders approved a long-term plan for an African Economic Community. In the first five-year stage, the emphasis was to be on strengthening regional organizations within the continent such as the Economic Community of West African States and the Southern African Economic Development Conference. Over the longer term, the plan called for moving step-by-step to a continent-wide African common market.

The United Nations, reporting on the special program for African recovery and development (1986-1990), noted that the outcome was clearly unsatisfactory, with economic growth rates averaging only 2.3 percent per annum in real terms, resulting in a per capita decline of 0.7 percent per annum. A fall in commodity prices alone cost Africa $50 billion over the program period, while Africa's debt rose to $271.7 billion in 1990, and debt servicing took up over 30 percent of export earnings.

Through the OAU and other regional agencies, African leaders pledged greater support for democracy and resolution of regional conflicts—support demonstrated through such actions as the West African peacekeeping role in Liberia. A nonofficial gathering of African leaders, including incumbents and former office holders, met in Kampala, Uganda, in May and issued proposals for greater cooperation on security, stability, development, and cooperation. The proposals included strengthening peacekeeping mechanisms for both civil wars and wars between states.

The choice of a new UN secretary-general shaped up as, in large part, a race between three Africans—Boutros Ghali of Egypt, Bernard Chidzero of Zimbabwe, and Olusegun Obasanjo of Nigeria. The winner was Ghali, who took office on January 1, 1992, becoming the first African to hold the post.

**Southern Africa.** In South Africa the white-minority government of President F. W. de Klerk abolished many apartheid laws, including the Land Act restricting ownership of land by race and the Population Registration Act classifying South Africans by race, and it released additional political prisoners. Anti-apartheid critics noted, however, that hundreds of political prisoners remained behind bars and that race continued to be fundamental in determining political rights, government services, pension rights, and economic position. In July the African National Congress (ANC) held its first open conference inside South Africa and elected a strong multiracial leadership, blending leaders from exile and those from grass-roots groups inside the country. In late December, the government and various political groups, including the ANC, met in Johannesburg at a Convention for a Democratic South Africa, and began efforts aimed at framing a nonracial constitution for South Africa. Working groups were established to report back to the next session.

A cease-fire was finally achieved in May in the civil war in Angola, with an agreement providing for creation of a new nonpartisan national army and for multiparty elections. In Mozambique, however, talks between the

*Supporters of the Islamic Salvation Front, which seeks to turn Algeria into an Islamic republic along the lines of Iran, take to the streets in December to celebrate the front's success in the first round of parliamentary elections.*

tion Front took charge. Both groups agreed to resolve the dispute over the status of Eritrea through a peaceful referendum. In Somalia, however, the ouster of Siad Barre led not to peace but to disintegration, with two separate rebel groups claiming control in the north and south of the country and Siad Barre's backers still continuing to resist.

In Sudan, the civil war continued unabated, as the southern Sudan People's Liberation Army fought an Islamic fundamentalist regime accused of numerous human rights abuses.

Despite peace in some areas, as many as 22 million people in the Horn remained threatened by famine.

**East Africa.** Campaigns for democracy in East Africa were most intense in Madagascar and in Kenya. Massive demonstrations in Madagascar during the year were met by violence; in October, President Didier Ratsiraka agreed to an 18-month transitional administration bringing in the opposition, and to a referendum on a new constitution, but the stability of the agreement was in doubt. In Kenya, President Daniel arap Moi came under strong internal and international criticism for suppression of dissent, for corruption, and for refusal to abandon one-party rule. In December he agreed to new multiparty elections in 1992, but critics still questioned whether they would be fair.

In Rwanda, rebel forces opposing President Juvénal Habyarimana clashed with government troops, despite Habyarimana's agreement to schedule elections.

**West and Central Africa.** In French-speaking countries, a wave of demands for democracy reached a peak during the year. Mali leader Moussa Traoré was ousted in March, after violent confrontations. However, the changeover in Congo, from a Marxist-oriented regime to a pluralistic one under interim Prime Minister Andre Milongo, was peaceful. In August a national conference in Niger stripped power from President Ali Seybou and placed Andre Salifou at the head of a transitional government. There were also several attempts to restore the military regime in Togo. A move toward democratic reform proceeded in Benin, where the prime minister and former opposition leader, Nicephore Soglo, won election against incumbent President Mathieu Kérékou.

government and the rebel group Renamo repeatedly stalled.

In Zambia, President Kenneth Kaunda was ousted by trade union leader Frederick Chiluba in multiparty elections in November. Kaunda was blamed for economic problems. He made a graceful exit.

**Horn of Africa.** The Horn of Africa saw its most dramatic changes in decades, with the overthrow of Somali leader Muhammad Siad Barre in January and then of Ethiopia's Mengistu Haile Mariam at the end of May. Mengistu fled the Ethiopian capital as troops of the Tigre People's Liberation Front advanced and resistance by government forces collapsed; the TPLF, a coalition based primarily in Tigre province, had been fighting a guerrilla war for greater regional autonomy. In the disputed territory of Eritrea, the Eritrean People's Libera-

A prodemocracy movement in Cameroon faced resistance from President Paul Biya, but he did agree late in the year to hold multiparty elections.

Most active in resisting the prodemocracy currents was Zaire's Mobutu Sese Seko. Despite agreement to a national conference in August and even to a coalition government in October, Mobutu continued to cling to power. Foreigners were evacuated as indiscipline within government security forces mounted. Much of the country's economic infrastructure was destroyed by looting. While Belgium and France supported opposition demands that Mobutu leave the country, the United States held out hope for a compromise government bringing Mobutu together with some opposition figures.

In Liberia, prolonged negotiations between Liberian groups and West African states led to a November agreement for disarmament of the rebel forces that had controlled much of the countryside. The agreement also provided for maintenance of order by the West African peacekeeping force until a new Liberian government is elected.

**North Africa.** In Algerian parliamentary elections on December 26, the fundamentalist Islamic Salvation Front won a majority in nearly 200 of the 430 races, securing those seats, and was ahead in about 150 others, with a runoff election scheduled for mid-January 1992. The secular ruling National Liberation Front secured only 15 seats in the December elections. Islamic fundamentalists thus appeared, at year's end, assured of a substantial majority in the new Parliament. In neighboring Western Sahara, a United Nations plan finally resulted in a cease-fire in September between Saharan rebels and Moroccan troops. A UN-observed referendum to decide the territory's status was planned.

See also separate articles on many of the individual countries mentioned.     W.M.

**AGRICULTURE AND FOOD SUPPLIES.** As the Soviet Union struggled during 1991 to keep food distribution systems from collapsing, U.S. corn and wheat farmers were stymied by drought.

**Food Problems.** Although the world grain harvest was slightly below 1990's, it was enough, when combined with adequate stockpiles, to meet food needs in most of the industrialized world, with the dramatic exception of many of the republics of the Soviet Union. The collapse of the centrally directed Communist economy (and, by year's end, of the union itself) brought Western nations together to provide food imports on a scale reminiscent of that needed to deal with African famines in the

*Citizens of Mogadishu, Somalia's capital, survey the extensive damage that was left after rebel forces entered the city and forced the exile of President Muhammad Siad Barre in January.*

*Fish farming has grown impressively in recent years in Atlantic Canada, where the high tides in the Bay of Fundy provide nearly ideal conditions for commercial salmon farms like this one in St. John, New Brunswick.*

1970s. The United States granted $3.1 billion in government credit guarantees to the Soviet Union to import grain and feed. Western Europe, Japan, and the United States agreed in principle to provide credit and food donations totaling $10 to $12 billion, as well as grain and protein meal for livestock feed.

The main Soviet food problems were two-fold: first, bad weather diminished the grain harvest to 175 million metric tons, compared with 1990's near-record 235 million metric tons; and second, the state grain-buying apparatus was unable to get enough grain from farms to mills or livestock operations. The wheat harvest was off 28 percent, and the feed-grain output fell 25 percent. Some farms withheld grain, others bartered or sold for higher prices, and many republics prevented grain from moving outside their borders. U.S. Department of Agriculture (USDA) experts on the Soviet Union expected that Soviet government agencies would procure only 40 million metric tons of grain in 1991, only slightly more than half of normal.

While fruits and vegetables appeared adequate or, in some regions, in surplus, Western experts and Soviet officials noted shortages of meat, bread, potatoes, eggs, sugar, and milk. Much of the shortfall was expected to be made up by commercial imports, financed by Western banks and governments, while direct food donations were expected to be minimal.

Elsewhere in the world, slightly better crops as compared to 1990 only partly relieved sub-Saharan Africa's famine. The USDA expected that international food aid in 1992 would be about the same as the previous year's 3.6 million metric tons. Donated food was expected once more to fall short of need.

**World Output.** Sharply lower Soviet, U.S., and Chinese harvests were responsible for a projected 4.8 percent decline in world grain production and an expected decline of about 6 percent in grain stocks. Although grain harvests rebounded throughout Europe, in the United States greater planted acreage was unable to offset the effects of drought. World output of oilseeds (soybeans, rapeseed, cottonseed, flaxseed) gained slightly over 1990; cotton production was up 4.4 percent; and world sugar production was forecast to set a record.

**Trade Negotiations.** Major agricultural exporters faced off in the fifth straight year of a stalemate in efforts to negotiate more open food and agricultural trading rules. A ministerial-level meeting of more than 100 nations was called in late 1990 to ratify a new charter for international trade rules under the auspices of the General Agreement on Tariffs and Trade (GATT). It broke up in failure when the European Community, supported by Japan, refused to accede to demands by the United States, Australia, Canada, and other agricultural exporters to slash agricultural supports and phase out agricultural export subsidies. In December 1991 the GATT director general presented a sweeping plan to break the stalemate by, among other actions, cutting subsidies to farmers worldwide.

**United States.** At a projected 1.98 billion bushels, U.S. wheat production was down 28 percent from 1990. The corn harvest, estimated at 7.48 billion bushels, was down 5.5 percent, and soybean output of 1.93 billion bushels was up fractionally. The U.S. cotton crop of 17.7 million bales, up 14 percent from 1990, was the largest since 1937. Drought struck the eastern Corn Belt in July and early August, reducing the yields of corn and soybeans, but rain later in the year prevented a disastrous crop shortfall.

The USDA estimated consumption of red meat (beef, pork, and lamb) and poultry at 216 pounds per capita, up 2.46 percent from 1990, and forecast a gain of nearly 3 percent for 1992. Red meat production was estimated at 39.4 billion pounds, compared with 1990's 38.6 billion pounds, while poultry output was estimated at 24.9 billion pounds, up from 23.6 billion pounds the year before. The USDA forecast that 1991 milk production would decline fractionally to 148 billion pounds, due chiefly to declining milk prices.

The USDA count of 2.1 million farms as of June 1, 1991, down from 2.44 million ten years earlier, demonstrated the continuing trend toward fewer but larger farms. The largest 2 percent of the farm units (those with sales of $500,000 or greater) farmed 13.5 percent of all U.S. farmland. People who lived on farms made up 1.9 percent of the U.S. population in 1990; census data showed that the 674 most "farm-dependent" counties lost 4.6 percent of their population during the 1980s.

After 1990's record cash farm income of $59.7 billion, an estimate by the USDA in October forecast 1991 cash farm income in the range of $54 to $59 billion, largely because of lower prices of livestock. Farm real estate

prices increased for the fourth consecutive year, to an average of $682 per acre.

**Europe.** With both food exports and food stocks on the rise, farmers in Western Europe objected to efforts to reduce price support programs and permit more imports from newly democratized Eastern European countries.

**Canada.** Wheat production was up 1 percent, but other grain output fell. The federal and provincial governments introduced emergency price and income relief programs for grain and oilseed producers who claimed they were victims of the price-depressing U.S.-EC wheat trade war. A devastating potato virus affected production in the Maritime Provinces.

**Asia and Australia.** China's grain harvest fell around 4 percent, chiefly because of a decline in feed grain production, while India and other Asian producers saw production hold even or increase. Thailand, which recovered from a 1990 drought, made major gains, but Australia saw wheat production off 29 percent from the previous year as the planted area shrank and bad weather reduced yields.

**Biotechnology.** Consumers of the future could see fresher fruit and vegetables—even flowers—all year round because of a genetic engineering discovery at a laboratory operated by the USDA and the University of California in Albany, Calif. An experimental tomato was bred to continue growing on the vine but not ripen or age. The tomato produces no ethylene, a gas that ripens and ultimately rots the fruit of many plants. Crops that do not produce ethylene could be shipped and stored at room temperature and ripened with an application of ethylene gas when ready for sale. At present, up to half of all fresh produce harvested in the United States is lost to spoilage, much of that due to ethylene.

**Fisheries.** The 1991 world commercial fishing catch was expected to just equal the 1990 total of 100 million metric tons live weight, indicating a continued leveling off in yearly catches. Further increases to supply the accelerating consumer demand for fish must come primarily from a restructuring of national fishery management systems or from fish farming (the cultivation of fish for sale or conservation). The world's oceanic commons, which are being freely exploited by fishing fleets competing with each other, are substantially over-fished and are producing smaller amounts of traditional stocks than they would with en-forceable regulations that allowed for effective reproduction and growth of the fish.

Aquacultural or fish farm production of food species in fresh and estuarine waters world-wide has been increasing at annual rates of about 20 percent for carp, salmon, and trout; nearly 30 percent for shrimp; and 40 percent for sea scallops. The traditional farm opera-tions for marine shellfish continue to expand but at less rapid rates. Much of the expansion has been occurring in China and Japan.

Marine recreational anglers in the United States caught about 270 million fin fish weigh-ing about 170 million pounds on an estimated 40 million fishing trips in 1990. The major species included rockfish, sea bass, tuna, mackerel, and bluefish.

W.F.R. (Fisheries) & J.C.W.

**ALABAMA.** See STATISTICS OF THE WORLD.

**ALASKA.** See STATISTICS OF THE WORLD.

**ALBANIA.** The political monopoly wielded by the Albanian Party of Labor (APL, or the Communist Party) since 1944 ended in 1991, as Albania joined other former Eastern Euro-pean Communist states in embracing political pluralism.

**Initial Reforms.** In late 1990, after student demonstrations and violence, Albanian Presi-dent Ramiz Alia granted demands for opposi-tion parties; the Democratic Party emerged, followed by others. Alia also replaced conser-vative APL leaders with young reform-minded Communists and induced Nexhmije Hoxha, widow of Albania's longtime dictator, Enver Hoxha, to resign as president of the Demo-cratic Front (a political organization controlled by the APL). After a massive student-led rally in Tirane on February 20, 1991, Alia dismissed the cabinet of Adil Carcani, a holdover from the Hoxha era, and appointed a government headed by Fatos Nano, from APL's reformist faction, to remain until spring elections.

In Albania's first multiparty election since 1924, the APL won 169 of the 250 seats in the People's Assembly, while the Democratic Party elected 75 members, and two minor par-ties captured the rest. Alia was defeated in his first contested bid for office.

**Aftermath.** The new People's Assembly offi-cially renamed the country the Republic of Albania. Despite his defeat at the polls, Alia was elected president of the republic by the assembly. He reappointed Nano as prime minister, and on May 12 the new cabinet re-ceived the assembly's vote of confidence. However, the anti-Communist independent trade union organization instigated a general strike, the nation was gripped by economic paralysis, and on June 4 the Nano cabinet re-signed. President Alia then appointed a gov-ernment of "national stability" headed by Ylli Bufi, another APL reformist. Albania's first non-Communist government since 1944, it was empowered to serve until the next elec-tions, planned for mid-1992.

At the Tenth Congress of the APL, delegates repudiated the policies of Enver Hoxha and expelled several former close associates of the dictator. They also changed the party's name to the Socialist Party and elected Nano as party leader. But after the congress, a coalition of major opposition parties pressed for President Alia's resignation and for legal proceedings against the Hoxha family and others for cor-ruption. In response the government arrested several former Communist leaders, including Nexhmije Hoxha.

On December 4 the Democrats quit the cab-inet, saying that the Socialists were hindering reforms and delaying elections. Three days later, amid riots over food and fuel shortages in which 40 were killed, Prime Minister Bufi re-signed and was replaced by Vilson Ahmeti. Late in the month, Alia responded to continued opposition pressure by moving up the elections to March 1, 1992.

**The Economy.** The nation's combined indus-trial and agricultural output declined 50 per-cent in the 12 months ending in July 1991. Unemployment continued to rise, and the in-flation rate was projected to be at least 30 per-cent. Albania's foreign debt soared, and food production fell dramatically. Italy, especially concerned by a vast influx of Albanian refu-gees, donated food, medicine, and economic aid. In July the United States airlifted 125 tons of military rations left over from the Persian Gulf War, and in August the European Com-munity offered $2.4 million in emergency aid.

**Foreign Relations.** In March, U.S.-Albanian relations were restored after a 52-year hiatus. British-Albanian ties resumed in June, and Albania later established diplomatic relations with Israel, Cyprus, and the Vatican. Albania was also admitted to the Conference for Security and Cooperation in Europe and established relations with the European Community. In October Albania was granted membership in the International Monetary Fund and the World Bank. The Albanian regime was, however, embarrassed by massive illegal emigration of its citizens to Greece and to Italy.

See STATISTICS OF THE WORLD.          N.C.P.

**ALBERTA.** See STATISTICS OF THE WORLD.

**ALGERIA.** A breakdown of civil order led President Chadli Benjedid to declare martial law on June 5, 1991, for the second time in three years; the crisis was triggered by the approach of national legislative elections that promised a showdown between the former single party, the National Liberation Front (FLN), and its fundamentalist rival, the Islamic Salvation Front (FIS), which had been victorious in 1990 local elections. Elections were postponed; when the first round of elections eventually took place in December, the FIS took a commanding lead.

**Political Unrest.** The parliamentary elections, originally scheduled for June 27, were the first contests for national office held under a multiparty system since Algeria's independence in 1962. They were initially planned under an election law passed by the FLN-controlled National Assembly, which opposition parties criticized as gerrymandering. The FIS took its protest to the streets at the end of May; when the government took measures to clear the streets, violence broke out, causing Benjedid to declare martial law. At the behest of the army, he appointed a new prime minister, Sid Ahmed Ghozali, who pledged "free and clean" parliamentary elections.

Despite such concessions, violence flared again at the end of June. The Army arrested two of the FIS's most prominent leaders, and announced they would be tried for incitement to rebellion. Several hundred other party activists were also taken into custody. Meanwhile, Ghozali appointed a transitional cabinet and held talks regarding procedures for a fair election, pushing a bill revising the electoral law through the National Assembly.

**Elections.** In the first round of elections, held on December 26, the FIS fell just 28 seats short of a majority. It was expected to win these easily in the second round, scheduled for January 16, 1992. But, while the election was widely seen as free and fair, there were indications that something might be done to prevent the FIS from gaining victory.

**Economy.** In September, Algeria's monetary authorities, hobbled by a $25 billion debt, devalued the dinar. In December, the Parliament agreed to Ghozali's proposal that Algeria reopen its oil fields to foreign companies as a means of raising some $7 billion. Earlier in the year the government had announced the establishment of a stock market as a step toward a market-oriented economy.

**On the World Stage.** The war against Iraq aroused great anger among Algerians. In postwar diplomacy, Algeria emphasized the right of the Palestinians to representation in any Middle East peace conference. Algeria gave its full support to UN peacekeeping efforts in the Western Sahara.

See STATISTICS OF THE WORLD.          R.A.M.

**AMERICAN SAMOA.** See STATISTICS OF THE WORLD.

**ANGOLA.** A cease-fire initialed on May 1, 1991, between the government and the former guerrilla opposition Unita (National Union for the Total Independence of Angola) brought peace to Angola for the first time since independence in 1975.

**Peace Settlement.** The agreement concluded at peace talks in Portugal, after more than one year of grueling negotiations, laid out highly detailed provisions for ending the civil war, including a cease-fire to begin on May 15, monitoring by a Joint Political Military Commission and foreign observers, merger of the two contending armies into a nonpartisan national army, and elections to take place in late 1992.

Concessions which made possible the final accord included the government's agreement to shorten the period before elections and Unita's consent to a merger of the armies before elections. These measures allayed both the government's fear that Unita would use its

# ANGOLA

guerrilla army to intimidate voters and Unita's fear that the government would delay elections and pressure voters into supporting the ruling MPLA (Popular Movement for the Liberation of Angola).

Initial implementation of the cease-fire was successful, as joint teams began de-mining roads, and people and goods began moving freely in most areas of the country. However, there were delays in regrouping troops to assembly points, in release of some prisoners, and in beginning the merger of the two armies. **Political Developments.** The MPLA made significant adjustments in its top leadership and party platform at a special congress in April, abandoning a Marxist orientation in favor of a democratic socialist position, with a strong emphasis on the free market and political pluralism.

More than ten new parties registered under a new multiparty law. None immediately garnered widespread support, but they drew on strong popular feelings against abuses by both sides during the war, disillusionment with the incumbent regime's serious economic failures, and fear of the brutal tactics employed by Unita's guerrilla army. Meanwhile, Unita held its own congress in March, reelecting Jonas Savimbi as president.

**Foreign Relations.** Although both the United States and the Soviet Union reportedly kept the peace agreement's injunction to stop military supplies to either side, the United States continued covert "nonlethal" aid to Unita and pledged not to establish formal diplomatic relations with Angola until after the 1992 elections. The last contingent of Cuban troops left Angola on schedule at the end of May.

Angolan President José Eduardo dos Santos visited Washington, D.C., for the first time in September, obtaining a personal pledge from President George Bush of U.S. neutrality in the upcoming elections. Savimbi, visiting Washington in October, argued successfully that the United States should maintain sanctions against Angola until after the elections.

**Economic Developments.** The Angolan government's structural adjustment program, carried out with World Bank assistance, gained momentum with a devaluation of the kwanza, tight budgetary controls, and plans for further devaluations and privatization of state firms. But implementation of reforms was still slowed by bureaucratic inertia and by fears of political backlash.

The increase in freedom of movement following the peace agreement facilitated relief convoys for up to 800,000 people seriously threatened by famine, but there was still an estimated food aid deficit of 130,000 tons for the 1990-1991 season.

*See* STATISTICS OF THE WORLD.     W.M.

*After 16 years of war the government of Angola, represented by President José Eduardo dos Santos (left), agreed to a peace pact with the former guerrilla opposition, led by Jonas Savimbi (right). Overseeing the signing in Lisbon was Portuguese Prime Minister Aníbal Cavaço Silva.*

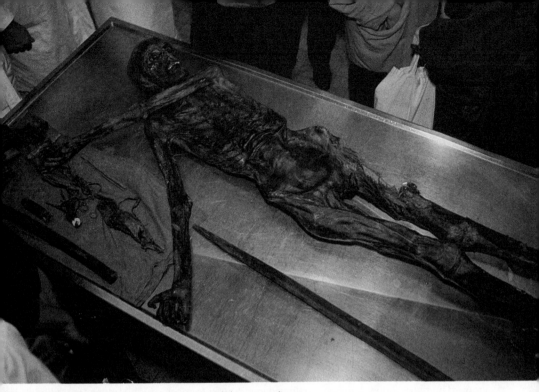

*The "Iceman" is what the Austrian press named the extraordinary find made by two Alpine hikers—the remarkably intact mummified body of a man who died on a glacier at least 4,600 years ago. He was clad in a leather jacket and boots and surrounded by tools, trinkets, and weapons, including a copper-headed ax.*

**ANTHROPOLOGY.** In 1991 anthropologists felt concern over threats to world food supplies and to vanishing populations of indigenous peoples, coupled with excitement over discoveries about prehistoric ancestors of the human race.

**World's Food Supply at Risk.** Worldwide, farmers are planting modern, high-yield crops for market, abandoning traditional varieties of wheat, corn, potatoes, millet, and rice their ancestors cultivated for generations. The resulting genetic uniformity of agriculture threatens the human food supply, according to a report by University of Georgia anthropologist Robert E. Rhoades in the April issue of *National Geographic*. Genetically similar plants are identically vulnerable to pests, disease, and drought. Rhoades stressed the need to rediscover and protect hardy old strains of germ plasm (the genetic material that dictates each plant's development) to help ensure future harvests. Rhoades and his colleagues have identified regions on every continent, except Antarctica, where pockets of traditional agriculture with genetically diverse food crops still exist for scientific study and preservation.

**A Body From the Neolithic Age.** The discovery in late September of a remarkably well-preserved body of a man who apparently died some 4,600 years ago is expected to give scientists valuable insights into life in the Neolithic Age. The body—clad in what scientists believe to be a well-insulated leather coat and boots and surrounded by late Neolithic paraphernalia, including a backpack, a copper-headed ax, a flint lighter, kindling, a bow, and more than a dozen arrows—was found encased in ice by two German mountain climbers in the Tyrolean Alps, which run between Austria and Italy.

The appearance of the body an estimated 46 centuries after the man's death was attributed to the partial thawing of Alpine glaciers after several years of above-average temperatures. The "Iceman," as he was dubbed by the Austrian press, was flown to the University of Innsbruck, Austria, for scientific tests, including radiocarbon dating to determine the exact age of the body.

**Hominid Finds in Ethiopia.** Two U.S. research teams reported fossil findings in Ethiopia that might push back the date for the existence of *Australopithecus afarensis*, the earliest true hominids (humanlike beings) known. According to an article in the March 22 issue of *Science*, John Fleagle and Solomon Yirga of the State University of New York at Stony Brook found an assortment of *A. afarensis* teeth at Fejej dating back 3.7-4.4 million years, the oldest dates yet recorded for these hominids. And Donald C. Johanson of the Institute of Human Origins in Berkeley, Calif., discoverer of the previously oldest-known hominid remains (the small female *A. afarensis* known as "Lucy"), announced that his team had found the bones of at least 15 *A. afarensis* individuals at Hadar, site of the Lucy find. Among Johanson's newest discoveries is a large, deeply grooved humerus (upper arm bone) believed to have been attached to very strong shoulder muscles, a clue that *A. afarensis*, who was thought to have been exclusively a ground dweller, may also have spent at least some time in trees.

**Yanomami Indian People.** In the mid-1980s, at nearly 10,000 strong, the Yanomami were the largest group of indigenous people living in the Amazon rain forest of Brazil. Yet by early 1991, a fact-finding commission sent by the American Anthropological Association (AAA) reported that the Yanomami could become extinct before the year 2010. The anthropologists found that many Yanomami were sick or starving because gold and tin miners had polluted their water supplies, scared away game, and left behind pools of stagnant water that attracted malaria-carrying mosquitoes.

The AAA commission, led by University of Chicago anthropologist Terence Turner, brought media attention and political pressure to bear on Brazilian President Fernando Collor de Mello, who responded by expelling all miners from Yanomami lands and providing medical assistance to deal with the malaria epidemic. In November, Collor de Mello designated a portion of Amazonian rain forest as a Yanomami reserve. This area, plus a

smaller park just across the border in Venezuela, provides a 68,331-square-mile protected homeland for the tribe.                D.G.

**ANTIGUA AND BARBUDA.** See STATISTICS OF THE WORLD.

**ARABIAN PENINSULA.** The nations of the Arabian Peninsula experienced a turbulent year in 1991, as the Persian Gulf War and the far-flung scandal of the Bank of Credit and Commerce International (BCCI) focused worldwide attention on the region.

**Gulf War.** Diplomatic efforts by countries in the peninsula to secure Iraq's withdrawal from Kuwait, which it had invaded and occupied in August 1990, continued through early 1991. At the December 1990 summit of the Gulf Cooperation Council, leaders of Bahrain, Kuwait, Oman, Qatar, Saudi Arabia, and the United Arab Emirates (UAE) unanimously demanded Iraq's withdrawal from Kuwait. Oman, alone among the GCC members, and Yemen, Iraq's only ally in the peninsula, continued to receive high-ranking Iraqi officials in hopes of a negotiated settlement. Yemen also sought compromise through its seat on the Security Council in the United Nations.

Not counting Kuwait and Saudi Arabia, the GCC states contributed some 10,000 ground troops as well as ships and airplanes to the U.S.-led alliance against Iraq, with Qatari military units the most active once combat began in January. Six soldiers from the UAE were killed during the assault that achieved the liberation of Kuwait. Qatar also hosted U.S., Canadian, and French fighter planes, pilots, and support staff. Another 8,000 allied troops and a British air force squadron were based in Bahrain, which served as the center for allied naval operations; American K-135 air tankers and a British Jaguar squadron flew out of bases in Oman; and the UAE provided some $3.6 billion toward U.S. war expenses.

Immediately following the war, American officials began discussions with their Gulf allies about an increased U.S. presence in the region. In October, Bahrain signed an agreement allowing the United States to pre-position military equipment there; a similar agreement already existed with Oman. In August the U.S. government agreed to sell 20 Apache attack helicopters to the UAE and 8 to Bahrain.

Yemen's support of Iraq during the crisis cost the newly unified state dearly. The United States cut a proposed $30.5 million humanitarian aid program to $2.9 million for the 1990-1991 fiscal year. Saudi Arabia's expulsion of a million Yemeni workers in late 1990 created hardship, and the UN-imposed economic boycott of Iraq greatly reduced crude oil supplies to the Aden refinery.

**BCCI Scandal.** Sheikh Zayed bin Sultan al-Nahyan, ruler of Abu Dhabi, and his government found themselves in the center of the BCCI scandal when it was revealed that "senior" government officials of the sheikhdom, which controlled a 77.4 percent share of the bank and was the site of its headquarters, had been paid to buy BCCI shares since 1986 and had known about the fraud going on within the bank as early as 1990. In May the government agreed to refinance some $3 billion in bad loans made by BCCI and promised a reorganization of the bank. Despite these efforts, authorities in the seven countries with the largest BCCI operations on July 5 seized the bank's assets on their territory. Later in the month a British judge ordered the Bank of England to delay liquidation of the British operation so that Abu Dhabi could complete its reorganization plan. Abu Dhabi agreed to establish a £50 million fund to cover borrowings by British depositors and salaries for BCCI employees during this period. In September more than two dozen former BCCI officials were detained in Abu Dhabi.

By October, Abu Dhabi's efforts to rescue BCCI appeared doomed to failure, as most of the bank's staff in the UAE were put on three-month unpaid leave and most of the staff at BCCI headquarters were dismissed. According to a November report, BCCI allegedly stole more than $2 billion from Sheikh Zayed's personal account.

**New Yemeni Constitution.** The citizens of Yemen were scheduled to vote on a new constitution in March, but the vote was postponed until May after conservative Muslims, who objected to a provision that the sharia, the code of Islamic law, would be the "main source" rather than the sole source of Yemeni law, called for a boycott and organized street protests. Half the registered voters partici-

pated in the referendum, in which the constitution was overwhelmingly approved.

See STATISTICS OF THE WORLD. See also KUWAIT; SAUDI ARABIA.                    C.H.A.

**ARAB LEAGUE.** See INTERNATIONAL CONFERENCES.

**ARCHAEOLOGY.** In 1991, events showed that archaeology is very much a part of the present. From the threat posed to ancient ruins by the Persian Gulf War to the discovery of new sites and the exposure of forgeries, archaeology has been in the headlines.

**Persian Gulf War.** With the outbreak of hostilities in the Persian Gulf, concern mounted for the region's archaeological treasures. Iraq engaged in archaeological blackmail to further its military policy by parking MIG fighters next to the ziggurat (ancient Mesopotamian temple tower) at Ur, assuming that the coalition forces would not risk destroying the monument by attacking the fighters. Earlier, Iraqi forces had plundered Kuwait's national museum and taken many artifacts to Iraq; by late in the year only some had been returned.

The extent of damage to Iraqi archaeological sites as a result of the air war was uncertain. Early reports indicated damage to Islamic ruins at Samarra, Parthian ruins at Hatra, the Iraq Museum and the 12th-13th century Mustansiriyah School in Baghdad, and the Ctesiphon Arch outside Baghdad. Later reports suggested, however, that damage was limited.

**Guatemala Ban.** At the Guatemalan government's request, the United States imposed an emergency import ban on Maya artifacts from the Peten region. The U.S. President's Cultural Property Advisory Committee found that the record of the Lowland Maya civilization was in jeopardy from unbridled looting; of the more than 2,200 archaeological sites in the Peten, nearly 85 percent of those inspected had been looted.

**Dead Sea Scrolls.** In September the Huntington Library in San Marino, Calif., created a stir when it agreed to allow all scholars access to its virtually complete set of photographs of the so-called Dead Sea Scrolls. It was one of a series of key developments involving research into the famous scrolls, discovered in caves and ruins near the Dead Sea between 1947 and 1956 and consisting of some 800 Hebrew

# ARCHAEOLOGY

and Aramaic documents bearing on the formative years of Christianity and modern Judaism. Access to copies had long been limited to a small group of international editors designated by the Israeli Antiquities Authority. In response to the Huntington move, the Israeli Antiquities Authority, in October, agreed to let other researchers examine scroll photographs elsewhere, but "for personal research only" and not for publishing a text of the scrolls. These restrictions were later dropped. Meanwhile, two American scholars, who gained access to photographs of what they believed to be all the unpublished scrolls, announced plans to publish them in a two-volume edition.

The Antiquities Authority had earlier agreed

*Researchers around the world suddenly gained access to the Dead Sea Scrolls, a collection of manuscripts and fragments dating from the second century B.C. to the first century A.D. Discovered in the 1940s and 1950s, the scrolls had for decades been under the control of a small group of scholars—until September, when the Huntington Library decided to make available its photographs of the documents.*

to allow carbon-14 determinations—using a new, nondestructive method—to aid in dating the Dead Sea Scrolls. A Swiss laboratory in Zurich tested 14 manuscripts, which proved to date from the mid-second century B.C. to the late first century A.D.

**Pipeline Fine.** Transcontinental Gas Pipeline Corporation agreed in May to pay $25.5 million to the U.S. Treasury and the state of Alabama in connection with damage to 48 archaeological sites in Alabama during the construction of gas pipelines. Although Transcontinental had hired an archaeological consulting firm to survey the 139 miles of routes, it constructed the pipelines before the survey was completed and before Alabama's State Historic Preservation Office could review the findings. Of the 77 sites on the pipeline routes, 49 were listed on the National Register of Historic Places, and 48 of these sites were damaged or destroyed during construction.

**Getty Kouros.** A marble sculpture thought to be the work of a late sixth-century B.C. Greek artist may be a modern forgery. The object—a kouros, or stylized statue of a naked youth—was purchased in 1985 by the J. Paul Getty Museum for a reported $9 million from a Swiss art dealer despite some initial suspicions. Papers accompanying the kouros said it had been acquired by a Geneva physician in 1930 from a Greek dealer. Later the museum learned these documents were fraudulent.

More doubts were raised when the torso of a second kouros, obviously a fake, surfaced in Basel in 1990. According to a rumor, both the Getty kouros and the second torso were produced in the early 1980s in a Rome workshop. To compare the two, the museum purchased the second torso, and conducted a series of studies that indicated similarities. The new evidence suggests to some scholars that both are modern works.

**German-owned Treasures Returned.** While most archaeological treasures and art works taken from European museums by Nazi troops were recovered after World War II, the whereabouts of many objects that later disappeared from occupied Germany have remained unknown. It now appears that many were acquired by the advancing Soviet army. Chief among these is the so-called Priam's Treasure,

*Several hoards of Celtic gold and silver artifacts, uncovered in 1990 and 1991 at Ken Hill in southeastern England, were declared the property of the crown and turned over to the British Museum. The discovery was said to be the biggest of its kind in Britain in the 20th century.*

a collection of gold jewelry discovered by Heinrich Schliemann at Troy. The jewelry, which is of Early Bronze Age date—and is unrelated to the Trojan King Priam, Homeric Troy, or the Trojan War—disappeared from Berlin at the end of the war. Soviet officials, admitting that the jewelry was in the Pushkin Museum, arranged for its return to Germany.

**Celtic Hoard.** At an inquest in March, a large collection of Celtic gold and silver first uncovered in August 1990, with the aid of a metal detector, at Ken Hill in southeastern England was declared the property of the crown. Following C. A. Hodder's discovery of the initial hoard, the British Museum, with the Norwich Castle Museum and Norfolk Archaeological Unit, had excavated the site and found several additional hoards—containing hundreds of rings, bracelets and other artifacts, apparently buried around 70 B.C. Archaeologists suspect that the site may have been the treasury of a Celtic tribe.                                    M.R.

**ARCHITECTURE.** During 1991 some important buildings were completed and work on others was begun—although architecture in the United States that year was most notable for a palpable downturn, and many architects were unemployed.

**Museums.** The Solomon R. Guggenheim Museum took the most daring steps. A major renovation and expansion of its flagship Frank Lloyd Wright building in New York was in progress under the direction of the local architectural firm Gwathmey Siegel. The addition features a huge vertical rectangular volume set behind Wright's famous spiral showcase, a startling geometric juxtaposition that caused an outcry from neighborhood preservation groups. The project was also plagued by delays, attributed to the special quality of the building materials and unusual construction methods, as well as to changes in plan resulting from study of the original plans. Late in the year, reopening of the museum was postponed until May 1992.

The most celebrated museum venture was Robert Venturi and Denise Scott Brown's seemingly self-effacing addition to London's National Gallery of Art, which opened during the summer to praise and controversy. The addition, known as the Sainsbury Wing, houses Early Renaissance art in a structure that pays homage to Sir John Soane's 1814 Dulwich Picture Gallery—as well as to Mies van der Rohe. Venturi also designed the tile and terra-cotta ornamented Seattle Art Museum, which opened in December.

Canadian architect Moshe Safdie's vast expansion of Montréal's Museum of Fine Arts opened in October, neatly interweaving new construction and a grand entrance with its existing rowhouse neighborhood.

**Design Competitions.** Important competition winners included Spanish architect Rafael Moneo, for the Palazzo del Cinema in Venice; Kuwabara Payne McKenna Blumberg for the Library of Queen's University in Kingston, Ontario; and Michael Graves and the Klipp

73

The Sainsbury wing, an addition to London's National Gallery of Art, attracted attention for its sheer restraint, as it merged unobtrusively with its neighbor and blended into Trafalgar Square (left). Its interior (shown at right) allows for wide spacing of the paintings, and the high ceilings permit natural light to flood in from above.

Partnership for a new public library in Denver. In New York, Spanish architect Santiago Calatrava won an international competition to design a so-called Bioshelter for the city's huge Cathedral of St. John the Divine. Responding to the cathedral's predominantly Gothic form, Calatrava proposed a series of vaulted glass-and-steel spaces attached to the exterior, with rows of trees along the roofline of the nave.

**Environmental Emphasis.** After four years of construction, eight scientists moved into Biosphere 2, a 3.15-acre concrete, glass, and steel enclosure of 7 million cubic feet in southern Arizona designed by Sarbid Corporation to mimic the Earth's climatic zones, from rain forest to desert, in miniature.

Architects were also paying increasing attention to the ecological effects of materials. In retrofitting an eight-story, century-old George Post building in lower Manhattan for the National Audubon Society, the Croxton Collaborative used new heating, cooling, lighting, and glazing technology to reduce energy needs dramatically. In addition, the architects installed recycling chutes, called for recycled materials wherever possible, and used natural-fiber carpeting and sealed wood products to reduce the volatile organic compounds, or VOCs, that environmental scientists say contribute to poor air quality in many older office buildings.

**Other New Buildings.** Among other noteworthy new buildings was the Oregon Convention Center in Portland, designed by the Portland firm of Zimmer Gunsul Frasca, which was awarded the AIA's 1991 Firm Award. The hallmark of the center's design, inspired by a 1948 Frank Lloyd Wright suspension bridge in Pittsburgh, is a pair of glass and steel towers at either end of the complex that rise 250 feet above its roofline. In Chicago, a new Comiskey Park by Hellmuth, Obata & Kassabaum's Sports Facilities Group supplanted the beloved Chicago White Sox park of the same name at the beginning of the baseball season. The stadium received mixed reviews: praise for its excellent sightlines and intimate feel, criticism for its steep upper deck and "suburban" isolation amid acres of parking spaces. In Tokyo, a 33-story twin-tower City Hall complex by Kenzo Tange brought an impressive new feature to the city's generally low skyline.

**Exhibitions, Prizes, Personalities.** Two Japanese architects were the subjects of major traveling exhibitions at American museums. The life's work of 60-year-old Arata Isozaki was displayed at the San Francisco Museum of Contemporary Art, even as several of his projects were moving ahead or reaching completion in the United States. A show devoted to the work of Tadao Ando opened in October at New York's Museum of Modern Art.

Charles W. Moore won the AIA's Gold Medal, and his firm received the AIA Twenty-Five Year Award for the design of the Condominiums at Sea Ranch in northern California. Robert Venturi won architecture's highest international honor, the Pritzker Prize. But the exclusion of Denise Scott Brown, his wife and longtime partner, from the award raised questions about attitudes toward women within the profession. On the other hand, Susan Maxman was elected first vice president of the AIA, putting her in line to become, in 1993, the body's first female president.

**Urban Planning.** The Miami firm of Andrés Duany and Elizabeth Plater-Zyberk continued to plan new towns based on principles of "traditional neighborhood design." New Duany Plater-Zyberk towns were begun in Orange Beach and Blount Springs, Ala., and in Vero Beach, Fla.

Perhaps the most controversial urban planning debate concerned the 72 acres of land on the West Side of Manhattan owned by developer Donald Trump. Lean economic times in general and Trump's in particular forced him to yield to critics who called his original designs grandiose; he hired Skidmore, Owings & Merrill to work on a smaller-scale proposal.

**Preservation.** As the World Monuments Fund set in motion efforts to develop a master plan to preserve the Cambodian temple city of Angkor, heavy war-caused destruction of historic sites occurred in Yugoslavia and in the Euphrates River valley of Iraq. Among important preservation projects completed in the United States were two historic residences: Henry Hobson Richardson's Stoughton House in Cambridge, Mass., and Frank Lloyd Wright's Dana House in Springfield, Ill.          P.S.

**ARGENTINA.** The year 1991 began with military unrest and political scandal, but late in the year the government had high hopes for its new economic policies.

**Military Affairs.** When rebellious officers led an uprising in the Argentine capital during December 1990, President Carlos Saúl Menem's conciliatory relationship with the armed forces paid off: Loyal troops isolated and overwhelmed the rebels, whom the Menem government, with strong support from the officer corps, sternly punished.

Having extinguished the threat from the right, the administration announced reductions in military personnel and spending expected to put some 40 percent of the Argentine military and state security personnel out of work. The government also cut off funding for development of the controversial Cóndor II missile, a medium-range surface-to-surface ballistic missile developed by the Argentine Air Force with initial support from Iraq and Egypt. Argentina later joined Brazil in an accord allowing international inspection of their nuclear sites.

**Scandal in High Places.** Menem began the year with an attack against government corruption. Ironically, Labor Minister Jorge Triaca, slated to head the anticorruption campaign,

Soccer superstar Diego Maradona was questioned by Italian police in connection with a prostitution and drug-smuggling operation; then he tested positive for cocaine—which led to his suspension from international soccer for 15 months. Finally, he was arrested in Buenos Aires for cocaine possession and hauled off by police (he is in the center of the rear seat).

revealed in a January interview that corrupt practices had aided his personal career as a union official. This led to Triaca's dismissal and a thorough cabinet shuffle. In July, journalists uncovered evidence of bribes and kickbacks in past military procurement programs.

After years of highly publicized marital troubles, Menem's wife filed for divorce in March. Prior to that, her brother, an economic adviser to the president, had been accused of soliciting a bribe from the U.S.-controlled Swift-Armour Meat Packing Company, and her sister's ex-husband, the director of Customs at Ezeiza International Airport, had been implicated in money-laundering and drug trafficking operations funneled through the airport.

Another scandal involved soccer superstar Diego Maradona, who tested positive for cocaine and was suspended from international soccer. He was arrested by both Italian and Argentine authorities for cocaine possession, drawing suspended sentences. In October he announced plans to leave Argentina.

**Economic Growth.** Currency speculation and the failure of anti-inflation programs forced Economics Minister Antonio Erman González to resign at the end of January. But negotiations to create a common market with Brazil, Paraguay, and Uruguay ended successfully with the signing of a treaty on March 26, and a deal for the sale of Aerolineas Argentinas, the country's largest publicly owned airline, was concluded on July 4. Fiscal re-

forms also yielded returns. Sweeping payroll and employee cuts and a new currency plan, with the austral's value pegged to the dollar at a set exchange rate of 10,000 to 1, brought inflation down below 2 percent a month.

On October 31, Menem announced a sweeping deregulation of the economy. Circumventing the Congress, he issued an executive decree that, among other things, eliminated government organizations controlling production and sale of beef, grain, sugar, tobacco, and wine.

**Foreign Relations.** The Menem government's standing abroad improved through the year. Strong support for the U.S. cause in the Persian Gulf conflict, efforts to fight international drug trafficking, and active support of the U.S.-backed Brady debt plan drew praise from the Bush administration. An invitation to Menem to address a joint session of the U.S. Congress during his state visit in November reflected the improved relations between the two countries.

After a year of negotiations, the government signed an agreement with Chile in August settling 22 lingering border disputes that had nearly caused a war between the two neighbors in the recent past. Later in the year, Argentina and Great Britain reached an agreement concerning oceanic traffic around the disputed Falkland Islands.

**Electoral Victories.** Menem's Peronist party won significant victories in congressional and gubernatorial elections in San Juan and San

Luis provinces in August, then captured the governorships in all the remaining provinces in September. This result allowed the party to increase its majority in Congress.

See STATISTICS OF THE WORLD.          D.L.

**ARIZONA.** See STATISTICS OF THE WORLD.

**ARKANSAS.** See STATISTICS OF THE WORLD.

**ART.** In 1991 some major exhibitions questioned the ways in which American art has traditionally portrayed the nation's people and their histories, while retrospectives showcased such artists as Georges Seurat, Albert Bierstadt, William Johnson, and John Constable.

**Annenberg Bequest.** Publishing magnate Walter H. Annenberg left his $1 billion collection of more than 50 works from the late 19th and early 20th centuries to the Metropolitan Museum of Art in New York City. Annenberg, who had been wooed by several museums, based his decision on his belief in "strength going to strength." The Metropolitan Museum is the largest in the United States (rivaling the Louvre as the largest museum west of the Hermitage in St. Petersburg), and its Department of European Paintings, which will receive the Annenberg gift, is one of its strongest components. The gift promises to cement the Metropolitan's strengths as well as fill some gaps—

for instance, in the lack of major paintings from the end of Cézanne's and Monet's careers.

**Notable Anniversaries.** The National Gallery celebrated its half-century of existence and gave tribute to its benefactors with an exhibition entitled "Art for the Nation: Gifts in Honor of the 50th Anniversary of the National Gallery of Art." Though day-to-day operations are federally funded, the nation's art museum has relied upon philanthropic generosity ever since it was conceived and initially funded by Andrew W. Mellon. A diplomat and onetime U.S. treasury secretary, Mellon was the first of many donors who built up the museum's impressive array of works.

To mark the anniversary, Paul Mellon, a current trustee and son of Andrew W. Mellon, promised to give 31 wax sculptures by Edgar Degas; with this gift, the National Gallery will own the world's most important collection of Degas sculpture. Representing the 20th century, Richard Diebenkorn, Jim Dine, Helen Frankenthaler, Jasper Johns, Ellsworth Kelly, Roy Lichtenstein, and Robert Rauschenberg all enriched the permanent collection with pieces from their own oeuvres, which also were shown in the exhibition.

The National Gallery looked forward to the

A contemporary black artist virtually forgotten at his death in 1970, William H. Johnson was the subject of a major exhibition organized recently by the National Museum of American Art. His painting Going to Church is typical of his style and use of color.

77

*Japanese fishermen's flags made up one of the most colorful displays in a show at the Victoria and Albert Museum—part of London's "Festival of Japan," a citywide celebration of Japanese culture that included 15 separate exhibitions from various periods.*

500-year anniversary of the European discovery of the Americas in "Circa 1492: Art in the Age of Exploration." A compendium of works meant to illustrate the state of culture throughout the world in that watershed year, the exhibition included not just paintings, sculptures, prints, and decorative objects, but maps, globes, and scientific instruments as well. The show spotlighted the cultural production of Africa, Asia, the Americas, and Europe in the 15th century; thus, Yoruba terra cottas, Benin metalwork, and Aztec stone carvings shared billing with Korean porcelain, Chinese bronzes, and paintings by Japanese and European masters from Sesshu to Leonardo to Bosch. Though criticized as something of a hodgepodge, the exhibition delighted viewers, and certain sections of the show poignantly evoked cultures long since wiped out by European domination.

**Reexploring the West.** Images of the western frontier dominated two major exhibitions. "The West as America: Reinterpreting Images of the Frontier, 1820-1920" ran from March through July at the National Museum of American Art (a branch of the Smithsonian Institution) in Washington, D.C., and created a furor. A revisionist examination of images by several artists—from Frederic Remington and George Caleb Bingham to relative unknowns like Irving Couse—the exhibition highlighted ways in which American art appeared to promote the notion of Manifest Destiny (a belief in the God-given right of European Americans to seize and settle the North American continent).

A more benign view of the American West was presented in "Albert Bierstadt: Art and Enterprise," which was organized by the Brooklyn Museum in association with the National Gallery. Born in Germany, Bierstadt was brought to America as a toddler and conceived a deep passion for its broad vistas. The photos and sketches gleaned from an 1859 expedition to the Rocky Mountains served as the basis for monumental landscapes that established Bierstadt's reputation.

**Japan Comes to London.** A citywide "Festival of Japan" dominated London's art scene in the last months of 1991. Fifteen separate exhibitions were mounted, including sculpture from the Kamakura period (the 12th century to the 14th century) at the British Museum, a survey of Japanese design at the Design Museum, an exhibition of Japanese robotics at the Science Museum, and a retrospective devoted to Hokusai, a famed 19th-century printmaker, at the Royal Academy. The most sweeping exhibition, however, was "Visions of Japan" at the Victoria and Albert Museum, a wide-ranging show conceived by contemporary architect Arata Isozaki.

**Major Retrospectives.** In commemoration of Georges Seurat's untimely death 100 years ago, the Réunion des Musées Nationaux in Paris and the Metropolitan Museum of Art in New York organized a retrospective look at the artist's brief but extraordinary career. Since *Sunday Afternoon on the Grand Jatte*, Seurat's most famous painting, now in the collection of the Art Institute of Chicago, is deemed too large and too important to travel, the retrospective relied on smaller pictures, drawings, and numerous studies to evoke the range of Seurat's interests and talent. Two successful demonstrations of his investigations of color and light that figured prominently in the retrospective were the dark and somewhat eerie *Invitation to the Sideshow*, a scene of nighttime music-making, and the upbeat, warm-toned *Circus*, which features performers cavorting in a brightly lit ring.

John Constable, foremost painter of the English countryside, was the subject of an exhaustive retrospective organized by the Tate Gallery in London. Some 350 works were displayed—from the lively oil sketches Constable made outdoors, directly from nature, to the more contrived large exhibition pieces that the artist called his "ten-footers."

The Casa Buonarotti in Florence hosted an enormously popular exhibition of the works of Artemisia Gentileschi, a Roman painter of the 17th century. Another woman artist, 20th-century Russian avant-gardist Liubov Popova, was the subject of a retrospective organized by the Museum of Modern Art in New York.

The work of a heretofore underappreciated 20th-century American painter was brought to the public's attention by "Homecoming: William H. Johnson and Afro-America, 1938-1946," an exhibition mounted by the National Museum of American Art in Washington, D.C. Johnson's paintings explored contemporary and historical events and evoked the life-styles of fellow African-Americans, from sharecroppers to urbanites.

The art of Romare Bearden, another innovative chronicler of the African-American experience in the 20th-century United States, was presented in an exhibition organized by the Studio Museum in Harlem and scheduled to travel on to Chicago, Los Angeles, Atlanta, Pittsburgh, and Washington, D.C. A jazz

*Invitation to the Sideshow, a somewhat eerie scene of nighttime music-making by French painter Georges Seurat, was one of the highlights of a major retrospective of the artist's work held in Paris and New York to commemorate the centennial of his untimely death at the age of 32.*

musician as well as a visual artist, Bearden, who died in 1988, is particularly known for his work in the medium of collage.

**Contemporary Art.** A panorama of contemporary art was presented in Berlin by "Metropolis," an exhibition that included works by 72 artists from more than 20 countries and featured photographs, installations, and video displays, as well as painting and sculpture. An even broader view of the contemporary art world was provided by the 21st São Paulo Bienal in Brazil, which showed works by almost 300 artists from 50 countries. Contemporary art with roots in the cultures of sub-Sarahan Africa was the subject of "Africa Explores: 20th-Century African Art," a show launched by New York's New Museum of Contemporary Art and its Center for African Art. A presentation of work by African-born artists living both at home and abroad, it surveyed modern reactions to traditional forms and concerns as well as contemporary experiences and dilemmas.

The Whitney Museum's Biennial in New York City showcased the work of living American artists. While well-known, established names were exhibited on the second and third floors, the fourth floor featured artists who had never shown at the Biennial before. The ground floor gallery was devoted to the *AIDS Timeline*, a visual chronicle created by Group Materials, an artists' collaborative.

**Christo Umbrellas.** In October the environmental artist Christo opened a colorful exhibit on two continents consisting of huge 20-foot-tall umbrellas—1,340 blue ones placed in a meandering pattern across a dozen miles of rural Japanese plains, and 1,760 yellow ones on the hillside at California's Tijon Pass, along an interstate highway. The installation was praised as evocative by critics and drew large crowds. But it turned to tragedy when 40 mile-per-hour winds blew an umbrella loose from its foundations, crushing a California woman to death and injuring several others. Christo immediately ordered all the umbrellas taken down; in the process, a Japanese workman was electrocuted when the crane he was operating touched a power line.

**The Auction Market.** After a spate of record-breaking sales in recent years, major houses saw auction fever cool by the end of 1990. In one of the few signs of vigor during 1991, Robert Rauschenberg's *Rebus* sold for $7.3 million in May—$1 million more than it had brought just 18 months earlier.

**A Renewed Museum.** The Jeu de Paume in Paris, once home to the collection of Impressionist and Post-Impressionist works now hung in the Musée d'Orsay, opened its doors in June for the first time since closing for remodeling in 1986. Its 11,000 square feet will now function as a space for temporary exhibitions. The inaugural show was a selection of drawings and paintings from the last decade in the career of Jean Dubuffet, who died in 1985.        J.Su.

**ASTRONOMY.** The premier astronomical event of 1991 was a total solar eclipse. Scientists also got their first closeup view of an asteroid—as well as new looks at the planet Venus and Halley's Comet.

**Darkness in Daytime.** The total eclipse of the sun on July 11 was seen by more people than any in history. Despite unusual weather that turned forecasts topsy-turvy, most observers within the long but narrow path of the moon's shadow got a clear view of the spectacle. Watchers were thrilled by a very bright and far-flung example of the corona, our star's outer atmosphere. An added bonus was the presence of two huge, fiery prominences, glowing clouds of hot gas lying just above the solar surface and clearly visible to the unaided eye.

The eclipse was memorable for another reason. For the first time, the moon's shadow passed over major astronomical observatories. Scientists on Mauna Kea and Mauna Loa on the island of Hawaii battled high clouds and dust from the eruptions of Mount Pinatubo volcano in the Philippines to make their observations. Many sky watchers elsewhere on the Big Island got good views of the celestial spectacular, but on the normally clear west coast of the island—the area where most of the press had gathered—the eclipse was clouded out.

As the shadow sped eastward, conditions got better, and most viewers at the southern tip of Mexico's Baja California peninsula saw totality clearly. Across central Mexico and in Mexico City itself skies were clear in large part. This good luck generally continued along the rest of the path of totality over Central America

*Observers on Hawaii's Kohala coast, equipped with protective glasses, enjoy the spectacle of the July 11 solar eclipse; besides the halo-like corona, they were treated to a view of two enormous prominences, glowing clouds of hot gas appearing just above the solar surface (left).*

and northern South America. Outside of the thin strip where the eclipse was total, tens of millions of persons in the Americas saw a partial solar eclipse.

**Gaspra Encounter.** Scientists got their first closeup look at an asteroid in November, when the U.S. space probe *Galileo*, launched in 1989, transmitted to earth a picture taken at a distance of about 16,000 kilometers (10,000 miles). *Galileo* had sped by the tiny world on October 29. The minor planet was revealed to be an irregularly shaped hunk of rock about 20 km (12 mi.) long and 13 km (8 mi.) wide and pitted with craters from collisions with interplanetary debris over previous aeons. *Galileo* itself was hampered by a balky main antenna

that would not open fully. This problem did not seriously affect the Gaspra encounter but threatens, if not corrected, to doom the mission to failure when the probe makes its scheduled rendezvous with the planet Jupiter and its moons in December 1995.

**Other Solar System News.** Data from the U.S. space probe *Magellan* orbiting Venus reinforced the idea that the cloud-shrouded planet is quite active geologically. Images made from high-resolution radar scans revealed evidence of meteorite impacts, large volcanos, vast lava flows, extensive faulting, and folding of surface rocks, in addition to a wide variety of unusual features and terrains that are currently unexplained. The findings suggest that the surface of Venus may be surprisingly young by geological standards, only some 200 to 400 million years old.

Images produced by Belgian astronomers in February showed that Halley's Comet was then some 300 times brighter than expected. The cause was a vast cloud of dust that suddenly appeared and surrounded the comet's nucleus. Astronomers were surprised by this outburst because Halley is currently outbound in its orbit and well beyond the orbit of Saturn, where the effects of solar heating are very small. The cause of the flare-up is uncertain.

**New Planet?** British astronomers announced the discovery of what seemed to be a planet circling a highly compressed neutron star far from our own solar system. The discovery was hailed as the first strong evidence of other planetary systems, but scientists questioned how a planet so near a star that originated in a supernova explosion could survive such a blast, or how, if the planet was created after the explosion, it might have condensed from the rapidly expanding debris. Such suspicions were confirmed in January, 1992, when the astronomers admitted their calculations had been off; when adjusted, "the planet just evaporated," said one. Nevertheless, two American astronomers stuck by a claim to have discovered at least two planets orbiting another neutron star.

**New Astronomical Satellites.** On April 7, NASA deployed the Gamma Ray Observatory satellite in orbit from the space shuttle *Atlantis*. The $550 million spacecraft was at first threatened with failure, as its main communications antenna failed to deploy properly. Astronauts freed the antenna and saved the mission during a dramatic and unscheduled space walk. The observatory behaved well after that, and scientists now have a powerful new tool for studying the very energetic radiation from some of the universe's most exotic and powerful objects.

The European Space Agency's *Rosat* satellite completed its planned survey of the X-ray sky early in February and since then has been observing specific astronomical targets. Severe problems with the gyroscopes that help point *Rosat* in the right direction severely slowed, but did not halt, the latter program. On August 30, Japan launched the Solar-A spacecraft, a joint project of Japan, the United States, and Great Britain, which is designed to make a three-year study of solar flares in visible light and X rays.

**Astronomy in the 1990s.** The U.S. National Research Council issued the findings of a special blue-ribbon panel of astronomers established to set priorities for the science in the 1990s. Chaired by John N. Bahcall of Princeton University, the group recommended four large programs of instrument development. The first was the Space Infrared Telescope Fa-

---

### Why the Sky Is Dark

When your six-year-old asks, "Why is the sky dark at night?" you might reply, "Because the sun's gone down." Yet, when you think about it, that's no real answer. Since the number of stars in the universe is, for all practical purposes, infinite, one would expect the night sky to be a continuous curtain of light. The fact that it isn't has become known as the Olbers paradox, after German astronomer Heinrich Wilhelm Olbers (1758-1840).

One common explanation is that, as distant galaxies speed away from the earth, their light is "shifted" toward the red end of the spectrum. Those that are farther away are receding faster and have greater red shifts; in the most distant galaxies the light shifts right out of the visible spectrum into the infrared or radio spectrum, rendering it invisible. A second explanation is based on the distance and life span of galaxies. Some galaxies may be so far away that their light just hasn't had time to reach the earth, and they can emit only so much light before burning out. Both explanations are compelling, but which best explains the Olbers paradox?

Astrophysicist Paul S. Wesson recently used a computer analysis to calculate the expected radiation fields of different models of the expanding universe. He concluded that while both phenomena contributed to the blackness of the night sky, red-shifting alone would reduce brightness by a factor of around three—not enough to darken the heavens. It has to be the "finite galaxy" model that produces the required effect.

One problem does remain. How do you explain this to your six-year-old?

cility, an instrument with a main mirror 0.9 meter (3 feet) in diameter that would orbit some 100,000 km (60,000 mi.) above the earth's surface. In second place was an 8-m (26-ft.) optical telescope to be built on Mauna Kea and optimized for work at infrared wavelengths. The third spot went to the Millimeter Array, a collection of some 40 movable radio telescopes, each 8 m in diameter, with very accurate surfaces for working at very short radio wavelengths. The final big program was an 8-m optical telescope in the southern hemisphere.                                    R.A.S.

**AUSTRALIA.** Australia's battered economy continued to shrink in 1991. Prime Minister Bob Hawke withstood one bruising challenge to his leadership but failed to survive a second.

**Economic Woes.** In October, for the first time since the severe 1982-1983 recession, unemployment passed the 10 percent mark. Foreign debt by 1991 had reached $120 billion (Australian dollars used here and throughout), and the economy was registering negative growth. Half of the Commonwealth Bank of Australia was sold to the public in a hugely successful stock market offering, and the government achieved a dramatic reduction in inflation, which fell to an annual rate of below 3 percent. The lower inflation rate, however, came at a terrible price in terms of unemployment, negative growth, and business failures.

To add to the problems, Australia's 125,000 farmers faced a drought covering more than 400,000 square miles of eastern Australia. Lost rural production as a result of the drought was valued at more than $1.4 billion and still rising. Government officials estimated that at least 25 percent of the nation's 23 million cattle—the basis of a $2.5 billion industry— were at risk.

**Leadership Battle.** For eight years Bob Hawke and Treasurer Paul Keating had been a formidable political partnership, but their relationship began to show strains in February, when Keating in effect publicly criticized Hawke's leadership abilities. Then on June 3, Keating mounted an extraordinary leadership challenge, calling for a vote against Hawke in the Labor caucus (the 110 Labor members of Parliament). This was preceded by revelations that before the 1990 election, Hawke had

A devastating drought afflicted vast areas of eastern Australia. Wheat production fell to a fraction of normal levels, and sheep and cattle ranchers watched helplessly as their stock—such as this sheep— starved for lack of grass.

promised Keating he would step down from the prime ministership "a reasonable time" before the 1993 election, thus allowing Keating to establish himself as prime minister beforehand. Hawke said he had decided to break his promise because he believed Labor stood a better chance of winning in 1993 with him as leader.

Hawke won the caucus-room ballot, 66 votes to 44, and Keating resigned as treasurer, retreating to the back benches. Keating said he would not mount another challenge, but he made a series of speeches across the country questioning the government's economic policies. Then, in the fall, John Hewson, leader of the opposition Liberal Party, released an alternative economic program that included plans for an across-the-board 15 percent goods and services tax, steep income tax cuts, and cuts to social welfare programs. The Hawke government did little to counter the proposals effectively, and a series of opinion polls in early December showed that Hawke's approval rating had fallen to 31 percent, his lowest rating since he became prime minister.

In a desperate effort to shore up his leadership, Hawke removed John Kerin, the person he had chosen to follow Keating as treasurer, and replaced him with the dour but more economically literate finance minister, Ralph Willis. But in the Labor Party the move was seen as too little too late. When a group of senior pro-Hawke ministers decided it was time for Hawke to go with dignity, and approached the prime minister with this suggestion, he refused to resign, saying Keating would have to challenge him for the job.

On December 19, Hawke announced that he would that evening declare the party leadership vacant and recontest it at a caucus meeting. Keating quickly announced that he too would stand for the leadership. This time Keating won 56 votes to Hawke's 51. For the first time in Australian history, a Labor prime minister had been voted out of office by his own party. Keating, who became the country's 25th prime minister, had until March 1993, when the next general election was due, to turn around the Australian economy and so give Labor some chance of holding on to office after a decade in power.

**State Politics.** Labor remained in power in South Australia, Western Australia, Victoria, and Queensland. In New South Wales the Liberal-National Party coalition government led by Premier Nick Greiner suffered a surprising setback, failing to win a majority of legislative seats in May elections; Greiner formed a minority government with four independents to give him a slender hold on power.

**Foreign Relations.** Australia's two Navy frigates, committed by Prime Minister Hawke to help with the blockade of Iraq in the wake of the Iraqi invasion of Kuwait in August 1990, were part of the international naval task force in the Persian Gulf during the Gulf War.

### New Leader Down Under

On December 19, Paul Keating, 47, was elected in a party poll as leader of Australia's governing Labor Party, and thus prime minister, ousting Bob Hawke. Keating, who until recently had been treasurer in Hawke's cabinet, said his major priorities would be to heal the rifts in the Labor Party, come up with new policies to counter the recession, and "get the country cracking again."

The son of a boilermaker, Keating left school at 14 but took night classes and later attended college. He worked first as a clerk and for two years managed a rock group called the Ramrods. By the time he was 18, Keating was already a party activist, and at 25 he was elected to Parliament, becoming the nation's youngest legislator. Articulate and witty, Keating became known as the outstanding performer in federal parliamentary debates. Before recession hit the country, Keating was also regarded as a highly successful treasurer, but he never had any of Hawke's natural affinity with the people and clearly is no baby-kissing populist.

*Paul Keating*

Foreign Minister Gareth Evans visited South Africa in June and made headlines when he cursed a security official assigned to escort him to the black township of Soweto. Evans, who had asked for low-key security arrangements, was instead assigned a convoy of troops and armed guards. He also clashed with Zulu Chief Mangosuthu Buthelesi, leader of the Inkatha movement, who accused the Australian government of interfering in South Africa's internal affairs by funding projects involving the more radical African National Congress. On a more positive note, Evans's plan for a cease-fire in Cambodia, to be overseen by the United Nations and followed by UN-supervised elections, formed the basis of the Cambodian peace accords signed in Paris at the end of October.

Relations with Malaysia were tense. The Malaysians were particularly upset by an Australian Broadcasting Corporation television series, *Embassy*, set in an Australian embassy in a fictitious Muslim Asian country; Malaysian Prime Minister Mahathir Mohamed said the series made fun of Islam and ridiculed Malaysians. However, tensions were reduced after Evans went to Kuala Lumpur and met with Mahathir.

**The Arts.** The renowned historian Manning Clark died in May. Clark's six-volume *A History of Australia* is considered an extraordinary work of scholarship and the defining text on Australia's heritage.

An important breakthrough in the arts was the increasing emergence of Aboriginal music as a major force in Australian culture. The Aboriginal rock band Yothu Yindi had a hit single, *Treaty*, the first Aboriginal-band record to reach the Top 10. The group, from Arnhem Land in the Northern Territory, played a mix of traditional Aboriginal music and modern rock and was leading the way for around 50 Aboriginal bands whose music was becoming increasingly popular in Australia.

*See* STATISTICS OF THE WORLD. M.G.

**AUSTRIA.** In 1991 the right-wing Freedom Party suffered some embarrassment when its leader made an apparently pro-Nazi statement, and the Austrian government of Chancellor Franz Vranitzky finally apologized for Austria's role in World War II.

On June 13, Jörg Haider, right-wing populist, leader of the Freedom Party, and governor of the province of Carinthia, said to his legislature, "In the Third Reich they had an orderly employment policy, something the government in Vienna cannot accomplish." The Socialists promptly persuaded the People's Party to join them in ousting Haider from office on June 21; however, Haider remained in the government as Carinthia's deputy governor. In the election that immediately followed in the province of Burgenland, Haider's Freedom Party took only one seat from the People's Party. In later local elections, however, the Freedom Party made a strong showing.

Haider's outburst had one important consequence. On July 8, Chancellor Vranitzky acknowledged to Parliament that many Austrians had welcomed the *Anschluss* (the merger with Nazi Germany) of 1938, supported National Socialism, held positions in its hierarchy, and participated in its persecutions, and he apologized "to the survivors and the descendants of the dead."

This declaration was preceded by President Kurt Waldheim's decision not to seek a second term. Waldheim, accused—falsely—of having been a Nazi but—rightly—of having lied about his knowledge of atrocities committed during World War II, had kept the People's Party, which had elected him in 1986, on tenterhooks about his intentions. Many felt that he was hurting Austria's prestige by the ostracism imposed on him by a host of nations worldwide.

Changes in Eastern Europe were a mixed blessing for Austria. While the official figures on entering refugees were not alarming, there was a widespread feeling that a great number of Eastern Europeans, especially Romanians, illegally entered Austria, and Haider fanned a xenophobic response.

Austria was strongly affected by the civil war in Yugoslavia. Parties on the right came out for the recognition of an independent Slovenia and Croatia, while the Social Democrats urged waiting to see what the other European nations did. On September 17 a free vote in Parliament supported a waiting stance proposed by both coalition parties.

*See* STATISTICS OF THE WORLD. F.C.E.

**AUTOMOBILE INDUSTRY.** The year 1991 was a painful one for automakers both in the United States and elsewhere. For the first time since 1980, Ford, Chrysler, and General Motors all lost money, as sales in the United States plunged a huge 11.5 percent, thanks to the combined effects of the Persian Gulf War and the recession. But Chrysler, Ford, and General Motors were not alone in their troubles. A new U.S. tax on luxury cars hurt European importers, and a growing chorus on Capitol Hill and in Europe called for limits on Japanese expansion.

**Sales.** U.S. car and truck sales dropped for the third straight model year, but 1991 was the most difficult of the three. Nearly all of the 41 volume car makes saw sales fall. The Big Three fared slightly worse than the industry average. Most Japanese brands also declined, but not as much as the competition. As a result, late in the year, one-fourth of all cars and trucks sold in the United States carried Japanese labels, while many others had been built by Japanese firms and sold by the Big Three.

The new "luxury" tax on cars over $30,000, combined with competition from Japan's new luxury cars, hit European brands hard. High-priced lines such as Audi, Porsche, and Jaguar saw sales drop by about 40 percent each. France's Peugeot and Britain's Sterling pulled out of the U.S. market altogether.

**Products.** Japanese carmakers continued to pepper the U.S. market with new entries, especially sports and luxury coupes. Mitsubishi brought Japan's car of the year, the Diamante, to America. And Mazda replaced its boxy 929 with a stylish successor featuring solar cells to power fans that automatically vent heat from the interior when the car is parked in the sun.

The Big Three lagged in replacing old models as quickly as the Japanese, but they did create improved successors to their current lines. GM's 1992 replacement for the Cadillac Seville was touted as an American luxury entry that could finally stand up to the best from Japan and Europe, and Chrysler's stylish 1993 LH models were anticipated as challengers to such popular midsized cars as the Ford Taurus, Honda Accord, and Toyota Camry.

Known as a "yuppie" trophy in the go-go 1980s, BMW's new 325i was positioned as a safe, socially responsible, and environmentally sound car for the 1990s. Mercedes-Benz, meanwhile, charged into Rolls-Royce territory with its new S-class line. Mercedes' flagship, the V-12 powered 600SEL, began at $127,800. For the commoners, Volkswagen's Golf and GM's Opel Astra each vied to become the best-selling car in Europe.

**Prices and Earnings.** Slumping sales had helped put General Motors in the red in 1990 for the first time in a decade; in 1991, Ford and Chrysler also posted losses. Sales were at their lowest since the early 1980s. In December, GM announced plans to close 21 plants, eliminate over 70,000 jobs, and cut 1992 capital spending by $1.1 billion. Still, the Big Three appeared in better shape than during their money-losing years a decade before: They had more cash and far more competitive products, and cost-cutting and modernizing had made them more efficient.

---

**Vanity of Vanities**

It's the kind of thing that, when you see it in the store, you slap your forehead and say, "Why didn't I think of that?" It's a board game called "Vanity Chase" from Select Creations of Milwaukee. Players move car-shaped tokens along a board bearing a fanciful depiction of California by deciphering those oh-so-clever vanity license plates that real drivers have been puzzling out for years. For example, IXLR8 is "I accelerate." Try these samples to test your plate-decoding skills. For the last five, you have to figure out not only what the plate means, but also the occupation of the driver. (But first cover up the answers below.)

1. CRAZL80  2. IW84NO1  3. WZNUN82  4. JOBNJOB  5. NNNNR  6. 10ERSAX  7. RUN2RT  8. WEMO4DO  9. OLDNACL  10. CMEB4DK

**Answers:** 1. Crazy Lady  2. I Wait for No One  3. Was New in '82  4. In Between Jobs  5. Foreigner  6. Tenor Sax—Saxophone Player  7. Are You Into Art—Artist  8. We Mow for Dough—Gardener  9. Old Salt—Sailor  10. See Me Before Decay—Dentist

*Among the year's classier new models, the Cadillac Seville (top) was promoted as a rival to the best luxury cars of Europe and Japan, while the Mercedes 600SEL came with an 11-speaker audio system, a 12-cylinder engine, and a price tag over $125,000.*

Price increases on 1992 models averaged nearly 5 percent among the Big Three. In many cases the hikes helped cover the cost of additional standard equipment, such as air bags and antilock brakes. At the very low end, the $4,825 Yugo GV Plus remained the least expensive car on the U.S. market—and one of the least popular. At the other extreme, Rolls-Royce sold out its allotted share of 90 Bentley Continental R models even before they arrived. Its price: $261,800—before taxes.

**Cars and the Environment.** Just a few years after embracing hopped-up horsepower with renewed passion, the auto industry adopted a "greener" posture for the 1990s. Most companies expanded their fleets of cars capable of running on such "clean" fuels as methanol or natural gas. Electric car projects became so commonplace that they merited their own exhibit at the Tokyo Motor Show, but significant technological hurdles remained. Most prototypes required hundreds of pounds of batteries and still needed to be recharged after 100 miles.

**Trade.** The United States and Japan held talks in an attempt to reduce the $41 billion automotive trade deficit with Japan. But there was little apparent progress, and on Capitol Hill legislators prepared measures that would re-strict Japan's automotive presence. Japanese automakers built more than 1.5 million cars and trucks in North America during 1990, but they were criticized for using too many Japanese-made parts. (Nearly every Japanese maker announced plans to boost purchases from U.S. suppliers.) Meanwhile, Europe, too, wrestled with the "Japanese question," and decided to allow the Japanese market share to rise to no more than 16 percent by the end of the decade.

**Global Markets.** The Trabant and Wartburg, two pollution-spewing symbols of East Germany's manufacturing inefficiency, went out of production, marking an end of an era. After the fall of Communism in Eastern Europe, such makers as General Motors, Volkswagen, and Mercedes-Benz quickly staked out a presence there. Germany's new sales strength helped offset steep declines in such markets as the United Kingdom.

Sales in Japan were down, in part because of global automotive recession. Auto sales also suffered when a new law required proof of a parking space before a car could be registered.

Mexico provided a bright spot on the world automotive map. The country appeared poised to become a manufacturing power, while a rising standard of living was expected to boost domestic demand. Mercedes-Benz said it would join Ford, Chrysler, General Motors, Nissan, and Volkswagen in 1993 to become Mexico's sixth producer of passenger cars.                                              D.V.

**AVIATION.** The political turbulence of 1991 was reflected in virtually every aspect of aerospace activities, from air travel to manufacturing. The U.S. industry suffered heavy financial losses, largely because of increased fuel costs due to the Iraqi invasion of Kuwait and subsequent Persian Gulf War. A trend of consolidation in the industry intensified, as losses pushed several once-powerful carriers into bankruptcy.

On January 8, Pan American World Airways filed for bankruptcy. Long the leading U.S.-based international airline and a pioneer in intercontinental flight, Pan Am was eventually brought down by competition from both U.S. and foreign airlines, together with the growing pressures of fuel costs and recession. After months of spirited negotiations, the airline agreed to sell Delta Airlines dozens of routes

worldwide, as well as its East Coast shuttle. Pan Am survived for a time as a regional carrier, with service to the Caribbean and Latin America. But in December, Delta backed away from its promise to help finance Pan Am's remaining routes, and the airline was forced to shut down. After a fierce bidding war with American, United Airlines bought Pan Am's assets, subject to federal approval.

Eastern Airlines was also unfortunate. The former giant, which in 1986 became part of the empire built by Texas Air Corporation and Frank Lorenzo, went into Chapter 11 proceedings in 1989, but pressure from creditors and the financial maneuverings of Lorenzo prevented it from effecting a reorganization. Eastern shut down for good in January 1991, after 62 years of operations.

Other U.S. airlines also faced deep problems. Trans World Airlines defaulted on a $75.5 million bond payment in February. Chicago-based Midway Airlines filed for Chapter 11 in March; Phoenix-based America West Airlines followed suit in June. In mid-Novem-

*Pan Am, once the glamorous carrier to exotic destinations with planes like this Clipper III (below), which inaugurated translantic passenger service in 1937, fell on hard times and was forced to shut down. Its familiar logo (left) will be seen no more.*

ber, Midway shut down operations, filing suit against Northwest Airlines, which had pulled out of negotiations to acquire it. Meanwhile, Continental Airlines was forced to put up some of its route authority assets for sale and began discussing a possible merger with Northwest, and USAir announced it would try to obtain union consent to a temporary cut in salaries. (Despite its difficulties, USAir bought 108 arrival and departure slots at New York City's LaGuardia Airport from Continental and agreed to run the Trump Shuttle.)

A report by the Transportation Research Board, an agency of the National Academy of Sciences, concluded that deregulation of the industry had not compromised safety in airline operations but warned that the benefits of lower fares from deregulation might soon disappear as consolidation continues.

**U.S. Manufacturers.** Boeing Corporation, which remained bullish about the future, announced a trend-setting new airliner, the 777, scheduled to fly in mid-1994. The largest twin-engine jet in Boeing's inventory, the 375-passenger 777 was being developed as a replacement for aging McDonnell Douglas DC-10 and Lockheed L-1011 planes. It was Boeing's first plane to be completely developed with the "design/build concept," in which prototype tooling and mock-up aircraft are essentially eliminated and the complete plane is designed and manufactured to final specifications the first time, thereby eliminating costly changes later on. The 777 is also a "paperless" airplane; designers, manufacturing engineers, suppliers, and launch operators are tied together in a comprehensive computerized network that virtually eliminates engineering drawings and manuals.

On September 15 the McDonnell Douglas C-17 military transport plane made a successful test flight, amid continuing debate about the over-budget C-17 development program. Any reduction of C-17 orders would put severe pressure on the company, already struggling with a debt of over $5 billion. At the same time, however, McDonnell Douglas looked forward to better economic performance from a reasonably healthy order book.

The MD-11, a three-engine wide-body airliner produced by the Douglas Aircraft Company division of McDonnell Douglas, went into service early in the year on U.S. and foreign airlines. Douglas also began tests on a model of the wide-body MD-11 airliner reconfigured to hold 410 seats instead of the original 287. But in October two drills to determine whether the increased number of passengers could be evacuated within the Federal Aviation Administration's time limit not only failed to meet the standard but resulted in dozens of injuries. Blaming the FAA's strict rules for realistic evacuation conditions, Douglas announced it would seek safety certification for its planes using other methods.

In November, Douglas announced a preliminary agreement to sell 40 percent of its commercial aircraft division to the Taiwan Aerospace Corporation for $2 billion.

**Airbus Dispute.** In Toulouse, France, Airbus Industrie completed final assembly of the A340, a midsize four-engine long-range jet that made its first flight in late October, and the growing subsidy dispute between Airbus Industrie and U.S. manufacturers began to take on crisis proportions. The European consortium now accounts for some 30 percent of all new airliner orders in competition with McDonnell Douglas and Boeing, and the U.S. manufacturers claim that Airbus has benefited from government subsidies of over $13 billion. In June the United States placed the issue before an arbitration panel under the General Agreement on Tariffs and Trade.           R.E.B.

**AWARDS AND PRIZES.** The following is an annotated listing of selected prizes awarded during 1991. Some awards in specific fields are covered in separate articles such as BROADCASTING, LITERATURE, MOTION PICTURES, MUSIC, and THEATER.

## NOBEL PRIZES

The Norwegian Nobel Committee made a clear political statement in awarding the 1991 peace prize to dissident leader Daw Aung San Suu Kyi of Myanmar (formerly Burma), under house arrest by the military leaders of her country. Nadine Gordimer became one of only seven women ever to have won the prize in literature. The prize money for each of the Nobel awards in 1991 was valued at nearly $1 million. Prizes were given out on December 10, the anniversary of Alfred Nobel's death.

*The 1991 Nobel Peace Prize went to the leader of the opposition to the military regime in Myanmar (Burma), Aung San Suu Kyi, who remained under house arrest in Yangon, the country's capital. She is seen here with a portrait of her father, Aung San, considered the father of modern Burma.*

**Peace.** *Daw Aung San Suu Kyi* (born 1945 in Yangon [Rangoon], Myanmar), leader of the opposition to the military government of Myanmar. She was placed under house arrest in July 1989 for criticizing the country's former leader, military strongman Ne Win, and remained in isolation, unable to communicate with even her husband and two teenage sons, in October 1991 when the Nobel Prize was announced. Although she had not addressed the people of Myanmar since her arrest, she remained for them a powerful symbol of the democracy movement. The Nobel Committee cited her "nonviolent struggle for democracy and human rights" against "a regime characterized by brutality."

The daughter of Aung San, a revolutionary leader regarded as the founder of modern Myanmar who was assassinated in 1947, Aung San Suu Kyi left her home in 1960 and stayed abroad (and uninvolved in the country's politics) until 1988, when she returned to care for her sick mother. As protests against military leader Ne Win and harsh crackdowns by the military rocked the country, she began speaking out for democracy and human rights, eventually becoming secretary-general of the strongest party in the democracy movement, until her arrest in 1989. During her imprisonment, her party captured almost 80 percent of the parliamentary seats in the 1990 multiparty elections. The military then made it impossible for the party to take power.

Although the government offered to let Aung San Suu Kyi leave the country, she refused to do so unless the regime freed all political prisoners, turned power over to civilians, allowed her to address the country over radio and television for 50 minutes, and permitted her to make a public procession to the airport.

**Literature.** *Nadine Gordimer* (born 1923 in Springs, South Africa), South African writer praised by the Swedish Academy as being "of very great benefit to humanity." Born in a provincial mining town near Johannesburg, Gordimer began writing at age 9 and was first published at age 15. Much of her work contains themes of exile and alienation. She writes without sentimentality, in a precise yet lyrical style. Among her ten novels and nine volumes of short stories are *July's People* (1981), the story of a white family fleeing a civil war with the help of their black servant; *The Conservationist* (1975), about a self-deceived industrialist on a 400-acre Transvaal farm; *Burger's Daughter* (1979), the story of a white girl coming to terms with the radical activities of her father; and the recent *Jump and Other Stories*.

Gordimer plans to use some of her prize money to help the predominantly black Congress of South African Writers, of which she is a founder. She is also a member of the African National Congress.

**Economics.** *Ronald H. Coase* (born 1910 in Willesden, England), an influential thinker who achieved important breakthroughs in economic thought, particularly on how people organize to advance their economic interests and when government intervention is needed. A graduate of the London School of Economics, Coase emigrated to the United States in 1951 and spent his teaching career at the University of Chicago.

Coase's 1937 study entitled *The Nature of the Firm* explored why companies exist, as opposed to a decentralized market of individuals buying and selling skills and products. A second study, entitled *The Problem of Social Cost* (1960), enraged other economists when it was first published, although it has since become one of the most cited works in modern economics. In it Coase challenged the effectiveness of defining precise property rights, arguing that in the case of damage, what matters is low-cost resolution, not assignment of blame.

**Physiology or Medicine.** For research in cell physiology, *Erwin Neher* (born 1944 in Landsberg, Germany), of the Max Planck Institute for Biophysical Chemistry in Göttingen-and *Bert Sakmann* (born 1942 in Stuttgart, Germany), of the Max Planck Institute for Medical Research in Heidelberg. Neher and Sakmann proved the existence of tiny pores, or tubelike channels, that dot the outer membranes of cells and allow cells to take up and excrete charged atoms, or ions. Such ion channels regulate a cell's internal levels of sodium, potassium, calcium, or chloride ions. Defects in ion channels underlie disorders such as diabetes, epilepsy, cystic fibrosis, and some forms of heart disease.

*Nadine Gordimer became the first South African to win the Nobel Prize for literature, when the Swedish Academy awarded her the honor, citing her "very great benefit to humanity."*

The committee awarding the prize said the researchers' contributions "have meant a revolution for the field of cell biology for the understanding of different disease mechanisms, and opened a way to develop new and more specific drugs."

**Chemistry.** *Richard R. Ernst* (born 1933 in Winterhut, Switzerland), of the Federal Institute of Technology in Zurich. He was honored for refinements in the techniques of nuclear magnetic resonance spectroscopy, first developed in 1945, that led to the tissue-scanning method known as magnetic resonance imaging (MRI), now a standard medical procedure. Additionally, his work made it possible to determine the three-dimensional structure of complex molecules containing hundred of atoms, to study interactions between molecules, and to study molecular motions and rates of chemical reactions.

In work done in 1966, Ernst improved the existing technology by bombarding tissue samples under study with short, intense pulses of radio waves.

**Physics.** *Pierre-Gilles de Gennes* (born 1932 in Paris, France), a professor at the University of Paris. He was honored for discovering mathematical methods to describe phenomena of order and chaos in such widely differing materials as liquid crystals, superconductors, and polymers.

De Gennes's research has focused on phase transitions, in which atoms or molecules in a material shift between ordered and disordered states. In the 1950s he studied how tiny atomic magnets alter their alignment with changes in temperature, and in the 1960s he began working with liquid crystals, which have characteristics of both solid and liquid phases.

## PULITZER PRIZES

John Updike won his second Pulitzer when the prestigious awards were announced April 10. The year's fiction award for his *Rabbit at Rest* followed the 1982 prize for *Rabbit Is Rich*, another in his series of novels about a Pennsylvania car salesman. The drama prize went to Neil Simon, for his 26th Broadway play, *Lost in Yonkers*, a look back at adolescence in the 1940s. The general nonfiction award went to a book on insect life—*The Ants*, by Bert

Holldobler and Edward O. Wilson. Steven Naifeh and Gregory White Smith authored the biography winner, *Jackson Pollock: An American Saga*. Poetry winner was Mona Van Duyn, for her seventh collection of verse, *Near Changes*. Shulamit Ran, a native of Israel, won the music award for her *Symphony*, which was commissioned by the Philadelphia Orchestra. The biography award went to Laurel Thatcher Ulrich for *A Midwife's Tale: The Life of Martha Ballad, Based on Her Diary 1785-1812*.

In the journalism categories, Caryle Murphy of the Washington *Post*, who covered the Iraqi invasion of Kuwait, sometimes from hiding, shared the international reporting award with Serge Schmemann of the New York *Times*, who reported on the dissolution of East Germany. The public service award went to Jane Schorer of the Des Moines (Iowa) *Register* for a series of articles about a rape and its aftermath, and the award for feature writing was given to Sheryl James of the St. Petersburg (Fla.) *Times* for a four-part series on a woman who abandoned her baby.

Other Pulitzer Prizes awarded in journalism follow:

**Reporting, Beat.** Natalie Angier, New York *Times*.

**Reporting, Investigative.** Joseph T. Hallinan and Susan M. Headden, Indianapolis *Star*.

**Reporting, National.** Marjie Lundstrom and Rochelle Sharpe, Gannett News Service.

**Explanatory Journalism.** Susan C. Faludi, *The Wall Street Journal*.

**Commentary.** Jim Hoagland, Washington *Post*.

**Criticism.** David Shaw, Los Angeles *Times*.

**Editorial Cartooning.** Jim Borgman, Cincinnati *Enquirer*.

**Editorial Writing.** Ron Casey, Harold Jackson, and Joey Kennedy, Birmingham (Ala.) *News*.

**Photography, Feature**. William Snyder, Dallas *Morning News*.

**Photography, Spot News**. Greg Marinovich, Associated Press.

## OTHER PRIZES AND AWARDS

Among many other significant awards were:

**Academy of American Poets**. Fellowship to J. D. McClatchy; Walt Whitman Award to Greg Glazner for *From the Iron Chair*.

**American Academy and Institute of Arts and Letters**. Gold medals to David Diamond (music) and Richard Wilbur (poetry). Arnold W. Brunner Memorial Prize in Architecture to Tadao Ando. Award of Merit for the Novel to Walter Abish. Witter Bynner Prize for Poetry to Thylias Moss. Jimmy Ernst Award in Art to Peter Agostini. E. M. Forster Award in Literature to Alan Hollinghurst. Walter Hinrichsen Award in Music to Marjorie Merryman. Charles Ives Fellowship in Music to Nathan Currier. Louise Nevelson Award in Art to Gabor Peterdi. Jean Stein Award for Fiction to Cormac McCarthy. Harold D. Vursell Memorial Award in Literature to Ursula K. LeGuin. Morton Dauwen Zabel Award in Poetry to Gordon Rogoff. Award for Distinguished Service to the Arts to Alexander Schneider.

**Grawemeyer Award**. For original musical composition, $150,000 to John Corigliano for his *Symphony No.1*.

**Kennedy Center Honors**. For lifetime achievement in the performing arts, to country and western singer Roy Acuff; musical comedy writers Betty Comden and Adolph Green; the tap-dancing brothers Fayard and Harold Nicholas; movie star Gregory Peck; and choral and orchestral leader Robert Shaw.

**Robert F. Kennedy Human Rights Award**. $30,000 divided between Avigdor Feldman, an Israeli lawyer, and Raji Sourani, a Palestinian lawyer from the Gaza Strip, for work in human rights and nonviolence.

**Albert Lasker Medical Research Awards**. $15,000 research award split between geneticists Edward B. Lewis of the California Institute of Technology and Christiane Nüsslein-Volhard of the Max Planck Institute in Tübingen, Germany. Clinical Medical Research Award to Yuet Waikan of the University of California at San Francisco. Public Service awards to Thomas P. O'Neill, former speaker of the House of Representatives, and Robin Chandler Duke, of the Population Crisis Committee.

**MacArthur Foundation**. A total of 31 awards, worth between $150,000 and $375,000, given to: chemistry professor Jacqueline K. Barton, cultural critic and political commentator Paul Berman, mathematician James F. Blinn, historian Taylor Branch, dancer and choreographer Trisha Brown, historian Mari Jo Buhle, philosopher Patricia Smith Churchland, statistician David Donoho, anthropologist Steven Feld, literary critic Alice Fulton, theorist and performer Guillermo Gomez-Pena, drama theorist Jerzy Grotkowski, artist David Hammons, child care specialist Sophia Bracy Harris, author W. Lewis Hyde, composer Ali Akbar Khan, mathematician Sergiu Klainerman, biologist Martin E. Kreitman, historian Harlan Lane, community revitalization specialist Monsignor William J. Linder, Native American linguist Patricia Locke, choreographer Mark Morris, film maker Marcel Ophus, English professor Arnold Rampersad, composer and conductor Gunther Schuller, environmental toxologist Joel Schwartz, jazz composer Cecil Taylor, puppeteer Julie Taymor, world healthcare advocate David Werner, planetary scientist James A. Westphal, poet Eleanor Wilner.

**National Book Awards**. Fiction prize to Norman Rush for *Mating*; nonfiction prize to Orlando Patterson for *Freedom*; poetry prize to Philip Levine for *What Work Is*; National Book Foundation Medal for Distinguished Contribution to American Letters to Eudora Welty.

**National Medal of the Arts**. Awarded by the White House to: Maurice Abravanel, conductor emeritus of the Utah Symphony; country musician Roy Acuff; architect Pietro Belluschi; J. Carter Brown, director of the National Gallery of Art; tap dancer Charles (Honi) Coles; Santa Fe Opera founder John Crosby; painter Richard Diebenkorn; R. Philip Hanes, Jr., founder of the American Council for the Arts; actress Kitty Carlisle Hart; choreographer Pearl Primus; and violinist Isaac Stern.

**Pritzker Architecture Prize**. $100,000 to Robert Venturi.

**Samuel H. Scripps American Dance Festival Award**. $25,000 to Anna Sokolow.

**Templeton Prize for Progress in Religion**. $820,000 to Rabbi Immanuel Jakobovits of Great Britain.

**Wolf Prize in Physics**. $100,000 shared by Maurice Goldhaber of New York and Valentine L. Telebdi of Zurich, Switzerland.

**World Food Prize**. $200,000 to Nevin S. Scrimshaw, professor emeritus, Massachusetts Institute of Technology, for nutrition field work in Central America.

# B

**BAHAMAS.** *See* Statistics of the World.
**BAHRAIN.** *See* Statistics of the World.
**BANGLADESH.** The year 1991 was memorable for "free and fair" elections and for the conversion from a presidential to a parliamentary form of government. Another major occurrence was the catastrophic cyclone and tidal surge that devastated the country's southeastern coastal areas.

**Transition.** Late in 1990, former President Hussain Muhammad Ershad had resigned under pressure from widespread pro-democ-

## *In the Path of Destruction*

*"One woe treading upon another" is how a government official described the devastation heaped upon Bangladesh by a cyclone that hurled 20-foot waves into densely populated lowlands on the Bay of Bengal. This view of the village of Madarbari suggests the extent of destruction. Survivors (right) had the task of disposing of the dead, then faced problems of hunger, homelessness, and disease.*

racy demonstrations; pending elections, power went to a caretaker government headed by the chief justice, Shahabuddin Ahmed. Ershad himself was arrested and charged with illegal possession of firearms and embezzlement of public funds. Tried and convicted on the weapons charge, he was sentenced in June 1991 to ten years in prison.

**Parliamentary Elections.** In democratic elections on February 27, the Bangladesh Nationalist Party (BNP), led by Begum Khaleda Zia, won 169 seats out of 330, giving it a small majority. The Awami League, led by Sheikh Hasina Wazed, was second with 87, followed by Ershad's Jatiya Party with 35 and the Islam-based Jamaat-i-Islam with 20. The remaining seats were scattered among smaller parties. Numerous non-Bangladeshi observers pronounced the election to be "free and fair."

Acting President Shahabuddin swore in a new government headed by Begum Zia as Bangladesh's first woman prime minister (although under the continuing presidential system power remained with Shahabuddin).

**Parliamentary System.** After the election, the Awami League remained steadfast in demanding change to a parliamentary system of government, while the BNP began to waver in its opposition to changing. Both parties ultimately introduced differing bills to establish a parliamentary system. A compromise measure was worked out, enacted by Parliament, and ratified by voters in a September referendum. The role of head of government was then transferred from the president to the prime minister, and Begum Zia was formally reappointed to that position. On October 8, Abdur Rahman Biswas was elected by Parliament to the now ceremonial post of president; he had been speaker.

**Cyclone.** On April 30 the southeastern coast was hit by a cyclone and tidal surge of enormous proportions. Deaths totaled more than 125,000, and property damage was estimated by the United Nations at $1.78 billion. Shelters erected following earlier devastating storms, along with an early-warning system, did prevent some casualties. Relief efforts were mounted quickly by neighboring Pakistan and India as well as many more distant nations. A group of United States Marines was

diverted to Bangladesh on their return to Pacific stations from Operation Desert Storm.

**The Economy.** The new government attempted to meet requirements of the International Monetary Fund by introducing a new value-added tax. This met with opposition but survived with some modifications. However, the economy remained very much in deficit both internally and externally. The foreign debt burden was reduced somewhat when several countries forgave government-to-government debt.

*See* STATISTICS OF THE WORLD.          C.B.

**BANKING AND FINANCE.** In 1991, with the U.S. economy weathering a recession, many commercial banks seemed in poor shape. The rash of major bank mergers continued. Congress approved legislation providing $100 billion to bolster the Federal Deposit Insurance Corporation (FDIC) and help bail out troubled U.S. savings and loans institutions. The biggest international story was the collapse, amid fraud allegations, of the Bank of Credit and Commerce International (BCCI).

**Banking Legislation.** In February the administration of President George Bush proposed a sweeping overhaul of the U.S. banking system, removing many barriers and regulations imposed after the banking crisis of the 1930s. The proposal was advertised as an attempt to strengthen the system while providing more services to the consumer. Among other things, the deregulatory legislation would allow industrial companies to own banks and permit banks to open or buy branches in other states. Well-capitalized banks could underwrite corporate securities and sell mutual funds, and financial firms would be allowed to own banks with a strong capital base. Stricter limits would be imposed on deposits covered by federal deposit insurance.

Critics of the proposal charged that deregulation could damage commercial banks as it did savings and loan institutions (S&Ls) in the 1980s. Ultimately, Congress enacted what was in large part a bailout bill stripped of most other features. The new legislation increased the amount that can be borrowed by the FDIC from $5 billion to about $70 billion. (Congress also approved $25 billion, in addition to a previous $80 billion, for bailing out S&Ls.

# BANKING AND FINANCE

Despite the size of this figure, there were fears that more money would before long be needed.)

Under the new banking legislation, regulators received greater authority to seize banks before they become insolvent. Regulators were required to make more frequent examinations, and regulation of foreign banks was made stricter. Higher deposit insurance premiums were to be required for banks involved in high-risk practices. The rights of banks to underwrite insurance were restricted. The legislation did not incorporate Bush administration proposals to allow banks to affiliate with industrial companies or to expand their operations across state lines.

Meanwhile, banks continued to get around geographic restrictions on banking activities.

By October, 34 states had legislation allowing unlimited nationwide banking or permitting out-of-state banks to enter on a reciprocal basis. Another 15 had regional reciprocal regulations.

**Mergers.** Among other U.S. bank acquisitions or mergers, NCNB Corporation of North Carolina announced a plan to acquire Georgia's C&S/Sovran, expecting to become the fourth-largest bank in the country. Chemical Banking agreed to merge with Manufacturers Hanover, making the New York combination the third largest in the country. BankAmerica, by acquiring Security Pacific as planned in 1992, would become the second-largest bank in the nation.

**Profits and Losses.** Although newspaper headlines highlighted some major losses

*Those implicated in the wide-ranging Bank of Credit and Commerce International scandal included (above, left to right), Saudi Arabian financier Gaith Pharaon, BCCI founder Aga Hassan Abedi, former U.S. Defense Secretary Clark Clifford (who was chairman of First American Bank, secretly owned by BCCI), and acting BCCI President Swaleh Naqvi. At left, guards enforce the closing of BCCI's main operations center, in Karachi, Pakistan.*

among prominent U.S. banks, the industry as a whole reported first-half profits in 1991 of $9.75 billion, down about 12.3 percent from the first half of 1990. Of the 12,138 banks in the United States as of mid-1991 (down 185 from December 1990), 89 percent were profitable. Bank assets were virtually the same as at the end of 1990. However, banks did boost their equity capital in the first half of 1991 by 3.6 percent, to $225.5 billion.

Nonperforming loans increased 6.4 percent from the end of 1990, to $82.6 billion, or 4 percent of all loans outstanding. Loan-loss reserves decreased 2.4 percent, to $53.6 billion. Real estate mortgage loans accounted for about half of the bad credits at banks, and were a major reason why the nation's largest bank, Citicorp, declared an $885 million loss in the third quarter of 1991.

**S&L Cleanup.** The U.S. savings and loan industry continued to shrink. In the first half of 1991, industry assets declined by $84 billion, or 7.5 percent, to a total of $1.026 trillion. About three-fourths of the nation's 2,532 thrifts were profitable, earning $2.6 billion in the first half. However, the 24 percent of thrifts that were unprofitable lost $4.7 billion. Some 300 were expected to fail and be turned over to the Resolution Trust Corporation for disposal of their assets.

The RTC, formed in 1989, had seized more than 650 insolvent thrifts by October 1991, and it had sold or closed nearly 550 of these. The agency liquidated more than half the $330 billion in initial assets it had seized, about half of them from failed Texas thrifts. L. William Seidman, outgoing chairman of the FDIC, predicted the total government outlay for bailing out S&Ls would reach $225 billion to $250 billion, or as much as $700 billion if interest charges on that amount of fresh federal debt were added over several decades ahead.

The RTC also helped in more than 600 convictions for major thrift crimes. Among the most notable of those convicted was Charles H. Keating, Jr., found guilty on state charges connected with the collapse of the Lincoln Savings and Loan Association. He also faced federal charges.

**Credit Crunch.** Many U.S. banks seemed reluctant to make loans. Some economists ar-

*In an effort to jump start the U.S. economy, the Federal Reserve moved aggressively to lower interest rates during the year. While this presumably helped businesses that needed to borrow money, it left average savers in some dismay at the slow growth of their bank accounts.*

gued that this "credit crunch" was more a case of poor demand for loans than a hesitancy on the part of financially troubled banks to make loans. Nonetheless, President Bush announced a program of technical measures to spur bank lending, such as easing the limits on the amount of preferred stock banks could sell to raise capital. Also, new guidelines were issued to liberalize real estate valuation and loan-loss reserve rules.

In another attempt to stimulate the demand for loans, the Federal Reserve gradually lowered its discount rate (the rate it charges banks for loans) from 7 percent in December 1990 to 4.5 percent by early November 1991. The rates that banks charged their customers also dropped. As economic recession continued, a further, sizable drop in the discount rate, to 3.5 percent, was announced in December; this was the lowest level since 1964.

Savers saw interest rates on their bank accounts decline. Interest rates on credit cards, however, largely resisted the downward trend. Efforts in Congress late in the year to limit the rates to 14 percent drew sharp criticism from bankers and ultimately failed.

**BCCI Scandal.** The scandal involving the Bank of Credit and Commerce International broke on July 5, when, in a coordinated swoop, authorities seized BCCI's assets in the seven countries or territories with its largest operations—Great Britain, Luxembourg, the Cayman Islands, the United States, France, Spain, and Switzerland. The seven governments acted after a special audit commissioned by the Bank of England uncovered huge losses by the bank. By July 29, when a Manhattan grand jury indicted BCCI, its founder, and its former chief executive on charges of fraud, money laundering, bribery, and theft, a total of 44 countries had closed BCCI offices in their jurisdictions. Total claims against the bank worldwide were estimated at $20 billion, while its total assets were believed to be less than $10 billion.

BCCI had been founded in 1972 by a Pakistani banker, Aga Hassan Abedi, and a handful of compatriots whose ambition was to create a world-class Muslim bank. Having little actual capital, BCCI gambled on futures and options trading and extended high-risk loans. It raised millions of dollars through bookkeeping tricks that inflated profits and helped cover massive trading and loan losses. The bank built up a corporate structure so complex that it could operate virtually unregulated all over the world with more than 400 shell companies, offshore banks, branches, and subsidiaries. Among its depositors were at least 20 central government banks, mostly in developing countries. Funds were shifted around or paid out when necessary to maintain the bank's credibility in financial markets, but huge sums disappeared by means of outright theft or "loans" on which the interest or even the principal was not collected. A separate set of books kept by BCCI's top management concealed these activities from auditors. Dictators, drug dealers, and terrorist groups allegedly used the bank to loot national treasuries, launder drug profits, or conduct clandestine arms deals.

*U.S. Activities.* U.S. regulatory authorities never gave BCCI permission to operate a branch or accept deposits in the United States. For a time, BCCI was able to maintain state-licensed agencies or representative offices in a number of U.S. cities. BCCI also used sham stockholders to illegally acquire three American banks, the largest being First American Bankshares in Washington, D.C. And BCCI bought prestige for itself by cultivating influential people—for example, donating $8 million to former President Jimmy Carter's public policy center at Emory University.

First American Chairman Clark Clifford and President Robert Altman resigned their First American jobs on August 13 and appeared in the fall before congressional subcommittees investigating the scandal. Clifford, a former secretary of defense and adviser to Democratic presidents, and Altman, Clifford's protégé and junior law partner, denied that they had known of BCCI's secret ownership of their bank. However, Abdur Sakhia, a former BCCI executive, testified that he believed Altman must have known and noted that many important executive decisions were ultimately made by BCCI. Clifford described as "legal and proper" a deal in which he and Altman used a loan from BCCI to buy stock in First American, which they sold two years later at a profit of several million dollars.

Many observers suggested that BCCI's abundance of friends in high places helped to explain why it had been allowed to go unchecked for so long. There were charges that federal officials, including then-Attorney General Richard Thornburgh, had ignored repeated warnings about illegal activities in the United States by BCCI and its customers and had blocked investigations. The acting director of the CIA, Richard Kerr, admitted to the Senate that the CIA had failed to tell the Federal Reserve or the Justice Department what it knew about BCCI's secret control of First American.

In mid-November the Justice Department indicted Abedi; Gaith Pharaon, a Saudi Arabian financier who ostensibly owned one of the U.S. banks actually controlled by BCCI; and BCCI's acting president, Swaleh Naqvi, for racketeering in a conspiracy to take over the Independence Bank of Encino, Calif. They were also charged with fraud in a stock scheme involving the Centrust Savings Bank in Miami.

The following month BCCI agreed to plead guilty to federal and New York State criminal charges and to forfeit more than $550 million (all of the bank's known U.S. assets). About half of the funds were used to shore up First American and the Independence Bank, half to help reimburse BCCI depositors worldwide.

*British Developments.* Meanwhile, in Britain, as in the United States, the scandal touched prominent figures in both major political parties. Under Britain's deposit insurance system, depositors stood to recover 75 percent of amounts up to £15,000, and no portion of deposits in excess of that amount. The government of Abu Dhabi—which, along with Sheikh Zayed bin Sultan al-Nahyan, owned 77 percent of the bank—protested the July seizure of BCCI's assets, saying it had been trying to implement its own rescue plan. A British judge delayed until early 1992 a decision on whether to liquidate BCCI operations, and Sheikh Zayed offered to supply up to $2 billion to help pay off creditors (including the more than a million depositors around the world) under a plan that might give them perhaps 40 cents on the dollar.

*Third World Impact.* Nowhere was the BCCI collapse more devastating than in Africa, where the bank obtained about 11 percent of its $20 billion in nominal assets. The government of Cameroon, for example, had reportedly deposited one-third of its reserves with BCCI in London. The disgraced bank, however, retained a reservoir of good will in its original home. In Pakistan, where BCCI had cultivated intimate connections with a wide spectrum of political parties and leaders, its troubles were widely seen as part of a Western or Jewish conspiracy to destroy an upstart Muslim-owned rival.

**Other Developments.** Japan's banking and financial community was shaken by revelations of fraud and other irregularities at some of the country's most prestigious banks and securities firms. Several top executives resigned, including the heads of the Sumitomo Bank, Fuji Bank, and Industrial Bank of Japan.

The six largest banks in the world were Japanese at the end of 1990. Japan's largest bank, Dai-Ichi Kangyo, had $428 billion in assets, larger than the three largest U.S. banks combined. Only 2 U.S. banks made it into the top 50 banks: Citicorp, as number 21, and BankAmerica, as number 45.

In October the International Monetary Fund gave the Soviet Union special association status. After the dissolution of the Soviet Union

in December, the IMF continued talks with the individual republics, which were expected to eventually become members. Latvia, Lithuania, and Estonia, which left the Soviet Union earlier in the year, had already applied for membership.                          D.R.F.

**BARBADOS.**  See STATISTICS OF THE WORLD. *See also* CARIBBEAN BASIN.

**BEHAVIORAL SCIENCES.**  Studies published in 1991 examined a possible new explanation for early puberty, evidence for a relation between stress and resistance to infection, and a possible physiological factor in homosexuality, among other topics.

**Early Puberty.**  Is the timing of puberty determined partly by the stresses experienced in childhood? It may be, according to a controversial new theory propounded by Jay Belsky and Patricia Draper of Pennsylvania State University and Laurence Steinberg of Temple University. They theorize that children who experience stressful, negative, insecure childhoods tend to enter puberty relatively early as evolution's way of ensuring that they pass their genes on to future generations. However, Belsky and Draper concede that nutrition and health are still key factors in determining the onset of puberty (which is why the average age for first menstruation has dropped steadily since the early 19th century).

Basically, the theory predicts that children who live in poverty; whose parents are harsh, insensitive, inconsistent, or abusive; whose parents' relationship is stormy or ends in divorce; and who develop behavioral problems will tend to enter puberty earlier. Though the theory focuses on females—since it is easier to accurately determine the onset of puberty in women than in men—Belsky feels it should hold for both sexes.

Depending on childhood experiences, Belsky says, evolution can send the child down either of two evolutionary paths—that of quantity or that of quality. Girls whose early childhood experiences have taught them that the world is insecure and risky will begin menstruating early and also having sex early, with a greater number of partners. This is the quantity strategy, in which more energy is put into mating than into parenting. In contrast, girls who are brought up in stable homes, where their emotional and material needs are met, are more likely to have learned that the world is a welcoming place, people are trustworthy, and relationships stable. They will enter puberty later and delay having sex until they have

**A Game That's Really Catching**

*Thunk. R-r-r-rip! Thunk. R-r-r-rip! Thunk. R-r-r-rip!* If that sound is unfamiliar, you couldn't have spent much time at the beach; it's the sound made by the year's hottest fad—Super Grip Ball. This clever new plaything, which could be the klutz's best friend, consists of a ball and two circular mitts, all covered in Velcro. When a tossed ball strikes any part of the mitt, it sticks—a boon both to small children, who lack adult coordination, and to grown-ups who want to pretend they're big-league Golden Glovers.

Invented in Korea, Super Grip Ball never really caught on in the United States until a young entrepreneur named Mark Paliafito bought the U.S. marketing rights in January 1991. A zealous promotional campaign, which included giving away sets to beach-going collegians on spring break, paid off, and by September Paliafito's company had sold some 1.2 million sets, at a price tag of $15 to $20 each. Imitators sprang up, but Paliafito's biggest problem was keeping pace with the demand. The big stores, like Toys "R" Us and Kaybee, couldn't get enough of the sticky mitts, and the gadget emporiums Brookstone and Sharper Image were selling them by the truckload. After all, fads don't last long, so when you find one you have to catch it quickly, and stick with it.

found the right mate. This is the quality strategy, in which more energy is put into parenting to ensure a child's survival.

Critics of the theory note that there is no real proof that early puberty is related to psychological stress in childhood, and offer alternate explanations for the early onset of sexual activity in many teenagers, including lack of parental supervision and the sense that there is little to look forward to.

**Stress and Resistance to Infection.**  A recent study conducted by Sheldon Cohen, David Tyrrell, and Andrew Smith at the Medical Research Council's Common Cold Unit in Salisbury, England, provided evidence of stress as a strong risk factor for development of the common cold. The researchers gave 420 subjects a series of questionnaires relating to behavior, personality, psychological stress, and health practices, then quarantined them for two days. A nasal spray containing one of five different respiratory viruses was then administered to all but 26 (who were given plain saline nasal sprays and studied as controls). The quarantine continued for another week, as the volunteers were watched and tested for viral infection and the development of cold symptoms.

When Cohen, Tyrrell, and Smith analyzed the data by grouping the volunteers according to their tested levels of stress, they found infection rates ranging from 74 percent in the group with the lowest stress level to 90 percent in the group with the highest. The percentages of patients actually developing colds also rose with the tested stress levels. When the data were reexamined—grouped and regrouped according to age, sex, education, allergic status, weight, the season, smoking, alcohol consumption, exercise, quality of sleep, dietary practices, and personality traits such as self-esteem—not one of these factors showed a relationship with viral infection or with actually catching a cold.

However, another study, conducted by psychologist Judith G. Rabkin and colleagues at the New York State Psychiatric Institute and the College of Physicians and Surgeons at Columbia University, found that, among 124 HIV-positive homosexual men, there was no relationship between depression or stress and the number of immune cells or how far the disease

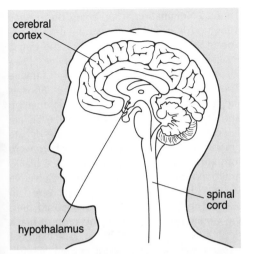

cerebral cortex

spinal cord

hypothalamus

*A provocative report on autopsy studies of the brains of heterosexuals and homosexuals seemed to lend support to the hypothesis that homosexuality has a biological basis. It was found that a particular cluster of cells in the hypothalamus—a portion of the brain that, among other things, plays a role in sexual behavior—was twice as large in the heterosexual men examined as in the homosexual men or heterosexual women.*

had progressed. While Rabkin did find some association between depression and the number of symptoms a patient exhibited, she called the connection "small" and "tentative."

**Homosexuality and the Brain.** While most scientists agree that both psychology and biology probably play a role in homosexuality, nobody has been able to come up with evidence of a biological basis for homosexual behavior. This summer, however, a study by neurobiologist Simon LeVay of the Salk Institute in La Jolla, Calif., provided possible evidence of a physiological difference between gay and heterosexual men. (The sample from which the evidence was derived was small, however, and did not include any homosexual men who had not died of AIDS.)

The study, published in August, was based on an analysis at autopsy of the brains of 41 different people: 19 homosexual men who had died of AIDS, 16 presumed heterosexual men, and 6 presumed heterosexual women. LeVay looked at small clusters of cells known as nuclei in a portion of the brain called the anterior hypothalamus. He found that one particular

nucleus was one-quarter to one-half as big in the homosexual men as in the heterosexual men, while it was the same size in the homosexual men and heterosexual women. Past studies had shown that this same nucleus is twice as big in heterosexual men as in heterosexual women and that, at least in rats, it is responsible for typically male sexual behaviors such as mounting.

LeVay remained cautious, urging that more studies be done before any final conclusions are drawn—in particular, studies examining larger numbers of brain samples, including samples from homosexuals who did not die of AIDS and from the brains of homosexual women. L.O.

**BELGIUM.** The government of Prime Minister Wilfried Martens, a Christian Democrat, collapsed in October 1991. The four-party center-left coalition fell after the Flemish telecommunications minister, without cabinet approval, signed lucrative telecommunications contracts benefiting only Flemish companies and outraging the French-speaking Walloons. All parties in Martens's center-left coalition lost seats in the ensuing November 24 elections, with parties in the far right and environmentalists making substantial gains. Pending formation of a new coalition government, the Martens government continued in a caretaker capacity.

In early January the Martens government had dispatched 18 Mirage fighter-bomber aircraft as part of a NATO force to protect Turkey from possible attack by neighboring Iraq, as tensions in the Persian Gulf region increased. Belgium also deployed six transport aircraft and five warships for support operations in the Gulf region. After the U.S.-led air war against Iraq began, Belgium agreed to supply the United States with nearly 1,000 automatic weapons and granted more than $30 million in aid to Britain and France.

In January, four Belgian hostages detained in the Middle East since 1987 were freed in conjunction with the release by Belgian authorities of a convicted Palestinian terrorist. The action appeared to violate the official policy of not negotiating with terrorists. In addition, Walid Khalid, a known terrorist, had been allowed into the country on a tourist visa to facilitate secret negotiations for the hostages' release. Two top Foreign Ministry officials resigned to take responsibility for allowing Khalid to enter, and Martens acknowledged that the secret negotiations had been "an error of discretion."

In September, Belgium and France sent troops to Zaire, a former Belgian colony, to protect and evacuate their citizens in the wake of rioting by Zairian soldiers protesting low pay. The action was described as purely humanitarian.

The Organization for Economic Cooperation and Development projected slow economic growth in 1991, with a 1.8 percent increase in gross domestic product, compared to 3.5 percent in 1990. Consumer prices were likely to rise by a little over 3 percent; the unemployment rate was projected to drop slightly below 8 percent.

See STATISTICS OF THE WORLD. W.C.C.

**BELIZE.** See STATISTICS OF THE WORLD.

**BENIN.** See STATISTICS OF THE WORLD.

**BHUTAN.** See STATISTICS OF THE WORLD.

**BLACKS IN THE UNITED STATES.** The confirmation battle over Supreme Court nominee Clarence Thomas and the passage of a civil rights bill were among the events that most concerned African-Americans in 1991. Earlier in the year, the issue of police brutality to blacks gained prominence. (See also CIVIL LIBERTIES AND CIVIL RIGHTS; CRIME; UNITED STATES: Supreme Court.)

**Thomas Nomination.** Supreme Court Justice Thurgood Marshall, a staunch civil-rights advocate and the first black to sit on the Court, resigned in June after 24 years of service. President George Bush nominated Clarence Thomas, a 43-year-old U.S. Court of Appeals judge, to fill the empty seat. The nomination and confirmation hearings before the Senate Judiciary Committee touched off debate among black Americans, many of whom were torn between supporting Thomas, as a black, and opposing him because of his conservative views. Black and civil rights groups were also split. The NAACP and others opposed him; the Council of 100, an organization of black Republicans, supported him; and the National Urban League and the American Civil Liberties Union remained officially neutral. The debate intensified when Anita Hill, a black law professor at the University of Oklahoma, came forward with allegations that Thomas had sexually harassed her when they both worked at the U.S. Department of Education and the U.S. Equal Employment Opportunity Commission during the early 1980s.

While some black Americans saw Thomas's Senate confirmation hearings as beneficial exposure for a large number of black professionals, many were distressed by the divisiveness of the controversy and the sensational nature of the charges. In the end, Thomas was narrowly confirmed by the Senate, 52-48.

Rosa Parks, whose 1955 refusal to give up her seat to a white passenger on a Montgomery, Ala., bus helped spark the civil rights movement, was commemorated with a bust in the National Portrait Gallery. Parks (right) was embraced by the sculptor, Artis Lane, during the unveiling ceremony in February.

**Civil Rights Bill.** After two years of debate, Congress passed and Bush signed a civil rights bill. The measure was intended to reverse several recent Supreme Court decisions that made it more difficult for women and minorities claiming job discrimination to bring and win damage suits. Bush had criticized previous versions of the bill on the grounds that they could lead to minority quotas in hiring and promotion. After he agreed to a compromise bill, the White House counsel issued a controversial draft executive order requiring federal agencies to phase out racial preferences in hiring. Bush disavowed it, but his statement at the formal signing of the bill appeared to narrow the administration's interpretation of certain provisions. In December the U.S. Equal Opportunity Commission ruled that the measure did not apply to discrimination claims filed before it was signed into law.

**Persian Gulf War.** Black Americans were, as a whole, less enthusiastic about the U.S. participation in the Persian Gulf war than were whites. A poll taken January 17-20 found that 47 percent of blacks supported military action against Iraq, as opposed to 80 percent of whites. Representative Gary Frank (R., Conn.) was the only one of the 25 black U.S. House members to vote for the authorization of military force on January 12. Many blacks believed funds spent on the war would be better devoted to problems at home, and many also feared that African-Americans would suffer a disproportionate share of the casualties, since although only 12 percent of the population, they made up about 25 percent of the troops. Blacks actually accounted for 17 percent of the 375 U.S. fatalities in Desert Shield and Desert Storm.

**Police Brutality.** In March, a videotape of Los Angeles policemen brutally beating and kicking black motorist Rodney King drew national attention to the issue of police brutality. A possible racial motive for the beating was revealed when transcripts of conversations between officers who were pursuing King were found to contain racist epithets. As a result of the incident, the Justice Department launched a nationwide investigation into reports of police brutality, and Los Angeles Police Chief Daryl Gates responded to pressure from local civil rights groups by announcing he would resign in April 1992.

**Politics.** During the year, Kansas City, Mo., and Denver elected their first black mayors. On the national scene, Virginia Governor L. Douglas Wilder, the nation's first black elected governor, declared his candidacy for the 1992 Democratic presidential nomination. Jesse Jackson, the "shadow senator" from Washington, D.C., who garnered millions of votes in two previous presidential elections, announced in November that he would not be a candidate in 1992. In September, Representative William Gray III (D., Pa.), the third-ranking Democrat in the House and the highest-ranking black member of Congress, resigned his seat to become head of the United Negro College Fund. Gray said he wanted to spend more time with his family and his church.

**Population.** According to census figures released early in 1991, there were 30 million blacks in the United States in 1990, an increase of 13.2 percent since 1980. A survey released in August found an increase in the proportion of black American families earning more than $50,000 a year—1 in 7 black families as of 1989, compared with 1 in 17 in 1967. At the same time, however, the percentage of blacks living in poverty declined only slightly, from 32.2 percent in 1967 to 30.7 percent in 1989.

**Health.** In November, basketball star Magic Johnson's revelation that he had tested positive for the AIDS virus focused widespread attention on the disease, especially among minority, inner-city youth for whom Johnson is a role model. Blacks suffer from AIDS at a disproportionate rate—as of December 1991, they made up 29 percent of the 202,800 Americans diagnosed with the disease.

A report released in April found that higher cancer rates for blacks were due to poverty, not race. The cancer rate for African-Americans is 383 per 100,000, versus 358 for whites. When compared with whites of similar income, education, and neighborhood, however, blacks were found to have a slightly lower incidence of cancer.

**Arts.** Whoopi Goldberg won the Academy Award for best supporting actress in March for her performance in the film *Ghost*. Goldberg became only the second black women to win an acting Oscar, after Hattie McDaniel, who won the same award for her role as Mammy in *Gone With the Wind* (1939).  M.M.D.

**BOLIVIA.** In February 1991 the government of President Jaime Paz Zamora and opposition groups agreed on a compromise plan for reforming the judicial system and methods for counting election votes, among other reforms. Charges were also dropped against nine Supreme Court justices indicted because the court had struck down a government-approved beer tax as unconstitutional.

Claiming that Peru's Shining Path (Sendero Luminoso) guerrillas had made incursions into Bolivian territory, armed forces commanders implemented a counterinsurgency strategy based on intensified rural operations. Meanwhile, other terrorist groups, such as the so-called Ayllus Rojos, emerged.

Facing drastic cutbacks in U.S. assistance if Bolivia failed to meet its 1991 coca-leaf voluntary eradication target of 7,000 hectares (about 17,000 acres), the government began a controversial program of forced eradication. In late August confrontations took place between zealous government officials, anxious to forcefully eradicate coca bushes, and peasant unions. At U.S. insistence, the government stepped up interdiction efforts, moving the Army into a key region, the Beni Department, on October 1.

Relations with the United States in fact were dominated by the war on drugs, as 56 U.S. military advisers began training two Bolivian army battalions. On July 29 the government announced a decree granting drug traffickers 120 days to avoid extradition to the United States by turning over their assets and collaborating with Bolivian authorities in capturing other traffickers. By October, under the terms of the decree seven of the top ten traffickers had turned themselves in.

The New Economic Policy, Bolivia's stabilization program initiated in 1985, is the longest-running program of its kind in Latin America. In continuing the program the government focused on implementing a 1990 decree permitting foreign investment in mining and oil drilling and paving the way for the privatization of state enterprises.

Hydrocarbon and mineral exports were expected to exceed the $918 million achieved in 1990, and nontraditional exports were expected to surpass the 1990 figure of $276 million. Moreover, the gross domestic product was projected to rise for the fifth consecutive year, reaching 2.7 percent. Government officials pointed to the repatriation of capital, measured by a significant increase in U.S. dollar and dollar-linked time deposits in the banking sector, as a sign of public confidence in the economy. Bolivia's efforts to resolve its debt problems with the help of structural adjustment loans from the Inter-American Development Bank and the International Monetary Fund resulted in a total foreign debt reduction of $900 million.

See STATISTICS OF THE WORLD.  E.G.

**BOTSWANA.** See STATISTICS OF THE WORLD.

**BRAZIL.** The radical economic program announced by President Fernando Collor de Mello after coming to office in March 1990 experienced setbacks in 1991, as high inflation rates and unemployment eroded popular support. Some progress seemed to be made in protecting the environment.

**Collor's Program.** President Collor managed to reduce inflation from an annual rate of 1,765 percent in 1989 to 400 percent during the first 12 months of his term, although during 1991 inflation rose again. Plans to trim 360,000 jobs from the government payroll saw little success. The government's efforts to sell state enterprises met with violent resistance, although its controlling interest in the Usiminas steel company was successfully sold at a premium of 11 percent over the asking price.

In late January 1991, the economics minister, Zélia Cardoso, announced new measures, including wage and price freezes, but these were widely ignored, and Cardoso resigned in May. President Collor named a former banker and diplomat, Marcílio Marques Moreira, to replace Cardoso. Meanwhile, frustrated by congressional opposition, Collor sidestepped the Congress repeatedly, issuing numerous presidential decrees to implement his programs and proposing constitutional changes that would strengthen the power of the executive branch.

Collor was most successful in opening up

the highly protectionist economy. Hundreds of tariffs on imports were reduced or eliminated. The move toward freer trade eased the once tense trade relations with the United States.

**Key Problems.** The major international problem of the Collor administration was the difficulty of forging a workable accord with commercial banks on nearly $60 billion in medium-term and long-term loans. The debt crisis considerably slowed the flow of foreign investment into Brazil. More than $1 billion left Brazil in capital flight in 1990, a trend that continued in 1991.

The war in the Persian Gulf created problems by closing down one of Brazil's most important foreign markets (Iraq), and the disruption of oil markets forced Brazil to ration gasoline.

**Social Tensions.** The continuing economic crisis worsened the plight of the millions of slum dwellers *(favelados)* in Brazil's major cities. In March, hundreds of *favelados* invaded and occupied several unfinished high-rise apartment buildings in Rio de Janeiro. A wave of kidnappings largely directed at the wealthy highlighted the growing social problems.

In early February the president of the Rural Workers Union, Expedito Ribeiro de Souza, was murdered in Rio Maria, Pará. De Souza was reportedly the fifth union leader assassinated in Rio Maria in a 12-month period. Violence between small farmers and large cattle ranchers continued, and several other rural labor leaders were wounded or killed.

**The Amazon.** Although massive burning of the Amazon rain forest continued, the pace of the destruction slowed, in part because of government measures that eliminated tax breaks for cattle ranchers in the Amazon basin. Collor also revoked decrees that had reduced Yanomami Indian lands by 75 percent and opened virgin forest to mineral prospectors. Late in the year, the government announced the creation of rain forest reserves for the Yanomami and other Indian groups.

*One of the world's largest hydroelectric dams was dedicated by the presidents of Brazil and Paraguay in May. The Itaipu Dam across the Paraná River, which separates the two countries, had been under construction for 18 years.*

In June, Collor announced a plan to allow foreign financing of environmental projects. The Brazilian government also took steps to halt the spread of the cholera epidemic from Peru into the Amazon basin.

**Regional Cooperation.** On March 26 the presidents of Argentina, Brazil, Paraguay, and Uruguay signed an agreement to form a four-country free-trade zone by 1995. On May 6 the presidents of Brazil and Paraguay dedicated the final turbine in the huge Itaipu Dam hydroelectric power complex on the Paraná River between the two countries. In December, Brazil and Argentina agreed to set up a joint agency aimed at putting their nuclear sites under international inspection.

See STATISTICS OF THE WORLD.        M.C.E.

**BRITISH COLUMBIA.** See STATISTICS OF THE WORLD. See also CANADA.

**BROADCASTING.** In the United States, the year 1991 saw some of the most dramatic live coverage of public affairs in television's history, starting with the Persian Gulf War in January and February, continuing through the Clarence Thomas confirmation hearings in the fall, and ending with William Kennedy Smith's rape trial in December. Broadcast and cable networks alike felt not just the pinch of a slumping economy, but also the pressure of trying to stay profitable as the viewing audience continued to fragment.

**Home Video Makes News.** The spread of affordable video technology has turned millions of people into potential producers of programming. This was dramatically demonstrated by an incident in Los Angeles in March, when motorist Rodney G. King was brutally beaten by Los Angeles police after they pulled his car over for speeding. A video enthusiast named George Holliday who happened to be on the scene captured the incident on his camcorder, and his tape ended up being shown on almost every newscast in America. This exposure sparked a national debate about police brutality and prompted an inquiry by an independent commission, which recommended sweeping changes including replacing the Los Angeles chief of police.

**1990-1991 Season.** NBC won the September-to-April prime-time season ratings contest for the sixth consecutive year, but it was almost the closest three-way race in the history of network television; less than half a ratings point separated NBC from third-place CBS. NBC averaged a 12.7 rating; ABC, a 12.5 rating; and CBS, a 12.3 rating. Fox Broadcasting, which programmed at least a portion of five nights weekly, finished with a 6.4 average rating. The combined audience for the three major networks continued to erode, dropping to a new low of only 63 percent of all prime-time viewers.

**Top Banana**

In June, NBC named Jay Leno as the fourth permanent host of the *Tonight Show*, taking over when veteran Johnny Carson retires in May 1992. The genial comedian had been attracting younger viewers than Carson and keeping himself in line for what he has called "the only job in television."

Leno, who will be 42 when he takes the helm, began performing professionally as a college student in Boston. His labors to succeed were hindered by his appearance (Leno has a chin that won't quit), but he honed his comedy on the road, tirelessly playing big clubs, small clubs, any club to try new material on different audiences. Comedy is like lifting weights or jogging, says Leno. You have to do it every day.

*Jay Leno*

The highest-rated series of the season was NBC's award-laden barroom comedy *Cheers*, then in its ninth year. The venerable CBS magazine series *60 Minutes* finished second. The rest of the top ten slots went to *Roseanne* (ABC); *A Different World* (NBC); *The Cosby Show* (NBC); *NFL Monday Night Football* (ABC); *America's Funniest Home Videos* (ABC); *Murphy Brown* (CBS); and *America's Funniest People* (ABC), *Designing Women* (CBS), and *Empty Nest* (NBC), all tied.

The season saw *Family Matters*, an ABC situation comedy about a middle-class black family, develop into a top 20 hit, largely because of the unexpected popularity of the character named Steve Urkel, a superbright "nerd" portrayed by Jhaleel White. Meanwhile, CBS's *Northern Exposure*, a whimsical comedy-drama about a city-bred doctor forced to work off his medical school loans in an Alaskan hamlet populated by eccentrics of assorted ethnic heritage, became the new cult show of the season. The program edged up the Nielsen chart and became a top 20 performer during the summer.

*Northern Exposure* was in a sense a sunnier, more accessible successor to ABC's *Twin Peaks*, which lost viewers steadily. ABC canceled the serial at season's end, along with two other dramatic series that had been widely acclaimed: *thirtysomething* and the Vietnam series *China Beach*. CBS's *Dallas* ended its internationally popular 13-year run.

The most impressive made-for-TV movies of the season were CBS's *Sarah, Plain and Tall*, starring Glenn Close as a New England woman who journeys to Kansas in answer to a widower's advertisement for a mother for his children; NBC's *Switched at Birth*, a fact-based drama that transcended its tabloid possibilities; and ABC's *Separate but Equal*, a dramatization of the U.S. Supreme Court's historic school desegregation ruling, with Sidney Poitier portraying lawyer (later Supreme Court Justice) Thurgood Marshall.

On the late-night front, NBC announced Johnny Carson's retirement from *The Tonight Show*, naming guest host Jay Leno to succeed him, effective in May 1992.

**1991 Fall Season.** In response to soaring production costs and the ratings failure of the pre-

Northern Exposure, a comedy-drama series revolving about the adventures of a young city doctor who takes up his practice in a remote Alaskan town, made an impact with its fanciful tone and its zany cast of characters.

vious season's more ambitious series—such as the musical drama *Cop Rock*, the medical anthology *Lifestories*, and the action series *The Flash*—the three major networks retreated to familiar formats and faces. Three months into the season, only one series, *Home Improvement* (ABC), had emerged as a top ten hit; it starred comedian Tim Allen as the host of a TV fixit show whose overzealous use of power tools at home drove his wife up the sheetrock.

Only a few dramatic series made the network schedules. These included NBC's *I'll Fly Away*, about a small Southern town during the early days of the civil rights movement; *Homefront*, about American soldiers and their families readjusting after World War II; and *Reasonable Doubts*, a crime drama in which Academy Award-winning actress Marlee Matlin, who is deaf, played a deaf prosecuting attorney. The most acclaimed new series was CBS's *Brooklyn Bridge*, an autobiographical series by producer-writer Gary David Goldberg (*Family Ties*) about growing up in an extended Jewish family in Brooklyn in the mid-1950s. ABC's *FBI: The Untold Stories* and *American Detective* continued the trend of low-cost so-called "reality" programs.

**Fox Broadcasting.** Fox's big programming gamble of the 1990-1991 season—shifting its most popular show, *The Simpsons*, to Thursdays, head to head against NBC's *Cosby Show*—paid off in the long run. Still a solid ratings performer, though not the top-20 show it had been on Sundays, *The Simpsons* enabled the "fourth network" to establish a full-fledged lineup on Thursdays. It included *Beverly Hills 90210*, a dramatic series about high school students in Los Angeles's ritziest residential section, which by season's end had become the most popular show on television among teens and young adults. In addition to successful returning series such as *The Simpsons*, *Married . . . With Children*, and *In Living Color*, Fox's schedule in the fall of 1991 included *Herman's Head*, a comedy that took viewers inside the lead character's head; *Drexell's Class*, in which veteran actor Dabney Coleman played an irascible elementary school teacher; and *Roc*, a comedy about a Baltimore sanitation worker.

**Public Television.** Public television experienced trying times, with competition from some cable networks in such programming areas as nature, culture, and public affairs. Cuts in state and local funding resulted in job and programming cutbacks at some of the nation's most productive public TV stations, notably New York's WNET and Boston's WGBH. Meanwhile, the Public Broadcasting Service (PBS) and its loose confederation of 341 stations came under increased scrutiny by right-wing watchdog groups. The program that ignited the greatest furor was *Tongues Untied*, a film by Marlon Riggs about being a gay black man in America, which included explicit language and a scene of two men kissing. Partly because of pressure from the right-wing, pro-Christian American Family Association, public TV stations in 18 of the 50 largest markets re-

Michael Landon, one of television's most beloved performers, died in July. He is seen at right in his role as Little Joe in Bonanza, with costars Lorne Greene (center) and Dan Blocker (right). He later played the rugged but sensitive father in Little House on the Prairie (above), a family-oriented show which he also created and produced.

fused to carry the program. When similar complaints subsequently arose about *Stop the Church*, a film about a demonstration by AIDS activists against policies of the Roman Catholic Church, PBS removed it from the schedule. Public broadcasting also drew criticism from left-wing watchdog groups, such as Fairness and Accuracy in Reporting, for its increased efforts to court conservative viewers and corporations to make up for shortfalls in state funding.

PBS still managed to present another impressive "showcase week" to launch its 1991 fall season. *Columbus and the Age of Discovery*, a seven-hour documentary series exploring the "collision" of Western Europe and the Americas, won healthy ratings. Other notable fall programming included *Childhood*, a series that traced the growth of children from 12 families on five continents; *LBJ*, a four-hour biography of former President Lyndon Johnson; and *Land of the Eagle*, an eight-hour survey of North America's wildlife and wild places.

**Cable Television.** In July three major television companies—NBC, Time Warner, and Cablevision Systems—launched the Court-

room Television Network, a cable channel devoted to coverage of criminal and civil trials. Its programming included live coverage of the Senate confirmation hearings of U.S. Supreme Court Justice Clarence Thomas and the rape trial of William Kennedy Smith. The *Christian Science Monitor* launched the educational-informational Monitor Channel in May.

There were several mergers: Discovery Networks, which owns the Discovery Channel, bought the Learning Channel, and the NBC-owned CNBC (Consumer News and Business Channel) absorbed its rival Financial News Network (FNN). The Comedy Channel, owned by Home Box Office, and HA! TV, owned by MTV Networks, Inc., merged their programming into a single service dubbed Comedy Central, which presented a 24-hour schedule. The year also saw the advent of broadcast-cable production partnerships.

**News.** The Cable News Network, which in 1991 celebrated its 11th anniversary, made a giant leap into public consciousness on January 17, when the Persian Gulf War began with the allied bombing of Iraq. Although ABC's Gary Shepard was the first to report antiaircraft fire, it was CNN's Peter Arnett, John Holliman, and Bernard Shaw, watching the bombing from the Rashid Hotel in downtown Baghdad, whose reports mesmerized America (*see also* PEOPLE IN THE NEWS: Peter Arnett). For almost two days, only CNN was able to get live reports out of Baghdad, thanks to a "four wire"— a private, dedicated phone line that does not go through normal telephone switching systems—arranged with the Iraqi government before the war started. Frustratingly scooped, the broadcast networks complained CNN had made some kind of special, perhaps unethical, deal with the Iraqis. CNN officials said they had simply lobbied harder.

CNN's coverage remained controversial throughout the war. After Holliman and Shaw left Baghdad, Arnett stayed on with a producer and a small satellite dish. Some officials suggested he was being used to transmit enemy propaganda, and a conservative coalition tried to get CNN to pull the plug on him. CNN not only stood by Arnett but also gained prominence and prestige from its war coverage. The first night, CNN's cablecast was watched in 11 million homes, an all-time high. And CNN's

*Courtroom fanatics got all they could wish for with the launching of the Courtroom Television Network, a cable channel devoted exclusively to actual trials. Its virtually complete coverage of the William Kennedy Smith rape trial brought high ratings and national publicity; here, prosecutor Moira Lasch is seen during a broadcast.*

reports got additional exposure on its 225 broadcast subscribers, 130 of which have primary affiliations with CBS, ABC or NBC.

Throughout the war, the networks wrangled with Pentagon officials over what they considered restrictive rules governing media coverage, including requirements that reporters be accompanied by military guides. For viewers, the "live television war" was a lesson in the messy process of journalism. They saw network correspondents fumbling with gas masks as Iraqi Scud missiles approached and heard them ask questions at military briefings that sometimes sounded dumb or antagonistic. They also saw in large part a bloodless war; footage provided by the military of bombing missions looked as abstract as a video game.

Although the war made the network news divisions the center of attention for a while, it came back to haunt them as the year wore on. Along with other breaking news that demanded extensive coverage, particularly the failed coup in the Soviet Union and the Clarence Thomas confirmation hearings, the war coverage pushed them over budget. Only CNN was expected to top its 1990 profits in 1991. CBS News and NBC News anticipated losses. ABC, CBS, and NBC closed some of their national and international news bureaus to save money.

The year also brought the death of two distinguished television journalists. Harry Reasoner, one of the original *60 Minutes* hosts and a former ABC News anchor, and veteran NBC correspondent Douglas Kiker both died in August.

**Emmy Awards.** The Academy of Television Arts and Sciences Awards were presented in Pasadena, Calif., in August. Emmy winners included *L.A. Law* for best drama series, *Cheers* for best comedy series, and *Separate But Equal* for best miniseries or special. James Earl Jones won as best actor in a drama series for his role in *Gabriel's Fire*, Patricia Wettig was named best actress in a drama series for her role in *thirtysomething*, and Burt Reynolds in *Evening Shade* and Kirstie Alley in *Cheers* were voted best comedy actor and actress, respectively. Sir John Gielgud in *Summer's Lease*, shown on *Masterpiece Theater*, and Lynn Whitfield in *The Josephine Baker Story* were named best actor and actress in a miniseries or special. Colleen Dewhurst won a posthumous Emmy for her role in *Murphy Brown*.

**Regulation.** In response to the Children's Television Act of 1990, the Federal Communications Commission adopted rules governing commercial content of programs "produced and broadcast primarily" for children under age 12. The FCC limited commercials in weekday programming to 12 minutes per hour and in weekend programs to 10½ minutes per hour. It also forbade "program length commercials"—shows inspired by toys or other merchandise—from containing advertisements for the merchandise and urged stations to increase the amount of educational programming for children.

The agency also sought to strengthen AM radio's appeal. It voted to add new AM frequencies, which would be available only to existing stations willing to change wavelengths, in a move to reduce interference caused by an overcrowded dial. It also relaxed its limits on radio station ownership; from 1992 there would be no limit on the number of stations a company could own nationwide, and a company could own up to two FMs and two AMs per market.

**Canadian Developments.** Canada's three big television companies—the publicly run Canadian Broadcasting Corporation, the privately owned CTV, and the Canwest-Global System—aired only four new prime-time dramatic series among them. Early in the year CBC debuted the teen soap opera *Northwood* and the saga of an inner-city journalist, *Urban Angel*. In September, Global introduced *Sweating Bullets*, a Canadian-Mexican coproduction set in the Florida Keys. In November, CTV launched the action-adventure series *Counterstrike*, a coproduction with French and American networks. In September, CBC introduced *Newsmagazine*, a half-hour current affairs show on weeknights.

On September 5, Viewer's Choice Canada, a pay-per-view service, premiered in major cities in Ontario, Québec, and the Atlantic provinces. It was expected to become available across the country in 1992.

In radio, the regulatory Canadian Radio-Television and Telecommunications Commission increased Canadian content requirements on most FM stations from 20 to 30 percent, while at the same time loosening restrictions on both advertising and programming.

N.W.H.

**BRUNEI.** *See* STATISTICS OF THE WORLD.

**BULGARIA.** As it struggled to establish a free-market economy and bolster relations with other countries, Bulgaria in late 1991 installed a non-Communist government.

**Political Change.** The fairly even split in the Grand National Assembly between the Bulgarian Socialist (formerly Communist) Party and the Union of Democratic Forces (UDF), a coalition of over a dozen parties ranging from social democrats to conservatives, made a consensus on policy difficult for the government of Dimitur Popov, installed in late 1990.

When Bulgaria's new constitution was presented by the Grand National Assembly on July 14, some UDF members staged a hunger strike, claiming that the constitution would consolidate the power of the Socialists. Nevertheless, the constitution went into effect, and on October 13, after several postponements, elections took place.

In the elections, the UDF won by a slight plurality, edging out the Socialist bloc (which included five minor parties in addition to the Bulgarian Socialist Party) and winning 110 seats, 6 more than the Socialists. The Movement for Rights and Freedom, an ethnic Turkish party, garnered 8 percent of the vote, winning the remaining 24 seats. UDF leader Filip Dimitrov was named prime minister; at 36, he was the youngest in the country's history. The new Parliament passed a law mandating confiscation of the Socialist Party's property.

**Zhivkov Trial.** The trial of former Communist leader Todor Zhivkov, charged with corruption and the abuse of power, opened in February in Bulgaria's Supreme Court. In March the prosecutor added the charge that Zhivkov was primarily responsible for Bulgaria's anti-Turkish policies. Zhivkov entered a plea of not guilty. The trial was unresolved at year's end.

**Foreign Policy Efforts.** Ever since the collapse of hard-line Communism in Bulgaria, the country had been endeavoring to improve its standing in the international community. Improved relations with Washington led to a new U.S.-Bulgaria trade policy in January 1991, but relations between Sofia and Ankara remained strained as a result of past human rights abuses directed at Bulgaria's ethnic-Turkish minority. The specter of boundary revision shadowed

Todor Zhivkov (center), former Communist leader of Bulgaria, went before the nation's Supreme Court in February, charged with abuse of power and corruption.

Sofia's relations with Yugoslavia and Romania. Speculation that Bulgaria might acquire Yugoslav Macedonia fueled a century-old dream among right-wing expansionists. And Romanian Foreign Minister Adrian Nastase made some Bulgarians nervous when, in a speech in June, he referred to the issue of Southern Dobruja, a territory acquired by Bucharest from Sofia in 1913 and returned to Bulgaria in 1940.

In August, Israeli Prime Minister Yitzhak Shamir made a state visit to Bulgaria. In exchange for $3 million in credit from Jerusalem, Sofia agreed to allow Soviet Jews emigrating to Israel to travel through Bulgaria.

**Turkish Rights.** The extension of civil, cultural, and religious rights to the Turks and other minorities continued. Parliament granted Turkish communities the right to have schools in which some classes were taught in Turkish, although many Turks were dissatisfied with this partial concession.

**Economic Problems.** The Popov government instituted draconian measures to speed the transition to a market economy, including the elimination of price subsidies. Prices rose steeply, and unemployment increased. Work stoppages were frequent. Energy was in short supply, necessitating the rationing of electricity. Bulgaria's nuclear power plant at Kozloduy on the Danube was shut down completely in September, following months of safety warnings from international experts. Sofia's decision to suspend payments on its $11 billion foreign debt made new aid hard to find, but the World Bank and the Group of 24 wealthy countries extended loans, while the European Community approved food and medical aid.

See STATISTICS OF THE WORLD.        F.B.C.

**BURKINA FASO.** See STATISTICS OF THE WORLD.

**BURMA.** See MYANMAR.

**BURUNDI.** See STATISTICS OF THE WORLD.

# C

**CABINET, UNITED STATES.** *See* UNITED STATES OF AMERICA: *The Presidency.*

**CALIFORNIA.** *See* STATISTICS OF THE WORLD.

**CAMBODIA.** After more than two decades of civil war, Cambodia's opposing factions signed a peace treaty in October 1991. The parties to the treaty were the regime installed by Vietnam in 1979, led by Premier Hun Sen; the Chinese-backed Khmer Rouge (in power from 1975 to 1979, under the leadership of Pol Pot); and two non-Communist groups, the followers of Prince Norodom Sihanouk (ousted in a 1970 coup), and the Khmer People's National Liberation Front, an independent group led by former Premier Son Sann. However, the future of the peace plan remained in some doubt.

The treaty, signed in Paris on October 23, was sponsored by the UN Security Council and witnessed by representatives of 18 nations. It provided for an immediate cease-fire; formation of a transitional coalition government, the Supreme National Council (SNC), representing all four factions, with Sihanouk serving as chairman and interim head of state; and free national elections in 1993. The transition phase and election process was to be monitored by the UN, which would run certain key ministries for a time. Memories of the terrors and "killing fields" massacres of the Pol Pot regime remained vivid, however, and there was anxiety that the Khmer Rouge would regain a dominant role.

Although Prince Sihanouk received a tumultuous welcome when he returned to Phnom Penh on November 14, thousands of angry demonstrators met the Khmer Rouge delegation headed by Khieu Samphan when it returned later in November, and some of them attacked Khieu Samphan physically, forcing him to flee to Thailand. Violent demonstrations in December in Phnom Penh, partly to protest Khieu Samphan's expected return, led Hun Sen to declare that he could not guarantee safety for the Khmer Rouge officials. Amid heavy security—and restrictions by the Hun Sen regime on freedom of expression—Khieu Samphan returned at the end of the month, and the Supreme National Council held its first meeting in Cambodia.

The war left Cambodia with a debilitated populace, a shattered economic and social infrastructure, and a legacy of fear and suspicion. Cambodia's gross domestic product had

*Prince Norodom Sihanouk, Cambodia's former ruler who spent most of the previous 20 years in exile, returned in November to Phnom Penh, where he was welcomed by enthusiastic crowds. Sihanouk headed a new Supreme National Council, established under a UN-supervised peace plan for the war-torn nation.*

fallen to among the lowest in Asia. Runaway military expenditures and monetary expansion had fueled inflation and debased the local currency. A cut in trade credits from the Soviet Union had created shortages. A scarcity of food was aggravated by drought and cutbacks in foreign aid.

See STATISTICS OF THE WORLD.          G.H.

**CAMEROON.**   See STATISTICS OF THE WORLD.

**CANADA.**   As 1991 began, Canadians were apprehensive about events in the Persian Gulf. The country was divided about the wisdom of committing its limited air force and meager navy to an American-led military adventure. Most Canadians considered the shrinking economy and the rancorous debate over French-speaking Québec's place—if any—in the federation to be more pressing problems. Polls conducted throughout the year showed that more than 80 percent of Canadians consistently disapproved of the performance of Prime Minister Brian Mulroney (see profile in PEOPLE IN THE NEWS) and his Progressive Conservative government.

**The Gulf War and the Military.**   In the final hours before the Persian Gulf War began in

January, Canada's Parliament formally debated the call to arms. The narrow majority that spoke in favor of war reflected a national ambivalence about that course. Just over 50 percent of all Canadians polled opposed the decision to place the country on the offensive.

For the Canadian military, peace brought more attrition than the battlefield. None of the 2,000 troops who served in the Gulf were lost. But federal Defense Minister Marcel Masse announced in September that the size of the armed forces would shrink from 87,000 to 76,000. Masse also said that Canada would withdraw its 6,600-person tank and air forces under NATO command in Germany, effectively ending a 40-year presence there.

**Divisions Over the Future.**   The 1990 failure of the Meech Lake accord had left Canada's future as a united nation in more doubt than ever. That agreement would have acknowledged Québec to be a "distinct society" within Canada and secured Québec's recognition of changes to the Canadian constitution, formally withheld since 1982. But the accord fell apart when Manitoba and Newfoundland failed to ratify it. Québecers perceived the Meech Lake

As Canada was strained by separatist sentiment in Québec and a widespread desire for political reform, Constitutional Affairs Minister Joe Clark (right) oversaw the drafting of proposed constitutional changes. His plan, hammered out over the summer, was submitted to a parliamentary panel headed by Senator Claude Castonguay (left) and MP Dorothy Dobbie.

collapse as, in effect, a stinging rebuke from English Canada.

As the year 1991 began, two groups in Québec were studying that province's options, one on behalf of its National Assembly (as the provincial legislature is called), the other on behalf of the governing Liberal Party. Both committees found that sentiment was running strongly in favor of outright independence if English Canada did not agree to cede large areas of federal power to Québec within a year. The National Assembly committee concluded by recommending that Québecers be allowed to choose by referendum between independence and a new Canadian federation in which their province would have vastly greater powers.

But it was the report Liberal lawyer Jean Allaire presented to his party in late January that defined just what Québecers expected any new federal deal to include. The Allaire Report called on Ottawa to relinquish broad areas of its present authority to the provinces, keeping charge of the Canadian currency, the national debt, the existing system of revenue equalization among the provinces, and protection of the country's borders. In concert with the provinces—and subject to provincial veto—the federal Parliament would also be permitted a share of authority over some additional areas, including amendments to the Criminal Code of Canada. But the Canadian Charter of Rights and Freedoms would have no force in Québec.

The last exemption was a critical one. The Charter, adopted as a part of the Canadian constitution in the 1982 amendments that Québec rejected, had quickly acquired a central place in most Canadians' sense of citizenhood and become a powerful legal weapon on behalf of individual rights. Among Québec's political leadership, however, the Charter was viewed as a threat, partly because of its origins in the contested amendments and partly because it favored legal challenges to the province's language laws, which restrict the use of English in Québec.

Allaire's vision became the official policy of Québec's Liberal Party in March. In June the National Assembly voted that the government should hold a referendum no later than Octo-

ber 1992 in which Québecers would be given a choice between independence and any Canadian offer of additional power.

Meanwhile, two federal groups were also examining the constitutional question. One was a parliamentary committee led by Québec Senator Gerald Beaudoin and Alberta Conservative Member of Parliament Robert Edwards. After holding hearings around the country, in July the Beaudoin-Edwards committee urged Mulroney to put any new proposals for amendments to the constitution before the Canadian people in a nonbinding referendum.

The full measure of Canadians' anger at their federal leaders surfaced before the other federal panel—the 12-member Citizens' Forum on Canada's Future. Appearing before the forum in large and small groups across the country, Canadians unleashed a torrent of criticism. They demanded that politicians at every level consult the public closely in the next round of constitutional negotiations. But beyond demanding an early settlement of the long-standing grievances of Canada's native peoples, they offered little specific guidance.

**New Reform Proposals.** Recognizing that his own deep unpopularity had cast a pall over attempts to arrest the country's slide toward division, in April Prime Minister Mulroney named former Foreign Minister Joe Clark to head the newly created portfolio of constitutional affairs. In his new role, Clark had the unpromising task of formulating a compromise that would bridge the differences between the wholesale national devolution that Québec envisaged and the quite distinct ideas for reform emerging from consultations in other provinces.

On September 24, after a summer of intense battles within the federal cabinet between ministers from Québec and those from the rest of Canada, Clark presented the government's proposed constitutional compromise. It envisaged a far more sweeping overhaul of the Canadian confederation than the six-point Meech Lake accord. But it was far from the full retreat from federal power that Allaire had called for. Under the compromise plan the constitution would recognize Québec as a "distinct society"—the wording used in the Meech Lake accord—but define that distinction as deriving from Québec's language, culture, and civil law; this change was intended to forestall use of the "distinct society" clause to justify unacceptable restrictions on civil liberties. The plan would also reshape Canada's Senate into an elected chamber with members more equitably distributed among Canada's provinces and territories and with some representation guaranteed for aboriginal peoples.

Among other provisions, native Canadians would achieve an undefined right to self-government in ten years if they failed to negotiate a settlement of the governance issue before then. But native governments would remain subject to Canadian laws and the Charter of Rights and Freedoms. Provincial barriers to the free movement of goods, services, capital, and labor would become unconstitutional. The federal government would transfer to the provinces authority over only a handful of the 22 areas that the Allaire Report had demanded—among them tourism and manpower training—but would agree to reach "constitutional agreements" with provinces like Québec, giving them federal authority in the areas of culture and immigration.

While most provincial leaders muted their criticism of Clark's proposals, in Québec, Jacques Parizeau, leader of the separatist opposition Parti Québécois, denounced them, and Premier Robert Bourassa declared them to be unacceptable in their existing form. The proposals were put before a parliamentary panel, which was to report its conclusions in early 1992.

**Opposition Parties.** Although polls indicated that the federal Liberals were far more popular than the ruling Conservatives, the party's organization and leadership remained weak. Jean Chrétien, a Québec lawyer and former cabinet minister in several Trudeau governments who won his party's leadership in June 1990, proved to be a poor performer in English, and Québec critics tied him to the failure of the Meech Lake accord, effectively discrediting him in his home province. The federal New Democrats, meanwhile, lost momentum.

The federal force displaying the most momentum was the barely four-year-old Reform Party of Canada. The party, which espouses a neoconservative program of balanced public budgets and smaller government—and a hard line toward Québec—won only 2 percent of the votes in Canada's 1988 general election. By June 1991, however, Gallup polls found that Reform and its slight, scholarly leader, Preston Manning, had as much public support as Mulroney's ruling Conservatives.

**Provincial Fortunes.** In British Columbia, Dutch-born Social Credit Premier William Vander Zalm resigned in April amid allegations of personal corruption, and in October, after a disastrously inept election campaign, the conservative Social Credit Party saw its long dominance at the ballot box come to an end. Voters elected a majority of New Democrats to the legislature under the leadership of moderate Michael Harcourt, a former mayor of Vancouver. The provincial Liberals—moribund for most of the years of Social Credit Party rule—captured second place to become the official opposition party.

Voters in Saskatchewan replaced the aging Conservative government of Premier Grant Devine, which had borrowed heavily, as low world wheat prices wracked the prairie province's grain-based economy. In an election on October 21, the NDP, under lawyer Roy Romanow, a minister in several NDP governments in the late 1970s, won a majority.

In New Brunswick, however, Premier Frank McKenna's Liberals comfortably retained a majority after late September elections. What startled analysts there was the performance of the right-wing Confederation of Regions party, which outpolled both the Conservatives and the NDP to elect eight members—enough to form the official opposition. The party, known by its acronym, CoR, advocates withdrawing language protection from the roughly one-third of New Brunswick's 750,000 people who speak French.

**Indian Affairs.** Manitoba lawyer Ovide Mercredi's election in June as the national chief of the Assembly of First Nations attracted great attention in Canada and marked a year in which relations between natives and the Canadian government seemed to improve. Northern Québec's Cree forced the province's Liberal government to delay its planned $13 billion expansion of an already massive hydroelectric project, pending an environmental

*The New Democratic Party won two provincial elections in October. Above, Saskatchewan NDP leader Roy Romanow (right) celebrates with former NDP Premier Allan Blakeney; at right, Michael Harcourt, British Columbia's new premier.*

review. And in August, NDP Premier Bob Rae of Ontario signed an agreement with leaders of the province's 175,000 native residents acknowledging that they possess an inherent right to self-government.

The most striking development of 1991 was the agreement by the federal government to grant control over 770,000 square miles—equal to one-fifth of Canada's land area—to the 17,500 Eskimos, or Inuit, living there. The area, to be carved out of the Northwest Territories and to be known as Nunavut, would have territorial status to start with but might eventually become a province. The Inuit would have outright title to about one-sixth of Nunavut and mineral rights over 14,000 square miles. Rights to the rest of the area would stay with the federal government, with the Inuit being paid resource royalties from any development. The accord was to be submitted to Parliament for approval, with a plebiscite in the Northwest Territories to follow.

**A Weak Economic Recovery.** Canada's gross domestic product grew by almost 1 percent in April 1991—the first significant growth since the country's economy fell into recession in the second quarter of 1990. But despite a continuing drop in interest rates, there was little strength in the recovery. Unemployment remained over 10 percent throughout the year, and many analysts predicted that few of the 250,000 jobs lost in Canada's manufacturing sector would ever return.

The economic year got off to a bad start as Canadian consumers reacted to the imposition on January 1 of a 7 percent national value-added tax on almost all goods and services (food, rent, and financing charges are exempt) by severely restraining their spending. Those consumers who did spend often sought out perceived tax-free bargains across the Canada-U.S. border. When appeals to patriotism failed to reduce the massive weekend exodus of millions of Canadian shoppers, the government responded by cracking down on Canadians who failed to report their purchases—and pay duty and tax on them—at border points.

The three-year-old Free Trade Agreement with the United States continued to produce uneven benefits. Canadian truckers organized blockades that tied up major Toronto and Ottawa highways to dramatize their claim that crippling Canadian taxes on fuel and tires left them unable to meet competition from American-owned rigs. The agreement also failed to protect potato growers in Prince Edward Island

117

The Prince and Princess of Wales, Charles and Diana, brought their royal presences to Canada in October. They are seen here with Ontario Premier Bob Rae (far left) at the Science North Center in Sudbury, Ont.

and lumber producers in British Columbia from losing export orders to American competitors, who benefited from protectionism.

**Law and Diplomacy.** If support for the Gulf War was ambivalent, the Canadian government took clear stands elsewhere. In the wake of the failed August coup attempt in the Soviet Union, Canada was among the first nations in the West to recognize the independent governments of the Baltic states. And when Haiti's military toppled the country's first democratically elected president in September, Canada took a leading role in organizing diplomatic resistance to the coup.

At home, Parliament rejected a law permitting abortions at any stage of pregnancy if a woman's physical, mental, or psychological health was endangered by the pregnancy, thus effectively leaving any future regulation of abortion up to the provinces. Parliament also adopted a bill tightening Canada's already strict gun control provisions.

**Royal Visit.** During a week-long visit to Canada in October, the Prince of Wales made a strong plea for national unity, endorsing the status of Québec as a "distinct society." Prince Charles was accompanied by his wife, Princess Diana, and by their sons, William, 9, and Henry, 7.

**Sports.** Heads snapped to attention across North America when the Toronto Argonauts of the eight-team Canadian Football League signed Notre Dame running back Raghib "Rocket" Ismail to a four-year contract for $30.1 million (Canadian dollars). Baseball's Toronto Blue Jays provided both excitement and disappointment, as they captured the American League Eastern Division title but fell in the playoffs.

*See* STATISTICS OF THE WORLD. C.W.

**CAPE VERDE.** *See* STATISTICS OF THE WORLD.

**CARIBBEAN BASIN.** Leaders of the 13 English-speaking Caribbean Community (Caricom) countries met twice during 1991, in Trinidad in late February for their first regional economic conference and in St. Christopher and Nevis (St. Kitts and Nevis) in July for their 12th annual heads of government summit. At the July summit, the British Virgin Islands and the Turks and Caicos Islands were granted associate Caricom membership; Anguilla and Colombia received observer status. Caricom officials also approved a framework agreement providing for a joint U.S.-Caricom council to negotiate on trade and investment matters.

The Persian Gulf War and North American recession dealt a severe blow to tourism, the region's main revenue producer, especially in the peak early months of 1991, resulting in discounted hotel rooms and personnel layoffs across the Caribbean. Recovery during the summer was slow.

The Windward Island nations of Dominica, Grenada, St. Lucia, and St. Vincent and the Grenadines inched closer toward political union, as details of a proposed unification plan were considered by a Regional Constituent Assembly. The unity proposal, when completed, was to be submitted to a referendum in the four island nations.

**Barbados.** Prime Minister Erskine Sandiford's governing Democratic Labor Party began the year with a clear-cut victory in January 22 elections, winning 18 parliamentary seats, to 10 for the Barbados Labor Party. In August, Sandiford announced an austerity program.

**Belize.** In January, Belize was admitted as a full member of the Organization of American States, where it had had observer status since 1989. In September, Guatemala recognized Belize's right to self-determination and independence; Belize, in turn, offered Guatemala the use of its ports.

**Dominican Republic.** In February, octogenarian President Joaquín Balaguer resigned as president of the Social Christian Party; he later fueled speculation that this would be his last term in office by declaring that he "could not repeal the laws of nature." The recession continued and labor unrest led to periodic strikes. Austerity policies succeeded in lowering both inflation and the state-sector deficit. However, sugar production declined and tourism slumped.

**Guyana.** Guyana's President Desmond Hoyte and his ruling People's National Congress postponed elections until 1992. In the meantime, with a foreign debt in excess of $1.7 billion, Guyana continued with the aus-

terity policies required under a three-year plan negotiated with the International Monetary Fund.

**Jamaica.** The year brought continued evidence of Prime Minister Michael N. Manley's conversion from a dedicated socialist of the 1970s to an ardent advocate of free-market economic policies. While the country's foreign exchange policy was liberalized to encourage exports, the government offered for sale 64 wholly or partially owned government enterprises. Despite a downturn in tourism early in the year, signs of a turnaround were apparent by late summer.

Howard Felix Harlan Cooke, 70, a senator and former education minister, became the island's governor general in August, replacing Sir Florizel Glasspole, 82, who retired.

**Montserrat.** The National Progressive Party, contesting its first general election, swept to power on October 8 in this tiny British crown colony. Under the leadership of Reuben Meade, a 37-year-old economist, the NPP won four of the seven seats at stake.

**Suriname.** In May, several months after the ouster of President Ramsenk Shawaar in military coup, new elections were held, and Ronald Venetiaan, of the New Front Party, became president of Suriname. An advocate of constitutional revisions designed to reduce the political influence of the military, Venetiaan was confronted by an ailing economy weakened by heavy debt and a drop in world prices for bauxite.

**Trinidad and Tobago.** The country elected a new prime minister, Patrick Manning, in December. Manning represented the People's National Movement, which won 21 of 36 seats in Parliament. In his campaign, Manning promised relief from austerity measures.

*See* STATISTICS OF THE WORLD. *See also* CUBA; HAITI; PUERTO RICO.

D.D.B., P.W., J.D.M., & T.P.A.

**CENTRAL AFRICAN REPUBLIC.** *See* STATISTICS OF THE WORLD.

**CEYLON.** *See* SRI LANKA.

**CHAD.** *See* STATISTICS OF THE WORLD.

**CHEMISTRY.** Researchers in chemistry explored a variety of new frontiers in 1991, among them properties of newly discovered molecules nicknamed buckyballs.

## CHEMISTRY

**Fullerenes.** Scientists made much progress in understanding fullerenes, all-carbon molecules whose atoms are arranged as hexagons and pentagons that fit together to make a cage. The spherical 60-carbon fullerene, called the buckminsterfullerene, or buckyball for short, because it resembles the geodesic dome made famous by the late U.S. inventor R. Buckminster Fuller, has undergone all kinds of experimental and theoretical studies as scientists try to understand its structure and properties and those of other members of the fullerene family. What practical applications there may be for these fascinating molecules remains unclear, although scientists speculate that there could be many.

Much, for example, was learned about fullerenes as superconductors—materials capable of transmitting electricity with zero resistance at extremely low temperatures. In April, R. C. Haddon and colleagues at AT&T Bell Laboratories in Murray Hill, N.J., announced the first superconducting buckyball material. This was a a film treated with a potassium additive, with a critical temperature of 18 kelvins. Over the next few months the temperature at which buckyballs remain superconducting increased as researchers experimented with different additives. In August, Zafar Iqbal from Allied-Signal Inc., in Morristown, N.J., reported that he and his colleagues had produced a thallium-rubidium buckyball film that remained superconducting to a temperature of 45 kelvins.

Meanwhile, Pierre-Marc Allemand and coworkers at the University of California, Santa Barbara, announced in July that they had made a buckyball compound that became magnetic at 16 kelvins. Several research groups showed that fullerenes exhibit nonlinear optical properties as well; that is, they multiply the frequency of light passing through them. John H. Holloway and his colleagues at Leicester University, England, heated buckyballs and fluorine gas to create a completely fluorinated fullerene. And Jack B. Howard and his colleagues at the Massachusetts Institute of Technology reported on a new technique for making large quantities of fullerenes by burning benzene to make soot. The standard method for producing fullerenes has been to vaporize graphite rods.

**Light From Silicon.** In May, British and French scientists announced they had excited acid-etched silicon wafers to emit visible light in response to illumination and that the color of light depended on the degree of etching. Later, researchers from Johns Hopkins Univer-

Buckyballs were much in the news as chemists such as Rice University's Richard E. Smalley, here holding a buckyball model, scrambled to find applications for these fascinating new carbon molecules, technically known as buckminsterfullerenes because their structure resembles the geodesic dome developed by the American inventor R. Buckminster Fuller.

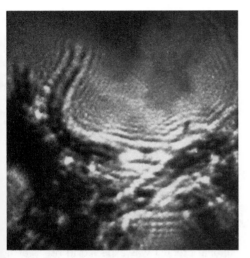

*Using an electron beam so fine that it is projected from a tip just one atom wide, scientists at IBM's Zurich Research Laboratory were able to create atomic-scale holograms of carbon fibers, gold films, and—seen here—DNA.*

sity in Baltimore, led by Peter Searson, achieved similar results by exciting wafers of porous silicon with a green argon laser. The silicon gave off reddish-orange light. In September the British group, led by Leigh T. Canham from the Defense Research Agency in Great Malvern, England, reported on transmission electron microscopy showing that the acid created quantum wires 3 nanometers (120 billionth of an inch) wide and that colors varied according to wire thickness. Silicon may thus take on an added role in the science of lasers and in the science of ultraminiaturized computer chips.

**Electron Holography.** Hans-Werner Fink, of IBM's Zurich Research Laboratory in Switzerland, and his colleagues reported in September on the use of a lensless electron projector to make atomic-scale electron holograms of carbon fibers, thin gold films, and DNA molecules. They produced the highly coherent electron beam needed for obtaining three-dimensional images by using an ultrathin tungsten tip, sharpened to one-atom width, that enables the projector to shoot out low energy electrons for seeing overall shape and structure and then high energy ones for resolving finer

details. This device minimizes beam damage and so can be used with biological molecules such as DNA.

**Superconductors.** Using scanning tunneling microscopy, U.S. and European research teams produced strikingly similar images of the surfaces of yttrium-barium-copper oxide ceramic films. The images showed that this superconductor contains several billion spiral defects, called screw dislocations, per square inch. Each research team—Cristoph Gerber and associates at the IBM Zurich Research Laboratory in Switzerland and Marilyn Hawley and her colleagues at the Los Alamos National Laboratory in Los Alamos, N.M.—reported independently in March that their results partly explained why these films make such good superconductors. They suggested that introducing these defects into bulk superconductors such as wires might improve their critical current densities, the maximum amounts of electricity they can carry with zero resistance. But in July, Sungho Jin, a materials scientist at AT&T Bell Laboratories in Murray Hill, N.J., found that even with equally high densities of these defects, superconducting wires still had critical current densities two orders of magnitude lower than those of thin films. He and his colleagues concluded that much higher densities of defects are required to pin down the stray magnetic forces that interfere with the free flow of electrons.                    E.J.P.

**CHILE.** Although the former dictator, General Augusto Pinochet, remained as head of the army, democratic reforms in Chile moved forward in 1991. Support for President Patricio Aylwin (inaugurated in early 1990) remained high. Chile's drought ended with heavy rains and mudslides that left more than 100 people dead and tens of thousands homeless.

**Domestic Politics.** Strains appeared in the ruling Coalition of Parties for Democracy (CPD) as the country began to prepare for 1992 municipal elections and a 1993 presidential race. The two largest parties in the coalition, the Christian Democrats and the Socialists, wanted to keep the coalition together, but some other parties, especially the Party for Democracy, were pushing for greater competition among members. In a historic break with the past, the Chilean Communist Party abandoned its advocacy of armed struggle and now favored the eradication of violence from all societies.

**Terrorism.** In April, right-wing Senator Jaime Guzmán was assassinated. Guzmán was the chief ideologue of the dictatorship's 1980 constitution, which remained in force. Responsibility for the assassination was claimed by the extreme left Lautaro Youth Movement, but there were also accusations that the far right was involved. In response to this and other terrorist violence, the government established a new Coordinating Office of Public Security.

**Human Rights.** Released in March, the long-awaited report by the National Commission on Truth and Reconciliation documented the deaths of 2,279 people from September 1973 until March 1990 as a direct result of the "systematic policy of extermination" carried out by the Pinochet dictatorship. Aylwin later warned that Chileans "must not think" about full justice for those guilty of past human rights violations because further scrutiny could destabilize the new democratic system, which is in itself "the best guarantee that there will not be violations of human rights in the future."

Retired General Manuel Contreras and Brigadier General Pedro Espinoza, who headed Pinochet's secret police, were indicted on charges of manslaughter and the use of false passports in the 1976 murders of Orlando Letelier, the former Chilean interior minister and ex-ambassador to the United States, and his associate, Ronni Moffitt, in a bomb explosion in Washington.

**Economic Gains.** Chile became eligible for preferential trading status with the United States. The government predicted that inflation would not rise above 18 percent in 1991, compared to 27.3 percent for 1990. Gross national product was expected to rise 5 or 6 percent. In August the unemployment rate was 7.4 percent, up from 5.3 percent at the end of 1990. External debt was declining.

President Aylwin announced a $2.35 billion four-year public works program. The World Bank granted a $1.8 billion loan for projects with a "strong social content."

*A disastrous mudslide brought on by torrential rains struck the town of Antofagasta on Chile's northern coast in June, killing over 100 people and destroying many homes.*

**Foreign Affairs.** Full diplomatic relations between Chile and the Soviet Union, interrupted for 17 years, were restored in May. Argentina, Brazil, and Chile agreed to ban the use or production of chemical weapons in their territories, and Chile and Argentina signed an agreement settling all but one of their historical border disputes.

*See* STATISTICS OF THE WORLD.          D.W.

**CHINA.** Chinese perceptions in 1991 were influenced by the superpowers—in this case, the loss of that status by the Soviet Union as contrasted with the impressive performance by the United States in the Persian Gulf War. Meanwhile, China's politics were dominated and stultified by roughly a dozen elderly, "retired" leaders with strong conservative views, chief among them Deng Xiaoping. While it was impossible to be sure of the real attitude of the less senior members of the top Communist Party leadership, the dominant octogenarians were concerned primarily with the maintenance of their own power and of the Communist Party's dictatorship.

At the annual session of the National People's Congress (March 25-April 9), Premier Li Peng accused "foreign hostile forces" (meaning mainly the United States, presumably) of working to promote "peaceful evolution" (meaning, essentially, political liberalization) in China. In this atmosphere, it was not surprising that the regime sternly forbade demonstrations in June in commemoration of the second anniversary of the Tiananmen Square demonstrations and massacre.

**Dissent and Repression.** Clearly there was widespread opposition, especially in the cities, to the Communist Party and its version of socialism. Active resistance was rare, however, because it was certain to be sternly repressed. Since the Tiananmen massacre of June 1989, the regime had considerably improved the discipline and efficiency of the People's Armed Police. Tight political controls prevailed on campuses, and the students were generally quiet.

In February, obviously taking advantage of the concentration of world attention on the Persian Gulf, the regime carried out a rapid series of trials involving people considered to have been actively involved in the 1989 demonstrations. Among the most widely publicized sentences were 4 years for student leader Wang Dan, and 13 years each for Wang Juntao and Chen Ziming. Pressure from former United States President Jimmy Carter secured the release of one dissident, Li Lin. A second, Wang Youcai, was freed in November.

China's ethnic minorities (about 7 percent of the population) had their own reasons for discontent with the harsh repression to which they were often subjected. In Tibet, demonstrations in late May on the 40th anniversary of the region's "liberation" by Chinese forces were met with a curfew and violent repression by police and troops. A wave of nationalism in Inner Mongolia, stimulated by reforms in the neighboring Mongolian People's Republic, was similarly repressed, and a British journalist was expelled for reporting on it.

**The Economy: A Mixed Bag.** The Chinese economy was rife with problems. An estimated 100 million people were unemployed. Severe flooding in July destroyed about 10 percent of the summer harvest and forced the government to appeal, for the first time since 1949, for relief aid from abroad. The regime found itself unable to hold down inflation without holding down growth. Official statistics showed that 70 percent of the industrial growth in 1990 had come from the private and cooperative sectors, and only 30 percent from the socialist (or state) sector.

The picture was by no means entirely bleak, to be sure. A limited degree of reform had long been in progress. In most areas consumer goods were in adequate supply. The coastal provinces, especially in the south, were showing great economic vitality.

**The Quest for Unification.** In July Beijing gave its indispensable approval to a badly needed new airport for Hong Kong, provided that at least $3.2 billion were left in the Hong Kong treasury in 1997, when the territory was to revert to China. In effect, Beijing had asserted its veto power over actions of the Hong Kong government.

Meanwhile, Taiwan's "flexible diplomacy" and its campaign for membership in the General Agreement on Tariffs and Trade (GATT) continued to perturb Beijing, as did the insertion by the main opposition party on Taiwan,

*One of the first visits by a foreign head of government to China since the Tiananmen Square massacre of 1989 was made in September by British Prime Minister John Major, seen here with Chinese President Yang Shangkun.*

the Democratic Progressive Party, of a demand for independence (from China) into its platform in October.

**Foreign Affairs.** The abrupt collapse of the Soviet Union left the United States as the only superpower and eliminated Beijing's former ability to play one against the other. Beijing viewed with disfavor a perceived tendency toward closer collaboration among the leading industrial democracies. Beijing also feared that ethnic unrest in the Soviet Union might spill over onto Chinese territory. In May an agreement was reached on the eastern (Manchurian) sector of the common border; its terms were believed to be preponderantly favorable to the Chinese side. Further talks were planned to settle the border in the western (Xinjiang) sector. In March, Beijing agreed to a $730 million commodity credit in support of the ailing Soviet economy. And in May, General Secretary Jiang Zemin visited Moscow. The two sides expressed agreement on a moderate approach to such major issues as the Middle East and Cambodia.

The May summit notwithstanding, the Chinese leadership was disgusted by Gorbachev's perceived weakness and his abandonment of Marxism-Leninism. Beijing's approval of the unsuccessful August coup appeared likely to cast a psychological pall over any relationship between China and the independent republics that succeeded the Soviet Union, although in late December China announced it was recognizing Russia.

In spite of its expanding ties with South Korea, Beijing continued to cultivate its difficult North Korean ally. In October President Kim Il Sung visited China. Reportedly, he was warned to reform his economy and to stop developing nuclear weapons, although in November, China refused to go along with the Bush administration's request that pressure be put on North Korea to stop its nuclear weapons research. Also in November, China restored relations with Vietnam. In Cambodia, Beijing appeared to be reducing its aid to its notorious allies, the Khmer Rouge, and cooperated with the other permanent members of the UN Security Council in working out a peace settlement there.

Two important powers with which China had long had significant relations, Japan and Britain, became the first two states to send their heads of government to China since the Tiananmen massacre.

Like the other permanent members of the Security Council, China had for some years been a leading seller of arms to Third World countries, reportedly including Pakistan, Syria, and Myanmar (formerly Burma). Beijing was also reported to have transferred nuclear technology to Iran, a rumor it stoutly denied. In addition, the Chinese were said to be helping Algeria build a nuclear plant.

Beijing had had fairly close ties with Iraq, which reportedly owed it $3-4 billion for arms and other items. Hence, although it felt compelled to join in the general condemnation of the Iraqi invasion of Kuwait, Beijing could not bring itself to support military action against

Iraq. By the summer there were reports that China and North Korea were shipping arms surreptitiously to Iraq by way of Singapore and Jordan.

**Relations With the United States.** The Bush administration continued efforts to cooperate with China: In opposition to a great deal of congressional sentiment, President George Bush extended China's most favored nation status for 1991-1992 without conditions, arguing that its cancellation would be an inappropriate form of pressure and would harm American, Taiwanese, and Hong Kong—as well as Chinese—interests.

In November, U.S. Secretary of State James A. Baker came to China, becoming the highest-ranking U.S. official to visit since the 1989 crackdown. He brought a list of requests which included the release of pro-democracy political prisoners and the halt in the sale of missiles and nuclear technology to other countries. He did succeed in getting the Chinese to

*An early monsoon brought flooding and devastation to southern China in July. With more than half of the nation's provinces affected and millions made homeless, the Communist government was forced, for the first time, to appeal to the international community for disaster aid.*

forgo the sale of missiles to Pakistan and Syria, but China made no pledge to halt its export of nuclear technology and refused to release political prisoners. The Chinese response to the Baker mission rekindled U.S. opposition to China's most favored nation status, and after negotiations to end pirating of U.S. patents, copyrights, and trademarks failed, the administration began a legal process to restrict some imports from China.

See STATISTICS OF THE WORLD.     H.C.H.

**CHINA, REPUBLIC OF.**  See TAIWAN.

**CIVIL LIBERTIES AND CIVIL RIGHTS.** Passage of a new civil rights bill and the confirmation battle triggered by a controversial nomination for Supreme Court justice were among the key developments relating to civil rights and civil liberties in the United States in 1991—a year that marked the 200th anniversary of the ratification of the Bill of Rights. Discrimination and First Amendment issues continued to command attention, and there were important court rulings on defendants' rights (see UNITED STATES: Supreme Court). Topics such as abortion, police brutality, and hate speech on campus also made the news (see CRIME AND LAW ENFORCEMENT; EDUCATION; STATE GOVERNMENT REVIEW; WOMEN).

**Civil Rights Bill.**  In November the U.S. Congress approved a civil rights bill intended to make it easier for people claiming employment discrimination to bring and to win damage suits. The new legislation was aimed at reversing several recent Supreme Court decisions that, in interpreting earlier statutes, had narrowed remedies available to those claiming job discrimination based on race, religion, national origin, or sex. Under the final bill, signed by President George Bush on November 21, hiring or promotion practices that have a "disparate impact" on women or minorities are illegal unless the employer can show they are "job related" and "consistent with business necessity." The right to sue for damages for discrimination or harassment is specifically applied to dismissals and promotions, not merely to hiring; victims can sue not only for back pay and rehiring, as under a 1964 law, but also (subject to some monetary limits) for compensatory and punitive damages.

The day before Bush signed the civil rights bill, White House Counsel C. Boyden Gray circulated a draft executive order requiring all federal agencies to phase out the use of racial preferences or quotas in hiring. Bush disavowed the plan, but some critics doubted the extent of the administration's commitment to affirmative action. In December the U.S. Equal Employment Opportunity Commission ruled that the measure did not apply to discrimination claims filed before it was signed into law.

**Confirmation Battle.**  In June, Thurgood Marshall, then 82, the former civil rights attorney who in 1967 became the first black to sit on the U.S. Supreme Court, announced his intention to retire. As chief counsel for the NAACP Legal Defense Educational Fund, Marshall played a key role in the 1940s and 1950s in getting the courts to strike down segregation laws—most notably in the landmark 1954 Supreme Court ruling outlawing segregated school systems. During his tenure on the Court, Marshall was known for his advocacy of free speech, affirmative action, and the rights of criminal defendants.

To fill the vacancy, President Bush nominated Clarence Thomas, 43, a judge on the U.S. Court of Appeals for Washington, D.C.; also a black, he was regarded as a conservative. The American Civil Liberties Union took a neutral position on the nomination, stressing that this should not be construed as an endorsement. Other civil rights groups announced opposition, including the Leadership Conference on Civil Rights and the NAACP. Besides citing Thomas's professional abilities, supporters stressed his strength of character in overcoming poverty and discrimination.

After hearings in which Thomas did not indicate a position on abortion and other issues of concern to civil libertarians, the Senate Judiciary Committee split, 7-7, on his confirmation. Charges of sexual harassment against Thomas, made by law professor Anita Hill (also a black), who had worked for Thomas at two federal agencies, then became public. The Judiciary Committee held three days of nationally televised hearings on these charges, during which Hill detailed her allegations and Thomas flatly denied them. The bitter confirmation battle ended in a narrow 52-48 Senate vote to con-

*After over two decades as a leading civil rights lawyer and nearly a quarter-century on the Supreme Court, Justice Thurgood Marshall announced his retirement at a press conference in June (right). Above, top (1954): Marshall flanked by fellow attorneys in the landmark* Brown v. Board of Education *desegregation case. Bottom (1967): President Lyndon Johnson nominates Marshall to the Court.*

firm Thomas. (*See also* PEOPLE IN THE NEWS: Anita Hill *and* Clarence Thomas.)

**Education.** In Detroit, a plan for an all-male public school focusing on discipline, high achievement, and development of a positive self-identity for black inner-city boys was blocked by a federal district court, which ordered the admission of girls as well. Under a compromise agreement, the schools were allowed to open for boys only at the beginning of the fall term, with girls entering as soon as their applications could be processed. In the area of higher education, however, a federal district court upheld the male-only admissions policy

at the state-supported Virginia Military Institute, ruling that maintaining the college's mission, built around highly rigorous military training, outweighed other factors.

In December a federal judge ordered Alabama's higher education system to remedy vestiges of racial discrimination by changing financing, admissions, and staffing policies.

The U.S. Department of Education had ruled in late 1990 that race-specific scholarships awarded by colleges and universities were illegal and that institutions continuing to award them would be ineligible for state aid. Following a major outcry, however, Secretary of Edu-

127

cation Lamar Alexander announced in March that the ruling would be put on hold. In December, Alexander proposed new rules regulating college scholarships based solely on race.

In April, Alexander delayed reauthorizing the Middle States Association of Colleges and Schools, one of six major regional accrediting agencies. He specifically objected to standards that appeared to require quotas based on race, ethnicity, and gender among students, faculty, administrators, and governing boards. In November an advisory panel recommended that the association be given a one-year renewal. In December, Middle States declared its diversity policy not mandatory.

**FBI.** The FBI announced disciplinary action against eight agents accused of being involved in death threats or other harassment against Donald Rochon, a black former agent who had filed civil suits against the agency and white agents in 1984. Rochon also was awarded more than $1 million.

**Housing.** A survey conducted for the Department of Housing and Urban Development found that black and Hispanic Americans faced discrimination nearly 60 percent of the time when trying to buy or rent housing in 25 metropolitan areas. Also, a Federal Reserve Board study found that banks were more likely to deny mortgage loans to blacks and Hispanics than to whites.

**Voting.** In an important interpretation of the Voting Rights Act of 1965, the Supreme Court ruled that it applies to the election of state and local judges as well as to other elections. The Voting Rights Act makes it illegal for states and localities to maintain electoral districts and voting practices that have the effect of discriminating because of race.

**Homosexuals.** The California legislature in September enacted a law outlawing job discrimination against homosexuals, but the measure was vetoed by Governor Pete Wilson. At the time, four states—Connecticut, Hawaii, Massachusetts, and Wisconsin—offered legal protection against job discrimination for homosexuals, while in California 17 cities had such legislation. In October the California Court of Appeals extended to private employers an earlier court ruling that had prohibited

public employers from discriminating against homosexuals.

There was increasing pressure on the armed forces to end the ban on the military enlistment of gays and lesbians. A study commissioned by the Defense Department concluded there was no connection between homosexuality and security risks. In December, however, a U.S. district court in Washington, D.C., upheld the ban.

**AIDS.** In May the Bush administration decided not to remove AIDS from the list of diseases for which persons can be denied entry to the United States; the only other disease on the list was tuberculosis, which (unlike AIDS) can be spread by casual contact. Harvard University later announced that the 1992 International Conference on AIDS would be moved from Boston to a site outside the United States because of the administration's policy.

**Boy Scouts.** The Boy Scouts of America announced a special new program called Learning for Life, serving girls, homosexual youth, and atheists. The action came about after legal challenges from former and would-be scouts opposing the organization's policy of banning such individuals.

**Arts and Media.** Debate continued over public funding, by the National Endowment for the Arts, of "obscene" art. An NEA requirement that grant recipients sign a pledge not to use NEA funds for materials the agency might consider obscene was dropped early in the year. Meanwhile, the U.S. Court of Appeals in Washington, D.C., declared unconstitutional a 1988 federal law banning "indecent" programming on radio or television regardless of time of day. The Federal Communications Commission had adopted rules to impose the full-time ban, but they were unenforced.

M.Gr.

**COINS AND COIN COLLECTING.** Several commemorative issues—coins made principally for collectors—were released in the United States in 1991. Early in the year, the U.S. Mint struck a three-coin set to mark the 50th anniversary of the completion of the Mount Rushmore National Memorial: a $5 gold piece, a silver dollar, and a half-dollar that was cast in an alloy of copper and nickel. Profits from the sale were to be shared equally

*In 1991 a U.S. silver dollar was issued to mark the 38th anniversary of the end of the Korean War. The rather awkward date is explained by the fact that sales will be used to finance a memorial in Washington to the war's veterans, who have long complained that they lacked one.*

by the U.S. Treasury and the Mount Rushmore National Memorial Society. The Treasury's portion was earmarked to help reduce the national debt; the balance was to go toward preservation of the memorial and toward restoration projects. In April the Mint issued a silver dollar honoring veterans of the Korean War. Proceeds from this sale were to help fund a Korean War veterans' memorial in Washington, D.C.

June marked the introduction of another silver dollar coin, this one to salute the 50th anniversary of the founding of the United Service Organizations (USO). Meanwhile, Congress authorized issuance of three coins commemorating the 500th anniversary of Christopher Columbus's first voyage to the New World.

A myriad of foreign issues flooded the U.S. market. Both France and Spain struck a large number of high-value commemoratives to help underwrite their respective Olympic Games of 1992. Spain, Italy, and Portugal all issued series of special coins in honor of Columbus's initial voyage.

Although the value of investment-grade silver dollars fell sharply in the recession climate of 1991, truly rare coins generally held their value. One of 12 known 1927-D Saint Gaudens $20 gold pieces brought a record $475,000 at auction in March. A chance find in an old potato field in Long Island, N.Y., brought to light the eighth known example of a 1652 New England sixpence. The last specimen of this scarce colonial coin sold at auction in 1980 for $75,000.

In early fall the U.S. Treasury released a new $100 note, the first of its long-awaited currency designed to foil would-be counterfeiters. New $50 bills were to be issued in early 1992, and $20, $10, and $5 bills were scheduled to make their debut over the next few years. The new currency features microscopic lettering and a narrow polyester filament that copy machines cannot reproduce. As the government prepared to change all currency notes except $1 bills (which are rarely counterfeited), debate began anew on the introduction of another minisized dollar coin to replace the dollar bill in circulation.

The American Numismatic Association observed its 100th anniversary in Chicago in August, attracting more than 22,000 collectors to the week-long event.                E.C.R.

**COLOMBIA.** In 1991 the government of President César Gaviria Trujillo sought to reduce the level of civil violence. The adoption of a new constitution, followed by new legislative elections, opened the way for major political changes. The economy, despite its problems, remained one of the healthiest in Latin America.

**Political Changes.** When the Assembly opened its deliberations in February, it moved toward reforms more far-reaching than had been anticipated. Momentum in favor of a true opening of the economy mounted. On June 8 the president and Assembly leaders agreed to dissolve the national congress and hold new elections in October. Legislative functions were handled during the interregnum by a special 18-member commission, which was drawn proportionally from the parties in the Assembly.

On Independence Day, July 5, a new consti-

129

tution was proclaimed, containing 380 articles and 59 transitory provisions. It provided for direct election of governors, popular referenda and plebiscites on public issues, the restriction of congressional privilege, and reorganization of the judicial system. Individual rights were spelled out, extradition was ruled out (thus meeting a major objective of the drug bosses), and a more refined and restricted set of emergency powers was adopted. While the four-year presidential term was retained, reelection was excluded.

In elections on October 27 the ruling Liberals won 57 of the 102 Senate seats and about half of the seats in the lower house. The Liberals also won 15 of the 27 governorships.

The elections were marked by low turnout, with only about one-third of eligible voters going to the polls. Prior to the elections, 12 people were killed in clashes between rebels and government troops; 3 more people died in Election Day violence.

**Drug War.** Gaviria had entered office in August 1990 pledging a renewed quest for internal peace. Offering preferential treatment to drug traffickers who surrendered to the government, Gaviria provided them an opportunity to avoid extradition to the United States. By mid-year several major drug dealers were in official custody, including the most notorious chief of the Medellín cocaine cartel, Pablo Escobar. The Gaviria administration was praised by many Colombians for significant results, while critics contended that drug dealers who surrendered under the program would merely receive minimal sentences before returning to their business operations.

**Guerrilla Activities.** Gaviria promised justice for all armed organizations accepting the authority of the state. By early 1991 the Popular Liberation Army (EPL) had agreed to terms and announced its commitment to a broad leftist alliance in lieu of armed struggle. However, the Revolutionary Armed Forces of Colombia (FARC) and the National Liberation Army (ELN) were less receptive. An informal umbrella organization of recalcitrant guerrilla groups, known as the Simón Bolívar National Guerrilla Coordinador (CNGSB), launched a new military offensive in July, but the organization later suspended hostilities.

**Military and Police.** Colombia's attorney general reported that in January-August 1991, some 1,880 people had died from political violence. Both the military and the police drew continual criticism for alleged human rights abuses. Gaviria sought to combat such changes by reorganizing security forces and strengthening government controls, naming Rafael Pardo Rueda as the new minister of defense, the first civilian to hold the post in nearly a half-century.

**Economy.** During the year the government sought to open the economy further to competition. A series of reforms announced in August included adjustments to the exchange rate and cuts in public expenditures, designed to tame inflation.

See STATISTICS OF THE WORLD.        J.D.M.

**COLORADO.** See STATISTICS OF THE WORLD.
**COMMONWEALTH OF INDEPENDENT STATES.** See UNION OF SOVIET SOCIALIST REPUBLICS.

**COMMONWEALTH OF NATIONS.** See INTERNATIONAL CONFERENCES.

**COMOROS.** See STATISTICS OF THE WORLD.
**COMPUTERS.** The computer industry in the United States struggled to recapture its lost luster in 1991. Despite bargain prices, sales lagged as corporate buyers cut back on purchases. Computers got smaller, lighter, and faster.

**IBM Stumbles.** Under siege from clone makers, market leader IBM found itself on the defensive. Nine-month sales slumped to $42.7 billion, down 7.1 percent from the $46 billion of the first nine months of 1990. IBM reduced PC prices by as much as 24 percent, but the move failed to reverse the trend. Late in the year, IBM was studying plans to break up into a family of smaller, more market-responsive subsidiaries and reduce its work force.

**The IBM-Microsoft Feud.** Thanks to the surging popularity of Microsoft Corporation's Windows 3.0, the trend toward graphical computing on the PC accelerated. A graphical computing environment like Windows acts as a buffer between the PC's underlying operating system and the user. In 1987, when IBM unveiled its PS/2 line of computers, it released an accompanying operating system codeveloped with Microsoft called OS/2. Early versions of

OS/2 received a chilly reception, but IBM promised that future upgrades would include powerful features no other operating system could match. While Windows was a 16-bit system, this new version of OS/2 would be a true 32-bit operating system. It would process data faster and more efficiently, and allow programmers to take fuller advantage of the Intel Corporation's more powerful generation of 386 and 486 microprocessors.

Most PC users, however, refused to abandon DOS for OS/2, and as the promised upgrade was repeatedly delayed, Microsoft began to encourage PC users and developers to move over to Windows. Microsoft convinced many of the software industry's key developers to design software only for Windows. Late in 1990, IBM and Microsoft had jointly announced that Windows would henceforth be marketed as an entry-level graphical environment and that OS/2 was the choice for jobs that required more sophisticated computing needs. But that neat theoretical division failed to work in reality. As Windows drained the attention of software developers away from IBM's OS/2 operating system, the chill between the two companies worsened. Meanwhile, IBM rescheduled shipment of OS/2 2.0 from late 1991 to early 1992.

*Software giant Microsoft, headed by William Gates (above), was once IBM's ally. When that relationship soured, IBM happily forged a pact with onetime archrival Apple Computer. At top, IBM President Jack Kuehler (left) and Apple chief John Sculley display the technology-sharing pact.*

**PC Wars and Casualties.** The soaring popularity of low-cost clones underscored the transformation of the PC industry into a commodity business. That spelled trouble for established brands such as IBM and Compaq, which could once charge premium prices. Compaq posted the first loss in its history and ousted its founder and chief operating officer. In a round of mergers and acquisitions, Businessland, the largest company-owned chain of computer stores in the world, was swallowed up by systems integrator JWP. Borland International became the third-largest software maker when it bought its archrival, Ashton-Tate, in a $439 million deal. And after five months of negotiations, AT&T landed NCR in a $7.48 billion deal that it was hoped would rejuvenate AT&T's flagging efforts in the computer market.

**Surprising Alliance.** IBM and Apple Computer stunned the computing world on October 2 when these two fierce rivals announced joint ventures to develop multimedia computers and object-oriented software. Along with Motorola, they unveiled plans to also make a microprocessor to be used in future Apple and IBM PCs and workstations. The alliance underscored the recent weaknesses of both companies.

**ACE Initiative.** Compaq Computer, Digital Equipment, Microsoft, and more than a dozen other manufacturers agreed to a common standard for building workstation architectures. The consortium, the so-called Advanced Computing Environment (ACE), promised to construct a new standard that would be founded upon a design for RISC-based computing. The unifying component was to be a high-powered, 64-bit chip designed by MIPS Computer Systems to power their machines. The MIPS chip offers twice the data processing capacity of Intel's top-of-the-line 32-bit chips.

**Chip Wars.** In March, Advanced Micro Devices (AMD) broke Intel's monopoly on the 386 chip market when it began shipping its own clones of the chip. Chips and Technologies joined the fray when it became the second company to manufacture clones of Intel's popular 386 chip. Later, Intel joined forces with IBM to cooperate in new chip design projects for the most powerful desktop and portable computers.

**On-line Bulletin Boards.** In October the Anti-Defamation League of the B'nai B'rith complained that Prodigy Services Company was allowing anti-Semitic messages to be posted on its electronic bulletin boards; Prodigy agreed to ban messages deemed "grossly repugnant to community standards." That same week, a federal judge ruled that CompuServe Information Service could not be held liable for the content of material distributed in an independent newsletter on its network.

**New Technologies.** "Multimedia" refers to the application of converging computer technologies that merge audio, motion video, still photos, graphics screens, and text on a computer. The computer industry had been slow to develop the appropriate hardware and software applications to generate quality multimedia presentations at reasonable prices for, for example, consulting, teleconferencing, and home use. But in 1991 Microsoft rallied a consortium of many vendors—excluding IBM—to agree upon technical hardware and software development standards.

The industry got its first look at pen-based computers that let people use a PC by writing on the screen by hand with a special pen, and NCR introduced a new implementation of parallel processing that offers up to four times the power of traditional mainframe machines at one-tenth the price. NCR's machine can deliver up to 2,000 MIPS (millions of instructions per second). Another machine featuring parallel processing, Thinking Machine Corporation's CM-5, was introduced in late October.

In November, Cray Research Inc. unveiled its most powerful supercomputer yet, the Y-MP C90, and Intel introduced the Paragon XP-S, a machine capable of doing 300 billion calculations a second. C.C.

**CONGO.** See STATISTICS OF THE WORLD.

**CONGRESS OF THE UNITED STATES.** See UNITED STATES OF AMERICA: *Congress.*

**CONNECTICUT.** See STATISTICS OF THE WORLD. See also STATE GOVERNMENT REVIEW.

**COSTA RICA.** Beset by economic problems due largely to poor prices for its exports, Costa Rica in 1991 continued its economic austerity program under President Rafael Angel Calderón Fournier, Jr., of the Social Christian Unity Party (PUSC). Thousands of government workers were laid off, and economic growth appeared slow.

On February 1, Calderón announced a "national plan in the battle against poverty," promising the creation of 200,000 private sector jobs in tourism, export farming, and fishing, financed with public and private money. Two weeks later, the International Monetary Fund signed on to provide $196 million in loans, and Costa Rica agreed in turn to reduce its fiscal deficit. On April 22, however, an earthquake that hit the Caribbean coast completely disabled the port of Limón and caused $30 million in damage to the banana industry. Inflation reached 13 percent by May; the IMF had hoped for 15 percent for the entire year.

Calderón, a strong believer in a free market economy, attempted to sell off such state industries as petroleum and the electric company, and in August he announced plans to unfreeze basic food prices. The government's economic policies drew harsh reactions from labor. On June 19 a 72-hour general strike was launched at the ravaged port of Limón. Two weeks later, two workers' organizations called a national strike, demanding an end to devaluation and to privatization.

Meeting in January with leaders of other Central American countries, Calderón negotiated a bilateral treaty liberalizing trade with Mexico. Negotiations with Venezuela later resulted in a treaty aimed at eventual free trade between the two countries, and Venezuela promised a loan of $9 million for earthquake relief and $35 million in additional loans.

On April 19, 20,000 members of indigenous tribes were accorded Costa Rican citizenship.

*See* STATISTICS OF THE WORLD.     T.P.A.

**CRIME AND LAW ENFORCEMENT.** In the United States in 1991, massacre and mass murder made headlines, as did the rape trial of William Kennedy Smith. There were new legal developments in the Iran-contra scandal, and police in Los Angeles were accused of racist practices.

**Multiple Murders.** During lunchtime on October 16, George J. Hennard drove his pickup truck through the glass front of Luby's cafeteria in Killeen, Texas, got out, and began shooting at patrons. By the time Hennard had emptied

Luby's cafeteria in Killeen, Texas, was the site of one of the worst mass killings in American history when George J. Hennard drove his pickup truck through the window, got out, and proceeded to open fire, killing 22 and wounding 23.

several clips from two semiautomatic pistols, 22 people were dead, including 14 women. During an exchange of fire with local police Hennard was wounded, whereupon he shot himself in the head.

On October 10, according to police, Joseph M. Harris, a 35-year-old Navy veteran who had worked as a mail handler for nine years before being fired in 1990, drove to the Wayne, N.J., home that his former supervisor shared with her boyfriend and fatally shot both. Harris allegedly then drove to the Ridgewood post office where he had been employed and killed two mail handlers. He surrendered to police after several hours of negotiations.

On November 14, 31-year-old Thomas

---

**Those Crime-Busting, Collectible Canines**

Ryne Sandberg, a second baseman, weighs 175 pounds, is 32 years old, and won the National League's Most Valuable Player Award in 1984. Bandit, a golden retriever, weighs 75 pounds, is 3 years old, and once sniffed out 1,488 pounds of marijuana hidden beneath the floor of a semi-trailer. What do they have in common? Both have their pictures on a collectible card. Glossy cards, now distributed in schools, bear photos of the drug-sniffing canines and list such facts as breed, age, weight, and "largest or most notable seizure."

The idea originated with U.S. Customs Service agents in Dallas. For some time, the Customs Service had been sending representatives into classrooms as part of its drug education program, and nothing aroused the children's interest more than a live demonstration of a drug-sniffing pooch in action. The first set of cards, released on a limited basis, were snapped up so avidly that the Customs Service soon expanded the program to cover the entire nation.

Other four-footed sleuths on the cards include Zoom, who once detected 80 pounds of cocaine in a car's gas tank; Red, who, after biting a car's tires, helped agents find 167 pounds of marijuana inside; and Bullet, who after a decade of smuggler busting, in which he turned up 1,297 pounds of cocaine and over 3½ tons of marijuana, was enjoying "a well earned retirement."

---

McIlvaine, a Michigan man who days earlier had lost his final appeal for reinstatement as a postal clerk, killed three postal supervisors and wounded six others in a post office outside Detroit, before killing himself.

In November a 28-year-old former graduate student shot six people at the University of Iowa, killing five before killing himself. Gang Lu, apparently angered that his dissertation had been passed over for a prize in favor of another student's, killed three faculty members, the winner of the prize, and the vice president for academic affairs.

Jeffrey Dahmer, a 31-year-old unemployed Milwaukee laborer, was arrested in July after a handcuffed man fled his apartment and told police Dahmer was trying to kill him. Searches of the apartment revealed the remains of 11 bodies of men and boys, some dismembered, along with photographs of some of the victims. Dahmer had reportedly enticed victims to his apartment with promises of money if they would allow him to photograph them, and then drugged and killed them. He confessed to committing 17 murders in Wisconsin and Ohio. Charged with 15 murders in Milwaukee, he pleaded not guilty by reason of mental illness.

The Milwaukee police department drew heavy criticism for its handling of the Dahmer case after it was learned that at least one of his murders could have been prevented. Weeks before Dahmer's arrest, neighbors had called the police to inform them that a teenage boy, naked and bleeding, was standing outside his apartment building. The police officers who responded to the complaint returned the boy to Dahmer; his body was later found with the others.

Nine people—six monks, a nun, and two young acolytes—were killed by gunshots in August at a Thai Buddhist temple in Phoenix. Two teenagers were held in connection with the crime after guns in their possession were linked to the slayings.

A siege of a Sacramento electronics store in April ended with the death of 6 people and the wounding of 11 others. Hostages said the gunmen, four Vietnamese immigrants, were angry over hardships they had endured after coming to America. Three of the four, all

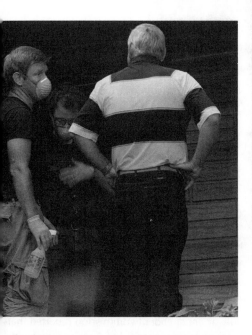

After dismembered remains of 11 bodies were found in his Milwaukee apartment, Jeffrey Dahmer (above, seated between his attorneys) was charged with murder. Police searched his previous residence in Ohio (left), where they found what they believed to be the remains of his first victim.

members of an Asian gang, and three hostages were killed as police stormed the store; the fourth gunman, who was critically wounded, was charged with murder.

In September, Julio Gonzalez, a 37-year-old immigrant from Cuba, was sentenced to 25 years to life in prison for murdering 87 people in March 1990 by setting fire to the Happy Land Social Club in New York.

**William Kennedy Smith Trial.** William Kennedy Smith, 30-year-old nephew of Senator Edward Kennedy (D, Mass.), was charged in May with the alleged rape earlier in the year of 29-year-old Patricia Bowman, whom he had met at a bar and invited back to the family compound in Palm Beach, Fla. Fascination with the Kennedy clan led to heavy media coverage of the trial, which was televised in its entirety with Bowman's face electronically blurred. After nine days that included compelling testimony by both accuser and accused, the jury deliberated a scant 77 minutes and declared Smith not guilty, apparently unconvinced there was sufficient evidence to counter his claim that his sexual relations with Bowman had been consensual. Besides focusing attention on the issue of date rape, the case revived controversy over whether the plaintiff's name should be publicly revealed. Most of

the media did keep her identity confidential, but after the trial she went public with a television interview.

**Iran-Contra Affair.** The prosecution dropped its case against former national security aide Oliver North, whose conviction on several charges relating to the Iran/contra scandal, including mutilating government documents and obstructing Congress, was overturned by an appeals court in 1990. North's case was abandoned in September after the special prosecutor, Lawrence E. Walsh, said he would be unable to prove that testimony in North's criminal trial had not been tainted by statements the former Marine lieutenant colonel had given to Congress under limited immunity.

In July a former CIA official, Alan D. Fiers, Jr., admitted in federal court that, under orders from superiors, he had concealed information about North's activities from House and Senate intelligence committees. One of those superiors was Clair E. George, who was the third-ranking official in the CIA before retiring in 1987. George was indicted in September on ten felony counts of perjury and obstruction, stemming from testimony he gave before three congressional committees in 1986; he pleaded not guilty. A month later, as part of a plea bargain, Elliott Abrams pleaded guilty to mis-

demeanor counts that he had lied to two congressional committees about his participation in discussions on funding. Abrams was an assistant secretary of state under President Ronald Reagan. Later in the year, another former high-ranking CIA official, Duane Claridge, was indicted for perjury for allegedly misleading Congress about his role in secret arms shipments to Iran; he pleaded not guilty.

In November a federal appeals court overturned the convictions of John M. Poindexter, who had served as national security adviser under Reagan and was the highest-ranking White House official to be found guilty of participation in the Iran-contra affair. The appeals court threw out the convictions on the same grounds as in the North case. Walsh was expected to appeal.

**Police Brutality.** Motorist Rodney G. King was stopped by Los Angeles police in March after his car was reported to be speeding. Several police officers kicked King repeatedly, clubbed him more than 50 times, and shot him with a stun gun. Several other officers stood by. After the beating, King was hog-tied, dragged to the side of the road, and left bleeding until an ambulance arrived; he was hospitalized for two days.

An amateur videotape of the assault was broadcast on television news programs, sparking wide public concern and protests from civil rights groups. Four members of the Los Angeles police were subsequently indicted on charges of assault with a deadly weapon and misuse of authority; all pleaded not guilty. In July an independent commission reported that a significant number of Los Angeles police officers used excessive force and demonstrated overt racism; the commission recommended that Police Chief Daryl F. Gates be replaced and that police officers spend more time patrolling the streets. Gates eventually said he would resign in April 1992.

**Mafia Trial.** A long-running Mafia case came to an end in New York in October with all defendants acquitted of the most serious charges against them. The "windows trial" featured several defendants alleged to be high-ranking members of organized crime families, including Peter Gotti, brother of John Gotti, reputed boss of the Gambino crime family. The case centered around accusations that the window replacement industry in New York City was controlled by the Mafia through a complex system of bid rigging and union payoffs. The main prosecution witnesses were former Mafia associates who had become informers as part of plea bargain arrangements.

**Crime Bill.** A compromise anticrime bill endorsed by many House and Senate Democrats sparked heated debate before Republicans shot it down. The measure called for, among other things, extending the death penalty to cover 52 more federal crimes; mandating a five-day waiting period for handgun purchases, to allow police time to conduct background checks (as promoted by former White House press secretary James Brady, shot and seriously wounded in the 1981 assassination attempt against President Reagan); and imposing tighter restrictions on habeas corpus appeals. President George Bush threatened to veto the bill, saying it needed even stricter restrictions on habeas corpus and a provision making some evidence obtained without a search warrant admissible in court. Democrats accused Bush of seeking to appease the strong anti-gun-control lobby, which objected to the Brady provisions. The House narrowly passed the bill on November 27, but Senate Republicans killed it by threatening to filibuster if it was brought to a vote there.

**War on Drugs.** After President Bush announced in 1989 his national strategy to combat drug abuse, spending on drug control rose by more than $4 billion to an estimated $10.4 billion in 1991. But while casual use of cocaine and marijuana was declining among the affluent, the middle class, and students, little progress was seen among the homeless and minorities. There were reports that heroin was being sold more cheaply and was being used to mitigate the effects of crack, a cocaine derivative, and that former addicts were returning to the drug. In November federal agents seized 12 tons of cocaine in Miami, in the second-largest cocaine bust ever in the United States.

**Noriega on Trial.** Deposed Panamanian dictator Manuel Antonio Noriega went on trial in Miami in September on charges of drug trafficking, money laundering, and racketeering. Several witnesses testified that Noriega, then head of intelligence for the Panamanian military, had allowed drug shipments from Colombia into Panama in the early 1980s and had protected illegal drug profits. After calling 46 witnesses, the prosecution rested in mid-December, with the defense scheduled to begin presenting its case in January.

**Financial Scandals.** Scandal tarnished the reputation of one of the most prestigious Wall Street brokerage houses, Salomon Brothers Inc., in mid-1991. The firm came under federal investigation after some of its traders in government securities violated U.S. Treasury bidding rules by purchasing more than the legally permitted 35 percent of several issues of Treasury notes offered at auction. Four traders were fired in August. But then Salomon Brothers admitted that its chairman and two other top managers had known of the improper transactions and failed to inform federal regulators. All three resigned their posts.

Phoenix financier Charles Keating was convicted of securities fraud in a state court in December in connection with the collapse of his California-based Lincoln Savings and Loan Association. He also faced federal charges.

**Kahane Verdict.** El Sayyid Nosair, an Egyptian immigrant, was acquitted in December of the 1990 murder of Rabbi Meir Kahane, founder of the extremist Jewish Defense League, though he was convicted on lesser charges. Kahane was shot to death in November 1990, at a crowded meeting in a Manhattan hotel.                                    L.S.G.

**CUBA.** In 1991, President Fidel Castro maintained a tight hold on the helm of government, seeking to weather economic crisis and the impact of the Communist breakdown in the Soviet Union and Eastern Europe.

**The Changing International Scene.** Dissolution of the Soviet-led trading group Comecon, which had included Cuba, meant a loss of 15 percent of Cuba's trade. Chaos in the Soviet Union made Moscow unable to keep its commitments to Havana. The final collapse of Soviet Communism took Cuba's leaders by surprise, as did the announcement that Moscow would withdraw troops and halt military and economic aid. In response to intensified U.S. hostility, Cuba liberalized its exit visa policies and relaxed its pursuit of those fleeing the island by boat. An increase in the number of Cubans entering the United States was agreed to by Washington but slowed by U.S. fears of a mass exodus.

Havana signed a trade pact in September with Byelorussia (Belarus), a republic that declared independence on August 25. Relations with the remaining Communist states—China, Vietnam, and North Korea—were reinforced. The presence of Spanish tourists, trade, and investment assumed a growing importance, and French and German companies agreed on a joint venture to explore for oil off the Cuban coast.

Castro was a conspicuous participant at the first summit of Ibero-American heads of state, held in Mexico in July, but he came away empty-handed. In October, Castro met with the presidents of Mexico, Colombia, and Venezuela, who promised closer relations but no economic aid. He got a diplomatic boost in August from the Pan American Games, which Cuba hosted for the first time.

**Economic Crisis.** Shortfalls in the delivery of Soviet oil, foodstuffs, and machinery caused severe economic dislocations. Factories closed and consumer shortages became acute. Food was fully rationed, as was gasoline. Although basic needs were still being met, public anxiety was growing. The government took steps to conserve energy and promote food self-sufficiency. Priority was given to the development of tourism and the pharmaceutical and electronics industries. Equally significant was Cuba's new openness to joint ventures with foreign capital. The year's excellent sugar crop was a bright spot. Nevertheless, late in the year the deepening crisis led Havana to consider a "zero option" emergency austerity plan.

**Political Developments.** Although there was widespread consumer discontent, most of the population seemed to accept the official explanation that the economic crisis was caused by a combination of Soviet difficulties and U.S. hostility. There were, however, criticisms of the bureaucracy and demands for greater popular participation in decision-making. A reform faction within the Communist leadership proposed a return to homegrown revolutionary models. The collapse of Soviet Communism lent a new urgency to the oft-postponed party congress, which was finally held in October, but the limited reforms it endorsed failed to meet popular expectations and were soon followed by a crackdown on political dissidence.

*See* STATISTICS OF THE WORLD. P.W.

**CYPRUS.** In 1991, Greek Cypriots elected a new legislature, and prospects for a resolution of the dispute dividing the island seemed to recede.

In the elections on May 19, 6 parties competed for the 56 seats allocated to the Greek community. The right-wing Democratic Rally Party gained 1 seat, for a total of 20. The center-right Democratic Party dropped 5 seats, to 11. The Communist Party won 18 seats, up from 15; the Socialist Party gained 1 seat for a total of 7.

The election campaign had focused on finding a political solution to the island's 17-year division into Greek and Turkish sectors. The Democratic Rally and the Communists supported the goals and methods of President George Vassiliou, who envisioned a single federal republic achieved by negotiations through United Nations channels with support from Athens. The Democrats and the Socialists, by contrast, criticized UN efforts and attributed the problem to the 1974 Turkish occupation.

During a May visit to the United States, Vassiliou discussed the Cyprus problem with U.S. President George Bush and UN Secretary-General Javier Pérez de Cuéllar. During a July visit to Greece and Turkey, Bush urged the leaders of Greece, Turkey, and the Greek and Turkish Cypriot communities to take part in a UN-sponsored conference in the United States in September to resolve the Cyprus dispute. After preliminary talks with government leaders, however, UN officials reported that the Greek and Turkish Cypriots were in disagreement on important aspects of a federal solution. Secretary-General Pérez de Cuéllar subsequently announced that the September conference on Cyprus could not be held because the parties remained too far apart.

*See* STATISTICS OF THE WORLD. P.J.M.

**CZECHOSLOVAKIA.** In 1991 the democratically elected Czechoslovak government sought to forge ties with Western nations while dealing with the trauma of conversion to a free-market economy and containing rising nationalist passions.

**Economic Reform.** On January 1 central planning was abandoned and subsidies dismantled on about 85 percent of goods sold, thus putting industrial enterprises under pressure and forcing some into bankruptcy. Agricultural and industrial production declined and unemployment rose, especially in the eastern, or Slovak, part of the country. Foreign trade declined sharply, primarily because the Soviet Union—the country's primary foreign customer—was itself hard-pressed and could afford far fewer imports.

*Two Soviet soldiers stationed in Czechoslovakia tote their bedrolls as they prepare for the trip home. The withdrawal of all Soviet troops was completed in June.*

However, Czechoslovakia's foreign debt remained lower than that of other East European countries, as did the inflation and unemployment rates. Efforts to attract foreign investors resulted in some 3,000 joint ventures by the fall. The process of so-called small privatization was well underway, with more than half a million small businesses in private hands by midyear, but privatization of state-owned enterprises was delayed.

**Political Developments.** The Civic Forum, an umbrella organization that brought down the Communist regime in 1989 and won the 1990 general election, splintered into three factions: a left-leaning group, called the Civic Movement, and two groups with right-of-center orientation—the Civic Democratic Alliance and the Civic Democratic Party. Numerous small parties continued to crowd both ends of the political spectrum. The Communist Party, stung by the loss of most of its membership and property, quietly retrenched, skillfully securing important administrative positions and penetrating the emerging private economic sector. The government moved to counter this trend in October by ousting former Communist Party officials from high and middle-ranking administrative posts. In December the National Assembly passed a law imposing jail terms for supporting or promoting Communism.

**Slovakia.** Slovakia and the Czech lands are divided by two different political cultures and mentalities. During World War II, the Czech part of the country was Hitler's victim, whereas the officially independent Slovakia was Hitler's ally. Surveys showed that, while most Czechs in 1991 accepted the move toward a free-market economy, most Slovaks preferred a modified socialist system.

President Vaclav Havel, a Czech, was spat upon on March 14 by Slovak nationalists commemorating the anniversary of the declaration of a separate Slovak state in 1939. Passions were inflamed further when Vladimir Meciar, the popular premier of the Slovak Republic, was removed from office on April 23 by a group of Slovak parliamentary leaders. No supporter of economic reform, Meciar was dismissed in the wake of allegations that he had exploited his access to secret police files, had secretly negotiated with Soviet generals without the knowledge of the federal government, and had become involved in what appeared to be a planned leftist putsch along the lines of

139

the 1948 Communist takeover of Czechoslovakia. The new Slovak premier, Jan Carnogursky, expressed support for preservation of the Czechoslovak federation, albeit in a diluted form.

**Changing Ties.** Czechoslovakia was accorded the status of a full member in the Council of Europe in February. The next month, President Havel became the first representative from a former Soviet-bloc state to visit NATO Headquarters in Brussels, where he spoke of the need for closer ties with Western nations. On June 21, the last units of the Soviet armed forces left Czechoslovakia after 23 years of occupation. The event was celebrated with a huge rock concert, with President Havel in attendance.

*See* STATISTICS OF THE WORLD.        O.U.

# D

**DAHOMEY.** *See* BENIN.

**DANCE.** A hugely successful new work by master choreographer Paul Taylor brightened a year in which some companies' financial problems continued to make headlines.

**Triumph for Taylor.** Commissioned jointly by Washington's Kennedy Center and Houston Ballet Director Ben Stevenson as part of a program to nurture American choreography and American companies, Paul Taylor's *Company B* was an immediate success at its June premiere. Set to hit songs of World War II days sung by the Andrews Sisters, *Company B* also alluded to a desert war not unlike the one in the headlines at the time it was created. Audiences and critics were rapturous, and President George Bush, in attendance at the world premiere, invited the entire cast around for breakfast at the White House the following morning.

**Revivals.** Peter Martins, director of the New York City Ballet (NYCB), crafted a costly ($2.8 million) staging of the complete *Sleeping Beauty*. He insisted on controversially quick tempos, used exceptionally lavish, ornate decor, and reinterpreted the ballet's closing moments by literally having crowns pass to a new generation. The production was a tremendous box office hit.

Another notable event was the restoration of Balanchine's own 1927 ballet *La Chatte* undertaken by Les Grands Ballets Canadiens. Ballet and art historians Millicent Hodson and Kenneth Archer worked with Dame Alicia Markova to capture the memory of this supposedly lost work before it was gone forever. Their research recovered the vital, experimental modernism of Balanchine's youth (he was 23 when he choreographed the Greek fable of a cat transformed into a woman and, when she scampers after a mouse on her wedding day, back into a cat). The constructivist aesthetic of the designs and the inspiration of illustrations on Greek vases combined to create a daring investigation of linear and profile elements in duets and group dances.

**Mark Morris.** The activities of Mark Morris, the Seattle-born choreographer based at the Brussels Théâtre de la Monnai since 1988, continued to make news. Morris failed to ingratiate himself with the European press and public, and with his European tenure nearing its end, he teamed up with superstar Mikhail Baryshnikov to form a small touring ensemble, the White Oak Project, which traveled to many cities around the United States. In January 1991, Morris finally had the success in Belgium that until then had eluded him: he presented an avant-garde version of *The Nutcracker*, retitled *The Hard Nut*, that included, among other things, a snowflake waltz for men in toe shoes and tutus. The production was judged both witty and thoughtful, but it came too late to save Morris's career in Brussels, and he returned to the United States the richer for having received one of the year's MacArthur awards.

**East-West Exchanges.** The interpenetration of Soviet and Western ballet accelerated during the year. Hitherto unthinkable exchanges included Vladimir Vasiliev's production of *Don Quixote* for American Ballet Theatre (ABT), Galina Ulanova's coaching the Boston Ballet in *Giselle*, and guest appearances with Western companies throughout Europe and North America by such dancers as Nina Ananiashvili, Andris Liepa, and Faruk Ruzimatov.

Meanwhile, the Kirov Ballet, which first danced American choreography in 1989, added Balanchine's *Apollo* and *Tchaikovsky Pas de Deux* as well as Tudor's *Jardin aux Lilas* to its repertoire. At the Jacob's Pillow Dance Festival, 12 American and 12 Soviet dancers exhumed Massine's *Choreartium* and *Les Présages* (both from 1933), before taking them to be seen in the Soviet Union in September.

**American Companies.** Among the troupes imperiled by financial and/or succession problems, ABT stood out. Founded by Lucia Chase and Richard Pleasant in 1939, ABT had not yet settled down under new permanent leadership since Chase was forced to step down at age 87 more than a decade earlier. The troupe's new artistic director, Jane Hermann, inherited huge debts from Mikhail Baryshnikov's 1981-1989 administration and so aroused Baryshnikov's hostility that he withdrew the performing rights to all ballets personally produced by him during those years. In the depressed economic climate, appearing opposite the New York City Ballet's popular *Sleeping Beauty*, ABT played to a scandalously empty Metropolitan Opera House; its new productions were rejected by press and ticket buyers alike. As the end of the year approached, ABT, without the resources to produce a new *Nutcracker*, was forced to cancel December engagements; it also scaled back its annual spring season at the Metropolitan Opera House.

The Alvin Ailey American Dance Theater, where former company star Judith Jamison took the helm, introduced new dancers and repertory and revived several Ailey works not seen for decades. Following the 1990 dissolution of its board of directors, the Joffrey Ballet regrouped under a new executive director, Robert Yesselman. Though the company's decade-old "life blood" connection to the Los

*Peter Martins's interpretation of Tchaikovsky's* The Sleeping Beauty *at the New York City Ballet was notable for its imaginative staging, lavish decor, and the exceptional dancing of ballerina Kyra Nichols, seen here performing the role of Aurora with Lindsay Fischer as Prince Désiré.*

Angeles Music Center was canceled, the Joffrey signed a long-term agreement with the Wiltern Theatre in Los Angeles for annual spring appearances. However, the company canceled its winter season in New York City.

**Deaths.** With the death at age 96 of Martha Graham, the modern dance world lost its foremost artist. Graham, who began dancing at age 22, created a series of 180 works that helped define modern dance. Her work was a radical departure from the ethereal grace of classical ballet, ranking her in the eyes of many as an artistic pioneer. Graham taught not only choreographers and dancers—from Erick Hawkins (her husband at one time) to Baryshnikov—but also actors like Gregory Peck and Bette Davis. Her influence extended far beyond dance, encompassing also theater and stage and costume design.

Dame Margot Fonteyn died of cancer at 71. As the prima ballerina of Britain's Royal Ballet, Fonteyn dazzled audiences and inspired cho-

141

With Martha Graham's death in April, modern dance lost its most famous pioneer. As both dancer and choreographer over a span of more than 60 years, she created roles that defined the vocabulary of her art. An outstanding triumph was Appalachian Spring (left), choreographed in 1944 to music by Aaron Copland. Below, in Clytemnestra (1958), she danced with Paul Taylor, one of many students who went on to greatness in their own right.

reographer Sir Frederick Ashton to many of his finest creations, including *Ondine* (1958). At 42 she teamed up with Nureyev, then a 23-year-old recent defector from the Soviet Union; the partnership lasted 15 years and became legendary around the world.

**Stars of the Future.** Among young dancers the most outstanding was 22-year-old Elizabeth Loscavio of the San Francisco Ballet, who made her first New York appearances when that troupe gave a one-week season at City Center in October. The petite Loscavio struck many longtime dancegoers as a young Gelsey Kirkland or Fonteyn. Also striking was the Royal Ballet's 22-year-old Darcey Bussell, a leggy, eager, technically and lyrically admirable discovery of choreographer Kenneth MacMillan. Leaping to stardom at New York City Ballet were Margaret Tracey and Wendy Whelan, the company's new principal women, and Nilas Martins, son of Peter Martins, who proved to be an interesting heir to his father's roles in Balanchine's *Diamonds* and *Apollo*.　　　　　　　　　　　　A.F.

**DELAWARE.** See STATISTICS OF THE WORLD.
**DEMOCRATIC PARTY.** See UNITED STATES OF AMERICA: *Political Parties.*

**DENMARK.** In February 1991 the Danish coalition government, under Prime Minister Poul Schlüter, secured parliamentary backing for its budget by moderating some personal income tax reductions. Supporting the budget were the three center parties and the two governing parties. The main opposition party, the Social Democrats, abstained rather than opposing the government and causing an election. Voting against the government were the leftist Socialist People's and rightist Progress parties.

The ensuing parliamentary climate was warm enough for a major reform of unemployment and job training legislation to pass in May. Equally important were measures to stabilize local taxes and provide greater municipal subsidies from the central government.

The Danish government's long-term efforts to reduce inflation, eliminate the perpetual balance of payments deficit, and lower interest rates all made progress. Inflation was running at around 2.5 percent. Overall economic growth was expected to decline slightly, by 1.6 percent, for 1991. However, the unemployment rate rose to over 10 percent. Nearly all political parties were committed to new initiatives to reduce unemployment.

In August, Parliament approved plans for a road and rail bridge nearly 11 miles long to connect Denmark (just south of Copenhagen) with southern Sweden. Another massive project, for a bridge-tunnel crossing the Great Belt (a strait separating two major Danish islands) was underway.

Movements toward European troop reductions, in reaction to changes in the Soviet Union and Eastern Europe, produced a positive response in Denmark. Danish defense efforts, already minimal, were modestly scaled back, but Denmark did support plans for a NATO emergency force under British command. There was broad public support for Denmark's quick recognition in late August of restored sovereignty in the Baltic states. Despite Danish support for European economic integration, opinion remained divided over ambitious plans for a European monetary union and over foreign and defense policy integration.

Danish support of culture and the arts was symbolized by the dramatic expansion of the Louisiana Art Museum just north of Copenhagen. Another museum in the same area, Rungstedlund, the estate of Danish author Isak Dinesen (Baroness Karen Blixen-Finecke), was reopened to the public after undergoing extensive restoration.

See STATISTICS OF THE WORLD.        E.S.E.

**DISTRICT OF COLUMBIA.** See STATISTICS OF THE WORLD.

**DJIBOUTI.** See STATISTICS OF THE WORLD.

**DOMINICA.** See STATISTICS OF THE WORLD.

**DOMINICAN REPUBLIC.** See STATISTICS OF THE WORLD. See also CARIBBEAN BASIN.

# E

**EARTH SCIENCES.** In 1991 Mount Pinatubo, a long-dormant volcano on the Philippine island of Luzon, exploded in one of the largest eruptions of the century. Bangladesh was devastated by a cyclone. Earth scientists were concerned about global warming.

## CLIMATOLOGY

Allied forces fighting in the Persian Gulf War found that weather played a significant role in the course of events. The year saw many weather extremes.

**Persian Gulf War.** In the air campaign waged by U.S.-led allied forces against Iraq in the Persian Gulf War, rain clouds made it difficult to pinpoint targets and assess the success of strikes. Low cloud cover offered protection on several occasions for Iraq to launch Scud missiles at Saudi Arabia and Israel. On February 24, as the ground war began, strong southerly winds hindered Iraq from possibly using chemical weapons, since the chemicals would have blown back on Iraqi troops.

# EARTH SCIENCES

Before leaving Kuwait, the Iraqi forces ignited hundreds of oil wells. Thick smoke from the fires blocked the sun over much of Kuwait for weeks. Analyses showed that very little was reaching the stratosphere, where it could affect the earth's temperature by reflecting sunlight away from the earth. However, scientists in China claimed that particles from the fires had seeded clouds over southwest China, triggering extensive flooding. There were also reports of oily black rain or snow falling on Iran, Pakistan, Bulgaria, Turkey, the southern Soviet Union, Afghanistan, and India.

**Winter Extremes.** Exceptionally heavy rain fell along the U.S. Gulf Coast starting in January, which was the wettest on record from Beaumont, Texas, to Wilmington, N.C. Meanwhile, during the first ten days of February, more than 170 daily record maximums were set across the nation. Drought conditions continued in California, alleviated somewhat by heavy rains in March.

*Unusually frigid and snowy weather in England in February disrupted daily routines to such an extent that the celebrated changing of the guards ceremony outside London's Buckingham Palace had to be canceled pending a thaw.*

**Spring Storms.** Shreveport, La., was the wettest place in the world in the middle of April, as more than 19 inches of rain fell in just five days. A large tornado in late April destroyed a southeast neighborhood of Wichita, Kan., with at least 25 people killed. More than 70 tornadoes touched down on that same day from Texas to Minnesota.

**Summer Heat and Hurricane.** Record heat hit the Middle Atlantic states in late spring and then in the summer. The weekend of July 19-21 brought temperatures over 100°F to three state capitals: Harrisburg, Pa., Providence, R.I., and Hartford, Conn. Philadelphia had its hottest summer ever. Hurricane Bob formed near the Bahamas, and by August 19 it was lashing eastern Long Island, N.Y., and raking across Rhode Island and Cape Cod, Mass. Damage was estimated at over $2 billion.

**Volcanic Disruption.** Mount Pinatubo, a volcano dormant for 600 years on the Philippine island of Luzon, began a series of violent eruptions in June that devastated the surrounding countryside, ejecting twice as much dust into the stratosphere as Mexico's El Chichón in 1982. The dust partially obstructed the view of a total solar eclipse on July 11 at the Mauna Kea Observatory in Hawaii. By early autumn the dust cloud had spread into the middle latitude's stratosphere, making for unusually colorful sunsets.

**Wild Weather.** Wild weather occurred from October 28 to November 6, beginning with an ocean storm that formed near Nova Scotia and rapidly strengthened while moving toward the southwest, causing extensive tidal flooding. A severe winter storm brought the greatest single snowfall yet recorded in Minneapolis (28.2 inches) and Duluth (36.4 inches). The mercury fell to −17°F at Pueblo, Colo., on November 3, and snowflakes were seen in Brownsville, Texas. The following day there were record lows in 100 U.S. cities.

**Bangladesh Cyclone.** In late April, an intensifying tropical cyclone pushed into the southeast corner of Bangladesh, killing over 120,000 people in the path of the cyclone. Winds exceeded 125 mph, and waves and tides rose more than 20 feet above sea level.

**Weather Satellites.** The launch of a new generation of U.S. weather satellites, originally scheduled for 1990, was further delayed by revelations of mismanagement and serious developmental obstacles. Documents gathered by the General Accounting Office showed that NASA, the agency purchasing the satellites for the National Weather Service, may have wasted more than $300 million by failing to work out a cost capping agreement with the main contractor.                    P.G.K.

## GEOLOGY

Objects of interest in the geological sciences included huge outpourings of volcanic material on the earth's surface millions of years ago and a new view of the planet Venus.

**Superplumes.** The earth's mantle (the layer just below the crust) may have experienced a tremendous upwelling of material over 120 million years ago, sending up hot jets of material called plumes. Scientists have suggested that large plumes, perhaps 1,000 miles across, may have formed continental flood basalts, large outpourings of dark volcanic rocks such as the Columbia Plateau in Washington State and the Siberian Traps in the Soviet Union. Roger L. Larson of the University of Rhode Island recently went further, postulating that a superplume, perhaps over 3,500 miles across between 124 and 83 million years ago, correlated with increases in world temperature, oil formation, and sea level, as well as with a period in which the normal processes of reversal of the earth's magnetic field ceased.

**Planetary Geology.** The *Magellan* spacecraft was providing an unsurpassed view of Venus's geology, revealing numerous impact craters, highly fractured terrain, and evidence of widespread volcanism. The *Galileo* spacecraft, on its way to Jupiter, sent back images of the moon that enabled scientists to determine the mineralogical composition of the moon's far side. The *Galileo* flyby also revealed the largest lunar impact crater ever seen, over 1,200 miles in diameter. In October the spacecraft took the first close-up image ever of an asteroid, Gaspra.

**Earthquakes.** In Asia a February 1 quake with a magnitude of 6.8, centered in the Hindu Kush region of Afghanistan, killed at least 1,000 people, and an October 20 earthquake of magnitude 6.1 in the foothills of the Himalayas killed over 2,000. On April 29 a magnitude

A river of hot ash pouring down the side of Mount Unzen sent a fire truck and a fire fighter fleeing in the Japanese town of Kita-Kamikoba as 43 people were killed. During more than a month of activity, the volcano destroyed hundreds of buildings and forced the evacuation of thousands.

7.1 shock occurred in the western Caucasus region of the Soviet Union, killing over 100 people. And a magnitude 6.4 earthquake at Timor, Indonesia, on July 4 also caused casualties.

In the Americas, a magnitude 6.7 earthquake shook northern Peru on April 4, killing at least 100 and causing extensive damage. In Costa Rica a magnitude 7.6 earthquake on April 22 killed 76 and left another 9,800 homeless. On June 28 in southern California, a magnitude 5.8 quake killed 2 people and injured at least 100.

**Volcanoes.** Scientists from the National Oceanic and Atmospheric Administration and Oregon State University have discovered a new line of volcanoes, off the Oregon coast. This is

145

*The worst earthquake to hit Costa Rica in more than 80 years struck near the coastal city of Limón in late April. Besides its human toll, the tremor, which measured over 7 on the Richter scale, destroyed thousands of homes, damaged bridges, and tore huge cracks in vital roads and highways.*

the first direct evidence of historic volcanism on the midocean ridges, where plate tectonic theory holds that the oceanic crust is actively forming.

At Mount Pinatubo in the Philippines, an explosion on April 2 ejected steam and ash 2,000 feet high. On June 12-15 many large explosions sent ash clouds 15 miles high, culminating on June 15 with an ash column reaching over 20 miles high and continuing for 11 hours. In terms of sulfur dioxide emissions, Pinatubo may have been the largest eruption of the century. Although hundreds of people were killed, 200,000 lives were saved because of timely evacuations.

A dome of lava began to build at the Unzen volcano on Kyushu Island, Japan, on May 20 and partially collapsed on May 24, producing hot ash flows down the mountain and prompting the evacuation of thousands. A major collapse on June 3 caused hot ash to surge into a populated district, killing 43 people, including three volcanologists. Hundreds of buildings were damaged by continuing mud and ash flows.

After ten years of quiescence, one of Iceland's most active volcanoes, Hekla, erupted

with an ash cloud 7 miles high on January 17; the eruption lasted until March 11. The eruption of Kilauea, on the island of Hawaii, entered its ninth year, although activity was subsiding somewhat. A lava dome began to grow at Colima Volcano in Mexico on March 1, and on April 16 the dome collapsed, accompanied by lava flows and avalanches.　　　　E.S.

## OCEANOGRAPHY

The Persian Gulf War resulted in a huge oil spill in the Gulf. There were new findings on global warming.

**Kuwait Oil Spill.** The world's largest oil spill was due primarily to Iraqi-caused discharges from Kuwaiti oil facilities during the Gulf War. Estimates of the quantity of oil released ranged up to 6 million barrels. In addition, the fires set to Kuwaiti oil wells led to the release of substantial quantities of pollutants into the Gulf. Late in the year, after the last oil well fires were extinguished, vast amounts of oil still remained on the beaches.

**Global Warming.** The permanent ice cover over the Arctic Ocean shrank by about 2 percent between 1978 and 1987, according to a study by Per Gloersen of NASA's Goddard Space Flight Center and William J. Campbell of the U.S. Geological Survey. The reduction may be an early indication of a global warming trend. The study found no reduction in the coverage of antarctic sea ice, but this may be due to the greater area of open ocean near Antarctica, which would delay warming. In any event, confirmation of global warming effects will require long-term observations—30 years or more—even in the arctic region. But several disturbing bits of evidence have been reported recently. The sea ice northeast of Greenland was substantially thinner in 1987 than 1976. Also, snow-covered areas of the northern hemisphere continents were smaller during the winter of 1990 than in any previous winter on record.                    M.G.G.

**ECONOMY AND BUSINESS, U.S.** The U.S. economy was generally sluggish in 1991. The number of unemployed workers grew. And despite low inflation and interest rates, wary consumers held back on spending—hurting manufacturers, home builders, retailers, and the travel industry.

The first quarter of the year saw the bottom of the recession that began in 1990. As the year wore on, continuing economic weakness made the economy an increasingly important 1992 presidential campaign issue. Senate Majority Leader George Mitchell (D, Me.) charged in late October that the record of growth under the presidency of Republican George Bush was the worst since that of Herbert Hoover in the Great Depression of the 1930s. The economic news was not all bad, however: The stock market ended the year at a record high.

**Recession.** According to many economists, the recession started in July 1990 and ended in the spring of 1991. But the subsequent increase in output of goods and services was small compared to most economic recoveries. The fourth quarter brought evidence that the economy was slowing again. The Commerce Department's Index of Leading Indicators, designed to point to future economic activity, declined 0.2 percent in September—the first drop in eight months. The index rose 0.1 percent in October, then dropped 0.3 percent in November. Industrial output declined in the fourth quarter and, for the whole year, averaged 1.9 percent less than in 1990.

### Sit Down, Pump Up

In this bustling world it's common for office workers to eat at their desks. As for exercise—well, until recently those harried employees could always plead "too busy."

Now you can not only eat at your desk, you can work out there too, with the Nordic Fitness Chair. Produced by NordicTrack—those people who, with their well-known cross-country ski exerciser, helped a generation to pretend their living rooms were Scandinavian forest trails—it looks like an ordinary chair but conceals a system of arms that, when unfolded, allow for 20 different exercises (some models have an optional leg attachment for the lower body).

In recent years fitness experts have concluded that aerobic exercise—jogging, swimming, bicycling, cross-country skiing—is not enough to give balanced fitness. Also needed is upper-body strength training. Of course, one can utilize an array of weights and dumbbells, but those can prove obtrusive, and they don't have the glitz of high-tech ingenuity. Nor will they arouse the same envy in the neighbors.

The fitness chair comes in five models ranging in price from around $500 to more than twice that. It's the kind of thing that could give new meaning to the term "power lunch."

*With the U.S. economy mired in recession, unemployment offices, such as this one in New Bedford, Mass., were among the few places where business was brisk.*

Unemployment in December reached 7.1 percent, the highest rate in 5½ years, and the number of unemployed rose to 8.9 million, the highest in nearly eight years. A sharp drop in the stock market in mid-November was also interpreted by many analysts as an indication that the economy was not yet building toward a recovery, although the Dow Jones average revived and surged to a record high.

By mid-December, Federal Reserve Board Chairman Alan Greenspan admitted that the recovery was in serious trouble. The White House, reversing a policy of downplaying the economic sluggishness, began speaking of a continuing recession and a need for presidential action to reverse the trend.

**National Versus Domestic Product.** The federal government late in the year changed its preferred method of characterizing the nation's output of goods and services. For half a century the government had used the gross national product, or GNP, for this purpose; under the new policy, the government used gross domestic product, or GDP. While the GNP covers production by American residents or corporations anywhere in the world, the GDP measures goods and services produced by

workers and capital within U.S. borders. Most economists regard the GDP as a better indicator of a country's economic performance, and most industrialized countries were already using it.

As a result of the recession, the GDP declined in the last quarter of 1990 and the first quarter of 1991 by an annual rate of 3.9 percent and 2.5 percent, respectively, based on 1987 dollars. It grew 1.4 percent in the second quarter and 1.8 percent in the third.

**Interest Rates.** The Federal Reserve acted a number of times to reduce the interest rates under its control, in the hope of pushing down other interest rates as well, taking its strongest action late in the year. On October 30, the Fed lowered its target for the federal funds rate to 5 percent, down 0.25 percent from the previous day. That rate, which commercial banks charge each other on overnight loans, had been 8 percent a year earlier. The prime rate, which banks charge their better customers, was 8 percent at the end of October, down from 10 percent a year earlier. Other interest rate reductions followed.

On December 20, the Fed knocked an entire percentage point off the discount rate (which it charges banks for loans), bringing it to 3.5 percent, its lowest level since 1964. This rate had been 7 percent in December 1990 and was cut six times in 1991. The funds rate was cut to 4 percent. By year's end, major banks had dropped the prime to 6.5 percent, its lowest level since 1977.

Householders who had taken out equity loans against their homes rejoiced at the lower costs. Holders of savings accounts, however, were not so pleased with the low rates offered by banks.

**Government Budget Woes.** The recession hurt government revenues. For the 1991 fiscal year (October 1, 1990, through September 30, 1991), the federal government suffered a record $268.7 billion budget deficit. Total federal outlays in fiscal 1991 were $1.323 trillion, up 5.7 percent from the previous year. Revenue totaled $1.054 trillion, compared to $1.031 trillion the year before. The fiscal 1991 deficit approximated 4.8 percent of the gross national product, one measure economists use to gauge the importance of a deficit. That was up from 4.1 percent in 1990 but well below the 6.3 percent level hit in 1983.

**Consumer Confidence Weak.** Slow growth did not help consumer confidence, which had tumbled badly after Iraq invaded Kuwait in August 1990 and the armed forces of the United States and its allies moved into the Persian Gulf region. Confidence revived with the quick winter victory of the allies, then took a sharp dip later in the year, indicating that consumers believed the country was still in recession or heading into one. The news worried retailers concerned about their Christmas trade, and was not a good sign for the economy generally, since consumers buy two-thirds of the nation's output. After a promising rise in September, retail sales actually dropped in October, rose only slightly in November, and were disappointing in December.

Sales of homes weren't greatly helped by a drop in housing prices. Nor did buyers respond to low mortgage rates. (By the end of the year the average interest rate for 30-year fixed-rate mortgages had fallen to 8.35 percent, the lowest level in more than 18 years.) Single-family housing starts, which had been running at about a 1.1 million annual rate at the beginning of 1990, plunged to a 790,000 annual rate by February 1991. However, housing starts appeared to be recovering late in the year.

Automobile sales did poorly as well. For calendar year 1991, sales of cars and light trucks reached only 12.3 million units, down 11.2 percent from 13.9 million in 1990; this was their lowest level since the recession of the early 1980s. Slow sales particularly hurt American car companies. The economic impact of the losses took on a vivid form in December, when General Motors announced it would close 21 U.S. and Canadian plants and cut 74,000 jobs by the end of 1995.

One positive result of the economy's lack of vibrancy was lower inflation. Consumer prices rose 3.1 percent during 1991, down from 6.1 percent in 1990 and the lowest rate since 1.1 percent in 1986. And many experts expected the downward trend to continue in 1992.

**Retailing.** Household names in retailing continued to file for bankruptcy with depressing frequency, although a plan was announced to bring the Campeau Corporation's Federated and Allied department store chains out of Chapter 11 bankruptcy by February 1992. The Sunbelt's Carter Hawley Hale department store operator filed for court protection under Chapter 11 and was bailed out by Zell-Chilmark Fund of Chicago. And in June the Lionel Corporation, operator of Kiddie City, also filed for Chapter 11. Following a weak Christmas sales season, many analysts predicted thousands more retail bankruptcies in 1992.

Overall, department stores were the big losers in retailing, while the big winners were the discounters like Wal-Mart and K Mart. Specialty apparel shops presented a mixed picture—if only because The Gap Inc. showed such strength.

Specialty stores were the locus of much of the new thinking in other areas. For example, when the price of coffee beans rose substantially in the mid-1980s, the big coffee makers turned to cheap beans, and gourmet coffee shops began to bloom. Retail sales of what is called "specialty" coffee more than tripled in the last six years. And, whereas overall furniture sales in the United States were flat, the

Swedish firm of Ikea had customers standing in line for furniture that was simple, moderately priced, and just rugged enough to do the job. **Income Trends.** The proportion of the U.S. population whose income fell below the federal poverty level rose to 13.5 percent in 1990, up from 12.8 percent in 1989. Although Census Bureau numbers were not available for 1991, most economists assumed the poverty rate rose another notch, owing to the slow pace of the recovery. The number of people receiving federal food stamps reached a record 23.6 million in August, an increase of more than 3 million over the same month in 1990; and there was a rise in the number of applicants in relatively well-to-do suburbs. The recession also led to a drop in the birthrate. The U.S. Department of Health and Human Services reported that 2,361,000 babies were born from January through July, 50,000 below the seven-month figure for 1990.

Meanwhile, a study by the Economic Policy Institute, a liberal Washington think tank, found that the economic position of the typical young family had deteriorated in the 1980s. The median income of a family in which the parents were aged 25 to 34 declined in constant 1989 dollars from $31,544 in 1973 to $30,873 in 1989. Minorities were hit harder, as were families headed by a worker without a college education.

**Corrective Moves.** On October 8 the Bush administration announced a round of regulatory measures meant to encourage banks to make new loans and stimulate the economy. One change was to ease the limits on how much preferred stock banks could sell to raise capital. Another was to allow bank officers who believed that their institutions had been unfairly treated by examiners to circumvent the usual process and appeal directly and secretly to the examiners' supervisors in Washington.

An effort by the Democrats to extend unemployment benefits by 20 weeks after the first 26 weeks of state-provided payments expired was vetoed by the president, who said the $6.4 billion measure was too expensive. He asked Congress to adopt a less generous bill that would extend benefits for up to ten weeks at a cost of $3 billion. In the end a compromise acceptable to Bush was enacted. At a cost of about $5.3 billion, it extended benefits for up

*While most furniture dealers suffered flat sales, the Swedish firm Ikea flourished with its offerings of simple, moderately priced goods sold in a self-service format.*

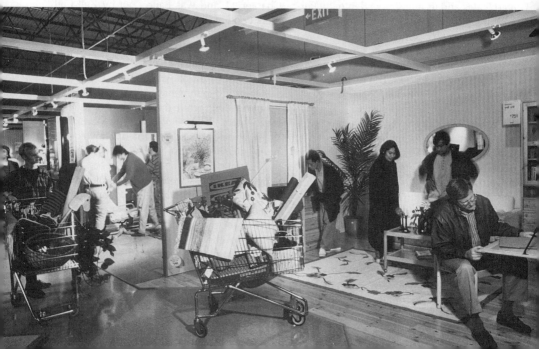

*Some of the freshest-brewed ideas in retailing are being found in specialty shops such as Gloria Jean's, a chain of gourmet coffee stores with over 100 outlets in the United States. Shown here, company founders Edward and Gloria Jean Kvetko.*

to 20 weeks, depending on the state. The extension was to be financed partly by speeding up estimated tax payments from some upper-bracket taxpayers and extending a surcharge on employers' unemployment insurance taxes.

As the year drew to a close, there was much talk of a tax cut to stimulate the economy. Various plans were put forth in the hope of enacting legislation by early in the upcoming election year. Texas Senator Lloyd Bentsen (D), for example, proposed to reduce taxes by $72.5 billion over five years by providing taxpayers a $300 credit for each child under 18. Senator Daniel Patrick Moynihan (D, N.Y.) revived his idea of trimming the Social Security payroll tax. Senators Phil Gramm (R, Texas) and Robert W. Kasten (R, Wis.) and Representative Newt Gingrich (R, Ga.) proposed reducing the capital gains tax and boosting the tax deduction for individual retirement accounts. Representative Dan Rostenkowski (D, Ill.), the chairman of the House Ways and Means Committee (where federal tax legislation is initiated), proposed a two-year tax cut for working-class and middle-income families via an income tax credit equal to 20 percent of the Social Security and Medicare taxes paid. Economists noted, however, that any economic stimulus from such tax measures would not occur for many months, perhaps when the recovery was moving ahead and would not need it.

**Foreign Exchange, Trade.** The foreign exchange market appeared relatively calm. At the close of December 31 it took 1.52 German marks to buy a dollar, compared with 1.49 marks a year earlier; the dollar's value in British pounds was 0.54, up from 0.52 the year before. The dollar fetched 124.85 Japanese yen, down from 134.80 a year earlier.

In the first ten months of 1991, the U.S. merchandise trade deficit averaged $65 billion at an annual rate. That was down sharply from the full-year 1990 merchandise trade deficit of slightly over $100 billion. Because of cash contributions from coalition partners in Operation Desert Storm, the broader current account, which also includes trade in services, investment income, and unilateral transfers, showed a surplus of $10.5 billion in the first quarter of 1991 and another surplus of $3 billion in the second quarter. In the third quarter, however, there was a $10.5 billion deficit in the current account, and the fourth quarter was also expected to show a deficit.

D.R.F. & W.K.W.

**ECUADOR.** President Rodrigo Borja Cevallos and his ruling Democratic Left (ID) party faced unremitting political opposition in 1991. In a special legislative session in mid-February, the opposition launched a major offensive against the Borja government, attacking key economic measures that included currency devaluation and domestic price increases.

During that session and later, conservative parties joined with Ecuador's three Marxist parties to pass votes of censure against a number of cabinet members, thus removing them from office.

For a time, congressional opposition leaders called for the impeachment of Vice President Luis Parodi Valverde. They charged that, as acting president during Borja's temporary absence from Ecuador, Parodi had authorized the printing of currency to pay a private building firm and had altered regulations governing contracts with private companies.

At the start of the year, Ecuador's inflation rate was running above 50 percent, renegotiation of the foreign debt had floundered, and living conditions were worsening. Street demonstrations erupted in January over the size of the monthly minimum wage. After four days of protests resulted in dozens of injuries and nearly $500,000 in damage, the United Workers' Front (FUT) called a 24-hour general strike for February 6. During this action, the FUT was joined for the first time by the increasingly vocal Indian organization, the Confederation of Ecuadorean Indigenous Nationalities (Coniae).

In late May, under Coniae leadership, Ecuadorean Indians occupied the legislature in Quito for two days as a symbol of resistance. Two specific demands were put forward: a constitutional amendment declaring Ecuador to be a "multiethnic and pluricultural nation" and amnesty for some 1,000 Indian militants who appropriated land they claim was stolen from their ancestors by European colonizers. At an Indian national assembly on September 6-9 in the Amazon town of Puyo, the Indians continued their protests, demanding autonomy in their own traditional territories. They expressed particular concern over exploration of the Amazon by foreign oil companies.

On May 18 the presidents of the five Andean states—Bolivia, Colombia, Ecuador, Peru, and Venezuela—met to confirm plans to create regional common market by 1995.

See STATISTICS OF THE WORLD.          J.D.M.

**EDUCATION.** In 1991, President George Bush offered a series of proposals to improve education in the United States and appointed a new education secretary, Lamar Alexander, a former Tennessee governor known for dedication to education reform. However, reform efforts in the United States met with limited success. The academic performance of U.S. students was not improving, and fiscal constraints throughout the nation made it hard to implement new programs in the public schools. Higher education had troubles of its own, ranging from heated debates over "political correctness" to controversy involving alleged improper use of government research funds.

**America 2000.** In April, President Bush unveiled America 2000, a "nine-year crusade" to achieve six education goals adopted by the state governors and the president at a Charlottesville, Va., education summit in 1989. The goals, which had been reiterated by Bush in his 1990 State of the Union address, were that, by the year 2000, all children will start school ready to learn; the high school graduation rate will increase to at least 90 percent; students will demonstrate, through testing, competence in critical subjects; American students will be first in the world in mathematics and science; every adult will be literate and skilled to compete in a global economy; and all schools will be drug-free and safe

Bush's America 2000 plan called for student achievement in five core subjects—English, history, geography, mathematics, and science— to be monitored by voluntary American Achievement Tests. It also envisioned private-sector funding to jump-start at least 535 high-performance "New American Schools" by 1996, as well as a highly controversial "choice" plan, which would subsidize education at the public or private school of choice.

In drafting the America 2000 strategy, the education secretary consulted closely with business leaders. David T. Kearns, former chairman of Xerox Corporation, was appointed deputy secretary of education and named administration liaison to the New American Schools Development Corporation, whose mission was to raise up to $200 million to fund innovative schools. Critics charged that America 2000 could derail existing reform efforts and that it failed to address the most dire issues facing schools, such as race, class, economics, and decaying facilities.

### High-Profile Schoolmaster

Unanimously confirmed by the U.S. Senate in March, former Tennessee Governor Lamar Alexander, 52, quickly became a high-profile education secretary. Known for his interest in such concepts as tougher standards for students and merit pay for teachers, he soon saw many of his ideas taken up by President George Bush as part of Bush's "America 2000" program, setting forth educational goals for the future. Many ideas attracted controversy—including a recommendation that laws be changed to allow parents a greater ability to choose which schools their children attend. Alexander also took issue with the Middle States college accrediting agency for "cultural diversity" standards he claimed undermined academic freedom and encouraged the use of quotas. And in December he proposed regulations that would generally bar college scholarships based solely on race.

A Tennessee native, Alexander graduated from Vanderbilt University and earned a law degree from New York University. He coordinated Howard Baker's successful 1966 U.S. Senate campaign, became a White House aide, and served two terms as governor of Tennessee, where he implemented many of his reform ideas. He became president of the University of Tennessee in 1988.

*Lamar Alexander*

**Progress Report.** The first report card on the six U.S. education goals adopted at Charlottesville painted a somber picture of how far the public schools still had to go. According to the report, released in October by a National Education Goals Panel, high school completion rates were at an all-time high, and drug use in schools was down. But U.S. students continued to lag academically behind counterparts in other nations. And, while most Americans had mastered basic functional literary skills, far fewer could perform such tasks as interpreting the main argument of a lengthy newspaper column or using a shopping catalog to fill out an order form and calculate the cost of several items.

Recognizing that close to 30 million American adults have serious literacy problems, Congress enacted the National Literacy Act. The measure provides for research and financial aid to establish adult and family literacy programs at the federal, state, and local level.

**Budgets and Recession.** According to the Goals Report, 26 federal agencies spent about $59 billion in fiscal year 1991 for activities to support national education goals, in such programs as higher education loans and job training, subsidized school lunches, special programs for disadvantaged students, and Head Start. Critics said the statistic disguised a decrease in federal funding.

Paying for school reforms proved a formidable challenge for legislatures and school boards scrambling—not always successfully—to balance budgets without laying off teachers and cutting programs. Meanwhile, litigation in over 20 states challenged funding inequities between rich and poor districts, fueling debate over the use of property taxes as a basic means to finance public education.

153

# EDUCATION

**Standards and Testing.** Student accountability was a key issue. In June, Congress created a National Council on Education Standards and Testing to study means of measuring student achievement. In a draft report issued in December, the council recommended voluntary national curriculum standards and national tests, but left the details unclear. Meanwhile, some 450 educators and policymakers met in August in Snowmass, Colo., to discuss creating a national examination system based on performance. The effort became known as the New Standards Project. Similar efforts were made by, among others, Harvard University, the College Board, and several states. The testing council's congressional members maintained that the nation was moving too quickly to testing, as the field became cluttered with testing proposals.

A report released by the U.S. Education Department in the fall concluded that, despite some encouraging trends, overall student performance had not improved over the past two decades, with losses during the 1970s being offset by gains in the 1980s. The report was based on findings from standardized tests in mathematics, science, reading, and writing under the congressionally mandated National Assessment of Educational Progress (NAEP). Whites continued to outperform blacks and Hispanics, but the gap showed narrowing.

In June the NAEP released data from math tests administered in 1990. In these tests, more than 25 percent of the fourth-graders tested failed to show proficiency in simple arithmetic calculations, and only 5 percent of the high school seniors showed a sufficient knowledge of advanced mathematics to prepare them for college-level work.

Meanwhile, on the Scholastic Aptitude Test, used for screening college applicants, average verbal scores dropped to an all-time low. Average scores on the Test of Standard Written English, a 30-minute, multiple-choice test administered along with the SAT, also declined, as did average math scores (for the first time since 1980). On a positive note, the proportion of the senior class that performed at high levels on the exam rose once again, as it has since 1983, and the substantial gap between white and black students' performance continued to narrow.

**School and Work.** Increased attention was paid to the plight of the so-called "forgotten

*A contentious issue in U.S. education was multiculturalism, or the extent to which textbooks and curricula should be overhauled to reflect the nation's racial and ethnic diversity. In Oakland, Calif., the school board, claiming state-approved textbooks lacked a multicultural point of view, rejected them, forcing some teachers, like Cheryl R. Washington, to do without textbooks and rely on homemade materials.*

half" of students who finish high school but do not go on to college. Efforts to integrate vocational and academic instruction, to eliminate the general education track, to link classroom learning to the worksite and community, and to move vocational education from narrow, skill-based training to "all aspects of the industry" appeared to gain some momentum. Congress was considering action calling for such things as school-to-work programs for all students and corporate support for worker training programs.

In July the Secretary's Commission on Achieving Necessary Skills outlined the basic skills, cognitive abilities, and personal qualities high school graduates need to succeed in career-ladder jobs. The report found that "more than half of our young people leave school without the knowledge or foundation required to find and hold a good job." The report found, particularly, that the nation was "utterly failing the majority of poor, disadvantaged, and minority youngsters."

**Higher Education.** In June the American Federation of Teachers, the National Education Association, and the American Association of University Professors jointly noted that "higher education is facing an unprecedented financial crisis" following a decade of reduced federal support combined with severe state recessions. State-resident tuitions and fees at public four-year institutions rose 13.2 percent for the 1991-1992 academic year; the figure for private four-year colleges was 9.4 percent. In their book *Keeping College Affordable: Government and Educational Opportunity*, Michael S. McPherson and Morton Owen Schapiro concluded that many colleges and universities would have to either adopt even more dramatic tuition increases or accept a decline in quality because of an inability to attract and keep top scholars on the faculty or offer a sufficient range of courses.

Higher education's image suffered from revelations that questionable or unallowable charges had been billed to the government in connection with federal research conducted on campus. Stanford University president Donald Kennedy resigned amid allegations of overbilling for research "overhead" expenses such as costly furnishings for the president's official residence. Several other universities gave back some funds, including the University of Pennsylvania, which returned about $900,000.

Campuses across the United States debated the issue of "political correctness," or efforts to proscribe speech or behavior offensive to particular groups such as women, racial minorities, and homosexuals, in response to signs of an increase in bias-related incidents on U.S. college campuses in recent years. A Brown University junior was expelled in January for having allegedly shouted racist and homophobic slurs in a dormitory courtyard in defiance of an antiharassment code adopted by the university in 1989. In October, a federal district court struck down the University of Wisconsin's rule against hate speech, as an unconstitutional abridgement of free speech. The rule had prescribed a range of penalties, up to expulsion, for speech demeaning of an individual's sex, creed, race, disability, ancestry, or sexual orientation.

Meanwhile, at the City College of New York, Leonard Jeffries, a tenured professor and chairman of the school's black studies department, became a center of controversy for making public comments at a state-sponsored cultural conference that were deemed racist and anti-Semitic; his term as chairman was renewed by the college for an eight-month period only, pending further consideration of the matter.

L.C.-K.

**EGYPT.** The Persian Gulf War and its ramifications dominated events in Egypt during 1991. Following Iraq's invasion and occupation of Kuwait in August 1990, Egyptian President Hosni Mubarak had attempted to defuse the crisis through diplomacy. When these efforts failed, Egypt committed the second-largest allied army contingent (about 45,000 troops) to the U.S.-led coalition deployed in the Arabian Peninsula.

While Egyptian casualties were minimal (only ten Egyptian soldiers were killed in action), the scope of Iraqi casualties inflamed public opinion in Egypt, stirring protests especially by fundamentalist Islamic forces. The relatively quick conclusion to the war by no means pacified opposition forces. Members of the Jihad (Holy War), as well as scores of other

*Egypt's position in the Arab League, to which it returned in 1989, was enhanced at this May 1991 meeting in Cairo, where Egyptian Foreign Minister Esmat Abdel Meguid was elected secretary-general of the organization.*

groups, carried on repeated battles with Egyptian security forces.

**Improved Foreign Relations.** Diplomatic exchanges, coupled with a meeting between Mubarak and Soviet President Mikhail Gorbachev in September, resulted in increased cooperation with the Soviet Union prior to its disintegration at year's end. Relations with Libya also continued to improve. Meanwhile, Egypt remained a close U.S. ally and the second-largest recipient of U.S. foreign aid.

Although the Gulf War pitted Egypt against Iraq and strained relations with Iraq's principal supporters (Jordan, the Palestine Liberation Organization, Yemen, and Sudan), cooperative relations with all but Iraq and Sudan were soon restored.

In May, Foreign Minister Esmat Abdel Meguid was elected secretary-general of the Arab League. Later in the year, Deputy Prime Minister Boutros Ghali was elected secretary-general of the United Nations.

**Internal Affairs.** The trial of Gamal Abdel Nasser's son, Khaled, and other members of the "Egypt's Revolution" group, accused of assassination attempts against U.S. and Israeli officials in Egypt, came to an end in April. Khaled Nasser was acquitted, while several others were found guilty and sentenced to long prison terms.

The Gulf crisis caused hundreds of thousands of Egyptian expatriate workers in Iraq and the Arabian Peninsula to scurry home to safety, signaling an end to billions in hard currency earnings that they had previously repatriated to Egypt and greatly boosting the ranks of the unemployed. In addition, the crisis frightened away huge numbers of foreign tourists. Dire economic circumstances were averted by massive assistance and debt reductions from Western and Far Eastern donors as a reward for Egypt's political and military support during the crisis. It also helped that Egypt's oil exports for fiscal 1990-1991 were 70 percent higher than projected. Tourism rebounded strongly late in the year, and Mubarak maintained price freezes on a list of heavily subsidized basic commodities.

In March a memorandum of understanding was signed with the World Bank. The agreement cleared the way for a $300 million structural reform loan from the International Monetary Fund in April, as well as for promises of $4 billion in aid over the next two years by the Paris Club, an international consortium of Egypt's creditors.

See STATISTICS OF THE WORLD.        K.J.B.

**ELECTIONS IN THE UNITED STATES.** In 1991 elections, American voters expressed discontent by defeating some key incumbents and insiders, including Governors Ray Mabus (D) of Mississippi and Buddy Roemer (R) of Louisiana—the latter in a first-round election. In the Louisiana runoff, voters chose scandal-tainted former Governor Edwin Edwards (D) over David Duke, a former Ku Klux Klan leader.

**Thornburgh vs. Wofford.** The antiestablishment theme dominated the U.S. Senate race in Pennsylvania between Harris Wofford (D) and Dick Thornburgh (R), to replace the late H. John Heinz. Thornburgh, a former governor and U.S. attorney general, was perceived as a Washington insider. Wofford, a former college president, aide to President John F. Kennedy, and state party chairman, ran a populist campaign that emphasized the declining economy and the need for national health insurance. He came from far behind to win with an impressive 55 percent of the vote.

**State Elections.** David Duke gained nationwide attention when he outpolled incumbent Governor Roemer and ran a close second to former Governor Edwards in Louisiana's first-round election on October 19. But in the November 16 runoff, a heavy turnout of blacks swamped Duke, who polled only 39 percent, to 61 percent for Edwards. White voters did give Duke a majority of their vote, responding to his campaign attacking rising crime, unemployment, welfare abuses, and affirmative action.

In Mississippi businessman Kirk Fordice (R) was aided by the anti-incumbent mood; he

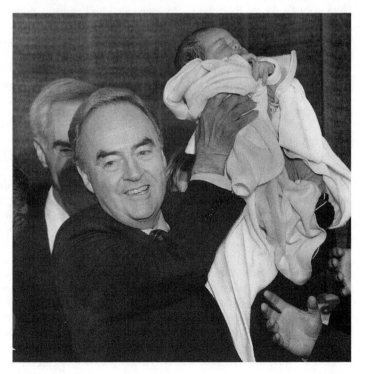

*Democrat Harris Wofford, who had never run for elective office before, won a stunning upset over former Attorney General Dick Thornburgh on November 5 in Pennsylvania's U.S. Senate election. Wofford holds up his ten-day-old grandson, Nathaniel, after being declared the winner.*

*Dogged by his racist past, Louisiana State Representative David Duke (right), running as a Republican, was soundly defeated by former Governor Edwin Edwards, a Democrat, in the November 16 runoff election for governor of the state. Here, the candidates meet in a pre-election debate.*

also made some use of racially charged issues in his successful effort to defeat Governor Mabus on November 5. Democrats picked up a governorship in Kentucky, however, where Lieutenant Governor Brereton C. Jones overwhelmed Larry J. Hopkins, a seven-term U.S. representative linked to check bouncing at the U.S. House bank. Earlier, the Arizona gubernatorial runoff election was won by J. Fife Symington (R), a real estate developer, over former Phoenix Mayor Samuel (Terry) Goddard, a Democrat.

In New Jersey a tax revolt swept Democrats from control of the legislature; Governor Jim Florio (D), elected in 1990 with 62 percent of the vote, faced GOP majorities of 27-13 in the Senate and 58-20 in the House. Democrats almost lost their majority in the Virginia legislature; voter anger there was thought to be focused on Governor L. Douglas Wilder, a candidate for the Democratic presidential nomination.

**Municipal Elections.** Among mayoral incumbents, Kathryn Whitmire, Houston's mayor since 1981, was outpolled on November 5 by land developer Bob Lanier and black State Representative Sylvester Turner; in the runoff Lanier won with 54 percent, carrying a majority of both white and Hispanic voters. In San Francisco Mayor Art Agnos came in second to his former police commissioner, Frank Jordan, in a five-candidate race; in the runoff Jordan gained enough support among the city's gay and minority populations to win with 52 percent. Both elections were nominally nonpartisan, with no one running under a party label. The same was true in Boston, won handily by incumbent Raymond I. Flynn; in Dallas, won by former U.S. Representative Steve Bartlett; in Fort Worth, where Kay Granger became the first woman mayor; in Memphis, where former Superintendent of Schools Willie Herenton became that city's first black mayor, defeating incumbent Richard Hackett by fewer than 200 votes; and in Salt Lake City, where Deedee Corradini became the first woman mayor.

In Indianapolis, Steven Goldsmith (R) defeated Louis Mahern (D). Regular Democrats were easy victors in Baltimore (incumbent Kurt Schmoke) and Philadelphia (former District Attorney Edward Rendell). In Chicago, Richard M. Daley, son of former Mayor Richard J. Daley, scored an impressive victory—63 percent of the vote in the February primary, 71 percent in the April general election—over a divided black opposition.

In other spring elections the Reverend Emanuel Cleaver became the first black mayor in Kansas City, Mo., and Wellington Webb the first in Denver. Two members of the San Antonio City Council, Maria Berriozabel and Nelson Wolff, outpolled Mayor Lila Cockrell in the first-round election, and Wolff won the runoff. **Referenda.** The state of Washington was a focus of attention for its ballot initiatives. Led by Speaker of the House Tom Foley, who has been reelected to the U.S. Congress from eastern Washington since 1966, opponents of a measure to limit the terms of all elected officials succeeded in defeating it, 54 percent to 46 percent. (Elsewhere, voters in Cincinnati, Houston, and Worcester, Mass., all set some limits on local officeholders.) Washington voters agonized over, and ultimately defeated, another ballot initiative that would have allowed doctors to end the lives of terminally ill patients who ask to die. A third referendum in Washington proposed to guarantee a woman's right to an abortion in the state even if the U.S. Supreme Court modified its 1973 decision in *Roe* v. *Wade*; it passed by a margin of less than 1 percent.

San Francisco voters approved a measure forbidding the city to cut the child-welfare budget below its 1991 level, and the electorate in Washington, D.C., approved a measure to hold the manufacturers and sellers of certain assault weapons financially liable for deaths resulting from their use.               J.B.

**ELECTRONICS.** Few groundbreaking consumer electronic products actually made it onto retailers' shelves or into American homes in 1991. The most significant developments occurred behind the scenes, setting the stage for a new generation of technologies and home entertainment devices.

A pair of new digital recording formats were announced: digital compact cassette machines and Sony's Mini Disc (*see* MUSIC: Classical Recordings). Two new interactive multimedia formats were launched: compact disk-interactive (CD-I) and Commodore Dynamic Total Vision (CDTV). In video games the focus turned from the 8-bit Nintendo Entertainment System (NES) to a trio of 16-bit successors. "Multimedia" became the order of the day, with computer makers rolling out low-priced systems that could meld high-quality audio, video, and text into a seamless package.

"Home theater" continued to flourish as Americans bought larger and larger TV sets and began to link them with their audio systems. **VCRs and Camcorders.** The videocassette recorder evolved from a machine that revolutionized home entertainment—by late 1991 it was in eight of every ten U.S. households—into the butt of a national joke. You know, the one about the VCR that does nothing but flash 12:00 because its owner cannot program it. Late in 1990, VCR Plus, a device that allows people to program a VCR simply by punching in a short code number, became a surprise best-seller for Gemstar Development Corporation, an entrepreneurial California company. In the fall, RCA began marketing VCRs that had the VCR Plus system built in.

Just as VCRs were getting easier to use, so too were camcorders. Well over half the camcorders sold were in one of the two compact formats—8-millimeter or VHS-C. Canon's UC1 weighed in as the year's lightest, at 1.28 pounds.

**Television.** The U.S. Federal Communications Commission embarked on the nitty-gritty job of testing proposed high definition TV sys-

*By taking advantage of the huge information storage capacity of compact disks, Sony's Data Discman displays electronic books contained on 3-inch disks that are capable of holding up to 100,000 pages of print.*

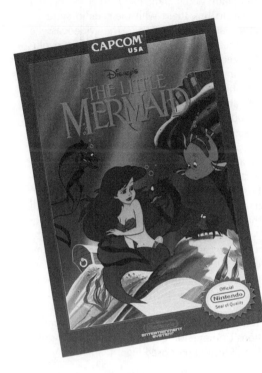

*Makers of video games woke up to the fact that girls play them too. New Nintendo games geared to girls included* Barbie, *based on the pre-teen icon, and* The Little Mermaid, *derived from the hit Disney film.*

tems and working toward the formulation of a U.S. standard. Although HDTV was not expected to be widely available in the United States until the late 1990s, televisions that can display pictures in the wide-screen 16:9 aspect ratio were being prepared for 1992 release. Japan, meanwhile, began broadcasting 8 hours of HDTV daily; at $30,000 each, the TV sets were to be found only in hotel lobbies and large public buildings.

Zenith became the first company to sell a line of TV sets with built-in closed caption decoders, which, under U.S. law, will be mandatory in all sets built after mid-1993 with screens 13 inches or larger.

**Interactivity.** Consumers got their first look at interactive multimedia when Commodore's CDTV and Philips's CD-I hit the stores. Part CD player and part computer, both systems let the user shape the how a program runs. On a CD-I tour of the Smithsonian, the user could call up an ancient musical instrument to view, read a description of it, and even hear what it

sounded like. On a photography workshop disk, the user can view a scene, choose the aperture and shutter speed, and see what the results would have been.

CDTV, which actually works off the same operating platform as Commodore's Amiga computer, first hit a limited number of stores in mid-April, but problems with both hardware and software stunted initial sales. Commodore was unable to entice other major hardware companies to support its format. But CD-I, launched by Philips in October, expected supporting hardware from such companies as Sony, Matsushita Electric, and Yamaha.

An interesting entry employing CD technology was Sony's Data Discman Electronic Book Player, a portable reader using disks that can hold up to 100,000 pages of text.

**Video Games.** Nintendo, whose popular 8-bit Nintendo Entertainment System (NES) had long dominated the video game market, unleashed the Super NES, which had twice the horsepower. Nintendo was relying on a $25 million Christmas marketing campaign, as well as the latest Mario Brothers cartridge (called Super Mario Brothers and available for Super NES only), to win market share. But Sega, whose Sega Genesis machine commonly sold for $50 less than Super NES's $200, competed fiercely, inspired by Sonic the Hedgehog, star of the year's most popular video game. Meanwhile, new video game stars—Barbie and the Little Mermaid—tried to capitalize on the growing enthusiasm of girls for electronic games. M.Br.

**EL SALVADOR.** For much of 1991 El Salvador's civil war dragged on, but peace negotiations led to a suspension of hostilities late in the year.

**War and Peace.** In December 1990 the rebel Farabundo Martí National Liberation Front (FMLN) had added a new weapon, ground-to-air missiles, to its arsenal. The following month a government helicopter carrying three U.S. military passengers was downed by a missile, killing one of the airmen; the two survivors were executed on orders of the local FMLN commander. U.S. President George Bush used the deaths as a reason to unfreeze $42.5 million in military aid to the Salvadoran government that had been suspended by Congress in November 1990.

As the ground war progressed, the FMLN invaded the capital, San Salvador, in February, inflicting considerable damage before withdrawing. In March rebels attacked the vital Cerrón Grande dam. The Salvadoran Army struck back in June with heavy offensives in the east and north. Subsequently, the FMLN launched a retaliatory offensive; and despite some initial progress in peace negotiations, the government made an attack on the long-held rebel stronghold of Guazapa Volcano. Fighting continued until mid-November, when the rebels announced a unilateral cease-fire after a breakthrough in the talks. The government then announced a suspension of bombings and heavy artillery assaults.

At the tenth round of UN-mediated peace talks, held in Mexico City in April, the parties had signed an agreement to limit the powers of

With Secretary-General Javier Pérez de Cuéllar seated at the head of the table, guerrilla leaders (left) and Salvadoran government negotiators signed an agreement at the United Nations in September providing the framework for a peace accord to end their long civil war. A detailed accord was signed on January 1, 1992.

the Salvadoran armed forces, strengthen the judiciary, and alter election laws. When the two sides met at the United Nations in September with Secretary-General Javier Pérez de Cuéllar, they agreed, among other things, that the armed forces would be purged and cut back, a new civilian police force would be created with rebel participation, and land reform and social programs would be implemented. Under prodding from Pérez de Cuéllar, who was ending his term as secretary-general, the two sides reached a basic agreement in the final minutes of the year. Signed early on January 1, 1992, it fleshed out the September accord. A cease-fire was set to begin on February 1, 1992, about two weeks after the scheduled signing of final peace accords.

**Human Rights.** Death squad and extralegal executions carried out by the Salvadoran Army continued. In April the warring parties agreed to the establishment of a UN observer commission to monitor progress on human rights.

In September, Salvadoran Army Colonel Guillermo Alfredo Benavides Moreno was convicted on charges of murder and terrorism that stemmed from the 1989 massacre of six Jesuit priests and two others. A lieutenant was also found guilty in one of the murders; seven other defendants were acquitted. Although the investigation and trial left questions about the involvement of higher-ranking officers, the verdict marked the first time in recent memory that a Salvadoran army officer was convicted of killing a civilian.

**Congressional Elections.** In March legislative elections the ruling right-wing National Republican Alliance (Arena), the party of President Alfredo Cristiani, lost its absolute majority, winning 39 of 84 seats in the National Assembly. Even after the elections, however, Arena could still control the assembly with the aid of other conservative parties.

**Mixed Economic Signs.** In January the International Monetary Fund approved a $50 million loan to El Salvador. From July to the end of the rainy season, El Salvador was beset by the most devastating drought in recent history, affecting an estimated 75 percent of its crops. Massive poverty and high inflation continued. Cristiani continued his policy of privatization, encouraging the division of farming communes set up by previous regimes and privatizing six banks expropriated by the government in 1980.

See STATISTICS OF THE WORLD.          T.P.A.

**ENERGY.** The war in early 1991 in the Persian Gulf, one of the world's major oil-producing regions, had a transient effect on oil production and prices. Political disintegration and economic collapse in the Soviet Union threatened to turn what had been a major exporter of oil into a net importer in the near future. In the United States, natural gas attracted increasing attention as an alternative to gasoline, and Congress resisted a package of energy proposals advanced by the president.

**Oil and the War.** The start of the Persian Gulf War in mid-January temporarily plunged world oil markets into turmoil. Reports of the outbreak of fighting caused the spot price of West Texas intermediate crude to jump more than $6 per barrel, to as much as $40. But after early reports of success by the U.S.-led coalition forces indicated that Saudi Arabian oil facilities were probably not in danger, the spot price dropped, plunging more than $10 per barrel in a single day, and it continued to fall as the threat of a wider war faded.

The war itself had very little effect on world oil production. The invasion of Kuwait by Iraqi forces on August 2, 1990, and a subsequent United Nations embargo against Iraqi oil exports decreased oil production in both countries sharply, and the outbreak of the war brought it to a virtual halt. But other countries, especially Saudi Arabia, boosted production enough so that the loss was barely noticed. In fact, total production by members of the Organization of Petroleum Exporting Countries (OPEC) declined by only 388,000 barrels per day—or about 13 percent—between first quarter 1990 and first quarter 1991.

In the closing days of the war, retreating Iraqi troops set on fire or otherwise sabotaged about 750 of Kuwait's 940 producing wells. Control of the fires was complicated by the presence of unexploded ordnance, booby traps, minefields, and large lakes of crude oil surrounding some of the wells. Nevertheless, the last burning well was capped in early November. By the end of the year, Kuwait's oil production had risen to nearly 600,000 b/d, and Kuwait Oil Company predicted production would regain its prewar level of 2.1 million b/d before the end of 1992.

Still, the long-term effects of the well blowouts and fires on Kuwait's oil resources may not be known for some time. Uncontrolled flow from each damaged well averaged 10,000-15,000 b/d. When all the damaged wells were flowing wide open, Kuwait was losing a billion barrels of oil, or 1 percent of its reserves, every 2½ months. In addition to these irrecoverable losses in reserves, the uncontrolled flow resulted in lower reservoir pressure, reducing long-term productivity.

**OPEC.** In mid-March, two weeks after the cease-fire in the Persian Gulf War, with oil prices down below $18 a barrel (as opposed to a $21 target price), 12 of the 13 OPEC nations (excluding Iraq) informally agreed to cut production by 5 percent, to 22.3 million b/d. At a meeting in Geneva in September, the OPEC states fixed a somewhat higher production ceiling, of 23.65 million b/d; at this point, oil prices were around $19-$20 per barrel. The new ceiling allowed for a small amount of Kuwaiti output, but none from Iraq.

In late November, at a Vienna meeting, with prices slumping to a little below $19 a barrel and Kuwaiti output rising, OPEC members deferred making any change in production ceilings, citing uncertainties in the market. The UN sanctions against Iraqi oil exports had been modified to allow exports on a conditional and limited basis, but Iraq had not accepted any conditions. Baghdad was known to have exported some oil, but in amounts too small to affect world markets. Observers noted that future market conditions were highly unpredictable, being dependent on such factors as whether Iraq would resume large-scale exports and whether recession would continue in industrialized nations.

**Soviet Oil.** An 826,000-b/d decline in total world oil production between the first quarter of 1990 and the first quarter of 1991 could be attributed essentially to the 10.5 percent decline in output by the politically and economically disintegrating Soviet Union. By June 1991, Soviet oil production was only 9.47 million b/d, a 20 percent drop from its 1988 peak. Early in the year, approximately 20,000 Soviet

oil wells were reported to be idle because of a lack of equipment. Because of the production decline, oil exports were expected to drop to about 1 million b/d for the year as a whole, compared with 2.9 million b/d in 1988. The energy situation was further complicated by a 12 percent drop in coal production in the first half of 1991, as a result of labor strikes. However, oil production in the region that was the Soviet Union had apparently stabilized by the end of 1991.

*The Yankee Rowe plant in Rowe, Mass., the oldest operating nuclear power plant in the United States, was shut down in October, as recommended by the staff of the federal Nuclear Regulatory Commission. The fear was that the reactor's containment vessel might crack in the event of an accident and release radiation into the environment.*

**U.S. Oil Trends.** Final statistics showed that petroleum production in the United States declined 3.4 percent in 1990, to 7.355 million b/d. Because domestic consumption declined 1.9 percent in that year, total net imports remained flat, at 7.161 million b/d. Crude oil reserves were declining, mostly because of a decrease in Alaskan reserves. Oil drilling activity in the United States was slumping to the lowest level since 1942, with the number of active rigs in 1991 down by nearly 15 percent from 1990.

**Natural Gas.** U.S. natural gas reserves rose 1.3 percent, to 169.3 trillion cubic feet at the end of 1990, but the natural gas surplus appeared to be nearing an end, and shortages could develop by 1995. Concerns about acid rain produced by coal-fired electrical generating and about the safety of nuclear plants were likely to lead to increased natural gas use by electrical utilities. In March 1991 the Midland Cogeneration Venture in Midland, Mich., the world's first conversion of a nuclear power plant to a gas-fired cogeneration plant, completed its first year of operation.

Natural gas also appeared destined to play a significant role as a motor vehicle fuel, as it produces a much lower level of smog-forming emissions than gasoline. In 1992, General Motors was scheduled to introduce a version of its Sierra pickup truck fueled with compressed natural gas (CNG), Ford planned to introduce a demonstration fleet of about 100 CNG-fueled light-duty pickups for use by gas utilities and customers, and Chrysler Corporation and the Gas Research Institute were to test 25 CNG-fueled Dodge vans for possible introduction in the 1994 model year.

Pacific Gas and Electric Company (PG&E), which provides electricity and natural gas service to most of northern and central California, opened 7 CNG refueling stations in early 1991. The utility also signed an agreement to construct CNG refueling facilities at the Chevron Corporation's service stations within PG&E's service area. Meanwhile, Southern California Gas Company in Los Angeles asked regulators to approve a program for the installation of 51 CNG refueling stations by the end of 1993.

Additionally, demand for methanol, which is commonly made from natural gas, was expected to rise sharply, because of its increasing use as a motor fuel and as the feedstock for methyl tertiary butyl ether (MTBE), a gasoline additive that reduces pollution.

**Nuclear Energy.** Nuclear generation of electricity in the United States appeared destined to begin a long-term decline. At the beginning of 1991 there were 114 commercial nuclear power reactors that had received full-power operating license from the U.S. Nuclear Regulatory Commission (NRC). Three of these units—Pennsylvania's Three Mile Island Unit 2, New York's Shoreham plant, and California's Rancho Seco plant—had licenses but were not actually in operation. No new nuclear reactors had been ordered by U.S. utilities since 1977, and only three of the eight units in the construction pipeline at the beginning of 1991 were likely ever to be completed.

On October 1, Yankee Atomic Electric Company shut down the Yankee Rowe nuclear plant in Massachusetts after the NRC staff recommended its immediate closure for safety reasons. The 31-year-old plant was the oldest operating commercial nuclear power plant in the nation. Critics had maintained that the reactor containment vessel had become brittle and could crack, a possibility that in a worst-case scenario could result in a meltdown of the reactor core. The NRC action suggested that many of the nation's aging nuclear power plants could face much stricter review.

**Energy Policy.** Consumption of all forms of energy in the United States increased a scant 0.07 percent in 1990, to 81.405 quadrillion British thermal units (Btu). Energy efficiency improved slightly, as consumption per dollar of gross national product decreased to 19,600 Btu.

In February the Bush administration unveiled its National Energy Strategy, aimed at reducing oil consumption by 3.4 million b/d below the level projected for the year 2010. The plan was also intended to increase domestic oil production by 3.8 million b/d over the same period, largely through federal tax incentives to promote enhanced oil recovery in existing fields and through opening the coastal plain of the Arctic National Wildlife Refuge in Alaska to oil and gas production.

The National Energy Strategy also sought to accelerate the process for licensing a nuclear power plant and provided additional incentives for utilities to use clean coal technologies. It proposed that by the year 2000, nine out of ten nondiesel vehicles bought by federal and state governments and seven out of ten such vehicles bought by private companies be required to use alternative fuels. Research and development on electric vehicles and on technologies to convert biomass feedstocks to alcohol fuels would be expanded. All new buildings subsidized by federal funds or with federally insured mortgages would be required to meet energy efficiency standards, and the Corporate Average Fuel Economy (CAFE) program would be reviewed to determine if its standards, which require automakers to achieve a certain minimum gasoline mileage in their vehicles, should be revised.

Most of the legislative proposals in the National Energy Strategy were incorporated into an omnibus energy bill that reached the floor of the U.S. Senate in early November. Opponents began a filibuster, and after a cloture vote fell 10 votes shy of the necessary 60, the bill was withdrawn. The opposition focused on the prospect of commercial oil and gas drilling in the pristine Arctic National Wildlife Refuge and on the CAFE proposals, which critics contended were too weak because they favored large domestic car models; the critics said technology now available would permit boosting the CAFE standards immediately.

D.F.A.

**ENVIRONMENT.** Heightened public interest in environmental matters and reduced international tensions at one time led optimistic observers to predict that the 1990s would be a true Environmental Decade, in which dramatic new measures would at last bring U.S. and global environmental problems under control. However, the events of 1991 showed that the environment still had to compete for center stage with a host of other issues.

**Oil Spills and Fires.** The Gulf War produced two of the biggest environmental disasters of the year: a large oil spill in the Persian Gulf and hundreds of oil well fires and leaks in Kuwait. Beginning in late January, about a week after the U.S.-led allied forces began their bombing campaign to drive Iraqi troops out of Kuwait, the Iraqis apparently opened valves at the Al-Ahmadi refinery complex on the Kuwaiti coast and at the Sea Island Terminal, 10 miles offshore, which is connected to the complex by underwater pipelines. Crude oil poured into the Gulf for a week, until allied bombers were able to destroy the mechanisms that released it. In June the British Foreign Office estimated that about 88 million gallons had been discharged into the water.

The resulting oil slick, estimated at 350 square miles in area, moved south toward Saudi Arabia and the coastal desalination plants that country relies upon to supply fresh water. The oil also menaced hundreds of miles of coastline and many small islands that serve as refuges for wildlife, including rare turtles and dugongs (sea cows). Although booms and other equipment protected much of the endangered area, many animals, especially sea birds, died after being coated with oil.

The Iraqis began to set Kuwaiti oil wells on fire a few days before allied forces launched their ground offensive on February 24 (Gulf time). By the time those forces seized the oil fields, 640 of Kuwait's 940 producing wells were ablaze, and oil was leaking from many others damaged by either the Iraqis or allied military action. About 150 wells were left to burn themselves out; the remainder had to be extinguished and capped. Using mostly conventional firefighting methods, 10,000 workers from more than 30 countries managed to put out the last fires by early November.

Although it was first speculated that the masses of dense, oily smoke produced by the fires would cause global climatic changes, most scientists later concluded that the smoke had not risen high enough to cause more than local or at most regional problems. However, the smoke lowered surface temperatures in Kuwait and Saudi Arabia by as much as 25 degrees Fahrenheit during the summer, killing or injuring desert plants and animals and aggravating people's respiratory problems. Pools of unburned oil and the heavy soot resulting from the fires increased the acidity of the soil and were potential contaminants of food and water.

In April the 1989 *Exxon Valdez* disaster, in

which 11 million gallons of petroleum had spilled into Alaska's Prince William Sound, drew renewed attention. A federal judge in Alaska rejected a proposed settlement of state and federal cases against Exxon, calling the $1 billion settlement offer insufficient punishment for the giant oil company. But in October the same judge approved a settlement that was just $25 million more than the original proposal and, because more of it would be tax deductible, would cost Exxon less. The judge said the company was "sensitive to its environmental obligations," citing its cleanup work since the spill and its voluntary payment of some civil claims. Hundreds of lawsuits by private parties awaited action.

**Global Warming.** International cooperation was missing in a series of talks aimed at producing an agreement limiting emissions of carbon dioxide, methane, and other so-called greenhouse gases. (Many scientists believe these emissions cause a gradual warming of the earth's climate by trapping heat from the sun in the atmosphere.) Negotiators from more than 100 nations met three times during the year to seek agreement on a global warm-

ing treaty. Japan and the European Community nations favored concrete targets to stabilize greenhouse gas emissions at 1990 levels by the year 2000, but the United States, the world's largest emitter of such gases, continued to resist specific timetables. The Bush administration maintained that too little was known for certain about global warming to take measures that would cost hundreds of billions of dollars worldwide and threaten economic growth.

**Antarctic Treaty.** The United States had been at odds with other nations regarding a proposed treaty protocol to ban mining and oil exploration in Antarctica for 50 years. Environmental groups and most nations that had signed the 1959 Antarctic Treaty, which bars military forces from the frozen continent, argued that such a ban was necessary to maintain at least one place on earth in a near-pristine condition. As developing nations increase their demand for raw materials in the coming years and industrial nations search for new sources of energy and minerals, many feared Antarctica would be turned into a vast mining camp.

*The Persian Gulf War produced two of the year's greatest environmental disasters. When Iraqi forces in Kuwait opened refinery pipelines, million of gallons of oil spilled into the Gulf, creating a slick that clogged shores and threatened wildlife (at right, dead sea birds are removed from a Saudi beach). And when Kuwaiti oil fields were set ablaze (left), clouds of black smoke hung over the country, causing respiratory problems and lowering temperatures by blocking out sunlight.*

In July, after two years of negotiations, President George Bush announced his support for such a ban, in return for which other nations agreed to a U.S. proposal that would make it easier for mining to begin after the 50-year moratorium. Under the revised treaty, the ban can be lifted in 2041 if three-fourths of those nations with full voting rights under the 1959 treaty so agree. The treaty was signed in Madrid in October.

**Ozone Depletion.** For the third year in a row, a major hole opened in the stratospheric ozone layer over Antarctica during the southern hemisphere's spring, the National Aeronautics and Space Administration reported in October. One of the space agency's satellites recorded the lowest ozone levels over Antarctica in the 13 years it had been monitoring stratospheric ozone, which protects the earth from ultraviolet solar radiation that can cause skin cancer and cataracts in humans and damage to crops. Depletion of the ozone layer has been blamed on synthetic chlorine compounds, especially chlorofluorocarbons (CFCs), used in air conditioners and refrigerators. An international agreement provides for most CFC production to end by 2000, but in 1991 new findings of accelerating ozone depletion over the earth's temperate zones intensified calls for a faster phaseout.

In April the U.S. Environmental Protection Agency (EPA) reported that the amount of stratospheric ozone over the middle latitudes of the northern hemisphere in late fall, winter, and early spring declined about 5 percent over the previous decade; the loss in the corresponding latitudes and seasons in the southern hemisphere was even greater. Even more serious, an international study covering roughly the same period and reported in October found a 3 percent depletion over the middle latitudes of the northern hemisphere during late spring and summer, when ultraviolet rays are strongest and pose the greatest danger; again, the rate in the corresponding latitudes and seasons in the southern hemisphere was higher.

**Lead.** The EPA issued new rules intended to reduce the concentration of toxic chemicals in drinking water. In May the agency's previous standard for permissible levels of lead, 50 parts of lead per billion parts of water (50 ppb), was changed to 15 ppb for tap water and an average of 5 ppb throughout a water supply system. By mid-1992 all water suppliers in the United States will have to begin testing tap water in homes for lead levels; water with levels exceeding the EPA limits will have to be treated with chemicals that lower its acidity and thus reduce the leaching of lead from pipes, solder, and brass plumbing fixtures. Where such treatment proves insufficient, systems must begin in 2000 to replace underground lead pipes with nonlead ones.

**Dioxin.** In April, EPA administrator William Reilly said his agency would conduct a one-year review of recent evidence indicating that dioxin may be less toxic than originally thought. Dr. Vernon Houk of the Federal Centers for Disease Control—one of the leading proponents of the government's decision in 1982 to buy out the property owners of Times Beach, Mo., when it was revealed that the town had been widely contaminated with dioxin—conceded in May that the decision had probably been a mistake. Houk said he was now convinced that while dioxin may be a potent toxin in some animals, it is at worst "a very weak carcinogen." Environmentalists called the EPA's review premature.

**Asbestos.** The future of a seven-year program by the EPA to eliminate most asbestos use in the United States was uncertain after future stages of it were struck down by a federal appeals court in October. The court ruled that the agency had violated the Toxic Substances Control Act of 1976 in imposing the asbestos ban without adequately considering "less burdensome alternatives," providing an opportunity for opponents to challenge EPA conclusions, or evaluating the hazards of products likely to be substituted for those banned. The ruling upheld the first stage of the ban, which as of 1990 prohibited new uses of asbestos, imports of asbestos products, and use of asbestos in such U.S.-made products as clothing. But it sent the next two stages back to the EPA for reconsideration.

**Air Pollution.** During the year, 11 eastern states and Washington, D.C., accepted a regional agreement to follow California's preexisting standards for reducing the motor vehicle emissions that are the major cause of smog in urban areas. Under the revisions of the federal Clean Air Act approved by Congress in 1990, states were allowed to choose between federal regulations to reduce such pollution and California's stricter rules, which require new emission control equipment on gasoline-powered cars sold in the late 1990s and stipulate that a small but steadily increasing percentage of new cars must run on fuel other than gasoline. In November, California adopted new standards on gasoline, requiring cleaner fuel by 1996.

**Wetlands.** President Bush announced in August a proposal to narrow the government's definition of wetlands (the marshes, swamps, and similar habitats that provide flood control, filter pollution from water, and shelter a host of plant and animal life). Although Bush had campaigned on a promise of "no net loss" of U.S. wetlands, he said the government's field manual gave such sweeping definitions that many tracts of dry land were classified as qualifying for federal wetlands protection under the Clean Water Act.

Field tests revealed late in the year that the less rigorous standards would leave "many obvious wetlands" unprotected. Officials of the Army Corps of Engineers, the EPA, and the Fish and Wildlife Service called the proposed definitions unworkable and scientifically unsound. While waiting for Bush's decision on whether to modify them, the agencies responsible for protecting the nation's wetlands used a modified 1987 field manual to determine wetland status.

**Waste Disposal.** Controversy continued to surround the Waste Isolation Pilot Plant in Carlsbad, N.M., the proposed burial site for radioactive waste produced by U.S. nuclear-weapons production programs. In October, as the U.S. Department of Energy (DOE) prepared to ship the first of up to 8,500 drums of plutonium-contaminated waste to the site for a five-year trial period, New Mexico sued to block the shipment, and in November, a federal district court judge issued an injunction that temporarily barred the DOE from opening the repository.

In September the EPA issued regulations intended to make the nation's 6,000 garbage dumps less of a threat to the groundwater beneath them. Among other things, dumps will

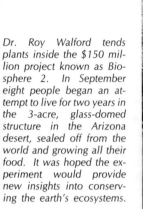

Dr. Roy Walford tends plants inside the $150 million project known as Biosphere 2. In September eight people began an attempt to live for two years in the 3-acre, glass-domed structure in the Arizona desert, sealed off from the world and growing all their food. It was hoped the experiment would provide new insights into conserving the earth's ecosystems.

have to install monitoring wells to detect any garbage-tainted liquids leaking into the groundwater, and new dumps will have to have clay or synthetic liners. The regulations, issued only after a lawsuit by environmental groups, were likely to result in the closing of many small, poorly run dumps and to boost business for big garbage companies able to afford the expense of complying.

With the number of dumps likely to decline 50 percent by 1995, either because of the new rules or because they have reached their legal capacity, the need to save dump space by recycling such things as newspapers, metal cans, and glass and plastic containers became more apparent. In 1988 there were only about 600 programs to collect recyclables from households; by 1991 there were an estimated 2,700. Even in communities where recycling was voluntary, studies showed that up to 95 percent of

the households put recyclables at the curb at least once a month.

**Drift Nets.** After considerable pressure from the U.S. government, Japan agreed in November to abide by a UN moratorium and halt the use of drift nets in the North Pacific by the end of 1992. Japanese fishermen use the huge nets, which stretch as far as 40 miles, to catch squid, but they also kill large numbers of whales, dolphins, seabirds, turtles, and fish. Taiwan and South Korea previously agreed in principle to phase out their use.

**Biosphere 2.** On September 26, four men and four women were sealed into Biosphere 2 (the researchers label the earth as Biosphere 1), near Oracle, Ariz. In an area of 3.15 acres completely sealed off under an airtight glass dome, with only sunlight, electricity, and electronic communications to connect it to the rest of the world, the eight people, living in com-

At a song festival in the capital city of Tallinn in early September, joyous Estonians acclaim their country's new independence. Estonia had been a republic of the Soviet Union since 1940.

As the push toward independence quickened during the first half of 1991, Estonia was more inclined than its fellow Baltic republics to rely on negotiation with the Soviet Union, partly because it put a higher priority on preserving existing economic ties with Moscow. The drive for independence was also slowed down by deep strategic divisions within the country, with one side stressing gradualism and the other demanding independence before all else. However, after the August coup attempt against the government of Soviet President Mikhail S. Gorbachev, the two camps united against Soviet pressure. On August 20, even as Soviet tanks were rolling toward the capital city of Tallinn, Estonia's national legislature passed a full declaration of independence from Moscow. The European Community extended diplomatic recognition on August 27, the Soviet government followed suit on September 6, and on September 17, Estonia was admitted to the United Nations.

The unity of the two political camps was short-lived, and bitter disputes broke out over the membership of the Constituent Assembly that was given the task of creating a new constitution. The issue of whether citizenship should be granted to all long-time residents was also a major source of conflict, since ethnic Estonians had declined to around 60 percent of the population. Most of the remainder of the population were ethnic Russians who did not speak Estonian or know the country's history and culture.

Many observers saw Estonia as the Baltic nation most likely to successfully establish a market economy. It started off with a somewhat higher living standard than the other former Soviet republics, and its policies revealed a realism that may encourage entrepreneurs to invest.

See STATISTICS OF THE WORLD.        L.T.L.

**ETHIOPIA.** Threatened by increasingly successful rebel attacks, President Mengistu Haile Mariam stepped down and fled to Zimbabwe on May 21, 1991; a week later Ethiopian rebels captured the capital, Addis Ababa, and established full control over the country.

The Marxist government, in power for 17 years, had begun to crumble earlier, when the Tigre People's Liberation Front (TPLF) captured

pany with some 3,800 other species of animals and plants, were expected to grow all of their own food during a two-year stay, using only recycled air, water, and plant nutrients. The $150 million project, an attempt to duplicate conditions on earth in miniature, attracted interest among ecology-minded gardeners and environmentalists, who hoped it would lead to improved methods for growing healthy crops.        S.S.

**EQUATORIAL GUINEA.** See STATISTICS OF THE WORLD.

**ESTONIA.** In 1991, Estonia regained its independence. Estonia had been part of the Soviet Union since 1940 as a consequence of the Hitler-Stalin nonaggression pact, in which Germany gave Moscow the right to annex the three Baltic states.

the regions of Gojam and Gonder. The government's last air base at Bahir Dar was taken and the capital was sealed off from the north. On May 19 the TPLF took the Wollo region; a few days later, the Eritrean People's Liberation Front (EPLF) captured Eritrea's capital, Asmara, and then its port of Assab, shutting off supplies from Ethiopia's only remaining sea outlet. As Ethiopia's northern army collapsed, hundreds of thousands were captured, many died, and some 35,000 Ethiopian soldiers and civilians fled to Djibouti. Following the TPLF's May 28 takeover of Addis Ababa, the remaining Ethiopian troops melded into the population.

After Mengistu fled, Vice President Tesfaye Gebre-Kidan had become acting president. Representatives of all parties were attending peace talks in London, mediated by the United States, when the TPLF moved into Addis Ababa and a new interim government was established by Meles Zenawi, leader of the Ethiopian People's Revolutionary Democratic Front, a coalition of groups dominated by the TPLF. A former Marxist from Tigre, Meles promised "a democratic and peaceful transition." Captured officials of the former Marxist government were interned; some were subsequently released, but others were held for trial. In June the temporary government was confronted by violent anti-American demonstrations in Addis Ababa, with the United States being called the "midwife" of the new Tigrean rulers.

On July 5 a conference of 24 political groups, with U.S. Assistant Secretary of State for African Affairs Herman Cohen attending as an observer, created a transitional government to prepare the country for democratic elections. The new government—an 87-member Council of Representatives—was made up of 27 ethnic and political groups. Meles was chosen as transitional president, and his party dominated the government. With U.S. approval, Eritrea's right of self-determination was recognized.

Beginning May 24, over 14,000 Ethiopian Jews were airlifted to Israel during a 36-hour period. In September, Ethiopia's new government allowed the emigration to continue; by year's end some 20,000 Ethiopian Jews had been flown to Israel. Meanwhile, the charity organization Oxfam America reported that 7 million Ethiopians were in urgent need of food relief, while the United Nations indicated that potential famine was as severe as in the 1980s. In September the United States allocated $22 million for refugees in the Horn of Africa; part of that money was allocated to Ethiopia, where 300,000 former Ethiopian soldiers had no means of subsistence.

*See* STATISTICS OF THE WORLD.          P.J.S.

*A rebel soldier keeps his rifle at the ready as he and his comrades enter Addis Ababa, Ethiopia's capital, in May, completing their victory over the country's Marxist regime.*

**EUROPEAN COMMUNITY.** Moving toward greater economic and political unity, the European Community (made up of France, Germany, Italy, Belgium, the Netherlands, Luxembourg, the United Kingdom, Ireland, Denmark, Greece, Spain, and Portugal) held a two-day summit meeting in December 1991 in Maastricht, the Netherlands, at which the 12 leaders agreed on treaties committing themselves to monetary union at the end of the decade and gave the community a clear political profile.

**Toward Economic Union.** During the year officials continued to draft, pass, and implement legislation removing obstacles to the free flow of goods, capital, and labor among member countries. A Community-wide standardization of value-added and excise taxes was agreed upon, and by the summer, 70 percent of the required liberalizing legislation for "Europe 1992" had been adopted.

In a series of meetings, EC finance ministers laid the foundations for an economic and monetary union (EMU) treaty, finally adopted at Maastricht. The 12 countries agreed to create a single currency and a regional bank by 1999 at the latest. However the British obtained the right to "opt out" and Denmark, which supported monetary union, was to hold a referendum on the issue.

**Beyond the Twelve.** A landmark treaty between the EC and the countries of the European Free Trade Association (Austria, Switzerland, Sweden, Finland, Norway, Iceland, and Liechtenstein) was signed in October. It created a "European Economic Area" in which, beginning January 1, 1993, there would be a free flow of most goods, services, capital, and peo-

*At a December summit in Maastricht, the Netherlands, leaders of the 12-nation European Community agreed to create a common currency and move toward greater political union. British Prime Minister John Major (right)—shown with his foreign secretary, Douglas Hurd (center), and Sir Leon Brittan, European Commission vice president—won Great Britain the right to "opt out" of certain provisions.*

ple across 19 countries. Meanwhile, Sweden announced it would seek admission to the EC. Poland, Czechoslovakia, and Hungary also desired full membership upon transformation into market economies.

**Political Disunity.** The EC had difficulty acting as a unified world power. Prior to the Gulf War, France broke rank to launch a solo peace initiative; later, some EC countries disapproved of the fighting in Kuwait and Iraq, while others participated in it.

After civil war erupted in Yugoslavia in the summer, the Community offered to mediate among contending forces, but had difficulty agreeing on policies. By November, however, after 12 EC-negotiated cease-fires had collapsed, EC countries were able to agree to place economic sanctions on Yugoslavia, to ask the UN to impose an oil embargo, and to investigate the feasibility of sending UN peace-keeping troops. In December, as fighting continued, the Community gave in to German pressure and said it would recognize the independence of Croatia, Slovenia, Bosnia-Hercegovina, and Macedonia, on the condition that they met certain standards of human and minority rights.

At the heart of negotiations over political union was the question of how to enable the EC to act as a unified force in political and military affairs. The French favored a European Community military force; Britain, Italy, and others pressed for a revitalized Western European Union closely attached to NATO. (The WEU has nine members—Britain, France, Italy, Germany, Belgium, the Netherlands, Luxembourg, Spain, and Portugal—all of whom also belong to the EC.) Constitutional proposals for a European political union included a Dutch proposal to establish a close federation of countries with a strong federal government and a competing Luxembourg plan for a loose confederation of states, where common policies would emerge from majority voting among member governments and from some variety of co-decision by an elected Parliament.

Under the treaty signed in December, member states agreed to strengthen the WEU while maintaining ties to NATO and seeking an eventual common defense policy. They committed themselves to common foreign and security policies, to be decided unanimously. While bowing to British fears that "federalism" means centralization and dropping plans to identify the Community's "federal" vocation, member states gave the Strasbourg-based European Parliament new powers to monitor the Community budget, as well as veto power over certain areas of EC legislation.          D.J.P

# F

**FASHION.** "This season you can be sure there will be a zippered leather jacket and a tartan pleated skirt in your fashion future," the New York *Times* predicted on September 17, 1991. The next day *Times* columnist Anna Quindlen derided the motorcycle jacket/pleated skirt combo as "Terminator chic with parochial school overtones." It was that kind of year in U.S. fashion. There were complaints that designers were recycling the same old styles and headlines like this one from *USA Today*: "Women say new styles are ridiculous." One thing was nearly certain: People weren't buying.

**Spring 1991.** The gloomy retail climate put pressure on designers to come up with clothes women didn't already have hanging in their closets. With most working women wedded to suits and separates, designers proposed the return of spring dresses and were virtually unanimous in recommending shift or chemise dresses in bright colors, often shown with matching loose coats. Chemises came in sleeveless, cap-sleeved, halter-necked, and strapless versions. They were comfortable and—once lengthened to knee length—flattered a wide range of figures. But they were eerily reminiscent of the mini-chemises

*Oscar de la Renta was one of many designers who featured plaid as a predominant theme in their fall collections; unlike some other de la Renta creations, this plaid was not made of mink.*

suaded great numbers of American women to wear them. In fact, many "city shorts" weren't all that short—only an inch or two above the knee.

**Fall 1991.** The defining look for fall was the short pleated skirt. Actually, any skirt with movement at the hem looked newer than the short straight skirts of previous seasons.

Fall's other major rage, tartan plaids, came in every imaginable version, including authentic Scots Highlander tartans and fantasy plaids in shocking pink and orange. Oscar de la Renta even showed plaid mink. Some criticized the plaid fad as silly, but it made economic sense. In tartan, designers were backing a classic fashion, acceptable to even the most conservative women.

The same couldn't be said for the motorcycle mama look, championed in Paris by Karl Lagerfeld for Chanel, who showed black leather jackets bedecked with gold chains and motorcycle boots with Chanel logos.

**Back to Basics.** Both men and women *did* seem willing to spend a certain amount of money on anything of proven quality and utility that seemed unlikely to go out of style.

The Champion reverse-weave sweatshirt, which for the first 50 years of its history had been worn mainly by athletes, emerged as status casual wear for children and adults.

Denim was another back-to-basics success story. Though basic five-pocket jeans topped the best-seller list, overalls worn with one shoulder strap dangling nonchalantly were a big urban success. Adding Spandex to denim produced pants that looked like jeans but fit like leggings. At the other extreme, many teenagers embraced jeans a couple of sizes too big. Hopping onto the baggy bandwagon, some manufacturers began cutting jeans looser to appeal to no-longer-lean baby boomers.

**Footwear.** Comfortable, lightweight walking shoes cushioned with space-age foam made up the fastest growing segment of both the men's and women's shoe business. Coincidentally, Doc Martens—the clunky lace-up black oxfords and ankle boots that had been popular with punkers—won more adherents among people with avant-garde tastes. They were worn with jeans and even with delicate dresses and chiffon skirts.

worn by Jacqueline Kennedy and Babe Paley in the mid-1960s. To many women, the chemise seemed too much of a period piece to be enticing.

Leggings and unitards met with greater popular success. Women were used to wearing them for exercise or dance classes, and many were inexpensive—under $20. One fashion pundit predicted leggings would become "the jeans of the 90s."

Very short skirts looked new and fashionable but seemed impractical. Enter "city shorts." For decades designers had suggested that tailored shorts could be as appropriate for the office as skirts, but they had never before per-

**Menswear.** Several menswear manufacturers began marketing "athletic fit" suits—cut to fit men whose workouts had produced big shoulders, arms, and thighs to go with their small waists and hips. Sales of imported designer suits and of European-style suits from American manufacturers held up considerably better than sales of standard American sack suits. Men's ties exploded in whooshes of smoky color and in conversation-piece prints depicting theater tickets, athletic posters, or fish.

**Etc.** The zipper, celebrated its centennial. Probably entirely by coincidence, shapely zippered jackets appeared in many designer collections. Pajama sales increased, another de-

*Legwear in a wide array of fabrics, patterns, and colors made a splashy impact on the fashion scene; crochet leggings, like these by Hue, were airy and very much in style.*

velopment attributed to the aging of the baby boomers and the popularity of "cocooning."

Designer Oscar de la Renta became the first established New York designer to show his fall collection in Paris rather than in New York, perhaps the most notable move in the U.S. fashion industry's increasingly serious efforts to expand into the international market. The French department store Galeries Lafayette opened a branch on Fifth Avenue in New York and stocked it with clothes and accessories from a range of French designers.     P.McL.

**FIJI.** See STATISTICS OF THE WORLD.

**FINLAND.** In 1991, Finland's long-standing special ties with the Soviet Union ended. Early in the year, after Soviet troops stormed a television tower in Lithuania, killing more than a dozen people, Finnish President Mauno Koivisto, displaying extreme caution, had termed the bloodbath an "internal Soviet matter." But the decay of Communist authority in succeeding months had a profound impact on Finland's relationship with the Soviet Union. In September, Koivisto named ambassadors to the newly independent Baltic states. October talks in New York between Finnish Foreign Minister Paavo Vayrynen and his Soviet counterpart at the time, Boris Pankin, led to abandonment of the 1948 friendship treaty between the two countries. The Finns were thus challenged to reconsider their policy of neutrality. At year's end, with the Soviet Union dissolved, Finland was negotiating with Russia on trade and economic cooperation.

The Soviet Union's unilateral decision, effective January 1, to shift the foundation of Finno-Soviet trade from a barter system to convertible currency arrangements impelled Finland to secure fresh markets in Western Europe. In October the creation of a large new common market, called the European Economic Area, was agreed to by the European Community and the European Free Trade Association, to which Finland belongs.

Prime Minister Harri Holkeri's Conservative/Social Democratic-led cabinet resigned on March 15, just before scheduled elections. These were a clear defeat for the governing coalition, whose parties lost 22 seats in the Eduskunta (Parliament). The Center Party replaced the Social Democrats as the largest sin-

As hard times befell French farmers, demonstrations erupted around the country, with farmers demanding higher prices and greater protection from imported foodstuffs. Here, farmers in the Auvergne in October seize a truck carrying cows brought from Poland.

gle party. On April 25 a new coalition government was formed led by the Center chairman, Esko Aho.

In the autumn an austerity budget was approved, cutting public spending and increasing income taxes. Unions agreed to reduced salaries as an alternative to layoffs and bankruptcies. The government also devalued the Finnish markka by 14 percent.

In June the Eduskunta approved a law abolishing the college of electors, which was based on American practice, and introducing the French-style direct election of the head of state.

See STATISTICS OF THE WORLD.          D.A.

**FISHERIES.** See AGRICULTURE AND FOOD SUPPLIES.

**FLORIDA.** See STATISTICS OF THE WORLD.

**FORMOSA.** See TAIWAN.

**FRANCE.** As Socialist President François Mitterrand marked a decade in power, the French in 1991 became increasingly concerned about the revolutionary events occurring in the Soviet Union and Eastern Europe. Europe's center of gravity seemed to be shifting toward a united, powerful Germany, and the emergence of the United States as the only global superpower meant that Paris could no longer expect to serve as a bridge, or mediating force, between Washington and Moscow.

Clashes between police and North African immigrants highlighted the growing problem of racial conflict in France between the predominantly white, Catholic population and black and Arab workers seeking better lives in France. Meanwhile, farmers demanded higher prices for their products, and strikes by nurses, transport workers, and police showed that prosperity was still unevenly distributed after ten years of Socialist rule. On October 24 a general strike of state employees severely hampered the transportation system.

Mitterrand tried to galvanize his European Community partners to achieve greater progress toward political and economic union, but some wondered if the 75-year-old leader's energy and vision were failing. Conservative opponents picked up the same rallying cry—"Ten Years is Enough!"—that left-wing protesters used in 1968 to help bring down Charles de Gaulle. Speculation grew that Mitterrand would not serve out his second seven-year term, due to expire in 1995.

**Politics.** Mitterrand accepted the resignation in May of Prime Minister Michel Rocard and replaced him with Edith Cresson, a staunch supporter, who thus became France's first woman prime minister. Rocard, a centrist who had often sparred with Mitterrand, was known to harbor presidential ambitions. Cresson's appointment was seen as more acceptable to Mitterrand's traditional left-wing constituency, but it also appeared to be a shrewd effort to capture new support from women.

Cresson's brutal candor, in which she lambasted Japanese protectionism, did not help her overcome voter anxiety about high unemployment and the immigration problem. Within weeks her approval rating fell to barely 25 percent, and the public dismay also dragged down Mitterrand's standing in the polls. Surveys showed that the center-right opposition alliance, headed by former President Valéry Giscard d'Estaing and Jacques Chirac, could capture a majority of seats in Parliament if elections were held in 1991. But the mainstream opposition was still plagued by the perennial rivalry between Giscard and Chirac. In addition, the center-right opposition was still troubled about how to cope with the extreme right-wing National Front party of Jean-Marie Le Pen, which was gaining support for its anti-immigration message.

**Immigration.** The population of North Africans, estimated at between 3 and 4 million, continued to grow dramatically. The subsequent burden on the economy and the health and welfare systems generated alarm and exerted pressure on politicians to adopt less tolerant stands toward foreigners. Both Giscard and Chirac appeared to be striving to lure voter support from Le Pen's extremist National Front, which led ruling Socialists to cry shame on them for pandering to racist sentiment. Nonetheless, the Cresson government announced a crackdown on illegal immigration as part of a tough new program to alleviate public concern about France's role as a haven for exiles.

**Defense.** France contributed more than 10,000 troops to the Persian Gulf War effort, but the overwhelming technological prowess displayed by American military forces raised some concern about the antiquated nature of French equipment. With the Soviet military threat fading, Mitterrand decided that most of the future investment in modernizing French nuclear forces would be devoted to its submarine fleet, rather than air or land-based missiles. France suspended plans to deploy the new Hades missile, whose limited range meant that its nuclear payload could only reach targets on German territory. France also pledged to create a joint military force with Germany of 30,000 to 50,000 troops that officials said would serve as the nucleus of an independent European army.

**Foreign Policy.** French diplomacy was concentrated on achieving a blueprint for political

### Madame Prime Minister
France's first woman prime minister was no stranger to controversy when she took office in May. As a politician in various cabinet posts, Edith Cresson, 57, has spoken bluntly, once calling her male rivals "elephants" for their huge egos and deriding the Japanese as "yellow ants." When British tabloids recently headlined old remarks of hers questioning the virility of Anglo-Saxon men, she was ridiculed in the House of Commons. Meanwhile, Japanese protesters beheaded her in effigy. Back in France, high unemployment stirred workers' resentment, and her popularity ratings were plunging, but she refused to curtail her frank style. The wife of a retired auto executive, Cresson insisted she wanted to continue her mandate, if only to prove women can accomplish as much as men in the often sexist world of politics. "Men are not in any sense irreplaceable," she says, "except in one's private life."

*Edith Cresson*

and economic union that heads of government in the European Community approved at a summit meeting in December. Poland, Czechoslovakia, and Hungary, granted associate status in the fall, demanded early EC membership to seal their transition to free markets and free elections, but France was more concerned with "deepening" the EC's institutions by gaining the further surrender of national sovereignty. France participated in the Western financial and food rescue effort to help the people of the former Soviet Union to survive the winter, but its assistance was largely channeled through the EC and was dwarfed by Germany's multibillion-dollar payments to aid Moscow.

In the Middle East, France supported U.S. efforts in the wake of the Gulf War to promote negotiation of a lasting peace between Israel and its Arab neighbors, but it did not play a key role in this area. Relations with Lebanon,

*Lebanese Christian General Michel Aoun, ousted from his Beirut stronghold after opposing a Christian-Muslim power-sharing agreement, was given refuge in France in 1991. He is seen here on the balcony of his new home in Marseille.*

frosty since France allowed Christian strongman General Michel Aoun to take refuge in its Beirut embassy in 1990, improved as the two countries reached an agreement that allowed Aoun to live in exile in France. France also hosted the conference that ended civil war in Cambodia.

France joined Belgium in rushing troops to Zaire to protect Western citizens after riots threatened to topple the dictatorship of Mobutu Sese Seko; later, France urged the shaken African leader to move toward democracy or risk the total collapse of his regime.

Relations with Iran were injured by the assassination in Paris on August 8 of Shahpur Bakhtiar, a former Iranian prime minister. A French investigation led to the issuing of an arrest warrant on October 22 for one official in the Iranian government, and later for extradition from Switzerland of another Iranian suspect. However, France and Iran in late October announced the settling of a dispute stemming from an unpaid $1 billion loan made to France in 1974 by the shah of Iran.

**Economy.** France achieved a major economic milestone when its rate of inflation fell below 3 percent in 1991. The success was largely attributed to Finance Minister Pierre Bérégovoy. But the number of jobless was still expected to surpass a record 3 million, or about 10 percent of the work force, by the end of the year.

When Cresson succeeded Rocard as prime minister in May, she appointed Bérégovoy as the head of a "superministry" in charge of economics, foreign trade, industry, and telecommunications. His mandate was to modernize the French economy and help it compete more effectively with such industrial rivals as Germany and Japan. Indeed, Cresson claimed that the very survival of France's automobile and electronics industries was at stake as Japan's largest and most ambitious companies began taking aim at the single European market set to open at the end of 1992. France still maintains one of the Western Europe's highest levels of state involvement in private enterprise, and companies such as the Peugeot car manufacturer have received massive infusions of state aid to stave off bankruptcy. To help curtail those costs the government recently agreed to offer an expanded stake to private companies.

**Culture.** France reaffirmed its restored status as one of the great art capitals of the world with an impressive retrospective of the great French postimpressionist Georges Seurat on the centenary of his death. Seurat's path-breaking experiments in color and light opened the door for Picasso, Matisse, and other pioneers of modern art. Similarly, a major Paris showing of the work of Théodore Géricault on the 200th anniversary of his birth demonstrated the range and depth of an over-looked native painter.

In music Paris paid homage to Wolfgang Amadeus Mozart on the bicentennial of his death. The highlight of the celebration was a clever, controversial production of *The Magic Flute* by the American stage director Robert Wilson.

The futuristic Pompidou Center changed directors as it passed through a wrenching identity crisis. Hélène Ahrweiler, who retired, was replaced by Dominique Bozo, the noted curator who assembled the Picasso Museum in Paris. Bozo made his initial mark with two impressive shows depicting the work of André Breton and Max Ernst and launched a major renovation of the 14-year-old complex.

**Architecture.** After inaugurating the pyramid built by the American architect I. M. Pei at the Louvre art museum and the soaring cubist arch at La Défense business center, Mitterrand insisted on pushing ahead to finish a new national library known as TGB, or "très grande bibliothèque," the largest of its kind in the world. Squatters protesting the lack of adequate low-income housing occupied the chosen site along the Seine River, and architects and intellectuals urged that construction should be stopped so that drastic changes could be made in architect Dominique Perrault's design. But Mitterrand demanded that the library be completed promptly, before his second presidential term ends in 1995.

**Life-style.** A serious freeze struck many of France's finest vineyards in the Bordeaux region, but after several bumper crops of high quality grapes in previous years, the damaged harvest was not expected to cause a sharp rise in wine prices. France celebrated the apotheosis of a new star chef, Bernard Loiseau, whose Côte d'Or restaurant in the Burgundy town of Saulieu was crowned with its third star in the Michelin Guide. Loiseau, renowned for his wizardry with fresh vegetables, often features potatoes cooked in creative ways, using such exotic flavors as truffles and sea urchin juice.

Yves Montand died at age 70 on November 9. For nearly half a century the popular singer and actor had enthralled audiences with his suave renditions of ballads and his more than 50 film roles. Known for his outspoken political views, he evolved from a Communist fellow traveler in the 1950s to a critic of the Stalinist French left and then, in recent years, to a position right of center.

*See* STATISTICS OF THE WORLD. W.D.

# G

**GABON.** *See* STATISTICS OF THE WORLD.
**GAMBIA, THE.** *See* STATISTICS OF THE WORLD.
**GEORGIA.** *See* STATISTICS OF THE WORLD.
**GERMANY.** Chancellor Helmut Kohl began 1991 in a politically dominant position. After December 1990 elections, the first national elections of the newly unified German state, his Christian Democratic Union and its Bavarian sister party had, in coalition with the Free Democrats, 398 of the 662 seats in the Bundestag. However, the government's popularity declined in subsequent months.

**State Elections.** January elections in the state of Hesse brought defeat to the Christian and Free Democratic coalition that had governed there since 1987, though the two parties' losses were slight, and the Kohl government was not the issue. An environmental, or "green," party supplied the margin of victory for a new coalition government with the Social Democrats.

The next two months saw a precipitous drop in the popularity of the Kohl government, which resulted in April in the Christian Democrats' first-ever defeat in the chancellor's home state, Rhineland-Palatinate; the Social Democrats won 44.8 percent of the vote to 38.7 percent for the Christian Democrats.

A major theme of the 1990 national campaign had been that the economic rebuilding of the former East Germany would be carried out with no new taxes, or by private investment alone. But Kohl had grossly underestimated economic deterioration in the East and, therefore, the enormous costs reconstruction would entail. In February his government was forced to ask for some $18 billion in new taxes for 1991 through a 7.5 percent increase in income taxes, plus hikes in tobacco and fuel taxes. The dream of a cost-free German unification vanished, and Rhineland-Palatinate had its first Social Democratic premier. The Christian Democratic loss in Rhineland-Palatinate

appeared to shift control of the Bundesrat, the upper house of the national Parliament, away from Kohl's government; Christian Democratic premiers now governed in only 7 of the 16 German states that together controlled 32 of the 69 Bundesrat votes.

A June election in Hamburg again resulted in a marked drop in the Christian Democratic vote. The Social Democrats, governing with the Free Democrats since 1987, won 61 of 121 seats in the state assembly and formed a single-party government.

**Rebuilding the East.** A major reason for underestimating the costs of reconstruction was the leading role in the Soviet bloc once played by East Germany. As in other Soviet-bloc countries, East German leaders overemphasized the production of heavy industrial goods, such as steel, machinery, and arms. When the 1970s brought huge increases in the cost of energy, a continued emphasis on heavy industry meant almost no spending on transportation, telecommunications, housing, the environment, or research on new and laborsaving technologies. Demands for increased production were traditionally met by adding to the labor force, so that in the 1980s, East Germany had the world's highest employment rate.

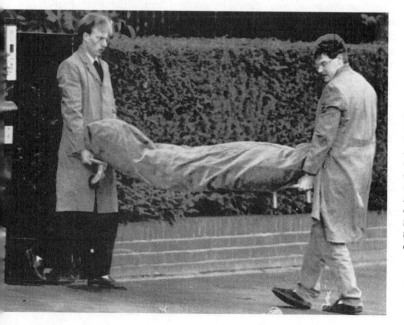

*"The manager of German unity," as Detlev Rohwedder was known, was killed in April by assassins from Germany's radical Red Army Faction. As the official in charge of selling or dismantling the property of the former East German state, Rohwedder had become the focus of the anger felt by those who suffered the shocks of the shift to capitalism.*

Eastern Germans, therefore, faced enormous economic problems. Because of price as well as mediocre quality, their goods could not compete in world markets. Even their consumer products were unwanted at home because those of western Germany, although higher priced, were better. To turn the situation around, the Kohl government in 1991 mounted a massive campaign, "Upswing East," which built on changes already undertaken. Some $84 billion in public funds were made available for expenditures in the east. One type involved direct investment in new or upgraded highways, railroads, telecommunications, and housing. The government also provided funds and loaned officials to state and local governments in the east to improve their administrative capabilities.

A second type of expenditure concerned enterprises once managed by the East German state. In June 1990 a government-owned, but independent, Trustee Agency had been created that instantly became the world's largest holding company. Taking charge of over 10,000 enterprises, its mission was privatization. Public funds were available for both capital improvements and subsidies to German and foreign investors to motivate them to make purchases. As of July 1991 the Trustee Agency had sold about 3,000 enterprises, including all department stores, 70 percent of restaurants and shops, and half the hotels.

A third type of expenditure was directed toward those who lost their jobs as excess labor was cut to make the eastern economy more efficient. Unemployment in the east in July went over 1 million for the first time, a rate of 12.1 percent.

The German government was also granting and loaning billions of dollars worth of foodstuffs and goods to the Soviet Union and a number of East European countries. Whenever possible, aid was given in the form of eastern German exports. In October, with a booming construction industry pointing to the future, analysts indicated the corner had been turned and predicted in place of the steep economic decline of 1991 an eastern economy growing at a rate of about 10 percent in 1992.

The economy of western Germany in 1991 began to cool a bit. The drop from a growth rate of 4.6 percent in 1990 to an estimated 3.5 percent in 1991 was attributed to a softening domestic demand and a huge increase in imports. Aided by the strong German mark, imports into western Germany were $225 billion through July, compared with $158 billion for the same period in 1990. The strong mark, in turn, was based on the highest interest rates in nine years. Concerned with inflation (which, as of September was 9.1 percent in the east and 4.0 percent in the west), the Federal Bank raised the discount rate three times, to reach 8 percent.

**"Inner Unity."** By October 1991, on the first anniversary of unification, the "inner unity" of the two German states remained in question. Germans of the east felt western Germans blamed them as a people for the extreme economic degradation of their society. Western Germans questioned in surveys saw easterners as lazy, passive, and unreliable. The two groups referred to each other pejoratively as *"Ossis"* and *"Wessis"* ("easties" and "westies"), with the easterners seeing the latter as arrogant know-it-alls. The German president, Richard von Weizsäcker, found himself forced to lecture his countrymen about a "Wall in people's heads."

Adding to a depressed atmosphere in the east was increasing right-wing violence among youthful males, who, having expected a beautiful life under capitalism, found themselves without jobs. Another problem was the growing numbers of public figures of the recent reform period who were found to have been collaborating in the past with the "Stasi," the notorious East German political police. In November the Bundestag approved a law allowing the estimated 6 million people spied on by the Stasi to see their files. The law also contained provisions for the government to release information about Stasi informers and agents. It was expected to go into force early in 1992 after approval by the Bundesrat.

There still were some hopeful signs. In addition to promised economic growth in the east in 1992, an August survey indicated that a majority of Germans still had positive feelings overall toward unification.

**New Capital.** A major controversy arose about relocating the German capital from

Bonn to Berlin. When the West German state came into being in 1949, Bonn—a sleepy, provincial town—was made the capital to underscore its temporary nature. In the next 42 years, however, government became a major industry in Bonn. About one-third of its 276,500 inhabitants would have to leave if the change were made. And the move would cost tens of billions of marks.

Proponents of Bonn cited the great success of West German democracy in that location. Those favoring Berlin were moved by a sense of history and by the city's location in the east, where the great challenges facing Europe were currently taking place.

In the June Bundestag vote, although small majorities in the two largest parties, Christian and Social Democrats, voted to stay in Bonn, large majorities in other parties tipped the balance to Berlin. To lessen financial problems and the negative effects on the city of Bonn, it was agreed that the move would take place over 10 to 12 years. The Bundestag itself, however, would move within 4 years.

**Anti-foreigner Violence.** In one month beginning in mid-September, young men across Germany—mainly skinheads and neo-Nazis—committed over 500 acts of violence against foreigners. The attacks were reminiscent of the kind of violence that swept Germany in the early 1930s before Hitler seized power.

Most foreigners in Germany were workers and their families who migrated to labor-short West Germany in the 1960s. They numbered about 4.5 million, with the largest group—about 1.5 million—coming from Turkey. But most victims in the east were among some 200,000 Vietnamese and black Africans from Mozambique who were imported in 1989 as contract laborers.

Extremists throughout Germany found targets primarily in three other categories: recent illegal immigrants, mainly fleeing from the poor economies of Poland and Romania; legal ethnic German immigrants from Poland, Romania, and the Soviet Union; and about 900,000 people who had come from various countries seeking asylum. Most were running

*The Brandenburg Gate, which once stood as the symbol of Berlin's division, began undergoing a restoration to serve as a new symbol— of the city's unity. Here, workers prepare to remove for cleaning the famous statue of a horse-drawn chariot.*

*The emergence of groups of neo-Nazis and skinheads, such as these at a rally in Dresden in June (above), brought an ominous and unsettling element to German society. Anti-Semitism once again raised its ugly head, now abetted by high technology, such as this video game (right), which invites players to become the manager of a concentration camp.*

away from poverty, not political persecution, and few applicants were actually granted asylum. But they were cared for at state expense during the long application process, and most of those denied asylum were never deported.

Voter resentment regarding the situation was well demonstrated in late September elections in the city-state of Bremen. The ruling Social Democrats, who took a liberal stance on the asylum issue, dropped from 50.5 percent of the vote in 1987 to 38.8 percent. A right-wing party, the German People's Union—campaigning with slogans like "the boat is full"—gained seats in the state assembly for the first time. The Social Democrats continued to govern, however, by negotiating a red-green-yellow "traffic light" coalition with the Greens and Free Democrats.

Party leaders meeting with Chancellor Kohl in October agreed on legislation to shift responsibility for caring for asylum-seekers to the federal government and to reduce the time taken to process applications to six weeks.

The government also won the approval of its European Community partners, Switzerland, Austria, and 13 Eastern European countries for tougher border controls to check illegal East-West migration. It was unclear how these controls would be enforced.

**European Community.** At a European Community summit meeting in Maastricht, the Netherlands, in December, Kohl played a critical role in building a consensus that made possible agreement on steps toward economic and political union. The Community agreed to adopt a single currency by 1999 at the latest (with Britain retaining the right to opt out), to work toward common foreign and security policies, and to adopt as a long-term goal a common defense policy.

*See* STATISTICS OF THE WORLD. R.J.W.

**GHANA.** *See* STATISTICS OF THE WORLD.

**GREAT BRITAIN.** For Britain, 1991 began on a note of wary uncertainty. War was looming in the Persian Gulf region. And the British had a virtually untested prime minister, who had taken over from his Conservative colleague Margaret Thatcher little more than a month before. Although John Major (*see profile in* PEOPLE IN THE NEWS) seemed less dogmatic than his formidable predecessor, no one knew how he would handle the chief policies that had led to her downfall: the highly unpopular poll tax and a stubborn resistance to European monetary and political union. The country also was in deep recession, and the prospect of a general election was never far away.

**Major's Decision.** Major had until July 1992 to call an election. Speculation that he would call an early election in 1991 persisted until early October, when he ruled out a 1991 date.

**Gulf War and Aftermath.** Britain's forces in the Persian Gulf region—45,000 of the allied total of around 700,000 by the outbreak of war—acquitted themselves well, particularly in the air war, where they launched 4,000 combat missions and 2,500 support sorties against Iraq. Six Tornado GRI ground attack aircraft were lost in combat and only 24 lives, though accidental casualties before hostilities began brought the death toll up to 47. Financial contributions from Japan, Germany, and Gulf states minimized the cost to a defense budget already under pressure.

Politically, the war consolidated support for the new government; economically, it intensi-fied the recession in the travel, entertainment, and tourism industries. As soon as the fighting started, public opinion, which had been evenly divided, swung heavily—to some 80 percent—in favor of military action. So did the official Labor opposition in Parliament.

After the conflict, Major scored a diplomatic success in persuading initially skeptical allies, notably the United States, of the need to provide a "safe haven" on both sides of the Iraqi-Turkish border for Kurdish refugees fleeing Saddam Hussein's vengeance. Soon after the war, Roger Cooper, a businessman jailed in Iran on charges of espionage, was released, and in the second half of the year, the remaining British hostages in Lebanon—John McCarthy, Jackie Mann, and Terry Waite—were freed, as was businessman Ian Richter, who had been jailed in Iraq.

**The Poll Tax.** The unpopular community charge, or poll tax, a uniform charge imposed on all adults within a local government district and set by local councils under tight restraints from the central government, had been adopted by the Thatcher government as an alternative to property taxes, but remained widely resented as unfair—and widely evaded. Michael Heseltine, the minister appointed by Major to examine the problem, finally announced in March that the poll tax

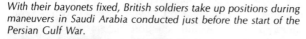

*With their bayonets fixed, British soldiers take up positions during maneuvers in Saudi Arabia conducted just before the start of the Persian Gulf War.*

would be replaced by a new "council tax" lev-
ied primarily on the basis of the value of the
property occupied by a household, but with a
50 percent discount for single-occupied
homes. To ease financial burdens on districts,
it was also agreed to shift the cost of postsec-
ondary education to the central government
and increase the national sales tax to pay for
it. However, the council tax could not be introduced before 1993, and municipal treasur-
ers were left to threaten up to 7.5 million of
those subject to the poll tax with prosecution
for nonpayment.

**Continued Recession.** As inflation fell from
9.7 percent when Major took over to 4.3 percent by the next November, interest rates
dropped from 14 to 10.5 percent. Meanwhile,
the recession appeared to linger, with Britain's
gross domestic product projected to fall a full 2
percent in 1991. Business bankruptcies continued at record rates, conspicuously among
service industries, as did personal bankruptcies
and home repossessions.

**Banking and Finance.** The government
feuded with major banks, which it accused of
failing to pass interest rate cuts on to small
businesses, currently failing at a rate of up to
50,000 a year. Bad debts and deregulation
had hurt the banks' own profits. Meanwhile,
on July 5, the Bank of England revealed it was
leading a worldwide seizure of the Arab-
backed Bank of Credit and Commerce International (BCCI) on the grounds of what others
called "the largest bank fraud in world financial history." BCCI had tentacles everywhere;
it had 24 branches in Britain and held large
accounts for local governments. Many observers believed that the Bank of England could
have stepped in sooner and should have done
more to rescue BCCI, whose assets amounted
to less than half of liabilities.

**Labor Slippage?** Labor Party leader Neil Kinnock stressed the importance of better education of British workers and tax breaks for industrial development, to prepare for the vast
European Community free-trade zone due to
take effect by the end of 1992. He also continued his purge of Trotskyite "Militant Tendency" party members, expelling from the
party two members of Parliament suspected of
such allegiance. His success in refashioning

the party in a more moderate image kept the
Tories on the defensive for most of the year.
But Kinnock trailed badly behind Major in
polls of voter preference for prime minister.
By late fall most polls put Labor narrowly
ahead, with just over 40 percent for both main
parties, though the Tories enjoyed a year-end
surge. Labor remained handicapped by fears
that it would raise taxes too much and fail to
keep British defenses strong enough in the
post-cold-war era. Meanwhile, the Liberal
Democrats, the third party led by Paddy Ash-
down, were doing fairly well in the polls.

**Citizen's Charter.** Chief among Major's
domestic initiatives was the Citizen's Charter,
a blueprint for empowering the citizen to obtain better treatment from public services such
as British Rail and the Royal Mail. Legislation
was promised to implement wider competition
in the provision of services now provided by
government, reduce hospital waiting times,
and monitor the performance of government
employees. The public gave the charter a
skeptical welcome.

**Courts and Crimes.** Efforts to uphold the convictions of six people, all Irish, found guilty of
causing 21 deaths in the 1974 bombing of two
Birmingham pubs by the Irish Republican
Army (IRA) finally collapsed. As with similar
cases in the past, the miscarriages of justice
stemmed from faulty forensic evidence and
dubious "confessions," many allegedly extracted through police beatings.

With reported crime at a record level, Home
Secretary Kenneth Baker also faced criticism
over prison suicides, escapes from custody by
IRA terrorists, and, in the fall, the worst outbreak of urban rioting since the early 1980s.
There were disturbances in Cardiff, Oxford,
Birmingham, and Newcastle-upon-Tyne, some
related to the practice of stealing cars for joy-
riding, racing, or even "ram-raiding" department store windows to steal goods.

In late October there was widespread welcome for the decision by the Law Lords, Britain's highest court, to overturn the 255-year-
old English legal ruling that a husband cannot
be found guilty of raping his wife.

In May a War Crimes Act, which would
allow the prosecution of suspected Nazi war
criminals who had slipped into Britain after

*In February, three mortar rounds were fired from a van parked near the prime minister's residence in central London. The shells missed their target, and the van, seen here in the foreground, burst into flames. The Irish Republican Army claimed responsibility for the attack.*

1945, was passed into law without the consent of the House of Lords, the first time in 40 years the House of Commons had enacted a bill over the Lords' opposition.

**Northern Ireland.** On February 7, from a van in the heart of tourist London, halfway between Trafalgar Square and Parliament, IRA terrorists fired three mortar bombs 200 yards over the roofs of Whitehall toward the Cabinet Room in the prime minister's house in Downing Street, where Major and his colleagues were deliberating. One mortar exploded in the garden behind the house, shattering windows but injuring no one. Eleven days later, bombs went off at two of London's major railway stations during the morning rush hour. One person was killed and 40 injured at Victoria Station.

Painstaking efforts to get all parties in Northern Ireland around the same negotiating table

for the first time since 1974 collapsed in July. In place of talks came a surge of sectarian killings in which Protestant paramilitaries began to show the ruthless organizational efficiency of the IRA. The need to maintain military strength in Northern Ireland contributed to Britain's decision to cut its post-cold-war armed forces by only 20 percent, compared with up to 30 percent among its neighbors.

**Race and Refugees.** Bill Morris was elected leader of the giant Transport and General Workers' Union, becoming the first black to head a British union. Lawyer John Taylor became the first black Conservative to win his party's endorsement for a parliamentary candidacy in a winnable seat.

Labor MPs, whose ranks already included four nonwhites, were quick to attack as racist a government bill introduced in the fall to restrict the admission of political refugees to Britain. Most of the cases that would be affected by the legislation involved Africans or South Asians. The bill followed close on the heels of an agreement between Britain and Vietnam that would allow the forcible repatriation of many of the more than 60,000 Vietnamese refugees confined in detention centers in Hong Kong. The agreement was criticized by Labor and the Liberal Democrats as well as by the U.S. government and the refugees themselves, who threatened suicides, hunger strikes, and riots. The first groups were repatriated in November and December.

**Hong Kong Transition.** Also controversial was an accord with Beijing, signed in September, allowing greater control by Chinese authorities over direction of the new airport to be built in Hong Kong, in return for Beijing's willingness to honor approved debts accumulated to construct the facility. China assumes sovereignty over the British colony in July 1997; the airport construction is intended to boost confidence in Hong Kong's future after that time. The accord also committed British Hong Kong authorities to leave Hong Kong with a least $25 billion in reserves as of July 1997.

**European Union.** At a European Community summit at Maastricht in the Netherlands in December, Britain obtained the right to "opt out" of an agreed-upon timetable to create (for member nations meeting certain conditions) a common currency by 1999. Greater political convergence was also sought. Yet here again the British resisted, and the "federal goal" in the draft agreement was weakened to "an ever closer union" in the political union treaty that was signed. To accommodate Britain, the so-called social chapter—in effect, laws to enhance worker rights and employment protection—was dropped from the political union treaty; the other EC countries decided to sign a separate treaty on this issue.

Major kept crucial areas of policymaking in the hands of intergovernmental procedures between the 12 countries rather than conceding them to the machinery of the European Commission. But he was forced to concede enhanced cooperation in the foreign policy field, so that if the 12 could agree unanimously on a common policy, a single country would not have an absolute veto power over certain measures to implement it. Britain—cool to the French-German idea of a "European Army"—persuaded the other countries to enhance the semimoribund Western European Union as the European defense mechanism, in a fashion that made it complementary to NATO and "subordinate" to the EC. EC powers of common action were extended into such fields as consumer protection, health, education, and transportation and telecommunications networks. And Britain agreed, reluctantly, to give the European Parliament a veto over certain Community legislation.

**Royal News.** In May, Queen Elizabeth II and Prince Philip made their first official U.S. visit since 1976. During their stay in Washington the queen became the first British monarch to address a joint session of Congress. The royal couple went on to Florida, where the queen conferred an honorary knighthood on General H. Norman Schwarzkopf, Jr., the allied field commander in the Persian Gulf War.

The Prince of Wales, whose marriage was persistently reported to be in trouble, aroused controversy by condemning educational experts for ignoring Shakespeare in schools and the private car for being a "gas-guzzling" beast. The tabloids also reported gleefully on the claim by Heather Tonkin, a New Zealand nurse, that Mark Phillips, estranged husband of Princess Anne, had fathered her five-year-old daughter. And they prominently covered as well disagreements between Diana, the Princess of Wales, and her father over costly renovations at the family's stately home.

*See* STATISTICS OF THE WORLD.          M.C.W.

**GREECE.** During 1991 the conservative government of Prime Minister Constantine Mitsotakis moved slowly to reverse policies instituted under Socialist rule.

**Domestic Politics.** The new government, in office since April 1990, started the year with a series of political retreats, including reversing the decision to pardon those serving life sentences for instituting the military dictatorship of 1967-1974 and withdrawing a controversial education reform bill.

The government proceeded slowly in shifting to a more market-oriented economy. Early in the year the executive commission of the European Community took the unusual step of withholding approval of a critical loan of 2.2 billion ECUs (European currency units), worth $3 billion, until Greece agreed to reduce the public sector borrowing requirement, lower inflation, and improve the balance of payments, among other steps.

**Foreign Relations.** In July, President George Bush arrived in Greece for a two-day visit, the first by a U.S. president since 1959, and pledged U.S. help in resolving the long-standing Greek-Turkish dispute over Cyprus. But a meeting outside Paris in September, chaired by the UN secretary-general, revealed that Mitsotakis and Turkish Prime Minister Mesut Yilmaz were too far apart to warrant a formal peace conference.

Increasingly cordial relations with the Soviet Union were marked by the April visit of the Soviet foreign minister to Athens and by Mitsotakis's official visit to the Soviet Union in July. After the unsuccessful August coup in the Soviet Union, Greece promised Moscow $100 million in commercial credits.

The massive influx of Albanian refugees continued. By August, the number had risen to an estimated 50,000, almost half of whom were ethnic Greeks. In May the government announced plans to resettle in Greece the tens of thousand of Pontians, ethnic Greeks from the Soviet Union, who had fled to Greece since 1988, fearing rising nationalism in several Soviet republics. Most were to be settled in the northern province of Thrace, where they would reduce the relative size of the Turkish Muslim population.

**Corruption Proceedings.** A special 13-member tribunal convened on March 11 in Athens to initiate the long-awaited trial of former Prime Minister Andreas Papandreou and three of his senior cabinet officials during the 1981-1989 period of Socialist rule. The four officials were accused of involvement in a $210 million bank embezzlement scandal run by George Koskotas, former owner of the Bank of Crete. Koskotas was extradited from the United States to stand trial himself; he appeared as a star witness.

**Terrorism.** After a week-long trial in September, the editors of seven Greek newspapers were sentenced to jail terms ranging from five to ten months for publishing without government permission a proclamation by terrorists. The newspapers' action violated a stringent new antiterrorism bill passed by Parliament at the end of 1990.

A Greek guerrilla organization claimed responsibility for the death of a U.S. Air Force sergeant in a bomb explosion in March. In April seven Greek bystanders were killed in the port city of Patras when a bomb intended for the British consulate exploded in the hands of a Palestinian terrorist. Seven Palestinians were jailed, pending trial for murder, and 26 Palestinian diplomats and students were subsequently expelled from Greece.

*See* STATISTICS OF THE WORLD. J.A.P.

**GRENADA.** *See* STATISTICS OF THE WORLD.

**GUAM.** *See* STATISTICS OF THE WORLD.

**GUATEMALA.** As there was no clear winner in the November 1990 presidential election, a runoff was held on January 6, 1991, between the two highest vote getters: Jorge Carpio Nicolle of the National Union of the Center and Jorge Serrano Elías of the Solidarity Action Movement. Serrano won with 68 percent of the vote and was sworn in on January 14. A coalition consisting of the Solidarity Action Movement, the Christian Democrats, and the National Advancement Movement controlled the Congress, with a combined total of 57 seats. Serrano's new cabinet contained only three Solidarity Action Movement members, the other seats going largely to his coalition

*A visit to Crete was one of the stops for U.S. President George Bush as he made the first trip to Greece by an American president in over 30 years.*

partners. In his campaign, Serrano had accused the former government of massive corruption, and he began large-scale investigations soon after taking office.

Figures released in July showed that 89 percent of Guatemalans live in poverty. Other figures put inflation in the 10 to 15 percent range. Faced with a staggering foreign debt, the congress in July passed an emergency bond act to help meet overdue obligations. Certain types of businesses were virtually forced to buy these bonds on a one-time basis. In a late September visit to the United States, Serrano and his finance minister persuaded the International Development Bank to reopen lines of credit cut off during the previous regime.

Several Marxist revolutionary movements, banded together as the Guatemalan National Revolutionary Union (URNG), negotiated with representatives of the government, through the mediation of a National Reconciliation Commission (CNR), then met in Mexico City in April and signed the so-called Mexico Accord; in it, both sides declared a willingness to find a political solution to the war and established a procedure for sustained dialogue. Talks broke

down in late October over resolution of human rights issues.

In August the private Guatemalan Human Rights Commission declared that human rights violations under Serrano were as bad as in the worst period of the previous regime. The Mutual Support Group for Families of the Disappeared reported 547 political murders and 118 disappearances through June. In October a military tribunal investigating a massacre of Indians at Santiago Atitlán on December 2, 1990, sentenced two soldiers to prison. The Atitlán massacre and other human rights violations had convinced the United States to cut off military aid.

In July, Guatemala fell victim to the South American cholera epidemic, experiencing its first outbreak in 134 years. A state of emergency was declared in September. As of November 30 there had been almost 3,000 cases and 42 deaths.

See STATISTICS OF THE WORLD.          T.P.A.

**GUINEA.** See STATISTICS OF THE WORLD.

**GUINEA-BISSAU.** See STATISTICS OF THE WORLD.

**GUYANA.** See STATISTICS OF THE WORLD.

# H

**HAITI.** In February 1991 a democratically elected government was inaugurated in Haiti for the first time in the country's history; eight months later it was overthrown.

The activist priest Jean-Bertrand Aristide, whose fiery anti-Duvalierist sermons and demands for reform had made him a hero to Haiti's poor majority, had been elected president in a landslide on December 16, 1990. In early January, a coup attempt was launched by Duvalierists led by ex-Tonton Macoutes head Roger Lafontant, but it was defeated by loyal army units. The interim president, Ertha Pascal-Trouillot, handed over power to Aristide, who was inaugurated as scheduled on February 7. But the National Assembly was still controlled by conservatives. Over the legislature's objections, Aristide named a cabinet

composed of inexperienced members of his inner circle, headed by Prime Minister René Préval, a businessman and human rights activist. Aristide also retired senior military officers and promoted General Raoul Cedras, who had overseen his election, to army chief.

In July, Aristide defused one coup plot, and a sailors' mutiny halted another, which was intended to prevent Lafontant's trial. With menacing Aristide supporters surrounding the court, Lafontant was sentenced in August to life imprisonment. By then, however, Aristide's position had weakened considerably. His efforts to circumvent opposition control of the National Assembly were denounced as unconstitutional. His failure to condemn the vigilante actions of his supporters led to criticism, as did an apparent failure to focus on the country's grave economic problems. Food riots revealed an erosion of support among poor Haitians.

On September 30, shortly after Aristide's return from addressing the United Nations, he was overthrown in a violent military coup that claimed more than 300 lives; he was replaced by a junta headed by Cedras. Aristide, in exile in Venezuela, asked the Organization of American States to restore him to power; the OAS endorsed him, imposing economic sanctions and sending a diplomatic mission to Haiti in October. But Haitian soldiers installed an interim government, which announced in November that a new presidential election would be held in January 1992, with Aristide ineligible to run because of a constitutional provision banning a president from succeeding himself.

As violence increased and OAS and U.S. sanctions began to bite, thousands of Haitians fled to the United States. Hundreds died at sea. After the coup, the U.S. government suspended its decade-old policy of forced repatriation for Haitians, then reinstated it, on the grounds that the Haitians were economic, not political, refugees. By year's end thousands of refugees were living in a camp at the U.S. military base in Guantánamo Bay, Cuba, as immigrant rights advocates fought in court for the refugees' right to asylum.

The inauguration of a democratic government had brought a restoration of foreign aid to Haiti. Most of this aid was suspended after the coup. The economy continued to stagnate, with tourism destroyed and economic sanctions adding to Haiti's woes.

See STATISTICS OF THE WORLD.    P.W.

**HAWAII.** See STATISTICS OF THE WORLD.

The tanks rolled in Haiti as the country's first democratically elected president was ousted in a violent military coup. A few days earlier, President Jean-Bertrand Aristide had made a triumphal visit to New York, where he addressed the United Nations (left).

# Health and Medicine

**In 1991 a basketball superstar revealed he had the AIDS virus, focusing new attention on AIDS prevention. Treatments for some forms of heart disease and cancer were in the news, as was the safety of silicone breast implants.**

The year saw some advances in drug treatments for AIDS, which continued, however, to spread throughout the world. Major concern focused on the role and responsibility of healthcare workers in the AIDS-affected treatment environment. Advances in biology yielded greater understanding of the genetic factors involved in Alzheimer's disease, cystic fibrosis, and other disorders (*see* LIFE SCIENCES).

**AIDS.** As the AIDS epidemic began its second decade, the disease, for many, hit closer to home than ever before; in November Earvin "Magic" Johnson announced that he had tested positive for the human immunodeficiency virus (HIV), which causes AIDS. The basketball star said he was retiring from the sport and would devote himself to efforts to promote "safe sex" practices to help people avoid the still-spreading disease. Meanwhile, as of November 30, 202,543 cases had been diagnosed in the United States, and the death toll stood at 130,687. Roughly 1 million Americans in all were believed to be infected with the virus. In Canada, 5,349 cases of AIDS had been diagnosed, and 3,192 people had died from it by early October.

Although the spread of infection appeared to be slowing somewhat in North America, it continued to increase in developing countries, especially in sub-Saharan Africa, South America, and the Caribbean. At the International Conference on AIDS in June, a World Health Organization official said more than 366,000 AIDS cases had been reported in 162 countries; many others remained unreported, and

an additional 10 million adults worldwide were believed to be infected with the virus.

Heterosexuals accounted for a rising proportion of new cases of AIDS in the United States. The main source of infection in large cities was intravenous drug users, who spread the virus by sharing needles and by having sexual intercourse without condoms. As a result, a growing number of women—and their babies—were becoming infected with the AIDS virus. On the basis of study findings published in April, researchers estimated that up to 2,100 HIV-infected babies will be born each year in the United States.

In August the U.S. Centers for Disease Control (CDC) expanded the definition of AIDS to reflect more accurately the extent of the epidemic. Effective in 1992, people will be considered to have AIDS if they are infected with HIV and have fewer than 200 CD4 cells per cubic millimeter of blood. (CD4 cells are white blood cells important in the immune system that are destroyed by the AIDS virus.) They need not have any other symptoms. The definition of AIDS in effect through 1991 included only HIV-infected people with any of a variety of AIDS-related infections and other conditions. The new definition was expected to increase the national count of AIDS patients by at least 50 percent.

*Commission Report.* After two years of study, the National Commission on AIDS, appointed by President George Bush and Congress, issued a report on the AIDS epidemic. It concluded that some progress against the disease had been made but that federal officials had

*Kimberly Bergalis (left), who was infected with the AIDS virus during dental treatment, appeared before a congressional committee in September to support mandatory AIDS testing of health workers; she is seen here with her mother arriving in Washington. Bergalis died of AIDS in December.*

failed to provide leadership, and that government funding for efforts to prevent the spread of the infection and take care of the sick was inadequate. The commission recommended that insurance coverage and treatment for drug abuse be made available to all who need it and that laws banning needle-exchange programs be eliminated. In December the Bush administration proposed rules meant to make it easier for some AIDS patients to get Social Security benefits.

*Treatment.* The U.S. Food and Drug Administration (FDA) approved several new drugs; by early October there were a total of nine drugs for AIDS patients, including those approved in earlier years.

In January the FDA approved a drug to treat anemia in people with AIDS. The drug, erythropoietin (brand name, Procrit), reverses the deficiency of red blood cells that is often caused by zidovudine (formerly called AZT), an antiviral drug taken to treat AIDS, and by drugs taken for AIDS-related conditions. Erythropoietin is a genetically engineered ver-

sion of a kidney hormone that stimulates the bone marrow to make red blood cells.

In September the FDA approved a drug that delays progression of a vision-threatening condition, cytomegalovirus (CMV) retinitis, which afflicts about 20 percent of AIDS patients because of their weakened immune systems. Foscarnet (brand name, Foscavir) is the second drug approved for use in AIDS patients with CMV retinitis. The other drug, ganciclovir, produces side effects that many patients cannot tolerate. In October it was announced that studies showed that foscarnet not only controlled CMV retinitis but allowed people with AIDS to live 50 percent longer than those treated with ganciclovir. However, foscarnet itself may also have side effects, including nausea, kidney damage, and seizures.

In October the FDA approved dideoxyinosine (DDI)—brand name, Videx—for treating patients in advanced stages of infection from the AIDS virus. The drug was simultaneously approved in Canada by the Health Protection Branch of the Canadian Department of Health and Welfare. DDI was approved for use in AIDS patients who cannot tolerate or do not respond to zidovudine (AZT). Because the need for an alternative drug was so great, the FDA set a precedent by approving DDI before the completion of long-term safety and efficacy tests. The drug's potential side effects include inflammation of the pancreas, which may be fatal, and painful nerve damage, and its use must be carefully monitored. Like zidovudine, DDI stops replication of the AIDS virus and slows decline of the immune system but does not cure AIDS.

A study conducted by the Department of Veterans' Affairs and made public in February found that people who began taking zidovudine before developing any symptoms lived no longer than people who began after they had symptoms. Additionally, black and Hispanic patients in the study did not experience a slowing in the development of symptoms when they took zidovudine. However, subsequent studies, published in November, in which the data from previous research on the drug was reanalysed, concluded that zidovudine has equal benefit for whites, blacks, and Hispanics.

*Prevention.* In August the National Commission on AIDS endorsed needle-exchange programs to reduce the spread of AIDS among intravenous drug users who may share contaminated needles and syringes. In several cities programs in which drug users exchange used needles for clean ones have suggested that the method stems the spread of disease: Yale University researchers reported that a needle-exchange program in New Haven, Conn., had reduced new HIV infections by one-third. Critics, including the Bush administration and many physicians, cited a lack of proof that such programs work and said they encourage drug abuse.

As part of an effort to prevent spread of the AIDS virus through sexual intercourse, high schools in New York City began distributing condoms to students. The school system was the first in the country to make condoms available to teenagers without any say by their parents, some of whom protested along with religious leaders and some members of the city's board of education.

In October an advisory panel to the FDA recommended that blood centers start testing for HIV-2 as well as the much more common strain of the virus, HIV-1, by June 1992. Although only 31 cases of HIV-2 infection had been reported in the United States since 1987, Health and Human Services (HHS) Secretary Louis Sullivan said that testing for both viruses could make the blood supply safer.

Scientists continued to search for a vaccine to prevent the spread of AIDS; by 1991, 11 experimental vaccines had been injected into uninfected human volunteers from low-risk populations to test their safety and ability to stimulate immune defenses.

*U.S. Immigration Policy.* In January, HHS Secretary Sullivan proposed that, as AIDS cannot be spread by casual contact, it should be removed from the list of communicable diseases that would bar foreigners from entering the United States. In May, however, the Bush administration halted the plan. Federal health officials later decided that some immigrants with AIDS would be admitted to the country, but that those seeking permanent residence would be barred, because of the potential cost burden on society.

*Naming of Discoverer.* A long, bitter dispute over who discovered the AIDS virus was put to an end in May when Dr. Robert Gallo of the National Institutes of Health dropped his claim. That gave the credit of discovery to Dr. Luc Montagnier of the Pasteur Institute in France. The two investigators had shared the credit since 1987.

*Healthcare Workers and AIDS.* In December the CDC dropped a plan to publish a list of procedures and types of surgery it considered too risky for AIDS-infected healthcare workers to perform. Instead the agency said the emphasis should be placed on identifying infected health workers who do not meet infection control standards or whose physical or mental state makes them unfit to practice. Several medical groups, as well as the largest organization of dentists, had refused to define any procedures as high-risk, saying there was no significant risk to patients and that guidelines would cause unnecessary alarm. According to the CDC, 6,000 U.S. healthcare workers have AIDS and perhaps 50,000 more may be infected with the AIDS virus.

The only healthcare worker known to have infected patients is Dr. David Acer, a Florida dentist. Five of his patients were found to harbor the same strain of the HIV virus that had killed him in 1990. The first of his patients to be diagnosed, Kimberly Bergalis, who became a symbol of the fight for mandatory testing of healthcare workers, died in December.

Late in the year, the federal Occupational Safety and Health Administration issued new regulations to protect workers from AIDS and other blood-borne viruses. Among other things, the regulations required employers to provide gloves, masks, mouth guards, and smocks for healthcare workers who might come into contact with blood or bodily fluids on the job.

**Speeding Drug Approvals.** The FDA announced plans in November to speed its drug approval process, as it did for the AIDS drug DDI. Highest priority was to be given to drugs for incurable or life-threatening diseases like AIDS and cystic fibrosis. The speeding-up program, which would take four years off the current ten required to move a drug from laboratory to pharmacy, was to be accomplished in part by using private contractors to review data for categories of drugs where there are likely to be backlogs of applications, such as painkillers and antibiotics. Drugs would continue to be thoroughly tested for safety before going on the market, but studies of effectiveness would continue after marketing, raising the possibility that some would later be withdrawn if found ineffective.

**Cancer Treatment Adjuncts.** Intensive chemotherapy (drug treatment) suppresses the production of infection-fighting white blood cells that normally occurs in the bone marrow. The resulting deficiency of white blood cells, called neutropenia, leaves patients vulnerable to infections. In February the FDA approved filgrastim (brand name, Neupogen), a granulocyte colony-stimulating factor that increases the number of white blood cells, thus decreasing the risk of potentially fatal infections. In a major study of patients with small-cell lung cancer, treatment with filgrastim halved the incidence of fever with neutropenia and of infections after chemotherapy.

In March the FDA approved a similar drug for speeding recovery of patients undergoing autologous bone marrow transplants (transplants from their own bodies) for non-Hodgkin's lymphoma, Hodgkin's disease, or acute lymphocytic leukemia.

Transplants using donated bone marrow, done mainly to treat leukemia, were helped by the antiviral drug ganciclovir (brand name, Cytovene), researchers reported in April. More than 15 percent of patients who receive transplants of donated bone marrow develop pneumonia caused by a common virus, cytomegalovirus (CMV), and most of them die of the infection. In controlled tests, 70 percent of untreated patients died or developed pneumonia over a four-month period, compared with only 25 percent of the patients who took the drug ganciclovir.

**Colorectal Cancer.** After rectal cancer is surgically removed, additional treatment consisting of chemotherapy and radiation can prolong patients' lives as well as reduce the likelihood that the cancer will reappear, researchers reported in March. The additional treatment is appropriate for people whose cancer has spread to neighboring tissue or lymph nodes

(stages II and III)—a group that includes almost half of the estimated 45,500 Americans afflicted with cancer of the rectum during 1991. The study compared the combination treatment with standard radiation treatment in 204 patients whose cancers had been surgically removed. After an average of seven years, 62 of the patients treated with radiation alone died, as opposed to 49 of the patients given the combination treatment. The difference represented a 36 percent reduction in cancer-related deaths and a 41 percent lower rate of local cancer recurrence.

In August investigators reported identifying a gene that, when mutated, initiates colon cancer. The gene, called APC (for adenomatous polyposis coli), should allow doctors to detect the cancer early and to identify people with a predisposition to colon cancer called familial adenomatous polyposis, which affects about 50,000 Americans. Some people may be born with varying degrees of mutation of the gene. In others, exposure to cancer-causing substances, radiation, or fatty food may produce genetic defects.

**Cholesterol Screening.** In April a panel of experts for the National Cholesterol Education Project urged doctors to test cholesterol levels of children whose parents or grandparents had heart attacks or signs of heart disease at or before age 55. The panel also recommended testing of children who have a parent with high cholesterol in the blood (over 240 milligrams per deciliter as defined by the panel, although many experts consider 200 milligrams to be the upper limit of normal). The recommendations, which were endorsed by 42 major health and professional groups, could apply to as many as a quarter of American children. Most children found to have high cholesterol could be treated through low-fat, low-cholesterol diets, although some might require treatment with a cholesterol-lowering drug.

**Heart Failure.** A pair of studies published in August showed that the drug enalapril (brand name, Vasotec) reduces deaths and hospitalization among people with mild or moderate chronic heart failure. Chronic heart failure, estimated to affect 2 million Americans, puts more elderly people in the hospital than any other condition. Fifteen percent of patients die within a year. In a study of more than 2,500 patients, enalapril was found to have reduced hospital admissions by 26 percent and reduced the risk of death by 16 percent. Enalapril is used to treat high blood pressure and relieve shortness of breath and other symptoms of heart failure. It works by dilating the blood vessels.

Another study on enalapril, reported in November, showed that the drug is effective not only in treating chronic heart failure but also in preventing the onset of symptoms. The five-year study involved more than 4,200 people with significant heart damage but with no symptoms of heart failure. It was found that enalapril reduced the risk of developing heart failure by 37 percent. Those taking the drug also had lower death rates and hospital costs and experienced fewer fatal and nonfatal heart attacks.

**Sepsis Treatments.** Two new drugs were developed that help prevent death from sepsis, an infection of the blood that kills 100,000 hospitalized Americans each year. The drugs are effective in treating sepsis caused by gram-negative bacteria, which accounts for about one-third of the cases. A February report showed that one of the drugs, nebacumab (brand name, Centoxin), reduces deaths by about 40 percent among patients with gram-negative infection, including serious cases in which patients have gone into shock. The second drug, E5, halved the number of deaths among patients in early stages of infection but not among patients in shock, it was reported in August.

In September an FDA advisory committee recommended approval of Centoxin but delayed action on E5 until study results could be analyzed further.

**Small Intestine Transplants.** Transplantation of the small intestine is becoming a practical treatment, University of Pittsburgh surgeons suggested in May when they reported the first successful series of such transplants. The operations were performed on three children and two adults with short gut syndrome, a condition caused when all or part of the small intestine is surgically removed or underdeveloped because of traumatic injury, inflammation, blood clots, or birth defects. People with the

syndrome must be fed intravenously. The surgeons attributed the success of the transplants to use of a powerful experimental immunosuppressive drug, FK-506, that helps prevent the body's rejection of a transplanted organ, a particularly prevalent problem in the case of the small intestine.

**Smoking.** In January the CDC reported an increase in the number of Americans who died from smoking. The death toll in 1988, the most recent year for which statistics are available, represented an 11 percent increase over the number of smoking-related deaths reported three years earlier. Of the more than 430,000 total deaths, about 200,000 were from cardio-

*Passive smoking, or the inhalation of cigarette smoke produced by others, was cited by researchers at the University of California as the cause of 53,000 deaths every year in the United States.*

vascular diseases like coronary heart disease and high blood pressure, over 110,000 from lung cancer, some 30,000 from other cancers, and over 80,000 from respiratory diseases like bronchitis and emphysema. The CDC attributed the rise to the results of high smoking rates in the 1960s, saying it takes 20 to 30 years for the effects of cigarette smoking to become apparent.

Agency officials said almost 4,000 non-smoking Americans died of lung cancer caused by secondhand smoke, but they did not estimate the number of deaths due to heart disease caused by secondhand smoke. University of California researchers estimated in January that

passive smoking causes 53,000 deaths annually among nonsmokers, including 37,000 from heart disease. The National Institute for Occupational Safety and Health recommended in July that employers ban smoking in the workplace.

The CDC estimated that about 28 percent of Americans smoked in 1988, down from 30 percent in 1985 and 40 percent in 1964, when the surgeon general first issued a warning against smoking.

In April HHS Secretary Sullivan asked owners of arenas and parks to deny the use of their facilities for sporting events sponsored by tobacco companies. He also asked sports promoters to stop accepting tobacco companies as sponsors, arguing that such sponsorships encourage children to smoke.

**Lead Poisoning.** The CDC in October announced it had lowered the blood lead level it considered to be "of concern," citing growing evidence that levels previously believed safe can cause developmental problems in children. In 1985 the agency defined lead poisoning as 25 micrograms of lead per deciliter of blood. In 1991 it urged blood lead screening for all children under age six and recommended that federal agencies launch lead-awareness programs in communities where many children have blood lead levels of 10 micrograms per deciliter or higher. For those with levels over 15 micrograms, efforts were urged to identify and remove sources of lead exposure. The CDC said children with levels over 20 should be treated by a doctor, while those with levels over 45 should undergo a procedure for removing excess lead from the body. High blood lead levels can cause women to deliver low-birthweight babies and result in intelligence deficits and nervous system damage in children.

**Women's Health.** Throughout the year, researchers added to the mounting evidence that women get less attention than men for certain medical problems. According to results of two studies of heart disease patients reported in July, women are half as likely as men to undergo cardiac catheterization, a common diagnostic procedure that helps to determine the severity of heart disease. In one of the studies, women were also half as likely to have bypass

### The Ultimate Try-on

It was high time, according to childbirth educator Linda Ware, that fathers-to-be really, *really* got to understand what their spouses go through during pregnancy. Solution: the Empathy Belly, the first-ever "try-on" pregnancy.

The Empathy Belly, which weighs in at 35 pounds, consists of a rib-constricting belt and a strap-on stomach and breast unit encasing water-filled bags plus a free-swinging weight (to simulate a baby's kicking) and lead balls and lead shot over the bladder, liver, and intestines (stand-ins for a baby's head, buttocks, and limbs).

Anyone man enough to try out the device promptly learns why pregnant women in the third trimester so often lose their pizzazz. An extra 35 pounds, most of it pointing forward, can quickly lead to an aching back, and a disinclination to bend down even to tie shoelaces. Constant pressure on the bladder means frequent trips to the bathroom. And constricted ribs lead to heartburn, shortness of breath, a rise in blood pressure, and fatigue. Not surprisingly, men who have endured the Empathy Belly are reported to be considerably more sympathetic toward their pregnant partners.

The Belly also has brought home some hard "facts of life" to teenage girls in sex education and pregnancy prevention programs. Being pregnant is no fun—added to which is the fact that one's boyfriend is quite likely to say: "If you looked like that, I'd dump you."

surgery or balloon angioplasty to open up clogged arteries. A study reported in November additionally found that men were twice as likely as women to receive "clot buster" drugs such as streptokinase and TPA that can stop heart attacks in progress. Heart disease is the leading cause of death for American women as well as men, although it generally strikes women about ten years later. The American Medical Association also reported that women have less access to kidney transplants and that they are less likely to have a diagnostic test called sputum analysis for lung cancer.

Pointing up another issue in women's health, a review of seven major studies in September suggested that drugs that lower high blood pressure in men may not work and may even be harmful in some women. Most methods of preventing, diagnosing, and treating medical conditions are based on studies that include only men. However, many in the medical community speculate that prescribing drugs for women on the basis of study results in men may be inappropriate because of women's hormonal and physiological differences. In response to increasing criticism that women are excluded from medical studies, the National Heart, Lung, and Blood Institute announced in October that it would launch a study to determine whether low doses of aspirin protect women against heart attacks and strokes. The study, to include more than 40,000 women, was to be similar to a 1988 study involving 22,000 male physicians, which showed that an aspirin every other day reduced the incidence of a first heart attack.

One important study directed toward the unique health problems of women found that taking the hormone estrogen after menopause reduces the risk of heart disease by 50 percent and lowers the risk of death from cardiovascular disease. The ten-year follow-up study of the Nurses' Health Study, involving some 48,500 women, was the largest to date on how estrogen affects heart disease in women. It showed that the benefits of estrogen in preventing heart disease outweigh any possible negative effects, such as increasing the risk of some types of cancer. Published in September, the study showed no association between estrogen use and strokes.

*An advisory committee of the Food and Drug Administration held hearings in November on whether silicone breast implants should be banned because of health hazards. Here, author Karen Berger holds up an implant at a news conference, after her group appeared before the committee to oppose a ban.*

**Breast Implants.** After complaints from some women who had received them, the FDA in November held hearings on whether to ban silicone breast implants. The implants are used both by women who have had breasts removed because of cancer and by those who wish to enhance their breasts for cosmetic reasons. While some women said they had experienced no problems with the implants, others blamed them for a number of health problems, including serious autoimmune diseases such as arthritis and scleroderma. The implants, which are made of silicone gel in a harder silicone bag, can rupture and leak into the body, with unknown effects, and they can also cause hard scar tissue to form. Critics say that the implants make it more difficult to detect breast cancer.

An FDA panel rejected manufacturers' safety data as inadequate and recommended requiring companies to establish permanent registries to list all women who receive implants and keep track of their condition. In addition the panel called for a series of studies testing the safety of the implants. A decision on the panel's recommendations was expected in early 1992.

**Photographing Memories.** In 1991 researchers for the first time took pictures of the human brain as it recalled a memory. The X-ray images revealed some surprises, among them that not all memory activity takes place, as long believed, in the hippocampus, the organ in the brain in which memory is formed. For some simple recall tasks the brain used the visual cortex, while for more complicated memory exercises the prefrontal cortex, a higher-thinking area at the front of the brain, was used. The study marked an additional breakthrough in that normal human brains were observed. Until now all knowledge of the anatomy of memory has come from research on people with brain injuries.

See also BEHAVIORAL SCIENCES; LIFE SCIENCES. L.C.H.

**HONDURAS.** Under President Rafael Leonardo Callejas, Honduras in 1991 saw a continuation of its decade-long movement toward democracy and a relatively low level of guerrilla and death-squad violence.

In January Colonel Luis Alonso Discua, the new commander in chief of the armed forces, ordered a number of transfers giving more power to junior officers. When Colonel Roberto Mendoza was removed as Air Force head, he seized the Tegucigalpa airport for ten hours on January 26 and urged a military rebellion; the coup attempt was unsuccessful.

Offered amnesty if they agreed to abandon their low-intensity campaign to overthrow the government, several prominent Marxist guerrilla leaders returned from exile and announced they were discontinuing their military campaign. But one faction of the Popular Liberation Movement (Cinchoneros) remained active, staging a series of bombings.

In early May, five squatters were killed and several others injured in a confrontation near the port of Tela between landowners and peasants claiming idle land. Peasant leadership came from the National Agrarian Workers' Central, which demanded a speedup of land reform and advocated continued peasant land seizures.

Despite damage to crops due to torrential rains and flooding, the export of bananas was projected to reach an all-time high in fiscal 1990-1991, but coffee exports were expected to be down substantially. In order to lessen Honduras's costly dependence on foreign oil, President Callejas ordered gasoline rationing in January. Other austerity measures included the dismissal of 9,000 government employees, increases in bus fares and electricity rates, and the removal of government price supports.

Such initiatives helped the government to secure large loans from the World Bank, the International Development Bank, and the International Monetary Fund. By August, however, Callejas's economic adjustment measures had resulted in a sharp decline in investment, unprecedented inflation levels, and popular unrest.

See STATISTICS OF THE WORLD. T.P.A.

**HOUSING.** See ECONOMY AND BUSINESS.

**HUNGARY.** With the departure of the last of the Soviet troops on June 19, 1991, Hungary became a truly sovereign state. The momentous event ended 46 years of Soviet occupation and was celebrated with concerts, sporting events, and the ringing of church bells.

**Political Developments.** A three-party coalition, dominated by the Hungarian Democratic Forum, governed the country. An important measure enacted in June offered full or partial restitution to those whose land, housing, or business had been expropriated by the Communists. Parliament also agreed to pass another law to deal with restitution to those citizens whose property had been expropriated between 1939 and 1949. A law on the restitution of former church property was passed in July, permitting churches to reclaim from local governments expropriated property needed for "nonprofit" activities.

In November, Parliament passed a measure designed to bring to trial those responsible for the murders of revolutionaries following the crushing of the 1956 revolution. It was under constitutional review.

**Economic Developments.** Hungary's attempt to shift from a planned economy to a market economy was more successful than that of other Eastern European countries. However, privatization was slowed by lack of financial resources, and only a fraction of the commercial assets offered found buyers. The state-owned industrial sector remained in a recession. Inflation rose by 35 percent. The number of the unemployed was expected to reach 300,000—6 percent—by year's end. The trade deficit was reduced, as exports to the West continued to grow, but exports to the East suffered a radical decline.

**Foreign Affairs.** Early in the year, a Hungarian-Czechoslovak-Polish summit conference took place in Visegrad, Hungary; a follow-up meeting took place in mid-October in Cracow, Poland. The conferees' goal was to work toward a free-trade zone in the area. In November the three countries were granted associate membership in the European Community. Regional cooperation was also the aim of the Hexagonale group, consisting of Hungary, Italy, Austria, Yugoslavia, Czechoslovakia, and Poland. A Dubrovnik (Yugoslavia) summit meeting held at the end of July led to agreements on commercial and military cooperation.

The harsh treatment of the Hungarian minority in Transylvania continued to poison relations with Romania, though some amelioration was noticeable. Czechoslovak-Hungarian relations were strained by Slovakia's ongoing construction of the Gabcikovo hydroelectric dam on the Danube. Aside from the ecological consequences, the Hungarians feared the dam could alter the course of the river, which marks the border, in favor of Slovakia.

Tensions between Yugoslavia and Hungary exploded in January when Hungarian officials denied, then admitted having sold 10,000 Kalashnikov rifles to Croatia, a breakaway member of the Yugoslav federation. In September, Serbia accused Hungary of allowing crop-duster planes to ferry arms to Croatia from remote airfields in southern Hungary. On the other hand, Hungary protested overflights by the Yugoslav air force. In late October a Yugoslavian plane accidentally dropped two bombs on a Hungarian village, causing injuries and property damage. As a result, an agreement was signed creating a security zone along the border. According to the Hungarian Red Cross, the number of Yugoslav refugees (mostly Croatian) had risen to 35,000 by the end of November.

Hungary's relations with the West continued to be good. A highlight was Pope John Paul II's first visit to Hungary, August 16-20.

*See* STATISTICS OF THE WORLD.        P.P.

# I

**ICELAND.** In general elections for the Althing (Parliament) on April 20, 1991, the conservative Independence Party won 26 seats, having gained 8 additional seats, including all 7 previously held by the Citizens' Party. Although the center-left coalition of Prime Minister Steingrimur Hermannsson retained a slender majority in Parliament, his government resigned, and President Vigdis Finnbogadottir then asked the Independence Party and the Social Democrats (who had 10 seats) to form a coalition cabinet. David Oddsson, head of the Independence Party, became prime minister; Jon Baldvin Hannibalsson of the Social Democrats remained foreign minister.

Iceland became the first nation to extend full diplomatic recognition to the three Baltic nations—Estonia, Latvia, and Lithuania. In October, at a meeting in Luxembourg, Iceland joined the other European Free Trade Association nations in agreeing to accept membership in a projected 19-nation European Economic Area.

During the year, Iceland, together with Norway, sponsored "Vinland Revisited," a Viking ship expedition from Norway to North America. The flotilla consisted of the *Gaia*, a replica of a Viking ship found in Gokstad, Norway, in 1880; the *Oseberg*, a replica of a Viking pleasure craft; and the *Saga Siglar*, a

The age of the Vikings seemed to come to life again when Iceland, in a joint venture with Norway, sent replicas of two Viking ships (the one seen here is the Gaia) on a cross-Atlantic voyage to commemorate the landing of the Norsemen in the New World some 1,000 years ago.

veteran arctic vessel. Leaving Norway on May 17, the ships visited Iceland on June 17 and continued on to several ports before arriving in Washington, D.C., for ceremonies October 9 (Leif Ericson Day).

See STATISTICS OF THE WORLD.          E.J.F.

**IDAHO.**  See STATISTICS OF THE WORLD.

**ILLINOIS.**  See STATISTICS OF THE WORLD.

**INDIA.**  The assassination of former Indian Prime Minister Rajiv Gandhi in May 1991 raised public anxieties, as did other violence, ongoing caste and religious tensions, economic hardships, and continuing insurgencies. But India came to the end of the year with a sense of confidence in the new prime minister, P. V. Narasimha Rao, and in the Congress Party government he headed.

**Gandhi Assassination.**  Gandhi had been prime minister from 1984 until 1989, when his Congress Party lost its majority and he assumed the role of leader of the opposition. At the beginning of 1991 a minority government was in power, headed by Chandra Shekhar of the

Janata Party Socialist. The Shekhar government fell in March, after Gandhi withdrew his support, and elections were called for May.

Gandhi was assassinated on the night of May 21 by a female suicide bomber at a campaign rally in the town of Sriperumbudur, 25 miles from Madras in South India. The Indian government determined that the killing was perpetrated by the Sri Lankan Tamil separatist group known as the Liberation Tigers of Tamil Eelam, which Gandhi had alienated with his 1987 military "peacekeeping" intervention in fighting between Sri Lankan government forces and LTTE guerrillas.

The most systematic and massive manhunt in India's history ended in August when the investigating team caught up with the alleged mastermind, Raja Arumianayagam, known as Sivarasan, or "One-Eyed Jack," outside Bangalore. He and six associates committed suicide before capture. The LTTE connection was corroborated electronically in mid-December when the Tamil Nadu Forensic Sciences Department matched the skulls of Sivarasan and others with photographs taken at the site of the assassination.

**Election Results.**  It turned out that Gandhi's death, which came a day after the first phase of voting, improved the Congress Party's fortunes at the polls. After a national mourning period, a second phase of voting took place on June 12 and 15. It saw a marked increase in voter turnout. The final outcome for the party was 225 seats in the 545-seat Lok Sabha (lower house of Parliament). With the support of 17 Lok Sabha members from small regional parties, the Congress formed a minority government in June. The new government benefited from the determination of all parties to see it succeed, to maintain a degree of stability, and to avoid yet another election—the voters were beginning to tire of campaigning.

Prime Minister Narasimha Rao, aged 70, is from the state of Andhra Pradesh in South India, where the Congress Party did extremely well. A respected elder statesman and veteran cabinet minister, he was named the party's interim president after Sonia Gandhi, Rajiv's widow, declined the position. The other claimant for the prime ministership was Sharad Pawar, chief minister of Maharashtra State,

As he was campaigning in May, India's former Prime Minister Rajiv Gandhi (right) was assassinated in a bomb attack (above). Three days later in New Delhi (below), his son Rahul, accompanied by a Hindu priest, lit the funeral pyre; Rajiv's wife, Sonia (right), and daughter Priyanka also took part in the ceremony.

The results of India's general election are posted outside a newspaper office in New Delhi in June. The Congress Party of recently assassinated leader Rajiv Gandhi won a plurality and was able to form a government, with Narasimha Rao as prime minister.

whose political base was in Bombay. He deferred to Narasimha Rao and subsequently resigned the chief ministership to become minister of defense in his cabinet.

An important political shift was the emergence of the right-wing Bharatiya Janata Party as the single largest opposition party, having grown from only 2 seats in 1984 to 119 seats in the Lok Sabha at the end of 1991. A party of Hindu fundamentalism, the BJP also emerged as the leading party in state legislative elections in Uttar Pradesh, and made inroads in South India and among middle-caste farming communities of the north. Higher-caste professionals in cities like New Delhi also voted solidly for the BJP.

**The Economy.** Late in the year, inflation was officially placed in the range of 13-15 percent but unofficially estimated at 20 percent—despite the year's bumper agricultural harvest. At the macroeconomic level, India faced a severe balance-of-payments crisis, partly as a result of an escalation in foreign-exchange costs caused by the Persian Gulf crisis. The price of imported oil went up, remittances from the 300,000 Indians who had been working in Iraq and Kuwait dropped precipitously, and exports of goods and services to those countries plummeted.

The Narasimha Rao government responded with plans to close money-losing public enterprises while abolishing export subsidies and reducing agricultural subsidies. Reaction from trade union leaders was predictable: a nationwide protest strike was called for November 29. Participation was widespread but far from complete.

Other fiscal measures introduced by New Delhi included the restructuring of the inefficient tax system, the devaluation of the rupee to make exports more attractive, and a general loosening of controls on domestic industry along with new opportunities for foreign trade and investment. In mid-November an agreement was signed to extend to India the European Community's International Investment Partner Scheme, which would encourage small and medium enterprises. A month later, U.S. corporate giants Hewlett Packard and Ford signed joint venture agreements with Indian companies.

The World Bank offered a $500 million loan to fund retraining programs for workers laid off in the process of retrenching public-sector industry. The International Monetary Fund offered a $2.3 billion loan.

**Foreign Affairs.** For India, the disintegration of the Soviet Union, long one of its staunchest supporters, ushered in a period of profound policy change. Evidence of the shift was India's vote with the United Nations majority in December to repeal the UN resolution equating Zionism with racism. During the Persian Gulf War, Prime Minister Shekhar had already permitted U.S. cargo planes to refuel at Bombay, thereby opening a new phase in Indo-U.S. relations.

In December, Chinese Prime Minister Li Peng became the first Chinese leader to visit India since Prime Minister Zhou Enlai in 1960. Specific agreements that resulted were limited to a modest resumption of local border trade, an exchange of consulates in Bombay and Shanghai, and bilateral cooperation in space-related research. India conceded full Chinese claim to Tibet, provoking widespread protest marches among Tibetan refugees long resident in India.

**Kashmir, Punjab, and Assam.** The Narasimha Rao government moved vigorously to revive the stalled political process in the insurgent states of Kashmir, Punjab, and Assam, while at the same time reinforcing its armed presence in these regions. This intense military crackdown, coupled with equally intense negotiations, apparently paid dividends in Assam, where the United Liberation Front of Assam declared an indefinite cease-fire in mid-December. In Punjab, up to 180,000 troops were brought in to root out terrorists in anticipation of elections scheduled to be held by mid-February 1992. The government of India proposed similar efforts in negotiations with Kashmir, but the Kashmir situation was complicated by Pakistan's encouragement of the insurgency.

*See* STATISTICS OF THE WORLD. W.H.

**INDIANA.** *See* STATISTICS OF THE WORLD.

**INDIANS, AMERICAN.** The acclaim given to the film *Dances With Wolves* was one prominent indication of a heightened public interest in the problems and concerns of American Indians in 1991.

**Growing Public Awareness.** The U.S. Census Bureau reported that 1,959,234 Americans classified themselves as American Indians, Eskimos, or Aleuts in the 1990 national census. This figure represented an increase of more than one-third over the 1980 enumeration of 1.4 million and apparently reflected a shift in identification as well as a rise in Indian fertility.

In one reflection of increased public sensitivity, the U.S. Congress approved legislation to rename the Custer Battlefield National Mon-

*Tourists explore the Custer Battlefield National Monument in Montana. Late in the year, Congress renamed the site the Little Bighorn Battlefield National Monument and authorized construction of a memorial to the Plains Indians who also fought there.*

ument in Montana the Little Bighorn Battlefield National Monument. Under the law, a monument to the Indians who fought Custer will be erected alongside the marker commemorating fallen members of the 7th Cavalry.

In March at the annual Academy Award ceremonies, *Dances With Wolves*, starring Kevin Costner, was named the best motion picture of the year. The film, which is about life among the Lakota Sioux, had won a vast audience following its release in the fall of 1990; it played in packed movie halls for more than six months and later found an even larger public when it was released on videocassette.

The "tomahawk chop" used by fans of the Atlanta Braves baseball team to express their support was an object of controversy. In this stadium ritual, fans, some wearing headdresses and war paint, brandish rubber tomahawks and intone an Indian melody of sorts. Many Indians have found this demeaning, and about 150 of them, some with placards reading "stop the chop," demonstrated outside the Minneapolis Metrodome before the first game of the World Series. The issue focused attention on long-held patterns of ethnic stereotyping and in particular on the practice of giving sports teams such nicknames as Braves, Indians, Chiefs, and Redskins.

Also in 1991 there were acrimonious discussions of how best to commemorate the quincentenary of the first voyage of Christopher Columbus to the New World—which began the wide-scale exploration and colonization of the Americas by Europeans.

**Artifacts.** New federal legislation providing for the return of ritual and tribal items does not apply to the private art market, and in May, Sotheby's auction house sold three masks— two Hopi and one Navajo—despite protests from the tribes. Following the auction, however, the purchaser, collector Elizabeth Sackler, announced she had bought the masks in order to return them to the Indians.

**Tribal Administration.** The inauguration in January of Peterson Zah as the first president of the Navajo Nation marked the beginning of a new, more democratic form of government for a tribe whose previous leader, Peter MacDonald, had been removed from office and convicted of corruption in the Navajo Tribal Court.

Early in the year, seven tribes embarked on an experiment in self-government, setting their own budgets for federal appropriations and running their own programs rather than relying on the U.S. Bureau of Indian Affairs. The experiment was intended to silence criticism of the BIA as well as to fulfill a general desire for greater self-determination on the part of tribal governments.

Representatives of six Chippewa communities agreed in May to limit their harvesting of off-reservation natural resources such as fish and timber, while the state of Wisconsin recognized the tribe's right to hunt, fish, and gather plants beyond the boundaries of their reservations.                                    F.E.H.

**INDONESIA.** Indonesia made efforts in 1991 to deal with increasing unrest, play a role in foreign affairs, and achieve economic reform. Official concern about the rising tide of popular political commentary was evident in increased censorship. In March this led 45 prominent personalities to form a new organization, Democracy Forum, to protest the suppression of popular dissent. On July 4, Indonesia's most celebrated dissidents, the Group of Fifty, testified before Parliament, where they criticized President Suharto's tenure as unconstitutional. There was also widespread criticism of the burgeoning business interests of the Suharto family.

On January 1, Indonesia joined the UN Human Rights Commission in Geneva; meanwhile, alleged human rights abuse in the territory of East Timor (annexed by Indonesia in 1976) was high on the commission's agenda. Protests continued in East Timor, and in November soldiers attacked a funeral procession there, claiming to have acted in self defense. At least 50 people were killed. There also was an increase in violent incidents in Aceh province, North Sumatra, with many killings attributed both to the Army and to rebel groups.

Indonesia continued to develop its role as regional mediator. As cosponsor (with France), Indonesia tenaciously fostered the Cambodian peace negotiations. In July Indonesia was host of a meeting on the disputed (and potentially oil-rich) Spratly and Paracel Islands, to which China, Taiwan, Vietnam, Malaysia, the Philippines, and Brunei all laid claim.

*A severe drought in Indonesia caused a drop in the rice harvest and, in some places, curtailed hydroelectric power. The dry land is apparent in this scene in Central Java, above. At left, Javanese boys fetch water from a distant well.*

In the Persian Gulf War Indonesia provided troops for the multination peacekeeping force on the Iraq-Kuwait border. Indonesia has the world's largest Muslim community, with strong anti-Israeli sentiments; for his part, President Suharto downplayed any religious and factional aspect of the war, stressing instead the UN's need to enforce the sanctity of national borders.

In its annual budget of January 7 the government stressed the need for economic caution and continuing austerity. Indonesia projected a 5 percent real growth rate for GNP in 1991 (down from 7 percent in 1990) and a 7 percent inflation rate (down from 9.5 percent). Falling oil revenues were expected, and severe droughts reduced rice harvests in many regions. To conserve energy, domestic oil prices were raised 22 percent in July, and electricity prices went up 20 percent in August.

The government continued its five-year economic reform campaign with a package of tariff cuts. In March a new set of rules was issued to curb currency and stock exchange speculation and improve the security of financial institutions. A floor of 21 percent was imposed on lending rates in September. Many smaller banks disappeared during the year, and tens of thousands of employees were laid off by larger financial institutions.

*See* STATISTICS OF THE WORLD. G.H.

**INTERNATIONAL CONFERENCES.** The dramatic and historic Mideast peace talks topped the list of international conferences in 1991. **Middle East Peace Conference.** For the first time since the creation of Israel in 1948, Israel and all the Arab nations around it attended an international conference, the first round of which was held in Madrid from October 30 to November 4. Representatives from Israel,

Egypt, Syria, and Lebanon, as well as a joint Jordanian-Palestinian delegation and observers from other Arab states, met at the conference, sponsored by the United States and the Soviet Union. The ultimate aim was to achieve a peaceful settlement between Israel and its Arab neighbors. After acrimonious opening statements, bilateral talks were held between Israel and Syrian, Lebanese, and joint Jordanian-Palestinian delegations. A second round of talks was convened in Washington, D.C., on December 10, after some delay by the Israeli delegation, which opposed the site. The talks adjourned December 18 after failing to advance beyond discussion of procedures, although both sides tentatively agreed to meet again in January.

**Group of Seven Summit.** Leaders of the world's seven major industrial democracies—the United States, Canada, Britain, France, Germany, Italy, and Japan—held their annual economic summit in London on July 15-17. Western relations with the Soviet Union dominated the agenda of the so-called Group of Seven. Soviet President Mikhail Gorbachev addressed the assembly, and Gorbachev and U.S. President George Bush, meeting separately, agreed to the terms of a strategic arms reduction treaty. The G-7 leaders vowed in principle to aid the Soviet Union. They also agreed on the possible use of force to prevent Iraq from obtaining nuclear weapons and backed an international arms registry.

**Commonwealth of Nations.** The Commonwealth of Nations held its biennial conference of national leaders October 16-20 in Zimbabwe. Delegates endorsed a plan for phased removal of sanctions against South Africa and issued a declaration endorsing human rights, democracy, and the free market.

**Organization of American States.** The Organization of American States met in emergency session in Washington, D.C., on October 2 to formulate a response to the coup in Haiti. The OAS voted to isolate the new Haitian military leaders politically, economically, and militarily, while still allowing humanitarian aid to reach the country. The move was the first test of the OAS's agreement reached in June in Santiago, Chile, to act against any regime that took power in a coup.

**Comecon and CSCE.** Following the democratization of Eastern Europe and the decision of many members to start trading in hard currency, the nine-member Soviet-bloc trade alliance known as Comecon (Council for Mutual Economic Assistance), at a meeting in Budapest in late June, voted to disband.

The Conference on Security and Cooperation in Europe got four new members—Albania and the Baltic states of Estonia, Latvia, and Lithuania—bringing the total membership to 38. The Baltic states were admitted at a CSCE foreign ministers' conference focused on human rights, which opened on September 10 in Moscow; members expressed concern over rising nationalism in Europe. At an emergency session held in Prague in August, the CSCE had offered to help mediate the escalating civil war in Yugoslavia.

**Arab League.** The Arab League elected Egyptian Foreign Minister Esmat Abdel Meguid as its secretary general in Cairo on May 15. It was the first time an Egyptian was chosen since the league cut ties with Egypt because of the 1979 Egyptian-Israeli peace treaty.

See also AFRICA; CARIBBEAN BASIN; ENERGY; EUROPEAN COMMUNITY; INTERNATIONAL TRADE; MILITARY AND NAVAL AFFAIRS; PACIFIC ISLANDS; UNITED NATIONS. M.M.D.

**INTERNATIONAL TRADE.** The world in 1991 continued to shift gears from Star Wars to trade wars, as the era of U.S.-Soviet military confrontation gave way to economic confrontation between trading groups. World trade volume grew only slightly, by an estimated 1 percent in 1991, according to the International Monetary Fund.

**GATT Talks.** As the year drew to a close, the 108 member nations of the General Agreement on Tariffs and Trade (GATT) again seemed to be approaching a deadlock in the so-called Uruguay round of trade negotiations. The talks had stalled the year before in a dispute (still to be settled) over agricultural subsidies by the 12-nation European Community (EC) that hurt farmers elsewhere. In a speech in The Hague in November, U.S. President George Bush warned that failure to conclude the five-year-old Uruguay round of GATT talks would plunge the United States and Western Europe into an "impoverishing rivalry."

Both sides in the agricultural trade dispute were taking more moderate positions than previously. The United States now called for a cut of 35 percent over five years in European export subsidies and 30 percent over five years in internal supports and barriers to market access. The Community proposed a 35 percent cut in its subsidies over six years. Major overall U.S. goals for the GATT talks included a one-third reduction in quotas, extension of the GATT system to include the one-third of world trade not covered by international rules of trade, protection for patents, copyrights, and trademarks, and the opening up of government procurement.

**European Trade Blocs.** After a marathon negotiating session in Luxembourg, the Community and the seven-nation European Free Trade Association—Iceland, Norway, Switzerland, Finland, Sweden, Liechtenstein, and Austria—agreed to form a free-trade zone that would constitute a market of 380 million consumers. The pact establishing the new common market, called the European Economic Area, would go into effect in 1993, if ratified.

**North American Trade.** Negotiations toward formation of a North American Free Trade Area (NAFTA) began in June. Canada joined the United States and Mexico in the goal of creating a market of 360 million consumers with a total output of $6 trillion. Proponents claimed the progressive elimination of barriers to the flow of goods, services, and investment would be a catalyst for growth in all three nations.

**Asian Groups.** The South Asian Association for Regional Cooperation discussed but post-

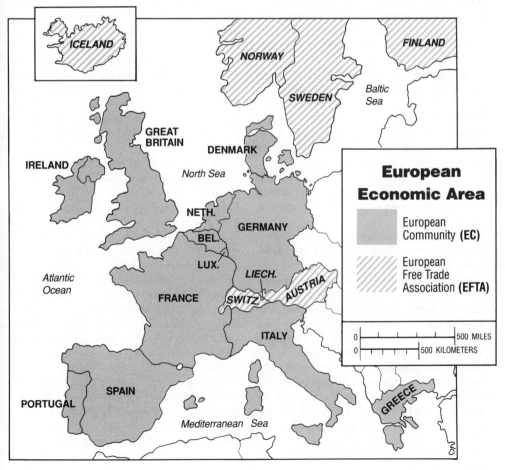

## European Economic Area

European Community **(EC)**

European Free Trade Association **(EFTA)**

poned action on establishing a regional free-trade zone to bolster the economies of its member nations (India, Nepal, Bangladesh, Bhutan, Pakistan, Sri Lanka, and the Maldives). Many members feared Indian dominance of a free-trade zone.

The Asia Pacific Economic Cooperation (APEC), at a meeting in mid-November in Seoul, declared itself committed to free trade and decided to establish a permanent secretariat along with a budget for several projects aimed at promoting regional cooperation and growth. The group's members include the United States, Canada, Japan, Australia, New Zealand, Singapore, Malaysia, Thailand, Indonesia, the Philippines, and Brunei. Taiwan, Hong Kong, and China became APEC members at the November gathering.        D.R.F.

**IOWA.** See STATISTICS OF THE WORLD.

**IRAN.** Iran managed to stay uninvolved, for the most part, in the Persian Gulf War. The long-stagnant Iranian economy in 1991 showed its strongest performance since the 1979 Islamic revolution.

**Economic Developments.** Tehran projected only a narrow government budget deficit for 1991-1992. Real growth in the gross domestic product stood at 7.5 percent in the 1990-1991 fiscal year, a gain of two percentage points over the previous year. Growing national income, however, did not result in an improved life-style for the mass of Iranians. Rising prices for food, transportation, utilities, and university tuition provoked popular protests and outbreaks of violence.

To rid itself of the worst industrial burdens undertaken when properties and businesses were confiscated after the 1979 revolution, the government proposed privatizing 400 state companies. The regime of President Ali Akbar Hashemi Rafsanjani also had to cope with rapid population growth; new birth control measures, including the distribution of free contraceptives, were adopted in July.

**Political Developments.** In a nationally televised Friday prayer in May, Rafsanjani specifically attacked radical leaders for their inability to address real concerns faced by ordinary Iranians. A principal target of the president was Ahmad Khomeini, son of the late Iranian leader Ayatollah Ruhollah Khomeini. The speech hinted at an upcoming political rout of radical elements, and several influential leaders, including Ayatollahs Reyshahri and Khalkhali, were in fact silenced by being implicated in embezzlement scandals.

In October Parliament passed an election reform bill. Candidates were to have identical time periods for their campaigns and were to be selected on their records. Control over nominations, however, remained in the government's hands, and only those nominations approved by religious figures, revolutionary organizations, or official agencies were to be accepted. In part to placate criticism touching on human rights violations, the government also pushed through a measure allowing individuals on trial to have defense lawyers of their own choice.

**Foreign Relations.** Iran and Iraq continued to normalize relations. In mid-January they signed an agreement to demilitarize their mutual borders. During the Persian Gulf War, Iran, despite its declared neutrality, allowed nearly 150 Iraqi planes to land in its territory. As a result of the conflict, Iran was flooded with an estimated 700,000 Kurdish and 500,000 Shiite refugees from Iraq. Tehran lacked the resources to cope with the onslaught of refugees and reluctantly accepted Western assistance.

Iran also sought to improve relations with the conservative Arab Gulf monarchies. In March it was announced that diplomatic relations with Saudi Arabia, broken in 1988, would be restored. Meanwhile, Iran increased its presence in Sudan, reportedly helping in the establishment of military training camps there for Islamic fundamentalist militants.

Relations with the United States improved when Iran assisted in the release of several hostages, including all the American captives, held in Lebanon. Diplomatic relations with Great Britain were restored in September, and all British hostages in Lebanon were eventually released.

On August 8 the former shah's last prime minister, Shahpur Bakhtiar, was found assassinated in Paris. France charged three Iranians with stabbing him. In December an Iranian allegedly involved was arrested in Switzerland under a warrant issued by France. Tehran re-

Iraqi President Saddam Hussein visits his troops stationed in Kuwait. The date: January 15—the last day for Iraq to get out of the emirate before the United Nations authorization of the use of force goes into effect.

acted by restricting movements of Swiss diplomats in Iran.

Reports surfaced alleging that China was helping Iran develop a nuclear capability. Tehran denied having produced nuclear weapons and said it sought nuclear technology for peaceful purposes only.

See STATISTICS OF THE WORLD.          J.A.K.

**IRAQ.** On January 17, 1991, after sanctions and diplomacy had failed to make Iraqi President Saddam Hussein undo his 1990 invasion of Kuwait, the United States and its allies launched a major air assault on Iraq, heavily damaging Iraq's infrastructure and taking many lives. A ground campaign begun February 24 brought the toll to 100,000-200,000 Iraqi soldiers, according to some estimates, plus an unknown number of civilians. (See the feature article WAR IN THE GULF.) Fighting ended on February 28, with Iraq driven out of Kuwait. But internal rebellions, massive destruction, shortages of food, clean water, and other civilian needs, political turmoil, war reparations obligations, and poor relations with many countries it had fought left Iraq in a state of social and economic devastation.

**Shiite Uprising.** In March, shortly after Iraq's defeat on the battlefield, reports emerged from Basra and other southern cities that Baghdad's authority was being challenged by Shiite Muslim dissidents as well as by disaffected army units, with Shiites gaining control in some southern towns. Within weeks, however, U.S. officials suggested that the revolt had failed in Basra, with Saddam Hussein's Republican Guard units regaining the city. Other key cities fell by early April, though clashes continued at various points in the south for months.

Hundreds of thousands of Iraqi Shiites fled their homes during the war and later, many going to Iran. Some headed south toward Kuwait, where the allied forces provided aid and comfort. In late April most of the refugees in Kuwait were airlifted to a refugee camp near Rafha, Saudi Arabia.

**Kurdish Revolt.** Meanwhile, Iraq's Kurds renewed their campaign for autonomy in northern Iraq. Guerrillas claimed to have taken control of Sulaymaniyah and other Kurdish towns, but heavy civilian casualties created a huge exodus—at its peak an estimated 2 mil-

Kurdish refugees by the hundreds of thousands fled from their homes to makeshift camps to escape the vengeance of Saddam Hussein's troops after their postwar rebellion against Iraqi rule collapsed. The map above shows the regions, in Iraq and neighboring countries, largely populated by Kurds.

lion people—into the inhospitable mountains of northern Iraq. After throngs crossed into Turkey, the Turkish government sealed its frontiers, leaving hundreds of thousands stranded between its forces and the advancing Iraqi Army from the south. The allies built (and provided military protection for) refugee camps and airlifted food and supplies.

In April, Kurdish leaders negotiated with Hussein an agreement to implement the autonomy agreement of March 1970 and called on the refugees to return to their homes. Many did, but little of the autonomy agreement was implemented. Instead, the violence continued. Autonomy talks with the government continued late in the year but were hindered by disagreements among Kurdish leaders. From October through December, some 200,000 Kurds fled their homes to escape attacks by the Iraqi Army.

**Political Response.** Hussein's reaction to the uprisings was a combination of repression and cooption. He appointed his cousin, hard-liner Ali Hassan al-Majid, as interior minister and later defense minister. Loyal troops were moved to both the north and the south to crack down severely on opposition movements. Meanwhile, on March 4 a general pardon was announced for all Iraqi Army deserters, provided they rejoined their units, and the government declared an increase in food rations and a big pay raise for the army.

**War Damage.** Although the declared allied objective was to force an Iraqi withdrawal from Kuwait, many targets inside Iraq were destroyed in the war, including the transportation infrastructure, oil refining and distribution sector, electrical power systems, and industrial production base. More than 30 major bridges across the Tigris and Euphrates rivers were totally destroyed. Much of the country's telecommunications capacity, including the telephone system and TV and radio broadcasting, was also destroyed. Iraqi officials estimated war damage to the civilian infrastructure at $200 billion.

The World Health Organization and the United Nations Children's Fund dispatched a joint damage assessment team into Iraq on February 28. The team reported that the lack of electrical power, leading to the failure of water purification and sewage treatment systems, was creating serious health hazards in the Baghdad area.

A March report by the Red Cross suggested that the situation in Basra was even worse. The Red Cross brought relief supplies and a mobile water treatment plant to serve the population of Baghdad. By April, fuel supplies were available, electric power was back, though not on a 24-hour basis, and television broadcasts had resumed.

**Postwar Economy.** During the war United Nations sanctions made the importation of food supplies next to impossible. The cease-fire agreement allowed Iraq to import food, and major deals were signed with Canada, Australia, and Thailand. In September the UN agreed to allow Iraq to sell $1.6 billion worth of oil, primarily to pay for food and civilian needs, on the condition that 30 percent of the revenues be set aside to pay reparations for damages wrought by the war. Iraq refused, saying the plan compromised its sovereignty. These decisions in effect continued the UN sanctions, even though Iraq resumed limited oil production and, illegally, exportation, with most of the oil being trucked to Jordan.

**Weapons Disclosures.** Under the cease-fire agreement to the Persian Gulf War, Iraq was required to help the UN remove or destroy all its nuclear, chemical, and biological weapons. Iraq destroyed at least some of its chemical weapons but claimed that its nuclear program was for peaceful purposes only. However, in September documents were found showing that Iraqi scientists were pursuing a program to produce weapons-grade, highly enriched uranium and reprocessed plutonium. This led to a stand-off in which Iraq detained 44 UN inspectors in a bus in a Baghdad parking lot for nearly a week. In October, Iraqi officials admitted they had conducted research on building an atomic bomb. Another UN team in November found chemical warheads. Investigations of a suspected biological weapons plant and of evidence suggesting a concealed quantity of enriched uranium continued late in the year.

*See* STATISTICS OF THE WORLD.      J.A.K.

**IRELAND, NORTHERN.** *See* GREAT BRITAIN.

**IRELAND.** The year 1991 was largely dominated by political and economic uncertainty and anxiety over public finances.

**Economic Affairs.** The budget, drawn up against the uncertain international background of the Persian Gulf War and recession in the United States and Britain, allowed for modest growth, a borrowing requirement of £460 million (Irish pounds), and a small increase in unemployment. By midyear targets had to be abandoned as too ambitious, and the government announced a package of emergency measures to cut public spending. The biggest disappointment was in unemployment, which soared to over 20 percent.

A ten-year program for economic and social progress was agreed on in January by the government, employers, trade unions, and farming organizations. The program laid down a basic pay increase of 10.75 percent over three years and a strategy for economic and social development, but it did not prevent stoppages in the state-owned electricity, transport, and postal sectors.

**Political Affairs.** Local elections in June produced losses for the ruling Fianna Fail Party. Talks began the next month between Fianna Fail and its junior coalition partner, the Progressive Democrats, to review the program of government agreed between them in 1989. By October the government was under severe pressure because of financial scandals in companies partly owned by the state. Fianna Fail's rating in the opinion polls and Prime Minister Charles Haughey's personal support had fallen sharply. But Fianna Fail and the Progressive Democrats succeeded in agreeing on a revised program of government that included reforms in taxation, local government, transportation, education, and agriculture. In November, Haughey survived a no-confidence motion on his leadership of Fianna Fail.

**IRA.** The Dublin City Council voted in November not to allow the outlawed Irish Republican Army's powerful counterpart, the Sinn Fein party, to hold its annual convention in a city-owned building unless the party denounced violence. The vote was seen as a reflection of growing public hostility toward the IRA. Later in the month the Haughey government made good on its promise to tighten the

211

extradition laws, announcing that it would close loopholes used by fugitive IRA members to avoid extradition to Britain.

**Foreign Affairs.** President Mary Robinson paid a state visit to the United States, where, among other activities, she addressed groups of Irish immigrants, many of them illegal aliens hoping to obtain legal status under a new U.S. immigration lottery held in October, allowing 16,000 places for Irish citizens.

Britain's Northern Ireland secretary of state, Peter Brooke, sought to negotiate a replacement for the problematic 1985 Anglo-Irish Agreement, which outlined for Ireland a formal consultative role in the administration of Northern Ireland, but talks led to no substantive progress and were abandoned in July.

*With the outbreak of hostilities in the Persian Gulf in January, Iraq began launching Scud missiles at Israel, forcing citizens to don safety gear against possible chemical attacks. This mother in Jerusalem is adjusting her five-year-old daughter's protective hood.*

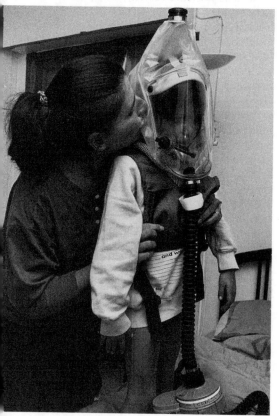

**National Notes.** The Roman Catholic Primate of all-Ireland, Archbishop Cahal Daly, was made a cardinal on June 28.

The 75th anniversary of the 1916 Easter Rising, which led to the establishment of an independent Irish state, was commemorated in a deliberately low-key fashion, in contrast to the widespread celebrations held for the 50th anniversary. The continuing troubles in Northern Ireland were mainly responsible for the change.

See STATISTICS OF THE WORLD.                    J.C.

**ISRAEL.** Dominating the news in Israel in 1991 were the Persian Gulf War, a continued high level of immigration, and the convening of a Middle East peace conference involving both Arabs and Israelis.

**Persian Gulf War.** In mid-January, after the United States and its allies began air attacks against Iraq, Israel found itself under bombardment by Iraqi Scud missiles, as Iraqi President Saddam Hussein sought to break the allied coalition by diverting its Arab members into a war with Israel. The Iraqis fired 39 Scud missiles at Israel between January 18 and February 25. Thirteen Israelis were killed by the missiles, either directly or indirectly; 200 were injured; 4,095 buildings were damaged; and 1,644 families were evacuated from their homes in Tel Aviv and Ramat Gan. Israeli Prime Minister Yitzhak Shamir persuaded his cabinet not to retaliate against the Iraqi attacks, and Israeli public opinion overwhelmingly supported the decision.

Within days of the first Iraqi missile attack, the United States sent four batteries of Patriot antimissile missiles to Israel, and the Patriots successfully intercepted some Scuds. Israel received a low-interest loan of $210 million from the European Community, as well as $670 million in military aid from Germany, including antichemical warfare equipment (there had been fear that the Scud missiles would have chemical warheads), two submarines, and Hawk and Stinger missiles. The United States provided $650 million in war damage compensation and $400 million in loan guarantees for the resettlement of Soviet Jews.

**Aftermath.** Much of the goodwill Israel had built up in the United States by not retaliating

*In a peace conference put together by the United States, Israel sat down with its Arab neighbors, including Palestinian representatives, to discuss ways of bringing peace to the Middle East. Here, Israeli Prime Minister Yitzhak Shamir addresses the conference's opening session in Madrid.*

against Iraq was dissipated in the occasionally bitter discussions leading up to the Middle East peace conference, arranged through diplomatic efforts by the United States. The central problem was an Israeli decision to step up housing and settlement construction in the occupied territories, regarded by the United States as an obstacle to peace talks. Housing Minister Ariel Sharon stood fast to an expansion of settlement and, in August, unveiled a housing plan that would link Jerusalem with Jericho—thus cutting in half any possible Palestinian self-governing entity on the West Bank. In response, President George Bush, in September, called on the U.S. Congress to delay for 120 days consideration of an additional $10 billion loan guarantee to help settle Soviet Jewish immigrants. Congress acceded to the delay.

**Peace Conference.** The peace conference, which opened in Madrid on October 30, included bilateral talks between Israel and Syria, Israel and Lebanon, and Israel and a joint Jordanian-Palestinian delegation—the first face-to-face peace talks between Israel and these parties. (During earlier negotiations with Israel, U.S. Secretary of State James Baker accepted Israel's conditions for the Palestinian members of the joint delegation—no Palestine Liberation Organization members and no Pal-

estinians from East Jerusalem or outside the Israeli-occupied territories.) After the first talks, the Israelis and the Jordanian-Palestinian delegation agreed that they would talk further on two tracks—an Israeli-Jordanian track and an Israeli-Palestinian track—and that the Palestinians and Israelis would soon begin negotiations on self-rule for the West Bank and Gaza. A new round of talks was held December 10-18 in Washington, D.C., with no substantive progress reported.

**Other Foreign Relations.** Soviet President Mikhail Gorbachev sent Foreign Minister Aleksandr Bessmertnykh to the region after the Gulf War—a trip that included the first visit ever by a Soviet foreign minister to Israel. Although Bessmertnykh condemned the settlements being built in occupied territories, Soviet Jewish immigration to Israel continued, with the pace reduced mainly because of the housing and job difficulties facing immigrants once they arrived. Following the Soviet coup attempt in August, Moscow agreed to direct flights between the Soviet Union and Israel for emigrants and ultimately agreed to resume full diplomatic relations with Israel, broken off in 1967. The Soviets also followed the U.S. lead in calling for the United Nations to repeal, as it did, a 1975 UN resolution equating Zionism with racism.

213

In the 36-hour "Operation Solomon" in late May, Israel brought some 14,000 Ethiopian Jews to Israel just before the collapse of the Ethiopian regime of President Mengistu Haile Mariam. The new regime allowed Jewish emigration to continue, and 20,000 had left by year's end.

There was a limited improvement in relations between Israel and its Arab neighbors. Kuwait announced plans to lift its boycott of Western companies with economic links to Israel. Israel's glacial peace with Egypt thawed somewhat as the Egyptians hosted visits by representatives of both the Labor and Likud parties. Israel also became involved in facilitating the release of Western hostages held in Lebanon, as it freed a number of Lebanese detainees.

**Party Politics.** In early February, Shamir brought the ultra-right-wing Moledet Party into the governing coalition, making its leader, Rehavam Ze'evi, minister without portfolio. Ze'evi's call for "transferring" Arabs out of Israeli-controlled areas alienated many members of the governing coalition. Moledet joined the other ultra-right-wing parties to threaten a departure from the government coalition if Shamir made substantive concessions to the Arabs in the peace talks. Joining the hardliners was Sharon, who also announced his decision to challenge Shamir for the party leadership in 1992. Shamir moved to protect his own political position by personally heading the Israeli delegation to the Middle East peace conference.

**Mixed Economic News.** While tourism recovered after the Gulf War, with 119,367 people visiting Israel in October, other aspects of the Israeli economy were not so positive. The inflation rate was running at an annual level of 18.1 percent as of November, and unemployment rose in August to record levels.

See STATISTICS OF THE WORLD.          R.O.F.

**ITALY.** During 1991, Italy attempted to tackle its $1 trillion national debt by substantially modifying public spending as the 1992 deadline for European Community economic integration drew nearer. Forced to economize after decades of pork-barrel spending, politicians played up the fear of being left out of the inner circle of European unity.

In February the Italian Communist Party, the largest in the West, changed its name and symbol. Meanwhile, more than 40,000 Albanians flooded southern Italy during the year, trying to escape Europe's poorest state.

**New Government.** Italy formed its 50th government since World War II, after Prime Minister Giulio Andreotti's five-party coalition government collapsed at the end of March. Socialist Party leader Bettino Craxi had sparked the crisis by demanding new initiatives to solve some of the country's pressing economic and social problems. A nearly identical cabinet was reformed in April, with the omission of the tiny Republican Party, which had resigned to protest the loss of a minister. The remaining four-party coalition included Andreotti's ruling Christian Democrats (the country's largest party and the consistent government leader since the republic was founded in 1946), the Socialist Party, and the small Social Democrat and Liberal parties.

**Communist Farewell.** The Italian Communist Party changed its name to the Democratic Party of the Left (PDS) and relegated its hammer and sickle symbol to the base of a massive oak tree, the new party symbol. A small group of hard-core party members led by Armando Cossutta resigned in protest and formed a new Communist party, Rifondazione Communista (Communist Renewal). Other tiny Marxist parties such as Democrazia Proletaria (Proletarian Democrats) dissolved and joined its ranks.

The fall of Soviet Communism after the abortive August coup was welcomed by the PDS, which remained the second-largest party in Italy. Its name change appeared to open the way for an eventual entry into government, as both Christian Democrats and Socialists alternately courted and criticized the party.

**Persian Gulf War.** On January 17 a deeply divided Parliament authorized a tiny Italian contingent of ten fighter planes and four ships to assist the Gulf allies in the war against Iraq. Massive antiwar rallies took place in Rome and other cities shortly before the outbreak of war in mid-January. On their first bombing mission over Kuwait (and Italy's first since World War II), all but one of the planes were forced to return to their base in Abu Dhabi for technical and refueling problems. The plane flown by pilot Major Giancarlo Bellini and navigator Captain Maurizio Cocciolone was shot down; Cocciolone, his face bruised and bloodied, was later one of the pilots featured in Iraqi "interviews" released to international television. Both men were returned safely to Italy in March.

**Economic Affairs.** After decades of heavy public spending, Italy finally faced making deep cuts to bring the economy into line with its European partners. A 1992 budget bill, proposing deep cuts in health spending, a freeze on public wages, and speeded-up efforts to partially privatize money-losing state industries, had to be approved by Parliament by December 31; otherwise, spending levels would be frozen at 1991 levels. Protests against the proposed budget rained in from all sectors. The three major labor unions held a general strike on October 22. However, the budget approved on December 29 was essentially the one presented.

In April the government admitted it had then already exceeded its 1991 target deficit of 132 trillion lire (about $101 billion) by at least 12 trillion lire, and the figure was continuing to rise. About 80 percent of the deficit was from servicing heavy debt charges. Inflation hovered at close to 7 percent and unemployment stood at around 11 percent. One reason for the growing deficit was the Italian tradition of tax evasion. In October the government offered partial amnesty: just pay 25 percent of past-due taxes and all would be forgiven.

**Albanian Invasion.** Southern Italy was inundated in the spring and summer with thousands of desperate Albanian refugees. In March, 25,000 "boat people" arrived in the southern port of Brindisi on stolen boats and hijacked ships. Overwhelmed and unprepared city officials tried to cope as refugees rioted over food. Then in August the *Vlore*, a rusty freighter carrying an estimated 19,000 people, broke through a government blockade and docked at Bari. Hundreds of refugees jumped ship and swam ashore, and thousands were herded into the dilapidated Della Vittoria soccer stadium, where they rioted for food. Within days, more than 17,000 had been sent back to Albania on government chartered planes and ferries. The remaining refugees, some armed with knives and pistols, held a standoff with police. They were bused in small groups to processing

*Albanian refugees by the thousands poured into southern Italy, straining local resources and prompting the Italian government to send many back home. Here, a pregnant woman is removed from an Albanian freighter in the Italian port city of Brindisi to be taken to a hospital.*

*The water was cascading once more in Rome's celebrated Trevi Fountain, which returned to operation in July after a three-year, $2.4 million restoration project.*

camps but were soon sent back to Albania.

Italy sent unarmed Italian soldiers into Albania to distribute food and basic goods there, and it pledged a total of more than $150 million in aid, more than any other country. The Italian Navy was patrolling the country's waters to help cut off further migration.

**Crime and Terrorism.** In October the Interior Ministry reported 1,636 murders in the preceding 16 months attributable to organized crime wars in Sicily and the southern regions of Calabria, Campania, and Apulia. The federal government also suspended town councils of 18 towns suspected of having been infiltrated by Mafia members.

A public outcry erupted after Libero Grassi, a prominent Sicilian businessman who had publicly condemned the "pizzo," or Mafia extortion, was gunned down in front of his Palermo home in late August. Also evoking an outcry was the move in August by President Francesco Cossiga to pardon imprisoned former Red Brigades' leader Renato Curcio. The effort failed when it was vetoed in September by Justice Minister Claudio Martelli.

Earlier in the year, a magistrate in Genoa released two Palestinians jailed in connection with the 1985 hijacking of the cruise ship *Achille Lauro*. The two, not part of the commando team that actually seized the ship, were freed about two years early under a broad government amnesty program.

**Refurbishings.** In July the water flowed once again in Rome's Trevi Fountain, after nearly three years of costly restoration work. The blinding whiteness of the fountain startled Romans used to its muted smog-gray tones. The $2.4 million restoration project involved shoring up the foundation of the building on which the fountain rests, repairing statues chipped by coin tossers, and clearing the pool of calcium deposits.

The Leaning Tower of Pisa remained closed while a restoration plan was devised. Experts, who said the tower could fall within 30 years, decided to apply steel cable rings to the first tier to relieve pressure on part of the building.

See STATISTICS OF THE WORLD.          P.H.

**IVORY COAST.** See STATISTICS OF THE WORLD.

# J

**JAMAICA.** *See* STATISTICS OF THE WORLD. *See also* CARIBBEAN BASIN.

**JAPAN.** During 1991, Japan experienced a change of government along with financial scandals, continuing (but apparently declining) economic growth, and closer relations with serveral nations.

**From Kaifu to Miyazawa.** On October 4, Prime Minister Toshiki Kaifu announced he would not seek a new term in office. Japan's ruling Liberal Democratic Party (LDP) chose senior party member Kiichi Miyazawa as his replacement; he was formally selected by the Diet on November 4.

Kaifu, 60, was forced to quit after losing the support of powerful faction leaders within the LDP by adamantly vowing to continue to seek political reform despite the defeat of reform legislation in late September. He had been plucked from relative obscurity two years earlier and chosen to lead the LDP largely on the basis of his "clean" public image, at a time when many senior party leaders, including Miyazawa, were linked to a scandal involving allegations of profiteering from insider stock purchases.

Former Deputy Prime Minister Miyazawa was chosen for his political influence and experience. Upon becoming prime minister he promptly installed a cabinet dominated by veteran politicians who had links to past scandals.

**Financial Scandals.** The most serious of a string of new financial scandals began in late June, when more than a dozen domestic securities companies were reported to have paid their most favored clients over 170 billion yen for losses on stock market investments in the 1980s and early 1990s. Hardest hit were Japan's "Big Four" securities companies, Nomura, Daiwa, Nikko, and Yamaichi. On June 27 the outgoing Nomura president, Yoshihisa Tabuchi, angered Finance Minster Ryutaro Hashimoto by saying that Finance Ministry officials had been aware of and had approved of stock loss compensation payments. In October, charges against Nomura Securities re-

*In a public apology at a Tokyo press conference, two officials of the Nomura Securities Company, new President Hideo Sakamaki (left) and company executive Naotaka Murazumi, acknowledge their company's role in the most serious, but by no means the only, financial scandal that rocked Japan in 1991.*

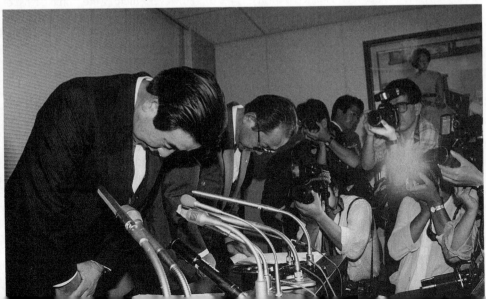

*Japanese tourists on Prince Edward Island pose for a snapshot in front of the house associated with Lucy Maud Montgomery's classic novel,* Anne of Green Gables. *The book, which has a devoted following among Japanese—especially women who, growing up during the bleak postwar years, identified with the heroine's spunk—has drawn thousands of visitors from Japan to the Canadian province.*

sulted in the company's receiving the most severe punishment ever given by the Finance Ministry, when it was ordered to close 79 of its 153 domestic branch offices for a month. The ministry also ordered temporary shutdowns of corporate sales divisions of all the Big Four securities firms.

Faced with mounting criticism of the apparently cozy relations between Finance Ministry officials and securities companies, the Diet hurriedly passed a bill on October 3 amending the Securities and Exchange Law to ban stock market loss compensation and impose stiff penalties on violators. Following the bill's passage, Finance Minister Hashimoto handed in his resignation. Meanwhile, Hashimoto's secretary admitted in August that he had helped arrange nearly $2 billion in illegal loans with the help of Fuji Bank, one of Japan's largest banks. Similar scandals were also discovered at two other major Japanese banks over the summer.

**Budget.** The budget for fiscal 1991 totaled 70.347 trillion yen, an increase of 6.2 percent over fiscal 1990. Public works spending rose 6 percent. Aid to developing countries in-

creased 8 percent, reflecting increased payments to Middle East nations as a result of the Persian Gulf War. Defense spending was up 5.5 percent. A budget deficit of 5.343 trillion yen was expected.

**Economic Trends.** In August the nation entered its 57th month of continuous economic growth, equaling a record stretch from 1965 to 1970. However, there were some signs of slowdown. Unemployment late in the year stood at slightly over 2 percent. The Tokyo Stock Market showed largely lackluster performance. Japan's current-account surplus was rising sharply, and its trade surplus also was rising.

**An Expanding Foreign Role?** On January 31, Prime Minister Kaifu's cabinet, with some reluctance, approved $9 billion in aid, in addition to the $4 billion previously contributed, to the multinational forces arrayed against Iraq. In a controversial move, the government also decided to send ships to help clear Iraqi mines. Late in the year, a measure that would allow Japanese troops to take part in UN peacekeeping missions abroad stalled in the Diet. In December, Japan cosponsored repeal of the

## Wrestling Robots

When you think of a Japanese sumo wrestler, you probably picture a beefy behemoth of 300-plus pounds with an intense stare and thighs the size of Toyotas. Yet in a hotly contested sumo tournament held in Tokyo at the end of December 1990, the contestants checked in at about 6 pounds. They were robots.

The All-Japan Robot Sumo Wrestling Tournament enabled the country's best robot technicians to match their computer chips, alloys, sensors, and, of course, their brains by flexing a little electronic brawn. Among the more than 300 contestants, some looked like little bulldozers, some like insects, others like floor-hugging metal wedges—all the better to get under and flip a rival. They were divided into two categories—half were radio controlled; the rest were on their own, using sensors to find opponents. Surprisingly, the entries from Japan's industrial powerhouses were upended in both categories by machines designed by students.

Other nations could hardly be blamed if they sized up robot wrasslin' as a foretaste of another Japanese technology poised to dominate global competition; Japan is already working on robots that can fight fires, drill tunnels, and explore the sea. But the mechanical sumos appear refreshingly useless. Indeed, the tournament's incentive—outside of the prestige and the first prize of about $8,000—seemed to be plain old fun. As one engineer put it, "I can't think of a single useful thing I could do with this robot. . . . Maybe I could teach it to attack my boss."

1975 UN resolution equating Zionism with racism.

*United States.* In contrast to previous years, official relations with the United States were largely low-key. In November President Bush, for domestic reasons, postponed a planned trip to Japan, but U.S. Secretary of State James Baker did visit. He urged the Japanese to expand participation in international affairs and to make trade concessions, including a lifting of the longtime ban on imported rice. Japanese and U.S. negotiators had earlier signed a

new five-year semiconductor agreement, to provide access for American chips into the Japanese market. In November the government also announced a program to encourage Japanese companies to buy more U.S. goods and enter into alliances with U.S. companies.

*Soviet Union.* The collapse of Communism in the Soviet Union revived hopes for the return of Japan's Northern Territories, three small islands and a group of islets off northern Hokkaido occupied by Soviet troops in the closing days of World War II. Soviet President Mikhail Gorbachev arrived in Tokyo April 16-19, in the first state visit of a Soviet leader to Japan. A dramatic round of unscheduled late night meetings ended with a disappointingly vague

*During a stop on his autumn tour of Southeast Asia, Japanese Emperor Akihito plants a tree at the cultural center of Chiangmai in Thailand. The trip was seen as an attempt to reassure Japan's neighbors that his country's intentions were peaceful and that it was time to bury the painful heritage of World War II.*

agreement calling for more work toward a future peace treaty. However, following the Moscow coup in August there was a flurry of activity, with both sides pledging to speed up negotiations. On October 8 the Japanese government announced a new emergency aid package of $2.5 billion, the largest it had ever given to the Soviets.

*Asian Relations.* Prime Minister Kaifu became the first major world leader to visit Beijing since the Tiananmen Square massacre. In a meeting with Kaifu on August 10, Chinese Premier Li Peng promised "in principle" to sign the nuclear nonproliferation treaty. Kaifu offered China new credit for loans.

Kaifu visited Seoul in January for talks with South Korean President Roh Tae Woo. He agreed to abolish fingerprinting requirements for ethnic Korean residents of Japan and to open jobs in local government and public schools to Japan's Korean residents. Relations with North Korea were shadowed late in the year by fears that the North Koreans were making significant progress toward the development of nuclear arms.

In late September, Emperor Akihito became the first Japanese head of state to visit Southeast Asia, a target of Japanese aggression during World War II. He expressed regret over the war.

**Endangered Marine Life.** The Ministry of International Trade and Industry announced in June that it would ban imports of endangered sea turtle species starting at the end of 1992. Bowing to pressure from the United States and other countries, Japan also agreed to comply with a UN moratorium on the use of huge drift nets in its fishing operations in the northern Pacific. The nets were widely criticized for killing enormous numbers of dolphins, whales, turtles, fish, and birds.

*See* STATISTICS OF THE WORLD. T.K.

**JORDAN.** The Persian Gulf War, major political reforms, and resumption of the peace process with Israel highlighted events in Jordan during 1991.

**Persian Gulf War.** King Hussein opposed both the Iraqi occupation of Kuwait and the American-led military buildup in the Gulf. As an alternative to war, he advocated an Arab-Israeli peace conference to be convened si-

multaneously with an Iraqi withdrawal from Kuwait. As the outbreak of the ground war approached, Jordan mobilized its armed forces and deployed 40,000 troops in the Jordan Valley to deter Israel from launching an attack on Iraq through the region. King Hussein condemned the fighting as a "brutal attack against an Arab and Muslim country and people."

Popular support for King Hussein's position was expressed through almost daily mass demonstrations. Coalition member embassies were stoned, diplomatic vehicles burned, a British bank bombed, and a German national murdered by pro-Iraqi terrorists. Iraq's defeat and the amount of damage caused by the war shocked the Jordanian population and left the kingdom politically isolated from its traditional Western and Arab allies.

*These Palestinian children in a camp near Amman were among hundreds of thousands of Palestinians and Jordanians who poured into Jordan from Kuwait and Iraq during the Persian Gulf crisis, overwhelming the country's resources.*

**Economy.** Jordan's economy, already in dismal shape, was devastated by the war. Impending International Monetary Fund reforms were delayed, and discussions on the rescheduling of loans and IMF disbursements were halted. Lost trade and an influx of 750,000 refugees from Iraq and Kuwait cost the kingdom $3 billion to $8 billion. The return of expatriates raised unemployment levels from 16 percent to 25 percent. Saudi Arabia and the Gulf states cut aid to Jordan, refused to provide much-needed petroleum, and banned the sale of Jordanian agricultural produce. U.S. economic and military aid was frozen.

After the war, Japan, Europe, and the United Nations all promised aid to offset Jordan's losses. Exports of agricultural products to Europe resumed in March, and President George Bush released $35 million in economic aid in July and an additional $22 million in October. However, Saudi Arabia, a major benefactor, continued to withhold assistance.

**Political Reshuffling.** Increasing Muslim influence and popular support for Iraq was reflected in a reorganization of the government on January 1. Mudar Badran continued as prime minister, while five moderate members of the Muslim Brotherhood and two members of the fundamentalist Islamic Bloc were named ministers. In June a national charter was approved that included provisions for political parties and established the sharia (Muslim Law) as the basic source of law.

In June, King Hussein accepted the resignation of Badran and asked Foreign Minister Taher al-Masri to form a new government. The American-educated Masri was viewed as both pro-Western and pro-Palestinian. The new government excluded all members of the Muslim Brotherhood and Islamic Bloc, who refused to serve if the government supported peace talks with Israel. Martial law, in effect since 1967, was ended in July.

**Peace Talks.** Despite popular opposition to the idea, the king agreed to participate in an international Arab-Israeli peace conference in a joint delegation with the Palestinians. The conference opened in Madrid on October 30. The parties agreed that further sessions would split into a Palestinian-Israeli track and a Jordanian-Israeli track. Further talks in Washington, D.C., in December foundered in disputes over the separate tracks.

See STATISTICS OF THE WORLD.     C.H.A.

# K

**KAMPUCHEA.** See CAMBODIA.

**KANSAS.** See STATISTICS OF THE WORLD. See also STATE GOVERNMENT REVIEW.

**KENTUCKY.** See STATISTICS OF THE WORLD.

**KENYA.** In December 1991 the governing council of the ruling Kenya African National Union (Kanu) agreed to scrap a 1982 constitutional provision and allow multiparty politics in Kenya. President Daniel arap Moi had proposed the reform, under increasing pressure from dissidents. Oginga Odinga, Kenya's first vice president, led the voices of opposition by forming two opposition groups, both of which were declared illegal. Other dissent came from religious leaders and from the Law Society of Kenya.

Meanwhile, a judicial investigation into the 1990 death of Robert Ouko, Kenya's foreign minister, led to charges against high-level officials close to Moi. Ouko's sister implicated Energy Minister Nicholas Biwott in the death, claiming Ouko had been killed for trying to expose government corruption. In late November, Moi relieved Biwott of his cabinet post and ordered him arrested, along with a former head of national security. But two weeks later, he released both men and dissolved the inquiry; a lesser official was then charged with the crime.

In a national tragedy, 19 girls were killed and 71 raped by male schoolmates on July 14 at the St. Kizito Mixed Secondary School. St.

*Schoolgirls at the St. Kizito Mixed Secondary School in Kenya attempt to retrieve their belongings in the wake of an assault by male schoolmates on a girls' dormitory, in which 19 girls were killed and 71 raped.*

Kizito's 271 girls had refused to participate in a strike organized by the school's 306 boys. The girls had sought protection by huddling together in a dormitory; those who died suffocated or were crushed to death in the pandemonium that resulted when the boys broke in. In all, 29 boys faced manslaughter charges, and 2 were also charged with rape.

Early in the year, the United States expressed appreciation for the use of Kenya's naval and air facilities during the Persian Gulf War, but in November, 12 major aid-donating countries, including the United States, warned that unless political and economic reforms were forthcoming, Kenya would face major aid cuts. The economy performed poorly, as the Gulf War reduced tourism and increased the cost of oil. Inflation remained well above 10 percent, and unemployment rose significantly. Prices for coffee exports were depressed.

See STATISTICS OF THE WORLD.    J.G.K.

**KHMER REPUBLIC.** *See* CAMBODIA.

**KIRIBATI.** *See* STATISTICS OF THE WORLD.

**KOREA.** In December 1991, representatives of North and South Korea signed a treaty of reconciliation and nonaggression, 38 years after the end of hostilities in the Korean War. Signing of the pact capped a year of intensified negotiations that earlier, on September 17, saw both Koreas admitted into the United Nations,

as both South Korean President Roh Tae Woo and North Korean Prime Minister Yon Hyong Muk visited New York to address the General Assembly. Individually, North Korea faced questions about the viability of its political and economic system in light of the collapse of Communism, and South Korea experienced internal conflict and slowing economic growth.

### SOUTH KOREA

While tensions within the country led to student violence, relations with foreign countries improved.

**Politics.** The ruling Democratic Liberal Party (DLP) won strong majorities in spring elections to take decisive control of local councils. However, President Roh's opponents pointed to the dismal participation rate in the elections, particularly among young people, as a sign of discontent. The main opposition party, the New Democratic Union led by Kim Dae Jung, was sobered by its defeat in the local council elections. Kim's group got together with the smaller Democratic Party led by Lee Ki Taek and merged into a reformed Democratic Party, hoping for better success in the 1992 national elections.

Meanwhile, student demonstrations accelerated in the spring. In April a clash between student demonstrators and police left one student dead, apparently of a metal-pipe beating by plainclothesmen. A number of students committed suicide in protest against government repression.

**Economy and Trade.** The gross national product was growing at an estimated 8.7 percent in 1991. Inflation was running at an annual rate of around 10 percent. South Korea's exports grew, but foreign debt rose to a projected $35 billion for the year. Trade with China, the Soviet Union, and North Korea grew significantly. South Korean firms signed agreements to help develop a variety of projects in the Soviet Union, from oil and gas exploration on Sakhalin to coal and metal mining near Khabarovsk and Chita.

**Evolving Foreign Relations.** South Korea sent a medical team to the Persian Gulf after hostilities broke out, in one sign of its emerging status on the world stage. Relations with the Soviet Union also improved early in the year.

In relations with the United States there was agreement over textile shipments and a civil aviation agreement permitting South Koreans access to more American cities. In January the United States and South Korea signed an agreement extending Korean criminal jurisdiction over American military personnel. The annual Team Spirit joint maneuvers went on as scheduled in March, scaled down in part as a favorable signal to the North Koreans. South Koreans agreed to take on a bigger share of the cost of supporting U.S. troops.

The problem of American tactical nuclear weapons in South Korea, a prime source of contention between the United States and North Korea, was disposed of by President George Bush in September when he declared his intention to eliminate all such weapons abroad. The United States also announced further reductions in troop strength.

### NORTH KOREA

North Korea's main problem was coping with the collapse of Communism. President Kim Il Sung turned 79 in April, and observers wondered if his son, Kim Jong Il (named military supreme commander in December), would be able to carry on after his father.

**Economic Problems.** During the year the grain ration was cut by an average 20 percent and North Korea was obliged to import as much as a million tons, most of it from Thailand but some via direct rice imports from South Korea. North Korea's efforts to pay for

*At a ceremony in Panmunjom, the remains of 11 U.S. servicemen killed in the Korean War were turned over by North Korea to the United States. The gesture followed an agreement by North Korea to cooperate with U.S. requests for information on over 8,000 servicemen unaccounted for in the conflict.*

its imports meant scraping for foreign exchange, including sales of Scud-B missiles to the Middle East.

**Nuclear Worries.** North Korea insisted that its 30-megawatt nuclear facility at Yongbyon was peaceful, and no issue loomed larger during the year than that of complying with international nuclear safeguards. The government first said that it would not permit inspection by the International Atomic Energy Agency. Then it agreed to permit IAEA inspection in principle, but not until American nuclear weapons were withdrawn from South Korea. When it seemed that the Americans would do this, the North Koreans held out for a "nuclear free zone" in which the Americans would not patrol with nuclear-armed ships and planes offshore. This demand was rejected.

In November, in face of rising fears that North Korea was nearer to being able to make a nuclear weapon than previously thought, the United States announced a halt to the long-planned pullout of U.S. troops in the South.

### NORTH-SOUTH RELATIONS

The nonaggression treaty, signed by the two Koreas on December 13 in Seoul, provided for the first mail, phone, road, and rail service between North and South Korea in 42 years. Both sides forswore terrorism and renounced the goal of overthrowing each other's government. The pact also called for a "phased reduction in armaments." Officials on both sides described the pact as a first step toward what they termed the inevitable reunification of Korea. On December 31 the two Koreas initialed an agreement banning nuclear weapons on the peninsula. However, provisions for ensuring compliance remained to be settled.

The new treaty culminated a year of high-level negotiations and also of increasing contacts between the two Koreas. Earlier in the year, the South Koreans eased their ban on

*A Kuwaiti desalination plant, wrecked by Iraqi sabotage, was just one of many damaged structures that needed rebuilding after the war, as Kuwait faced a reconstruction effort projected to cost billions of dollars.*

travel to the North somewhat, and students were emboldened to suggest new avenues of contact with their northern counterparts, such as inviting North Korean delegations down to watch sports festivals at southern universities. Meanwhile, combined North-South ping pong and soccer teams competed in international sports events.

*See* STATISTICS OF THE WORLD.     D.N.C.

**KUWAIT.** Liberated from Iraqi occupation in February 1991 by a U.S.-led multinational force in Operation Desert Storm, Kuwait went on to face severe economic, environmental, and reconstruction problems.

**Liberation.** Allied and Kuwaiti air forces began Operation Desert Storm with attacks on Iraqi military targets in occupied Kuwait on January 17. The Iraqis set fire to two refineries and an oil field and released oil from Kuwait's Sea Island Terminal into the Persian Gulf. The resulting oil slick forced the Iraqis to close two of Kuwait's four desalination plants. Coalition forces at first concentrated on targets in Iraq, although the allies liberated Qurah Island on January 24 and stopped the oil spill from Sea Island Terminal two days later. By early February, however, American B-52 bombers and battleships were attacking targets in the emirate. As the air war progressed, coalition forces concentrated on targets near the al-Jaber air base and increased pressure on Iraqi defensive lines. Iraqi forces retaliated by sabotaging Kuwaiti oil wells, initiating a new reign of terror on Kuwaiti citizens, and attempting to destroy Kuwait City.

On February 22, Marines crossed into Kuwait and penetrated Iraqi front lines, paving the way for the massive ground assault that began two days later. Syrian, Egyptian, Saudi, Kuwaiti, and American forces encountered little resistance. The allied advance prompted a massive Iraqi withdrawal as soldiers sought to flee Kuwait City in any vehicle available. After a two-day tank battle around Kuwait International Airport, Kuwait City was liberated on February 27.

The early days of liberation were chaotic as water and electricity were shut off and food was in short supply. Small pockets of Iraqis staged periodic attacks on Kuwaiti forces. Iraqis and suspected Iraqi sympathizers who

After the liberation of their country, Kuwaiti officials accused hundreds of people, such as these prisoners in a Kuwaiti courtroom in June, of collaboration with the Iraqi occupiers. The initial proceedings came under heavy international criticism for their legal deficiencies and harsh sentences.

were captured became early victims of retaliation from Kuwaitis.

Crown Prince Sheikh Saad al-Abdullah al-Salem al-Sabah arrived in Kuwait City on March 4 to assume his duties as martial law administrator. The next day Iraq announced that its annexation of Kuwait was void and that all Kuwaiti assets seized during the war would be returned. On March 14, Emir Jabir al-Ahmad al-Sabah returned.

**Cease-Fire and Security Arrangements.** After hostilities ceased, American troops occupied a 120-mile-long, 9-mile-wide cease-fire line between Iraq and Kuwai. The 1,440-person UN

Iraq-Kuwait Observation Mission (Unikom) replaced American troops in May, although about 1,500 U.S. soldiers remained in the emirate afterward.

Efforts to form an Arab security force to protect Kuwait after liberation collapsed. In September the United States and Kuwait signed a ten-year security pact that granted American access to ports and provided for storage of military equipment and joint military exercises. Kuwait and France signed a similar agreement in October.

**Reconstruction.** While most movable property had been carted off to Iraq, the country did not suffer major damage to its infrastructure. The U.S. Army Corps of Engineers restored electricity and water by the end of March. Kuwait International Airport reopened in June, and the main commercial port of Shuwaikh received its first shipments in August. By far the greatest damage was inflicted on Kuwait's oil industry, as over 700 oil wells were set ablaze by the Iraqis. By November all of the fires had been extinguished, although large oil lakes remained an environmental hazard. Oil production resumed in June. Exports reached 600,000 barrels per day by year's end, but Kuwait continued to import refined products since its refineries remained inactive.

Economic recovery was slowed by the general lack of capital, in part because of the large-scale Iraqi looting of banks and treasury reserves. The final cost of reconstruction was estimated to be $20 billion.

**Social Reconstruction.** Reports of human rights violations began in March with detentions, expulsions, and accusations of police and civilian brutality against the country's 400,000 resident Palestinians and other non-Kuwaiti Arab residents suspected of having collaborated with the Iraqi occupiers. Government officials indicated an intention to limit the number of non-Kuwaiti resident Arabs to about 80,000 and began to register all foreigners. Large-scale deportations, violating terms of the cease-fire agreement, began with the expulsion of approximately 1,000 people, some against their will. The government finally agreed to allow the Red Cross to monitor deportations, let deportees take their personal property with them, and let non-Kuwaiti Arabs who had remained in the country during the occupation take personal possessions and withdraw retirement savings accounts if they left the country. Meanwhile, the government barred entry to all non-Kuwaiti residents of the emirate, including 5,000 Bedoons (a stateless population who made up the lower class of the emirate) who were living in a refugee camp on the Iraqi border.

Trials of 630 people held on collaboration charges began on May 19 before martial law courts. In the earliest cases tried, no evidence was presented, no witnesses testified, the accused did not have access to lawyers, and no appeals were permitted. Furthermore, the sentences were excessive (in one celebrated case, a man was sentenced to 15 years imprisonment for wearing a T-shirt depicting Saddam Hussein). The procedural abuses were addressed in later trials, but the sentences remained harsh; 29 death sentences were issued, including 6 for journalists who worked for an occupation newspaper. International condemnation eventually led the government to commute all the death sentences and outlaw the indefinite detention of political prisoners.

**Domestic Upheaval.** Demands for political reforms that predated the invasion were resumed in the weeks following liberation, when various opposition groups organized under the umbrella of the Kuwaiti Democratic Front. In March public pressure resulted in the resignation of the government of Crown Prince Sa'ad. The resignation was celebrated by pro-democracy demonstrations in violation of martial law and a refusal by 96 political and business leaders to serve in any government until a date had been set for free parliamentary elections.

In April the emir announced that elections would be held during 1992 and that consideration would be given to revising the law restricting citizenship to literate males over 21 years of age whose families had lived in Kuwait before 1920. The opposition demanded even earlier elections and restoration of the 1962 constitution, which gave Parliament the right to censure the government and dismiss the prime minister. A new government was formed on April 20, but it differed only slightly from the previous one.

*See* STATISTICS OF THE WORLD.     C.H.A.

# L

**LABOR UNIONS.** The recession in the United States colored many of organized labor's activities in 1991. The unions saw some legislative victories, but lost on their opposition to a free-trade pact and on job protection for striking workers.

**Legislative Issues.** AFL-CIO supporters in Congress introduced a "workplace fairness" bill prohibiting the hiring of permanent replacements during strikes over wages and other economic issues. Employers have had the right to permanently replace economic strikers since a 1938 Supreme Court decision, but labor cited a 350 percent increase in the practice during the 1980s. The House passed the bill in July by a vote of 246 to 182, well below the two-thirds majority needed to override a promised presidential veto, effectively killing the measure.

Another legislative concern was the pending free-trade agreement with Mexico. In testimony before Congress, AFL-CIO Treasurer Thomas R. Donahue urged rejection of fast-track authority for the agreement. (Fast-track authority bars Congress from amending trade accords; legislators must either accept or reject them.) Labor opposed the proposed pact primarily because of experience with the *maquiladora* system, in which U.S. and other foreign firms have established plants in Mexico near the U.S. border. Low-wage Mexican workers use components and raw materials brought in duty-free to assemble finished goods, which are then shipped to the United States for sale. Despite labor's opposition Congress approved the measure in May.

Labor did see passage of a measure extending jobless benefits for workers and of a new civil rights law. The civil rights bill allowed victims of intentional job discrimination to sue for monetary damages applied to dismissals and promotion (not just hiring) and for compensatory and punitive damages. The unemployment insurance bill provided workers who had been jobless for 26 weeks with up to 20 additional weeks of compensation.

**Legal Developments.** In March the Supreme Court ruled unanimously that unions enjoyed broad protection from lawsuits by members dissatisfied with the outcome of labor-management negotiations. In another unanimous opinion, the Court upheld the National Labor Relations Board's rule-making authority in creating eight bargaining units in acute care hospitals. The American Hospital Association had pressed for broader, fewer groupings, which labor saw as an attempt to weaken unions. In June a narrow 5-4 majority ruled that employers did not have to take a dispute to arbitration as called for in a union contract after the contract has expired.

In an out-of-court settlement of two lawsuits, the Continental Can Corporation agreed to pay 3,000 present and former members of the United Steelworkers a record $415 million in pension benefits. The workers claimed that company officials had conspired to manipulate plant closings so that workers were laid off just before they became eligible for pension benefits. The case had dragged through the courts for ten years. Another long-standing labor-management battle ended in January when bankrupt Eastern Airlines finally shut down. A bitter 22-month strike by the machinists union, supported for the first eight months by the pilots and flight attendants, had helped seal the fate of the airline. In October the pilots gained a victory when the Supreme Court let stand a lower court ruling that the carrier had wrongly refused to reinstate hundreds of pilots after the Airline Pilots Association ended their strike. The award could come to nearly $75 million, but whether or not the pilots will collect—and how much—depends on other pending court cases and on the disposition of Eastern's assets as determined by the bankruptcy court.

**Leadership Changes.** In February President George Bush appointed a new secretary of labor, Lynn Martin, former five-term Republican congresswoman from Illinois. Martin replaced Elizabeth Dole, who had resigned. At the AFL-CIO convention in November, Lane

The freight stopped moving on railroads across the United States when members of 11 rail unions, including these strikers in Cicero, Ill., went out on strike on April 17. The prospect of national paralysis was averted when Congress quickly passed back-to-work legislation.

Kirkland and Thomas R. Donahue were re-elected to their seventh two-year terms as president and treasurer, respectively. In some other major changes, James R. Herman retired as president of the International Longshoremen's and Warehousemen's Union, to be replaced by David Arian. Nick Serraglio was elected president of the Allied Industrial Workers Union, succeeding Dominick D'Ambrosio. The United Transportation Union elected Thomas DuBose president, deposing Fred Hardin, who had led the union since 1979. And insurgent Ronald Carey, head of a local in Queens, N.Y., won 48 percent of the votes in a three-way race to replace William J. McCarthy as president of the International Brotherhood of Teamsters. The election was supervised by a federal court as part of the settlement of an antiracketeering suit brought against the union by the Justice Department.

**Mergers and Separations.** In an unusual reversal of the recent pattern of union mergers, Local 1199 separated amicably from the Retail, Wholesale, and Department Store Union effective January 1. Local 1199, which represents about 65,000 health care workers, wanted to devote all its energies toward organizing solely in that field.

**Collective Bargaining.** In June the U.S. jobless rate rose to 7.0 percent, as against 5.2 per-

cent in June of 1990, and average weekly earnings, adjusted for inflation, were 2.2 percent lower in April than one year earlier. Unions negotiated wage increases during the first quarter averaging 4.5 percent in the first contract year and 3.4 percent annually over the contract term. Data compiled by the Bureau of Labor Statistics in March showed that union workers retained a wide advantage in total compensation over nonunion employees. On average, union workers earned $19.77 an hour in pay and benefits, compared with $14.57 for nonunion workers. For blue collar workers the total compensation for union workers was $21.12 an hour, while for nonunion workers it was $12.40.

Bargaining was conducted in many areas, and most agreements were reached without major strikes. The Teamsters ratified a new master agreement in May that provided a total $2.50 per hour increase in pay and benefits for about 150,000 workers over a three-year period. Job security, safety, and equipment improvements were also part of the agreement. The International Ladies Garment Workers Union negotiated new contracts for 100,000 workers, gaining a 12 percent wage increase over three years. Unions representing 65,000 workers at General Electric negotiated a new three-year contract providing a pay increase o

3.5 percent in the first year, 2.25 percent in the second and third years. GE also agreed to discuss plant closings, transfer of work, and subcontracting decisions.

Unions representing some 560,000 U.S. Postal Service employees went to arbitration to obtain a four-year contract that included cost of living raises and a four-stage general wage increase totaling 5.8 percent by November 1993. The panel gave management more flexibility in hiring part-time workers and permission to hire new workers at 10 percent below the current starting wage. A nationwide rail strike by 230,000 workers in April was ended after one day by a federal back-to-work order that required a cooling-off period followed by a resumption of negotiations between management of the major railroads and the heads of the rail unions. By December three smaller unions had signed contracts with the employers. Caterpillar Inc., the heavy machinery company, closed two plants in Illinois after 8,000 United Autoworkers members went out on strike in November.

**International Activities.** The important role played by the AFL-CIO and its affiliated unions in providing technical assistance to his country's emerging free trade unions was acknowledged by Boris Yeltsin, president of the Russian republic, in a visit to Washington in June. The American labor delegation to the International Labor Organization Conference in Geneva, Switzerland, worked to stop employer groups from diluting the effectiveness of the ILO. In response to a complaint filed by the AFL-CIO with the ILO's Committee on Freedom of Association in 1990, the ILO's governing body rejected the practice of hiring permanent replacements for strikers.

**Union Membership.** At the AFL-CIO's biennial convention in November it was announced that membership in the 89 unions affiliated with the federation had increased by 377,000, to 13,933,000 from the 13,556,000 reported at the 1989 convention. The unions making the greatest membership gains in the two years since the last convention were the Service Employees, whose membership climbed by 119,000 to 881,000; the American Federation of State, County, and Municipal Employees, which increased by 101,000 to

1.19 million; and the American Federation of Teachers, which increased by 29,000 to 513,000.                                        G.B.H.

**LAOS.** The major political event in Laos during 1991 was the convening in March of the Fifth Congress of the Lao People's Revolutionary (Communist) Party. Former General Secretary Kaysone Phomvihan, 71, was elected party chairman. Nouhak Phongsavan, 77, was reconfirmed as number two on the Politburo. Souphanouvong and Phoumi Vongvichit, both 82, formerly third and fourth on the Politburo, stepped down to a newly designated "Advisory Board of the Party Central Committee." Disturbed by the collapse of Communism in Eastern Europe and the Soviet Union, the Lao party leadership indicated it would follow Vietnam and China in asserting the party's right to rule without competition, although Kaysone pledged to continue the drive to establish a free-market economy.

A draft constitution was adopted by the Supreme People's Assembly in August, 15 years after the founding of the Lao People's Democratic Republic. Following promulgation of the constitution, the SPA named Kaysone president, and he was then replaced as prime minister by General Khamtay Siphandone.

Laos continued to sustain a growing independence from its former mentor, Vietnam. By contrast, the influence of Thailand was rapidly increasing, largely through an expanding commercial role. Agreements were reached to permit the shipment of Lao agricultural goods into Thailand without import tax, to withdraw Lao and Thai troops from disputed areas, and to ensure the cooperation of Thailand in limiting resistance activities against Laos from refugee camps in Thailand.

Rapprochement with China continued. In January, Nouhak Phoungsavan, as chairman of the Supreme People's Assembly, met with Chinese President Yang Shangkun and Prime Minister Li Peng to discuss improvement of relations and an increase in trade, and a joint Lao-Chinese technical team was engaged in demarcating the common border. Meanwhile, Soviet interest in Laos was fading.

Lao relations with the United States improved. Early in the year, President George Bush agreed to the certification of Laos as eligible to receive U.S. economic aid, following two years of decertification because of the country's failure to meet minimum U.S. standards for control of narcotics production and trafficking. Laos continued to cooperate in the search for information about missing American airmen from the Vietnam War.

See STATISTICS OF THE WORLD.          J.J.Z.

**LATVIA.** More than five decades of Soviet rule—which began when the Soviet Union was allowed to annex Latvia in 1940 as part of the Hitler-Stalin nonaggression pact—ended in August 1991 with Latvia's formal declaration of independence. Unlike Lithuania, its Baltic neighbor to the south, Latvia had not proclaimed its independence in 1990, indicating instead that a transition to full independence was in progress.

Latvia's go-slow attitude spared it Soviet military reprisals, but Latvian nationalists did face armed pressure as the independence movement gained strength in 1991. Four people were killed in January in a Soviet attack on government buildings in Riga, the capital, and later in the year Soviet authorities destroyed what they regarded as illegal customs posts.

The leaders of the short-lived August coup against President Mikhail S. Gorbachev's government in Moscow found some of their most enthusiastic supporters in Latvia's Communist Party. But the Latvian government and its leader, Anatolijs Gorbunovs, staunchly opposed the coup, which had barely collapsed before Latvia declared its independence on August 21. The European Community extended diplomatic recognition six days later, and the Soviet government followed suit on September 6. On September 17, Latvia joined the United Nations.

One of the most difficult issues facing Latvia was the problem of who should qualify for citizenship. Only 52 percent of Latvia's population were ethnic Latvians; most of the rest were Russians who arrived after the Soviet annexation. In some large cities, including Riga, Russian-speaking people actually outnumbered ethnic Latvians. After considering various proposals, the Latvian Parliament passed a measure in October that granted full citizenship to ethnic Latvians and offered other residents the right to apply for naturalization before July 1992, but only if they had lived in Latvia for 16 years and could communicate in the Latvian language.

See STATISTICS OF THE WORLD.          L.T.L.

**LEBANON.** With Beirut reunited under their joint control after peaceful evacuation by rival militias, Syrian-backed President Elias Hrawi, a Maronite Christian, and Prime Minister Omar Karami, a Sunni Muslim, started 1991 ready to recover more of Lebanon's territory as part of the 1989 Taif peace plan for putting a permanent end to the civil war that began in 1975. With Muslims and Christians represented in equal numbers and seven militia heads included, the 30-member cabinet received a parliamentary vote of confidence on January 9, albeit by a slim margin because of its reputedly pro-Syrian orientation.

**Government Advances.** On January 29, during the Persian Gulf War, fighting between Israel and the Palestine Liberation Organization (PLO) broke out in Israel's self-declared security zone in southern Lebanon. Pro-Iraqi guerrillas fired unguided rockets at northern Israel, but these may have fallen instead in the security zone in southern Lebanon. Israel retaliated by heavily attacking Palestinian sites north of the security zone. When the operation ended on February 7, Lebanese government troops moved into the area for the first time in 15 years, taking over positions formerly held by the PLO.

In March the government ordered the disarmament of all Lebanon's militias. Most turned in their heavy armaments by the May 1 deadline, making possible the deployment of government troops in roughly one-quarter of Lebanon: north and south of Beirut along the coast and toward the southeast in the Shuf Mountains. The government then established its control over the southern coastal region of Sidon by forcibly disarming and disbanding some 6,000 PLO guerrillas on July 4. In October, Iran was reported to have decided on a phased withdrawal of its approximately 1,500 Revolutionary Guards, who had been stationed in eastern Lebanon since 1982.

**Relations With Syria.** A cooperation treaty signed on May 22 provided official Syrian recognition of Lebanon as a separate and independent state for the first time since the end of

*After complex negotiations, several hostages long held in Lebanon gained their freedom. Above, former U.S. hostages (left to right) Joseph Cicippio, Terry Anderson, and Alann Steen celebrate their release. At right, former Archbishop of Canterbury Robert Runcie (left) greets Terry Waite, who originally went to the Middle East as the archbishop's special envoy.*

French rule in 1943. In addition, the two countries agreed to coordinate their foreign, economic, defense, and internal security policies. A second accord, signed in September, was alleged by its critics to give Syria virtual control over Lebanon's internal affairs. It authorized each country to act against any military or political activities within its borders that could threaten the other country and allowed the security forces of each to arrest and prosecute "criminals" in the other.

**Increasing Tensions.** In May, Israel had sent additional tanks and infantry to its security zone in southern Lebanon, reportedly in reaction to Lebanon's cooperation pact with Syria. Even after the Lebanese government disarmed PLO forces in early July and was on its way to bringing southern Lebanon under its control, a long-standing Israeli condition for withdrawal, Israel continued to deploy troops in the area.

As Lebanon prepared for the Mideast peace conference on October 30, the government's decision to participate remained controversial, and the level of tension and violence in the country intensified. Most of the violence was centered around southern Lebanon, as mem-

231

bers of Hezbollah, the militant Shiite militia, stepped up hit-and-run raids inside the Israeli security zone. In response, Israel attacked guerrilla targets inside the zone and to the north. After the government participated in a second round of peace talks, held in Washington, D.C., in mid-December, a car bomb was set off in Beirut, killing 20 people.

**Release of Aoun.** On August 29, General Michel Aoun, the renegade Christian leader who had been ensconced in the French embassy in Beirut since the defeat of his forces in October 1990, left with two aides for France. As he left, France unfroze $45 million in economic aid to Lebanon.

**Release of Hostages.** Associated Press correspondent Terry Anderson, the last of the American hostages held by extremists in Lebanon, was released on December 4. Five other Americans, four Belgians, three Britons, and a Frenchman had already been let go in 1991. The bodies of two American hostages were returned in December. Two West Germans were thought to be the only remaining Western hostages. Meanwhile, in exchange for confirming the deaths or returning remains of missing Israeli soldiers, Israel freed 91 Lebanese and Palestinian guerrillas and returned the remains of others.

The releases resulted from complex negotiations mediated by the United Nations secretary-general and involving the governments of Iran, Israel, and Syria. Since the first was abducted in 1984, a total of 17 Americans were taken hostage in the Middle East.

See STATISTICS OF THE WORLD.          J.A.P.

**LESOTHO.**  See STATISTICS OF THE WORLD.

**LIBERIA.**  Although a fragile truce continued to hold during much of 1991, the civil war that had beset Liberia since 1989 still seemed a long way from resolution.

After a number of false starts, the two major actors in Liberia's conflict, interim President Amos Sawyer, backed by the West African peacekeeping force, and Charles Taylor, the main rebel leader of the National Patriotic Front of Liberia (NPFL), agreed in June to hold elections under international supervision. The Economic Community of West African States (Ecowas), which established the peacekeeping force, gave the agreement its backing in July.

A further agreement on the disarmament of each faction was arrived at in a mid-September conference, but elections, which were originally to take place by the year's end, were postponed.

Interim President Sawyer was steadily gaining legitimacy in the world community. In June, for example, the Organization of African Unity chose to seat Sawyer at its annual summit meeting, rejecting Taylor's two delegates. Because of his military strength, Taylor, whose NPFL forces controlled most of Liberia outside Monrovia, had much to lose as a result of progress toward a negotiated settlement. Observers speculated that his new willingness to negotiate was motivated by a loss of backing from Libya, which was apparently supplying him with arms through Burkina Faso. Taylor had also depended heavily on U.S. financial support, which dwindled as sentiment grew in favor of disarmament and free elections.

In March, a group of NPFL rebels and Sierra Leonean malcontents attacked Sierra Leone territories along the Mano River. The Sierra Leone army, bolstered first by a contingent of Guinean troops and then by 1,200 Nigerians, retook many of the large border towns in May, and the conflict dragged on throughout the year.

The civil war in Liberia was taking an incalculable toll in human suffering. Some 10,000 persons were killed in the two years of the conflict, and estimates of the number of refugees ranged up to 700,000. The economy also suffered serious dislocation. For example, no banks were operating in Liberia from July 1990 until mid-June of 1991, when the first of 13 banks reopened its doors. Liberia's banks were all looted by one armed group or another, but those thefts were small compared to the wholesale looting of the Liberian treasury by the country's former leader, Samuel Doe, whom the rebels had overthrown and killed in 1989.

See STATISTICS OF THE WORLD.          G.L.

**LIBRARIES.**  Although U.S. libraries in 1991 suffered from financial constraints, some were able to expand facilities or offer new services to readers.

**Advocacy and Activism.**  Designated the "Year of the Lifetime Reader" by Librarian of

Congress James H. Billington, 1991 was marked by a major yearlong campaign launched by American librarians to foster literacy and the love of reading.

The campaign also was an occasion to promote public and political support for libraries at a time of dwindling or threatened government funding. At the annual summer conference of the American Library Association, held in Atlanta, the keynote speaker, Reverend Jesse Jackson, criticized what he characterized as the federal government's weak commitment to libraries. A "Rally for America's Libraries" caravan left Atlanta on July 4, two days after the conference ended, and traveled on to Washington, D.C., stopping in several cities along the way.

President George Bush's 1992 budget proposal cut federal funding for libraries by more than 75 percent, with most of the library money he did request earmarked for literacy programs. Much of this cut, however, was restored by Congress, which also passed a Literacy Act, providing $1.1 billion over four years for a wide range of literacy efforts.

In July, 697 delegates gathered in Washington, D. C., for the second White House Conference on Libraries and Information Services. The proposals adopted included establishment of an office within the Department of Education to promote school and public library services for children and funding of a proposed National Research and Education Network, which would link scholars via computer.

**Fiscal Challenges and Physical Changes.** San Francisco voters approved a $105 million bond issue to finance a new central library. Among other communities planning new library facilities were Tulsa, Okla.; Jacksonville, Fla.; Naperville, Ill.; and Loudoun County, Va. Two large library systems completed major expansions of their central facilities. Chicago opened a new 750,000-square-foot neoclassical structure, and the New York Public Library completed an underground extension of its elegant central building, adding 121,500 square feet of storage.

Almost everywhere, however, frugality was the watchword. In New York, the three public library systems serving the city's five boroughs suffered sharp cuts in staffing, services, and

hours. Sacramento, Calif., postponed the opening of its new central library, citing budget problems; Newport, R.I., nearly lost its bookmobile, which was finally saved by a donation from the Ben & Jerry's ice cream company; and many other public and academic libraries endured hiring freezes or budget cuts.

**Reagan Library.** The $60 million Ronald Reagan Presidential Library in Sun Valley, Calif., was dedicated in November at a ceremony attended by all four living U.S. ex-presidents. The 153,000-square-foot facility, the largest of the ten presidential libraries, contains 47 million documents and 22,000 square feet of exhibition space. It was paid for by private funds, after Stanford University rejected a plan to build it there.

**New Services.** Many interesting service initiatives were reported. For example, the Buffalo and Erie County Public Library staff offered to select books for children younger than 12 that time-stressed parents could pick up on the way home from their jobs. In California the Monte-

*The New York Public Library, one of the largest research libraries in the United States, found more space for its rapidly growing collection by opening a stack extension beneath the lawn of adjacent Bryant Park. When fully utilized, the facility will almost double the library's previous storage capacity.*

rey County Free Libraries offered special services for migrant farm workers and their families, including library orientations and summer reading programs. And the Baltimore County Public Library coproduced, with the Baltimore Coalition for the Homeless, a "street card" for homeless adults—a pocket-sized pamphlet listing helpful agencies and programs.

**Controversies and Closings.** In *Kreimer v. Morristown*, a federal district court ruled that the Joint Free Library of Morristown and Morris Township (N.J.) had violated the rights of a homeless man by barring him on the basis of policies the court found too vaguely and broadly worded. These included rules against "noisy or boisterous behavior" and body odor "so offensive as to constitute a nuisance to other persons."

Many librarians criticized a decision by the Carnegie Corporation of New York to give its rich archives and a $470,000 endowment to Columbia University. In 1990, Columbia had created a furor by announcing the 1992 clos-ing of its School of Library Service, one of the oldest and most distinguished in the United States. Meanwhile, Brigham Young University announced that its library school would close as of 1993. M.B.

**LIBYA.** In 1991, Libya continued its efforts to lessen the country's diplomatic isolation. Efforts to improve relations with the West had limited success.

Libyan leader Muammar al-Qaddafi tried to maintain a neutral position during the Persian Gulf crisis. Initially playing peacemaker, he offered a plan to resolve the dispute. Qaddafi criticized Iraq's Scud missile attacks on Israel and blamed Saddam Hussein for opening the door to a western military presence in the region. During the crisis oil prices surged temporarily, and Libya also briefly increased its daily oil production.

Qaddafi's posture during the Gulf crisis was partly attributable to the restraining influence of Egypt, with which relations continued to improve. On March 28, Qaddafi drove a bull-

*The Great Manmade River, an immense pipeline project to bring water from Saharan wells to Libya's coastal cities, prompted wet and wild rejoicing when Libyans frolicked in the project's reservoir at Surt as Libyan leader Muammar al-Qaddafi inaugurated the second phase of construction in September.*

dozer into a customs post at the Egyptian border and declared that there would no longer be a border between the two countries. Qaddafi hoped a union with Egypt would lend his regime respectability and offer access to Egyptian labor and technology. Egyptian President Hosni Mubarak was notably less enthusiastic about uniting the two countries, though an alliance would offer investment opportunities and provide an outlet for a burgeoning population. To some extent Libya's blossoming relationship with Egypt also came at the expense of its ties with Algeria, Mauritania, Tunisia, and Morocco, its partners in the Arab Maghreb Union.

Libya's relations with Chad improved after the overthrow of Hissène Habré's pro-Western regime in December 1990. Idriss Déby, the new Chadian president, was widely believed to have received assistance from Libya in the takeover. However, the dispute over the status of the mineral-rich Aozou Strip, claimed by Chad but occupied by Libya, remained unresolved. In addition, Déby refused to hand over to Qaddafi some 600 former Libyan soldiers trained by the United States in a covert plan to destabilize the Libyan regime.

Relations with the West showed little improvement. The United States renewed economic sanctions for 1991, citing Libyan support of international terrorism. Britain reiterated that relations would not improve until Libya renounced terrorism. On the other hand, Roland Dumas, the French foreign minister, visited Tripoli in April, and in June, Italian Prime Minister Giulio Andreotti made an official visit.

In midyear, the U.S. Central Intelligence Agency linked Libya to the explosives used to destroy a Pan Am Boeing 747 over Scotland in December 1988 and a French DC-10 over Chad in September 1989. In October a French judge issued arrest warrants for four Libyan officials, and the United States later issued indictments against two suspects. The United States and Britain demanded that Libya turn over the suspects in the Pan Am bombing and compensate the victims' families. Libya at first denied involvement in either bombing, then said that suspects in the Pan Am bombing would be tried in Libya.

See STATISTICS OF THE WORLD.    A.D.

LIECHTENSTEIN. *See* STATISTICS OF THE WORLD.

**LIFE SCIENCES.**    Research published in 1991 included new discoveries about causes of various genetic defects and about sounds made by different animals.

## *BIOLOGY*

New studies uncovered information about the biochemical and genetic underpinnings of many diseases in humans and explored new approaches to gene therapy.

**Alzheimer's Disease.**    Evidence continued to accumulate that Alzheimer's disease, the most common cause of memory loss and dementia in the elderly, may be caused by the abnormal processing of a brain protein called amyloid. In February, John Hardy, Alison Goate, and their colleagues of St. Mary's Hospital in London announced they had found a genetic defect on chromosome 21 shared by two families suffering from an inherited form of Alzheimer's disease. Several more afflicted families with the identical mutation were reported later in the year by other researchers.

The defect resided in the gene for the amyloid precursor protein. This precursor protein gives rise to fragments of beta-amyloid protein that accumulate in numerous plaques in the brains of Alzheimer's disease patients. The chromosomal location of the defect was particularly telling because people with Down syndrome, who are born with three copies of chromosome 21, also exhibit mental deficiencies and abundant amyloid plaques. Although the specific defect is not a universal cause of Alzheimer's disease, its discovery hinted that changes in the amyloid precursor protein or in the system of enzymes that normally cleave it to produce beta-amyloid might be sufficient to cause some cases.

In April biochemist Eugene Roberts and his coworkers of the City of Hope Medical Center in California began to tie the effects of beta-amyloid to the neurological deficits of Alzheimer's disease. By injecting beta-amyloid into the brains of mice, the researchers showed they could cause the mice to forget maze-learning tasks that they had recently learned. Neil W. Kowall of the Massachusetts General Hospital, Bruce A. Yankner of Children's Hospital in Boston, and their colleagues carried the proof still further with a report published during August. Using rats, they demonstrated that injections of beta-amyloid caused the death of cells in the hippocampus, a brain center crucial to memory. Furthermore, this damage could apparently be prevented by first injecting the animals with substance P, a chemical that carries signals between nerve cells. Because it resembles a portion of the beta-amyloid molecule, substance P may be able to protect vulnerable brain cells by binding with them, thereby shutting out interactions with the more dangerous beta-amyloid.

In July researchers at California Biotechnology and the Miles Research Center of Bayer AG announced independently that they had successfully inserted genes for human beta-amyloid protein into mice. The mice developed plaques of the protein in their brains similar to those seen early in human Alzheimer's disease, although it was not clear that the mice suffered any analogous losses of mental acuity.

**Cystic Fibrosis.** In February two groups of researchers, led respectively by Michael J. Welsh of the University of Iowa College of Medicine and by John R. Riordan of the Hospital for Sick Children in Toronto, identified precisely how the malfunctioning of a key protein in the cells of cystic fibrosis patients causes the disease. Cystic fibrosis is a disorder that makes breathing perilously difficult; the problem is linked to a flaw in the cystic fibrosis transmembrane conductance regulator (CFTR) protein. As the new research showed, CFTR normally acts as a self-regulating channel that governs the flow of chloride ions through the cell membrane. In cystic fibrosis the protein is defective, which causes an imbalance in the concentrations of ions inside and outside cells. As a result, mucus produced by the body becomes dangerously thick and collects inside the lungs, leading to destructive inflammation. CFTR is the first discovered example of an ion channel that controls its own activity.

**Other Genetic Defects.** In June the gene responsible for fragile X syndrome, the most common inherited form of mental retardation, was discovered by C. Thomas Caskey of the Baylor College of Medicine and his collaborators. Late in the year, teams of scientists in

*A technician feeds a pig that, as a result of genetic engineering, can produce human hemoglobin, the oxygen-carrying component of blood. The breakthrough may make it possible for pigs to serve as living factories that produce a substitute for human blood.*

### Whistle Blower

In spring 1986, Margot O'Toole, a researcher at the Massachusetts Institute of Technology, reported suspicions that her supervisor, Thereza Imanishi-Kari, had falsified important scientific data. O'Toole's suspicions centered on a groundbreaking paper coauthored by Imanishi-Kari and four other microbiologists, including Nobel laureate David Baltimore, published in the scientific journal *Cell*. A panel of eminent scientists commissioned by the National Institutes of Health at first found no evidence of wrongdoing. But after an investigation by a congressional subcommittee, the NIH panel reopened its probe. In a 1991 draft report, panelists concluded that crucial data had indeed been falsified. Imanishi-Kari protested her innocence, and the report had to go through a complex review.

After O'Toole challenged Imanishi-Kari's research, and eventually left her position, she had difficulty for a long time finding a job in her field. But the 39-year-old Irish-born researcher now works at Genetics Institute, a biotechnology firm, on research relating to the immunology of breast cancer.

*Margot O'Toole*

France and Australia announced they had developed tests to show whether prospective parents carry this gene.

Meanwhile, Francesco Ramirez of the Mount Sinai School of Medicine in New York City and his colleagues in the United States, Japan, and France found a gene that produces a defective version of fibrillin, a structural protein, in patients with a congenital disorder related to Marfan's syndrome, an abnormality in connective-tissue development that can lead to serious heart and vision problems. Harry C. Dietz and his team at Johns Hopkins University also described two cases of people who developed Marfan's syndrome itself because of spontaneous mutations in their fibrillin genes.

**Gene Therapy.** New experiments in which genes were inserted into human subjects to cure diseases were undertaken during the year. In January, Steven A. Rosenberg and his colleagues at the National Cancer Institute began experiments in which genes for tumor necrosis factor, a cancer-killing protein produced by the body, were inserted into white blood cells called tumor infiltrating lymphocytes. The modified cells were then returned to the four cancer patients who donated them in the hope that these cells would be more efficient at destroying tumors. In yet another gene therapy trial, which started in October, Rosenberg removed tumor cells from cancer patients, inserted genes for either tumor necrosis factor or interleukin-2 (an immune response booster) into the cells, then returned them to the patients. The modified cells may excite a greater immune response against all tumor cells—in effect, acting as an antitumor vaccine.

In April a gene therapy technique with potential applications for treating cystic fibrosis emerged. Ronald Crystal, a director of the National Heart, Lung, and Blood Institute, announced that his laboratory had placed a functioning human gene into the lung cells of laboratory rats. The standard gene therapy techniques, involving the insertion of genes into blood cells that are then returned to the donor, could not have accomplished that end.

The small bats known as microbats (above) employ echolocation—the use of ultrasound to orient themselves and locate prey. Megabats (right) do not. This difference has led some biologists to the controversial hypothesis that the two types of bats are not related in the way once thought but have evolved from different ancestors.

Instead, Crystal and his coworkers altered an adenovirus, a virus of the type that causes the common cold, so that it would introduce the human gene when it infected cells in the respiratory system. The gene with which Crystal's group worked manufactured the protein alpha-1-antitrypsin, deficient in many people with a hereditary form of emphysema. The same technique could theoretically cure cystic fibrosis by introducing a working copy of the gene for the defective CFTR protein.

**Transgenic Animals.** At the World Congress on Cell and Tissue Culture in June, researchers at the DNX Corporation of Princeton, N.J., announced they had created three genetically engineered pigs that produced human hemoglobin, the iron-based pigment that carries oxygen inside red blood cells. There were hopes that hemoglobin could serve as a substitute for blood in emergency situations, since it can be stored at room temperature for months and infused into any patient, regardless of blood type. "Transgenic" pigs carrying the gene for human hemoglobin could function as living factories, producing huge volumes of the molecule without the need for human donors. DNX also reported a technique for purifying the human hemoglobin from the swine blood—a step as critical as creating the transgenic animals. Many questions remain, however, about whether the purified hemoglobin would be safe. FDA permission is required before human trials can begin.

**Virus Synthesized.** Biologists from the State University of New York's Stony Brook campus announced in December that they had synthesized the polio virus in a test tube by mixing human cell proteins and polio virus genetic material. This was the first time an entire virus had been created outside of living cells. The achievement should make it possible for scientists to look at how viruses put their components together and eventually to develop methods for blocking the replication of disease-causing viruses.                                J.R.

**BOTANY**

Among other topics, botanical research focused on iridescent plants and on the use of plant oils as replacements for some petroleum products in industry.

**Iridescent Fruit.** Iridescence is not an unusual trait for bird and butterfly wings, but it is rare in higher plants. One exception is the iridescent blue fruit of the tropical tree *Elaeocarpus angustifolius*. A blue color in fruit is usually due to anthocyanin pigment, but ripe *E. angustifolius* fruit has none of this pigment. Instead, according to a recent report, the skin of the ripe fruit contains iridosomes, stacks of fibers of the right thickness to reflect blue light.

The reason for this rather complex replacement for a pigment is actually rather simple. A bright color is useful because it attracts animals that, in eating the seed-containing fruit, aid in seed dispersal. But if the color were due to blue pigment, the pigment would absorb most of the light used in photosynthesis, the process by which the plant traps the energy in sunlight. Since photosynthesis in fruit can contribute significantly to the plant's energy supply, and since *E. angustifolius* must compete for sunlight in the dense growth of the tropics, it benefits from having iridescent fruit that can continue to photosynthesize when ripe, even under shady conditions.

**Plant Oils.** Plants use the sun's energy to make not only sugars but also oils. Besides the familiar edible oils produced by corn, olive, and peanut plants, oils that could be of industrial use are produced by wild plants that have yet to be exploited commercially. A recent study noted that if oils from plants such as *Crepis foetida* or those of the Flacourtiaceae family could be produced as efficiently as edible oils, they could replace petroleum products in the manufacture of many chemicals. Also, genetic engineering of plants could lead to plant production of useful oils. Sunflowers produce an oil—oleic acid—in large quantities. A single genetic alteration could allow the sunflower to convert some of its oleic acid to ricinoleic acid, an extremely versatile oil that has numerous industrial uses.      M.C.F.

## ZOOLOGY

Among other things, zoologists studied echolocation by bats, rumbling by rhinos, and purring by cats.

**Wall Bangers.** Hitting one's head against a wall is considered the essence of futility, but for mole rats of the "super species" *Spalex ehrenbergi* it is like using the telephone. These mole rats are blind and live in underground tunnels they have excavated, relying on scent and vocalization to communicate. But those senses function only over short distances. To communicate at a distance, the mole rats use wall banging, thumping their flattened heads against the tunnel walls. New research from Israel shows that they do not so much hear these messages as feel them through their skin. The exact receptor system involved has not been identified, but such "seismic sensitivity" is found in other mammals and in insects, amphibians, and reptiles. In the mole rats head banging seems to be a rather precise method of communication. Each of the four species in *S. ehrenbergi* has its own thumping rhythm, which may help prevent mating between individuals of different species. Wall-banging may also serve as a territorial signal, thus helping mole rats to avoid overcrowding, competition for food, and aggression.

**Crying Bats.** The small bats known as microbats use echolocation with ultrasound as a means to orient themselves and to locate prey: the sound waves bounce off the victim and indicate its location. Experiments on stationary microbats have shown that producing ultrasonic cries requires a lot of energy. If the energy costs of flying are added to those of echolocating, it would seem that searching for prey is an energy-expensive activity. However, new experiments on the costs of echolocation during flight show that the energy expended when the two activities are done simultaneously is not additive. Since the microbat must breathe to get the oxygen needed to power flight muscles, it can use the exhaled air pulses to carry its ultrasonic cries.

If this two-for-one deal makes echolocating so economical, why don't all bats take advantage of it? Most of the bats classified as "megabats" do not use echolocation, except for a crude form employed by one group of cave-dwelling megabats. This has led some biologists to the controversial idea that bats did not all evolve from the same ancestral species. Some researchers have maintained that the visual system of megabats has traits similar to those found in primates and have contended that megabats are an early offshoot of the primate family tree. Other scientists have used the similarity between the nerve patterns in the wings of microbats and megabats to argue for a common ancestor.

**Purring Cats.** Everyone has heard a cat purr, but no one has come up with an adequate explanation for how the sound is made. New research indicates that the vocal folds above the larynx, not the vocal cords, are involved. This would explain why cats can purr and meow at the same time. The purring sound results from the oscillation of the vocal folds as the cat inhales and exhales. Meowing, on the other hand, occurs only during exhalation, when the vocal cords vibrate. According to the research, the diaphragm and the muscles between the ribs do not seem to be necessary for purring. (The work of other scientists, however, disputes this point.) Most of the new research was done on domestic cats, and it shows that the characteristic purring sound remains the same as a cat gets older and that the sound is unrelated to weight, sex, and size. Less thorough research on cheetahs and pumas suggests that the same mechanism is involved in purring in these wild cats.

**Rumbling Rhinos.** The rumble is an animal sound of such low frequency that humans cannot hear it. Whales communicate by rumbling; elephants do too. The latest animal to be added to the rumbling list is the rhinoceros. Individuals from four rhino species were tested, and all rumble; they also make audible moans and grunts. Elephants use rumbles to communicate over long distances, and researchers suspect that rhinos do the same. Even where the rhino population density is very low, groups of female white rhinos can be found in the same vicinity, perhaps drawn by beckoning rumbles.

**Insect Invasions.** While the British and the French are working on the tunnel under the English Channel, biologists continue their studies, begun in 1987, of the tunnel's environmental impact. They recently reported the presence of a new spider species in Great Britain near the tunnel entrance: *Minicia marginella*. The species is common in northern Europe but had never before been seen in Britain. Since both a male and female were found, the spider may become a permanent resident rather than just a "tourist."

Across the Atlantic, biologists are studying another insect traveler, *Aedes albopictus*, an Asian mosquito species that recently arrived in the United States. This species grows well in water-filled tree holes or old tires and probably entered the country in used automobile tires imported from Asia. In Houston, where it was first spotted in 1985, it has already become the dominant mosquito species in artificial containers. This is particularly worrisome because *A. albopictus* can transmit serious diseases, such as dengue fever. To help predict how much of a problem this mosquito might become, researchers studied the competition between *A. albopictus* and the native American mosquito species usually found in water containers and tree holes, *A. triseriatus*. The native species held its own in tree holes but was wiped out by the newcomer in water-filled tires, thus indicating that competition from native mosquitoes will not be able to prevent the permanent establishment of *A. albopictus* in the United States.

**Red Wolves.** An interesting finding emerged from genetic analysis of the endangered red wolf (*Canis rufus*). Studies on mitochondrial DNA from captive animals, from blood samples gathered in the 1970s, and from museum specimens collected between 1905 and 1930 indicated that the red wolf may not be a distinct species, as has been assumed, but instead may merely be a hybrid between the gray wolf and the coyote. (Its recognition as a separate species has long been controversial.) This could pose a problem for conservationists because the U.S. Fish and Wildlife Service (USFWS) does not grant protection to hybrids. The researchers who did the genetic analysis argued that the captive population of red wolves seem to be similar to the wolves that once existed in the southeastern United States and should be reintroduced into the wild. The USFWS released the first such wolves at Alligator River National Wildlife Refuge, an island reserve in North Carolina, in 1987. Since then, researchers have established additional small populations on islands off South Carolina, Florida, and Mississippi. In November 1991, four red wolves were set free in Great

Smoky Mountains National Park, the first release on the U.S. mainland.

**Sibling Rivalry.** Sibling rivalry is common in many animal species, including humans. Among spotted hyenas (*Crocuta crocuta*), however, the competition can be fatal. Female hyenas usually give birth to twins, and researchers found that the first-born twin often attacked the second shortly after birth with bites to the neck and back. If the twins were of the same sex, the fighting was more severe and usually resulted in the death of one of the siblings. Such "siblicide" is common in predatory birds, but this was the first reported case in mammals.

Two factors make such behavior possible. First, spotted hyenas are well developed at birth, with fully erupted teeth and good coordination; they are ready for a fight. Also, female spotted hyenas usually give birth at the entrance to a den, often an abandoned aardvark burrow, which is too small for the mother to enter. The infants have to emerge to nurse, so the dominant sibling can prevent its rival from nursing. The resultant starvation, combined with wounds, leads to the weaker sibling's death.

But what advantage is there to this type of behavior? Spotted hyenas have a hierarchical social system in which rank affects reproductive success. For a female, elimination of a sister means the removal of a future competitor for rank—and thus for access to males. For a male, large size is an advantage in gaining rank, so elimination of a brother means more food available for growth.                  M.C.F.

**LITERATURE,** The year 1991 saw the publication of many new works by both both distinguished and lesser-known authors.

### AMERICAN

There were interesting books of poetry and criticism in 1991, as well as several fine literary biographies, but fiction—especially quite long novels—grabbed most of the headlines.

**Novels and Short Stories.** Norman Mailer has never been a minimalist; he likes space to move around in. Even by his standards, though, his new novel, *Harlot's Ghost,* is massive: it checks in at 1,334 pages and ends with the words "TO BE CONTINUED." In this novel Mailer attempts to tell the secret history

of the Central Intelligence Agency and, through it, the true history of our times. Reactions varied: Anthony Burgess praised its ambition and scope in the Washington *Post*, while Louis Menand in the *New Yorker* shredded it as bloated and pretentious.

Similar uncertainty accompanied the reviews of Harold Brodkey's long-awaited personal epic, *The Runaway Soul.* For 30 years Brodkey has been highly praised, partly for his short stories but mainly for this novel, versions of which previously circulated in manuscript to distinguished critics, editors, and writers. When *The Runaway Soul* finally appeared in 1991, notices were generally respectful, if somewhat muted, but a few were savage, principally because the book is a sequence of relentless self-analyses. Each chapter examines a typical moment of crisis in the life of Wiley Silenowicz and then squeezes every possible meaning out of the event.

*Critics were divided over the merits of Norman Mailer's hefty new novel,* Harlot's Ghost. *Some praised the 1,334-page tome's scope; others found it pretentious and were dismayed by its ominous final phrase: "TO BE CONTINUED."*

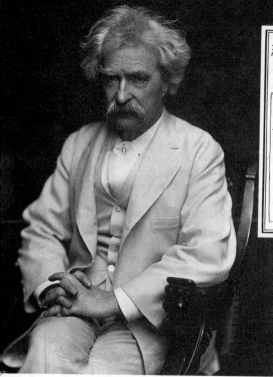

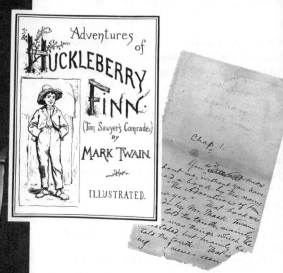

*Missing for over a century, the first half of Mark Twain's original manuscript for Huckleberry Finn, widely considered the greatest American novel, was found in a trunk in an attic in California. The manuscript, different from the published text in places, gives scholars an illuminating look at the evolution of Twain's style.*

The third big power hitter of the season was Don DeLillo's *Mao II*, the latest from a writer who has grown from a coterie favorite to one of the most admired novelists active today, mainly for his cutting edge focus on such matters as terrorism, conspiracy, media manipulation, and absurd violence. The main character in *Mao II* is a reclusive novelist named Bill Gray who stops cocooning only to land in the middle of a terrorist plot. With a downbeat ending, the novel teaches the dire lesson that "the future belongs to crowds."

John Barth remains one of the best American novelists. In *The Last Voyage of Somebody the Sailor*—the tale of a modern American who finds himself caught up in the world of the Arabian Nights—he displays his trademark wit and taste for fantasy, sexy encounters, sly political relevance, and linguistic exuberance. Another demanding novel, albeit one that nearly everyone praised, was Richard Powers's *The Gold Bug Variations*. Powers, a novelist in his early thirties and author of two well-received previous books (*Three Farmers on Their Way to a Dance* and *Prisoner's Dilemma*), managed to pack computer science, love affairs, and the secret of consciousness, as well as much else, into this tale of a pair of researchers who try to understand why a young genius suddenly chucked his career to spend his life in a dead-end job. Equally ambitious, Mark Helprin's *A Soldier of the Great War* recasts the European historical novel as it depicts an old Italian nobleman who looks back on his life, reflecting on the vanished pomp of yesteryear, the sweetness of youth, lost love, and the horrors of the 20th century.

Anne Tyler brought out her latest novel, *Saint Maybe*, to great popular success, though critics suggested it was not her best work. Set in Baltimore as usual, *Saint Maybe* is a novel about responsibility: after he causes the death of his brother and sister-in-law, a young man gives up his career dreams to take charge of the orphaned children. Eventually, he is led into a mission church, where he finds new meaning to his life. Up there with Tyler in the beloved writer category, Amy Tan could hardly hope to equal the runaway success of *The Joy Luck Club*. But her second novel, *The Kitchen God's Wife*, matches some of the flavor of the first book, relating magical tales of love and life in China, of daughters, mothers, and grandmothers. Meanwhile, Louis Begley's *Wartime*

*Lies*, an original and affecting novel about the Holocaust, was considered for several major awards.

Russell Banks has written gritty novels of the way Americans live now (*Continental Drift*) and brilliant pastiches of 17th-century prose (*The Relation of My Imprisonment*). In *The Sweet Hereafter*, he takes on a subject as brutal as any in the newspaper: a school bus crash that kills or maims nearly all the children in a small New England town. Jane Smiley's *A Thousand Acres* also evokes small-town life, as she retells the story of King Lear and his three daughters, updating the tragedy to Iowa farm country. Surprisingly the conceit works, as Smiley shows how a once-proud all-American clan gradually falls apart when the patriarch announces that he is divvying up the land.

A brighter, happier evocation of American life can be found in Garrison Keillor's *WLT: A Radio Romance*. A behind-the-scenes history of a small Minnesota radio station from the late 1920s to nearly the present, the book is as filled with characters as a high school stadium at the homecoming game.

When it comes to depicting the lingo of the land, the argot of the disc jockey or bail bondsman, Stanley Elkin is a master. In *The MacGuffin*, Elkin creates an aging commissioner of streets in a town much like St. Louis who, in the course of a day, makes love to a beautiful woman, stumbles onto a mystery surrounding the murder of a young Lebanese exchange student, remembers his courtship of his wife, nearly loses his job, and, chastened by events, finally comes home. Equally adept at catching the talk on the street are Pete Dexter and Elmore Leonard. Dexter's *Brotherly Love* depicts the seamy side of Philadelphia, in the tale of two cousins caught up in union corruption and violence. Elmore Leonard's *Maximum Bob* focuses on a corrupt judge and the good and evil characters who surround him.

Regarded as an "experimental" writer, Gilbert Sorrentino also possesses perfect pitch for the way language is flattened out in ordinary talk. In *Under the Shadow* he offers a spare, poetic text, made up of two-page or three-page sections with enigmatic leitmotivs, such as a woman, only partly clothed, glimpsed through a window leaning over a sink.

In the short-story field, Marianne Wiggins issued a fine collection, *Bet They'll Miss Us When We're Gone*. Michael Chabon, author of *The Mysteries of Pittsburgh*, returned with *A Model World and Other Stories*, a likeable collection of tales about mildly disaffected youth. The 90-year-old Nina Berberova—a Russian émigré to the United States—found herself newly celebrated when her long stories, collected as *The Tattered Cloak*, were translated into English and praised for their evocation of the shadowed world of Russian exiles in Paris. Fred Chappell brought out *More Shapes Than One*, witty, learned stories of the fantastic and down-home.

The most eagerly awaited science fiction novel of the year was probably *The Difference Engine*, by William Gibson and Bruce Sterling. Gibson and Sterling imagine an alternate 19th century in which Lord Byron has become prime minister and scientists have invented a primitive computer, the "difference engine" of the title.

**Nonfiction.** Perhaps the year's most electrifying book was *The Journals of John Cheever*, edited by Robert Gottlieb, drawn from the pocket notebooks of the late novelist and short-story master. Cheever presents himself as an all-too-human being, adulterous, homosexual, alcoholic, self-pitying.

Every year there's a John Updike book, sometimes two. This season belonged to *Odd Jobs*, his fourth collection of essays, addresses, and reviews. Once again, cavils and caveats notwithstanding, Updike shows himself to be just as good a literary journalist as he is a novelist. In *Patrimony* another admired novelist, Philip Roth, focuses his gifts on portraying the last days of his father. In *Broken Vessels*, short-story writer Andre Dubus speaks movingly about the accident that cost him a leg (he was helping a stranded motorist).

Perhaps the finest literary biography of the year was Brian Boyd's *Vladimir Nabokov: The American Years*, a follow-up to *The Russian Years*, which traces with scholarly passion and artistic exactness the career of this admired prose stylist.

**Poetry.** Two of the most widely noticed books of the year—John Ashbery's *Flow Chart* and Philip Levine's *What Work Is*—espouse

It was a banner year for Australian writer Elizabeth Jolley. Among other things, her ninth novel, Cabin Fever, won the Australian Natives Association Literature Award, and the first book-length critical study of her works was published.

radically different notions of poetry. Ashbery practices a gnomic autobiographical verse, nearly impenetrable at times but woven of beautiful word music. Levine prefers simple, clear lines that movingly evoke the lives of the poor, the disenfranchised, the forgotten.

**Prizes.** The 1991 Pulitzer Prize in fiction went to John Updike for *Rabbit at Rest*; Mona Van Duyn won the poetry Pulitzer for *Near Changes*. The National Book Critics Circle honored Updike's *Rabbit at Rest* in the fiction category and Amy Gerstler's *Bitter Angel* in poetry. The 1991 National Book Award was won by Norman Rush's *Mating* in fiction and Philip Levine's *What Work Is* in poetry; a special National Book Foundation Medal for Distinguished Contribution to American Letters was awarded to Eudora Welty. The PEN-Faulkner award went to John Edgar Wideman's *Philadelphia Fire*. M.D.

## AUSTRALIAN

Many fine works of literary criticism and biography were published in Australia during 1991, as well as some good novels and collections of poetry by established writers.

**Nonfiction.** A great publishing success story was David Marr's revealing biography *Patrick White: A Life*, which benefitted from the access Marr gained to the Nobel Prize-winning novelist. Geoffrey Dutton's *Kenneth Slessor: A Biography* is an excellent life of Australia's first great modernist poet. David Martin's autobiography, *My Strange Friend*, depicts the respected novelist, journalist, and poet's eventful career. Colin Roderick, the editor of the short-story writer and poet Henry Lawson's collected works, published *Henry Lawson: A Life*. Another noted turn-of-the century literary figure, Ada Cambridge, is commemorated in two biographies: Audrey Tate's *Ada Cambridge: Her Life and Work 1844-1926* and Margaret Bradstock and Louise Wakeling's *Rattling the Orthodoxies: A Life of Ada Cambridge*. And the first book-length critical study of Elizabeth Jolley's novels, *Elizabeth Jolley: New Critical Essays*, was edited by Delys Bird and Brenda Walker.

Several distinguished poets also received critical attention. Alison Hoddinott wrote *Gwen Harwood: The Real and the Imagined World*. Michael Griffith reestablished Francis Webb's stature as a major poet in *God's Fool: The Life and Poetry of Francis Webb*, and S. Walker published *Flame and Shadow: A Study of Judith Wright's Poetry*.

A radical assessment of Australian literature appeared in the Australian Cultural Studies series. Nearly half of Bob Hodge and Vijay Mishra's *Dark Side of the Dream: Australian Literature and the Postcolonial Mind* deals with aboriginal texts and issues, while John Docker tracks back and forth between Australian, British, and American literature and intellectual history in *The Nervous Nineties: Australian Cultural Life in the 1890s*.

**Fiction.** Thomas Keneally's *Flying Hero Class* is an action-packed thriller about an aircraft hijack. *The Tax Inspector* by Peter Carey, though received less warmly by critics than his previous works, is still a highly competent novel. *Cabin Fever*, Elizabeth Jolley's moving sequel to *My Father's Moon*, chronicles the life and hard times of a woman on her own. *Mates of Mars* by David Foster delves into the martial arts to explore Australian male culture. Jack Hibberd's comic *Life of Riley* follows a similar theme. In contrast, Rod Jones's *Prince of the Lilies* is a cerebral novel about an Australian archaeologist and his family in Crete. In *The Second Bridegroom*, Rodney Hall continues his preoccupation with Australian history and its relevance to Australians.

**Poetry.** Bruce Beaver's *New and Selected Poems*, Rosemary Dobson's *Collected Poems*, and A. D. Hope's *Orpheus* were especially strong. Other books of note included Les Murray's *Collected Poems* and Mark O'Connor's *Firestick Farming: Selected Poems 1972-90*.

**Awards.** Australia's most prestigious literary prize, the Miles Franklin Award, went to David Malouf for the novel *The Great World*. The Barbara Ramsden Award went to Gerald Murnane's book of short stories, *Velvet Waters*. Novelists Glenda Adams and Tim Winton shared the National Book Council's Banjo Award for fiction, Adams for *Longleg* and Winston for *Cloudstreet*. The Banjo Award for nonfiction went to Drusilla Modjeska's *Poppy*. Murray's *Dog Fox Field* won the poetry award. I.K.

### CANADIAN

Canadian writing in 1991 reflected Canadians' current anxiety and disillusionment.

**Nonfiction.** "Inside/Outside," Mordecai Richler's detailed article about Québec's language laws in the September 23 issue of the *New Yorker*, inflamed several prominent French-

*With his first novel,* Lives of the Saints, *31-year-old author Nino Ricci of Toronto (right) won the Governor-General's Award, Canada's most coveted literary prize.*

Canadian journalists and sparked editorials protesting or supporting Richler's portrayal of anti-Semitism in the province.

More than 30 biographies and books on current affairs were released in the fall, most of them marked by a lack of faith in Canada's political leadership. Nationalist Mel Hurtig's angry denunciation *The Betrayal of Canada* attacked the Conservative government of Brian Mulroney and big business for selling out the national interest, a theme vigorously pursued by Linda McQuaig in *The Quick and the Dead*. Mulroney's own background was laid bare in John Sawatsky's painstaking biography, *Mulroney: The Politics of Ambition*, and the lives of Canadian prime ministers' wives were traced by Heather Robertson in *More Than A Rose: Prime Ministers, Wives, and Other Women*.

With *Merchant Princes*, Peter C. Newman completed his three-volume history of one of Canada's most fabled institutions, the Hudson's Bay Company. The business interests controlling Canada's national sport were revealed in *Net Worth: Exploding the Myths of Pro Hockey* by David Cruise and Alison Griffiths. One of their main targets was Alan Eagleson, who defended his record as an agent for stars like Bobby Orr in *Power Play*.

**Fiction.** Two of Canada's best-known writers, Margaret Atwood and Robertson Davies, published new works. Davies's novel *Murther and Walking Spirits* is narrated by a deceased journalist who has been murdered by his wife's lover. Compelled to attend a phantasmagorical film festival that documents his forebears' lives, the narrator-spirit learns much about the shape of his own. *Wilderness Tips*, Atwood's third collection of short stories, presented ten pieces immediately recognizable for the spare and deadpan style that Atwood deploys in her stark revelations of contemporary mores. These stories, many of them set in Toronto, often depicted isolated women reflecting on the progressive diminution of their lives.

Other noteworthy fiction included Rohinton Mistry's first novel, *Such a Long Journey*, nominated for England's Booker Prize. Mistry, originally from India and now living in Toronto, vividly evoked the tortuous existence of a Bombay bank clerk. Alberto Manguel's first novel, *News From a Foreign Country Came*, explored the paradoxes that allow a seemingly civilized man to torture his fellow human beings. And Margaret Sweatman's first novel, *Fox*, was an evocative recreation of the social and historical climate of the Winnipeg General Strike of 1919.

**Poetry.** A welcome contribution to the standard editions of major poets was Zailig Pollock's two-volume edition of A. M. Klein's *Complete Poems*. Klein, a Jewish Montrealer, was the first Canadian writer to draw both on his Jewish heritage and on his Canadian experience. Roy Miki's first collection, *Saving Face: Poems Selected 1976-1988*, attested to his talent for drawing on his Japanese-Canadian background to create memorable images. Language poet bill bissett's new book, *hard 2 beleev*, won the 1990 Milton Acorn People's Poet Award. At a far remove from bissett's playful experiments with the vernacular, Louis Dudek's *Continuation II* and Ralph Gustafson's 32nd book of poems, *Shadows in the Grass*, were the latest contributions of two of Canada's most venerable men of letters. And the strong tradition in Canadian poetry of drawing on experiences abroad continued with works like Jan Conn's *South of the Tudo Bem Café*, and Lake Sagaris's *Circus Love*.

**Awards.** The Governor General's Awards went to Nino Ricci for *Lives of the Saints* and Gérald Tougas for *La mauvaise foi* (fiction), to Margaret Avison for *No Time* and Jean-Paul Daoust for *Les cendres bleues* (poetry), to Ann-Marie MacDonald for *Goodnight Desdemona (Good Morning Juliet)* and Jovette Marchessault for *Le voyage magnifique d'Emily Carr* (drama), and to Stephen Clarkson and Christina McCall for *Trudeau and Our Times* and Jean-Francois Lisée for *Dans l'oeil de l'aigle* (nonfiction).

Children's literature (text) winners were Michael Bedard for *Redwork* and Christiane Duchesne for *La vraie histoire du chien de Clara Vic*. The illustrators' prizes for children's books went to Paul Morin for *Orphan Boy* (text by Tololwa Marti Mollel) and Pierre Pratt for *Les fantaisies de l'oncle Henri* (text by Bénédicte Froissart).

**Obituary.** Northrop Frye died in Toronto on January 23 at the age of 78. He was the most

*The surprise winner of the 1991 Booker Prize, Britain's top fiction award, was* The Famished Road, *Nigerian-born author Ben Okri's story of an African spirit child with magical powers.*

widely known and cited critic of his time and Canada's most eminent educator. Frye published his first major work, *Fearful Symmetry,* a study of William Blake, in 1947; other works include *Anatomy of Criticism* (1957) and his two-part study of the Bible in Western literature, *The Great Code* (1982) and *Words With Power* (1990). *The Double Vision: Language and Meaning in Religion* was published posthumously.                                 N.K.B.

### ENGLISH

In 1991, Great Britain's most prestigious fiction award, the Booker Prize, went to the Nigerian-born Ben Okri for his novel *The Famished Road,* about a spirit child in a world where vision and reality are indistinct. Among the other final nominees for the Booker were Martin Amis's *Time's Arrow,* Roddy Doyle's *The Van,* and Rohinton Mistry's *Such a Long Journey.* Several noteworthy literary biographies also appeared.

**Novels.** Stylish, cool, and clever, Julian Barnes in *Talking It Over* unfolded his tale of amorous betrayal between friends through the medium of three ironically self-justifying monologues. In its stark portrayal of the brutal realities of war in the Far East, Timothy Mo's *The Redundancy of Courage* (another final nomi-

nee for the Booker Prize) also employed a three-section structure, effectively communicating the contrasted experience of invaders, conquered, and guerrillas.

In her moving novel *Regeneration,* Pat Barker, too, unflinchingly confronted the horrors of modern warfare. Set in 1917 and based on a real encounter in a war hospital near Edinburgh, it explored the developing relationship between the protesting officer-poet Siegfried Sassoon and a psychiatrist who treated him and became his friend.

Penelope Lively in *City of the Mind* and Maggie Gee in *Where Are the Snows* shared a common interest in the time theme. But whereas Lively alternated her central, contemporary narrative with excursions back into the past—from the experiences of an Elizabethan seaman to those of an air-raid warden in the London blitz—Gee moved forward to the year 2007 and the destruction of the ozone layer in the atmosphere.

Anita Brookner's *A Closed Eye* was perspicacious and stylistically elegant, yet bleak in vision, as it probed the sensibility, relationships, and ironies of existence for Harriet, Brookner's shrinking, immature heroine. Fay Weldon's collection of short stories *Moon Over Minne-*

247

apolis abounded in oppressed wives suffering from brutal, unfaithful, or otherwise unsatisfactory partners. In Angela Huth's *Invitation to the Married Life* various contrasted marriages were anatomized with acerbic ironical wit. Also humorously shrewd, Nina Bawden in *Family Money* portrayed a spirited elderly widow inconveniently resisting filial pressure to sell her desirable Regency residence and distribute the proceeds.

In *Wise Children*, her first novel in seven years, Angela Carter moved away from her past realm of mystery and magic into theaterland—from music-hall song and dance to Shakespeare. The picturesque narrative flowed with a racy verve. Susan Hill published a novel after a still longer silence. *Air and Angels*, set in the Edwardian era, portrayed the emotional turmoil that erupts when a respected, elderly Cambridge cleric falls passionately in love with a young girl on vacation from India. Related by a disdainfully snobbish narrator, Margaret Forster's *The Battle for Christabel* introduced issues of class and color surrounding conflict over the future of an orphan child.

The impressionistic style of Jennifer Johnston's *The Invisible Worm* cleverly conveyed the schizophrenic dislocation of the heroine's mind, ceaselessly revolving between the present and a past that contained the terrible source of her inner conflict and sickness. Another distinguished Irish writer, William Trevor, depicted self-delusion as the common failing of a pair of lonely heroines in his *Two Lives*, as each fled from arid reality into the comforting safety of a fantasy world of naive romanticism. In William Cooper's *Immortality at Any Price*, the satirical targets included his fellow writers, wordy academics, publishers, literary agents, and young men fighting their way ruthlessly to the top. Set in Florence over 40 years ago, Francis King's *The Ant Colony* cast a coolly disenchanted eye over its Anglo-American expatriate community and an institution closely resembling the British Council, the independent organization that promotes the English language and British culture in dozens of countries.

**Biography.** In *Constance Garnett: A Heroic Life*, Richard Garnett offered a warmly affectionate portrait of his grandmother, the redoubtable translator who introduced great Russian literature to the English reading public. Equally meticulous, Jane Emery's *Rose Macaulay: A Writer's Life* penetrated to the fears, guilt, and griefs of the vulnerable girl and woman hidden behind a facade. *Samuel Butler*, by Peter Raby, illuminated Butler's continuing conflict with his father, authority, and Victorian values, as well as his influence on modern consciousness.

Robert Bernard Martin's *Gerard Manley Hopkins: A Very Private Life* was arguably the outstanding literary biography of the year. It offered a shrewd yet compassionate portrait of of this Jesuit priest for whom—as one reviewer put it—"the lure of earth always threatened to match the appeal of heaven." Martin was the first scholar to have had full access to Hopkins's surviving private papers.

Among autobiographies, the *Memoirs* of Kingsley Amis proved an embarrassment: full of sourness and spleen, their rancorous acrimony extended to include those the author named as friends as well as his many acknowledged foes. M.W.

## WORLD

On the international literary scene in 1991, the fiction selected for translation into English imaginatively projected social and political failures and hopes in transitional times.

**Czech.** *Love and Garbage* (*Laska a Smeti*, 1990), a novel by the noted writer Ivan Klima, reflects the dilemma of how to live a moral life in a disjointed world. The narrator steps from his ivory tower and takes a street cleaner's job to gain drastically new perspectives. The novel *Mendelssohn Is on the Roof* (*Na Strese je Mendelssohn*, 1960) by Jiri Weil is the posthumously published legacy of a Czech Jew who escaped death with the help of those hiding him in Prague during the German occupation; with black humor he records what those days were like.

**French.** Jean Raspail's *The Blue Island* (*Ile bleue*, 1988) takes as its canvas the life of old and young refugees in coastal France while occupied by the Germans after 1939. Claude Simon, who won the Nobel Prize in literature in 1985, takes a look at reformism in the Soviet Union and has a dim view of events and persons in his novel *The Invitation (L'Invitation*, 1953); a mordant satire, it compares the Soviet nation to a rouged corpse.

**German-Austrian.** A bouquet of 12 masterly stories by the late Marie Luise Kaschnitz is collected in a volume called *Circe's Mountain*. *Pigeons on the Grass (Tauben im Gras*, 1951) is a belated but welcome translation of a novel by Wolfgang Koeppen that paved the way for postwar German novels to explore the nightmare years of Hitler with honesty and artistic intelligence. Gert Hofmann's growing reputation is enhanced with his novel *Before the Rainy Season (Vor der Regenzeit*, 1988), which dramatically portrays the hidden life of a typical German war criminal hiding in Bolivia. *Precision and Soul*, literary and journalistic essays translated for the first time from novelist Robert Musil's *Gesammelte Werke*, offers sprightly and incisive views on European arts and politics between 1911 and 1937.

**Hebrew.** Translated from diverse languages but mainly from the Hebrew by I. M. Lask, *Mimekor Yisrael: Classical Jewish Folktales* is the most comprehensive and best-edited anthology of its kind to date. In Amos Oz's latest novel, *To Know a Woman (La-daat ishah)*, an Israeli intelligence officer is torn between the realistic necessity for his job and his psychological disinclinations; the inner dialogue is intense.

**Japanese.** *Monkey Brain Sushi: New Taste in Japanese Fictions* is a lively roundup of stories that irreverently expose the dilemmas of contemporary Japanese life: work mania, selected censorship, and change of traditional ways. Another anthology, *Unmapped Territories*, edited by Yukiko Tanaka, concentrates solely on new women's fiction surfacing in Japan.

**Russian.** Anatoly Naiman's cultural biography *Remembering Anna Akhmatova (Rasskazy ob Anne Akhmatova*, 1989) recounts in depth the life and times of a legendary lyric poetess and the tragic fate of the Russian elite among whom she made her mark. Yury Tynyanov, an important scholar and fiction writer, deserves rediscovery for his novellas *Lieutenant Kije (Podporuchik Kizhe*, 1927) and *Young Vitushnikov (Maloletny Vitushnikov*, 1933); both are historical fictions based on the difficult times intellectuals faced under the czarist regime

during the 17th and 18th centuries. Valentin Grigor Rasputin belongs to the so-called Russian village prose school. His post-Stalinist novel *Farewell to Matyora (Proshchanie s Materoi*, 1976) depicts the impact of industrialization on Siberian villagers in a haunting and humanly touching way.

**Spanish.** Probably the most intriguing recent title belongs to the experimental novel *The Palace of the White Skunks (El palacio de las blanquisinas*, 1980) by the Cuban exile writer Reinaldo Arenas. The hero experiences different lives under assumed names, each threatened by psychological chaos. No palace or refuge is in sight. A Spanish feminist writer highly regarded by critics, Esther Tusquets demonstrates her considerable skill in her psychological novel *Stranded (Varada tras el ultimo naufragio*, 1980), which uses a stream of consciousness technique to engage readers in the lives, loves, betrayals, and reconciliations of couples on the Costa Brava scene.       S.M.

## BOOKS FOR CHILDREN

Children's books, the fastest-growing segment of U.S. publishing, became a billion-dollar industry in 1991. As has always been true, many of the sales came from the backlist of books published in previous years. But the frontlist, the new children's books, offered some truly spectacular titles.

**Picture Books.** Changes in printing technology and striving on the part of publishers for the best possible reproduction of artwork have led to a picture book explosion, with every art medium being explored.

Using cut-paper collage, Sara chronicled the wordless story of a lone figure moving through dark streets in *Across Town*. In *Tar Beach*, Faith Ringgold created from one of her magnificent story quilts a tale about a young African-American girl in New York City. Arthur Geisert used his etchings to perfection in a one-word picture book, *Oink*, presenting the antics of a group of young piglets.

Watercolor still remains the favorite medium of most picture-book artists. Allen Say used his traditional watercolor and ink to brilliant advantage in *Tree of Cranes*, relating the story of a young Japanese-American boy and his first Christmas in the United States. Petra Mathers presented a beautiful love story of two shy

# LITERATURE

Abuela takes my hand.
"Vamos," she says.
"Let's go."

Projections indicate that by the year 2000 a majority of American children will be nonwhite, and quality books about children from a variety of cultures graced publishers' lists in 1991. Abuela (above) recounted the adventures of a Hispanic girl and her grandmother, while Tar Beach (below) dealt with a black family in New York City.

Tonight we're going up to Tar Beach. Mommy is roasting peanuts and frying chicken, and Daddy will bring home a watermelon. Mr. and Mrs. Honey will bring the beer and their old green card table.

mice in *Sophie and Lou*. And Kevin Henkes, in one of his funniest books to date, explored in *Chrysanthemum* the trauma of a young mouse's first days at school.

**Novels and Short Stories.** Paula Fox wrote one of her most moving and harrowing books, *Monkey Island*, in which she made totally believable the plight of a homeless boy and the people he encounters on the streets. Paul Fleischman turned to 19th-century Ohio for the setting of *The Borning Room*, as he chronicled the life and death of a woman and of the world in which she lives. The ever-popular Beverly Cleary created a sequel to *Dear Mr. Henshaw* in her novel *Strider*. And James Marshall kept everyone laughing with his collection, *Rats on the Roof and Other Stories*.

**Books for Young Adults.** Robert Cormier's *We All Fall Down* provided a frightening look at the victims and perpetrators of random violence. Avi's *Nothing But the Truth* explored morality and truthfulness in the setting of a typical school. And Robert Lipsyte's *The Brave* presented the saga of Sonny Bear, a Native American boy who becomes a boxer in New York City, and his struggles to deal with his own anger and rage.

**Books of Information.** Innumerable books about Christopher Columbus and the Age of Exploration began to appear, the best of which, Peter Sis's *Follow the Dream*, presented a wonderful vision of the problems—and the perseverance—of the explorer. In *The Wright Brothers*, Russell Freeman revealed the determination that eventually resulted in the birth of flight. In a biography of a larger-than-life president, *Bully for You, Teddy Roosevelt*, Jean Fritz managed to capture Roosevelt's memorable dynamism and charisma.

Scholastic released *Ladybug and Other Insects*, *Colors*, *Weather*, and *Fruit*, a set of four books first published in France that use color acetate overlays to brilliant advantage. Knopf's attractive Eyewitness Series and Eyewitness Junior Series explored such subjects as reptiles, crystals and gems, crocodiles, and fish—all with fine color photography.

**Books for All Children.** Farrar, Straus and Giroux introduced a new line of Spanish-language books called Mirasol: Libros Juveniles. The first list included some classic titles for children—*Brave Irene* by William Steig, *Tuck Everlasting* by Natalie Babbitt, and *The Fool of the World and the Flying Ship* by Uri Shulevitz—as well as new books from the Farrar list. Other publishers began issuing not only backlist titles but also new titles in simultaneous Spanish and English editions.

Illustrator Caroline Binch made a spectacular debut in *Amazing Grace*, Mary Hoffman's book about a young black girl who eventually gets to play the part of Peter Pan. *Abuela* by Arthur Dorros, illustrated by Elisa Kleven, chronicled the adventures of a young Hispanic girl and her grandmother, who fly and soar over New York City.

**Awards.** The winners of the 1990 Newbery and Caldecott awards were announced in early 1991. The Newbery Medal was given to *Maniac Magee* by Jerry Spinelli. *The True Confessions of Charlotte Doyle* by Avi was the only Newbery Honor Book. The Caldecott Medal was presented to *Black and White* by David Macaulay. Caldecott Honor Books were "*More More More," Said the Baby* by Vera B. Williams and *Puss in Boots*, written by Charles Perrault, translated by Malcolm Arthur, and illustrated by Fred Marcellino. Coretta Scott King Awards went to Mildred D. Taylor (text) for *The Road to Memphis* and Leo and Diane Dillon (illustration) for *Aïda*.     A.S.

**LITHUANIA.** On September 6, 1991, 18 months after Lithuania declared its independence from the Soviet Union, the Kremlin recognized Lithuania as a separate state. Forcibly

*Vast crowds of mourners turned out in Vilnius, Lithuania's capital city, for the funeral of victims of a Soviet attack on a television tower in mid-January. The assault, which appeared to be the beginning of a crackdown by Soviet security forces, instead turned out to be the first in a succession of events during the year that paved the way to Lithuanian independence.*

incorporated into the Soviet Union as a result of the 1939 Hitler-Stalin nonaggression pact, Lithuania had long maintained that its annexation was illegal. The Soviet Union, for its part, sought to hold onto the Baltic states.

Moscow's campaign to quash the Lithuanian independence movement had taken a tragic turn in January 1991 when Soviet troops stormed the television tower in Lithuania's capital city of Vilnius, killing over a dozen people and wounding about 100. The troops claimed to be acting at the behest of a shadowy anonymous National Salvation Committee, a hastily formed group believed linked to Soviet security forces and the Lithuanian Communist Party. The incident only strengthened the people's nationalist resolve.

Despite worldwide expectations that the Soviet government would oust Lithuania's government and occupy the country, only a few skirmishes followed during the spring and summer. One of the worst incidents was a July 31 attack on what Soviet authorities regarded as an illegal customs post; at least seven people were killed in the incident. Two days earlier, in Moscow, Lithuanian President Vytautis Landsbergis had concluded a bilateral treaty with Russian Federation President Boris Yeltsin in which Lithuania was recognized as a sovereign state.

When the leaders of the August coup in Moscow against Gorbachev attempted to impose a state of emergency in Lithuania, the Lithuanian nationalist group Sajudis, along with the country's legislature, vowed to resist the hard-line Communists. The rapid collapse of the coup also marked the end of Soviet resistance to Baltic independence. The European Community extended diplomatic recognition to Lithuania, Latvia, and Estonia on August 27; the Soviet government followed suit ten days later. On September 17, Lithuania was admitted to membership in the United Nations.

International recognition came so swiftly that many problems arose. Eager to deny the authority of Soviet courts, the government issued certificates of exoneration to Lithuanians accused of war crimes after World War II. The process was suspended when Jewish organizations protested that some of those pardoned had aided the Nazis in the mass murder of Jews during the German occupation of Lithuania from 1941 to 1944. Lithuania admitted it had acted too hastily, and Landsbergis promised to establish an independent commission to review individual cases more carefully.

See STATISTICS OF THE WORLD. L.T.L.

**LOUISIANA.** See STATISTICS OF THE WORLD.

**LUXEMBOURG.** In 1991, Luxembourg assisted the anti-Iraq coalition in the Persian Gulf War by pledging $2 million in aid. The government also made available its airport facilities for the transit of supplies, troops, and war casualties.

With Premier Jacques Santer occupying the rotating presidency of the European Community during the first half of the year, Luxembourg also took a prominent role in negotiations toward treaties providing for closer political and economic unions of EC members. At a meeting of EC foreign ministers in June, the government presented a draft treaty on political union that envisaged strengthening and expanding the functions of the existing economic community. The European Parliament would gain the right to veto national laws in specified areas, such as environmental policy, and the European Court of Justice would be empowered to impose fines on governments violating EC law.

The Luxembourg proposal was temporarily put aside when the Netherlands assumed the EC presidency in the second half of the year and advanced its own plan. However, by October, EC leaders had reverted to the Luxembourg draft as the basis for negotiations toward the agreements concluded at the EC summit in December.

The Organization for Economic Cooperation and Development projected in July that Luxembourg's gross domestic product would grow about 2.9 percent over the 1990 figure. Industrial production was projected to advance by 1.5 percent. Stronger consumer purchasing power produced by tax reform measures was likely to expand private consumption by over 4 percent, while consumer prices were expected to increase by over 3 percent. Unemployment was forecast to increase only slightly, to 1.4 percent.

See STATISTICS OF THE WORLD. W.C.C.

# M

**MADAGASCAR.** *See* STATISTICS OF THE WORLD.

**MAINE.** *See* STATISTICS OF THE WORLD.

**MALAWI.** *See* STATISTICS OF THE WORLD.

**MALAYSIA.** Much of the political spotlight in 1991 was on economic planning and on state elections.

In June, Prime Minister Mahathir Mohamed and his cabinet introduced the New Development Policy (NDP), officially called the Second Outline Perspective Plan for 1991-2000, to replace the New Economic Policy, in effect since 1970. The NDP backs away from the previous emphasis on Malay ownership of companies and offers incentives to attract foreign investment. The projections are rosy: 8 percent growth per year through 2000, just about the 1991 rate.

Mahathir agreed to let his finance minister, Daim Zainuddin, resign and return to his corporate empire. Education Minister Anwar Ibrahim succeeded Daim in March. A Mahathir favorite, Anwar seemed a likely successor when the prime minister steps aside. One of Anwar's main rivals, Abdullah Ahmad Badawi, rejoined the cabinet as foreign minister. Another possible successor, Suleiman Daud, moved from the Ministry of Trade and Industry into the influential Ministry of Education.

The main opposition party in the state of Sarawak, the Sarawak Dayak Party, suffered serious losses in state legislative elections in September. The Malay-based United Indigenous People's Party won 27 seats in the expanded 56-seat legislature; it and two other parties made up the ruling National Front government in the state.

In May the United Malays National Organization made its electoral debut in a state by-election in the East Malaysian state of Sabah; it won the election. The UMNO has for a number of years been seeking to supplant the United Sabah National Organization as the representative of Malays in the state.

Strained relations between the federal government and the state government in Sabah continued. In January senior state officials, including Chief Minister Joseph Pairin Kitingan, were charged with corruption. In May, Pairin's brother, head of the powerful Sabah Foundation, was detained without trial under the Internal Security Act.

On August 14 the government announced that Pulau Bidong, probably the most well-known refugee camp for Vietnamese boat people, would be closed. More than 260,000 refugees had passed through the island camp on Malaysia's east coast since 1975. The 5,200 refugees remaining in the camp were to be transferred to another transit camp, near Kuala Lumpur.

*See* STATISTICS OF THE WORLD.      K.M.

**MALDIVES.** *See* STATISTICS OF THE WORLD.

**MALI.** *See* STATISTICS OF THE WORLD.

**MALTA.** *See* STATISTICS OF THE WORLD.

**MANITOBA.** *See* STATISTICS OF THE WORLD.

**MARSHALL ISLANDS.** *See* STATISTICS OF THE WORLD. *See also* PACIFIC ISLANDS.

**MARYLAND.** *See* STATISTICS OF THE WORLD.

**MASSACHUSETTS.** *See* STATISTICS OF THE WORLD.

**MAURITANIA.** *See* STATISTICS OF THE WORLD.

**MAURITIUS.** *See* STATISTICS OF THE WORLD.

**MEXICO.** In 1991, the government of President Carlos Salinas de Gortari projected a budget surplus and estimated the annual inflation rate at 19 percent, the lowest in 13 years. Gross national product grew at a relatively healthy rate. Mexicans even won first and second place finishes in two U.S. marathons, and Mexican beauty Lupita Jones was crowned as Miss Universe.

Almost forgotten were Mexico's chronic problems, including the poverty and squalor in which 40 percent of the population lives. Late in the year, President Salinas, in a state of the union address, referred to the "great dividing line" of poverty holding the country back and said that profits from the sale of government enterprises would be channeled toward social problems; he also called for dialogue with opposition leaders to correct "deficiencies" in the electoral process.

**Economy.** Wages remained low, while profits soared. Several banks, nationalized in 1982, were sold back to private investors; the price for a controlling stake in the largest, Banamex, was $3.2 billion. Purchase of a controlling interest in the telephone company brought in $1.76 billion. Windfall profits from oil exports as a result of the Persian Gulf crisis also brought in revenues. Efforts continued to negotiate a North American Free Trade Agreement with the United States and Canada, which, it was hoped, would bring in new industry, creating steady jobs for the underemployed 40 percent of the labor force.

**Foreign Relations.** A public relations campaign enhanced the country's image abroad, which in turn inspired domestic confidence in the government. Salinas met frequently with foreign leaders, traveling in Central America during January, visiting Canada in April and the United States in December, and hosting a meeting with Pacific Basin leaders during May. In July he made a European tour that took him on state visits to Germany, Czechoslovakia, the Soviet Union, Italy, and Vatican City, then hosted the first summit conference of Iberian-American nations. A bilateral trade pact was concluded with Costa Rica, and negotiations were opened with Guatemala, Nicaragua, Costa Rica, Colombia, and Venezuela. In September, Salinas traveled to Chile to sign his first free trade treaty.

**Environmental Concerns.** In January all motor vehicles were banned from in the center of Mexico City, regarded as the most polluted metropolis on earth. In March the government ordered the closing of a major oil refinery in the capital, and additional measures to restrict emissions there were announced in November. Unleaded fuel became available, and all 1991 cars sold in Mexico were required to be fitted with catalytic converters. A program to battle pollution along the U.S.-Mexican border was undertaken jointly with the U.S. Environmental Protection Agency. In September, responding to criticism that Mexican fishing boats were slaughtering dolphins, Salinas announced stricter regulations governing tuna

fishing. He later proposed a bill setting prison terms for those who intentionally kill dolphins and other protected species.

**Disputed Elections.** There were charges of fraud and chicanery during elections in August. Voters elected an all-new Chamber of Deputies, half the members of the Senate, and several governors. The governing Institutional Revolutionary Party (PRI) won 62 percent of the total vote, but in several districts its victories were questioned.

Apparently dismayed by reports abroad of irregularities in the voting, Salinas persuaded the governor-elect of the state of Guanajuato to refuse his mandate and call for new elections. In October the governor of San Luis Potosí resigned only days after his inauguration, evidently also under presidential pressure.

**Human Rights.** Early in the year, apparently stung by charges that Mexican federal police routinely torture prisoners, the president dismissed his attorney general, bringing in a replacement who promised reforms. Thereafter, more than 70 federal police officers were dismissed for abuses of authority, and many of

them were remanded for trial. However, reports from human rights organizations charged that abuses were continuing.

**Church and State.** In December, Mexico's legislators approved constitutional changes giving legal recognition to religious institutions. The measure was intended primarily to end decades of conflict between the government and the Roman Catholic Church. Mexico is over 90 percent Catholic.

See STATISTICS OF THE WORLD.     J.H.B.

**MICHIGAN.** See STATISTICS OF THE WORLD.
**MICRONESIA.** See STATISTICS OF THE WORLD. See also PACIFIC ISLANDS.
**MIDDLE EAST.** See INTERNATIONAL CONFERENCES; articles on individual countries.
**MILITARY AND NAVAL AFFAIRS.** For the United States military, 1991 was a bittersweet year. The swift and stunning success of the U.S.-led allied forces in the Persian Gulf War in January and February won worldwide acclaim and restored Americans' faith in the prowess and professionalism of their defense establishment. (See the feature article WAR IN THE GULF.) At the same time, President

*A worker in a U.S.-owned assembly plant in Mexico (at right) makes electronic relays. A growing number of U.S. companies have built plants in Mexico, where they benefit from low wages and weak environmental regulations. If a proposed North American Free Trade Agreement is concluded, the trend is expected to accelerate, worsening environmental problems like this industrial waste in Tijuana (left).*

George Bush announced a sweeping reduction in U.S. strategic forces, citing the collapse of the Soviet empire. The final disintegration of the Soviet Union, however, raised concerns about the disposition of its nuclear arsenal.

**Bush Initiative.** In a televised address on September 27, President Bush said he was ordering the worldwide withdrawal and destruction of all U.S. ground-launched, short-range nuclear weapons—missiles and artillery shells—as well as all short-range nuclear weapons carried by U.S. submarines and surface warships. He said he was canceling the alert status of B-1 and B-52 strategic bombers and of 450 Minuteman II intercontinental ballistic missiles (ICBMs) and canceling the development of a mobile version of the MX land-based missile and of a replacement for the short-range nu-

clear attack missile carried by U.S. strategic bombers. However, development of the Strategic Defense Initiative (SDI), the system popularly known as Star Wars, and of the B-2 (Stealth) bomber were to be continued.

Bush challenged the Soviet Union to match his unilateral cuts and proposed accelerated negotiations to eliminate all multiple-warhead ICBMs and find ways to guard against an unauthorized or accidental launch of nuclear weapons. His initiative was received favorably by most world leaders, including Soviet President Mikhail Gorbachev, who said the Soviet Union would essentially match the U.S. cutbacks.

**Arms Control Agreements.** On July 31, Bush and Gorbachev signed a complex arms reduction treaty sharply curtailing their strategic, or long-range, nuclear arsenals. If ratified by the

The U.S. military presence in the Philippines seemed to be ending after nearly a century. A treaty to extend the U.S. lease on the Subic Bay naval base was opposed by protesters (left) and killed by the Philippine Senate. And the destruction wrought by a volcano led the United States to give up Clark Air Base; below, a color guard lowers the flag there, signaling the withdrawal.

two countries, the Start accord would require an overall reduction of approximately 30 percent in their strategic nuclear inventories. The accord, which would be in effect for 15 years, did not cover space-based systems such as those envisioned for SDI.

The United States withdrew its last medium-range nuclear missiles from Europe in March, in accordance with a 1987 treaty. The last of 846 Pershing and ground-launched cruise missiles once based in Europe was destroyed on May 6. Among other developments, in June the United States and the Soviet Union resolved their differences over a treaty reducing conventional forces in Europe; the agreement cleared the way to implement the Conventional Forces in Europe (CFE) treaty signed in November 1990. The successors of the Soviet Union said they would observe existing arms agreements.

**Conventional Weapons.** In June the Pentagon disclosed new details of a $15 billion radar-evading cruise missile that could be launched from the ground or the air. The Air Force in April awarded a contract for the F-22 Advanced Tactical Fighter plane, which would replace the F-15 Eagle as the primary jet fighter by the late 1990s. The Army awarded a contract for a new light helicopter in March, and the first of the Burke-class guided missile destroyers was commissioned in July. The maiden test flight of the Air Force's C-17 cargo plane occurred in September.

Technical problems continued to dog the B-1B bomber. A government investigator told Congress in March that it might require $1 billion and ten years of repairs and redesign to correct the plane's defects. The future of the B-2 bomber was also in doubt because of skyrocketing costs and technical difficulties.

**Overall Retrenchment.** In May the North Atlantic Treaty Organization announced a massive reorganization of military forces in Western Europe that could cut the American troop presence there in half. New cuts in U.S. troop strength would result from a U.S. defense reorganization plan unveiled in April, designed to eliminate 94,000 military and civilian jobs and save $70 billion over seven years. In December the government also announced it would close several nuclear weapons plants.

In July, Congress voted to shut down 34 domestic military bases and cut back or realign operations at 48 others. The Pentagon also planned to reduce overseas bases, particularly in Germany.

In September the Air Force announced a sweeping reorganization. The Strategic Air Command's nuclear-armed bombers would be merged with tactical air forces into a new Air Combat Command, the number of four-star generals would be reduced, and thousands of staff jobs would be eliminated in favor of operational assignments in the field.

**Defense Budget.** The Pentagon asked for $278.3 billion in spending authority for the 1992 fiscal year, a decrease of $5.3 billion from the previous year. The defense budget bill finally approved by Congress and signed by Bush matched the request in total spending authorization but not in details. The bill authorized the purchase of only 1 B-2 beyond the 15 already ordered, rather than the 4 requested, and made even that purchase contingent on both technical improvements in the plane and another congressional vote. However, Congress did provide $1.8 billion for materials to keep the B-2 production line "warm" and $4.15 billion for a version of SDI.

*Iowa* **Explosion.** A $2.35 billion lawsuit was filed against the Navy in April by families of 38 of the 47 sailors killed when a gun turret exploded aboard the battleship *Iowa* in 1989. New investigations of the incident failed to establish the cause, and in October the chief of naval operations formally apologized to the family of Clayton Hartwig, the gunner's mate who a Navy review panel had initially said "most probably" deliberately caused the explosion, in which he was killed.

**Sex and Gender Issues.** The controversy over women in combat intensified as a result of the deployment of more than 32,000 women soldiers to the Persian Gulf during Operation Desert Storm. In the defense budget bill Congress authorized but did not require the Pentagon to permit women pilots to fly combat missions in future conflicts.

A Navy Department study, commissioned in 1990 after a series of incidents involving sexual harassment and alleged rapes at the U.S. Naval Academy and other naval installations, was made public in April. It found that three-fourths of the women and half the men interviewed reported that they had experienced or knew of sexual harassment in their commands. Assignment policies were found to be inconsistent and frequently detrimental to the careers of women sailors.

In a sex discrimination suit begun 18 years before, a federal district judge in November awarded $670,000 in back pay to 67 female civilian employees of the Navy's computer operations center who had claimed they had been discriminated against in hiring and promotions. The judge had ruled in favor of the women in 1981, but the Navy used delaying tactics to prolong the litigation.

Despite growing criticism from gay rights advocates, the Pentagon maintained its policy of discharging homosexuals, concluding that they were not security risks but could still be removed from the military because they threatened morale. A federal judge upheld the Pentagon's policy.

**MIAs.** The issue of American soldiers missing in action during the Vietnam War was rekindled with the emergence of a mysterious photograph purportedly showing three Caucasian men living somewhere in Southeast Asia. The Pentagon said the photograph was a forgery and continued to insist there was no credible evidence that U.S. soldiers were being held prisoner in the region, but some family members of MIAs disagreed. The Pentagon increased the number of employees involved in MIA matters and established a joint office in Hanoi, Vietnam's capital, to intensify efforts to resolve cases.

**Philippine Pullout.** In September the Philippine Senate rejected a treaty which would have allowed the United States to operate its naval base at Subic Bay for ten more years. The Philippine government ultimately said that U.S. withdrawal from the base must be completed by the end of 1992. The Pentagon had already announced it would abandon its other major Philippine facility, Clark Air Base, as a result of millions of dollars' worth of damage from the volcanic eruption of Mount Pinatubo in June.                                             T.D.

**MINNESOTA.** *See* STATISTICS OF THE WORLD.
**MISSISSIPPI.** *See* STATISTICS OF THE WORLD.

**MISSOURI.** *See* STATISTICS OF THE WORLD.
**MONACO.** *See* STATISTICS OF THE WORLD.
**MONGOLIA.** Throughout 1991, Mongolia continued to distance itself from its Communist past. A draft constitution calling for a parliamentary system was under consideration by the national assembly. Among other actions, the country's official name was changed from the Mongolian People's Republic to the Republic of Mongolia. In October there was a reported discovery near Moron of a mass grave containing the remains of thousands of Buddhist monks who had been massacred in the late 1930s by the Communists.

As of January 1, foreign trade was transferred to a hard currency basis, which cut trade with the Soviet Union, Mongolia's main trading partner, by two-thirds. There were acute shortages of gasoline, spare parts, foodstuffs, and medicines. Rationing of basic foods was introduced in major cities. As state property privatization got underway, foreigners were permitted to buy shares or complete properties. "Little" privatization was launched with the auctioning of several Ulan Bator shops and restaurants; "big" privatization of large state industrial enterprises was due to start later.

Former Mongolian leader Yumjaagiyn Tsedenbal, who was ousted in 1984 and blamed for the country's "stagnation," died in exile in Moscow on April 21 and was buried with military honors in Ulan Bator.

*See* STATISTICS OF THE WORLD.        A.J.K.S.
**MONTANA.** *See* STATISTICS OF THE WORLD.
**MOROCCO.** The United Nations took potentially decisive steps in 1991 to end the dispute over the Western Sahara, the former Spanish territory claimed by Morocco. Western Sahara residents were to be able to choose by referendum between independence and Moroccan sovereignty in a 1992 plebiscite. In May the UN General Assembly voted to finance a special peacekeeping force, the UN Mission for the Referendum in Western Sahara (Minurso). In June Johannes Manz, the personal representative of UN Secretary-General Javier Pérez de Cuéllar, met separately with representatives of the Moroccan government and of the Polisario Front, the national liberation movement which has been fighting for an independent Saharan state.

*Any doubts that Mongolia's orientation had turned decidedly westward were, one might say, stamped out with the country's issuing of a set of stamps depicting the American cartoon characters the Flintstones on a visit to the Gobi Desert.*

Both sides accepted September 6 as the date for a permanent cease-fire, but preparations for the referendum bogged down. Morocco had already submitted some 120,000 names of Sahrawis (residents of the Sahara) it wanted to add to the UN electoral register, which totaled some 70,000 names. Meanwhile, for several weeks after the cease-fire, tens of thousands of Moroccans crossed into the region and claimed voting rights. At the end of the year, the UN Security Council endorsed the broad outlines of the referendum plan.

Morocco continued to support efforts toward Maghreb (North African) unity, giving increasing substance to the Arab Maghreb Union (UMA), the regional grouping established in 1989 by Morocco, Algeria, Mauritania, Tunisia, and Libya. At the fifth UMA summit, held in Casablanca in September, agreement was reached to locate the UMA headquarters in Morocco.

The Persian Gulf crisis created tensions in Morocco. King Hassan had lined up solidly with the international community opposing Iraq's invasion of Kuwait and had sent a "limited symbolic contingent" of 1,300 troops to Saudi Arabia in August 1990. But in the following months, expressions of Moroccan public sentiment were overwhelmingly pro-Iraqi. The king rejected a demand by several political parties to bring the Moroccan troops home from the Persian Gulf but made a concession to public sentiment by pledging that the troops would not engage in combat against Iraq. Tensions reached a peak in a huge pro-Iraqi demonstration of over 300,000 people in Rabat on February 3. But Hassan's judgment was vindicated by the rapid defeat of Iraq, and he rode out the Gulf storm successfully.

*See* STATISTICS OF THE WORLD. J.D.

**MOTION PICTURES.** In 1991 the once-dominant tendency to target teenage audiences continued to weaken, as movie-makers increasingly relied on attracting adults through mature themes, serious dramas, and comedies with dramatic overtones.

**Blockbusters.** To be sure, action-style blockbusters often did extremely well at the box of-

*A trend toward tough, savvy female characters was noticeable in several popular 1991 films. In* Silence of the Lambs *(above), Jodie Foster played a sharp young FBI agent who tracks down a serial killer. In* Terminator 2: Judgment Day, *Linda Hamilton (right) showed she could blow away her adversaries with the same lethal power wielded by her muscular co-star, Arnold Schwarzenegger.*

fice. *Terminator 2: Judgment Day*, a sequel starring muscular Arnold Schwarzenegger, led the pack, amassing more than $200 million. *Robin Hood: Prince of Thieves*, with Kevin Costner in the lead role, took in more than $180 million. On the other hand, an intended action-oriented blockbuster, *Hudson Hawk*, starring Bruce Willis and reported to have cost as much as $60 million to make, flopped disastrously.

Brandon Tartikoff, the newly appointed chairman of the Paramount Pictures Corporation, said his company would again emphasize youth-oriented films in the face of the box office fizzle of two high profile releases, *Frankie and Johnny*, which teamed Michelle Pfeiffer and Al Pacino, and *The Butcher's Wife*, which starred Demi Moore. But that was not the general situation in 1991.

**Strong Themes.** Many of the films for mature audiences encompassed arresting subjects. In *Billy Bathgate,* an intelligent interpretation of E. L. Doctorow's novel about a youth who attaches himself to the Dutch Schultz gang in the mid-1930s, Schultz was interestingly portrayed by Dustin Hoffman as a self-righteous, shrewd gangland tyrant with a murderous temper and a knack for manipulating corrupt officials. *Little Man Tate* was an unusual drama about the adjustment problems of a seven-year-old genius and the tug-of-war between his mother, expertly portrayed by Jodie Foster (also making her directorial debut), and a gifted child expert, effectively played by Dianne Wiest. Foster also gave a powerful performance in *The Silence of the Lambs* as an FBI agent assigned to catch a psychopathic killer, brilliantly played by Anthony Hopkins. Jonathan Demme directed the thriller with Hitchcockian flair; it took in more than $130 million at the box office.

Callie Khouri scored strongly as a woman screenwriter with *Thelma and Louise,* which featured Susan Sarandon and Geena Davis as friends turned into desperados by unexpected events. Many women saw the film as a reflection of their grievances, while others felt it was merely manipulative. Although *Thelma and Louise* dealt with the viewpoint of women, the directorial assignment went to one of Hollywood's most skillful male directors, Ridley Scott.

Director Martin Scorsese brought his expertise to a remake of *Cape Fear,* the haunting 1962 film about an ex-convict who seeks revenge on the man responsible for his imprisonment. This time Robert De Niro was cast in the role once played by Robert Mitchum, but Mitchum was given a cameo role, as was Gregory Peck, who also had a key part in the original.

The greed that marked the 1980s was dramatized in *Other People's Money,* about a sleazy corporate raider seeking to take control of a staid old company. The movie provided a vehicle for Danny DeVito to play a character somewhat more complex than his usual roles. The medical profession was examined critically in *The Doctor,* starring William Hurt as a surgeon who learns he has cancer. Though the film ended conventionally, it made sharp points along the way about the callousness with which patients can be treated.

Questions about who really killed John F. Kennedy were raised anew in Oliver Stone's explosive and controversial *JFK,* which starred Kevin Costner. The Hollywood blacklist era was the subject of Irwin Winkler's *Guilty by Suspicion,* in which Robert De Niro played a director denied work for refusing to name colleagues as Communists. Hollywood was also the setting for *Barton Fink,* a highly stylized offering by the brothers Joel and Ethan Coen. The movie stars John Turturro as an idealistic New York playwright lured to Hollywood, where he is subjected to a nightmarish experi-

### Kane Is Fifty

Novelist John O'Hara said it was "the best picture he ever saw" and had "the best actor in the history of acting." That could be only one motion picture—*Citizen Kane.* To mark the 50th anniversary of the Orson Welles classic, a new, sharper print was released to theaters in nine major U.S. cities on May 1, 1991, with national distribution following. A video version followed, which included a documentary on Welles and tributes from leading directors.

When Hollywood was stormed by the 25-year-old *wunderkind* Orson Welles, fresh from triumphs in theater and radio (including a pseudodocumentary about an invasion from Mars that sent panicked listeners fleeing into the streets), many had hoped the cheeky outsider would fail. And when word leaked out that his chronicle of a power-hungry tycoon was based on newspaper magnate William Randolph Hearst, the Hearst newspapers, through threats and refusal to accept advertising, tried to squelch the picture.

Welles nevertheless forged ahead, employing astonishing cinematic techniques that would later become part of every filmmaker's vocabulary. The picture was a financial flop, but critics remained impressed; in the 1950s *Citizen Kane*'s reputation began its ascent. Perhaps its renown explains why Turner Entertainment, which took flak for adding color to such movies as *Casablanca,* announced that *Citizen Kane* would *not* be colorized.

ence, some of it real and some of it fantasy. *Barton Fink* was chosen best film at the Cannes Film Festival.

Conflict over ethnic identification provided the basis for David Mamet's unsettling *Homicide*, in which a detective, convincingly depicted by Joe Mantegna, rediscovers his Jewish heritage in the process of solving a murder. In *The Fisher King*, directed by Terry Gilliam, Jeff Bridges goes through a catharsis of another sort after he befriends Robin Williams as a troubled derelict. Director Gus Van Sant looked at the alienation of two male hustlers in *My Own Private Idaho*, starring River Phoenix and Keanu Reeves.

Other films of note included Barbra Streisand's directorial effort *Prince of Tides*; John Sayles's pessimistic *City of Hope*, starring Vincent Spano; Martha Coolidge's *Rambling Rose*, with both Laura Dern and her mother, Diane Ladd; Istvan Szabo's delightful *Meeting Venus*, presenting Glenn Close as an opera diva; Lawrence Kasdan's ambitious *Grand Canyon*, starring Kevin Kline, Steve Martin, Mary McDonnell, and Danny Glover; and

Warren Beatty's superior *Bugsy*, in which he gave one of his best performances as the gangster Bugsy Siegel.

**Ethnic Progress.** Spike Lee set the pace for an upsurge of African-American oriented films with *Jungle Fever*, a volatile drama tackling the subject of an interracial romance. Other notable black-oriented films included the dramatic and moving *Straight Out of Brooklyn*, in which 19-year-old Matty Rich drew upon his own family life and observations as he and various acquaintances coped with poverty, and *Boyz N the Hood*, a first feature directed by John Singleton. The latter, set in a gang-ridden part of Los Angeles, also was a story of struggle against the odds of growing up black. Another director to watch was Mario Van Peebles, whose *New Jack City* was an action film about city drug warfare.

**Mixed Fare.** Among comedies, *City Slickers* was a pleasing vehicle for Billy Crystal as a husband in midlife crisis. Bill Murray found a suitable vehicle in *What About Bob?*, in which he played a frenetic, phobia-ridden patient of a psychiatrist (Richard Dreyfuss), whose life he

**An Actress with Character**

To movie audiences, she first gained wide fame in the role of Annie Wilkes, the crazed, sledgehammer-wielding romance-novel fan in the hit horror film *Misery*, which brought her sudden celebrity and an Academy Award in 1991 as best actress. But Kathy Bates was already a distinguished theater actress when director Rob Reiner chose her for the part.

Born in Memphis she graduated from Southern Methodist University in Dallas. As a member of the Actors Theater of Louisville in 1979, she created the role of Lenny McGrath in the Beth Henley play *Crimes of the Heart*. Bates won wider acclaim, including a Tony nomination, for her portrayal of a suicidal woman in the play *'night Mother*, which moved to Broadway in 1983. In 1987 she won an Obie for her role as Frankie in the off-Broadway hit *Frankie and Johnny in the Clair de Lune*.

Now, with the success of *Misery*, Bates, at 43, has at last begun to get important film parts, including appearances in the December releases *At Play in the Fields of the Lord* and *Fried Green Tomatoes*.

*Kathy Bates*

turns topsy-turvy. *The Naked Gun 2 1/2: The Smell of Fear* reprised the earlier popular slapstick detective spoof to the tune of more than $86 million at the box office. *Hot Shots!*, a spoof of flyboy movies, garnered more than $68 million. Mel Brooks served up comedy and a social message in his *Life Stinks*, about a greedy real estate developer who bets he can live on the streets for a month.

Steven Spielberg directed the somewhat disappointing *Hook*, an expensive project derived from *Peter Pan* and filled with the star power of Dustin Hoffman, Robin Williams, and Julia Roberts. The entertaining *For the Boys*, starring Bette Midler and James Caan and directed by Mark Rydell, waxed nostalgic about the USO during wartime, while also making points about war. Liza Minnelli played a dance teacher honing amateur talent in *Stepping Out*. Director John Frankenheimer offered a new thriller, *The Year of the Gun*, involving terrorism in Italy. *Father of the Bride*, a remake of the 1950 Spencer Tracy vehicle, was a showcase for Steve Martin, with Diane Keaton co-starring. Macaulay Culkin, Hollywood's most bankable child star ever since *Home Alone*, returned in *My Girl*.

One of the year's most offbeat and lucrative films was *The Addams Family*, in which Anjelica Huston and Raul Julia played the devilish Morticia and Gomez. *Freddie's Dead: The Final Nightmare* held out the promise that this would be the last of Freddie Krueger, but it would be foolish to bet on it. There was yet another *Star Trek* film—*Star Trek VI: The Undiscovered Country*. Sean Penn made a stab at becoming a director with *The Indian Runner*. Lily Tomlin parlayed her stage show into a film version with *The Search for Signs of Intelligent Life in the Universe*, featuring her assortment of funny characterizations. Also transferred from stage was Eric Bogosian's tour de force *Sex, Drugs, Rock & Roll*. Harrison Ford played a lawyer who suffers brain damage when shot in a holdup, in *Regarding Henry*.

Evidences of a new trend toward animation were Disney's enjoyable *Beauty and the Beast* and Spielberg's animated sequel *An American Tail: Fievel Goes West*. Disney rereleased *101 Dalmatians*, which turned out to have enormous box office strength.

*The year came to a spooky finish with the release of* The Addams Family, *a hit film starring Raul Julia and Angelica Houston (center) as everyone's favorite weird couple.*

Among works by independent producers, Henry Jaglom's *Eating* featured a large group of actresses whom he assembled to create fictional discourse based on some of their real life experiences involving dieting and binging. Hal Hartley's *Trust* dealt with the alienation of a young man and woman in a community on Long Island.

Among documentaries, Jennie Livingston's *Paris Is Burning*, about cross-dressing dance competitions in New York, gained particular attention.

**Canadian Films.** By far the most stunning Canadian success was *Black Robe*, the epic based on Brian Moore's 1985 novel about a Jesuit missionary among the Algonquin Indians during the 17th century. By year's end, *Black Robe* had grossed more than Can$7 million in North America—more than any previous domestic feature with a Canadian story. It drew high praise from critics, many of whom saw the film's stark realism as a welcome antidote to the romanticizing of Indians in *Dances With Wolves*. French-speaking actor Lothaire Bluteau starred as the priest, but for commer-

Black Robe, a Canadian film directed by Bruce Beresford, starred
Lothaire Bluteau (center) as a 17th-century French priest who, as a
missionary to the Algonquin Indians, makes an epic 1,500-mile
canoe journey across northern Québec.

cial reasons the movie was shot in English with
subtitled Indian dialect.

Among other films, Québec's Lea Pool created a quiet masterpiece with La demoiselle
sauvage, about a romance between a female
fugitive and a dam engineer in the Swiss Alps.
Filmmaker Atom Egoyan refined his pet themes
of voyeurism and alienation in The Adjuster.
Deepa Mehta's Sam and Me, a bittersweet
drama about a disillusioned immigrant, received honorable mention at the Cannes Film
Festival. And documentary veteran Sturla
Gunnarsson made his first dramatic feature,
Diplomatic Immunity, a kinetic film about a
Canadian envoy in war-torn El Salvador.

**From Abroad.** Polish director Agnieszka Holland won praise for Europa, Europa, about the
real-life struggles of a Jewish boy during World
War II. Brigitte Roüan, a French actress directing for the first time, made the sensitive Overseas, about three sisters living in Algeria during
the turbulent 1950s. French director Jacques
Rivette spent four fascinating hours telling the
story of an artist trying to paint a masterpiece in
La belle noiseuse. Claude Chabrol's Madame

Bovary starred Isabelle Huppert. Additional
notable entries from France included Uranus,
Cross My Heart, My Father's Glory, and My
Mother's Castle.

Other significant foreign films included Pupi
Avati's The Story of Boys and Girls and Giu-
seppe Tornatore's Everybody's Fine, starring
Marcello Mastroianni, both from Italy. Akira
Kurosawa's Rhapsody in August effectively
examined the residue of World War II in Japanese-American relationships.

Many foreign imports in English proved
noteworthy. Let Him Have It, directed by
Peter Medak, was a powerful drama about a
man unjustly hanged for murder. Alan
Parker's The Commitments was an exceptionally good and earthy movie about a rock band
in Dublin. Actor-director Kenneth Branagh
uncorked Dead Again, a stylish mystery.
Prospero's Books was Peter Greenaway's
wildly imaginative version of Shakespeare's
The Tempest, with John Gielgud at the center
of the elaborate affair.

**Business Side.** According to the Motion Picture Association of America, the average cost

of making a film rose to $26.8 million. Marketing and distribution costs rose to another $11.6 million. Not only were costs high, but business was down.

Orion Pictures, known as a caring company that seeks worthwhile projects, filed for bankruptcy in December, as it continued to attempt to reorganize in the face of deep financial problems that had precluded it from releasing 12 films scheduled for 1991.

**Deaths.** David Lean, who made *Bridge on the River Kwai*, *Lawrence of Arabia*, and other admired works, died at the age of 83. Frank Capra, who had his name above the title of films that he directed long before that became fashionable, died at 94. Actress Jean Arthur, who appeared in three hit films directed by Capra, died at 90. Director Don Siegel, known for his cult classic *Invasion of the Body Snatchers*, died at 78. Many other film notables died during the year, among them actors Ralph Bellamy, 87, Klaus Kinski, 65, Fred MacMurray, 83, and Yves Montand, 70; actress Gene Tierney, 70; director Tony Richardson, 63; and screenwriter Robert Kaufman, 60.

**Awards.** Kevin Costner triumphed with his *Dances With Wolves* at Hollywood's Academy Award ceremony. Although he had been derided for daring to make a lengthy western film partly in the Sioux Indian language Lakota—and in his debut as a director at that—*Dances With Wolves* won the Oscar for best picture. Costner also won for best director, and the film was awarded Oscars for screenplay, cinematography, editing, original score, and sound. Jeremy Irons won the Oscar as best actor for his performance in *Reversal of Fortune*, and Kathy Bates was named best actress for her work in *Misery*. The supporting actor award went to Joe Pesci for *Goodfellas*, and the supporting actress award was won by Whoopi Goldberg for *Ghost*.

The Berlin International Film Festival gave its top honor, the Golden Bear, to *House of Smiles*, a film from Italy. The British Academy of Film and Television Arts chose *Goodfellas* as best film, and the French Cesar Academy Awards designated *Cyrano de Bergerac* as France's best film, with America's *Dead Poets Society* taking honors as the best foreign film.                    B.D.J. (Canadian) & W.W.

**MOZAMBIQUE.** War continued to be the dominant issue for Mozambique in 1991, as continuing peace talks between the Mozambican government and the Mozambican National Resistance (Renamo) made only halting progress. Although a partial cease-fire, providing for the restriction within fixed corridors of the Zimbabwean troops supporting the Mozambican government and for an end to Renamo attacks within those corridors, had been reached in late 1990, Renamo repeatedly violated the agreement and continued attacking civilians, the economic infrastructure, and government outposts.

Government troops scored several major victories against Renamo bases, but Renamo was able to regroup in unprotected rural areas. Documents captured in April, together with reports in the South African press, indicated that Renamo was continuing to receive covert support from South African special forces, from Kenya and Malawi, and from right-wing supporters in South Africa, Europe, and the United States.

Several new opposition parties made their official appearance. None of the new parties gained widespread support, but debate in Maputo, the capital, and in the Mozambican media was lively. Groups formerly affiliated with the ruling Frelimo party, such as the trade unions and the Organization of Mozambican Women, set up independent organizations. Meanwhile, at its Sixth Congress in August, the Frelimo party affirmed national reconciliation, political pluralism, market principles, and a democratic socialist concern for social justice as the basis for its future policies.

The nation's economic growth slowed in 1990 and 1991. Industrial growth was particularly hard hit by repeated power cuts due to Renamo attacks on power lines, while agricultural recovery was still hampered by the pervasive insecurity in rural areas. The government was forced to impose further austerity measures because of a reduction in Soviet economic support, and Mozambique remained highly dependent on food aid and other support, particularly from the United Nations, Sweden, the European Community, the United States, and Italy.

*See* STATISTICS OF THE WORLD.          W.M.

# MUSIC

**MUSIC.** Popular music saw the transformation of a country music star into a pop superstar, and a growing mainstream interest in jazz. In classical music, 1991 was the year of Mozart.

## POPULAR MUSIC

The shift away from rock continued in 1991. An increasing number of teenagers and young adults gravitated toward rap and dance music, while more older people bought country, gospel, and jazz.

**Shaky Rock Sales.** While established rock bands ranging from Guns N' Roses and Van

*The rock event of the year was the simultaneous release in September of two albums by the hard-driving Guns N' Roses, with lead singer Axl Rose—Use Your Illusion I and Use Your Illusion II. Hundreds of record stores opened at midnight to accommodate the group's many fans.*

Halen to Tom Petty and Bob Seger sold large numbers of albums, few new rock groups fought their way up the ranks. The more forward-looking acts tried to increase their appeal. Some remixed their singles for dance-club play. Others had success with a new "funk'n'roll" sound that combined rock, funk, metal, rap, and dance elements. A funk'n'roll band named Jane's Addiction headlined the summer's most successful package tour, which also featured black rockers Living Colour, postpunk band Siouxsie & the Banshees, industrial rockers Nine Inch Nails, and "gangsta" rapper Ice-T.

The most popular of the "alternative" rock bands with a college base was R.E.M., which sold more than 3 million copies of its *Out Of Time* album. There were also pop breakthroughs for a pair of new British acts, Jesus Jones and EMF. Two of the year's biggest pop hits by rock groups were Extreme's *More Than Words* and Queensryche's *Silent Lucidity*. Their melodicism and acoustic instrumentation—both in contrast to the snarling brand of hard rock for which the two groups were better known—seemed to mirror a popular MTV program called *Unplugged*, featuring top rock and rap acts in acoustic performances.

Two other rock veterans chalked up solid if unspectacular successes with their latest albums. Sting's jazz-tinged *The Soul Cages* sold a million copies, and Paul Simon achieved twice that with his Brazilian-themed *Rhythm of the Saints*.

In May, R.E.M. became the first rock act to reach No. 1 on the *Billboard* 200 Top Albums chart in a year and a half. But *Billboard* changed its method of calculating pop-album sales rankings, basing them on actual electronic piece counts of retail sales instead of on store reports, and the pattern of rock record sales appeared to change. During the summer months, new rock titles by Skid Row, Van Halen, and Metallica all debuted at No. 1, but the Skid Row and Van Halen albums quickly fell to lower chart levels.

The biggest rock event of the year was the release of the Guns N' Roses studio albums *Use Your Illusion I* and *II* at the end of September. The two shipped more than 4 million units upon release, despite the refusal of the

Wal-Mart and K Mart retail chains to carry these profane opuses. Several hundred record stores around the country opened at midnight to cater to the demand for the dual paeans to excess. But they were soon dethroned—by a mild-mannered country vocalist named Garth Brooks.

**Country Climbs.** In mid-September, Brooks's third outing, *Ropin' The Wind*, became the first country album to enter the *Billboard* 200 at No. 1. Retail orders of 2.6 million units in the title's first week of release showed there was a huge potential audience for traditional country music. (In November, capitalizing on this breakthrough, NBC launched *Hot Country Nights*, a prime-time, Sunday evening television show devoted to country music.) Country stars Clint Black, Travis Tritt, Vince Gill, Dolly Parton, Alan Jackson, and Trisha Yearwood also had albums certified either gold or platinum. And Nashville continued to develop new stars: Besides Yearwood, there were Diamond Rio, a sextet combining bluegrass, country, jazz, and rock, and Doug Stone, a new traditionalist.

**Gospel and Christian Revival.** Christian artists began to make bigger inroads than ever in the mainstream audience. Amy Grant scored a No. 1 hit with *Baby, Baby*, a nonreligious number that garnered lots of airplay and club play, along with some backlash from the Christian community. Other Christian acts included Michael W. Smith with his tuneful *Go West Young Man* and Carman with his more message-oriented *Addicted to Jesus*. BeBe & CeCe Winans and Sounds of Blackness, a 40-member gospel choir from Minneapolis, did quite well in the R & B market.

**Jazz Comes Back Big.** Jazz crossed over into the mainstream market to a greater degree than it had for many years. A big impetus was provided by Natalie Cole, an accomplished R & B singer who recorded a "standards" album as a tribute to her late father, Nat King Cole. That set, called *Unforgettable*, rode at No. 1 on the pop album chart for five weeks and sold more than 2 million units. A "duet" blending Nat King Cole's recording of the title track with his daughter's rendition went top 10 on the *Billboard* Hot 100 Singles chart.

A major hit was scored by Harry Connick,

*Garth Brooks's new release* Ropin' the Wind *went right to the No. 1 spot on* Billboard's *list of most popular albums, becoming the first country album ever to start at the top.*

Jr., with *Blue Light, Red Light*, an album of his own big-band-with-vocal compositions in the style of 50 years ago. It reflected the fan base he had created with two previous platinum albums and near-nonstop touring, as well as his sex-idol status.

**Dance Pop.** Many of the year's biggest sellers were the light, danceable pop records that still dominated pop radio, the easiest route to establishing familiarity among album buyers. Among the variations on this theme were titles by Janet Jackson, Mariah Carey, Paula Abdul, Madonna, Karyn White, Cathy Dennis, C&C Music Factory, and Londonbeat.

Coming straight out of the clubs were several off-the-wall smashes. Enigma (actually German producer Michael Cretu) created a pop hit, *Sadeness, Part I*, by setting Gregorian chants to a dance beat; and P.M. Dawn, a British dance act, moved the masses with an odd mix influenced by the Jackson 5, George Clinton, and Spandau Ballet. Ballad singers also had their share of hit recordings. Michael Bol-

**The Q Factor**

More than 30 years after releasing his first album, pop musician Quincy Jones, aged 58, is still going strong. In February his album *Back on the Block*—which spans just about every style of black music of the past 40 years and spotlights an astonishingly diverse array of guest artists—won him his latest Grammy, as Album of the Year.

As a composer, performer, arranger, and record producer, Quincy Delight Jones, Jr.—friends call him Q—is nothing if not eclectic. He has dabbled in big-band jazz, bossa nova, pop-rock, classical, funk, soul, doowop, African, Brazilian, disco, and hip-hop, taking them in fresh but always commercially viable directions. He produced Michael Jackson's first three solo albums, including *Thriller* (1982), the top-selling album of all time, and was the creative catalyst behind USA for Africa's fund-raiser *We Are the World*.

Through it all, Jones has been nominated for more Grammys (76) than any other artist and ranks second among all Grammy winners, with a grand total of 25—so far.

*Quincy Jones*

ton topped the pop albums chart with *Time, Love and Tenderness*. Whitney Houston attained triple-platinum status with *I'm Your Baby Tonight*, and Wilson Phillips continued to rack up No. 1 smashes with starry-eyed harmonies. Folk-rocker Bonnie Raitt sold a million of her latest album, and Bryan Adams scored a huge hit with his pop ditty *(Everything I Do) I Do It for You*, from the soundtrack to the film *Robin Hood*.

**Rap in Black and White.** Vanilla Ice's *To The Extreme* sold 7 million copies—the largest number for any album during the year—and opened the doors for many other white rappers on the pop charts. Among the most popular were 3rd Bass (which had actually preceded Vanilla Ice) and Marky Mark & The Funky Bunch, led by Mark Wahlberg, brother of New Kids On The Block's Donny.

Meanwhile, black rappers—who tended to dismiss the white rap acts as imitators—rang up plenty of sales themselves. Under *Billboard*'s new piece-count system, an album by N.W.A debuted at No. 2 without benefit of airplay. New efforts by Ice-T, LL Cool J, and Pub-

lic Enemy also sold strongly. The Geto Boys broke through with their very graphic tales of street life. And Hammer, who had been 1990's biggest star, debuted at No. 3 with his fall release, *Too Legit to Quit*. Hammer and LL Cool J aside, many of these acts' lyrics were so raw that neither pop nor urban radio stations would play their records.

A new crop of female rappers arrived. Some of them, such as Shazzy, Yo-Yo, and Bytches With Problems, criticized the sexism they saw around them. Others, like Queen Latifah and Sister Souljah, addressed other social problems as well.

**Strong R & B.** In the R & B area, both veterans and newcomers scored high marks during the year. In late November, Michael Jackson released *Dangerous*, his first album in four years; it spawned a No. 1 single, *Black or White*, and shipped 4 million copies in the United States alone. Luther Vandross enjoyed both urban and pop success, selling a million of his *Power Of Love* album. The durable Gladys Knight had a No. 1 R & B single with *Men*, 30 years after she first topped that chart with the Pips. Other established R & B acts that stood out were Peabo Bryson, Roberta Flack, the O'Jays, Surface, and Prince, who came back strongly with *Diamonds & Pearls*.

Among newer black acts were Hi-Five, a teenage hip-house group; two preteen acts, Another Bad Creation and Boyz II Men; and Color Me Badd, a kind of hip-hop doowop group that clicked with *I Wanna Sex You Up* from the *New Jack City* soundtrack and their No. 1 single, *I Adore Mi Amor*.

**Grammys.** Among Grammy award winners, Mariah Carey was recognized as Best New Artist and won for the Best Female Pop Vocal (*Vision of Love*). The Best Male Pop Vocal was Roy Orbison's *Oh Pretty Woman*. Phil Collins took the honor for Record of the Year, for *Another Day in Paradise*. The Album of the Year was Quincy Jones's *Back on the Block*, and the Song of the Year was Julie Gold's *From a Distance*, performed by Bette Midler. Eric Clapton's *Bad Love* was voted Best Male Rock Vocal and Alannah Myles's *Black Velvet* as Best Female Rock Vocal, with Aerosmith's *Janie's Got A Gun* winning the honors in the group category.

**Final Bows.** Trumpeter Miles Davis, who had been a major influence on the jazz scene from the late 1940s to the early 1970s, died in September at the age of 65. Tenor saxophonist Stan Getz, one of the most melodic improvisers in modern jazz, died at 64 in June. In March, tenor saxophonist Bud Freeman died at 84, and pianist Jimmy McPartland at 83. These two stars of an earlier era helped create the Chicago style of jazz in the 1920s. Country Music Hall of Fame member Tennessee Ernie Ford passed away in October at 72. Songwriter Doc Pomus died March 14 at age 65; his partner, Mort Shuman, died at 52 in November. Country music singer Dottie West, the first female country singer ever to win a Grammy, died at 58 in September, after a car accident. Freddie Mercury, lead singer for the rock group Queen, died in November, aged 45, of AIDS. Rock promoter extraordinaire Bill Graham was killed at 60 in an October helicopter crash. And Clarence Leo Fender, whose solid-body electric guitars ushered in a transformation in rock music, died in March, aged 81.                            K.T.

## CLASSICAL MUSIC

The bicentennial of the death of Wolfgang Amadeus Mozart prompted celebrations around the world, while in New York a legendary concert hall was also feted.

**Carnegie Hall Hits 100.** Carnegie Hall, the grande dame of U.S. concert halls, celebrated its centennial with a season-long parade of international talent. The activity culminated in a ten-day festival in the spring, in which soprano Kathleen Battle performed her Carnegie recital debut (to mixed notices), Van Cliburn made a rare return to play his trademark Tchaikovsky Concerto No. 1, and soprano Jessye Norman sang with the Metropolitan Opera Orchestra. The orchestras of Cleveland, Boston, and Philadelphia also participated. Also featured in concerts, among other luminaries, were singers Placido Domingo, Marilyn Horne, and Samuel Ramey; cellists Yo-Yo Ma and Mstislav Rostropovich; and violinists Isaac Stern (Carnegie's president), Pinchas Zukerman, and Midori.

**Mozart Magnified.** Virtually every musical organization celebrated the bicentennial of Mozart's death. New York's Lincoln Center vowed that its 11 constituents would collectively perform all 835 of Mozart's works by August 1992; the festivities started on January 27, 1991, Mozart's birthday, with a replica of a program Mozart himself had put together in 1783.

The Tokyo and Juilliard string quartets embarked on the complete Mozart quartets and quintets. Meanwhile, the Metropolitan Opera opened a new *Die Zauberflöte*, with Kathleen Battle as Pamina and few-frills sets and costumes by David Hockney. The Lincoln Center season also saw the 25th anniversary of the Mostly Mozart Festival.

Pianist Mitsuko Uchida performed the complete cycle of Mozart sonatas in a series of recitals that solidified her reputation as one of the supreme Mozart interpreters. Milwaukee's Florentine Opera presented a new *Le Nozze di Figaro*, while the Seattle Opera offered a *Don Giovanni*. At Aix-en-Provence, France, the Vienna Festival offered 12 different productions of 8 Mozart operas, including a new *Le Nozze di Figaro* conducted by Claudio Abbado. The Vienna State Opera presented a new *La Clemenza di Tito*, designed by Hans Schavernoch, while in Madrid, the Liceu and the Teatro Lírico Nacional La Zarzuela coproduced a new *Idomeneo* with Montserrat Caballé as Elettra. In Paris, the Opéra Bastille premiered director Robert Wilson's offbeat interpretation of *Die Zauberflöte*.

**Other Anniversaries.** The year also marked the bicentennial of the birth of French composer Giacomo Meyerbeer, who composed the operas *L'Africaine* and *Les Huguenots*, among other important works.

The Seattle Opera honored the centenary of Russian composer Sergei Prokofiev's birth by showing his *War and Peace* in high definition television. It was the first complete staging of the work by an American opera company. Another rarely performed Prokofiev opera, *The Gambler*, was unveiled in November by the Lyric Opera of Chicago.

**Opera.** The Bolshoi Opera performed at the Metropolitan Opera House in June, marking its first U.S. visit in 16 years. The Komische Oper Berlin came to the Brooklyn Academy of Music with Gluck's *Orpheus und Eurydike*. The Vancouver Opera performed a new, feminist production of Richard Strauss's *Salome*, directed by Glynis Leyshon. Pacific Opera offered a new production of Gounod's *Romeo et Juliette*. The Met presented a winning staging of Puccini's *La Fanciulla del West*, with Sherill Milnes, Placido Domingo, and Barbara Daniels; Janacek's *Kat'a Kabanova*; and Wagner's *Parsifal*. Notable debuts at the Met included those of sopranos Ruth Ann Swenson and Deborah Voigt, as well as that of conductor Leonard Slatkin.

Across the Lincoln Center plaza, the New York City Opera was up to its usual innovations, presenting the North American premiere

*The 100th birthday of Carnegie Hall in New York City was celebrated with a season-long parade of international talent. At this concert in May, Zubin Mehta conducts the New York Philharmonic with Isaac Stern on violin and Yo-Yo Ma on cello.*

of Bill T. Jones's dance opera *The Mother of Three Sons*, riveting for Jones's choreography, less so for Leroy Jenkins's score. Bernd Alois Zimmermann's *Die Soldaten* was criticized in the New York *Times* for "its screaming, pounding music" but praised as "a powerful, affecting work." City Opera's bows to traditional musical theater included Frank Loesser's *The Most Happy Fella* and Lerner and Loewe's *Brigadoon*. The company also brought back Erich Korngold's eerie, romantically scored *Die tote Stadt* after 13 years.

**New Stage Works.** Houston Grand Opera presented two world premieres, Carlisle Floyd's dissonant *The Passion of Jonathan Wade* and Meredith Monk's *Atlas*. The New Jersey State Opera presented the world premiere of Ulysses Kay's *Frederick Douglass*, the story of a runaway slave who became an abolitionist. England's Covent Garden premiered Harrison Birtwistle's *Gawain*.

Certainly the most controversial new work was *The Death of Klinghoffer*, a collaboration of composer John Adams, librettist Alice Goodman, choreographer Mark Morris, and director Peter Sellars. The work is based on the 1985 hijacking of the Italian cruise ship *Achille Lauro* by Palestinian terrorists and their subsequent murder of a wheelchair-bound Jewish passenger, Leon Klinghoffer. Premiered in Brussels in March, it came to the Brooklyn Academy of Music in September. Goodman's preachy libretto is unworthy of Adams's neo-Romantic score; Sellars's stage is busy, filled with Morris's dancers, video close-ups, and supertitles (sorely needed). Most critics did not take to the opera; neither did the public. John Corigliano's *The Ghost of Versailles* was heard in its world premiere at the Metropolitan Opera House in December. The opera is an entertaining rumination on art and history involving the ghosts of the beheaded Queen Marie Antoinette and the playwright Beaumarchais as well as the fictional characters in his most famous plays. Produced by Colin Graham and conducted by James Levine, with a stellar cast that featured Marilyn Horne and Teresa Stratas, the opera was generally welcomed.

**Concert Premieres.** Tod Machover's computer-assisted *Begin Again Again . . .*

premiered at Tanglewood. *Immigrant Voices*, performed at New York's Ellis Island in June, is a quasi-oratorio by Ellen Taaffe Zwilich that traces immigrants' paths to the New World using actual accounts and letters. William Bolcom's *I Will Breathe a Mountain* is a compelling song cycle written for Marilyn Horne, who premiered it at Carnegie Hall in March. Paul McCartney's *Liverpool Oratorio*, written with Carl Davis, came to Carnegie Hall in November. Davis conducted the Royal Liverpool Philharmonic, vocal soloists, the 180-member Collegiate Chorale, and the Boys Choir of Harlem. One U.S. critic judged the production "musically primitive."

**Orchestra News.** The Chicago Symphony celebrated its centennial and music director Sir Georg Solti's final season. A strike in September caused the cancellation of the first three weeks of the orchestra's new season—Daniel Barenboim's first as music director.

Both the St. Louis Symphony and the New York Philharmonic canceled European tours because of the Persian Gulf War. Zubin Mehta, then music director of both the New York Philharmonic and the Israel Philharmonic, canceled concerts with the U.S. orchestra in January in order to be in Israel during the war.

In September, German maestro Kurt Masur took over from Mehta as the New York Philharmonic's music director. Known as a disciplinarian and orchestra builder, the 63-year-old conductor has helped generate a new esprit de corps.

**Musical Chairs.** Among other changes, Catherine Comet announced that she would step down as music director of the American Symphony Orchestra; she was to be succeeded in 1992 by Leon Botstein. Chicago Symphony music director Daniel Barenboim became artistic director of Berlin's Deutsche Staatsoper. American conductor Kent Nagano became music director and principal conductor designate of England's Hallé Orchestra. Charles Dutoit, music director of the Orchestre Symphonique de Montréal, became music director of L'Orchestre National de France.

**Awards.** Composer and educator Gunther Schuller received a $374,000 MacArthur fellowship, and composer John Corigliano was

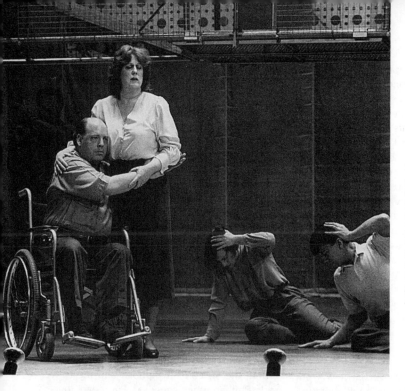

The Death of Klinghoffer, a controversial new opera from composer John Adams, librettist Alice Goodman, choreographer Mark Morris, and director Peter Sellars, was based on the 1985 hijacking of the cruise ship Achille Lauro by Palestinian terrorists and the murder of a wheelchair-bound passenger.

the winner of the prestigious $150,000 Louisville University Grawemeyer Award for his Symphony No. 1. Shulamit Ran became the second woman ever to win the Pulitzer Prize for music, for her symphony.

**Losses.** Three grand masters of pianism died in 1991: German Wilhelm Kempff, 96; Rudolf Serkin, 88, who began his career in Vienna in 1915; and Chilean pianist Claudio Arrau, 88. Others who died included Ernest Krenet, a Viennese-born American avant-garde composer; Anthony Bliss, onetime Metropolitan Opera executive director; and Polish-born British composer and conductor Andrzej Panufnik.

S.E.

## CLASSICAL RECORDINGS

The 1991 classical recording scene was dominated by Mozart mania. The bicentennial year of Mozart's death on December 5, 1791, was accompanied by a deluge, with Philips assembling—and 40,000 fans buying—every last note by Mozart in a mammoth collection running to 180 compact disks in 45 volumes. Still, the classical record business confronted reality as recession belt-tightening and a glutted market brought about an alarming downturn in sales.

The video medium offered long-range hope

to the industry. In the battle of the formats, tape was still outselling laserdisks, but promotion stressed the laserdisk's technical superiority to tape.

As hardware manufacturers and recording companies resolved their legal dispute over digital recording with an agreement (expected to be voted into law by Congress) allowing record makers and music publishers to collect royalties from the sale of blank tapes and disks, Sony unveiled its new Mini-Disc. This player, the size of a Walkman, can record onto a small magneto-optical disk, producing perfect sound. Philips demonstrated a related product, the digital compact cassette, that uses new perfect-duplicate technology in the form of tape.

**The Crossover Band-Aid.** Casting classical artists in popular roles remained lucrative. Top-selling crossover CDs included divas Kathleen Battle and Jessye Norman singing Spirituals in Concert (DG audio and video), baritone Thomas Hampson's crooning Night and Day and other Cole Porter songs (EMI), tenor José Carreras interpreting Hollywood's Golden Classics (Atlantic), and Placido Domingo and Itzhak Perlman Together (EMI). Crossover also worked the other way: Sting narrated Prokofiev's *Peter and the Wolf* (DG), and jazz pianist Keith Jarrett collaborated with recorder virtuoso Michala Petri in Handel sonatas (RCA). EMI scored a coup with ex-Beatle Paul McCartney's *Liverpool Oratorio*, his first classical venture.

**Welcome Reissues.** A steady stream of the industry's finest hours continued to pour forth. From EMI, recordings by Otto Klemperer, Maria Callas, Sir John Barbirolli, Artur Schnabel, Wilhelm Furtwängler, and others reminded listeners of the character, imagination, and grasp of style so often missing in contemporary performances. From BMG (RCA), the complete Arturo Toscanini Collection continued with Verdi's *Otello*, *Un ballo in maschera*, and *La traviata*, Puccini's *La Bohème*, Beethoven's *Fidelio*, and the maestro's famous New York Philharmonic recordings; also from BMG, the complete recordings of Enrico Caruso, history's most famous tenor, were released in a set of 12 CDs.

From Sony came a monumental 22-CD set of Stravinsky's stereo recordings of his own music and all of the "Copland Conducts Copland" series. Philips released two distinguished symphony cycles: Igor Markevitch's Tchaikovsky and Witold Rowicki's Dvorak. Koch International's historical series unearthed all the recordings by Richard Strauss of music other than his own, Furtwängler's earliest recordings on a pair of two-CD sets, and early Dvorak symphony recordings and the 1929 Smetana *Ma Vlast* conducted by Vaclav Talich.

**Opera.** James Levine's *Götterdämmerung* (DG) and Bernard Haitink's *Siegfried* (EMI) brought each conductor to within striking distance of completing his Wagner *Ring* cycle. Charles Dutoit led a French cast in Debussy's *Pelléas et Mélisande* (Decca/London), and Sir Georg Solti bid farewell to the Chicago Symphony Orchestra after 22 years as music director with a concert recording of Verdi's *Otello*, featuring Luciano Pavarotti in his first performance of the title role (Decca-London).

**Recording of the Year.** The Chicago Symphony itself produced the year's most impressive release—12 CDs of live broadcasts and out-of-print recordings dating from 1916 to 1988, crackling with a spontaneity and verve rarely heard on record. S.C.

**MYANMAR.** Repressive military rule continued in Myanmar (the official name for Burma) in 1991. The award of the Nobel Peace Prize to dissident leader Aung San Suu Kyi focused world attention upon her imprisonment and the political and economic environment of Myanmar. In July, Aung San Suu Kyi's house arrest was extended for three more years, although she has never been formally charged or tried in court. Antigovernment demonstrations in the capital city around the time of the Nobel award ceremonies in December (which Aung San Suu Kyi was unable to attend) resulted in the closing of the universities and numerous arrests.

The military government persisted in arresting, imprisoning, or ignoring the civilians who were elected to the proposed national Parliament in May 1990. A group of the elected representatives who were still free had formed the National Coalition Government of the Union of Burma (NCGUB), based in rebel-held territory. Its leader, Sein Win, a cousin of Aung San Suu Kyi, met with U.S. government officials and human rights groups to lobby for support for the restoration of democracy. He also warned that the military government was building up a formidable arsenal.

The military had offered minority groups the opportunity to keep their weapons, pursue their economic interests, and even continue to participate in the narcotics trade in exchange for halting their military resistance to Army rule. Some accepted, but other minorities continued to resist. In October the Kayin (formerly Karen) recovered Wa Paw Koe, one of the border enclaves they had lost in 1989-1990. In October, then again in late November and early December, the Kayin launched new offensives in the country's heartland, in the Irrawaddy delta area near Bogale. More than 1,000 were reported killed. In Kachin State the Army forced thousands of Kachins to move into temporary shelter to be used as human shields in case of attack.

In April the Kachins issued a new law calling for the total elimination of all cultivation, use, or trade of opium in their state by January 1, 1992. Under the new law convicted crop financiers and traders would be subject to the death penalty.

The economy of Myanmar saw little growth. The nation spent heavily on arms purchases, but little or no investment in productive areas was noted. Inflation ran between 40 and 60 percent, new jobs were scarce, and flooding in the 1991 rainy season was expected to reduce the rice crop by 300,000 tons. In July, the United States said it would not renew its $9 million textile trade agreement with Myanmar because of political abuses.

See STATISTICS OF THE WORLD: *Burma*.

J.S.

# N

**NAMIBIA.** In 1991, its first full year of independence, Namibia was able to boast of political stability and reconciliation but of only limited progress in addressing long- term issues of economic inequality and underdevelopment.

**Domestic Affairs.** The ruling South West African People's Organization (Swapo) pursued a course of compromise with opposition groups and of gradualism in addressing racial inequalities within the country.

A week-long conference on land reform in July discussed the problems of concentration of ownership. Whites, who are approximately 5 percent of the population, own 60 percent of the land and 95 percent of the commercial farmland. The conference, representing all sectors of Namibian society, reached a consensus on the need for action to redress the inequality, with specific proposals introducing taxes on commercial farmland, protective measures for farmworkers, expropriation of land with absentee foreign owners, and reallocation of underused land. The conference rejected nationalization of farms owned by Namibian citizens. In December, Swapo's first full Congress elected a mix of former exiles and internal leaders to the Central Committee and overwhelmingly reelected Sam Nujoma as party president.

With falling prices and production cutbacks for mineral exports such as uranium, drought in some parts of the country, and rising costs for oil imports, the Namibian economy went into recession. The government made some progress in eliminating wasteful separate racial and ethnic bureaucracies, and it resisted pressures to utilize the so-called peace dividend, some $114 million of annual budget savings, to provide tax cuts for the white commercial sector. Instead, budget allocations for health, education, and assistance to black farmers all increased substantially.

The government also began expanding veterinary services in order to improve the standard of black farmers' cattle and thus move farther north the "red line" south of which cattle meet European Community health standards. Eventually this should enable more blacks to sell their cattle in the commercial market, which produces beef for export to Europe and South Africa.

**Foreign Relations.** Namibian and South African delegations met in March to discuss the disputed status of Walvis Bay, Namibia's only significant port, where South Africa maintains military bases as well as a stranglehold over Namibia's foreign trade. Although the talks were inconclusive, observers reported that South Africa had tacitly agreed that eventually, once the issue was no longer politically sensitive for its white minority government, the port would revert to Namibian control.

There were a number of incidents along the Angolan border, especially when troops of the Angolan government or the rebel National Union for the Total Independence of Angola (Unita) crossed into Namibia in search of their opponents. But Namibia allowed the passage of UN relief convoys to territory controlled by both sides, even before a cease-fire in the conflict was declared at the end of May.

Despite its unique status as a former United Nations ward, Namibia found itself with only limited international support in the form of postindependence aid. One reason was Namibia's failure, because of the relatively high per capita income, to gain classification by international financial institutions as a "least developed country."

See STATISTICS OF THE WORLD.　　W.M.

**NAURU.** See STATISTICS OF THE WORLD.

**NEBRASKA.** See STATISTICS OF THE WORLD.

**NEGROES IN THE UNITED STATES.** See BLACKS IN THE UNITED STATES.

**NEPAL.** On May 12, 1991, Nepal held its first multiparty parliamentary elections since 1959. K. P. Bhattarai, appointed in 1990 as head of an interim coalition government, resigned as prime minister after losing his seat in the new House of Representatives; however, his party, the moderate Nepali Congress Party (NCP), emerged as the majority with 110 of the 205 seats. The United Marxist-Leninists (UML), composed of several relatively moderate Communist factions, became the second-largest party.

The elections resulted in the dissolution of an informal working arrangement between the NCP and the UML; those groups had led the movement in 1990 that pressured King Birendra into accepting a new political system based upon the principles of a democratic constitutional monarchy. After the elections the NCP formed a government headed by Prime Minister G. P. Koirala.

The Nepali economy continued to flounder, despite efforts by the new government to introduce reforms. The primary problem was the weak state of the Indian economy, about which Nepal's government could do little.

The government did move quickly and firmly to repair the damage done to Indo-Nepali relations in 1990, when New Delhi imposed a temporary blockade on trade with landlocked Nepal, then placed tight limits on trade. Real negotiations on several critical issues now seemed possible, and in December new trade and transit agreements between the two countries were concluded.

See STATISTICS OF THE WORLD.　　L.E.R.

**NETHERLANDS, THE.** In 1991 the Netherlands participated in the U.S.-led coalition against Iraq in the Persian Gulf War. The government sent two squadrons each of Patriot and Hawk missiles in January to help defend NATO ally Turkey against a possible air attack from neighboring Iraq. In the Gulf itself, two Dutch frigates and a supply ship, which had been in the region as part of the allied contingent enforcing the trade embargo against Iraq, were placed under U.S. military command when the war broke out in mid-January. The Netherlands also provided Israel with eight Patriot missile batteries. After the war, the Netherlands sent troops, engineers, medical personnel, and supplies as part of a Western plan to establish protected camps for Kurdish refugees in northern Iraq. The Dutch government also pledged financial assistance for Kurdish refugees in neighboring Iran.

In March, responding to the end of the cold war, the government announced plans to reduce the country's armed forces to 40,000 people over ten years, just under one-third of their present strength.

In domestic politics, elections for the 12 provincial legislatures on March 6 resulted in losses for both governing parties, the Christian Democratic Appeal (CDA) and the Labor Party (PvdA). The election was widely seen as an indication of voters' displeasure with austerity measures proposed by the government in February. On September 18, Dutch unions held a national strike in protest. Despite the election outcome, CDA and PvdA party leaders reaffirmed their commitment to the coalition and its program.

The Netherlands chaired the European Community's rotating presidency during the second half of 1991 and hosted an EC summit meeting in December at Maastricht at which treaties marking steps toward closer political and economic union were finalized.

See STATISTICS OF THE WORLD.　　W.C.C.

**NEVADA.** See STATISTICS OF THE WORLD.

**NEW BRUNSWICK.** See STATISTICS OF THE WORLD. See also CANADA.

**NEWFOUNDLAND.** See STATISTICS OF THE WORLD.

**NEW HAMPSHIRE.** See STATISTICS OF THE WORLD.

**NEW JERSEY.** See STATISTICS OF THE WORLD. See also STATE GOVERNMENT REVIEW.

**NEW MEXICO.** See STATISTICS OF THE WORLD.

**NEW YORK.** See STATISTICS OF THE WORLD.

**NEW ZEALAND.** The popularity of Prime Minister Jim Bolger's newly installed National Party government fell steeply in 1991 as measures to restructure New Zealand's economy intensified.

**Postelection Developments.** Bolger's new government got off to a slow start. In forming his cabinet, in late 1990, he had given Winston Peters, a Maori member of Parliament, responsibility for Maori affairs and a cabinet seat. Following months of vocal criticism from Peters, he dropped him from the cabinet in an October 1991 reshuffle. Debts exceeding $600 million (New Zealand dollars) incurred by the state-owned Bank of New Zealand aggravated budgetary pressures. A financial package designed to reduce expenditures through administrative savings and social welfare cuts went into effect in April.

**Tough July Budget.** In July, Finance Minister Ruth Richardson unveiled what she described as "the mother of all budgets." Besides seeking savings on pensions, the new budget fell short of fulfilling spending commitments previously made to the elderly and left intact a much-criticized surtax on additional income earned by recipients of state pensions. The state-funded universal healthcare system was modified, as steep increases were made in hospitals' and doctors' fees; however, more than half of the population were classified as low-income families, eligible for discounts on health and social services. The budget forecast virtually no economic growth until 1993, with the unemployment rate rising to around 12 percent.

**Opposition Parties.** As the new National government began to organize, the defeated Labor Party moved quickly to regain its traditional position on the left, endorsing new policies on many issues, including a "negotiated" rather than a "market" economy for New Zealand. A new party, the Liberals, came into existence in August.

**New Legislation.** The Employment Contracts Act, passed in May despite union protests, permitted groups other than trade unions to represent workers in negotiations with employers.

Legislation regulating New Zealand's broadcasting services was amended in the spring to permit 100 percent foreign ownership of radio and television companies. A few days later, an American consortium consisting of Ameritech and Bell Atlantic—owners since 1990 of New Zealand's principal telephone company, Telecom—and Time Warner purchased control of Sky Entertainment, a three-channel network relying on satellite transmissions for sports, cable news, and movies.

**Foreign Affairs.** Prime Minister Bolger dispatched 112 New Zealand medical and air force personnel to join the U.S.-led coalition

**Prime Minister Under Siege**
In his first year in office, New Zealand Prime Minister Jim Bolger saw his popularity plummet. Bolger, 56, had been leader of New Zealand's National Party since March 1986 and became prime minister after the October 1990 elections. In the face of rising unemployment and a much larger than anticipated budget deficit, Bolger's government introduced major cutbacks in New Zealand's "cradle to grave" welfare system. Among the changes were cuts in unemployment and health benefits, state-funded pensions, and housing assistance. After 14 months in office Jim Bolger's popularity was at only 5 percent, which was a record low for a New Zealand prime minister.

*Jim Bolger*

*Dame Catherine Tizard reads the Speech From the Throne at the opening of New Zealand's Parliament in January. With her swearing in the previous month, she became the first woman governor-general in New Zealand's history.*

against Iraq. The move was criticized but won Labor Party endorsement once hostilities started in January. Ultimately, New Zealand's medical teams had no part to play, but the country's two Hercules transport planes flew frequent missions moving troops and supplies.

Diplomatic relations with Namibia were established in January. French Prime Minister Michel Rocard visited New Zealand in the spring in a bid to repair relations damaged in 1985, when French security agents sank a Greenpeace vessel in Auckland harbor. New Zealand denounced the abortive coup in the Soviet Union and recognized the independence of Latvia, Lithuania, and Estonia in late August.

See STATISTICS OF THE WORLD.          S.L.

**NICARAGUA.** In 1991 the reconstruction of Nicaragua's government, economy, and society continued, in an atmosphere made tense by threats of renewed civil war.

**Tense Political Situation.** April 1991 marked the first anniversary of the national elections in which the Sandinistas, the revolutionary liberation front that won power in 1979, lost to a U.S.-backed coalition led by Violeta Chamorro. Under the 1990 transition accord, however, the Sandinistas continued to control the army, security forces, and important unions. Meanwhile, the governing coalition was divided into two principal factions. One stressed a cooperative approach to relations with the Sandinistas—much to the dismay of the other.

In February, Enrique Bermúdez, a former military leader of the anti-Sandinista guerrillas, or contras, was assassinated in Managua. A presidential commission was unable to unearth any suspects. Bermúdez's widow charged that the government, along with the Sandinistas, was conspiring to suppress evidence and delay the investigation.

The International Commission of Support and Verification (CIAV), the joint United Nations-Organization of American States team formed under the 1989 peace initiatives, reported that groups of contras had begun to rearm, attacking police stations and Sandinista-run farm cooperatives in retaliation for the government's failure to redistribute Sandinista-held land and to remove Sandinista officers from the military.

In June former President Daniel Ortega, now the secretary-general of the Sandinista party, warned that civil war could break out again if the legislature repealed the Sandinista government's transfer of millions of dollars worth of government-controlled property to supporters, by means of controversial legislation enacted just before its term ended. Sandinista sympathizers occupied at least six city halls and three radio stations in a protest against the proposed repeal, and bombs went off at the headquarters of pro-government parties. In August the ruling coalition pushed a repeal bill through the legislature, applying only to property above $11,600 in value, but it was vetoed by Chamorro. The veto was sustained in a December vote.

The Sandinistas held their first party congress in July. Seven members of the previously self-appointed National Directorate nominated

*The victim of an assassin, former Nicaraguan contra leader Enrique Bermúdez was laid to rest in February. The slaying, which some ascribed to the Sandinistas, was a clear indication that political tensions were still running high in Nicaragua.*

themselves for election as a group and were confirmed on that basis, despite reformist proposals that nominees compete individually on an open ballot.

**Search for Economic Stability.** Gross national product continued its fall in 1991. On March 4 the government began a new economic stabilization program based on devaluating the currency, which was anchored to the dollar. The new package included increases in state salaries, wholesale prices of basic foods and fuel, and costs for public transportation and utilities. Over 45,000 workers went on strike to protest the plan. The government also began a privatization program.

After a direct appeal by Chamorro in an April address to the U.S. Congress, the United States agreed to deliver aid that had been held up, and Nicaragua repealed a law requiring it to press for payment by the United States of claims assessed by the World Court for war damages. The United States forgave most of Nicaragua's debt to Washington.

**Foreign Affairs.** The Chamorro government renewed relations with El Salvador and was asked by the Salvadoran guerrillas to help mediate an end to the civil war in that country. Over U.S. objections, Salvadoran guerrillas were permitted to remain in Nicaragua. Relations with Costa Rica were strengthened by the formation of a binational commission and by Nicaraguan aid after the Costa Rican earthquake in April.

In September an accord was signed with the United States to combat the use of Nicaragua's Atlantic coast as a transfer point for cocaine.

*See* STATISTICS OF THE WORLD. J.F.A.

**NIGER.** *See* STATISTICS OF THE WORLD.

**NIGERIA.** The military regime of President Ibrahim Babangida proceeded with plans for a guided transition to civilian government. In December 1990 the two government-designated political parties, the Social Democratic Party (SDP) and the National Republican Convention (NRC), had competed in local elections, with the former winning a few more seats than the latter. In August 1991, Babangida announced a realignment of Nigeria's federal structure, creating nine new states to give representation to several ethnic minorities. Within this 30-state system more than 130 new local governments were formed. In addition, a number of state ministries were to be consolidated. Party primaries were finally conducted in October; in the elections, held in December, the NRC did well among the Ibos in the southeast and also in the Muslim north, while the SDP enjoyed success in the Christian and Yoruba-dominated west.

In April, Shiite Muslims clashed with police in the north, climaxing a growing strain between Shiite leaders and the military governor of Katsina State, a Christian. Christians and Muslims also rioted in Bauchi State, leaving more than 80 people dead. In October, Muslims attacked Christians in the northern city of Kano; at least ten people were killed.

There were student protests at several college campuses in May. In Lagos police killed two students during a campus riot, and three other universities were closed by demonstrations. Unrest spread to other campuses, and the government arrested student activist leaders. Meanwhile, riots erupted in Lagos in February after police demolished illegal shops and trading stalls in the central market; and workers staged several strikes during the year.

Although foreign earnings increased as a result of oil prices during the Persian Gulf crisis, the overall economy suffered from high debt and fiscal expansion. As part of an effort to close a high fiscal deficit, debt service on external loans was limited to 30 percent of foreign exchange earnings. The minimum wage was set at around $25 per month. Interest rates were lowered and regulations on the foreign exchange market tightened. In February the International Monetary Fund approved a new standby credit for Nigeria, facilitating the rescheduling of foreign debt. On the negative side, it was estimated that Nigeria had been swindled of some $200 million by the Bank of Credit and Commerce International, a long-time presence in the nation's banking sector.

Nigeria continued its leading role in the regional peacekeeping force dispatched to war-torn Liberia and acted to improve relations with other African states. In June, Babangida assumed the chairmanship of the Organization of African Unity.

See STATISTICS OF THE WORLD.        P.M.L.

**NORTH ATLANTIC TREATY ORGANIZATION.** See MILITARY AND NAVAL AFFAIRS.

**NORTH CAROLINA.** See STATISTICS OF THE WORLD.

**NORTH DAKOTA.** See STATISTICS OF THE WORLD.

**NORTHERN MARIANA ISLANDS.** See STATISTICS OF THE WORLD.

**NORTHWEST TERRITORIES.** See STATISTICS OF THE WORLD.

**NORWAY.** Olav V, king of Norway since 1957, died on January 17, 1991, at the age of 87. Born a Danish prince in 1903, Olav acquired a new homeland in 1905 when his father, Haakon VII, became the first king of newly independent Norway. In 1929, Olav married his Swedish cousin Princess Martha, with whom he had three children. (She died in 1954.) During World War II, Olav played a key role in leading from exile the Norwegian resistance to the Nazi occupation.

Upon the death of his father, Crown Prince Harald assumed the throne. Born in 1937, Harald received a military education in Norway and later attended Oxford University in England. In 1968 he married Sonja Haraldsen, a Norwegian commoner; they have two children. On June 23 the new king and queen were consecrated in a magnificent ceremony in the Nidaros Cathedral in Trondheim.

Meanwhile, local and regional elections on September 9 dealt a painful blow to the governing Labor Party. Nationally, the party received 30.5 percent of the vote, a decline of 5.4 percent since the previous elections in 1987. The number of Labor representatives on the 18 provincial councils was reduced by approximately one-fourth. The principal winners of the elections were the agrarian Center Party and the Socialist Left, whose unexpectedly strong showings seemed to reflect opposition on the part of many to Norwegian membership in the European Community.

Oil revenues increased significantly, and inflation continued to fall. Yet these positive developments were offset by unusually high unemployment rates of 7 to 8 percent and a significant increase in small business bankruptcies. All three major Norwegian commercial banks reported huge losses, prompting large government infusions of capital. In October the government released a budget designed to substantially reduce tax rates on personal income and containing the largest government deficit in Norwegian history. The budget was approved in December.

The head of the Norwegian National Security Police, Svein Urdal, resigned on October 11 following disclosures that his agency had allowed Israeli intelligence agents to interrogate Palestinian refugees seeking political asylum in Norway. The Israeli agents had been presented to them as "language experts." No Arabic-speaking Norwegian police officers had been present during these interrogations, and no official records had been kept. These practices were roundly criticized by all major political parties.

See STATISTICS OF THE WORLD.        K.S.

**NOVA SCOTIA.** See STATISTICS OF THE WORLD.

**NUCLEAR POWER.** See ENERGY.

279

# O

**OBITUARIES.** The following are among notable figures who died in 1991.

**Abbott, Berenice**, 93, pioneer of modern photography who first gained acclaim for her portraits of writers and artists in Paris in the 1920s but was best known for her photographs of New York City in the 1930s. She also took scientific photographs, many of which appeared in the textbook *Physics* (1960). December 10 in Monson, Me.

**Anderson, Carl David**, 85, cowinner of the 1936 Nobel Prize in physics for his discovery of the positron, an atomic particle also known as the positive electron. January 11 in San Marino, Calif.

**Appling, Luke**, 83, Chicago White Sox shortstop (1930-1950) who hit over .300 in all but four seasons and was elected to the Baseball Hall of Fame in 1964. Known as Old Aches and Pains because of the numerous maladies he complained of, Appling said he played best when he felt worst. January 3 in Cumming, Ga.

**Arrau, Claudio**, 88, eminent Chilean-born pianist who gave his first public performance at age five, playing works by Mozart, Beethoven, and Schumann. Highly admired for his interpretations of Liszt and Beethoven, as well as of Chopin, Schumann, and Debussy, Arrau played with purity, precision, and, even in later years, energy and passion. June 9 in Mürzzuschlag, Austria.

**Arthur, Jean (Gladys Georgianna Greene)**, 90, spunky, amiable actress who starred in several Frank Capra comedy dramas, including *Mr. Deeds Goes to Town* (1936), *You Can't Take It With You* (1938), and *Mr. Smith Goes to Washington* (1939). She was widely praised for her 1950 Broadway performance as Peter Pan. A perfectionist, she was often suspended by Columbia Pictures for refusing to take roles. June 19 in Carmel, Calif.

**Ashcroft, Dame Peggy**, 83, acclaimed British actress whose career spanned nearly six decades, from the Old Vic to the TV screen. Colleagues praised her emotional identification with characters and her versatility, as she

**DAME PEGGY ASHCROFT**

evolved gracefully from Shakespearean roles to works by Shaw, Ibsen, and Beckett. Late in life she won international fame for her Oscar-winning role in the movie *A Passage to India* (1984) and her performance in the 1980s TV miniseries *The Jewel in the Crown*. June 14 in London.

**Ashman, Howard**, 40, lyricist, playwright, and director. In 1982 he cowrote and staged a musical version of the 1960 film *The Little Shop of Horrors*; it became Off Broadway's third-longest-running musical. He shared an Academy Award in 1989 for the song *Under the Sea*, from the film *The Little Mermaid*. March 14 in New York City.

**Atwater, Lee (Harvey LeRoy Atwater)**, 40, skillful political tactician who, as George Bush's campaign manager during the 1988 presidential campaign, helped badly defeat Massachusetts Governor Michael Dukakis, the Democratic nominee. Atwater's negative campaigning was exemplified in 1988 by advertisements recalling Willie Horton—a convicted black murderer who raped a white woman while on a Massachusetts prison furlough program—to charge that Dukakis was soft on crime and, critics said, capitalize on racial fears. Appointed chairman of the Republican National Committee in 1989, he resigned about a year later because of a brain tumor. March 29 in Washington, D.C.

**Bakhtiar, Shahpur**, 75, Iranian leader who, as prime minister of Iran for 39 days in early

1979 after the departure of Shah Muhammad Riza Pahlavi, sought unsuccessfully to avert an Islamic revolution spearheaded by Ayatollah Ruhollah Khomeini. After his ouster, he escaped to France and formed the National Iranian Resistance Movement. Found stabbed to death on August 8 in Suresnes, France.

**Barbie, Klaus**, 77, Nazi war criminal; known as the butcher of Lyon, he led the Gestapo reign of terror against Resistance leaders there and was found responsible for the torture and death of many thousands. After World War II, Barbie was used by the U.S. Army as a paid informer and was helped to escape to South America, where Nazi-hunters tracked him down in 1972; ultimately extradited to France, he was sentenced to life imprisonment in 1987. September 25 in prison in Lyons, France.

**Bardeen, John**, 82, physicist, inventor, and two-time Nobel laureate. In 1957 he shared a Nobel Prize in physics for his contribution to developing the transistor; in 1972 he was cowinner of the same prize for helping to develop a theory of superconductivity. January 30 in Boston.

**Bell, James ("Cool Papa")**, 87, star batter and base runner of the Negro leagues from 1922 to 1946, and regarded by many as the fastest man in the history of baseball. Although Bell retired a year before the major leagues ended their color barrier, he became a living legend and in 1974 was inducted into the Baseball Hall of Fame. March 7 in St. Louis.

**Bellamy, Ralph**, 87, character actor. In 1958 he won the Tony and Drama Critics best actor awards for his portrayal, in *Sunrise at Campobello*, of Franklin Roosevelt struggling to resume an active life after polio. He played the same part in the 1960 movie and in 1983 played Roosevelt again in the TV miniseries *The Winds of War*. Later movies included *Trading Places* (1983) and *Pretty Woman* (1990). November 29 in Los Angeles.

**Bigart, Homer**, 83, acclaimed newspaper reporter who in a 43-year career for the New York *Herald Tribune* and the New York *Times* covered World War II, the Korean War, and the civil rights struggle; he received two Pulitzer Prizes, in 1946 and in 1951. April 16 in Portsmouth, N.H.

**Brown, Paul**, 82, innovative football coach who scored successes at all levels, from high school to professional. He founded the Cleveland Browns in 1946 and led them to eight straight titles, also introducing such measures as diagrammed pass patterns. From 1968 to 1975 he coached the Cincinnati Bengals, building them into a powerful team. August 5 in Cincinnati.

**Capra, Frank**, 94, Sicilian-born Hollywood film director who captured the hearts of Americans with his fast-paced sentimental films about regular guys who courageously overcome evil and corruption. He won three Oscars, for directing *It Happened One Night* (1934), *Mr. Deeds Goes to Town* (1936), and *You Can't Take It With You* (1938); also highly acclaimed was *Mr. Smith Goes to Washington* (1939). His own favorite, *It's a Wonderful Life* (1946), was derided as oversentimental, but eventually became a holiday favorite on television. September 3 in La Quinta, Calif.

**FRANK CAPRA**

# OBITUARIES

**Caulfield, Joan**, 69, glamorous actress who was propelled to fame in the 1940s films *Monsieur Beaucaire*, *Blue Skies*, and *Dear Ruth*. On television she costarred in the situation comedy *My Favorite Husband* (1953-1957). June 18 in Los Angeles.

**Chandler, A. B. ("Happy")**, 92, former governor of Kentucky, U.S. senator, and baseball commissioner from 1945 to 1951. As commissioner he supported Jackie Robinson's entrance into the major leagues, breaking the color line, and fought for players' rights; ousted by dissatisfied owners, he was finally elected to the Baseball Hall of Fame in 1982. June 15 in Versailles, Ky.

**Clark, Manning**, 76, Australia's best-known historian. His landmark six-volume work, *A History of Australia* (1962-1987), became the classic account of how the Australian nation was shaped by the lives and character of its people. May 30 in Canberra.

## MILES DAVIS

**Convy, Bert**, 57, actor and television personality. Besides roles in numerous movies and Broadway shows, he hosted a TV variety show and several game shows, winning an Emmy award as best game show host for *Tattletales*. July 15 in Brentwood, Calif.

**Cooper, John Sherman**, 89, longtime U.S. senator from Kentucky. A liberal Republican, Cooper was one of the first of his party to oppose Senator Joseph McCarthy and coauthored a 1969 amendment barring U.S. troops from fighting in Laos and Thailand. February 21 in Washington, D.C.

**Croll, David**, 91, Liberal Canadian politician who, in a 60-year career as mayor, provincial legislator, member of the federal Parliament, and federal senator, waged a tireless battle to aid workers and the underprivileged. June 11 in Ottawa.

**Daly, John Charles, Jr.**, 77, radio reporter and correspondent who achieved his greatest fame as personable host of the highly popular game show *What's My Line?* (1950-1967); he also was a news executive at ABC. February 25 in Chevy Chase, Md.

**Davis, Miles**, 65, jazz trumpeter, considered a genius by his peers. His unmistakable, voicelike tone was imitated by countless trumpeters, as was his constantly evolving style: He began playing in the era of be-bop and subsequently switched to cool jazz, hard bop, modal jazz, jazz-rock, and jazz-funk, as he drew inspiration from blues and other sources. On-stage he could be arrogant and aloof; off-stage he was flamboyant and independent. September 28 in Santa Monica, Calif.

**De Castries, Christian de la Croix**, 88, aristocratic French brigadier general. He became a national hero for defending the fortress of Dien Bien Phu in the jungles of Vietnam for 55 days against a devastating siege by Communist guerrillas. His final surrender, on May 17, 1954, marked the end of French rule in Indochina. Death announced July 30 in France.

**Delacorte, George T.**, 97, founder of Dell Publishing, known for its pulp magazines and comic books and (after World War II) its literary paperback reprints. He was a major benefactor to New York's Central Park, where the famous Alice in Wonderland statue is just one of his contributions. May 4 in New York City.

**DAME MARGOT FONTEYN**

**Dewhurst, Colleen**, 67, distinguished Canadian-born actress of stage, screen, and television. A larger-than-life figure with a full, throaty voice, she often played tragic characters and was closely identified with the plays of Eugene O'Neill. In 1973 she received a Tony nomination for her role in O'Neill's *Mourning Becomes Electra*; the next year she won a Tony for her part in his *A Moon for the Misbegotten*. She earned three Emmy awards for work on television. August 22 in South Salem, N.Y.

**Dimitrios I (Dimitrios Papadopoulos)**, 77, ecumenical patriarch of Constantinople and spiritual leader of over 250 million Eastern Orthodox Christians around the world. A mildly liberal theologian, he became, in 1990, the first patriarch to visit the western hemisphere. October 2 in Istanbul.

**Dunnock, Mildred**, 90, superb character actress who originated the role of Willy Loman's wife in the 1949 Broadway production of *Death of a Salesman*; in 1951 she received an Academy Award nomination for her role in the film version. She originated other classic parts and excelled in portraying mothers and eccentrics. A second Oscar nomination came for her performance in *Baby Doll* (1956). July 5 in Oak Bluffs, Mass.

**Durocher, Leo**, 86, feisty, never-say-die major league baseball player and manager who fought to win and coined the phrase "Nice guys finish last." After playing shortstop for 17 seasons, he spent 24 years managing the Brooklyn Dodgers, New York Giants, Chicago Cubs, and Houston Astros, leading the Dodgers to a 1941 pennant and the Giants to pennants in 1951 and 1954, the year they won the World Series. October 7 in Palm Springs, Calif.

**Fender, Clarence Leo**, 81, codesigner and manufacturer of the first mass-produced electric guitars. The 1954 Fender Stratocaster became a standard among rock musicians. March 21 in Fullerton, Calif.

**Finkelstein, Louis**, 96, dominant leader of Conservative Judaism in the 20th century. He headed the Jewish Theological Seminary of America from 1940 to 1972, when the Conservative movement emerged as the largest branch of Judaism. He made interfaith dialogue a priority and was associated with several U.S. presidents. November 29 in New York.

**Fish, Hamilton, III**, 102, conservative Republican U.S. representative from New York (1919-1945); he opposed U.S. involvement in World War II until the attack on Pearl Harbor and was a vocal adversary of President Franklin D. Roosevelt's New Deal politics. January 18 in Cold Spring, N.Y.

**Fodor, Eugene**, 85, creator of the famous travel guides that bear his name; begun in 1936, the Fodor series grew to more than 140 titles, with 200 million copies being sold each year. February 18 in Litchfield, Conn.

**Fonteyn, Dame Margot (Margaret Hookham)**, 71, prima ballerina of Britain's Royal Ballet. For almost 50 years, Fonteyn personified elegance and refinement while redefining classical ballet with passionate and lyrical performances. She excelled as Odette/Odile in *Swan Lake* (1935) and Princess Aurora in *The*

**REDD FOXX**

Sleeping Beauty (1939) and won acclaim in challenging roles written for her by British choreographer Sir Frederick Ashton. At 42 she began a dynamic partnership with the 23-year-old Russian defector Rudolf Nureyev. February 21 in Panama City.

**Ford, Tennessee Ernie (Ernest Jennings Ford)**, 72, country and western singer and TV variety show host in the 1950s and 1960s with an endearing down-home, folksy manner. Besides 16 Tons (1955), one of the best-selling records of all time, his recordings included Mule Train, Smoky Mountain Boogie, and Hogtied Over You. October 17 in Reston, Va.

**Foxx, Redd (John Sanford)**, 68, comedian best known as the crusty junk dealer on the 1970s TV series Sanford and Son. During a long career on the black theater and cabaret circuit he made 54 "party records"—bawdy spoken comedy recordings—that sold 20 million copies. In 1991 he began a new TV series, The Royal Family. October 12 in Los Angeles.

**Franciscus, James**, 57, actor and producer best known for his title roles as the earnest, likeable teacher in the TV series Mr. Novak (1963-1965) and the blind investigator in Longstreet (1971-1972). As a producer he

brought such classics as Jane Eyre, Heidi, and The Red Pony to the small screen. July 8 in North Hollywood, Calif.

**Frisch, Max**, 79, Swiss writer whose work examined the struggle for individual identity in a changing world; his novels include I'm Not Stiller (1958) and Man in the Holocene (1980); among his plays was The Firebugs (1958). April 4 near Zurich.

**Frye, Northrop**, 78, Canadian literary critic and educator. He first set forth his principles for a literary criticism founded on archetypes and myths in his book Anatomy of Criticism (1957). Other important writings include Fearful Symmetry (1947) and The Great Code: The Bible and Literature (1982). January 23 in Toronto.

**Gandhi, Rajiv**, 46, former Indian prime minister. The son of Indira Gandhi and grandson of Jawaharlal Nehru, he entered politics only reluctantly, winning a parliamentary seat after the death of his brother Sanjay in 1980. Made general secretary of the Congress Party in 1983, he became prime minister in October 1984 after mother's assassination; in an election later that year his party won a record majority in Parliament. Strongly advocating integrity in government and reconciliation among ethnic groups, he had only limited success in calming ethnic strife and was tarnished by a party corruption scandal, although never personally accused of wrongdoing; he lost office in November 1989. Assassinated while campaigning for reelection, at a rally May 21 in Sriperumbudur.

**García Robles, Alfonso**, 80, Mexican diplomat and cowinner of the 1982 Nobel Peace Prize; his persistent efforts to ban nuclear weapons in Latin America came to fruition in 1967, when 22 Latin American nations signed the Treaty of Tlatelolco. September 2 in Mexico City.

**Geisel, Theodor Seuss (Dr. Seuss)**, 87, popular author of children's books. His whimsical, rhymed fantasies, peopled with fabulous animals and accompanied by lively drawings, sold more than 50 million copies and were translated into 20 languages. Geisel's first children's book, And to Think That I Saw It on Mulberry Street (1937), was followed by such zany favorites as Horton Hatches the Egg

(1940), *The Cat in the Hat* (1957), and *How the Grinch Stole Christmas!* (1957). His most recent book, *Oh, the Places You'll Go!* (1990), used his characteristic style to charm an adult audience. September 24 in La Jolla, Calif.

**Getz, Stan**, 64, influential jazz musician and tenor saxophonist. He was at the forefront of the "cool jazz" movement in the 1950s and the bossa nova style in the 1960s, when he recorded such hits as *Desafinado* and (with singer Astrud Gilberto) *The Girl From Ipanema*; in the 1980s he was a popular concert and recording artist, winning a Grammy (one of 11 in all) for *Anniversary*. An innovative soloist, he had a distinctive sound. June 6 in Malibu, Calif.

**Ginzburg, Natalia**, 75, internationally acclaimed Italian writer whose fiction deftly portrayed family life in a subtle, understated style reminiscent of Chekhov; her best-known works include the novel *Voices in the Evening* (1961) and an autobiography, *Family Sayings* (1963). October 7 in Rome.

**Gobel, George**, 70, television comedian and personality who achieved popularity in the 1950s with his self-effacing, folksy humor and trademark crew cut. He starred in *The George Gobel Show* from 1954 to 1957, winning an Emmy in 1954, and became a fixture on the game show *Hollywood Squares* in the 1970s and 1980s. February 24 in Encino, Calif.

**Goody, Sam (Samuel Gutowitz)**, 87, founder of the Sam Goody chain of record stores. He began the business in 1938, first selling out-of-print records, then, with the advent of long-playing records in the late 1940s, giving away record players to ensure future customers. Business was booming by the time he sold his chain in the 1970s. August 8 in New York City.

**Goren, Charles H.**, 90, world champion contract bridge player and foremost authority on the game. Widely known as "Mr. Bridge," he introduced the now standard point-count system to bid bridge hands. He wrote over 40 books on bridge, selling an estimated 8 million copies worldwide, and starred in his own TV show (1959-1964). April 3 in Encino, Calif.

**Graham, Bill (Wolfgang Grajonca)**, 60, rock music promoter and a developer of the mass rock concert. He organized shows by some of the biggest names in the business, including the Rolling Stones, Jefferson Airplane, the Doors, and the Grateful Dead. October 25 near San Francisco.

**Graham, Martha**, 96, choreographer, dance innovator, and teacher, considered to be among the most influential artists of the 20th century. A pioneer of modern dance, she created in more than 180 works a language of movement that was powerful, emotional, sexually charged, and imbued with psychological insights. Some of her most vivid themes came from Greek mythology, with its intimations of universal tragedy: *Cave of the Heart* (1946), *Night Journey* (1947), *Clytemnestra* (1958). Other works were inspired by fresh American themes: the poetry of Emily Dickinson (*A Letter to the World*, 1940); rural life (*Appalachian Spring*, 1944; scored by Aaron Copland). Graham made her professional debut as a dancer in 1920 and continued to guide her company until shortly before her death. April 1 in New York City.

**Grange, Harold ("Red")**, 87, football hero of the 1920s. He won legendary status in 1924 when, playing for the University of Illi-

**HAROLD ("RED") GRANGE**

# OBITUARIES

nois, he made four touchdowns and rushed for 265 yards in the game's first 12 minutes, earning the nickname Galloping Ghost. In 1926, Grange joined the Chicago Bears, bringing new credibility to the fledgling National Football League; he also played for the New York Yankees football team during his pro career. After retiring in 1934 he served as a sportscaster; in 1963 he became a charter member of the Professional Football Hall of Fame. January 28 in Lake Wales, Fla.

**Greene, Graham**, 86, British writer whose fast-paced novels of intrigue, deception, and good and evil won extraordinary critical and popular acclaim. The author of 24 novels, along with short stories, plays, essays, and two volumes of autobiography, Greene was a convert to Roman Catholicism, and many of his works examined spiritual themes, including *The Heart of the Matter* (1948), *The End of the Affair* (1951), and his most admired novel, *The Power and the Glory* (1940), about a "whiskey" priest on the run from government persecution in Mexico. Even Greene's "entertainments," such as *Brighton Rock* (1938) and *The Third Man* (1950), had a moral dimension. He explored political themes in *The Quiet Ameri-*

**GRAHAM GREENE**

**RICHARD HATFIELD**

*can* (1956) and *Our Man in Havana* (1958) and sometimes showed a light touch, as in *The Comedians* (1966) and *Travels With My Aunt* (1969). April 3 in Vevey, Switzerland.

**Guthrie, A(lfred) B(ertram), Jr.**, 90, writer whose stories realistically depicted the world of the early Western pioneers. His novels include *The Big Sky* (1947) and the Pulitzer Prize-winning *The Way West* (1949); among other things, he also published a collection of short stories (*The Big It*, 1960) and wrote the film scripts for *Shane* (1953) and *The Kentuckian* (1955). April 26 in Choteau, Mont.

**Hatfield, Richard Bennett**, 60, flamboyant former prime minister of New Brunswick; he served 17 years, until 1987, when personal scandals led to a crushing defeat at the polls. His fondness for parties and celebrities won him the nickname Disco Dick, but he was also widely known for his commitment to national unity and to broadened language rights. April 26 in Ottawa.

**Heinz, John**, 52, U.S. senator from Pennsylvania since 1977 and former congressman. A moderate Republican, well-known as heir to the Heinz food company fortune, he was a staunch advocate for the elderly and for trade laws to encourage exports. April 4 in a plane crash in Lower Merion Township, Pa.

**Honda, Soichiro**, 84, founder of the Japanese auto company that bears his name. He developed the Honda motorcycle shortly after World War II, then, in 1957, began making cars. Considered a maverick in Japan, he found his greatest success in the United States, winning over a generation of drivers in the 1970s with his innovative CVCC engine and becoming the first Japanese automaker to build factories in the United States. August 5 in Tokyo.

**Husak, Gustav**, 78, hard-line Czechoslovak Communist Party leader after the Prague Spring and president of the country from 1975 to 1989. A party member since 1933, he helped lead the antifascist Slovak uprising in 1944. In 1954 he was sentenced to life imprisonment after a party purge, but he was released in 1960 and reinstated into the party. He was a principal architect of Czechoslovakia's federated system. November 18 in Bratislava.

**Hyde-White, Wilfrid**, 87, English actor known for his urbane drollery in such roles as father in the play *The Reluctant Debutante,* which he performed in London and on Broadway in the 1950s. Other film credits include *The Third Man* (1950), *The Browning Version* (1951), and *My Fair Lady* (1964). May 6 in Woodland Hills, Calif.

**Irwin, James B.**, 61, former astronaut who explored the moon on the Apollo 15 mission in July 1971, using the first battery-operated Lunar Rover vehicle. He later founded an evangelical religious organization and led two expeditions to Mount Ararat in Turkey seeking evidence of Noah's ark. August 8 in Glenwood Springs, Colo.

**Jackson, Sir Robert**, 79, Australian diplomat who was under secretary-general of the United Nations from 1972 to 1987. He was known for his work relief programs in Bangladesh and Cambodia and his revamping of the UN economic aid system for developing countries. January 12 in London.

**SOICHIRO HONDA**

**Jagger, Dean**, 87, character actor whose more than 120 film roles include an Academy Award-winning performance as an Air Force officer in *Twelve O'Clock High* (1950). He appeared frequently on television, notably in the series *Mr. Novak* (1963-1965). February 5 in Santa Monica, Calif.

**Jiang Qing**, 77, widow of Mao Zedong and leader of the so-called Gang of Four, the group of Communist radicals that presided over China's brutal Cultural Revolution from 1966 to 1976. She and her allies were overthrown when Mao died in 1976. Sentenced in effect to life in prison after a show trial, she reportedly committed suicide on May 14.

**Johnson, Bob**, 60, hockey coach who led the Pittsburgh Penguins to the Stanley Cup in 1990, becoming the first American to coach a championship team since World War II. He also led teams to national collegiate titles and coached the U.S. Olympic team in 1976. November 26 in Colorado Springs.

**Kaganovich, Lazar Moiseyevich**, 97, longtime close aide to Stalin. He joined the Kiev Bolshevik organization in 1911 and achieved

287

growing prominence, becoming a party boss in the Ukraine and later in Moscow, a transportation commissar during World War II, and a vice-premier. In these and other posts he reconstructed Moscow, helped collectivize agriculture, and carried out party purges. After Stalin's death in 1953 he was named to the Soviet Presidium and became a first deputy premier, but he was purged in 1957, accused of plotting to oust Nikita Khrushchev. July 25 in Moscow.

**Kempff, Wilhelm**, 95, esteemed German Romantic pianist. Best known for his performances of Beethoven, Schubert, Schumann, Chopin, and Brahms, he recorded prolifically even into his 80s. He also composed four operas, two symphonies, and other ensemble pieces. May 23 in Positano, Italy.

**Kerr, Sir John**, 76, former governor-general of Australia. In 1975 he set off a political crisis by dismissing the Labor Party government of Prime Minister Gough Whitlam when Whitlam, in a deadlock with the opposition over government spending, refused to call for elections or resign. Kerr stepped down two years later. March 24 in Sydney.

**Kosinski, Jerzy**, 57, Polish-born American writer of surrealistic and often violent fiction. His best-known work, *The Painted Bird* (1965), is an autobiographical novel about the harrowing experiences of a young boy sent to the Eastern European countryside to escape from the Nazis. He also wrote the award-winning *Steps* (1968) and *Being There* (1971), which was made into a film, but his later works were often panned. An apparent suicide, May 3 in New York City.

**Land, Edwin H(erbert)**, 81, inventor holding over 500 patents and founder of the Polaroid Corporation. Inspired by his three-year-old daughter who asked why she couldn't see her picture right after it was taken, he invented the instant camera in 1948; his company developed instant color photography in 1963. March 1 in Cambridge, Mass.

**Landon, Michael (Eugene Maurice Orowitz)**, 54, boyishly handsome actor, writer, and producer, known for his primetime, family-oriented TV series. He made his film debut in the title role of *I Was a Teenage Werewolf* (1957), then won fame as Little Joe

Cartwright on the TV series *Bonanza* (1959-1973). He also created, produced, and played starring roles in *Little House on the Prairie* (1974-1982) and *Highway to Heaven* (1984-1988). While some called his brand of TV sentimental, others admired its portrayal of sincere, loving relationships. July 1 in Malibu, Calif.

**Lean, Sir David**, 83, masterful British movie director whose 16 films garnered a total of 28 Academy Awards, including best-director awards for the epics *Bridge on the River Kwai* (1957) and *Lawrence of Arabia* (1962). A meticulous craftsman, he personally edited his films and went to painstaking measures to get a shot exactly right. Some of his films, especially *Ryan's Daughter* (1970), were criticized as showy and insubstantial, but he rebounded in 1984 with the award-winning *A Passage to India*. Other films include *Brief Encounter* (1945), *Great Expectations* (1946), and *Dr. Zhivago* (1965). April 16 in London.

**Lefebvre, Marcel François**, 85, French-born prelate whose defiance of Pope John Paul II produced the first schism in the Roman Catholic Church since 1870. A traditionalist, he fought at the Second Vatican Council to retain the Latin Mass and rejected other changes, forming his own order of priests in 1969. He was excommunicated in 1988 when he consecrated four bishops against the orders of the pope. March 25 in Martigny, Switzerland.

**Le Gallienne, Eva**, 92, British-born American actress, producer, director, and teacher. She brought the house down in London with her role in *The Laughter of Fools* (1915), then, moving to New York, had hits in *Not So Long Ago* (1919), *Liliom* (1921), and *The Swan* (1923). In 1926 she founded the Civic Repertory Theater, where she directed and acted in classic revivals until it closed in 1933. In later years she toured frequently, scoring a major success in 1958 with a television production of *The Bridge of San Luis Rey* and in 1976 as the mother in a Broadway revival of *The Royal Family*. June 3 in Weston, Conn.

**Leger, Paul Emile**, 87, Canadian cardinal. Appointed archbishop of Montréal in 1950 and made a cardinal in 1953, he headed Canada's largest Catholic diocese for 17 years before leaving to work as a missionary among lepers and handicapped children in Cameroon. After returning to Montréal he established a relief agency, distributing $12 million a year to the poor in 60 countries around the world. November 13 in Montréal.

**Lewis, Sir Arthur**, 76, cowinner of the 1979 Nobel Prize in economic science especially for his research in the problems of developing countries, presented in *The Theory of Economic Growth* (1954) and other works; he was the first black to win a Nobel Prize outside of the Nobel Peace Prize. June 15 in Barbados.

**Luke, Keye**, 86, veteran Chinese-born character actor; among his many roles was that of No. 1 Son in the Charlie Chan detective movies. January 12 in Whittier Calif.

**Luria, Salvador E.**, 78, Italian-born biologist and physician who shared the 1968 Nobel Prize in medicine and physiology for discoveries concerning the replication mechanism and genetic structure of viruses. He won the 1974 National Book Award in the sciences for *Life: The Unfinished Experiment*, and he was an outspoken peace activist. February 6 in Lexington, Mass.

**MacMurray, Fred**, 83, affable actor who starred in many film comedies of the 1930s and 1940s and, as the widowed father on TV's *My Three Sons* (1960-1972), embodied the American ideal of a benevolent dad. In many of his later movies—including *The Absent-Minded Professor* (1960)—he portrayed a paternal, gently bumbling character, but he could also play darker characters, such as the murderer in *Double Indemnity* (1944). November 5 in Santa Monica, Calif.

**Manzu, Giacomo**, 82, prolific Italian sculptor; his work, ranging from religious sculptures to a monument to Lenin, often combined allegorical and sexual imagery. He is well known for the monumental bronze "Door of Death" he made for St. Peter's Basilica in Rome, which attracted controversy for its nonspiritual themes. January 17 in Ardea, Italy.

**Maxwell, Robert (Jan Ludvik Hoch)**, 68, Czechoslovakian-born British entrepreneur who built a multibillion-dollar international communications empire that collapsed in bankruptcy after his death. Escaping the Holocaust, he made his way during World War II to England, where he joined the British army.

After the war he founded Pergamon Press, and he later served as a Labor Party member of Parliament (1964-1970). Launching a rapid expansion of his business interests in the 1980s, he made a series of major acquisitions, including the *Daily Mirror* in Britain and the Macmillan, Inc., publishing company and Official Airline Guides in the United States. In 1991 he took over the New York *Daily News*. However, by the 1990s Maxwell was also selling major assets to help ease a heavy debt burden, and evidence emerged after his death that he had siphoned money from pension funds and publicly held companies in his empire to stave off the collapse of his deeply indebted private companies. November 5 while his yacht was sailing off the Canary Islands.

**McKissick, Floyd**, 69, attorney and maverick civil rights activist who, as director of the Congress of Racial Equality (CORE) in the late 1960s, focused on economic and political power for blacks. In the 1970s he founded Soul City, a rural North Carolina town to be controlled by blacks, but the project failed. A backer of President Richard Nixon, he was named a state district judge in 1990. April 28 in Durham, N.C.

**ROBERT MAXWELL**

**YVES MONTAND**

**McMillan, Edwin Mattison**, 83, physics and chemistry pioneer and cowinner of the 1951 Nobel Prize in chemistry for the discovery of plutonium and neptunium. A longtime professor at the University of California at Berkeley, and head of its Lawrence Berkeley laboratory for 15 years, he made key contributions to the development of sonar, the atomic bomb, and the particle accelerator. September 7 in El Cerrito, Calif.

**Mercury, Freddie (Frederick Bulsara)**, 45, flamboyant rock musician and lead singer in the band Queen. He and Queen created an image of playful decadence on stage in the late 1970s, while merging the styles of pop, heavy metal, cabaret, and even opera. November 24 in London.

**Michener, Daniel Roland**, 91, Canadian governor-general from 1967 to 1974. He brought dignity to the office while doing away with some of its traditional formality. He also served as ambassador to Nepal, high commissioner to India, and speaker of the House of Commons. August 6 in Toronto.

**Montand, Yves (Yvo Livi)**, 70, Italian-born French singer and actor remembered as the epitome of Gallic charm. As a young man in Paris he caught the eye of the singer Edith Piaf, who helped him become a music hall star and started him on a career that led to more than 50 movies, including *The Wages of Fear* (1953), *Z* (1968), *The Confession* (1970), and *Jean de Florette* (1986). He also stirred interest with his controversial politics (evolving from the far left to the right) and his women—an early relationship with Piaf, a 36-year marriage to actress Simone Signoret, and an affair with Marilyn Monroe. November 9 in Senlis, France.

**Motherwell, Robert**, 76, American painter, printmaker, collagist, and art writer and philosopher. An abstract expressionist, he used "artful scribbling" in his paintings, letting the brush or pen wander on the canvas, undirected by the conscious mind. His best-known series, *Elegies to the Spanish Republic*, contains over 170 paintings in which massive ovoids and rectangles appear over and over. In another series, *Open*, rectangles suggest windows cut into a field of color. He received many awards, including a National Medal of Arts (1989). July 16 on Cape Cod, Mass.

**ROBERT MOTHERWELL**

**ARTHUR MURRAY, dancing with his wife, Kathryn**

**Murray, Arthur (Arthur Murray Teichman)**, 95, the world's best-known ballroom dance instructor. Starting out in the 1920s with a mail-order dance course, using the easy-to-follow diagrams that became his trademark, he built up a network of over 300 franchised dance studios by the time he retired in 1964. He made extensive use of publicity, most notably through a TV variety show, *The Arthur Murray Party*, hosted by his wife, Kathryn. March 3 in Honolulu.

**Nemerov, Howard**, 71, poet laureate of the United States from 1988 to 1990. He won a Pulitzer Prize and a National Book Award for his collected poems (1977), which address a variety of contemporary topics, often in colloquial language, but with attention to form. He also wrote fiction and essays. July 5 in University City, Mo.

**O'Faolain, Sean (John Francis Whelan)**, 91, Irish writer whose acclaimed short stories realistically depicted lower-class and middle-class life with irony and compassion. An ardent nationalist, he awakened an interest in Irish culture through his stories, novels, and travel books, as well as a biography of Irish statesman Daniel O'Connell. April 20 in Dublin.

**Olav V**, 87, king of Norway since 1957. A congenial ruler and avid sportsman, Olav was well-liked by his subjects. At the beginning of World War II, with parliamentary leaders and his father, King Haakon, he hid out for two months in the north woods as invading Nazi troops advanced; after retreating to England at the insistence of government leaders, he made broadcasts to the Norwegian people and helped build a fighting force of free Norwegians. January 17 in Oslo.

**Page, Ruth**, 72, ballet dancer and choreographer. She performed worldwide, with Anna Pavlova's classical company and Serge Diaghilev's Ballets Russes, among other groups; but her ballets, such as *Hear Ye, Hear Ye* (1934) and the frequently revived *Frankie and Johnny* (1938), used distinctly American themes. In 1956 she founded the Chicago Opera Ballet, later known as Ruth Page's International Ballet. April 7 in Chicago.

# OBITUARIES

**Papp, Joseph (Yosl Papirofsky)**, 70, dynamic, influential theater producer whose plays won three Pulitzer Prizes and over 20 Tony awards. He founded New York City's Public Theater, birthplace of the musicals *Hair* (1967) and *A Chorus Line* (1975), and as director of the New York Shakespeare Festival brought Shakespeare to the masses for more than three decades. October 31 in New York City.

**Pomus, Jerome ("Doc")**, 65, rock-and-roll lyricist. He and Mort Shuman, who died in November at 52, wrote *Turn Me Loose* for pop star Fabian, *Teenager in Love* for Dion and the Belmonts, and *This Magic Moment* for the Drifters, among many hits. March 14 in New York City.

**Porter, Sylvia F(eldman)**, 77, author and newspaper columnist who presented business and financial topics in language aimed at the general public. Her column, begun in the mid-1930s, under a byline that concealed her gender, was syndicated in 1947 and was still going strong more than four decades later. June 5 in Pound Ridge, N.Y.

**Ray, Aldo (Aldo DaRe)**, 64, burly, gravel-voiced character actor known for tough-guy military roles in films of the 1950s, such as *Battle Cry* (1955) and *The Naked and the Dead* (1958). March 27 in Martinez, Calif.

**Reasoner, Harry**, 68, award-winning veteran television journalist. He spent most of career at CBS News, where he was a reporter and correspondent, an anchor on *60 Minutes*, and a frequent newscaster, but never a regular anchor for nightly news; during a hiatus at ABC, from 1970 to 1978, he coanchored the *Evening News*, eventually with Barbara Walters. He gained a reputation as an excellent writer, with a wry, unflappable on-screen presence. August 6 in Norwalk, Conn.

**Remick, Lee**, 55, popular actress who first attracted attention as a majorette in the film *A Face in the Crowd* (1957) but later succeeded in more dramatic roles, including the alcoholic wife in *Days of Wine and Roses* (1962) and the blind heroine in the Broadway production of *Wait Until Dark* (1966). July 2 in Brentwood, Calif.

**Richardson, Tony**, 63, British director. He began his career in the theater and then turned

**JOSEPH PAPP**

to directing movies, often with social themes. His best-known films include *Look Back in Anger* (1959), *The Entertainer* (1960), and the Oscar-winning *Tom Jones* (1963). November 15 in Los Angeles.

**Rizzo, Frank**, 70, controversial mayor of Philadelphia from 1972 to 1980 who had gained prominence as the city's police commissioner in the 1960s, earning a national reputation for his iron-handed approach to law and order. July 16 in Philadelphia.

**Roddenberry, Gene**, 70, writer and producer whose 1960s TV science-fiction series *Star Trek* led a generation of viewers (and many more in reruns) on a journey through "space, the final frontier." The series inspired six feature films, a sequel series in the 1980s, and many diehard devotees, known as Trekkies. October 24 in Santa Monica, Calif.

**Ruffin, David**, 50, an original member of the pop group The Temptations and lead singer for *My Girl* (1965) and other hits. In 1968 he began a modestly successful solo career that was marred by drug abuse. June 1 in Philadelphia, after an apparent drug overdose.

**Schaefer, Jack**, 83, journalist and author of westerns widely praised for their authenticity and tightly constructed plots; he is best remembered for his first novel, *Shane* (1949), which was made into a popular 1953 film. January 24 in Santa Fe, N.M.

**Serkin, Rudolf**, 88, Austrian-born classical pianist whose brilliant performances, a mixture of classical and romantic styles, were noted for their painstaking technical skill. After his Berlin debut in 1921 he performed widely in Europe, often teamed with the German violinist Adolph Busch, and eventually settled in the United States. As a founder of the Marlboro Festival in Vermont and as a longtime instructor and director at the Curtis Institute in Philadelphia, Serkin helped inspire and shape a younger generation of pianists. May 8 in Guilford, Vt.

**Siegel, Don**, 78, director of more than 30 often sardonic action-adventure films, two of which—*Invasion of the Body Snatchers* (1956) and *Dirty Harry* (1971)—became cult classics. April 20 in Nipomo, Calif.

**Singer, Isaac Bashevis**, 87, Polish-born Jewish author whose vivid, charming, slyly ironic stories and novels were often based on his own experiences as a rabbi's son in Poland and later as an immigrant in America. He explored the relationship between God and humans and dealt boldly with passions and emotions. His 1972 novel *Enemies: a Love Story* was made into an admired film of the same name. In 1978, Singer won the Nobel Prize in literature; other prizes include National Book Awards for *A Day of Pleasure* (a children's book) in 1970 and for his short story collection *A Crown of Feathers* in 1974. July 24 in Surfside, Fla.

**Smith, Cladys ("Jabbo")**, 82, innovative, energetic jazz trumpeter popular especially in the 1920s and 1930s and considered a rival to Louis Armstrong. January 16 in New York City.

**Stigler, George Joseph**, 80, economist. He won the 1982 Nobel Prize in economics for his life's work, which included *The Theory of Price*, an analytical book of free market economics that sets economics in a historical context, and theories on the economics of information and the causes and effects of public regulation. December 1 in Chicago.

**Tamayo, Rufino**, 91, prolific Mexican painter and printmaker known especially for his simple images and powerful use of color. Vilified by the great Mexican muralists because his art was nonpolitical, he survived them to become a continuing force in Mexican art for over 60 years. June 24 in Mexico City.

**ISAAC BASHEVIS SINGER**

**DANNY THOMAS**
**With TV daughter in *Make Room for Daddy***

**Thomas, Danny (Amos Jacobs)**, 79, veteran nightclub and radio comedian and storyteller best known as star of the television series *Make Room for Daddy* (later renamed *The Danny Thomas Show*), which appeared from 1953 to 1964. He also acted in films, became a highly successful TV producer, and devoted much of his energy to raising money for St. Jude Children's Research Hospital, which he helped found in 1962. February 6 in Los Angeles.

**Tierney, Gene**, 70, well-born Hollywood film star who won renown for her role as a bewitching beauty in the classic film *Laura* (1944) and an Oscar nomination for her performance as a pathologically selfish woman in *Leave Her to Heaven* (1946). November 6 in Houston.

**Tower, John G(oodwin)**, 65, influential Republican U.S. senator from Texas (1961-1984) who chaired the Armed Services Committee from 1981 to 1984. A key figure in the drive to modernize the U.S. military, he suffered a humiliating defeat in 1989 when the Senate rejected his nomination as secretary of defense because of alleged heavy drinking and womanizing, and charges he was too closely tied to weapons manufacturers. Killed in a plane crash April 5, near Brunswick, Ga.

**Tree, Marietta**, 74, patrician-activist. Born to wealth, she devoted herself to public service as a close aide to Adlai Stevenson in the 1950s, a representative to the UN Commission on Human Rights in the 1960s, and a social hostess and worker for New York City causes. August 15 in New York City.

**Wagner, Robert F(erdinand)**, 80, three-term Democratic mayor of New York City (1954-1966). Criticized by many for an overcautious approach to problems, he was, however, credited with initiating important reforms and with defeating the long entrenched party machine. February 12 in New York City.

**Welensky, Sir Roy**, 84, prime minister of the Central African Federation from 1959 until its collapse in 1963. The federation of British colonies—Southern Rhodesia, Northern Rhodesia, and Nyasaland—was governed by whites, but Welensky insisted on calling it a partnership with blacks; he was enraged when Britain withdrew support for the federation. December 5 in Blandford Foru, England.

**Werblin, David A. ("Sonny")**, 81, entertainment and sports entrepreneur. Under his presidency, MCA-TV became so successful it was considered a monopoly and was broken up by the U.S. Justice Department. In sports Werblin was remembered for paying football star Joe Namath the then-enormous sum of $427,000 to turn pro and join the New York Jets. November 21 in New York City.

**Wilson, Sir Angus**, 77, British writer whose often satirical fiction portrayed conflicts in contemporary social life. Besides such critically esteemed novels as *Hemlock and After* (1952), *Anglo-Saxon Attitudes* (1956), and *The Middle Age of Mrs. Eliot* (1958), he wrote biographies of Charles Dickens and Rudyard Kipling. May 31 in Bury St. Edmunds, England.

**OHIO.** See STATISTICS OF THE WORLD.

**OKLAHOMA.** See STATISTICS OF THE WORLD.

**OMAN.** See STATISTICS OF THE WORLD. See *also* ARABIAN PENNINSULA.

**ONTARIO.** See STATISTICS OF THE WORLD.

**OREGON.** See STATISTICS OF THE WORLD.

**ORGANIZATION OF PETROLEUM EXPORTING COUNTRIES.** See ENERGY.

# P

**PACIFIC ISLANDS.** During 1991, Pacific island parliaments and prime ministers, identifying with Kuwait's predicament in being invaded by a larger country, generally supported the United Nations action in the Persian Gulf crisis. Following the end of hostilities, Fiji agreed to send small contingents of police and army officers to Iraq at the request of the United Nations.

In regional developments, Henry Naisali resigned as secretary-general of the 15-nation South Pacific Forum. The forum appointed Ieremia Tabai, former president of Kiribati, as his replacement at its 22nd annual meeting, held in July in Palikir, the capital of the Federated States of Micronesia. Tabai himself was succeeded as Kiribati's president by Vice President Teatao Teannaki, who won election over three other candidates.

Concerns about violence influenced preparations for the ninth South Pacific Games, held in Papua New Guinea during two weeks in September. Kiribati pulled out, citing reports of public unrest in the nation, which remained divided by a conflict between the government and rebels of the Bougainville Revolutionary Army. A cease-fire had been signed in January; however, it did not hold. Meanwhile, Sir

Serei Eri resigned as Papua New Guinea's governor-general, in a dispute over his refusal to fire a deputy prime minister implicated in corruption. Wiwa Korowi was elected as the new governor-general.

The partial termination of the Trust Territory of the Pacific Islands in late 1990 left only Palau as part of the territory. The Federated States of Micronesia and the Marshall Islands, both now independent, were admitted to the United Nations in September. Pohnpei legislator Bailey Olter had been elected president of the FSM in May.

In French Polynesia, Gaston Flosse was elected president early in the year. But he was charged by a French court with misuse of public funds and also had to deal with popular riots over new taxes proposed by the territorial government.

In Tonga, 2,000 demonstrators took to the streets in March to protest the decision by King Taufa'ahau Tupou IV to grant citizenship to foreigners who had bought Tongan passports. Prime Minister Fatefehi Tu'ipelehake resigned after 26 years in the post and was replaced by Baron Vaea.

Donald Kalpokas became Vanuatu's second prime minister since its independence in 1980,

The South Pacific Forum held its annual summit meeting in July in Palikir, capital of the Federated States of Micronesia. Officials of the 15-member group appointed a new president, stated their opposition to nuclear testing in the region, and called for protection from the effects of global warming.

after Walter Lini was removed in a parliamentary vote of no-confidence in September. The vote followed a split in the ruling Vanua'aku party and Lini's dismissal of cabinet ministers and other officials.

In April, Western Samoa held its first general election under universal adult suffrage. The governing Human Rights Protection Party, led by Prime Minister Tofilau Eti Alesana, was returned to power. A December cyclone that also hit American Samoa destroyed most crops and left thousands of people homeless.

*See* STATISTICS OF THE WORLD.          S.L.

**PAKISTAN.** In 1991 the quality of life in Pakistan declined as the economy faltered and mounting lawlessness threatened many citizens' personal security. Political conflict intensified during the year.

**The Economy.** The economy grew at a rate of 5.6 percent in the 1990-1991 fiscal year. Exports increased by 22 percent, but the balance of payments still showed a deficit of $1.85 billion. The federal budget for 1991-1992 also

projected a deficit; however, the government reduced personal income taxes in the higher brackets and on corporate incomes. At the same time, the government cut back on subsidies for some consumer goods.

Prime Minister Mian Nawaz Sharif continued to support private enterprise, hoping to stimulate both domestic and foreign investment. He had some success, as domestic investment was estimated to have increased in 1990-1991 by about 16 percent, but there was no significant rise in foreign investment. A program to sell public corporations to private investors proceeded slowly.

**Domestic Developments.** Prime Minister Nawaz Sharif settled a long-standing dispute among the provinces over rights to the waters of the Indus River. He also persuaded the provincial governments to agree on a revenue-sharing plan, reducing their dependence on the central government. Parliament passed a bill declaring the sharia (Islamic law and injunctions) to be the supreme law of the land.

Determined to keep former Prime Minister Benazir Bhutto and her Pakistan People's Party (PPP) out of power, Sharif and President Ghulam Ishaq Khan helped Jam Sadiq Ali to form a coalition government in the province of Sind, backed by several anti-Bhutto parties. As Sind's chief minister, Ali jailed many PPP leaders and hundreds of its workers on charges generally believed to be bogus. The PPP leaders offered to "cooperate" with Prime Minister Sharif if his government would stop harassing them. At issue was not only the repression in Sind but also charges of malfeasance that President Khan had filed against Benazir Bhutto. If Bhutto were convicted on even one charge, she could be barred from holding elective office for seven years.

**Foreign Relations.** Pakistan's relations with China remained friendly, and there were reports that the military had acquired an undisclosed number of Chinese aircraft and missiles. American aid remained suspended because Pakistan was believed to be building up its capability for nuclear weapons.

Most Pakistanis had been critical of the Iraqi occupation of Kuwait in 1990. Reactions to the U.S.-led coalition's air and ground campaigns against Iraq varied, although both Sharif and Bhutto endorsed the American moves. Following a U.S.-Soviet agreement in September to cut off military aid to both sides in the Afghan civil war, a negotiated settlement became a viable option, slightly improving the prospect of ending Pakistan's involvement in that war.

The popular uprising in the Indian state of Jammu and Kashmir continued to be a subject of contention between Pakistan and India, which denounced Pakistan for aiding the Kashmiri rebels. Clashes between the Indian and Pakistani troops stationed along the border between the two countries occurred with increasing frequency.

*See* STATISTICS OF THE WORLD. A.Sy.

**PALAU.** *See* STATISTICS OF THE WORLD.

**PALESTINE LIBERATION ORGANIZATION.** *See* ISRAEL; LEBANON; SYRIA.

**PANAMA.** Nearly two years after U.S. forces stormed into Panama to overthrow General Manuel Noriega, Panama in 1991 still confronted a moribund economy and challenges from unemployment, poverty, and homelessness. A kind of post-Noriega lethargy settled over Panama, with the country dominated by the civilian families that ruled before the military took over in 1968. The alliance that had spearheaded Noriega's ouster began to fracture. The key Christian Democratic Party, which held 5 of 12 cabinet posts in the ruling government, was ousted by President Guillermo Endara in May.

Noriega went on trial in September in Miami, charged with accepting $4.6 million in bribes from drug lords to protect cocaine shipments flowing through Panama to the United States from Colombia. Federal prosecutors had admitted that Noriega received slightly more than $300,000 from the United States for information on the Panamanian government.

*A Pakistani boy at a rally protesting the allied air offensive against Iraq flashes a victory sign and a poster of Iraqi President Saddam Hussein. Many Pakistanis took Iraq's side in the Gulf War, though both the prime minister and former Prime Minister Benazir Bhutto endorsed the U.S. stand.*

The prosecution rested in mid-November after presenting 46 witnesses. New evidence later surfaced that Noriega had aided U.S. drug agents in the 1980s, but its value to the defense was not clear. The defense was to begin presenting its case in January 1992.

On April 11 the government signed a treaty giving American officials access to information about secret Panamanian bank accounts when investigating drug trafficking and money laundering. The treaty ended a bitter dispute that had prompted the U.S. government to freeze $84 million in economic assistance to Panama, but it still did not allow access to accounts in investigations of tax evasion cases, as the United States had originally sought. Panamanian officials opposed opening bank records in such cases because it would threaten their lucrative offshore banking industry. Meanwhile, money laundering activity declined, but the cocaine trade remained at levels comparable to earlier years and may even have increased.

In June the United States warned Panama that it intended to speed up the closing of several large U.S. bases. Panama was unprepared and reluctant to take them over. Some 6,000 workers and 5,000 contractors were employed on these bases, and their average salary was $1,200 a month—four times the national average.

Problems with the Panama Canal continued to fester. While Gilberto Guardia Fabrega, a civil engineer, was approved as the first Panamanian to head the Panama Canal Commission, international maritime officials expressed concern that the canal was slowly deteriorating and suggested that Panama would be unable to manage the waterway properly when it takes full control in 1999.

See STATISTICS OF THE WORLD.          D.N.

**PAPUA NEW GUINEA.** See STATISTICS OF THE WORLD. See also PACIFIC ISLANDS.

**PARAGUAY.** In 1991, Paraguay continued to confront the social and political demands that first came to the fore in 1989 with the demise of General Alfredo Stroessner's dictatorship.

Violence in land conflicts became a common occurrence. A February report by the New York-based human rights group Americas Watch asserted that police had burned squatters' homes, beaten peasants, and stolen their property. The government claimed that in order to encourage foreign and domestic investment in agriculture, it was necessary to ensure that property rights be respected. Amnesty International accused the government of detaining peasants so as to preempt possible land occupations.

In August the National Assembly approved the draft of a new constitution to replace the 1967 version. Under the proposed changes the president could no longer appoint members of the judiciary or council of state without the consent of Congress and would need congressional approval to declare a state of emergency. The president could be reelected for an indefinite number of successive terms. Rules governing freedom of expression and assembly would be liberalized. The proposals were to be taken up by an elected Constituent Convention in early 1992.

In municipal elections on May 26, with candidates no longer handpicked by the nation's ruler, the ruling conservative Colorado Party was victorious in 70 percent of the electoral districts, but this was considered a major electoral setback. An independent left-of-center candidate, Carlos Filizzola, was elected mayor of the capital city, Asunción. Voting had to be canceled in 21 of the 206 electoral districts because of irregularities.

The government pressed ahead with the privatization of state-owned industries. In October, President Andrés Rodríguez sought congressional approval for selling off the nation's domestic and international airlines and its cement, shipping, steel, and telecommunications industries, in addition to putting the national distillery on sale.

On March 26, a common market treaty signed by representatives of the governments of Paraguay, Argentina, Brazil, and Uruguay provided for lower tariffs between the four nations. In June the U.S. Congress restored Paraguay's eligibility for trade benefits, which had been suspended in 1987 because of human rights violations.

See STATISTICS OF THE WORLD.

A.O'R. & J.F.

**PENNSYLVANIA.** See STATISTICS OF THE WORLD.

# People in the News

**In 1991, various members of America's foremost political family were in the spotlight, a general became a knight, and a pint-sized actor took Hollywood by storm. A world-famous movie star tied the knot—again.**

In the largest gathering of presidents and their wives in U.S. history, **George** and **Barbara Bush**, **Jimmy** and **Rosalynn Carter**, **Gerald** and **Betty Ford**, **Richard** and **Pat Nixon**, and **Lady Bird Johnson** joined **Ronald** and **Nancy Reagan** in November to dedicate the $60 million Ronald Reagan Presidential Library at Simi Valley, Calif., about 50 miles northwest of Los Angeles. Also on hand were **John F. Kennedy, Jr.**, and **Caroline Kennedy Schlossberg**; a bevy of Reagan-era cabinet officials; and such showbiz luminaries as **Jimmy Stewart**, **Bob Hope**, and **Arnold Schwarzenegger**.

In February, Reagan had celebrated his 80th birthday with a library fund-raising gala, at which the guests included former British Prime Minister **Margaret Thatcher**, **Elizabeth Taylor**, and Vice President **Dan Quayle**. During the summer **Ron Reagan**, the former president's son, launched his own syndicated TV talk show.

Health problems bedeviled the Bush family, as the First Lady broke her left leg in January in a sledding accident and the ordinarily robust president was hospitalized in May with an erratic heartbeat. When doctors concluded that he was suffering from Graves' disease, a non-contagious thyroid disorder that had earlier

**At the library: Lady Bird Johnson, Jimmy and Rosalynn Carter, Gerald and Betty Ford, Richard and Pat Nixon, the Reagans, George and Barbara Bush**

been diagnosed in Barbara Bush, and that First Dog **Millie** was afflicted with lupus, sleuths began scurrying around the White House and the vice presidential residence (where the Bushes had lived from 1981 to 1989) for possible environmental causes.

The Bushes' son **Neil** received a reprimand from federal regulators for his role in the failure of the Denver-based Silverado Banking, Savings and Loan Association. He later signed on with TransMedia Communications, a television consulting firm.

In May, **William Kennedy Smith**, the nephew of Senator **Edward M. Kennedy** (D, Mass.), was charged with raping a woman at the Kennedy family's Palm Beach, Fla., compound; the two had met in a bar during a night of carousing that also included the senator and his son **Patrick**. In late October, as the Smith trial was about to begin, Senator Kennedy made a public apology to Massachusetts voters for the "faults" in the conduct of his personal life. That conduct had been the source of ad-

ditional embarrassment earlier in the month when, as a member of the Senate Judiciary Committee, he had been uncharacteristically reticent during the nationally televised investigation of sexual harassment charges made against Supreme Court nominee **Clarence Thomas** by law professor **Anita Hill**. In December, after a jury quickly acquitted Smith of the charges, his accuser identified herself publicly as **Patricia Bowman**; the earlier disclosure of her identity by some news organizations had prompted a heated debate about journalistic policies in rape cases.

On a more upbeat note, Caroline Schlossberg published her first book, *In Our Defense: The Bill of Rights in Action*, coauthored with her friend and fellow attorney **Ellen Alderman**. Sparked by **Oliver Stone**'s new film *JFK*, starring **Kevin Costner**, controversy continued to surround the 1963 assassination of President **John F. Kennedy**, but another long-standing presidential mystery was resolved. After unearthing the remains of **Zach-**

**William Kennedy Smith with his mother, Jean, and lawyer Roy Black**

**Queen Elizabeth, with Barbara Bush, at Baltimore baseball game**

**ary Taylor**, Kentucky's medical examiner declared in June that the 12th president had died of natural causes, not arsenic poisoning as some historians had alleged.

Plane crashes on successive days in early April claimed the lives of two prominent Republican politicians, Senator **John Heinz** (Pa.), 52, and former Senator **John Tower** (Texas), 65; in November former U.S. Attorney General **Dick Thornburgh** (R) lost to interim appointee **Harris L. Wofford, Jr.** (D), in the contest for Heinz's seat. Thornburgh's longtime aide **Henry G. Barr** was convicted in February of cocaine possession and lying about his drug use to federal authorities, and in October former Washington, D.C., Mayor **Marion S. Barry, Jr.**, began serving a six-month prison sentence for cocaine use. **Robert Jeffrey Lujan**, the son of Interior Secretary **Manuel Lujan, Jr.**, was sentenced to 20 years in prison for rape and burglary.

Former House Speaker **Jim Wright** agreed to pay $15,000 to settle charges that he had accepted illegal campaign contributions, and Senator **Alan Cranston** (D, Calif.) was formally reprimanded by the Senate Ethics Committee for interceding with banking regulators on behalf of **Charles H. Keating, Jr.**, a key figure in the U.S. savings and loan scandals of recent

years and a Cranston campaign contributor. Keating, whose Lincoln Savings and Loan Association failed at a cost to taxpayers of $2.6 billion, was convicted of securities fraud in a California court; he also faced federal charges.

The scandal surrounding the Bank of Credit and Commerce International claimed a prominent victim when **Clark Clifford**, a former defense secretary and a venerable figure in the Democratic Party, resigned as chairman of Washington's biggest bank holding company, First American Bankshares, after revelations that it had been secretly controlled by BCCI. Another noteworthy resignation in Washington was that of the contentious White House chief of staff, **John Sununu**, whose unpopularity had intensified after reports of political and personal travels at public expense that included a jaunt in a chauffeur-driven government limo to a New York City stamp auction.

After overseeing the ouster of Iraqi forces from Kuwait earlier in the year, General **H. Norman Schwarzkopf, Jr.**, received an honorary knighthood in May from **Queen Elizabeth II**, retired from active duty, and settled down to write his memoirs, for which Bantam Books reportedly agreed to pay him more than $5 million. Meanwhile, President Bush reappointed General **Colin L. Powell** to a second

301

two-year term as chairman of the Joint Chiefs of Staff. Journalists in the Desert Storm spotlight included CNN's **Peter Arnett**, whose broadcasts from Baghdad brought him under fire from some U.S. conservatives as well as allied bombs; veteran CBS reporter **Bob Simon**, captured by Iraqi troops and held prisoner for 40 days after he made an unauthorized foray to the Saudi-Kuwaiti border; and **Arthur Kent**, an NBC correspondent nicknamed the "Satellite Dish" and "Scud Stud" for his good looks.

By early December improved prospects for peace in the Middle East had led to the release from captivity in Lebanon of almost all remaining Western hostages—Americans **Jesse Turner**, **Edward Austin Tracy**, **Thomas Sutherland**, **Joseph Cicippio**, **Alann Steen**, and **Terry Anderson** and Britons **John McCarthy**, **Jackie Mann**, and **Terry Waite**. **Saddam Hussein** still clung to power in Iraq, but another much-publicized U.S. target, former Panamanian dictator **Manuel Noriega**, went on trial in Miami on charges of drug trafficking, money laundering, and racketeering. In South Africa, **Winnie Mandela**, the wife of African National Congress leader **Nelson Mandela**, was sentenced to six years in prison as an accessory to the kidnapping and beating of four youths in Soweto in 1988. A harbinger of changing times in that country was the reported engagement of **Willem de Klerk**, the younger son of President **F. W. de Klerk**, to **Erica Adams**, who is of mixed black-white ancestry. **Imelda Marcos** returned home to the Philippines in November to face more than 60 criminal and civil cases based on allegations that she and her late husband, **Ferdinand E. Marcos**, siphoned off billions of dollars for personal use during his 21-year presidential tenure.

In Argentina, **Zulema Yoma de Menem** filed for divorce from her husband, President **Carlos Saúl Menem**, citing a June 1990 incident in which, before live TV cameras, he used armed guards to bar her from the presidential residence in Buenos Aires. The most powerful woman in modern Brazilian history, former Economy Minister **Zélia Cardoso de Mello**, recounted her seduction and abandonment by a fellow cabinet officer, Justice Minister **Bernardo Cabral**, in an authorized biography by

Madonna

**Fernando Sabino**. Both **Raisa** and **Mikhail Gorbachev** published books during the year, hers a personal memoir, his a quickie account of the coup that sought his ouster in August.

Highlights of a two-week visit to the United States in May by Queen Elizabeth and her husband, **Prince Philip**, included a baseball game in Baltimore, a gospel music service in Houston, and an address by the queen to a joint congressional session, the first ever by a British monarch. In July, **Charles** and **Diana**, the Prince and Princess of Wales, celebrated—or at least observed—her 30th birthday and the tenth anniversary of their apparently troubled marriage. During the year Charles signed deals involving the publication of a book of his watercolors and the creation of a half-hour animated film based on his children's story, "The Old Man of Lochnagar," first issued in 1980. Meanwhile, that perennial royal pop hopeful,

Monaco's **Princess Stephanie**, recorded her first English-language album and launched a European tour.

In other pop news, **Madonna** starred in a raunchy new documentary film, *Truth or Dare*; **Amy Grant** proved (as she told *People* magazine) that "Christians can be sexy" with her crossover hit "Baby, Baby"; ex-Beatle **Paul McCartney** premiered his first full-length classical piece, *Liverpool Oratorio*; and the "Godfather of Soul," **James Brown**, got out of jail and hit the comeback trail. But the biggest splash in the music world was made by the **Jacksons**: **Janet** locked up a $32 million deal with Virgin Records, while brother **Michael** signed a $50 million contract with Sony and launched *Dangerous*, his first album in four years, with a controversial video, "Black or White." A Nashville auto accident claimed the life of country singer **Dottie West**. **Jay Leno** was named to succeed **Johnny Carson** when the venerable *Tonight Show* host retires in May 1992, and **Deborah Norville**, already

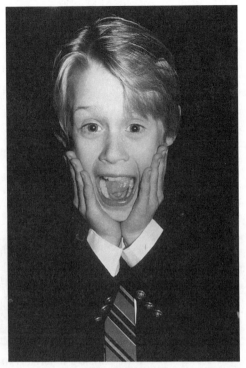

**Macaulay Culkin**

**Michael Jackson**

on maternity leave, was replaced as *Today* show cohost by **Katie Couric**.

Black directors were hot in Hollywood in 1991, as **John Singleton**'s *Boyz N the Hood*, **Spike Lee**'s *Jungle Fever*, **Mario van Peebles**'s *New Jack City*, and **Matty Rich**'s *Straight Out of Brooklyn* connected with both audiences and critics. Several actresses scored screen breakthroughs: **Geena Davis** and **Susan Sarandon** starred in *Thelma & Louise*, and **Jodie Foster** not only costarred with **Anthony Hopkins** in the supremely creepy *Silence of the Lambs* but also made her directing debut in *Little Man Tate*. But perhaps the biggest new figure in film and TV was only 4 feet 4½ inches tall—**Macaulay Culkin**. In 1991 he celebrated his 11th birthday and the fruits of his starring role in the hit 1990 movie *Home Alone*: his own TV cartoon show; a part in the 1991 film *My Girl*; appearances on a Michael Jackson video, a Bob Hope Christmas special, and *Saturday Night Live* (as its second-youngest host ever); and a contract for $5 million and 5 percent of the gross from *Home Alone 2*.

303

**The artist Christo's umbrellas (the California portion) on display**

In the literary world, Soviet émigré **Joseph Brodsky** was named U.S. poet laureate. **Christo**'s newest art venture, a $26 million extravaganza involving miles of massive umbrellas in California and Japan, ended tragically when wind uprooted an umbrella in the Tejon Pass north of Los Angeles and a 33-year-old woman was crushed to death; a Japanese worker was also killed as the project was being dismantled.

Even as **Anita Hill**'s allegations against Thomas focused attention on sexual harassment in the workplace, the 1992 Miss America, **Carolyn Suzanne Sapp**, asserted that she had been physically and emotionally assaulted by her football-player boyfriend, and **LaToya Jackson**, **Roseanne Barr Arnold**, and former Miss America **Marilyn Van Derbur** said that their parents had sexually abused them. In November actor-comedian **Paul Reubens**, the creator and host (as Pee-wee Herman) of the innovative children's TV program *Pee-wee's Playhouse*, pleaded no contest to charges of indecent exposure stemming from his arrest in a pornographic movie theater in Sarasota, Fla.

**Marlon Brando**'s son **Christian** received a ten-year prison term for voluntary manslaughter after admitting he had shot **Dag Drollet**, the lover of his half-sister **Cheyenne**; after two suicide attempts, she was charged in Tahiti with complicity in Drollet's death.

A Michigan medical board suspended the license of **Jack Kevorkian**, sometimes called Dr. Death, after he helped several women commit suicide. **Jim Bakker** had his prison sentence reduced from 45 to 18 years, while another fallen evangelist, **Jimmy Swaggart**, lost a $10 million slander suit and was arrested in the company of a prostitute. In Iran-contra cases, former National Security Adviser **John M. Poindexter** had his conviction overturned, and charges against **Oliver North** were dropped.

**Earvin ("Magic") Johnson**, three times Most Valuable Player in the National Basketball Association, saddened the sports world when he revealed he had tested positive for human immunodeficiency virus (HIV) and was retiring from professional basketball to become a spokesman for AIDS prevention through safe sex. Other sports shockers included the indictment of former heavyweight boxing champion **Mike Tyson** on a rape charge, the suspension of soccer superstar **Diego Maradona** from international competition because traces of cocaine were found in his urine, and the mysterious absence of **Monica Seles** from Wimbledon, the only 1991 Grand Slam tennis event she failed to win.

**Pete Rose**, already banned from baseball for betting on games, was declared ineligible for the Hall of Fame, but two likely future Hall of Famers—**Nolan Ryan**, who pitched his seventh no-hitter at the age of 44, and **Rickey Henderson**, who surpassed **Lou Brock** as all-time stolen base leader—solidified their hold on baseball immortality. Another aging pitcher, **Jack Morris**, led the Minnesota Twins to a World Series victory and then persuaded the Toronto Blue Jays to make him the highest-paid pitcher ever. Japanese fans were saddened when sumo wrestling champion **Chiyonofuji** announced his retirement from competition, after winning 1,045 matches and 31 tournament titles.

In the year's biggest celebrity bash, Elizabeth Taylor married construction worker **Larry Fortensky** (her eighth, his third) on Michael Jackson's 2,700-acre hideaway at Santa Ynez Valley, Calif.; they had met in 1988 while being treated for drug dependency at the Betty Ford Center. Among the 160 invited guests were Nancy Reagan, **Brooke Shields** (Michael's date for the day), **Quincy Jones**, **Gregory Peck**, movie executive **Barry Diller**, and gossip columnist **Liz Smith**. Although doing "the chop" together wasn't quite enough to help his Atlanta Braves win the World Series, **Ted Turner** and **Jane Fonda** got married on his 8,100-acre Florida spread in December, shortly before he was named *Time* magazine's Man of the Year; the honor recognized the (sometimes literally) revolutionary effect of the Turner-owned CNN on journalism and current events.

Others tying the knot included **John Travolta** and **Kelly Preston**, **Meg Ryan** and **Dennis Quaid**, film producer **Sherry Lansing** and director **William Friedkin**, New York City Ballet Director **Peter Martins** and prima ballerina **Darci Kistler**, and **Bruce Springsteen** and backup singer **Patti Scialfa**. Supermodels Ra-

chel Hunter and **Cynthia Crawford** married **Rod Stewart** and **Richard Gere**, respectively.

Senator **Strom Thurmond** (R, S.C.), 88, separated from his 44-year-old wife, **Nancy**. **Nick** and **Rebecca Nolte** filed for divorce, as did songwriters **Carole Bayer Sager** and **Burt Bacharach**, singers **Vic Damone** and **Diahann Carroll**, and novelist **Kurt Vonnegut, Jr.**, and photographer **Jill Krementz**.

**Bruce Willis** and **Demi Moore** had their second child; Moore had posed nude—and very pregnant—for the cover of *Vanity Fair*. **Maria Shriver** and **Arnold Schwarzenegger** also had their second, and **Tatum O'Neal** and **John McEnroe** their third, while legendary womanizer **Warren Beatty** was expecting his first, with **Annette Bening**, his costar in the hit film *Bugsy*.

G.M.H.

**Elizabeth Taylor, with new husband
Larry Fortensky**

**PETER ARNETT**

### PETER ARNETT

Covering the January 17 allied air attack on Baghdad from the heart of the Iraqi capital terrified Cable News Network (CNN) reporter Bernard Shaw, who later confessed, "It's the closest I've come to death." For his colleague Peter Arnett, however, it was all in a day's work. The Persian Gulf conflagration marked the 17th war or insurrection Arnett had covered up close, following the action through hamlets and jungles, reporting his personal observations, and often stirring up controversy in the process.

Peter Arnett was born on November 13, 1934, in Riverton, a whaling village in New Zealand. In his mid-20s the fledgling reporter landed in Thailand, where he took a job with a Bangkok English-language paper, and then in Laos, where he became the principal staffer for the Vientiane *World*. Arnett covered the Vietnam War for the Associated Press from 1962 through 1970, winning a Pulitzer Prize for his reporting, and returned to cover the fall of Saigon in 1975. He also covered the Jonestown massacre in Guyana and the Iranian hostage crisis, among other top stories, before leaving the AP for CNN in 1981. With CNN he has served as Moscow bureau chief (1986-1988)

and held plum assignments in Washington and in Jerusalem.

When his colleagues left Baghdad soon after the war began, Arnett's decision to remain as the sole Western correspondent in the embattled enemy capital and to submit his reports to Iraqi censors drew fire from some Americans, especially when he began sending back graphic accounts of civilian casualties from allied bombing. Arnett, who in April received an award from the Overseas Press Club for lifetime achievement in foreign reporting, took all the furor in stride. "I've been in much more dangerous situations in my career with much less attention than I'm getting now," he told one interviewer during the war. "It's just another story."

### JAMES A. BAKER III

During January and February, as war threatened and then raged over the Persian Gulf, U.S. Secretary of State James A. Baker III had to preserve UN backing for the policy of ousting Iraq from Kuwait, keep the fractious multinational alliance against Saddam Hussein from coming unglued, restrain the Israelis from retaliating against Iraqi Scud missile attacks, and prevent the Soviet Union from negotiating a

**JAMES A. BAKER III**

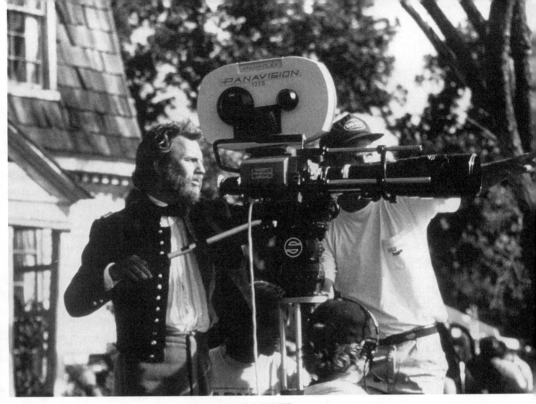

**KEVIN COSTNER**

diplomatic settlement that would have left most of Iraq's best troops and military hardware intact. That was the easy part.

In the wake of the U.S.-led military triumph in the Gulf, Baker took a key role in attempting to promote peace negotiations in the long conflict between Israel, the Palestinians, and Arab governments in the Middle East. Between March and October he made seven stops in Cairo, eight in Damascus, and nine in Jerusalem. He staked his personal prestige on a mediation effort, and the convening in October of talks in Madrid marked the most significant break in the Arab-Israeli impasse since the 1978 Camp David accords. Although Baker was unable to convince Israel to halt the construction of Jewish settlements on the occupied West Bank, his peace efforts did create a favorable climate for the release both of Western hostages held in Lebanon and of Palestinian detainees in Israel.

In December a second round of Middle East peace talks was held in Washington, where little progress was made. In any case, the major share of Baker's attention had to be turned toward the disintegrating Soviet Union. In a speech on December 12 at his alma mater, Princeton University, he outlined the Bush administration's plan for dealing with the Soviet crisis, including assistance in the dismantling of nuclear weapons, economic stabilization, and the creation of democratic institutions. He also pledged food and medical aid, but no significant increase in financial assistance.

A few days later the secretary left for Moscow and a meeting with Boris Yeltsin, president of the Russian republic, as well as with Mikhail Gorbachev in his last days as president of the rapidly dissolving Soviet Union. He went on to the central Asian republics of Kirghizia and Kazakhstan and then to Belarus and Ukraine, obtaining promises from the presidents of republics with nuclear missiles on their soil to adhere to arms reduction commitments made by Gorbachev.

### KEVIN COSTNER

In the early 1980s, Kevin Costner was virtually unknown. Cast as a suicide in *The Big Chill* (1983), he appeared only as a corpse—a 15-minute flashback showing him alive was cut at the last minute. But to compensate for this, director Lawrence Kasden wrote a good part specifically for him in the 1985 western *Silverado*. Other successes followed. In 1987, Costner starred in two consecutive hit movies— *The Untouchables* (playing federal agent Eliot Ness) and the political thriller *No Way Out*. He later appeared in two blockbusters about baseball, *Bull Durham* (1988) and *Field of Dreams* (1989).

In 1990 he clinched his reputation with the hit film *Dances With Wolves*. In this movie, the first released by his new film company, Costner directed for the first time and also starred. He spent $2.9 million of his own money to complete it and, in preparation for his role, studied the Lakota Sioux language (spoken by the Indians in the film, with subtitles) and learned to ride bareback. The film won seven Oscars in 1991, including best picture and best director.

More recently, Costner played the title role in the blockbuster *Robin Hood: Prince of Thieves* and starred as New Orleans District Attorney Jim Garrison in Oliver Stone's controversial *JFK*, a sharply opinionated probing into the 1963 assassination of President John F. Kennedy.

Kevin Costner was born on January 18, 1955, in Los Angeles. He attended California State University at Fullerton, majoring in marketing and finance. But his real interests pointed in a different direction, and before long he was appearing in community theater productions. Costner has been compared to such film greats as Gary Cooper and Jimmy Stewart. But he is usually photographed with an unsmiling, intense expression, and fans who see him in person often find him disappointingly ordinary.

## MIKHAIL GORBACHEV

Since coming to power as Soviet leader in 1985, Mikhail Gorbachev had taken dramatic initiatives. He began the titanic process of reform at home and played a key role in ending the cold war—a contribution that won him the Nobel Peace Prize in 1990. But in 1991, instead of his making things happen, things happened to Gorbachev. He was the target of an August coup attempt which, though unsuccessful, touched off a series of events culminating in his resignation from the presidency and the end of the Soviet Union.

When more than a dozen people in the independence-minded Soviet republic of Lithuania were killed by Soviet security troops in January, Gorbachev claimed he had not authorized the raid. But his refusal to condemn the troops' action and his subsequent calls for renewed press censorship brought demonstrators into the streets of Moscow and alienated many of his supporters abroad.

Meanwhile, elements of the Soviet leadership thought Gorbachev's reforms had already gone too far. On August 18 emissaries from a group of hard-line Communists came to his vacation residence in the Crimea and demanded that he sign a document transferring power to Vice President Gennadi Yanayev and the other members of a self-appointed State Committee for the State of Emergency. When Gorbachev refused, he and his family were placed under house arrest. Telephone communication was cut off, the dacha was surrounded by troops, and access roads were blocked by armed guards. While in captivity, Gorbachev prepared a written statement attest-

**MIKHAIL GORBACHEV**

ing to the illegality of the putsch, and he made a video to refute the plotters' claims that he had been removed because of illness.

With the coup's collapse on August 21, Gorbachev returned to Moscow—not as a hero but as a victim rescued by his former adversary Boris Yeltsin, president of the Russian republic. Gorbachev declared himself still a loyal Communist but had to repudiate the party and resign as its general secretary after massive complicity of party leaders in the coup became evident. He wrote a book about the putsch, *The August Coup: The Truth and the Lessons*, published in the United States in October, which, however, revealed little of substance.

For much of the fall Gorbachev continued efforts to enlist the Soviet republics in a treaty that would preserve something resembling an effective central government. But his plan for a Union of Sovereign States failed to garner sufficient support. In mid-December leaders of 11 of the republics agreed to form a loosely knit "commonwealth" and accepted Gorbachev's resignation from his remaining post as president—even though it had not yet been submitted. Accepting the inevitable, Gorbachev announced his resignation in a nationally televised address on December 25. In early 1992 he was to become head of a Moscow-based think tank, the International Foundation for Social, Economic, and Political Research.

## ANITA HILL

With apparent reluctance, Anita Hill moved into the national spotlight when she accused U.S. Supreme Court nominee Clarence Thomas of having sexually harassed her while she was his aide at two federal agencies in the early 1980s.

Anita Faye Hill was born on July 30, 1956, on a farm near Morris, Okla. The youngest of 13 children, she grew up in a poor, close-knit, deeply religious Baptist household and graduated from high school in 1973 as valedictorian and secretary of the student council. After graduating from Oklahoma State University, she attended Yale Law School on an NAACP scholarship, receiving her J.D. degree in 1980.

During a brief stint in private practice in Washington, D.C., Hill was introduced to Clarence Thomas, head of the Education Department's Office of Civil Rights. He became

**ANITA HILL**

her mentor, hiring her as his top assistant, and when he was appointed in 1982 to chair the Equal Employment Opportunity Commission (EEOC) she moved with him. When Hill left Washington in 1983 to join the faculty of the law school of Oral Roberts University, the initial contact came through Thomas. Three years later she moved to the University of Oklahoma law school, where she taught contract law and became a tenured professor.

Testifying in a clear, calm voice, Hill told the Senate Judiciary Committee in mid-October that despite her expressed discomfort, Thomas had repeatedly asked her for dates, tried to engage her in conversations about pornographic movies, and boasted "graphically" of his own sexual prowess. Four witnesses also testified that Hill had complained to them at the time about sexual harassment by her boss. But Thomas flatly denied all the allegations.

Republicans on the committee pressed Hill about why she had followed Thomas to the EEOC and had waited so long to make her charges. Her answer was that she had feared jeopardizing her career and sought to avoid embarrassment. To many, including experts on sexual harassment, the answer seemed plausible. But polls showed that a majority of Americans believed Thomas rather than Hill, and the Senate voted to confirm him by a 52-48 margin. To her supporters Hill remained a feminist heroine and martyr, while even her detractors acknowledged that her testimony had struck a nerve, focusing attention on an issue many would prefer to ignore.

### EARVIN ("MAGIC") JOHNSON

Earvin ("Magic") Johnson, who helped lead the Los Angeles Lakers and the National Basketball Association to unparalleled heights, retired prematurely after testing positive for the AIDS virus.

The basketball superstar, born August 14, 1959, in Lansing, Mich., broke the news on November 7, at a press conference at the Great Western Forum in Inglewood, Calif.—the arena where he had played 12 seasons and led the Lakers to 5 NBA championships. With flashes of his endearing boyish smile, Johnson said that, though he did not have symptoms of full-blown AIDS, doctors had advised him that the rigors of the sport could weaken his immune system. Only weeks before he had been

**MAGIC JOHNSON**

married to Earletha ("Cookie") Kelly, who he said had tested negative for the virus.

"Life is going to go on for me, and I'm going to be a happy man," said Johnson, who promised to become a spokesperson in the fight against AIDS. "I want people, young people, to realize they can practice safe sex."

In 1991, Johnson, who was voted the NBA's Most Valuable Player three times, established the ultimate record for a point guard, achieving a career total of 9,921 assists. But, Johnson's career cannot be measured merely by his individual statistics. He was the consummate team player. He revolutionized basketball. No one had ever seen a 6'9" player who was as versatile and could handle the ball as well.

The game that perhaps clinched his legendary status was the sixth game of the 1980 NBA Finals against the 76ers in Philadelphia. With Kareem Abdul-Jabbar resting a sprained ankle, Johnson delivered a championship for the Lakers by starting at center and then playing each of the other positions at various times, racking up 42 points, 15 rebounds, and 7 assists.

Following his grim announcement in November, Johnson became a hero to many. He accepted an invitation from President George Bush to join the 15-member National Commission on AIDS, formed a nonprofit foundation to support AIDS education, research, and therapy, and made a deal to write three books.

### JOHN MAJOR

It was never going to be easy for John Major to step into the shoes of Margaret Thatcher, the most powerful and prestige-laden British prime minister since Winston Churchill in his prime. But his first year in office revealed advantages as well as drawbacks in the situation.

Many people, both in Britain and other European Community countries, were grateful to be rid of Thatcher's dogmatic pronouncements and overbearing behavior. Major was self-deprecating and modest, a natural conciliator in public and around the cabinet table. Throughout 1991 he sought to reshape the Conservative Party into a visibly more caring one. He spoke of creating a "classless society" and of giving people "greater control over their own lives." His chief instrument toward these ends was a proposal for a Citizen's Char-

**JOHN MAJOR**

ter intended to give previously "powerless" individuals more rights and means of redress against large, faceless bureaucracies. He also played on his humble origins to stress his commitment to improving public education and the National Health Service.

The Labor opposition questioned whether the change from the Thatcher years was one of substance, especially since Major retained the central economic tenets of his patron. He did, however, respond to public hostility to the so-called poll tax, one of the key issues in Thatcher's downfall, by announcing that the uniform fee imposed on all adults by local governments would be replaced with a progressive tax based largely on property values.

Major's European Community partners found him personally warmer than his predecessor but, like Labor, were unsure how deep the differences really ran. At the December summit in Maastricht, the Netherlands, at which treaties on union were agreed to, he resisted committing Britain fully to all the accords. Unlike Thatcher, he did agree to a treaty establishing a single currency—but he

retained for Parliament the right to make the final decision on British participation. He also rejected Thatcher's call for national referenda on any European union treaties.

On a personal level, Major endeared himself to many voters by stopping his official car to dine in "greasy spoon" cafes and by displaying his passion for cricket. But Major's personal popularity could not offset the effects of deepening recession. He continued to put off the election that had to be called by July 1992. Until he could win an election, Major remained somewhat in Thatcher's shadow.

### BRIAN MULRONEY

For a week in late October, Canadians were bemused by a rumor—soon confirmed—that Brian Mulroney was a favorite of U.S. President George Bush to succeed outgoing UN Secretary-General Javier Pérez de Cuéllar. For every Canadian who responded that anything that got Mulroney out of Canada was a blessing, another Canadian worried that he would "do to the United Nations what he's already done to this country."

**BRIAN MULRONEY**

The reactions reflected the deep personal unpopularity that continued to dog Canada's prime minister, whose constitutional reform plan had collapsed in 1990. It was a better year than 1990 for the Québec-born lawyer, who turned 52 in March, but his image continued to suffer.

Controversy surrounded publication of the most detailed biography to date of the prime minister. John Sawatsky's *Mulroney: The Politics of Ambition* offered a generally well-balanced portrait of Mulroney's ascent to the top from his origins in a remote mill town. But it contained some unflattering revelations about Mulroney's youth, including his failure at Dalhousie Law School in Halifax (he flunked out and eventually graduated from Québec's Laval Law School) and allegations about a period of heavy drinking and womanizing after he failed to win the Conservative leadership on his first attempt in 1976.

Wisely, Mulroney scheduled few domestic public appearances during the year. He fared better on the international stage, playing an active role at meetings of the Group of Seven (leading industrial nations), the Commonwealth of Nations, and its French equivalent, La Francophonie, as well as in the tense diplomacy that surrounded the Persian Gulf War. In late October, British and American UN delegates proposed his name to the Security Council for secretary-general. But one week after his nomination became public, Mulroney issued a statement declaring that he would not accept the position if offered it.

In the end, by staying on and declaring himself eager to lead his party in another election, Mulroney took on not only those political adversaries among Québec's separatists who would like to tear the country apart, but also his personal critics.

## COLIN POWELL

When President George Bush nominated General Colin Powell for a second two-year term as chairman of the U.S. Joint Chiefs of Staff in May, his confirmation by the Senate was a foregone conclusion. Having long impressed his superiors as an exceptional soldier, Powell had just finished a bravura performance as head of the American military during its triumph over Iraq in the Persian Gulf War.

**COLIN POWELL**

Powell is the youngest man and the first black ever to chair the Joint Chiefs. He used his authority (newly expanded by law) to streamline the military and try to minimize the infighting that had frequently hampered its operations in the past. The swift victory of the U.S.-led coalition was a testament to his insistence that although combat is the least desirable alternative, war, once initiated, must be waged with overwhelming force and political resolve. As he described the Gulf operation, "Our strategy to go after this [Iraqi] army is very, very simple. First we're going to cut it off, and then we're going to kill it."

Powell was, however, thrust into unwelcome controversy in May, by the publication of *The Commanders*, a behind-the-scenes narrative of military decision-making in the Bush administration by Bob Woodward. It contended that Powell had favored a policy of sanctions and diplomatic pressure rather than military action to force Iraq out of Kuwait. Powell publicly denied any policy "distance" from Bush. But there were reports that Bush privately believed Powell had been a major source for the book and had spoken too candidly to Woodward.

Colin Luther Powell was born on April 5,

1937, in New York City, the son of Jamaican immigrants. In 1958 he graduated from the City College of New York, where he had been an ROTC officer, and was commissioned a second lieutenant in the army. His military career included two combat tours in Vietnam, where he was twice injured, and fast-track assignments in the army and joint commands. He served as a White House fellow in 1972-1973 and worked for two secretaries of defense on his way to becoming President Ronald Reagan's national security adviser in 1987. Bush first named him chairman of the Joint Chiefs in August 1989.

### DAN QUAYLE

In his third year in office, U.S. Vice President Dan Quayle appeared to be making an impact on administration policy. But his image problem surfaced anew when President George Bush was briefly hospitalized in May with an erratic heartbeat. News stories and polls focused on whether the 44-year-old Quayle was ready to assume the presidency; a majority of those interviewed felt Quayle was not qualified, prompting renewed speculation that he might be replaced on the 1992 Republican presidential ticket. As in previous instances, Bush rallied to Quayle's defense.

Before Bush's health episode, Quayle was a highly visible spokesman for U.S. policy during the Persian Gulf crisis, and he continued his work as chairman of the National Space Council, which was charged with reforming the troubled space program. As head of the Council on Competitiveness he enjoyed broad influence in shaping the nation's regulatory policies. Quayle also launched a much publicized attack on the legal profession. Speaking to the American Bar Association convention in Atlanta in August, he asserted that the United States had too many lawyers and too many lawsuits; not all agreed.

The vice president won some public sympathy in November when the satirical comic strip *Doonesbury* featured a series in which a fictional reporter investigated a supposed coverup of allegations of drug purchases by Quayle when he was a law student and a senator. In fact, such allegations had been made to the Drug Enforcement Administration in the early 1980s by two prison inmates, but the agency had found them to be groundless.

**DAN QUAYLE**

# PEOPLE IN THE NEWS

### H. NORMAN SCHWARZKOPF, JR.

In 1988, when "Stormin'" Norman Schwarz-kopf was named commander in chief of the United States Central Command, focusing on the Persian Gulf region, the appointment was seen as a comfortable prelude to his retirement in mid-1991. But when Iraqi dictator Saddam Hussein occupied Kuwait on August 2, 1990, Schwarzkopf was thrust into the crucible of history. President George Bush declared the occupation would not stand, and he ordered Schwarzkopf to Saudi Arabia to prepare for the possibility of war.

Less than six months later, more than half a million troops under Schwarzkopf's command launched Operation Desert Storm, the invasion of Kuwait and Iraq. In 43 days, culminating in a ground offensive that lasted only 100 hours, Schwarzkopf integrated troops from over two dozen nations into an effective force that liberated Kuwait and, using a dramatic flanking manuever, crushed Iraq's war machine. Allied casualties were minimal. Schwarzkopf was catapulted into the front ranks of American warrior-heroes.

Schwarzkopf's newfound fame brought him a Distinguished Service Medal from the Defense Department and an honorary British knighthood. It also made him a prized commercial property. Declining an appointment as army chief of staff, he retired on August 31 and contracted to write his memoirs for a reported advance of $5 million, besides signing on with a Washington speaker's bureau.

H. Norman Schwarzkopf, Jr., was born on August 22, 1934, in Trenton, N.J., where his father was superintendent of the state police. Graduating 42nd in his class of 485 at the United States Military Academy in 1956, he later earned a master's degree in guided missile engineering from the University of Southern California. His military service included two combat tours in Vietnam, where he was wounded several times; later, he was deputy commander of the U.S.-led invasion of Grenada. Schwarzkopf was the Army's deputy chief of staff for operations and had recently been promoted to four-star general when he was tapped for the Central Command.

In the Gulf War, Schwarzkopf may not have achieved the victory he had wanted; in March

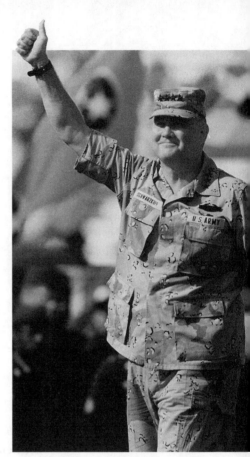

**H. NORMAN SCHWARZKOPF, JR.**

he told a television interviewer that his "recommendation" had been to continue the ground offensive longer. Administration officials insisted that Schwarzkopf had concurred in the decision to stop fighting, and Schwarzkopf apologized to the president for what he called a "poor choice of words."

### MONICA SELES

Monica Seles, the mercurial teenaged tennis star, put together a remarkable year, reaching the final of every one of the 16 tournaments she entered and winning 10 of them. She set a single-season mark for most money earned on the women's tennis tour ($2,457,758) and won three of the four Grand Slam tournaments—the Australian Open in January, French Open in May, and U.S. Open in September. And she defended her title at the season-ending Virginia Slims Championships, to close the year as the world's number-one woman player.

But at the other Grand Slam event—or rather

away from it—Seles put a serious dent in her popularity. Just before Wimbledon opened in June, she withdrew, citing medical reasons but opting not to make them public. Officials expressed dismay, demanding medical documentation. With rumors of pregnancy, career-threatening leg injuries, and knee problems headlined in British tabloids, public curiosity was further aroused when Seles showed up at the Florida mansion of real estate mogul Donald Trump. She came out of seclusion more than a month later, announcing to reporters that she merely had shin splints. Had she won Wimbledon, Seles would have become one of only four women in history to earn a Grand Slam.

Seles was born of Hungarian parents in Novi Sad, Yugoslavia, on December 2, 1973. At an

## MONICA SELES

early age she learned tennis from her father, an animator who drew the cartoon characters Tom and Jerry on tennis balls and instructed Monica to "first hit Tom and then hit Jerry." After turning pro in early 1989, Seles stunned the tennis world with her grunting ground strokes and her race to the top of the women's game. In 1990 she won six tournaments in a row and finished the year with a .900 winning percentage; the next year she took over the number-one ranking from Steffi Graf in March and solidified her position by midsummer.

## NEIL SIMON

Financially he is the most successful playwright in the history of the world—with a net worth estimated at up to $100 million—but Neil Simon has a hard time getting people to take him seriously. This is mainly because he is so funny. Even when writing about people who are unemployed and homeless, depressed, or in danger of being murdered, Simon makes audiences laugh.

For Simon, 1991 brought a happy end to years of feeling underappreciated. Months after telling an interviewer he despaired of ever winning the accolade he most wanted, the Pulitzer Prize in drama, Simon achieved that honor with his 29th play, *Lost in Yonkers*. The play, about two boys sent to live with eccentric relatives, also won the Tony Award for the year's best play and three of the four Tonys for acting in a nonmusical.

Simon was born on July 4, 1927, in New York City to Irving and Mamie Simon. He and his older brother, Danny, also a comedy writer, turned to show business as a way of breaking out of their working-class circumstances. Their apprenticeship was spent writing jokes for comics like Jackie Gleason, Sid Caesar, and Phil Silvers. By the late 1950s, Neil Simon had turned to the theater. Laboring nights and weekends for three years, he shaped a comedy based on his entering into adulthood. The result, *Come Blow Your Horn*, had a long run on Broadway, was sold to the movies, and is still widely produced by summer stock and amateur groups. More hits soon followed, among them *Barefoot in the Park*, *The Odd Couple*, *The Prisoner of Second Avenue*, and *Plaza Suite*.

In the 1980s, his reputation vaulted forward

**NEIL SIMON**

with an autobiographical trilogy. The first of the three plays, 1983's *Brighton Beach Memoirs*, was named best play of the season by the New York Drama Critics Circle. In 1985, *Biloxi Blues* became the first Simon work to win the Tony as best play, and in 1987, the third installment, *Broadway Bound*, nearly won the coveted Pulitzer.

### CLARENCE THOMAS

When President George Bush named Clarence Thomas, a conservative black federal judge, to replace Thurgood Marshall on the U.S. Supreme Court, the nomination was widely regarded as a political masterstroke that would split the nation's blacks and leave Democrats and liberal interest groups stymied. The scenario seemed to run as expected after Thomas testified for five days before the Senate Judiciary Committee. He stressed his up-from-poverty background, refused to say how he would vote on abortion, and appeared to soften some of his past stands on controversial issues. The committee deadlocked, 7-7, over whether to recommend his confirmation to the full Senate. While some senators expressed doubts about his qualifications and bridled over his refusal to air his views on abortion, the Senate was expected to confirm him by a comfortable margin.

Then the unexpected occurred. Anita Hill, a University of Oklahoma law professor who had worked for Thomas at two federal agencies in the early 1980s, had told the committee staff Thomas had sexually harassed her on the job. The committee did not pursue the charges until they were leaked to the media at the last minute. Then, in three days of sensational televised hearings, Hill repeated the allegations, replete with seamy details. Thomas denied the charges emphatically and accused the committee of a "high-tech lynching" that left his reputation in tatters. Polls showed most Americans believed him.

On October 15 he was confirmed as the 106th Supreme Court justice, by a 52-48 vote, receiving the largest number of negative votes of any successful Supreme Court nominee in history. He became the second-youngest justice in this century.

**CLARENCE THOMAS**

## BORIS YELTSIN

Thomas was born in poverty on June 23, 1948, in the segregated rural hamlet of Pin Point, Ga. His father left the family when he was a small child, and his maternal grandparents, with whom he lived in nearby Savannah for most of his childhood, sent him to a Catholic school run by nuns, whom he frequently credits for his later success. After graduating from Holy Cross College and Yale Law School, he became an assistant to John Danforth, then attorney general of Missouri. Danforth, who brought Thomas with him to Washington when he was elected senator, was a key supporter during the confirmation fight.

By the early 1980s, Thomas had experienced a conversion from his earlier liberalism and black nationalism; while still resentful of racism, he gained attention from the new Reagan administration as a prominent black conservative. In 1981 he was named head of the Office of Civil Rights in the Department of Education. The next year he became chairman of the Equal Employment Opportunity Commission, where he remained until he was appointed to the U.S. Court of Appeals for the District of Columbia in 1989.

### BORIS YELTSIN

On August 19, just a few hours after the public was told of a coup against the government of Soviet President Mikhail Gorbachev, Russian President Boris Yeltsin appeared outside the Russian Parliament building atop a tank and denounced the putsch as illegal and unconstitutional. His speech helped galvanize resistance and drew tens of thousands of people into the streets to protect him in the event of an armed assault. By the time the coup collapsed on August 21, Yeltsin had captured the imagination of the world and had eclipsed Gorbachev in stature. With the Soviet Union's final collapse in late 1991 and the formation of the Commonwealth of Independent States, Yeltsin, as head of the largest and most powerful former Soviet republic, emerged as the preeminent leader in the new confederation.

Yeltsin's transformation from regional party official to national reform leader began in 1985 when Gorbachev elevated him to Moscow party chief. While working to further Gorbachev's *perestroika* ("restructuring") reforms, Yeltsin demonstrated the crusading zeal that later made him a hero. He rode the subways instead of official limousines and denounced the privileges of party apparatchiks.

In late 1987 he and Gorbachev had a falling out—partly because Yeltsin was pressing for faster reforms. Yeltsin was dismissed, but this served only to increase his popularity and enhance his reputation as a maverick. He was elected a delegate at large to a special Communist Party conference in 1988. The following March, he was elected Moscow representative to the new national legislature, the Congress of People's Deputies, receiving a stunning 89 percent of the vote.

In July 1990, two months after the Russian Supreme Soviet voted him its chairman, making him the top leader in the Russian republic, Yeltsin quit the Communist Party—becoming the first prominent politician to do so. He also used his position in Russia to negotiate bilateral treaties with other Soviet republics, thus subverting the centralized structure that had characterized the Soviet government.

In June 1991, Yeltsin became the first popularly elected president in Russian history, garnering 60 percent of the vote in a field of six candidates. In November, as the central Soviet government continued to disintegrate, he moved to take over control of Soviet economic assets in Russia; by the end of the month the Soviet government seemed to be surviving only by the grace of Yeltsin, who agreed to have Russia finance the Soviet payroll.

Yeltsin faced great challenges as the year drew to a close—first and foremost the task of guiding Russia through a painful rapid transition to a free-market economy. In November he became prime minister of the Russian republic, to take personal responsibility for the economic program. In December, Yeltsin moved into Gorbachev's office shortly after the latter's resignation—even before the ex-Soviet president had had a chance to clean it out. He evidently had much work to do.

**PERSIAN GULF STATES.** See ARABIAN PENINSULA and individual countries.

**PERU.** In 1991, Peruvian President Alberto Fujimori sought to liberalize the ailing economy and combat the country's rampant terrorism. A cholera epidemic during the year struck a quarter of a million people, killing more than 2,000.

**Economy.** The rate of inflation fell from 7,650 percent in 1990 to about 100 percent in 1991. But economic output dropped for the fourth straight year, and a harsh austerity program brought great suffering. In June the government imposed a temporary "solidarity tax" on the wages of public employees who earned more than $240 per month, with the revenue to be redistributed to those earning less. Both before and after it was granted emergency powers by Congress in June, the government introduced measures to open Peru's economy to market forces, attract new investment, and reduce the budget deficit.

In September, seven industrial nations led by Japan and the United States loaned Peru $1.1 billion to repay its long-defaulted debts to the International Monetary Fund. Thereafter the so-called Paris Club of Peru's official creditors

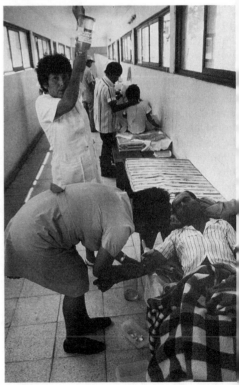

A cholera epidemic struck South America for the first time in nearly a century, beginning in Peru, the nation that was hardest hit. Here, nurses in a severely overcrowded hospital in Lima treat cholera victims in the corridor.

agreed to refinance $6.6 billion in loans falling due in 1991 and 1992.

**Terrorism and Drugs.** The insurgency of the Shining Path (Sendero Luminoso) rebels, which has cost more than 23,000 lives, entered its 11th year. After a sharp decline in terrorist activity, the rebels launched a wave of attacks in May and June, followed by another wave late in the year. In November the government used its emergency powers to issue a group of decrees which, among other things, allowed troops to seize property temporarily for use in the antiguerrilla campaign and force civilians to participate in it. Refusal to give information to government intelligence agents was declared to be treason.

The demoralized security forces made little progress against the international drug cartels, which, in tacit alliance with the Shining Path, obtain from farmers enough coca to produce more than half of the world's supply of cocaine. On May 15, Fujimori signed a controversial agreement under which the United States pledged $94 million to assist in fighting the drug traffickers and in financing a crop substitution program. Because of evidence of widespread corruption among the Peruvian military, however, the U.S. Congress withheld its portion of the aid as the year ended.

**Politics.** Premier Juan Carlos Hurtado Miller resigned from the cabinet in February in a dispute over economic policy. Carlos Torres y Torres Lara became premier, but in October he resigned unexpectedly, to be succeeded by Labor Minister Alfonso de los Heros.

In May and August, Congress indicted five members of former President Alan García's cabinet on charges of stealing millions of dollars through foreign exchange manipulations. The U.S. Department of Justice later accused two other García-era officials of accepting bribes to deposit government funds in the Bank of Credit and Commerce International. García was himself accused of defrauding Peru during his tenure from 1985 to 1990. In October, Congress stripped him of immunity from prosecution, and he was charged with embezzling government funds to build three houses for himself in Lima. But charges that he had stolen $50 million were dismissed.

See STATISTICS OF THE WORLD.          D.P.W.

**PETROLEUM AND NATURAL GAS.** *See* ENERGY.

**PETS.** At the beginning of 1991, cats once again outnumbered dogs in U.S. households. According to the American Pet Products Association, there were 52 million dogs living in 35 million U.S. households, and 60 million cats living in 31 million homes.

**Dog Stars.** The cocker spaniel remained the number-one breed in the American Kennel Club's registration ranking, with a total of 105,642 dogs registered in 1990. However, there were 5,994 fewer cockers registered than in 1989. Labrador retrievers and poodles ranked second and third, respectively, for the third year in a row.

The 115th Westminster Kennel Club show, held in New York City in February, was won by a white standard poodle, Ch. Whisperwind on a Carousel, who took home the Best-in-Show trophy. Britain's Crufts Kennel Club show, the world's largest dog show, celebrated its centenary early in the year. Top honors went to Ch. Raycroft Socialite, a clumber spaniel called Garfield by his owner.

This was also the year in which a canine "author"—Millie, the English springer spaniel owned by First Lady Barbara Bush—had her autobiography published by William Morrow & Company. *Millie's Book*, as told to Barbara Bush, made it to the New York *Times* bestseller list, where it stayed for 24 weeks. Proceeds were donated to the Literacy Volunteers of America.

**Feline Popularity.** In the world of purebred cats, the Persian remained on top in popularity, according to the Cat Fancier's Association. The registry showed 60,661 Persian cats registered in 1990, an increase of 3,814 cats over the 1989 figure. The Siamese ranked a distant second with 3,860 individuals registered, while the Maine Coon Cat was third with 2,727. The Maine Coon narrowly beat out the Abyssinian, 1989's third-place breed.

**Too Many Pets.** Once again there were more cats and dogs in the United States than there were available homes. The annual nationwide survey of animal shelters by the American Humane Association indicated that 7.2 million unwanted dogs and 7.6 million orphaned cats were put to sleep in 1990.

*Singer LaToya Jackson, with her pet snake, Adam, watches as a man digs in vain for his dog at the Long Island Pet Cemetery. Cemetery owners allegedly took money to cremate pets or bury them in individual graves, then dumped the animals into a pit.*

Pet overpopulation was such a problem that officials in California's San Mateo County drafted a strict—and controversial—ordinance that included a moratorium on dog and cat breeding, plus mandatory spaying or neutering of all dogs and cats in the county, whether or not they had homes. Breeders of purebred dogs, backed by the American Kennel Club, campaigned against the proposed law, and in November, the San Mateo Board of Supervisors adopted a modified ordinance. It eliminated the breeding ban and required the spaying and neutering only of animals adopted from shelters. Residents could keep unaltered pets but had to pay higher license fees for them, and breeders were required to obtain a special license. Other communities were considering similar legislation.

**Pet Scandal.** In July, proprietors of the Long Island Pet Cemetery in New York were charged with tossing some 250,000 dead animals into the woods and cremating thousand of others en masse, instead of providing the individual burials for which owners had paid hundreds, sometimes thousands, of dollars. Singer LaToya Jackson, wearing her pet snake, joined the angry pet owners at a demonstration over the empty graves. Later in the year, two members of the same family charged in the cemetery case were arrested and charged with selling rotten, pesticide-laden dog food at their chain of Bow Wow Meow pet stores.

**Humaneness for Horses.** The ongoing movement within the equine industry to promote humane treatment of horses was strengthened significantly. The American Horse Shows Association, which functions as the governing body for 24 breeds and disciplines of show horses, and sanctions 2,500 horse shows annually, passed several anticruelty amendments to its rules governing competitions. The changes permit the organization to deny or suspend membership privileges to individuals convicted of cruelty to horses.                    A.P.

**PHILIPPINES.** The year 1991 in the Philippines, like the preceding year, was fraught with natural disasters and economic crises. The defeat of a treaty extending the U.S. lease on Subic Bay Naval Station was a key landmark in U.S.-Philippine relations. The upcoming presidential elections were a focus of attention, as was the return of Imelda Marcos to Manila on November 4 after almost six years of exile in Hawaii.

**Aquino's Speech.** On July 22, in a state-of-the-nation address before Congress, an emotional President Corazon Aquino promised to conduct an orderly succession after the May 11, 1992, presidential elections. She said she herself would not seek a second term—though there still was speculation that she might run again in order to unify the ruling party, the LDP (Strength of Democratic Philippines). Aquino cited democracy as her major "steadfast and unalloyed" achievement. But though her place in history as a symbol of moral outrage and "people power" was secure, Aquino's lack of political savvy had hampered her ability to govern a long-troubled country of 66 million people, 60 percent of whom live in poverty. The economy was projected to grow at only .2 percent in 1991, and inflation and unemployment were high.

**Natural Disasters.** Mount Pinatubo, dormant for more than six centuries, erupted in mid-June, spewing volcanic ash over cities and villages in central Luzon. Hundreds of people died and hundreds of thousands were forced to flee. In early November, the islands of Letye, Samar, and Negros were devastated by the tropical storm Thelma, which left an estimated 7,000 dead in a fury of floods and mudslides.

**Philippine-American Relations.** In the fall U.S. troops turned Clark Air Base over to the Philippine government (the base had been rendered unusable by damage from the eruption of Mount Pinatubo). Also, the Philippine Senate voted against retaining the U.S. naval base at Subic Bay, effectively terminating the Military Bases Agreement signed in 1947 by the United States and the Philippines. Aquino, noting that a shutdown would remove millions of dollars each year from the economy and leave thousands of Filipinos unemployed, at first called for a referendum to circumvent the

Senate rejection of the treaty but later backed down. In October the Philippine Senate agreed to a three-year phase-out period for the naval base, but when subsequent negotiations reached an impasse the United States was told it must leave the Subic Bay base by the end of 1992.

**1992 Elections.** In November the ruling LDP selected Speaker of the House of Representatives Ramon Mitra as its presidential candidate for 1992. Senate President Jovito Salonga, who had led the Senate campaign to defeat the Subic extension treaty, was the front-runner for the nomination of the Liberal Party. He lost his Senate presidency in a political shakeup in December but was still expected to run. Other candidates included Senator Joseph Estrada, a

*A boy on the Philippine island of Leyte carries the marker to be placed on his sister's grave; she was a victim of a tropical storm that slammed into the region in November, killing some 7,000 people and leaving thousands more homeless.*

*Imelda Marcos, widow of former dictator Ferdinand Marcos, returned to the Philippines in November after nearly six years of exile. Immediately arrested on tax fraud charges, she is shown here being fingerprinted before her release on bail.*

film actor who bolted the Liberal Party to form his own Filipino Masses Party, and Miriam Defensor Santiago, formerly secretary of the Department of Agrarian Reform and commissioner of immigration.

**Imelda Marcos.** The return of Imelda Marcos and her son Ferdinand Marcos, Jr., added to the election fever that gripped the Philippine political scene. There was speculation as to whether she might seek the presidency herself or, if not, as to whom she would support. Late in the year, Marcos indicated she might run as she accepted the endorsement of her late husband's party, the New Society Movement, as its presidential candidate. Mrs. Marcos, who faced charges of tax evasion and graft, as well as more than 30 civil suits, was allowed to return by the Philippine government in the hope of recovering some of the millions of dollars believed to have been secreted in Swiss bank accounts by the Marcos family. She continued to spar with the government about the burial of

former President Ferdinand Marcos, who died in Hawaii in 1989 and whose body lay unburied in Honolulu; Imelda Marcos wanted her husband interred in a heroes' cemetery in Manila, while Aquino said the body could be interred only in Marcos's home town.

*See* STATISTICS OF THE WORLD.     B.A.A.

**PHOTOGRAPHY.** The year 1991 brought important changes at a major institution and continuing debate over photographs that feature controversial subject matter.

**MOMA.** John Szarkowski retired in July as director of the Department of Photography at New York's Museum of Modern Art, a post in which he had exerted unprecedented artistic influence through an important series of exhibitions and books. Peter Galassi, an associate director of photography at MOMA, was named as Szarkowski's successor. In September, Galassi assembled "Pleasures and Terrors of Domestic Comfort," an ambitious presentation of pictures by American photographers of the 1980s working in a wide variety of styles, from black-and-white documentary images to the staged tableaux of such artists as Cindy Sherman and Laurie Simmons.

**Controversy.** In July, Elizabeth Broun, director of the National Museum of American Art in Washington, D.C., sparked debate when she attempted to ban a work by Sol LeWitt from an exhibition highlighting the influence of Eadweard Muybridge, pioneering photographer and inventor of an early form of motion pictures. The LeWitt work, *Muybridge I* (1964), consists of a long black box with ten small holes cut into the side, through which the viewer sees images of a nude woman approaching the camera. Broun found it "degrading and offensive" to women. After protests from artists and curators, however, the work was restored to the exhibition.

In September a federal grand jury in San Francisco refused to return an indictment against Jock Sturges, whose studio had been raided by FBI agents in April 1990. Prosecutors had argued that Sturges's nude photographs of adolescent girls, widely exhibited in galleries and museums, were child pornography. Sturges said that he had photographed only his "naturist" friends and that he had always sought parental consent beforehand.

Photojournalism figured in debates during the Persian Gulf War. As a result of the U.S. government policy of assigning journalists to official press pools and controlling access to the front lines, few of the photographs that came back to the public depicted actual fighting. The most memorable images produced during the war itself were abstract ones, such as those showing the tracery of antiaircraft fire over Baghdad. Only after the war did Americans get to see much depiction of the destruction wrought by the Iraqi Army in Kuwait and by allied bombing in Iraq.

**Exhibitions.** Among major exhibitions during the year, "Appearances: Fashion Photography since 1945," curated by Martin Harrison, was presented during the summer at London's Victoria and Albert Museum. In September the

*Berenice Abbott, who died in December at the age of 93, was best known for her photographs portraying New York City in the 1930s; shown here, a view of the Flatiron Building, taken in 1938.*

International Center of Photography in New York offered a 20-year survey of the work of Annie Liebovitz, whose celebrity portraits have been featured in *Rolling Stone* and *Vanity Fair* magazines. Also in September, ICP presented a retrospective of the work of Mary Ellen Mark, whose photojournalistic projects have focused on such subjects as women in mental hospitals, homeless families, and Mother Teresa's mission in Calcutta, India.

**Losses.** Aaron Siskind, renowned photographer and teacher, died on February 8 at the age of 87. His closeup pictures of patterns of paint on walls, peeling posters, and strips of tar on roads transformed these objects into dramatic scenes, often suggesting human relationships.

Edwin H. Land, the inventor of the Polaroid instant photographic process, died on March 1 at the age of 81. Land, a Harvard dropout, founded the Polaroid Corporation in 1937 and developed the first instant film in 1948.

Berenice Abbott, 93, died on December 10. Beginning her work as a portrait photographer in Paris in the 1920s, Abbott returned to the United States in 1929 having purchased all the work of the still unknown, recently deceased Eugène Atget, whom she established as an important artist. Most prominent among her own works is a famous series of black-and-white photographs depicting New York City in the 1930s.

**Honors.** Harry Callahan, a leading figure in photography since World War II and widely known for his elegant black-and-white images, was honored as Master of Photography by the International Center of Photography. The $20,000 W. Eugene Smith Grant for Humanistic Photography went to Italian photojournalist Dario Mitidieri, for photographs of street children in Bombay, India. Fashion photographer Richard Avedon won the $43,000 Hasselblad Foundation photography prize.

**Technology.** In technical developments, a new top-of-the-line model of the medium-format Hasselblad camera, long a favorite of fashion and commercial photographers, was introduced. Designated the 205TCC, the new model featured its own system of three magazines, a motor winder, and six new lenses, as well as an improved method of measuring light automatically. C.H.

**PHYSICS.** Scientists discovered a technique for converting silicon into a light-emitting material and carried out new experimental demonstrations that atoms have wavelike properties. Plans for the Superconducting Super Collider were caught in a funding crunch.

**Silicon Light Emitters.** Despite its importance as the foundation of the microelectronics revolution, the semiconductor silicon has not been regarded as the key to the next step in digital information processing—the marriage of electronic and optical technologies—owing to its inability to emit visible light. But two groups of researchers, one British and one French, recently hit upon a technique for converting silicon into a comparatively efficient emitter of visible light. They immersed silicon in an acidic electrochemical cell. Holes were thus etched into its surface, making it porous. The British group increased this porosity by means of a second etching step, transforming the silicon surface into a large number of needlelike columns; when illuminated with laser light, the columns responded by emitting visible red, orange, yellow, and green light. The French group followed a slightly different procedure but had similar results, obtaining red, orange, or yellow light when illuminating silicon with ultraviolet light. The British group further claimed to have developed silicon structures that emit light when electric current passes through them, a behavior required for the integration of electronic and optical functions on the same chip.

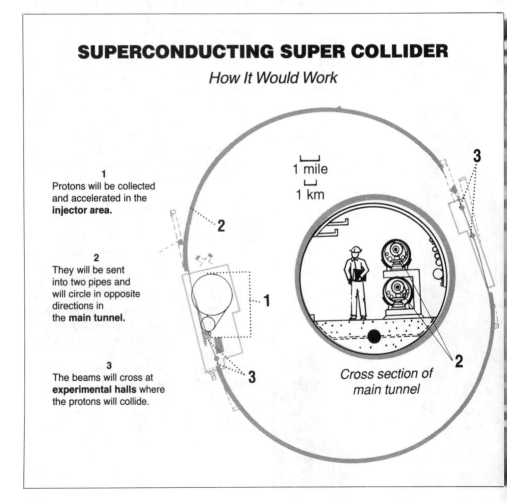

# SUPERCONDUCTING SUPER COLLIDER
## *How It Would Work*

**1**
Protons will be collected and accelerated in the **injector area.**

**2**
They will be sent into two pipes and will circle in opposite directions in the **main tunnel.**

**3**
The beams will cross at **experimental halls** where the protons will collide.

1 mile
1 km

*Cross section of main tunnel*

**Atomic Interferometers.** Interferometers split a wave—most commonly, a light wave—into two components. When the waves recombine, they form an "interference pattern" consisting of "light" and "dark" bands, or fringes, which are extraordinarily sensitive to anything that affects the paths of the light waves during the time they are split.

In 1991, research teams in the United States and Europe extended the demonstration of particle interferometry to atoms. The simplest experiment to visualize was one sending a beam of sodium atoms toward a diffraction grating that had a spacing of only 0.4 micrometer between the centers of the grooves. The atoms, split into beams with different directions, then passed through a second grating, which directed the split beams back together. A detector at the point of recombination recorded the interference pattern of light and dark fringes. Atomic interferometers may prove useful as navigation devices, as oil-field sensors, for use in scientific tests, and for verifying that atoms are electrically neutral.

**Heavy Neutrinos.** Physicists long tended to believe that neutrinos have no mass. But this assumption was challenged in 1985 by John Simpson of the University of Guelph in Ontario. Simpson studied the radioactive decay of tritium by the process of beta decay, in which one of the neutrons becomes a proton by emitting an electron and a neutrino. He concluded that about 3 percent of the time the emitted neutrino had a mass of 17,000 electron volts (17 keV). Attempts by other physicists to duplicate—or disprove—Simpson's findings were unsuccessful until recently, when two groups of physicists studied the beta decay of a sulfur isotope (sulfur-35) and carbon-14 atoms and found a 17-keV neutrino a very small percentage of the time. However, other researchers have failed to find any sign of the heavy neutrino.

**Super Collider.** The Bush administration in October redoubled its efforts to persuade Japan to invest more than $1 billion in the Superconducting Super Collider (SSC) project, for which cost estimates had skyrocketed to $8.4 billion. Large-scale financial support from overseas had failed to materialize. The state of Texas, however, pledged about $1 billion, and Con-gress appropriated $483 million for the super-collider for fiscal year 1992.

The 54-mile oval structure—planned to be built underground in Texas by 1999—would generate collisions between protons, the results of which, as measured by detectors, could answer fundamental questions of physics. In January the SSC Laboratory approved for further development a proposal by a 545-person team to design and build one of the collider's two planned main elementary-particle detectors; in July a collaboration of about 300 physicists was given the go-ahead to prepare a full proposal for the second.

**Fusion.** In November, for the first time ever, a significant amount of energy—about 1.7 million watts—was produced from controlled nuclear fusion. The reported breakthrough was achieved at the Joint European Torus (JET) laboratory in England. Researchers succeeded in fusing nuclei of two hydrogen isotopes—deuterium and tritium. The ability to handle radioactive tritium safely was regarded as a major step in the development of fusion as an energy source.　　　　　　　　　　A.L.R.

**POLAND.** During 1991, Poland continued to grope toward a market economy and a stable pluralist political system. But fall elections resulted in a Parliament of over 30 parties, and in December a critic of market reforms became prime minister, succeeding Jan Krzysztof Bielecki, a reformist.

**The Walesa Presidency.** President Lech Walesa lost a major political battle with the ex-Communist majority in the lower house of Parliament over a format for Poland's first fully free parliamentary elections. In early July he accepted a system of proportional representation that favored small parties. The elections, held on October 27, resulted in a chaotic situation, as 37 parties won seats in Parliament. The parties associated with Solidarity and economic reform received less than one-third of the vote. Turnout was low. The strongest showing was by the Democratic Union of former Prime Minister Tadeusz Mazowiecki, with 12 percent of the vote. The reformed Communists, under the banner of the Democratic Left Alliance, came in a close second.

In December five center-right parties agreed to form a government with Jan Olszewski, a

*Poland and Germany (historic enemies) signed an accord in June pledging cooperation and friendship. Attending the official ceremony were, from left to right, Polish Foreign Minister Krzysztof Skubiszewski, Polish Prime Minister Jan Krzysztof Bielecki, German Chancellor Helmut Kohl, former West German Chancellor Willy Brandt (initiator of a policy of closer ties with Eastern Europe), and German Foreign Minister Hans-Dietrich Genscher.*

constant critic of the economic reforms, as prime minister. He resigned within two weeks after clashing with Walesa on his cabinet choices and the pace of economic reform. But after Parliament gave him a vote of confidence, he put together—and Parliament accepted—a cabinet likely to soften the president's austerity program.

**Mixed Record for the Economy.** Instead of growing by 3-4 percent as predicted, the economy declined, with production falling an estimated 8 percent below 1990 levels, which themselves were 12 percent below those for 1989. The abrupt cessation of trade with the Soviet Union was a major factor. An estimated 200 to 300 Polish enterprises were on the verge of bankruptcy because their markets in the Soviet Union had disappeared.

On the positive side, inflation, which was running at an estimated 2,000 percent in 1989, was brought under control, with an annual rate of 40 percent in October 1991. In April the

Club of Paris group of Western creditor nations agreed to forgive half of Poland's $33 billion debt; also, 70 percent of Poland's $3.6 billion debt to the United States was forgiven, and the International Monetary Fund provided $2 billion in economic aid. Stock market volume rose with every session, and the influx of Western investment capital increased dramatically.

**Foreign Relations.** Poland pursued a dual foreign policy with a Soviet Union in the process of disintegration. It sought to normalize relations with Moscow while establishing relationships with the republics, especially the three Baltic states, whose independence Poland recognized almost immediately after the failed Soviet coup in August.

Early in the year, the Soviet Union refused Polish demands to hasten Soviet troop withdrawal from Poland, and Poland was under pressure not to join any alliances viewed as hostile by the Soviets. In October, however, it was announced that all Soviet troops would be withdrawn by the end of 1992. The Warsaw Pact was disbanded in two stages—the military elements in February, the political remnants in July—while Poland, Czechoslovakia, and Hungary sought to enter Western institutions, including NATO.

On June 17, Poland and Germany signed a treaty of friendship. Poland supported the U.S.-led alliance during the Persian Gulf War, sending a military hospital ship and a rescue ship to Saudi Arabia and committing staff for two land-based hospitals. Later, during a visit by Walesa to the United States, the United States committed additional resources for rehabilitation of the Polish economy.

See STATISTICS OF THE WORLD.          R.E.K.

**POPULATION.** The American people have never needed much urging to "go West," and, as the 1990 census clearly demonstrated, they are still on their way.

By law, the census's total U.S. population count by state had to be reported by December 31, 1990, as it was. Detailed population counts within each state were then steadily reported over the following weeks to meet an April 1, 1991, deadline, and the debate over the accuracy of the count went on throughout the year. Nevertheless, the figures showed that between 1980 and 1990, the population of California rose by a robust 25.7 percent, a rate nearly triple that of the nation as a whole. The fastest-growing state in the 1980s was neighboring Nevada, where the population spurted a full 50.1 percent, a rise largely fueled by a boom in the Las Vegas area. In 1980 the nation's second largest city (New York being number one) was Chicago; now it is Los Angeles. In all, the 13 Western states (including Alaska and Hawaii) had a population increase of 22.3 percent.

The American population has headed south as well as west. The South Atlantic region, which comprises the coastal states stretching from Delaware to Florida, witnessed a solid population boost of 17.9 percent, an increase in great measure driven by mushrooming growth in Florida. Further to the west, Texas, which experienced a 19.4 percent growth rate between censuses, now contains three of the ten largest cities in the United States—Houston, Dallas, and San Antonio.

## U.S. House Seats, by State*

| State | Number of Seats | Change From 1980 |
|---|---|---|
| Alabama (22) | 7 | — |
| Alaska (50) | 1 | — |
| Arizona (24) | 6 | +1 |
| Arkansas (33) | 4 | — |
| California (1) | 52 | +7 |
| Colorado (26) | 6 | — |
| Connecticut (27) | 6 | — |
| Delaware (46) | 1 | — |
| Florida (4) | 23 | +4 |
| Georgia (11) | 11 | +1 |
| Hawaii (41) | 2 | — |
| Idaho (42) | 2 | — |
| Illinois (6) | 20 | −2 |
| Indiana (14) | 10 | — |
| Iowa (30) | 5 | −1 |
| Kansas (32) | 4 | −1 |
| Kentucky (23) | 6 | −1 |
| Louisiana (21) | 7 | −1 |
| Maine (38) | 2 | — |
| Maryland (19) | 8 | — |
| Massachusetts (13) | 10 | −1 |
| Michigan (8) | 16 | −2 |
| Minnesota (20) | 8 | — |
| Mississippi (31) | 5 | — |
| Missouri (15) | 9 | — |
| Montana (44) | 1 | −1 |
| Nebraska (36) | 3 | — |
| Nevada (39) | 2 | — |
| New Hampshire (40) | 2 | — |
| New Jersey (9) | 13 | −1 |
| New Mexico (37) | 3 | — |
| New York (2) | 31 | −3 |
| North Carolina (10) | 12 | +1 |
| North Dakota (47) | 1 | — |
| Ohio (7) | 19 | −2 |
| Oklahoma (28) | 6 | — |
| Oregon (29) | 5 | — |
| Pennsylvania (5) | 21 | −2 |
| Rhode Island (43) | 2 | — |
| South Carolina (25) | 6 | — |
| South Dakota (45) | 1 | — |
| Tennessee (17) | 9 | — |
| Texas (3) | 30 | +3 |
| Utah (35) | 3 | — |
| Vermont (48) | 1 | — |
| Virginia (12) | 11 | +1 |
| Washington (18) | 9 | +1 |
| West Virginia (34) | 3 | −1 |
| Wisconsin (16) | 9 | — |
| Wyoming (50) | 1 | — |

*Subject to change as a result of litigation. Numbers in parentheses indicate 1990 population ranks. For 1990 census population of each state, see STATISTICS OF THE WORLD.

# POPULATION

The census revealed that the U.S. population is getting older—in 1980, 28 percent of the U.S. population was under 18; by 1990 that figure was down to 26 percent, while the proportion of people 65 and over rose from 11 to 13 percent. In 1980, 60 percent of U.S. households consisted of married couples, with or without children; in 1990 the figure was 55 percent. Women continued to outnumber men; according to the 1990 census, 51 percent of the population was female, the same proportion as in 1980.

**The New Congress.** The census's primary purpose, under the Constitution, is to provide the data for the distribution among the states of the 435 seats in the U.S. House of Representatives. Since the size of the House is fixed, states with small population gains or population losses will of necessity lose seats to states with greater gains. The first election held under the reapportionment occurring after the 1990 census will be the election of November 1992, which will involve many more House seats from the West and South and fewer from the Midwest and Northeast. After the 1980 census the Northeast and Midwest sent 208 representatives to the House; in 1993 the number will be 193. Florida will pick up four seats in the House; Texas, three. California will gain no less than seven, for a total of 52, more than any state has ever had. Moreover, with 54 electoral votes, it alone will have one-fifth of the total a presidential candidate needs to get elected.

## U.S. Cities—The Top Ten

| City* | 1990 Population | % Change From 1980 |
|---|---|---|
| 1. New York (1) | 7,322,564 | +3.5 |
| 2. Los Angeles (3) | 3,485,398 | +17.4 |
| 3. Chicago (2) | 2,783,726 | −7.4 |
| 4. Houston (5) | 1,630,553 | +2.2 |
| 5. Philadelphia (4) | 1,585,577 | −6.1 |
| 6. San Diego (8) | 1,110,549 | +26.8 |
| 7. Detroit (6) | 1,027,974 | −14.6 |
| 8. Dallas (7) | 1,006,877 | +11.3 |
| 9. Phoenix (9) | 983,403 | +24.5 |
| 10. San Antonio (11) | 935,933 | +19.1 |

*Number in parentheses indicates rank in 1980; Baltimore ranked 10th in 1980.

**The Decline of Rural America.** Four states lost population during the 1980s—Wyoming, North Dakota, Iowa, and West Virginia. All are predominantly rural. Fewer than one out of four U.S. residents now live in rural areas and small towns. Americans increasingly end up living in one of the 39 urban-suburban sprawls, termed by the Census Bureau "metropolitan areas," of more than 1 million people; these are now home to more than half the national population.

**Immigrants and Minorities.** On December 26, 1990, the Census Bureau reported that the population of the United States, as of April 1, 1990, was 249,632,692. This figure included almost a million overseas military personnel and civilian federal workers who were counted in the 1990 census under a new law; such people were not counted in 1980. The total was 22.2 million more than the 1980 figure, an increase of 10.2 percent. If, as in 1980, overseas personnel were left out, the population increase for the decade would be 9.8 percent, the smallest in any decade in U.S. history, except for the 7.3 percent recorded for the Depression years of the 1930s.

This slackened growth becomes even more meaningful in light of the fact that between 7 and 9 million immigrants entered the United States in the 1980s. In other words, as much as 40 percent of the U.S. population growth since the 1980 census was due to an influx of foreigners—largely from Asia, Latin America, and the Caribbean. The U.S. fertility rate actually dropped to an all-time historic low (1.86 children per woman).

Not since the World War I era has the population profile of the United States been so altered by immigration. While the U.S. population increased by around 10 percent, the Hispanic population went up over 50 percent, and the Asian population more than doubled. A quarter of all Americans now describe themselves as nonwhite or of Hispanic origin.

**The Undercount Controversy.** The largest minority group in the United States is still the black population, which, according to the 1990 census, constitutes 12.1 percent of the U.S. total—up from 11.7 percent in 1980. Blacks, however, represent one of the groups most likely to be undercounted, and many critics found fault with the Census Bureau's tally of the black population. After the release of the breakdown of the population by race and ethnic group in March 1991, U.S. Representative Thomas C. Sawyer, the Ohio Democrat who chairs the House subcommittee that monitors the census, charged that the bureau missed more than 2 million blacks. Big-city mayors complained that the underenumeration would seriously harm their already precarious financial situation.

The homeless are notoriously difficult to count. On the night of March 20, 1990, the Census Bureau sent out workers in an intensive effort to tally the homeless, but the effort was criticized by advocates for the homeless as missing vast numbers. The Census Bureau found some 230,000 homeless people; estimates of the actual number range as high as 3 million.

After the 1990 census the Census Bureau conducted its own Post Enumeration Survey, something routinely done after every census. This one covered 165,000 households, and the results, released in April 1991, indicated that between 4 million and 6 million people had been missed nationwide. Despite that finding, Secretary of Commerce Robert A. Mosbacher announced on July 15 that he would not adjust the 1990 census counts. His argument was that while the actual total count would be rendered more precise by the adjustment, statistics on how the population is distributed among states, cities, and neighborhoods might be made less accurate.

Mosbacher's decision immediately raised a furor among politicians whose constituencies would be most affected, primarily those representing big cities. If the adjustment had been made, for example, financially hard-pressed New York City would have stood to gain some 230,000 people—and millions of added dollars in federal aid. A U.S. House subcommittee issued a subpoena in an attempt to make the adjusted figures public. New York City and other plaintiffs who had filed suit in 1988 to require a recount revived their legal battle, and 12 other lawsuits were filed to force an adjustment, keep the current count, or at least make the Commerce Department release the adjusted figures. J.G.

*Portugal's Prime Minister Aníbal Cavaço Silva, with his wife, celebrates his party's sweeping victory in October elections*

**PORTUGAL.** Mário Soares was reelected to a second term in January 1991 as Portugal's president, and Prime Minister Aníbal Cavaço Silva was returned to office in October, as the Social Democratic Party (PSD) got a second consecutive absolute majority, with a mandate to govern until 1995.

**Political Developments.** A Socialist, Soares was elected in January to a second five-year term by an overwhelming 70 percent of the vote. Voter turnout was extremely low. After launching a bitter personal attack against Soares, Basilio Horta, the conservative candidate, received only 14 percent of the vote. Carlos Carvalhas, the Communist candidate, had 13 percent, and Carlos Marques, a leftist, received 3 percent of the vote. Soares declared in his campaign that he would take a more interventionist stance in dealing with the

329

Social Democratic government than he had in his previous term.

During the nine months that separated presidential from legislative elections, tensions between Cavaço Silva and Soares increased. Soares made good on his pledge to intervene in foreign affairs, where he sought to help mediate a peace settlement in the Persian Gulf War. The president also spoke out against many government positions.

Meanwhile, the Portuguese Communist Party, celebrating its 70th anniversary, kept on its Marxist-Leninist path rather than adapt to the changes sweeping Eastern Europe. The party clearly supported the failed coup in the Soviet Union in August, a position that fostered a new round of criticism from its less orthodox members.

The major victors in the October parliamentary elections were the Social Democrats, who received an absolute majority of the vote and 135 of 230 seats in the National Assembly. The Socialists captured 29 percent and 72 assembly seats. The major losers were the Communists, with 9 percent and a decline to 16 seats.

**Foreign Affairs.** The government was attacked for reacting too slowly to the Persian Gulf War. While most Portuguese parties were generally opposed to direct involvement in the hostilities, the country did provide logistical support and permission for U.S. use of the Azores air bases.

The government mediated an end to the 16-year-old Angolan civil war between the rebel Union for the Total Independence of Angola and the governing Popular Movement for the Liberation of Angola; both sides signed a peace accord in May, with supervised elections scheduled for 1992.

Pope John Paul II visited Fátima and the island of Madeira in May.

**Economy.** Finance Minister Miguel Beleza continued his free-market approach. His main goals were to reduce the government deficit and bring down inflation, creating the economic stabilization necessary for Portugal to join the European Monetary System. Among measures the government took to help bring down the deficit were continued privatization (of steel, bus, and brewing companies, among others), increased insurance rates, and increased taxes on alcohol, tobacco, and some automobiles.

In July thousands of small farmers placed tractor convoys across roads to protest low prices and increased competition from imports. They complained of paying three times as much interest on loans and up to twice as much for farming supplies as their counterparts elsewhere in the European Community.

See STATISTICS OF THE WORLD.          C.Cu.

**PRESIDENT OF THE UNITED STATES.** See UNITED STATES OF AMERICA: *The Presidency.*

**PRINCE EDWARD ISLAND.** See STATISTICS OF THE WORLD.

**PRIZES AND AWARDS.** See AWARDS AND PRIZES.

**PUBLISHING.** The U.S. publishing industry was hit hard by the recession in 1991. Book sales suffered. Debt-laden multimedia conglomerates, as well as smaller companies, were forced to lay off staff and shed holdings. Several newspapers and magazines went out of existence.

## BOOKS

Early in the year, at the height of the Persian Gulf War, some U.S. bookstores experienced the lowest rate of sales in their history. As a result, wholesalers and retailers cut inventory, and returns to publishers of unsold books reached unusually high levels. Still, there were several overnight best-sellers whose rates of sale surprised even the most seasoned industry executives.

**Nonfiction.** Kitty Kelley offered up a withering, sensationalized portrait of a former first lady in *Nancy Reagan: The Unauthorized Biography.* Other popular selections included *Me: Stories of My Life*, by actress Katharine Hepburn, and former producer Julia Phillips's savage look at Hollywood, *You'll Never Eat Lunch in This Town Again.* Best-sellers from the music world included Barbara Mandrell's *Get to the Heart: My Story* and LaToya Jackson's *LaToya: Growing Up in the Jackson Family.* *Madonna Unauthorized* by Christopher Andersen described the pop star's calculated climb to fame. Among sports books, *Bo Knows Bo*, Bo Jackson's autobiography, sold well at the same time the sports star suffered a career-threatening injury.

Best-sellers during the Persian Gulf War included Daniel Yergin's exhaustive history of the oil industry, *The Prize: The Epic Quest for Oil, Money and Power*, Albert Hourani's *History of the Arab Peoples*, and the paperback edition of *From Beirut to Jerusalem* by Thomas Friedman. After the war, U.S. commander General H. Norman Schwarzkopf, Jr., negotiated with at least five publishers for his autobiography, finally selling world rights to Bantam for an estimated $5 million.

Following the failed Soviet coup, Soviet President Mikhail Gorbachev offered *The August Coup,* a slim, impersonal tome about the coup attempt, along with several general essays, and Russian President Boris Yeltsin signed a contract for his story.

Former Marine Lieutenant Colonel Oliver North offered *Under Fire: An American Story*, an autobiographical work that included discussion of his role as a White House adviser in the Iran/contra affair. A surprise best-seller was *The Civil War: An Illustrated History* by Geoffrey C. Ward and others, a based on the popular Public Broadcasting System TV documentary that aired in 1990. With its $50 price tag, the book shot a hole in conventional industry wisdom about pricing.

*Den of Thieves* by *Wall Street Journal* editor James B. Stewart gave an account of the insider trading and junk bond scandals involving Michael Milken, Ivan Boesky, Martin Siegel, and Dennis Levine. Milken's lawyer, Alan Dershowitz, himself had a best-seller, *Chutzpah*, on the lists much of the year.

Robert Fulghum continued his best-selling ways with *Uh-Oh: Some Observations From Both Sides of the Refrigerator Door. You Just Don't Understand: Men and Women in Conversation* by Deborah Tannen was a steady best-seller. *Iron John: A Book About Men* by Robert Bly and *Fire in the Belly: On Being a Man* by Sam Keen also found strong readership. *Final Exit* by Derek Humphry, a controversial how-to suicide book, was given an unexpected publicity boost by the extensive

**Celebrity Muckraker**

Kitty Kelley's vituperative, no-holds-barred biography of Nancy Reagan variously shocked, disgusted, or confirmed Americans in their darkest suspicions of the former First Lady. The book's allegations, from charges of recycling unwanted gifts to marital infidelity, were privately denounced by Nancy Reagan's friends, and a steady parade of Kelley's "sources" insisted they had never said what was claimed. Amid the furor Kelley canceled her publicity tour for *Nancy Reagan: The Unauthorized Biography*. The book nevertheless became a runaway best-seller.

A free-lance writer who turned 49 in April, Kelley published her first book, *The Glamour Spas*, in 1975. Then she found her true vocation—writing racy unauthorized biographies of celebrities. Singer Frank Sinatra tried unsuccessfully to suppress her 1986 biography portraying him as a womanizer with underworld connections. Other subjects have included Jacqueline Kennedy Onassis and Elizabeth Taylor.

Most reviews of *Nancy Reagan* were vituperative, but some critics thought that the book contained a core of truth and could inspire a reexamination of the Reagan presidency.

*Kitty Kelley*

*Alexandra Ripley's* Scarlett, *the authorized sequel to Margaret Mitchell's classic 1936 novel,* Gone With the Wind, *did not impress many critics, but it chalked up sensational sales and soared to the top of best-seller lists. Here, the author autographs copies at a New York bookstore.*

media coverage of the October suicides of two women assisted by Dr. Jack Kevorkian, inventor of a "suicide machine."

**Fiction.** Many readers gave a damn about *Scarlett,* Alexandra Ripley's sequel to Margaret Mitchell's *Gone With the Wind.* The two largest U.S. bookstore chains, Barnes & Noble and Waldenbooks, reported record first-day sales. *Scarlett's* popularity helped *Gone With the Wind* itself to return to best-seller lists for the first time in years. Amy Tan's second book, *The Kitchen God's Wife,* climbed to the top of the fiction lists. Norman Mailer weighed in with a long tome, *Harlot's Ghost,* that was distinguished by a $30 price tag, long considered an insuperable barrier for works of fiction.

Other familiar authors on best-seller lists included Danielle Steel, *Heartbeat;* James Michener, *The Novel;* Stephen King, *Needful Things;* Robin Cook, *Vital Signs;* Michael Crichton, *Jurassic Park;* Sidney Sheldon, *Memories of Midnight;* Judith Krantz, *Dazzle;* Dick Francis, *Long Shot* and *Comeback;* Tom Clancy, *The Sum of All Fears;* Len Deighton, *MAMista;* Jean Auel, *The Plains of Passage;* Ken Follett, *Night Over Water: A Novel;* Robert B. Parker, *Pastime;* Elmore Leonard, *Maximum Bob;* and Peter Benchley, *Beast.*

Bret Easton Ellis's *American Psycho,* canceled for publication by Simon & Schuster in late 1990 after complaints about the novel's depictions of the brutalization and dismemberment of women, was published by Vintage in a paperback edition that spent a few weeks on the best-seller lists.

In a bizarre turn of events, the widow of Forrest Carter, whose *Education of Little Tree* won a major bookseller's award in 1991 and was a trade paperback best-seller, admitted publicly that her late husband had actually been Asa Carter, a Ku Klux Klan member and onetime speechwriter for former Alabama Governor George Wallace—and not an Indian orphan, as stated in the book. The book, originally published as autobiography in 1976, was reclassified as fiction by its publisher.

**Remainders, Returns, and Retrenchment.** Returns of books from bookstores to publishers were so high that several large publishers flooded markets with unprecedented levels of remaindered books. This, combined with high advances paid to authors in recent years by some houses, caused retrenchings at various publishers. The Doubleday division of Bantam Doubleday Dell announced that it would transfer all children's titles to another division and cut its annual titles to fewer than 200, down from more than 300 in recent years. After failing to find a buyer, 11-year-old North Point Press of San Francisco ceased publishing new books in June.

The only major expansion reported in trade publishing was made by the Walt Disney Company, which created an adult hardcover and trade paperback publisher, Hyperion, and aimed to put out 100 books annually within five years.

British-based Maxwell Communication Corporation, owner of the U.S. publisher Macmillan, sold several large parts of its publishing operations, such as Pergamon Press, the directories business of Maxwell Macmillan (including *Who's Who in America*), and Macmillan

Computer Publishing. Following the death of Maxwell Communication Chairman Robert Maxwell in November, the Maxwell empire was found to be in far deeper financial difficulty than had been believed, and evidence emerged that Maxwell had transferred assets out of Maxwell Communication and other publicly held companies, as well as pension funds, to shore up his private companies. Maxwell Communication filed for bankruptcy in both the United States and Britain.

Harcourt Brace Jovanovich, which had been saddled with huge debt after fending off Robert Maxwell's 1987 takeover attempt, was bought by General Cinema for some $1.5 billion.

J.M.

---

### According to Hoyle

What does a scorpion have in common with a comet, a hurricane, a frog, and a nap? They are all card games, and all are to be found in the latest version of *The New Complete Hoyle Revised*, published by Doubleday in 1991. The new 692-page volume contains the rules for nearly 600 games; it has 133 pages alone on bridge.

There really was a Hoyle—Edmond Hoyle (1672-1769), a British gamester who wrote treatises on five games (quadrille, whist, piquet, chess, and backgammon) that were bound under one cover in 1746. His name, like Noah Webster's, lived on long after he was gone; indeed, he still gets mail.

Besides setting forth rules for the major card games, the new edition describes scores of lesser-known but attractive ones. There is Oh Hell (or blackout) which, the authors say, "has the rare merit of being extremely simple to learn and play at, while affording extraordinary opportunity for skill in bidding and play." The section on children's games points out that "several of them are favorite 'minor' games among expert Poker and Bridge players." Among non-card games, there are entries on craps, roulette, baccarat, and many more. The new Hoyle makes no judgment on what is the best or most popular game, but for those who think of cards as a social event, it does offer one poignant reminder: "There are probably more Solitaires than all other card games together."

---

## NEWSPAPERS AND MAGAZINES

In 1991 many periodicals and multimedia conglomerates experienced troubles.

**Conglomerates Battle Debts.** The world's largest communications company, Time Warner, produces movies, television shows, books, records, and some two dozen magazines; it also has substantial cable television interests. But its 1990 merger left Time Warner saddled with $11.2 billion in debt. To pay down some of its debt in 1991, the company offered new common stock and negotiated a deal whereby two Japanese companies agreed to invest $1 billion in Warner Communications. Meanwhile, the company announced cost-cutting layoffs in its magazine division, which was suffering from significant declines in advertising revenue. About 600 people, or 10 percent of the work force, were let go. Hardest hit, apparently, was *Time* magazine, where senior management was also known to be considering major changes as it reassessed the role of newsweeklies.

Rupert Murdoch's debt-laden News Corporation's properties span the globe. The bulk of his holdings, however, are now concentrated in the United States, where his Fox subsidiary controls a film studio, a television network, and several television stations. In 1991, Murdoch changed the terms on much of his $8.2 billion in debt and raised some cash by selling eight American magazines and a newspaper, the *Daily Racing Form*, to a company called K-III Holdings for approximately $650 million.

British publisher Robert Maxwell's death in November came eight months after he had acquired the financially ailing New York *Daily News*, one of the largest-circulation dailies in the United States. Maxwell headed a communications empire that included newspapers worldwide. His purchase of the *News* in March from the Chicago-based Tribune Company ended an excruciating 21-week strike against the paper's previous ownership. The purchase was linked to an agreement with the striking unions providing for an estimated $70 million in savings on labor costs. Following the takeover, the *News's* circulation increased, but overall the paper was still losing money. After Maxwell's death the debts of his empire, including the privately held company that

333

owned the *News*, were found to be far larger than previously known, and allegations of improper financial manipulations emerged. In early December, as the Maxwell family began bankruptcy proceedings in the British courts for its private businesses, the *News* filed for protection under Chapter 11 of the U.S. bankruptcy law.

**The *Post*, *Tribune*, and Others.** In August, Peter Kalikow, publisher of the New York *Post*, filed for bankruptcy protection under Chapter 11; a spokesman claimed the *Post* would be unaffected. The news agency United Press International filed for bankruptcy in August and later announced plans to lay off about 150 people. On June 13 the *National* published its last issue, having lost about $100 million since

*The headline tells it all, as a pressman views the last printing of the Dallas Times Herald. The paper ceased publication in December after being bought out by the rival Dallas Morning News.*

its January 1990 launch as a daily national sports paper. In October the Gannett Company sold the Arkansas *Gazette* to the rival Arkansas *Democrat*, which promptly shut down the well-respected liberal newspaper. The Dallas *Times Herald* ended publication on December 9; it had fallen farther and farther in circulation and advertising behind the Dallas *Morning News*, which bought it out. The Hollywood (Fla.) *Sun* closed on December 24, and the Knoxville (Tenn.) *Journal*, an evening paper, announced it would cease publication as a daily on December 31, yielding to its morning rival, the *News-Sentinel*.

In May the New York *Times* announced a program to encourage early retirement by as many as 125 employees. Earlier in the year the *Times* had laid off 61 members of the Newspaper Guild. Also, the Atlanta *Journal* and *Constitution* announced plans to lay off 133 workers and leave another 122 jobs unfilled; the Miami *Herald* planned to cut about 150 jobs; and the Los Angeles *Times* launched an early retirement program for as many as 300 employees.

In April the *Telegram and Gazette* in Worcester, Mass., said that it was requiring all full-time employees to take a five-day unpaid furlough.

The 117-year-old *Hudson Dispatch* in Hudson County, N.J., was sold to the publisher of the rival *Jersey Journal* and ceased publication. And the Washington County *Post*, a weekly newspaper in Cambridge, N.Y., gave up the ghost after 192 years.

The Oakland *Tribune*, however, managed to squeak through, when financially strapped owner Robert Maynard swapped his debt for $5.5 million in preferred stock and a $2.5 million note guaranteed by the Freedom Forum, a nonprofit foundation. The *Tribune* continued to be the only black-owned metropolitan U.S. daily.

**Family Media Folds.** Family Media, publisher of six magazines, shut down and dismissed its 209 employees during the summer. One of the affected magazines, the science monthly *Discover*, was subsequently picked up by the Walt Disney Company.

**Cost-Saving Renewal System.** To cut down on the cost of printing, paper, and postage for subscription solicitations, renewal letters, and billing, more than 60 magazines started to test a new system called Auto Renew, under which a subscription continues, with the renewal charged to the subscriber's credit card, until the reader cancels. The American Express Publishing Corporation already had been using its own automatic renewal system, tied to the American Express credit card.          W.K.W.

**PUERTO RICO.** Puerto Rico's relations with the United States dominated the island's politics in 1991. Under the island's so-called commonwealth relationship with the United States, Puerto Ricans possess many powers of local self-governance but cannot conduct their own foreign relations (as they could if the island were independent) or participate fully in the U.S. political system (as they could if it were a state). All three major political parties on the island—which favor commonwealth status, statehood, and independence, respectively—supported in principle the idea of a plebiscite to determine the will of the Puerto Rican people.

Since the U.S. Congress failed to enact enabling legislation, the Puerto Rican legislature itself authorized a nonbinding referendum, asking voters whether they favored establishing a constitutional guarantee of their right to freely determine the island's political status "without colonial or territorial subordination to the full powers of the U.S. Congress." The bill was sponsored by Governor Rafael Hernández Colón's pro-commonwealth Popular Democratic Party, and by the pro-independence party, but was strongly opposed by advocates of statehood. They argued that a yes vote would alienate Congress, effectively blocking the direct vote on statehood that they favored. In the voting on December 8, the measure was defeated by 55 to 45 percent.

Meanwhile, in a move widely perceived as a blow to the statehood movement, the legislature eliminated English as one of the island's official languages. The action won the enthusiastic praise of many of the island's 3.6 million inhabitants, 90 percent of whom speak Spanish, but it was also denounced by some as a political ploy, designed to raise doubts in the United States about the wisdom of offering statehood to Puerto Rico. Nonetheless, the international Hispanic community reacted with applause, and for their defense of the Spanish language "the people of Puerto Rico" were named the recipients of the Prince of Asturias Literature Award, considered the most prestigious literary prize in the Spanish-speaking world.

Puerto Rico did not experience a recession in fiscal 1991, although several months of decline were registered. The large amount of federal funds transferred from Washington to the island served as a buffer against a general downturn. Close to $8 billion is injected annually into the Puerto Rican economy by the United States, accounting for almost one-quarter of the island's total personal income.
*See* STATISTICS OF THE WORLD.          M.J.C.

# Q

**QATAR.** *See* STATISTICS OF THE WORLD. *See also* ARABIAN PENINSULA.

**QUÉBEC.** *See* STATISTICS OF THE WORLD. *See also* CANADA.

# R

**RADIO.** *See* BROADCASTING.

**RECORDINGS.** *See* MUSIC.

# Religion

**Issues of human sexuality were a prominent subject of controversy. Political changes in the disintegrating Soviet Union and in Eastern Europe made the region a focus of attention for Protestants, Catholics, and Jews.**

At an assembly of the World Council of Churches, in February, the Persian Gulf War was a topic of concern, and some tensions were ignited between Orthodox and liberal Protestant groups. Pope John Paul II named 22 new cardinals and convoked an interfaith synod. Conditions improved for Soviet Jewry. Hindu-Muslim clashes continued in southern Asia.

## PROTESTANT AND ORTHODOX CHURCHES

Issues of human sexuality dominated the U.S. Protestant scene in 1991, with the ordination of practicing homosexuals a particular point of controversy.

**Sexuality.** The Presbyterian Church (U.S.A.) engaged the subject of sexuality in sweeping terms, issuing a 200-page report entitled *Keeping Body and Soul Together: Sexuality, Spirituality, and Social Justice.* The report, produced by a 17-member panel headed by a professor of religion at Agnes Scott College in Decatur, Ga., encouraged an ethic centered on the quality of relationships, endorsing "responsible" sex outside marriage and ordination of practicing homosexuals. Delegates to the denomination's June 4-12 general assembly in Baltimore overwhelmingly rejected the report and issued a pastoral letter to Presbyterians affirming the sanctity of "the marriage covenant between one man and one woman."

Later in June in Charleston, W.Va., delegates to the biennial meeting of the American Baptist Churches adopted a statement condemning the practice of homosexuality. At the Episcopal Church's July 11-20 general convention in Phoenix, delegates eventually opted for a statement upholding traditional church teachings on homosexuality but acknowledging a "discontinuity" between those teachings and the experience of many Episcopalians. (The choice of the convention site was also controversial; it was condemned by black Episcopalian groups because Arizona voters had recently rejected a proposal to create a Martin Luther King holiday in the state.) A United Methodist Church panel reported in August that it had failed, after hearings and deliberations over a three-year period, to arrive at a "common mind" on whether homosexuality is compatible with Christian faith.

At the general assembly of the Christian Church (Disciples of Christ) in October, delegates rejected the nomination of the Reverend Michael K. Kinnamon as president. Conservatives had mounted a massive campaign against Kinnamon, after he refused to condemn homosexual practice as sinful.

Bishop Lowell Mays of the Evangelical Lutheran Church in America resigned his post in January in the wake of sexual misconduct allegations and then gave up his clergy credentials two days before he was to go before a church disciplinary committee investigating the charges. In Denver a jury awarded a woman $1.2 million in damages after concluding that an Episcopal priest had taken advantage of her psychological problems when he seduced her. Television evangelist Jimmy Swaggart decided in mid-October to undergo medical care and counseling, after a California prostitute alleged that he had picked her up at a truck stop and asked for sex.

**Abortion.** Operation Rescue's multiweek siege on three abortion clinics in Wichita, Kan., during the summer highlighted tensions that continued to split the religious community. Operation Rescue's pro-life volunteers were given opportunities to speak at more than 40 area churches, and anti-abortion protesters disrupted an evening worship service at the city's Redeemer Lutheran Church, where Dr.

336

George Tiller, affiliated with one of the clinics, was a member.

At its August 28-September 4 Churchwide Assembly in Orlando, Fla., the Evangelical Lutheran Church in America adopted a statement that cast abortion in a mainly negative light but indicated that there could be "sound reasons" for ending a pregnancy under certain circumstances.

**Baptist Infighting.** In August the Reverend Jimmy Draper, a hard-line inerrantist, was inaugurated as president of the Southern Baptist Sunday School Board, succeeding the Reverend Lloyd Elder, who stepped down under pressure from conservatives. In June, messengers to the Southern Baptist Convention's annual meeting in Atlanta voted to cut funding to the Baptist Joint Committee on Public Affairs, a Washington-based watchdog agency whose stands on issues angered the convention's conservative majority. For their part, moderates sought to consolidate strength at a May meeting in Atlanta, where they elected officers and a coordinating council for their organization, the Cooperative Baptist Fellowship.

**Orthodox-Protestant Clash.** The Greek Orthodox Archdiocese of North and South America announced in June that it was suspending all activities in the National Council of Churches, pending deliberation with other Orthodox churches. The archdiocese was concerned about controversial trends in the liberal mainline Protestant community such as the ordination of women and of practicing homosexuals. After four more Orthodox denominations followed suit, the council named a panel of six high-profile church leaders to begin discussions with Orthodox representatives in an effort to heal the rift.

Orthodox concerns had ignited in February at the World Council of Churches Seventh Worldwide Assembly in Canberra, Australia, when a female South Korean theologian, Chung Hyun Kyung, delivered a dramatic keynote address that invoked a female Holy Spirit. Her talk culminated in the burning of bits of paper bearing the names of exploited spirits of the past said to be filled with "han," the Korean word for anger.

**Patriarchs.** On November 2, Metropolitan Bartholomew of Chalcedon, a 51-year-old

*Patriarch Bartholomew I holds his staff during a ceremony in November installing him as the ecumenical patriarch of Constantinople. With his elevation the 51-year-old leader became the spiritual head of about 200 million Eastern Orthodox Christians.*

Turkish prelate, was installed as the ecumenical patriarch of Constantinople, the spiritual leader of some 200 million Eastern Orthodox Christians around the world. He succeeded Dimitrios I, who had died in October. Late in the year, Russian Orthodox Patriarch Aleksi II made the first visit to the United States by a leader of the world's largest Orthodox church.

**NCC General Secretary.** On May 15, the Reverend Joan B. Campbell, a longtime ecumenist with ministerial credentials in both the Disciples of Christ and American Baptist Churches, was installed as the seventh general secretary of the National Council of Churches.

**The Former Communist Bloc.** Among other developments, a Ukrainian Bible Society was launched in the summer, the United Methodist Church established its first-ever congregation in the Soviet Union, and Methodists began a cooperative Christian education effort with the Russian Orthodox Church. As newfound religious freedoms in Eastern Europe and the Soviet Union opened the doors to evangelism from abroad, there was competition among Western groups that were frequently accused of "overevangelizing." Meanwhile, efforts to restore national churches to their pre-Marxist positions of prominence posed threats to other, less established religious groups.

**Persian Gulf War.** The Persian Gulf War dominated talk at the World Council of Churches assembly in Canberra, where delegates issued a statement calling for an immediate cease-fire and unconditional withdrawal of Iraqi troops from Kuwait. On January 15, the deadline set by President George Bush for Iraqi withdrawal from Kuwait, religious opponents of a war with Iraq held candlelight vigils, prayer services, and rallies across the United States. Evangelist Billy Graham, a supporter of the president's position on the war, was invited to lead White House officials in prayer the day

*At the World Council of Churches meeting in Australia in February, South Korean theologian Chung Hyun Kyung stirred debate with a keynote address which included the burning of lists of atrocities and oppression. Many praised the speech, but others, especially among Orthodox delegates, were disturbed by what they considered "pagan" and "unChristian" elements.*

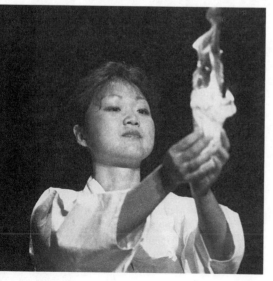

after the air offensive began. After the war ended, mainstream and evangelical churches alike focused on humanitarian relief operations in the Middle East, channeling food, medicine, and clothing principally through the Middle East Council of Churches.

**Financial Crises.** In October the Episcopal Church eliminated 52 staff positions at its national headquarters in New York, anticipating a $1 million budgetary shortfall in 1991. In May the Evangelical Lutheran Church in America eliminated 25 positions at its Chicago headquarters as part of a series of cutbacks to reduce spending in 1991 by $5.2 million. At the international level, the World Council of Churches approved a plan to reduce staff at the council's Geneva headquarters by 10 percent. The Lutheran World Federation announced it would cut its budget by 4 percent in light of an expected $1.7 million deficit in 1992.

**Columbus Anniversary.** Mainline church bodies made formal statements in advance of the 1992 commemoration of Christopher Columbus's first voyage to the New World. The National Council of Churches stated that invasion, genocide, slavery, and the destruction of nature had followed Columbus's arrival in the Americas and charged that churches by and large had "accompanied and legitimized this conquest and exploitation." G.D.S.

## ROMAN CATHOLIC CHURCH

Political and economic change set in motion by the collapse of Communism in Eastern Europe and the Soviet Union were major concerns of the Roman Catholic Church. Pope John Paul II named 22 new cardinals and convoked an interfaith synod.

**Collapse of Communism.** A synod of 137 European bishops, with observers from other faiths and continents, convened in Rome from November 28 to December 14, to discuss Christianity's role in the Europe taking shape after the fall of Communism. The synod was projected by John Paul II as a prelude for the laying aside of religious differences, but some Jewish groups felt its emphasis on the "Christian roots" of Europe slighted Jews. Also, five of eight Orthodox churches, notably the Russian Orthodox, spurned invitations to attend, thus exposing tensions arising from rival property claims and fear that Rome was viewing

*In May, on the tenth anniversary of the attempt to assassinate him, Pope John Paul II came to Portugal to pray at the shrine of Our Lady of Fatima, whom he has often credited with having saved his life. The bullet extracted from his body was placed in the crown of the Madonna's statue.*

traditional Orthodox territory newly freed from Communism as "mission lands." In a concluding statement the synod affirmed the church's commitment to a new evangelization countering the materialism of the West and Marxism's legacy in Eastern Europe.

Earlier, on May 2, Pope John Paul II issued a 25,000-word encyclical, *Centesimus Annus* ("The Hundredth Year"), dealing with questions raised by socioeconomic changes in Eastern Europe. *Centesimus Annus* broke new ground in citing "the free market [as] the most efficient instrument for utilizing resources and responding to needs." However, it warned against letting the collapse of Communism blind nations to the need to repair injustices in their own system.

The Vatican formally recognized Estonia, Latvia, and Lithuania in August; the following month, diplomatic relations were renewed with Bulgaria and Albania, completing the reestablishment of Vatican ties with Eastern-bloc countries. Bulgaria had been accused of complicity in the 1981 assassination attempt on the pope, though the charge was never documented. Earlier in the year, Bulgaria said it would open its intelligence files on the case to an international commission of scholars. In December the Vatican recognized the independence of Croatia and Slovenia.

In April, Pope John Paul named Monsignor Tadeusz Kondrusiewicz as the first Roman Catholic archbishop to serve in Moscow since 1936. He also appointed bishops in Siberia and Kazakhstan and created two new dioceses in Byelorussia (now called Belarus). In July,

Archbishop Miloslav Vik of Prague confirmed that during the Communist ascendancy as many as 300 secret ordinations to the priesthood had taken place in Czechoslovakia, involving some married men and one or two women. The ordinations, undertaken independently of Rome, were meant to insure the church's continuity in the face of Communist persecution. A Vatican commission was to evaluate each one.

**Papal Trips.** In May, John Paul II made a four-day visit to Portugal to pray at the shrine of Fatima on the tenth anniversary of the attempt on his life in St. Peter's Square.

John Paul made an eight-day visit to Poland, beginning June 1. Two weeks earlier, the Polish Parliament had rejected a ban on abortion; the pontiff scolded Poles for their tolerance of abortion and urged them to make their country an island of spiritual values. On August 13 the pope returned to Poland for the sixth Vatican-sponsored World Youth Day at the Marian pilgrimage center of Jasna Gora. Both there and at his next stop, in Hungary, he proposed religion as the binding force for the new foundations of Eastern Europe.

During a ten-day tour of Brazil in October, John Paul II denounced policies favoring rich landowners and warned against the "false mirages" of fundamentalist religious sects, which reportedly had made substantial inroads among the country's 130 million Catholics.

**The Vatican.** Pope John Paul published a 13,000-word encyclical on January 22 that encouraged Catholic evangelization in all parts of the world, even where Islamic laws forbid proselytizing. Entitled *Redemptoris Missio* ("Mission of the Redeemer"), the document was apparently aimed at areas of Asia, Africa, and the Middle East where Catholicism is lagging in growth behind Islam. The pope was critical of theological views that subordinate proselytism to ecumenical dialogue.

Presidents of bishops' conferences throughout the world were summoned to Rome in April to discuss the Vatican's chronic operating deficit, projected at a record $91.5 million for 1991. In March consideration of sainthood for Queen Isabella of Spain, sponsor of Christopher Columbus's voyages to America, was put aside. There were objections to her candidacy because of the denial of religious liberty and the persecutions of Jews and Muslims that marked her reign.

John Paul named 22 new cardinals in May, including a Romanian, a Czechoslovak, and a German from what used to be East Berlin, as well as two Americans (Archbishops Roger M. Mahony of Los Angeles and Anthony J. Bevilacqua of Philadelphia). The pope also revealed he had secretly named Bishop Ignatius Kung, 89, of Shanghai, whose Chinese name is Gong Pinmei, a cardinal in 1979. Kung was freed in 1985, after years in a Chinese prison.

**United States.** Hopes of reviving an eight-year effort by the American bishops to issue a pastoral letter on women's concerns encountered problems during a two-day Rome consultation in May. The U.S. bishops were advised to "walk cautiously."

In a draft of a pastoral letter in January, Milwaukee's Archbishop Rembert G. Weakland

*Gong Pinmei, who had spent 30 years in prison in China for refusing to renounce loyalty to the Vatican, formally received the red hat of a cardinal at a Vatican ceremony in June, 12 years after he was secretly elevated to cardinal by the pope.*

expressed readiness to ordain married men as a last resort if the current clergy shortage reaches crisis stage. Weakland later reported that the Vatican had rejected his idea as "out of place."

George A. Stallings, Jr., the Washington, D.C., priest excommunicated in 1990 after founding the breakaway African-American Catholic Congregation, further distanced himself from Rome on September 8 when he ordained Rose Vernell, a 50-year-old former Roman Catholic nun and a widow with two children, as a priest in his church.

**Latin America.** In Mexico constitutional changes were completed in December extending legal recognition to religious institutions for the first time since the Mexican Revolution and the constitution of 1917. Among other things, Mexico lifted property restrictions on the church, restored the clergy's right to vote, and permitted parochial education.

In El Salvador, an Army colonel and a lieutenant were found guilty in September of charges stemming from the 1989 murders of six Jesuit priests, their cook, and her daughter—the first time in memory that Salvadoran military officers had been convicted of killing civilians. Two lieutenants and four soldiers were found innocent. Meanwhile, an inquiry by a panel of U.S. House Democrats found strong circumstantial evidence suggesting that the crime was plotted by senior Salvadoran Army officers.

For the second time in six years the Vatican silenced the prominent Brazilian proponent of liberation theology, Franciscan Father Leonardo Boff. Boff was ousted in May as editor of the cultural magazine *Vozes* and ordered not to publish his theological views for a year.

**Transitions.** Archbishop Marcel Lefebvre, 85, died on March 25 in Martigny, Switzerland. His rejection of the reforms of Vatican Council II had spawned the church's first schism since 1870. Lefebvre was excommunicated in 1988.

Death also claimed Spanish Father Pedro Arrupe, 83, leader of the Jesuit order from 1965 to 1983, February 5 in Rome; 101-year-old German Jesuit author Oswald von Nell-Breuning, whose works on social justice were banned by the Nazis, August 21 in Frankfurt; France's Henri Cardinal de Lubac, 95, progres-

sive theologian who was under Rome's censure for eight years but then rehabilitated, September 4 in Paris; and Paul Emile Cardinal Léger, 87, who in 1968 resigned as archbishop of Montréal and spent 12 years working among lepers and poor children in Africa, November 13 in Montréal.

Jozsef Cardinal Mindszenty, implacable foe of Communism, who died in exile in 1975, was reburied on May 4 in the Hungarian basilica in Esztergom. He had said in his will that he wanted to be buried in his native land, after the "red star of faithless Moscow falls."

J.G.D.

## JUDAISM

Rapid political change put the spotlight on the status of Jews and Judaism in the Soviet Union and Eastern Europe.

**Soviet Jewry.** Jewish emigration continued at high levels, with nearly 180,000 Jews leaving the Soviet Union in 1991. The majority moved to Israel, although Soviet Jews postponed plans to emigrate because of the shortage of both jobs and housing there. In May the Soviet Parliament passed the country's first law granting citizens the right to travel and to emigrate freely, removing a barrier to U.S. trade and aid to the Soviets. Implementation was not immediate for fear of a "brain drain" and the economic costs of emigration.

Following the renewal of consular ties in January, the Soviet Union in mid-October reestablished diplomatic relations with Israel, after a 24-year break. In the religious and cultural spheres, cooperation between Jewish and Israeli groups and Soviet organizations increased. The government permitted representatives of the Va'ad, the representative body of European Jews, to become associates of the World Jewish Congress. New Jewish newspapers began to appear in many Soviet republics, and Jewish day schools opened in major cities.

In June, Soviet authorities opened their archives on the Holocaust to researchers from Yad Vashem, Israel's Holocaust memorial and museum. Later, the new head of the KGB, Vadim Bakatin, promised to provide access to agency files to a commission investigating the fate of Swedish diplomat Raoul Wallenberg, missing since 1945 after saving tens of thousands of Hungarian Jews during World War II.

# RELIGION

The breakup of the Soviet Union late in the year presented no immediate indication of any new change in policy toward Jews.

In late September the government of Ukraine officially acknowledged the massacre of an estimated 100,000 Jews by the Nazis at Babi Yar in 1941. The Kiev City Council declared September 29 an official "Day of Memory and Sorrow."

**European Jewry.** In January, German Chancellor Helmut Kohl and the prime ministers of the 16 German states agreed not to impose state or national quotas on Soviet Jews emigrating to Germany. In July, Chancellor Franz Vranitzky of Austria made a statement that for the first time accepted Austrian responsibility for its role in Nazi war crimes and pledged restitution to its victims.

Poland's President Lech Walesa made a state visit in May to Israel, the first ever by a Polish leader. In a speech to the Knesset (Parliament) he apologized for centuries of Polish anti-Semitism and urged renewal of links between Poles and Jews. Prime Minister Jozsef Antall of Hungary also visited Israel in May. At Yad Vashem, he accepted the Righteous Gentile Award conferred posthumously on his father, who during World War II was arrested by the Nazis for aiding hundreds of Polish Jews who had fled to Hungary.

Renewed outbreaks of anti-Semitism in Romania aroused concern during the spring, following the honoring of Romania's wartime dictator Marshal Ion Antonescu by Parliament. Antonescu had ordered the deportation to death camps of hundreds of thousands of Jews. The government denounced the resurgence of anti-Semitism and condemned Antonescu's rule, but threats against the chief rabbi and other incidents caused many Jews to fear that they might be made victims of bias.

**Ethiopian Jews.** In May, Israel secretly airlifted most of Ethiopia's remaining Jewish population to safety in a mission known as Operation Solomon. El Al Airlines brought more than 14,000 Ethiopian Jews to Israel, just days before rebel troops seized the Ethiopian capital. The new regime allowed the airlift to resume, and by year's end some 20,000 Ethiopian Jews had been flown to Israel.

**Relations With the Catholic Church.** In January a pastoral letter, signed by all of Poland's

*Operation Solomon was the name given to the secret airlift that safely brought more than 14,000 Ethiopian Jews to Israel over a 36-hour period in May. This elderly, half-blind woman was carried off the plane after her arrival.*

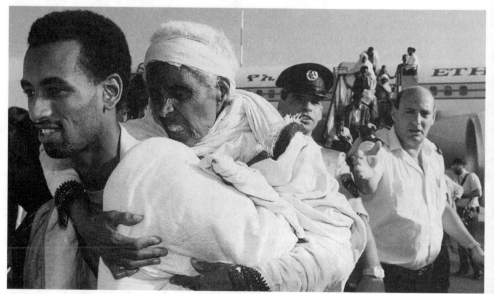

Catholic hierarchy, condemning anti-Semitism was read in Catholic churches throughout Poland. On several occasions during the year Pope John Paul II condemned anti-Semitism. However, a dispute between Catholics and Jews over the future of a Polish Carmelite convent established on the site of the Auschwitz concentration camp continued. In June, Jewish groups claimed no preparations were being made to build a promised interfaith center to which the convent would move.

**Nazi War Criminals.** Nazi war criminal Klaus Barbie, imprisoned in France, died at 77.

The newly independent state of Lithuania aroused controversy in September by its blanket exoneration of thousands of individuals convicted in Soviet courts of crimes committed during the Nazi era. Jewish groups alleged that among these individuals were mass murderers. The Lithuanian supreme court suspended the rehabilitation program after it confirmed that several individuals had been unjustly exonerated, and President Vytautas Landsbergis agreed to have an independent commission review cases of all Lithuanians suspected of war crimes.

In June, former Waffen-SS officer Josef Schwammberger was put on trial in Stuttgart, Germany, charged with the murder of thousands of Jews in concentration camps in Poland, where he was commandant.

**UN Resolution Repealed.** On December 16 the UN General Assembly repealed its 1975 resolution equating Zionism with racism. The vote was 111-25, with 13 abstentions and 17 other countries absent or not voting. Most of the former Soviet bloc and some African and Asian states reversed their former positions and voted for repeal.

**American Jewry.** In its annual survey of anti-Semitic incidents in the United States, published in January, the Anti-Defamation League of B'nai B'rith recorded an increase for the second year in a row.

**Culture and Education.** The first International Gathering of Children Hidden During World War II took place in New York City in May. An estimated 1,600 child survivors and others, including many of their Christian rescuers, came in the hopes of reuniting with rescuers or lost relatives. L.G.

## ISLAM

The Muslim world's most important annual gathering—the hajj, or pilgrimage, to Mecca, Saudi Arabia—took place without incident, despite the Persian Gulf War and the presence of close to a quarter of a million Western troops in the Saudi kingdom. Fears of a repetition of the 1987 tragedy—when an estimated 400 Iranian pilgrims were gunned down by jittery Saudi security personnel—proved unfounded, largely because the two governments had previously ironed out pilgrimage regulations.

For the second year in a row, specially chartered Aeroflot planes took pilgrims from several centers in the Soviet Union straight to Saudi Arabia, where they took part in the pilgrimage to Mecca. King Fahd of Saudi Arabia paid all pilgrimage expenses for approximately 5,000 Soviet Muslims. Several of the delegations of Sunni Muslims were received by high-ranking Saudi dignitaries, reflecting Saudi Arabia's interest in increasing its influence in the Central Asian republics.

**Central Asia.** With the breakup of the Soviet Union, all five Muslim republics in Central Asia (Kazakhstan, Kirghizia, Tadzhikistan, Turkmenistan, and Uzbekistan) declared independence and ultimately joined the new Commonwealth of Independent States. Opposition parties were emerging quickly, some of them led by Muslim clerics, or imams, who blended ethnic nationalism with strict religious strictures. In Tadzhikistan, Muslim leaders challenged state authority, sometimes through violent means, and there were clashes among Sunni Muslims, Tadzhik nationalists, and Communists. The Islamic Renaissance Party (IRP) of Tadzhikistan grew to, reportedly, close to a million people. After the failed August coup by hard-liners in Moscow, the Communist hierarchy in Tadzhikistan loosened somewhat its prior ban on IRP activities.

Throughout the region the mosque was the premier gathering place for Muslims to articulate opinions, vent frustrations against the authorities, and galvanize support. Campaigns to reconstruct ancient mosques and add new domes and minarets were in full force.

**Algerian Elections.** A first round of multiparty elections held in Algeria in late December resulted in a resounding victory for the Islamic

Salvation Front, virtually assuring the party of a parliamentary majority if runoff elections were held in early 1992. The strong showing of Muslim fundamentalists at the polls led many Muslims to predict a resurgence of Islamic power in other countries. Observers noted, however, that Islamic forces in Algeria differ significantly from those in Iran, since the former are Sunni, rather than Shiite, Muslims and do not have the same degree of anti-Western sentiment and intense devotion to religious leaders.                                              J.A.K.

### FAR EASTERN FAITHS

Conflict between Hindus and the Muslims colored Indian political life. In Tibet the Chinese government tightened restrictions on Buddhists. Symbols of the Shinto religion were reintroduced into Japanese public life.

**India.** India was shaken by the assassination of former Prime Minister Rajiv Gandhi, reportedly by the Tamil Eelam Tigers, a separatist Hindu terrorist group operating in both Sri Lanka and the South Indian state of Tamil Nadu, where Gandhi was campaigning in hopes of regaining his post in parliamentary elections. Gandhi had sent Indian troops in 1987 to aid the Buddhist-majority government of Sri Lanka in its civil war against the Tigers, who wanted their own independent homeland in Hindu, Tamil-speaking areas of Sri Lanka. Following a Hindu cremation ceremony held in New Delhi, Gandhi's ashes were sent across India and eventually immersed in the sacred Ganges River at Allahabad in North India.

Numerous disturbances were reported as the electoral campaign continued. For example, in June, over 100 persons were killed in simultaneous attacks by Sikh militants on trains in the northern Indian state of Punjab. In other areas of India more than 100 additional persons were killed in Hindu-Muslim riots during the campaign. In mid-June, P. V. Narasimha Rao became prime minister of a minority government, led by the secularist Congress Party.

**Tibet.** In May, on the 40th anniversary of the establishment of Chinese rule over Tibet, Chinese troops and police enforced draconian restrictions on the Tibetan capital of Lhasa. Monks and nuns were confined to their quarters or forced to participate in official celebrations of the anniversary events. Human rights

organizations reported an increase in the numbers of monks and nuns being jailed and tortured. Foreign tourists were denied access to religious centers and forbidden contact with nuns and monks. Earlier in the year, the Chinese government attempted to interfere in the contacts between the exiled Dalai Lama, Tibet's former temporal and spiritual head, and foreign governments during his travels abroad. He was received with great enthusiasm on visits to the United States in August and October.

**Japan.** In the summer the Japanese government permitted the official reintroduction into Japanese public life of two ancient symbols of imperial authority, both connected with the Shinto religion. The traditional *Hi-no-Maru* (round sun) flag, symbolizing Amaterasu, the Sun Goddess said to be the ancestress of the emperors, was declared the official flag of the nation. The national anthem, *Kimi Ga Yo* (Your Majesty's Reign), symbolic of the prewar status of the emperor as divine head of state, was also once more officially authorized. Although Emperor Akihito scrupulously maintained his role as constitutional monarch without reference to Shinto beliefs about his divinity, some critics voiced concern that these symbolic measures indicated dangerous right-wing tendencies.                                     C.S.J.W

**REPUBLICAN PARTY.** See UNITED STATES OF AMERICA: *Political Parties*.

**RHODE ISLAND.** See STATISTICS OF THE WORLD.

**RHODESIA.** See ZIMBABWE.

**ROMANIA.** In 1991, Romania saw continued unrest, economic hardship, ethnic rivalries, and political crisis, as the National Salvation Front (NSF), which had formed a government after the 1989 revolution, remained in power under President Ion Iliescu.

**Political Unrest.** A general strike that began in December 1990 in the western city of Timisoara lasted through January 1991 and sparked demonstrations in Bucharest and elsewhere, many organized by the opposition Civic Alliance. By April, Civic Alliance demonstrations had become massive affairs involving hundreds of thousands of individuals. In September thousands of coal miners hijacked trains and descended on the capital, joined by several other unions, to protest the erosion of

*Romanian miners storm the Parliament building in Bucharest during three days of demonstrations and rioting in September during which they demanded higher pay, lower prices, and the resignation of the government—a demand which was partly met when Prime Minister Petre Roman relinquished his office.*

their living standards and to demand the resignations of Iliescu and Prime Minister Petre Roman. On September 26, Roman, at least, complied. The violence reportedly left four people killed.

Roman's tenure, dating from May 1990, had been turbulent. At a March 1991 convention the National Salvation Front overwhelmingly adopted his reform program to complete the country's transition to a market economy. However, some cabinet members, including Finance Minister Theodor Stolojan, revolted, saying the changes were not radical enough. In April, Roman reshuffled his cabinet; Stolojan, an economist, became head of the government's privatization agency.

For Roman's replacement Iliescu turned to Stolojan, who announced that economic reform was his top priority. In November he initiated strict monetary controls, including a requirement that businesses keep accounts in lei, the Romanian currency.

**New Constitution.** On December 8, two-thirds of Romania's voters turned out for a referendum on a new constitution. The document, which guaranteed freedom of speech and assembly and banned censorship, proclaimed the country to be a multiparty, presidential republic. It was approved by a large majority, though many objected to key elements, such as the strong power given to the president. Two counties in Transylvania with ethnic Hungarian majorities voted overwhelmingly against the constitution, which recognized only Romanian as an official language.

**Economic Hardships.** In 1991, Bucharest's once fashionable shopping streets were coming to life again with private enterprises. Merchants readily found customers for wares unseen in Romania for years. Yet the overall economic situation was desperate. Cuts in state subsidies implemented by Roman in April sent consumer prices soaring. The government limited price rises on 11 essential food items to 125 percent and increased student grants and maternity and child benefits, but by December prices had risen 400 percent over December 1990 levels. Tens of thousands of workers were laid off. Food production plummeted. Romania's healthcare system was near collapse, and the country suffered several outbreaks of cholera. Energy supplies dwindled drastically, forcing many industrial plants to halt production. Violent crime rose sharply, and half a million Romanians left the country, many for Germany.

**Diplomatic Initiatives.** Romania strove to emerge from its Communist-era isolation, as President Iliescu visited India, Pakistan, China, Italy, the Soviet Union, and Israel. French President François Mitterrand became the first Western head of state to visit Romania since the fall of Nicolae Ceausescu, and Roman visited Washington, D.C. Japan pledged $1 billion for improvements in the country's transportation, and the United States promised humanitarian aid. The International Monetary Fund approved loans totaling more than $1 billion, contingent on some economic performance criteria.

*See* STATISTICS OF THE WORLD.        T.G.

**RUSSIA.** *See* UNION OF SOVIET SOCIALIST REPUBLICS.

**RWANDA.** *See* STATISTICS OF THE WORLD.

# S

**SAHARA, WESTERN.** *See* MOROCCO.

**ST. LUCIA.** *See* STATISTICS OF THE WORLD.

**ST. VINCENT AND THE GRENADINES.** *See* STATISTICS OF THE WORLD.

**SAMOA, AMERICAN.** *See* STATISTICS OF THE WORLD: *American Samoa.*

**SAMOA, WESTERN.** *See* STATISTICS OF THE WORLD: *Western Samoa.*

**SAN MARINO.** *See* STATISTICS OF THE WORLD.

**SÃO TOMÉ AND PRÍNCIPE.** *See* STATISTICS OF THE WORLD.

**SASKATCHEWAN.** *See* STATISTICS OF THE WORLD. *See also* CANADA.

**SAUDI ARABIA.** During 1991, Saudi Arabia played a key role in the Persian Gulf War, and the Saudi share of the world oil market increased during the crisis.

**Gulf War.** Late in 1990, as coalition forces gathered in the northern part of the kingdom, Saudi Arabia, Egypt, and Syria had agreed to try to dislodge Iraq from Kuwait through diplomacy. But Iraqi intransigence prompted King Fahd to affirm that Saudi Arabia would accept nothing less than a complete pullout.

Early on January 17, 1991, 150 Saudi Air Force fighters joined other coalition forces in the first phase of Operation Desert Storm, playing an active role in action against Iraq. Iraq responded with an artillery attack on the Khafji oil field. Saudi defenders withdrew. On January 30 four Iraqi tank battalions attacked along the Kuwaiti-Saudi border; meanwhile, Iraqi forces occupied the town of Khafji, but Saudi and Qatari mechanized forces, with U.S. Marine backing, promptly retook it. More than 400 Iraqis surrendered; 30 Iraqis and about half as many Saudis were killed. Small-scale skirmishing continued after that.

Iraqi Scud missiles were the major threat to security. By the end of the war, approximately 40 had been fired at the kingdom. The only Saudi casualties from Scuds came on January 25, when two office buildings in Riyadh were destroyed, with 1 person killed and 30 wounded. The most devastating attack occurred on February 25, when a Scud hit a barracks in Dhahran; 28 U.S. soldiers died.

During the conflict a massive oil slick in the Persian Gulf threatened four Saudi desalination plants. By the time the oil came ashore, much of it had evaporated and the plants were unharmed. The oil did, however, pollute beaches and harm wildlife.

Desert Storm came quickly to an end after U.S., Saudi, and other coalition forces flooded into Kuwait and Iraq on February 24. Subsequently, Allied field commander General H. Norman Schwarzkopf, Jr., became the first non-Saudi to receive that nation's Order of King Abd al-Aziz First Class.

**Security.** Although a $13 billion U.S. proposal to sell F-15 fighters, Apache helicopters, and battle tanks was postponed, $761 million worth of spare parts and $473 million worth of Humvees, laser-guided bombs, cluster bombs, and Sparrow air-to-air missiles were sold to the kingdom. A $3.3 billion sale announced late in the year would include 14 Patriot missile batteries and over 700 missiles.

**Oil.** Saudi petroleum production remained around 8.4 million barrels per day during the Gulf War, which had little impact on the oil industry. Following the war, the Saudis supported a stable oil price of about $21 per barrel. Oil prices dipped at the end of the year.

**Foreign Affairs.** Relations between Saudi Arabia and the Soviet Union showed improvement. The Soviets began permitting their nationals to perform the hajj, or pilgrimage, to Mecca, while Saudi missionaries were allowed to distribute Korans and operate in Muslim Soviet republics. The Saudis agreed to a $1.5 billion loan to the Soviet Union in August and extended an additional $1 billion in emergency aid in October.

The hajj saw the return of Iranian pilgrims— a sign of rapprochement between Iran and Saudi Arabia, which reestablished diplomatic relations in March.

**Finance and Politics.** Saudi expenditures during the Gulf crisis were estimated at up to $65 billion. For the first time in its history, Saudi Arabia made substantial borrowings— several billion dollars—from international banks. The government announced plans to issue treasury bills in October to help cover anticipated budgetary deficits.

On May 18, hundreds of university professors and religious leaders called for the convening of a consultative council, the revision of all laws to bring them into compliance with Muslim law, an end to corruption, a more equal distribution of wealth, an increase in military strength, and protection of human rights. Late in the year, King Fahd announced that laws would be introduced in early 1992 allowing the formation of a council and instituting other reforms.

See STATISTICS OF THE WORLD.        C.H.A.

**SENEGAL.** See STATISTICS OF THE WORLD.

**SEYCHELLES.** See STATISTICS OF THE WORLD.

**SIERRA LEONE.** See STATISTICS OF THE WORLD.

**SINGAPORE.** General elections in 1991 confirmed the ruling People's Action Party's (PAP) control of the Singapore government but saw some opposition gains in parliamentary seats and the popular vote.

On August 31, Prime Minister Goh Chok

*In some of the earliest ground action in the Persian Gulf War, Saudi troops patrol the streets of the Saudi town of Khafji, which they, along with U.S. and other allied forces, had just recaptured from invading Iraqi troops.*

*The exotic Raffles Hotel in Singapore—home away from home for Rudyard Kipling and Somerset Maugham, birthplace of the Singapore Sling cocktail—was restored to its former glory and recently reopened as part of Singapore's efforts to increase its tourist business.*

Tong, who had succeeded Lee Kuan Yew in November 1990, sought a mandate for his leadership by holding early parliamentary elections. The PAP was assured a majority, as 41 of its candidates for the 81 seats ran unopposed. It won 36 of the remaining 40 seats and about 60 percent of the popular vote, a margin that would be comfortable nearly anywhere but Singapore. Since full independence in 1965, the opposition had never won more than 2 seats in a general election. The biggest surprise was the defeat of the acting minister for community development, Seet Ai Mee, who only two months earlier had become Singapore's first woman cabinet member.

In March four Pakistani dissidents seized a Singapore Airlines flight from Kuala Lumpur to Singapore and ordered the pilot to fly to Australia. The plane landed at Singapore Airport, ostensibly to refuel, and local authorities began negotiations. After an eight-hour standoff, commandos stormed the plane and killed all four hijackers. None of the 118 passengers aboard was injured.

See STATISTICS OF THE WORLD.                K.M.

**SOLOMON ISLANDS.** See STATISTICS OF THE WORLD.

**SOMALIA.** The government of President Muhammad Siad Barre, in power since 1969, was toppled early in 1991, in a ferocious and destructive struggle for power.

On January 26 rebel forces identified with the United Somali Congress (USC) took control of the capital, Mogadishu, forcing the president to flee to his home village, in the southwest. The battle for Mogadishu had raged for a month, until the city lay in ruins without running water or electricity. Streets were littered with bodies; the USC estimated that some 4,000 civilians were killed. In the north, too, the destruction was striking. The Somali National Movement (SNM) battled the Somali military in the major towns, and Hargeysa, the former capital of northern Somalia, was destroyed. Thousands of refugees fled to neighboring Djibouti while hundreds of thousands crossed the border into Ethiopia, where they were later caught in the crossfire of that country's revolution. In March, 150 Somalis drowned while trying to cross into Kenya.

The USC established a new government, with its leader, Ali Mahdi Muhammad, as interim president, and Omar Arteh Ghaleb as prime minister. The regime faced virtually intractable problems and could not expect extensive international aid, as the attention of Western countries focused on the Soviet Union, Eastern Europe, and the Persian Gulf.

Shortly after the USC took control, disputes erupted among rival rebel groups. The Somali National Movement claimed control of the north and, refusing conciliatory efforts by Ali Mahdi, declared its secession in May. Meanwhile, fighting broke out in Mogadishu late in the year between rival factions of the Hawiye clan, one led by President Ali Mahdi, the other by General Muhammad Farrah Aideed. Both factions belonged to the USC. An estimated 4,000 men, women, and children—more than 90 percent of them noncombatants—were killed. In mid-December the Red Cross, the

United States, the United Nations, and the European Community began airlifting food and medical supplies to the city.

See STATISTICS OF THE WORLD.          P.J.S.

**SOUTH AFRICA.** The South African Parliament's repeal of major apartheid measures earned wide international approval in 1991. The white-minority government, the black nationalist African National Congress (ANC), and other groups began formal multiparty negotiations for a new South Africa, but continuing hostility among the major groups dampened hopes for an early, peaceful resolution of differences. South Africa's economy showed only tentative signs of recovery.

**Apartheid Acts Repealed.** In his address to Parliament on February 1, State President F. W. de Klerk advocated the repeal of the Population Registration Act, which classified all South Africans by race; the Group Areas Act, which designated where specific racial groups could live and work; and the Land Acts, which allotted 87 percent of the land in South Africa to whites. All 41 members of the Conservative Party walked out. By June, the government had achieved the repeal of these and numerous other acts. Other initiatives by de Klerk's government included limiting detention without trial to ten days, ending media restrictions, proposing a new South African constitution, and signing the Nuclear Non-Proliferation Treaty.

Although de Klerk's changes prompted the European Community, the United States, and other nations to lift numerous sanctions, the ANC and other opposition groups argued that the changes would not significantly aid South African blacks. Critics noted, for example, that while the Land Acts repeal allowed blacks to purchase land on the free market, few could afford to do so. They also noted that South African citizens born before the Population Registration Act's repeal would still be racially classified.

**Political Violence.** The three major political groups—the government, the ANC, and Chief

### A Figure of Controversy

While Nelson Mandela became a living symbol of the anti-apartheid movement, his wife, Winnie, who helped sustain him for his nearly 30 years as a political prisoner, came to be revered by South Africa's blacks as "mother of the nation." But a year after her husband's 1990 release, she went on trial for alleged involvement in the 1988 abduction and beating of four black youths, one of whom was later found dead. The judge concluded that she had authorized the abductions and had later covered up the affair. He sentenced Winnie Mandela, 55, to six years in prison; she was released on bail, pending an appeal.

An outspoken political activist, Mandela was frequently jailed and restricted in her activities during her husband's long imprisonment. Beginning in the late 1980s, she surrounded herself with the group of bodyguards known as the Mandela United Football Club, who reportedly terrorized anyone regarded as an opponent. Winnie Mandela thus lost stature in the eyes of many moderates within the anti-apartheid movement. In August she lost her post as head of the social welfare department of the African National Congress.

*Winnie Mandela*

*When State President F. W. de Klerk, in his speech at the opening of South Africa's Parliament, called for repeal of the legislation that upheld the country's apartheid system, Conservative Party members walked out in protest.*

Mangosuthu Buthelezi's Zulu-based Inkatha Freedom Party—worked to curtail violence. Early in the year, Mandela and Buthelezi met for the first time in 30 years and pledged to end fighting between their followers. The government agreed to accept the right of blacks to demonstrate peacefully and to expedite the release of political prisoners.

During the first seven months of the year, 5,000 incidents of political violence occurred, compared to 10,000 for the same period in 1990. Among the major incidents, unknown gunmen killed ANC activist Sam Ntuli in September; in addition, 13 mourners at his funeral were murdered.

**"Inkathagate."** In July Minister of Law and Order Adriaan Vlok said that individuals within the government had bankrolled Inkatha for anti-sanctions rallies. Foreign Minister Roelof "Pik" Botha admitted authorizing the payments for the rallies. De Klerk disclosed that the South African Defense Force had trained some Inkatha members. Buthelezi denied any knowledge of this assistance.

**Internal Negotiations.** On September 14, the government, the ANC, Inkatha, and some 20 other organizations signed a national peace accord. It stipulated codes of conduct for the South African police and for all political parties. The accord helped pave the way for multiparty negotiations on a post-apartheid political system for South Africa. At the first Convention for a Democratic South Africa, held in Johannesburg on December 20-21, representatives of the government, the ANC, and other groups agreed to create an undivided nation free of discrimination, with a multiparty democracy and bill of rights. De Klerk and Mandela argued publicly, but both declared at the end of the conference that progress had been made. Working groups were appointed to address such issues as drafting the new constitution, formulating transitional arrangements, and fostering a favorable climate for peaceful change.

**Opposition Groups.** At a July convention 2,500 delegates of the ANC elected the ailing Oliver Tambo as national chairman and Nelson Mandela as president. The ANC remained divided on a number of issues, including its policy of suspending violence. The May conviction of Winnie Mandela (wife of Nelson Mandela) on charges of kidnapping and being an accessory after the fact to four assaults also divided the ANC and hurt relations with the government. The charges stemmed from the activities of her bodyguards, who in late 1988 had apparently abducted, taken to Winnie Mandela's home, and beaten four youths, one of whom was later found dead.

In late October the ANC joined with some 40 other groups, including the Pan Africanist Congress (PAC) but not Inkatha, in a "Patriotic Front" against the government. The PAC soon dropped out, however, accusing the ANC of colluding with the government to share power, and then refused to take part in the December convention.

On November 4, about 4 million black workers staged a two-day strike, ostensibly against a value-added tax. Union and political leaders said, however, that the strike was also mounted to induce the government to incorporate the opposition into the decision-making process. Clashes between strikers and miners who attempted to go to work led to the deaths of 67 of the latter.

**Foreign Relations.** Early in the year, government officials held meetings with diplomats and business leaders from Gabon, Congo (a formerly harsh critic), Angola, France, and Zaire. In July, South Africa regained membership in the International Olympic Committee. In August, South Africa agreed to offer total amnesty to 40,000 political exiles, and the United Nations opened offices in South Africa to oversee the exiles' return—the first UN presence in South Africa in 30 years.

A number of countries lifted economic sanctions, while many others quietly increased trade. The European Community lifted its 1986 ban on importing South African gold coins, iron, and steel, and President George Bush lifted the U.S. sanctions imposed in 1986. Bush also announced he was doubling the current $40 million in aid to black South Africans.

**Economy.** In late 1991, South Africa had a zero economic growth rate and an inflation rate of about 15 percent. The balance of trade remained in surplus. Government revenues suffered from the continuing drop in gold revenues caused by high production costs and low gold prices. The lifting of sanctions encouraged South African business confidence, with the Johannesburg Stock Exchange industrial index jumping 50 percent between January and September.

See STATISTICS OF THE WORLD.          H.H.

**SOUTH CAROLINA.** See STATISTICS OF THE WORLD.

**SOUTH DAKOTA.** See STATISTICS OF THE WORLD.

**SOUTH WEST AFRICA.** See NAMIBIA.

**SOVIET UNION.** See UNION OF SOVIET SOCIALIST REPUBLICS.

**SPACE EXPLORATION.** Some notable successes in space flight punctuated 1991, a year in which the leaders of the world's major space programs were forced to defend, rework, or scale back their plans for the future. The United States conducted six space shuttle missions for the second year in a row, while the Soviet Union and its successors continued activities on the *Mir* space station. It was a good year for space science as earth-orbiting observatories and spacecraft elsewhere in the solar system advanced astronomy, astrophysics, and planetary sciences. Pentagon officials called the Persian Gulf War history's first space war because of the extensive use the U.S.-led coalition made of satellites for navigation, communication, electronic intelligence, surveillance, and reconnaissance.

***Magellan* and *Galileo.*** Spectacular images of Venus were produced as the U.S. spacecraft *Magellan*, launched from a space shuttle in 1989, completed the first phase of its mission of mapping the planet from a polar orbit with a synthetic-aperture radar. Previous spacecraft had produced images that penetrated the planet's thick carbon dioxide atmosphere but did not approach *Magellan*'s resolution of features as small as 120 meters (some 400 feet) across. *Magellan* yielded a substantial body of new information, sparking scientific debate on such questions as whether Venus's crust is composed of tectonic plates (like the earth's) and whether the volcano on the mountain Maat Mons has been active as recently as 1980.

*Nelson Mandela of the African National Congress (left) and Chief Mangosuthu Buthelezi of the Zulu-based Inkatha Freedom Party met in January for the first time in 30 years and vowed to end the violence between their followers.*

In April the main antenna refused to open on the U.S. space probe *Galileo*, also launched by a space shuttle in 1989. The problem threatened to disrupt the spacecraft's primary mission, a 22-month study of Jupiter's chemistry and magnetosphere planned to begin in 1995. The malfunction drastically slowed the transmission of data. *Galileo* was still able to produce the first close-up photo of an asteroid, taken from a distance of about 16,000 kilometers (10,000 miles), as it flew by Gaspra late in the year, but it took several weeks to relay the image.

**U.S. Space Shuttles.** In the first shuttle flight of the year, the 17-ton Compton Gamma Ray Observatory was placed in earth orbit—but

*The Spacelab, a laboratory designed to conduct research in space, returned to orbit in June inside the cargo bay of the space shuttle* Columbia, *this time to provide new data on the effects of weightlessness. Here, payload specialist Millie Hughes-Fulford checks some of the experimental animals aboard.*

only after two astronauts ventured outside the orbiter *Atlantis* on an unscheduled space walk. Jerome Apt and Jerry L. Ross manually swung into place a jammed boom that had an antenna on the end. On April 28, just 17 days after *Atlantis* landed, *Discovery* was launched with a crew of seven to carry out experiments for the Strategic Defense Initiative (SDI), the antiballistic missile research program known as Star Wars. It was the first shuttle flight conducted by the National Aeronautics and Space Administration (NASA) for the Defense Department not to be carried out in secrecy.

Four men and three women flew on *Columbia* in June on a mission dedicated to life sciences research in the long Spacelab module carried in the cargo bay. In August, *Atlantis* was used to launch a NASA satellite toward a geosynchronous orbit—an orbit synchronized with the earth's rotation—where it would relay data to the earth from spacecraft in low orbits. The first satellite in an international program called Mission to Planet Earth was placed into orbit by *Discovery* in September. The Upper Atmosphere Research Satellite's mission was to examine the chemistry, dynamics, and energy input of the atmosphere above 16 km (10 mi.).

The final shuttle flight of the year was a military mission on *Atlantis* late in November. The cargo was a "Defense Support Program" satellite, bound for a geosynchronous orbit to provide early warning of missile launchings. The crew successfully launched the missile, but a faulty navigation device on the shuttle forced them to cancel other planned experiments and return to earth three days early.

A new space shuttle orbiter, named *Endeavour*, was delivered to NASA in the spring, replacing *Challenger*, which was destroyed in a launch accident on January 28, 1986. According to the Bush administration, this was likely to be the last such vehicle purchased by NASA. Vice President Dan Quayle in July announced a new space launch strategy that "proposes to extend the life span of the shuttle fleet" but "does not envision acquiring new orbiters."

**Space Station Debate.** The most significant political debate on the U.S. space program in years unfolded when a subcommittee of the House Appropriations Committee voted in

Britain's first astronaut, Helen Sharman, a chemist in private industry, accompanied Soviet cosmonauts on a rendezvous with the orbiting Mir space station in May.

May to terminate NASA's project to develop and build a space station with the help of the European Space Agency, Japan, and Canada. The permanent orbital base, in which astronauts would live and work beginning around the year 2000, has been redesigned several times since it was proposed in 1984, in order to reduce its complexity and cost. Proponents argued it would help in maintaining the national technological base and, ultimately, in preparing for human exploration of Mars. Committee members and many scientists feared the project would jeopardize other civil space programs. In the end, Congress provided money for the space station for the 1992 fiscal year, but the overall NASA budget it approved was smaller than the Bush administration's request, which meant some research and development projects had to be cut.

**Soviet Space Activities.** Soviet programs already strapped for funds were further threatened by the collapse of central authority, which presented a special problem for space efforts because the launch sites and control and training centers are widely dispersed. Some projects were stretched out, and others canceled, to reduce costs. The Soviets also accelerated their efforts to market space products and services around the world and to di-versify into other fields. The U.S. government purchased a Topaz nuclear reactor (used to power spacecraft) so that U.S. engineers could study its successful design. The Soviets also struck a deal with a French company to sell pictures from the Almaz satellite, which is equipped with radar that can penetrate clouds and make detailed images at night. Other highlights included the launching of the first communications satellite dedicated to the Russian republic and of a weather satellite carrying a U.S. instrument to map the earth's depleted stratospheric ozone layer.

Non-Soviets again traveled aboard the space station Mir. In late 1990, Toyohiro Akiyama, whose employer paid more than $12 million for the ride, had become the first Japanese and the first journalist in space. A Soyuz transport that docked with Mir on May 20, 1991, carried Helen Sharman, a chemist with the Mars candy company, who became the first Briton in space. She conducted a limited number of experiments in a commercial program called Juno, which failed to attract sponsors and left its organizers in debt. Toktar Aubakirov, the first space traveler from Kazakhstan, and Franz Viehboeck, the first from Austria, visited the Soviet space station Mir in October.

After denying for more than 20 years that

they had been racing the United States to land humans on the moon, the Soviets revealed the secret design of their N1 moon rocket. The booster failed in four launch attempts.

**European and Asian Programs.** At a three-day meeting in Munich, science and technology ministers of the European Space Agency's 13 member nations trimmed the agency's budget for 1992 by 5 percent. The launching of Earth Resources Satellite 1 in July gave Europe its first spacecraft with radars for imaging and altimetry. The Ariane space consortium began marketing its next-generation Ariane 5 booster for flights beginning in 1995.

China and Japan also launched significant space missions. Japan suffered technical difficulties in developing the engines for its next generation of boosters, and the first flight was delayed until late 1993 or 1994. Nonetheless, the Japanese began marketing launch services of a large new vehicle, called H-2, signaling their intent to become a major player in the international market for delivering satellites into orbit. J.R.A.

**SPAIN.** An increasingly moderate Spanish Socialist Workers' Party (PSOE) continued to dominate the political landscape. The government of Prime Minister Felipe González Márquez, through tough economic policies and a pro-Western international stance, sought to bring Spain into closer alignment with its European Community (EC) partners.

**Resignation and Reshuffling.** Deputy Prime Minister Alfonso Guerra González resigned on January 12, under heavy criticism as a result of his brother's indictment on corruption charges. However, his influence in the party remained intact when he retained the post of deputy general-secretary. In March, González Márquez carried out a cabinet reshuffling; the new deputy prime minister was Narcís Serra. Carlos Solchaga, another moderate, retained the Ministry of Finance and the Economy.

**Elections.** Spaniards went to the polls on May 26 to elect all local as well as 13 of the 17 regional governments. Although the PSOE slightly increased its overall share of the popular vote, the Popular Party, a conservative group, loosened the PSOE's stranglehold in Spain's major cities. The once-powerful Democratic and Social Center, created by former

Prime Minister Adolfo Suárez in 1982, dropped to less than 4 percent of the vote, and Suárez resigned the party leadership.

In January, following 1990 Basque elections, the PSOE lost ground when nationalist parties, including the separatist Basque Left, formed a new Basque government excluding the regional wing of the PSOE.

**Separatism and Terrorism.** A September poll revealed that 39 percent of Catalonians and 33 percent of Basques favored separatism. In the meantime, the military wing of the ETA, the Basque separatist organization, continued its campaign of terror. On January 2 the lieutenant commander of the San Sebastián region was gunned down by a commando; on May 29, car bombs killed nine near Barcelona; and on June 12, two technicians attempting to dispose of bombs were killed in Madrid. Authorities prevailed, however, on May 30 when civil guards broke up Barcelona's ETA commando group, killing two. On August 17, police broke into a house in San Sebastián and fatally shot three leaders of the Basque organization.

**Gulf War.** Spain participated in the coalition that supported the allied campaign in the Persian Gulf War, although an early poll indicated that 71 percent of Spaniards opposed the war. In early February the news that U.S. B-52 bombers had carried out as many as 294 missions to the Gulf from their base in Morón near Seville provoked huge protest demonstrations in Madrid and elsewhere. Ironically, a poll taken after the war indicated that nearly two out of three Spaniards now agreed with Spain's role.

**The Economy and Labor Relations.** As Spain struggled with recession, steps were taken which reduced inflation to below 6 percent, partially by curtailing government expenditures. Gross national product grew at an annual rate of around 3 percent, while private investment shrunk. At 15.5 percent, Spain's unemployment rate remained one of the highest in the EC. In July, Solchaga announced a 1 percent increase in the value-added tax (VAT) for 1992 and a further reduction in government expenditures, including a 10.9 percent cut for defense.

**Looking Ahead.** Preparations were well under way to celebrate the quincentenary of

Christopher Columbus's first landfall in America, on October 12, 1492. Replicas of the *Niña, Pinta* and *Santa Maria,* the three ships commanded by the 15th-century Italian merchant, sailed from 20th-century Spain on October 12, 1991, bound for Miami and 16 other ports of call in the New World. Among other planned events, Spanish and American school children will meet in the villages of Balonas and Pontevadra, Spain, on December 14-15, 1992, and plant a "Columbus Grove" of 500 redwood seedlings, a gift from the New World to the Old. Meanwhile, Seville was preparing for its 1992 World's Fair, celebrating the theme of discovery.

*See* STATISTICS OF THE WORLD.                    M.S.

*The replicas of Columbus's original three ships weigh anchor in October in Huelva, Spain, to begin their re-creation of the explorer's original epic journey.*

# Sports

**In 1991 the Twins triumphed in perhaps the greatest World Series ever played, while in basketball the Duke Blue Devils and Chicago Bulls made it to the top for the first time ever. Tennis superstar Monica Seles captured three Grand Slam titles, and the most awesome record in track and field—the long jump—finally fell.**

### AUTOMOBILE RACING

Though he won the 1991 Indianapolis 500, for once Rick Mears was not the fastest driver at Indy. Gary Bettenhausen actually turned faster laps in time trials. Bettenhausen's Buick-powered Lola lasted 180 laps during the race, and Mears staged a dramatic battle with Michael Andretti, finally taking the lead for good with only 13 laps remaining. Though disappointed by not winning at Indy, Andretti went on to win 8 of the season's 17 races and the PPG Indy-car season championship.

Dale Earnhardt won his fifth Nascar Winston Cup Championship, although his spin into

*Ayrton Senna of Brazil won the Formula One driving championship for the third time. Here he is seen (in lead car) en route to victory in the Grand Prix of Brazil.*

Davey Allison only three laps from the end of the Daytona 500 helped Ernie Irvan win the most important event in stock-car racing. Earnhardt's steady, sometimes spectacular performances were also overshadowed late in the year when 51-year-old Harry Gant took an amazing four Winston Cup races in a row.

Ayrton Senna, a Brazilian driving for the McLaren-Honda team that has dominated recent Formula One seasons, opened the year by winning the Grand Prix of the United States, Brazil, San Marino, and Monaco and appeared ready to run away with the season championship. But then Nigel Mansell, a British driver for Williams-Renault, put together his own three-race winning streak. The turning point was the Portuguese race in mid-September; Mansell was leading when a wheel came off after a pit stop, and he was ultimately disqualified for the manner in which his crew had remounted the tire. Senna ended up with the season title. Between them, Senna and Mansell won 12 of the season's 16 races.

Six weeks after a crash in which he sustained broken ribs and vertebrae, Geoff Brabham came back to drive at DelMar and successfully defended his International Motor Sports Association Camel GT championship. The Camel GT season, dominated in recent years by Nissan, was marked by close competition this time, as Porsche, Nissan, Jaguar, Toyota, and Chevrolet all won races.

In international sports-car racing, Jaguar won both the manufacturers and drivers championships (the latter going to Teo Fabi of Italy). The 24 Hours of Le Mans was won by Mazda in the first victory there for a Japanese automaker and perhaps the greatest surprise of the entire racing season. Le Mans had been expected to be a battle between Mercedes-Benz and Jaguar. Mercedes did enjoy the lead for some 20 hours of the competition, with its cars sometimes running 1-2-3, and at the end of the race Jaguars were 2-3-4. But the first-place winner after two trips around the clock and 362 laps around the more-than-8-mile road course was Mazda.

In one event figured to have long-term importance for motor sports, the first Solar & Electric 500 event was conducted on the 1-mile oval at Phoenix. L.E.

## BASEBALL

It was the year of the underdog, as teams from the smallest markets triumphed over big-city clubs boasting big-name stars and salaries. The Minnesota Twins and the Atlanta Braves were the first teams in modern baseball to finish in last place one year and first place the next. They met in a tense, seven-game World Series narrowly won by the Twins.

**Individual Champions.** Terry Pendleton, a key contributor to the Braves' success in the National League West, took his first league batting title with a .319 average, and also won the league's Most Valuable Player Award. In the American League, the Texas Rangers' Julio Franco won his first batting crown with a .341 average. Howard Johnson of the New York Mets led the National League in home runs and runs batted in (RBIs), with 38 and 117 respectively, while the Detroit Tigers' Cecil Fielder

| NATIONAL LEAGUE | | | | |
|---|---|---|---|---|
| Eastern Division | W | L | Pct. | GB |
| Pittsburgh Pirates | 98 | 64 | .605 | — |
| St. Louis Cardinals | 84 | 78 | .519 | 14 |
| Philadelphia Phillies | 78 | 84 | .481 | 20 |
| Chicago Cubs | 77 | 83 | .481 | 20 |
| New York Mets | 77 | 84 | .478 | 20½ |
| Montréal Expos | 71 | 90 | .441 | 26½ |
| **Western Division** | | | | |
| Atlanta Braves | 94 | 68 | .580 | — |
| Los Angeles Dodgers | 93 | 69 | .574 | 1 |
| San Diego Padres | 84 | 78 | .519 | 10 |
| San Francisco Giants | 75 | 87 | .463 | 19 |
| Cincinnati Reds | 74 | 88 | .457 | 20 |
| Houston Astros | 65 | 97 | .401 | 29 |

| AMERICAN LEAGUE | | | | |
|---|---|---|---|---|
| Eastern Division | W | L | Pct. | GB |
| Toronto Blue Jays | 91 | 71 | .562 | — |
| Boston Red Sox | 84 | 78 | .519 | 7 |
| Detroit Tigers | 84 | 78 | .519 | 7 |
| Milwaukee Brewers | 83 | 79 | .512 | 8 |
| New York Yankees | 71 | 91 | .438 | 20 |
| Baltimore Orioles | 67 | 95 | .414 | 24 |
| Cleveland Indians | 57 | 105 | .352 | 34 |
| **Western Division** | | | | |
| Minnesota Twins | 95 | 67 | .586 | — |
| Chicago White Sox | 87 | 75 | .537 | 8 |
| Texas Rangers | 85 | 77 | .525 | 10 |
| Oakland Athletics | 84 | 78 | .519 | 11 |
| Seattle Mariners | 83 | 79 | .512 | 12 |
| Kansas City Royals | 82 | 80 | .506 | 13 |
| California Angels | 81 | 81 | .500 | 14 |

**PENNANT PLAYOFFS**
**American League**—Minnesota defeated Toronto, 4 games to 1
**National League**—Atlanta defeated Pittsburgh, 4 games to 3
**WORLD SERIES**—Minnesota defeated Atlanta, 4 games to 3

tied the Oakland Athletics' José Canseco for the most home runs in the major leagues (44). Fielder won the RBI crown outright, with 133. The Baltimore Orioles' Cal Ripken, Jr., won the AL Most Valuable Player Award.

Boston Red Sox star Roger Clemens, who picked up his third Cy Young Award, also copped both the earned run average (ERA) and strikeout titles for the AL. In the NL, the Montréal Expos' Dennis Martinez won the ERA crown, despite pitching for a club that finished 26½ games out of first place. New York's David Cone earned the strikeout title. Atlanta's Tom Glavine won 20 games and the NL's Cy Young Award.

**Milestones.** There were seven no-hitters, including the first multipitcher no-hitter in NL history. Oakland's Rickey Henderson stole 58 bases—tops in the AL—and became the all-time king of theft with 994, passing Lou Brock's 938 mark. St. Louis Cardinals' reliever Lee Smith saved 47 games, an NL single-season record. The Cardinals also played errorless baseball in 15 consecutive games, tying the record set by the 1975 Reds.

In another record, 13 managers were replaced during or shortly after the season.

**All Star Game.** The American League defeated the National League, 4-2, in the 62nd All Star Game, held on July 9 in Toronto's SkyDome.

**Hall of Fame.** Rod Carew, Gaylord Perry, and Ferguson Jenkins were inducted into the Hall of Fame. Carew, a seven-time American League batting champion, batted .328 during his 19-year career with the Twins and Angels. Jenkins played 19 years, with the Phillies, Cubs, and Rangers, compiling a 284-226 record with a 3.34 ERA. Over 22 years, Perry posted a 314-265 record and 3.10 ERA, playing for many teams. He was the only pitcher to win the Cy Young Award in both leagues.

**The Season.** The Toronto Blue Jays won the American League East title by seven games, led by Roberto Alomar, batting .295, and Joe Carter, who hit 33 home runs with 108 RBIs. The Minnesota Twins won the American League West division by eight games over the Chicago White Sox, relying on an offense led by Kirby Puckett. He batted .319 with 89 RBIs. The White Sox, finishing second for the second straight season, were paced by Frank Thomas, who batted .318 with 32 HRs and 109 RBIs.

The Pittsburgh Pirates won their second straight division title in the National League East, finishing a full 14 games ahead of the pack. Bobby Bonilla and Barry Bonds, with 43 HRs and 216 RBIs between them, along

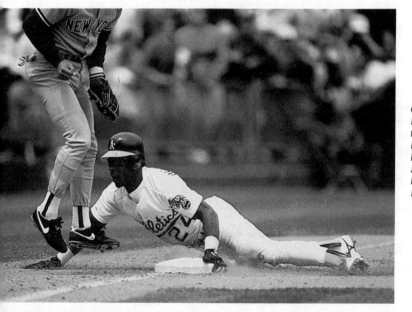

*Oakland's star outfielder Rickey Henderson broke the major league record for lifetime stolen bases when he swiped his 939th base, in a game against the Yankees, breaking the mark held by Lou Brock.*

*With his team down, three games to two, Minnesota's Kirby Puckett won the sixth game of the World Series with a dramatic 11th inning home run (above); in the final game, Gene Larkin (left) hit a bases loaded single in the bottom of the tenth, to give Minnesota a 1-0 win over the Atlanta Braves.*

with 43 stolen bases from Bonds, paced the Pirates. The St. Louis Cardinals, a surprising second, were led by Todd Zeile's 81 RBIs and Ray Lankford's 44 stolen bases. In the west, the Atlanta Braves relied on pitching—Tom Glavine, Steve Avery, John Smoltz, and Charlie Leibrandt combined for 67 wins—to take their first division title since 1982. The Los Angeles Dodgers finished a mere game behind; Brett Butler led the club with a .296 average and also had 38 stolen bases.

**Playoffs.** In the National League, the Braves defeated the Pirates in seven games. The Pirates won the first game, 5-1, at home, but in Game 2, 21-year-old lefthander Steve Avery outpitched Zane Smith, giving the Braves a 1-0

win. The Braves took Game 3, too, routing Pirates lefthander John Smiley in a 10-3 victory. The Pirates evened the series by winning Game 4, 3-2, then took the lead with Game 5, 1-0. But all was not lost for the Braves; Avery and Alejandro Peña shut out Pittsburgh for a 1-0 win in Game 6, and the Braves then captured the National League pennant in Game 7, thanks to John Smoltz's 4-0 shutout.

In the American League the Twins defeated the Toronto Blue Jays in five games. The Twins had narrowly taken Game 1, 5-4, in their Metrodome. Shocked by a loss in Game 2— their first postseason loss in the Metrodome in franchise history—they rebounded to take Game 3, 3-2, in Toronto's SkyDome with Mike

359

Pagliarulo's 10th-inning home run off Mike Timlin. The Twins also captured Game 4, 9-3, then sewed up the pennant with an 8-5 win in Game 5.

**World Series.** Commissioner Fay Vincent called the seven-game showdown between the Braves and Twins "the best World Series ever." Five of the games were decided by one run, four were decided in the winning team's final at bat, and three went into extra innings.

The Twins took the opener in the

**Play Ball!**

In 1980 ten sports fans, who hung around a now-vanished Manhattan restaurant called La Rotisserie Française, figured it would be fun if each of them pretended to own a batch of real baseball players—to hold a communal draft session and assemble make-believe teams. At the end of the season, they could, by comparing the players' actual statistics, see whose squad came out on top.

Today rotisserie baseball is a phenomenon, and every April fans gather in kitchens, saloons, and college dorms to set up leagues. Part of the fun is choosing a team name (Robert Barons, John Paul Popes, and Solly Manders are some examples). Participants don't *have* to put up money when they select players, but most do; this lets them sell players during the season in addition to trading them. Besides, if you think you're really smarter than your home club's general manager, this is your chance to put your money where your mouth is.

Rotisserie was played by at least a million Americans in 1991, says Greg Ambrosius, editor of *Fantasy Baseball* magazine. Not only are there books and even 900 numbers to supply tips on the most desirable players, but since standings need to be adjusted weekly by comparing statistics (each team has 23 players), there are computerized statistical services that do the number-crunching for a fee. "I would say $20 million to $50 million is generated by this hobby now," estimates Ambrosius. "But I think it will double, double, and double."

No wonder Steve Wulf, one of the original Rotisserie ten, says, "Now I know how Dr. Frankenstein must have felt."

Metrodome, 5-2, keyed by Greg Gagne's three-run home run off Braves' lefthander Charlie Leibrandt. In Game 2, Scott Leius's leadoff home run in the eighth inning broke a 2-2 tie and gave the Twins a 3-2 victory. Then Mark Lemke's 12th-inning single with runners on first and second gave the Braves a 5-4 win in Game 3. Avoiding a problem that had arisen in the playoffs, Dave Justice made sure to touch third base while scoring from second base; he ended a four-hour marathon, in which 42 players on the two teams saw action. The 12-inning contest represented the longest World Series game since Game 1 of the 1977 classic.

Jerry Willard's sacrifice fly in the ninth inning of Game 4 gave the Braves a 3-2 win, but not without controversy. In a hotly contested play at the plate, Atlanta's Mark Lemke— tagging up on Willard's fly ball—narrowly averted the tag from Twins' catcher Brian Harper and scored the winning run. In Game 5 the Braves enjoyed a 14-5 win—their easiest—mounting a 17-hit attack for their 14 runs, the most ever by a National League team in a World Series game.

The Twins scored a comeback in Game 6, as Kirby Puckett's leadoff home run in the 11th inning off Charlie Leibrandt gave them a 4-3 win, evening the Series. In Game 7, Gene Larkin hit a bases-loaded single in the tenth inning, giving the Twins a 1-0 win and the Series championship. Jack Morris, who was voted the World Series Most Valuable Player, pitched all ten innings for the Twins. The Braves will forever remember their failure to score in the eighth inning, after Lonnie Smith singled and Terry Pendleton lashed what appeared to be a run-scoring double to left-center. Smith stopped running near second base—later he admitted he had lost sight of the ball—and had to stop at third. Morris eventually pitched out of trouble, setting up the Twins' dramatic rally in the 10th.

**Baseball Riches.** In early December the Mets signed Bobby Bonilla to a five-year deal worth $29 million, making him the highest paid player in team sports. A short time later, the Blue Jays signed Jack Morris to a two-year deal guaranteeing him $10.85 million and making him baseball's richest pitcher.    B.K.

## BASKETBALL

In the 1990-1991 season, as basketball began to celebrate its centennial, Duke University won the National Collegiate Athletic Association (NCAA) championship, and the Chicago Bulls won the National Basketball Association (NBA) title, both for the first time. In late 1991 the basketball world was stunned by Los Angeles Laker star Earvin ("Magic") Johnson's announcement that he was retiring from professional basketball and had the AIDS virus (*see profile in* PEOPLE IN THE NEWS).

**Collegiate.** With the University of Nevada at Las Vegas's entire championship starting team returning, UNLV began the 1990-1991 season ranked unanimously as number one. That ranking changed abruptly on March 30, 1991, when Duke upset UNLV, 79-77, in the semifinal round of the NCAA tournament at the Hoosier Dome in Indianapolis. The stage was set for the Duke-Kansas final when the Jayhawks eliminated North Carolina, 79-73, in the other semifinal.

Duke had a disappointing Final Four record over the years, but the Blue Devils ended their long frustration by defeating Kansas, 72-65, on the big day. Duke quickly jumped to a 7-1 advantage and then thwarted several Kansas runs to lead the entire game. Center Christian Laettner, voted the game's Most Valuable Player, had 18 points and 10 rebounds.

Jerry Tarkanian, who built the Nevada-Las Vegas basketball program into a national power while battling the NCAA, announced he would step down as coach after the 1991-1992 season, in which UNLV began serving a one-year probation for recruiting violations. Tarkanian's announcement came in June, not long after the publication of photographs showing three Runnin' Rebels playing basketball and soaking in a hot tub at the home of Richard Perry, who had been convicted of sports bribery in the 1970s and 1980s.

In November the NCAA filed a suit seeking to overturn a Nevada law passed in an attempt to force the collegiate association to follow due process procedures in its investigations. Tarkanian countersued, accusing the NCAA of a 20-year vendetta against him.

In women's basketball, the University of Tennessee went into overtime for its 70-67 vic-

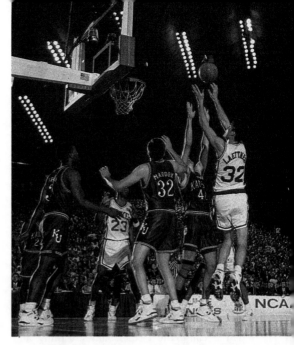

Led by center Christian Laettner, Duke's Blue Devils won the NCAA basketball crown by first upsetting undefeated defending champion UNLV and then (above) beating Kansas in the final game, 72-65.

tory over Virginia in the national championship game on March 31, in New Orleans. Dena Head and Dawn Staley each scored a tournament-record 28 points. It was the third championship for the Lady Vols.

Kevin Bradshaw, a 26-year-old, 6'6" United States International University guard, scored 72 points against Loyola Marymount on January 5 to establish an NCAA Division I record for the most points scored against a Division I school. He also won Division I scoring honors, averaging 37.6 points a game.

Larry Johnson completed his collegiate career at UNLV by winning four of the six major national player-of-the-year awards. The 6'7", 250-pound forward was also the first player to be taken in the NBA draft, by the Charlotte Hornets.

**Professional.** The Chicago Bulls began the season by junking their old offense and replacing it with a textbook system that required constant adjusting and readjusting to the situation on the court. Under the new system the younger, speedier Bulls got the ball into more hands for better shots. While superstar Michael Jordan won his fifth straight scoring championship, the Bulls also drew upon players like four-year pros Scottie Pippen and Horace Grant, sharpshooters John Paxson and Craig Hodges, veteran center Bill Cartwright, and key reserve Cliff Levingston to finish the regular season with a 61-21 mark.

The Detroit Pistons struggled by the Atlanta Hawks in five games in the opening round of the playoffs and got by the Boston Celtics in six before being swept by the Bulls in the conference final. The Portland Trail Blazers, who had lost only once in their final 17 regular season games, struggled in the playoffs from the outset, finally losing to the Los Angeles Lakers in six games.

The finals, featuring the two biggest names in the sport—Michael Jordan and Magic Johnson—was expected to be a seven-game series, but the Bulls won in five, perhaps in part because the Lakers' James Worthy and Byron Scott, who combined for an average of 35.9 points a game during the regular season, were sidelined in the final game with injuries. Jordan averaged 31.2 points while shooting .558 from the field and .848 from the free-throw line. He became only the second player in history to win the scoring title and to be selected as the most valuable player for both the regular season and the championship round.

On April 15, Johnson surpassed Oscar Robertson as the No. 1 assist man in NBA history, by reaching 9,888 assists; he finished the season with 9,921.

On September 18, 1985, Patrick Ewing, the Knicks' All-Star center, signed a ten-year, $32 million contract which stipulated that after his sixth season he could become a free agent if he was not among the four highest-paid players in the league as of June 1, 1991. Ewing claimed he was not; the Knicks contended he was. New York University law professor Daniel Collins, named as arbitrator in the case, ruled in the Knicks' favor.

The decision bound Ewing to play for New York for four more seasons, unless they chose to trade him. In November, however, Ewing agreed to a two-year, $18.8 million contract extension. Ewing's new deal, combined with what remains on his current contract, averages out to $5.5 million a year, making him basketball's highest paid player.

Susan O'Malley became one of the highest-ranking female executives in professional sports when she was named president of the Washington Bullets, succeeding owner Abe Pollin. She was the first woman in NBA history to hold that title.

**Hall of Fame.** Bobby Knight, the skilled but irascible Indiana University coach, was one of seven inductees into the Naismith Basketball Hall of Fame. In 26 years of coaching, including 20 at Indiana, Knight-coached teams accumulated 561 victories, and his Hoosiers won three NCAA titles. The other new members were Nate "Tiny" Archibald, Dave Cowens, Harry Gallatin, Larry O'Brien, Larry Fleisher, and Borislav Stankovic.                    S.M.G.

*Michael Jordan, long established as basketball's most exciting player, finally got the supporting cast he needed as the Chicago Bulls mastered the Los Angeles Lakers and Magic Johnson to win the NBA title.*

## NATIONAL BASKETBALL ASSOCIATION
### 1990–1991 Regular Season

**EASTERN CONFERENCE**

| Atlantic Division | W | L | Pct. | GB |
|---|---|---|---|---|
| Boston Celtics | 56 | 26 | .683 | — |
| Philadelphia 76ers | 44 | 38 | .537 | 12 |
| New York Knicks | 39 | 43 | .476 | 17 |
| Washington Bullets | 30 | 52 | .366 | 26 |
| New Jersey Nets | 26 | 56 | .317 | 30 |
| Miami Heat | 24 | 58 | .293 | 32 |

| Central Division | W | L | Pct. | GB |
|---|---|---|---|---|
| Chicago Bulls | 61 | 21 | .744 | — |
| Detriot Pistons | 50 | 32 | .610 | 11 |
| Milwaukee Bucks | 48 | 34 | .585 | 13 |
| Atlanta Hawks | 43 | 39 | .524 | 18 |
| Indiana Pacers | 41 | 41 | .500 | 20 |
| Cleveland Cavaliers | 33 | 49 | .402 | 28 |
| Charlotte Hornets | 26 | 56 | .317 | 35 |

**WESTERN CONFERENCE**

| Midwest Division | W | L | Pct. | GB |
|---|---|---|---|---|
| San Antonio Spurs | 55 | 27 | .671 | — |
| Utah Jazz | 54 | 28 | .659 | 1 |
| Houston Rockets | 52 | 30 | .634 | 3 |
| Orlando Magic | 31 | 51 | .378 | 24 |
| Minnesota Timberwolves | 29 | 53 | .354 | 26 |
| Dallas Mavericks | 28 | 54 | .341 | 27 |
| Denver Nuggets | 20 | 62 | .244 | 35 |

| Pacific Division | W | L | Pct. | GB |
|---|---|---|---|---|
| Portland Trail Blazers | 63 | 19 | .768 | — |
| Los Angeles Lakers | 58 | 24 | .707 | 5 |
| Phoenix Suns | 55 | 27 | .671 | 8 |
| Golden State Warriors | 44 | 38 | .537 | 19 |
| Seattle SuperSonics | 41 | 41 | .500 | 22 |
| Los Angeles Clippers | 31 | 51 | .378 | 32 |
| Sacramento Kings | 25 | 57 | .305 | 38 |

**PLAYOFFS**

**First Round**
Detroit defeated Atlanta, 3 games to 2
Portland defeated Seattle, 3 games to 2
Chicago defeated New York, 3 games to 0
Los Angeles defeated Houston, 3 games to 0
Boston defeated Indiana, 3 games to 2
Philadelphia defeated Milwaukee, 3 games to 0
Golden State defeated San Antonio, 3 games to 1
Utah defeated Phoenix, 3 games to 1

**Second Round**
Detroit defeated Boston, 4 games to 2
Portland defeated Utah, 4 games to 1
Chicago defeated Philadelphia, 4 games to 1
Los Angeles defeated Golden State, 4 games to 1

**Conference Finals**
Los Angeles defeated Portland, 4 games to 2
Chicago defeated Detroit, 4 games to 0

**Championship Finals**
Chicago defeated Los Angeles, 4 games to 1

## BOWLING

In the three major tournaments of the Professional Bowlers Association tour, Mike Miller of Albuquerque, N.M., won the PBA National Championship, Pete Weber of Florissant, Mo., took the United States Open, for his second time, and David Ozio of Vidor, Tex., won the Firestone Tournament of Champions. Ozio led the tour in earnings with $225,485. After the Tournament of Champions, Weber began serving a six-month suspension from the tour for losing his temper too often.

On the Ladies Pro Bowlers Tour, Nikki Gianulias won four tournaments and Leanne Barrette won three. Barrette led in earnings with $87,617. Dede Davidson of San Jose, Calif., took the Women's International Bowling Congress Queens tournament, and Anne Marie Duggan of La Habra, Calif., won the United States Open. On the seniors tour, John Handegard of Las Vegas won three tournaments and also led in earnings.            F.L.

## BOXING

Throughout 1991, Evander Holyfield maintained his hold on the title of world heavyweight boxing champion, as recognized by the three major governing bodies. He won memorable title defenses over 42-year-old George Foreman, a former champion, and over the little-known 25-year-old Bert Cooper.

The Holyfield-Foreman fight took place on April 19, in Atlantic City, N.J. Holyfield was 28 years old and trim at 208 pounds, while Foreman was an aging warrior, bulky at 257 pounds. Surprisingly, the fight went the full 12 rounds. There were no knockdowns, and Foreman won respect, if not the title.

Previously, on March 18, former champion Mike Tyson had scored a disputed knockout of Donovan ("Razor") Ruddock of Canada. In a rematch June 28 in Las Vegas, Tyson knocked Ruddock down twice, broke his jaw, almost closed his left eye, left his face bloody, and won a unanimous decision.

The next fight set up in the heavyweight sequence was a Holyfield-Tyson match November 8 in Las Vegas. However, after promoters said Tyson had suffered an injury in training, the bout was postponed. Holyfield signed for a November 23 defense against former European champion Francesco Damiani in Atlanta, but Damiani withdrew at the last minute and Cooper, a journeyman with a 26-7 record, was signed. Holyfield knocked Cooper down in the first round and stopped him in the seventh, but Cooper almost pulled off a stunning upset, nailing Holyfield in the third for a mandatory eight count.

*Despite predictions that he was too old, too slow, and too fat to have a chance against Evander Holyfield, George Foreman (right) took everything the heavyweight champ dished out and gave him the fight of his life before losing a 12-round decision in Atlantic City on April 19.*

Meanwhile, Tyson's personal trouble continued when the owner of the Miss Black America Pageant accused the fighter of having molested ten of the pageant's contestants. These charges were subsequently dropped, but Tyson still faced trial on separate charges that he had raped an 18-year old contestant in the pageant.

Sugar Ray Leonard, 34, came out of retirement, lost, and retired again; February 9, in New York City, 23-year-old Terry Norris knocked him down twice and won a unanimous decision to retain his World Boxing Council superwelterweight title. On June 3 in Las Vegas, Thomas Hearns won a unanimous decision over Virgil Hill and took Hill's World Boxing Association light-heavyweight title. And lightweight champion Pernell Whitaker outpointed the undefeated Policarpo Diaz of Spain and Jorge Paez of Mexico.

The Pan American Games, held in August in Havana, saw the Cubans win 11 of the 12 boxing gold medals.      F.L.

## CYCLING

Spaniard Miguel Indurain won the 1991 Tour de France, giving Spain its fourth victory in cycling's prestige event. Gianni Bugno of Italy came in second, followed by Claudio Chiappucci, also of Italy. The event, which began on July 6 in Lyon and ended on July 28 in Paris, produced the first Asian stage-winner, Djamolidine Abdujaparov from Tashkent. He won two stages and the green jersey for being the fastest sprinter. Italy won five stages, as did the Soviet Union and France.

In the World Cup series, 5 of the 13 rounds fell to Belgians, with 3 going to Eric van Lancker, but the overall series was won by an Italian, Maurizio Fondriest. Italy also won three of the Classics. Chiappucci took the Milan to San Remo; Bugno came in first in the San Sebastian Classic; and Moreno Argentin scored his fourth Liège-to-Bastogne-and-back win in seven years.

Indurain started the Tour of Spain as favorite but lost to an unexpected home rival, Melchor

Mauri. The Tour of Italy also provided a surprise success, in Franco Chioccioli.

Germany picked up six medals at the world cycling championships, where Australians Carey Hall and Stephen Pate were stripped of their gold and bronze medals for using steroids in the professional sprint.  M.P.

## FOOTBALL

In professional football the Washington Redskins dominated the National Football League's 1991 season and overwhelmed the Buffalo Bills in Super Bowl XXVI. In college football, for the second year in a row, two teams shared the number-one rating.

**Professional.** The National Football League endured a troubled year. Injuries struck many starting quarterbacks, and some teams with healthy quarterbacks tried to exercise ball control by running more, a style that took some of the excitement out of the game. Television networks lost millions of dollars in broadcasting NFL games and said that extending the season to 17 weeks in 1990 had been a mistake because they had to sell advertising for 15 more games per season during a recession, when advertisers were already cutting back. The league also faced renewed challenges to its restrictions on players' freedom to move from one team to another. And Lyle Alzado, an NFL defensive lineman for 14 years who had tried to make a comeback in 1990, announced he was suffering from inoperable brain cancer, which he blamed on years of steroid use.

Super Bowl XXVI matched the two NFL teams with the best 1991 season records, the Washington Redskins (14-2) and the Buffalo Bills (13-3). Also in the postseason playoffs were the other four division champions and six wild-card teams.

The National Conference playoffs started with upsets in both wild-card games, as the Atlanta Falcons beat the New Orleans Saints, 27-20, and the Dallas Cowboys defeated the Chicago Bears, 17-13. The Redskins then whipped Atlanta, 24-7, and the Detroit Lions routed Dallas, 38-6. In the conference final, the Redskins crushed Detroit, 41-10.

In the American Conference wild-card games, the Kansas City Chiefs beat the Los

*After Miami beat Nebraska in the Orange Bowl (right), and Billy Joe Hobert helped steer Washington to a trouncing of Michigan in the Rose Bowl (below), the two undefeated college teams shared the top ranking in the polls.*

### The Rocketeer

When Raghib "Rocket" Ismail spurned the National Football League—where he would have been the number one draft pick—and signed with the Toronto Argonauts of the Canadian Football League in April, it was the biggest deal ever made by a pro football rookie. Ismail, then 21, was guaranteed US$14 million over four years; with bonuses and endorsement deals, he could vault into the $25 million range.

A football superstar at his Wilkes-Barre, Pa., high school, Ismail went on to play for Notre Dame, where coach Lou Holtz, using him as a running back and wide receiver, was as impressed by Ismail's personality as by his amazing speed and blistering kick returns. Hopes were high in Canada that Ismail would revive the sagging fortunes of the Canadian Football League. His first season paid off for the Argonauts, as he led them to their first Grey Cup in eight years.

*Raghib Ismail*

Angeles Raiders, 10-6, by intercepting Todd Marinovich, the Raiders' rookie quarterback, four times. The Houston Oilers eliminated the New York Jets, 17-10. In round two, the Denver Broncos eked out a 26-24 victory over Houston and the Bills overran Kansas City, 37-14. The Bills edged Denver, 10-7, in the conference championship. It was the Bills' second consecutive trip to the Super Bowl.

Super Bowl XXVI, which was played indoors at the Minneapolis Metrodome, got off to a slow start; an apparent Washington touchdown pass was called back, and the first quarter ended 0-0. In the second quarter of the game, however, the Redskins, powered by their big offensive line nicknamed the Hogs, pulled ahead, 17-0. They scored again at the beginning of the second half, putting them ahead 24-0 before the Bills made their first points. The Washington defense intercepted Bills' quarterback Jim Kelly four times and had five sacks; Buffalo running back Thurman Thomas was held to only 13 yards in 10 carries. Washington quarterback Mark Rypien was named the game's Most Valuable Player.

The issue of free agency again made news in 1991. In 1989 a federal appeals court had ruled that the NFL was exempt from antitrust suits brought by players who wished to be free agents. In January 1991 the U.S. Supreme Court refused to hear the case, in effect upholding the earlier ruling. But in May a U.S. district court judge in Minneapolis ruled that there was no exemption because there was no existing collective bargaining agreement. That ruling cleared the way for a trial to begin in his court in early 1992 on an antitrust suit previously filed by Freeman McNeil of the Jets and six other players. Meanwhile, the league proposed an eight-year collective bargaining agreement that would include two-tier free agency. At year's end, the lawyers for the players were studying the proposal.

The Pro Football Hall of Fame added Texas ("Tex") Schramm, Earl Campbell, John Hannah, Jan Stenerud, and Stan Jones. The Toronto Argonauts beat the Calgary Stampeders, 32-21, to win the Canadian Football League's Grey Cup, with help from newly signed American star Raghib "Rocket" Ismail.

The NFL's grand experiment with a subsidiary springtime league, the World League of American Football, impressed its 26 sponsoring teams enough in its first season to keep going for another year. Every NFL team except Chicago and Phoenix invested $500,000 to start the ten-team league, which included six U.S. teams, one Canadian, and three European. The players were mostly NFL rejects. In its ten-week season from March to May the league gained attention with innovative rules, run-and-shoot offenses, helmet cameras, and dazzling uniforms.

**College.** After the dust had settled on another New Year's Day of college football, the University of Washington Huskies and the University of Miami Hurricanes had both emerged with 12-0 records. Washington finished on top of the final United Press International, *USA Today*/CNN, and *Football News* polls, while Miami garnered number one acclaim in the Associated Press poll and in the New York *Times* computer rankings.

The Huskies used a terrorizing defense, led by All-America tackle Steve Emtman, to stop the Michigan Wolverines in a convincing 34-14 Rose Bowl victory in Pasadena, Calif., on January 1, 1992. In Miami the hometown Hurricanes cruised past Nebraska, 22-0, in the first Orange Bowl shutout since 1963. The Nittany Lions of Penn State crushed the Tennessee Volunteers, 42-17, in the Fiesta Bowl to finish the season at 11-2 and number three in the polls. The Florida State Seminoles, the preseason favorite to win the national championship, finished a unanimous number four after topping Texas A&M in the Cotton Bowl, 10-2. And Alabama's Crimson Tide finished number five in most polls. The most exciting contest on New Year's Day 1992 took place in Atlanta at the Peach Bowl, where East Carolina erased North Carolina State's 34-17 second-half lead on its way to a 37-34 victory, capping an 11-1 Cinderella season.

The University of Michigan's Desmond Howard, a 5'9" receiver/kick returner, captured the 1991 Heisman trophy with the highest percentage of first-place votes (85 percent) since the award was first presented in 1935. Florida State's quarterback Casey Weldon finished second, and Brigham Young's Ty Detmer, the 1990 Heisman winner, placed third. Washington's Emtman made off with both the Outland Trophy, given to the best interior lineman, and the Lombardi Award, presented to the top lineman or linebacker. Emtman also was fourth in the Heisman voting, the highest finish for a defensive player since Pittsburgh's Hugh Green in 1980.

The Big East made its debut as a football conference with eight members—Miami (Fla.), Syracuse, West Virginia, Pittsburgh, Virginia Tech, Boston College, Rutgers, and Temple. South Carolina and Arkansas headed to the Southeastern Conference, Florida State to the Atlantic Coast Conference, Akron to the Mid-American Conference, and Fresno State to the Western Athletic Conference.

F.L. & M.M.

## GOLF

In September 1991, golfers from both the U.S. and European Professional Golfers' Association (PGA) tours competed for the biennial Ryder Cup. In the 12th and final match on the final day of competition, Hale Irwin of the United States defeated Bernhard Langer of Germany when Langer's 6-foot par putt slid by the lip of the cup, and the United States won, 14½-13½.

John Daly, a 25-year-old Tour rookie from Dardanelle, Ark., won the PGA Championship

*John Daly, in his first year as a touring pro, came almost out of nowhere to electrify golf fans with his fearless booming drives off the tee and win the PGA Championship by a margin of three shots.*

## It's a Broomstick! It's a Shovel!

On March 4, during the sudden-death playoff at the Doral-Ryder Open in Miami, Rocco Mediate stepped up to his ball on the first green and with one stroke started a controversy in the gentlemanly world of golf. The 28-year-old braced his left hand against his breastbone, clutched his 4'2" putter halfway down the shank, and coolly stroked the ball into the cup, taking the tournament (his first) and $252,000.

Breastbone? That's right. For the first time, a regular player won a Professional Golfers' Association (PGA) tour event while using the long-shafted putter.

Armed with high-tech drivers and wound balata balls, professional golfers have become such prodigious swingers that it is not unusual for them to reach 500-yard greens in two. But all too often the Superman then becomes afflicted with the "yips"—the dreaded waffling of a tense golfer's hands that causes an apparently easy putt to end up veering like a Frisbee. Hence, the long-shafted putter. It allows the player to rest one hand against the chest for stability; the club swings like a pendulum, and wrist and hand movement is minimal.

Many claim the newfangled club is illegal. But the rules are ambiguous, and the United States Golf Association, which regulates tournament play, has not taken a position. Meanwhile, a certain golfer who, while not the best player around, carries a lot of clout—George Bush—continues to knock home his putts with a Pole-Kat extralong.

and $230,000 with stunning ease, shooting a 12-under-par 276 for a three-shot margin over veteran Bruce Lietzke. At the Masters, held at the Augusta (Ga.) National Golf Club, Ian Woosnam of Wales won a three-way battle that came down to the 72nd hole, for $243,000 and his first major championship. The U.S. Open turned into a duel early in the fourth round between Payne Stewart, 34-year-old winner of the 1989 PGA Championship, and Scott Simpson, the 1987 Open champion. Simpson gained a two-shot lead but lost it on the final three holes; Stewart shot a 3-over 75 and defeated him by two shots.

Australian Ian Baker-Finch won the British Open at Royal Birkdale in Southport, England, with spectacular golf in the final round. Other stars included Steve Elkington of Australia, winner of the Players Championship; Tom Purtzer, the champion of the World Series of Golf; and Craig Stadler, who took the Tour Championship. Corey Pavin won the most money ($979,430), two tournaments, and the PGA Player of the Year Award.

Both the Open and the PGA suffered electrical storms in which a spectator was killed by lightning.

In his second year on the Senior tour, Jack Nicklaus, 51, won the PGA Seniors Championship and the U.S. Senior Open. Mike Hill, 52, won five tournaments, shared a sixth victory with Lee Trevino, and led in money earnings with $1,065,657. Chi Chi Rodriguez, 56, won four tournaments; he lost the Senior Open in an 18-hole playoff to Nicklaus.

The Ladies Professional Golf Association continued to lag third in attendance and prize money behind the PGA and Senior PGA tours. Pat Bradley, 40, now fully recovered from Graves' disease, became the 12th member of the Hall of Fame by winning her 30th tournament, and she led the tour in money earnings with $763,118. Meg Mallon, 28, won the Mazda LPGA Championship and the U.S. Women's Open. Amy Alcott won the Nabisco Dinah Shore Invitational. The other major, the du Maurier Classic, was captured by Nancy Scranton.                                    I.M.

### GYMNASTICS

When 15-year-old Kim Zmeskal of Houston won the women's all-around gold medal at the 1991 World Championships, she became the first American gymnast—woman or man—to capture any all-around medal in a world championships meet. The Soviet Union swept the other major honors.

The championships, held September 7-15 in Indianapolis, attracted 516 athletes from 52 nations. South Africa was allowed to compete for the first time in 25 years, and Germany competed under one flag. The Soviet men won their fourth consecutive team title, and Grigory Misutin gave them their eighth consecutive men's all-around title. The Soviet women took their fifth team title in six years.

The 4'7", 80-pound Zmeskal, who had been coached by Bela Karolyi (coach of Nadia Comaneci and Mary Lou Retton) since she was six years old, defeated 18-year-old defending champion Svetlana Bogunskaya of the Soviet Union.

In the men's team championship, the Soviet Union defeated China by more than seven points, a huge margin. En route to his victory in the all-around, the 20-year-old Misutin scored 9.9 in the floor exercise, 9.9 on the horizontal bar, and 9.85 on the parallel bars. With Vitaly Scherbo taking the silver and Valery Liukin the bronze, the Soviets swept the all-around medals.

In the U.S. championships, held in Cincinnati in June, Zmeskal won the all-around title for the second consecutive year. She finished second to 16-year-old Betty Okino in the McDonald's American Cup February 23-24 in Orlando, Fla. The men's winners were Chris Waller, a University of California at Los Angeles senior, in the national championships and Trent Dimas, a University of New Mexico sophomore, in the American Cup. F.L.

## HARNESS RACING

Peace Corps, a five-year-old mare, became the first female in 15 years to win the Elitlopp, held in May at the Solvalla racetrack in Stockholm. Meanwhile, harness racing's most prestigious event, the Hambletonian, was won in August by Giant Victory. In order to accommodate television, the conditions of the 66th Hambletonian were changed. There were now two elimination heats worth $119,000 each; the top five horses in each elimination heat then competed in the $1 million final heat to determine the winner.

In other trotting events, Crown's Invitation took the Yonkers Trot in July. A filly, Whiteland Janice, was the winner of the Kentucky Futurity in October.

In pacing, Precious Bunny took the North America Cup, the Meadowlands Pace, and the Art Rooney Memorial in June and July. Silky Stallone won the Cane Pace, while the Messenger was won by Die Laughing. Precious Bunny came back to take the Little Brown Jug in September and Windy City Pace two months later, setting a world record for earnings in a single year of $2,205,406.

In November, Nihilator, the richest pacer of all time, with earnings of $3,255,653, had to be destroyed because of laminitis, and Mack Lobell, the great trotter who earned a career total of $4,044,856, was retired from racing. W.L.

## HORSE RACING

In 1991 there were some major changes in U.S. horse racing, notably the launching of the American Championship Racing Series. Hansel and Strike the Gold were among the year's big stars.

**Early Races.** The top two-year-old of 1990, Fly So Free, rolled through Florida, winning the Hutcheson Stakes, the Fountain of Youth, and the Florida Derby. In California a new star named Dinard won three of his first four races

*The Breeders' Cup Classic, the world's richest horse race, was won in November at Churchill Downs in Louisville, Ky., by a horse from Ireland. Black Tie Affair, with jockey Jerry Bailey aboard, earned $1,560,000 for his owner, Jeffrey S. Sullivan, as he upset an all-star cast to win the event by a margin of 1 1/4 lengths.*

and then defeated Best Pal by a half-length in the Santa Anita Derby, but he had to be left out of the Kentucky Derby because of a pulled ligament in his left foreleg.

Cahill Road won the Wood Memorial Invitational impressively, but he was injured in the race and subsequently retired. Hansel got off to a good start, taking the Jim Beam and the Lexington Stakes. Meanwhile, Strike the Gold, with only one win from six lifetime starts, defeated Fly So Free by three lengths in the Blue Grass.

**Triple Crown Events.** It was Strike the Gold, the bettors' third choice, who won the Kentucky Derby, coming in 1¾ lengths in front of Best Pal. Mane Minister, an 87-1 shot, finished third. At the 116th Preakness, however, Strike the Gold finished sixth, running a disheartening race, as Hansel rolled to a seven-length victory over Corporate Report. (Once again, Mane Minister ran third.) Hansel covered the 1³⁄₁₆ miles in 1:54, which was only ⅗ of a second off Tank's Prospect's 1985 Preakness record.

Strike the Gold and Hansel put up a wonderful race in the Belmont Stakes. Hansel finished with a stirring head victory over Strike the Gold, also earning a $1 million bonus for best overall record in the Triple Crown. However, he subsequently lost the Travers by a neck to Corporate Report and, in the process, suffered a torn tendon sheath in his left front ankle, causing his retirement. Soon afterward,

Corporate Report was injured in a workout, and he, too, was retired.

Dance Smartly, a three-year-old filly, became the first female to win Canada's Triple Crown. Her bonus was $1 million.

**Older Horses.** In February the American Championship Racing Series was established for older horses, with all ten of its races valued between $500,000 and $1 million. Three horses—four-year-old Farma Way, five-year-old Festin, and four-year-old Marquetry—won two races each.

**Breeders' Cup.** On November 2, racing's $10 million day, the most brilliant winner was the two-year-old Arazi, who won the $1 million Juvenile by five lengths, the largest margin in the eight runnings of the Juvenile. Miss Alleged won the $2 million Turf. Dance Smartly, Canada's Triple Crown winner, took the $1 million Distaff, pushing her lifetime earnings to a female world record of $3,083,445. The $3 million Classic, the sport's richest race, was won by five-year-old Black Tie Affair.

**European Racing.** The three-year-old Generous won the Epsom Derby by five lengths, the Irish Derby by three, and the King George VI and Queen Elizabeth Stakes by seven, but finished eighth in the Prix de l'Arc de Triomphe at Longchamp. French Derby hero Suave Dancer won the Arc by two lengths over Magic Night and Pistolet Bleu. Arazi took first place in the Grand Criterium.

**Star on Ice**
A solidly built 5'10" 200-pounder with an uncannily quick and accurate shot, 27-year-old Brett Hull, son of hockey legend Bobby Hull, is a hockey star in his own right. A finesse player, he has a style of his own, with a knack for snaring a pass and sneaking through an opening. In 1989 he signed a four-year contract with the St. Louis Blues. In 1990-1991, playing right wing for the Blues, Hull racked up 86 goals—the third-highest season total for a player at any position. As a result, Hull was awarded the Hart Trophy as the most valuable player in the National Hockey League.

*Brett Hull*

**Milestones.** Laz Barrera, 66, a four-time Eclipse Award winner as the leading U.S. trainer, died in Downey, Calif., on April 25. Bill Shoemaker, who retired early in 1990 as the world's top-winning jockey (8,833 victories), was paralyzed in an April auto accident but was able to return to his job as a trainer in the fall. Pat Day established a record for the most stakes winners ridden in a year (58).

W.L.

## ICE HOCKEY

The Pittsburgh Penguins emerged as the champions of the National Hockey League in 1991 by claiming the first Stanley Cup in the 24-year history of the franchise.

The Penguins routed the upstart Minnesota North Stars, 8-0, on May 25 to clinch the best-of-seven final series for NHL superiority, four games to two. The Penguins had roared to a 3-0 lead in the first period and then coasted to victory behind superstar Mario Lemieux and goalie Tom Barrasso.

Lemieux, who missed more than half of the regular season because of a back problem, earned the Conn Smythe Trophy as most valuable player in the postseason. He amassed 16 goals and 28 assists in the playoffs. The Penguins' Mark Recchi had 10 goals and 24 assists in 24 playoff contests, while Kevin Stevens had 17 goals and 16 assists, and Barrasso posted a sparkling 2.60 goals-against average for 20 playoff games.

Sadly, the Penguins' coach, Bob Johnson, the first American to coach a cup champion since before World War II, fell ill in August; he died on November 26, at the age of 60.

Minnesota's story was strictly out of Cinderella. The North Stars had entered the Stanley Cup playoffs with 68 points during the regular season, the next-to-worst record of any of the 16 participating teams. Yet in the playoffs they defeated the Chicago Blackhawks, the odds-on favorites to win the cup, as well as the Edmonton Oilers, who had won five of the last seven Stanley Cups.

The Blackhawks earned the President's Trophy for the best regular-season record, with 106 points. Wayne Gretzky of the Los Angeles Kings wound up with 41 goals and 122 assists for 163 points and the NHL scoring title. Brett Hull of the St. Louis Blues exploded for 86 goals, which, along with 45 assists, gave him 131 points and the runner-up position. Hull was voted the Hart Trophy as the most valuable player in the NHL. Ray Bourque of the Boston Bruins won the Norris Trophy as best defenseman; Chicago's Ed Belfour garnered the Calder Trophy as best rookie and the Vezina Trophy as best goalkeeper. Gretzky received the Lady Byng Award for combining skill with gentlemanly play.

---

### NATIONAL HOCKEY LEAGUE
1990–1991 Regular Season

#### PRINCE OF WALES CONFERENCE

| Patrick Division | W | L | T | Pts. |
|---|---|---|---|---|
| Pittsburgh Penguins | 41 | 33 | 6 | 88 |
| New York Rangers | 36 | 31 | 13 | 85 |
| Washington Capitals | 37 | 36 | 7 | 81 |
| New Jersey Devils | 32 | 33 | 15 | 79 |
| Philadelphia Flyers | 33 | 37 | 10 | 76 |
| New York Islanders | 25 | 45 | 10 | 60 |

| Adams Division | | | | |
|---|---|---|---|---|
| Boston Bruins | 44 | 24 | 12 | 100 |
| Montréal Canadiens | 39 | 30 | 11 | 89 |
| Buffalo Sabres | 31 | 30 | 19 | 81 |
| Hartford Whalers | 31 | 38 | 11 | 73 |
| Québec Nordiques | 16 | 50 | 14 | 46 |

#### CAMPBELL CONFERENCE

| Norris Division | W | L | T | Pts. |
|---|---|---|---|---|
| Chicago Blackhawks | 49 | 23 | 8 | 106 |
| St. Louis Blues | 47 | 22 | 11 | 105 |
| Detroit Red Wings | 34 | 38 | 8 | 76 |
| Minnesota North Stars | 27 | 39 | 14 | 68 |
| Toronto Maple Leafs | 23 | 46 | 11 | 57 |

| Smythe Division | | | | |
|---|---|---|---|---|
| Los Angeles Kings | 46 | 24 | 10 | 102 |
| Calgary Flames | 46 | 26 | 8 | 100 |
| Edmonton Oilers | 37 | 37 | 6 | 80 |
| Vancouver Canucks | 28 | 43 | 9 | 65 |
| Winnipeg Jets | 26 | 43 | 11 | 63 |

#### STANLEY CUP PLAYOFFS

**Division Semifinals**
Pittsburgh defeated New Jersey, 4 games to 3
Edmonton defeated Calgary, 4 games to 3
Boston defeated Hartford, 4 games to 2
Washington defeated N.Y. Rangers, 4 games to 2
St. Louis defeated Detroit, 4 games to 3
Los Angeles defeated Vancouver, 4 games to 2
Montreal defeated Buffalo, 4 games to 2
Minnesota defeated Chicago, 4 games to 2

**Division Finals**
Pittsburgh defeated Washington, 4 games to 1
Edmonton defeated Los Angeles, 4 games to 2
Boston defeated Montreal, 4 games to 3
Minnesota defeated St. Louis, 4 games to 2

**Conference Finals**
Pittsburgh defeated Boston, 4 games to 2
Minnesota defeated Edmonton, 4 games to 1

**Championship Finals**
Pittsburgh defeated Minnesota, 4 games to 2

The 1991-1992 season marked the advent of a 22nd franchise, the San Jose (Calif.) Sharks.

Team Canada defeated the United States, two games to none, in the best-of-three final for the Canada Cup in September.　　　B.V.

## ICE SKATING

The International Skating Union eliminated competition in compulsory figures effective in 1991. In the first world championships without them, held March 12-16 in Munich, the United States won five medals, the Soviet Union four, Canada two, and France one. In men's skating, 24-year-old Kurt Browning, from Edmonton, Alta., outpointed Soviet Viktor Petrenko with six clean triple jumps, to win his third gold medal. U.S. champion Todd Eldredge won the bronze. In the women's competition, 19-year-old Californian Kristi Yamaguchi won the gold medal, her first, while her compatriots Tonya Harding and

*Kristi Yamaguchi placed first in the women's world figure skating championships, as her team from the United States swept the medals; it was the first time a single country had ever taken all three top spots.*

Nancy Kerrigan took the silver and bronze, in a U.S. sweep of the women's medals. Japanese skater Midori Ito, the 1989 champion, collided with another skater during warmups and was injured; she continued to skate but finished fourth overall.

Supple Natalya Mishkuteniok and partner Artur Dmitriev won the pairs title, the seventh straight for Soviet skaters. Isabelle Brasseur and Lloyd Eisler of Canada gained the silver medal; Californians Natasha Kuchiki and Todd Sand took the bronze. In ice dancing, French-Canadian brother and sister Isabelle and Paul Duchesnay, who represent France, won the gold. Soviets Marina Klimova and Sergei Ponomarenko took the silver, while the bronze medal went to Soviets Maia Usova and Aleksandr Zhulin.

In the U.S. championships held February 10-17 in Minneapolis, the winners were Eldredge in men's singles, Harding in women's singles, Kuchiki and Sand in pairs, and Elizabeth Punsalan and Jerod Swallow in dancing. Harding became the first American woman to land a triple axel in competition.

The four major world speed skating championships were all held in February in Northern Europe. The 22-year-old Norwegian Johann Olav Koss won the men's overall and set world records for 5,000 meters and 10,000 m. Germany's Gunda Kleeman captured the women's overall title. In the men's sprint competition, the Soviet Union's Igor Zhelezovsky won both 1,000-m races and Germany's Uwe-Jens Mey both 500-m races. Germany's Monique Garbrecht won the women's sprints, after Angela Hauck of Germany, the defending champion, fell and was injured during warmups. The World Cup circuit, which ran from November 1990 to March 1991, was dominated by Mey, Zhelezovsky, Koss, Garbrecht, Kleeman, Heike Warnicke of Germany, and Kyoko Shimazaki of Japan.　　　F.L.

## SKIING

In 1991, most of the ski world received snow. Indeed, February's Pre-Olympic Downhill in Val-d'Isère, France—a tuneup for the 1992 Winter Olympics—had to be canceled because the snow never stopped falling.

Austrian-born Marc Girardelli, who competes under the Luxembourg flag, had missed

*Petra Kronberger of Austria, seen here attacking the slope at the World Alpine Championships, so dominated women's skiing that she had the Alpine World Cup wrapped up with the season barely a month old.*

most of the 1990 Alpine World Cup season with an injury but managed to win the men's overall 1991 World Cup crown despite a balky knee that required surgery just days after the season ended. Girardelli's closest competitor was Alberto Tomba of Italy, who recaptured the form that had earned him two Olympic medals in 1988. Tomba was the men's giant slalom champion in 1991; Girardelli was the men's slalom champion. The top men's downhiller was Franz Heinzer of Switzerland.

Petra Kronberger of Austria compiled 312 World Cup points in winning the overall crown for the women's World Cup; her fellow Austrian Sabine Ginther was second, with 195. Other titles included Vreni Schneider (Switzerland), giant slalom; Carole Merle (France), super giant slalom; and Chantal Bournissen (Switzerland), downhill.

In the World Cup Finals at Waterville Valley, N.H., 19-year-old Julie Parisien of Auburn, Me., took the women's giant slalom; it was the first Alpine World Cup victory for an American since 1987. At the World Alpine Championships in Saalbach/Hinterglemm, Austria, the host Austrians won gold medals in five of the ten events; the top Austrian was Stefan Eberharter, who captured the men's super giant slalom and combined.

The Nordic World Cup was dominated by the Soviet Union. The men's cross-country overall title was taken by Vladimir Smirnov and the women's by Elena Vialbe, with the

men's and women's biathlon taken by Sergei Chepikov and Svetlana Davidova, respectively; all four were Soviets. The jumping title was won by Andi Felder of Austria, and the Nordic combined by Norway's Fred Boerre Lundberg.

The World Nordic Championships marked a swan song for the perpetual Swedish champion Gunde Svan, who won the men's 30-kilometer classic race and took home silver medals in the 15-km and 50-km freestyle races. The other top racer was Elena Vialbe, who garnered gold medals in the women's 10-km freestyle and 15-km classic.                                  E.P.

### SOCCER

In June 1991, Portugal won the under-20 World Cup with a victory over Brazil in the penalty kick tiebreaker, after the two teams had played a 0-0 overtime tie. The penalty kick shoot-out, and in particular its use to decide world championships, came under increasing fire. In August, Ghana took the under-17 World Cup, which was staged in Italy, by beating Spain, 1-0, in the final.

The first world championship for women, staged in China in November, was won by the United States with a 2-1 victory over Norway in the final game. The 1991 Toyota Cup, to decide the world's top club team, was won by Red Star of Yugoslavia, which beat Chile's Colo Colo, 3-0.

Qualifying games continued worldwide for the 15 berths (plus host nation Spain) in the

*The first women's soccer world championship was contested in a tournament in China in November; the winner, surprisingly, was the team from the United States, which was led by forward Carin Jennings (foreground).*

1992, concluded with France, England, Scotland, the Netherlands, Germany, the Soviet Union, and Yugoslavia qualifying to join the host nation in the final round. Which players would actually represent the former Soviet Union and Yugoslavia remained unclear because of the breakup of those countries.

In European club competitions, Red Star-Belgrade took the European Cup with a controversial penalty kick win over Olympique-Marseille. Manchester United celebrated the return of English clubs to European competition by beating Barcelona of Spain, 2-1, to win the Cup Winner's Cup. The UEFA Cup went to Inter-Milan, which beat another Italian club, Roma, by an aggregate score of 2-1. The West German midfielder and captain, Lothar Matthaus of Italy's Inter-Milan club, was voted European Player of the Year.

**North America.** Under its new president, Jack Warner of Trinidad, the Concacaf grouping (taking in countries in North and Central America and the Caribbean) held a championship for the region's national teams. Named the Gold Cup, it was staged in Los Angeles and won by the United States. The growing strength of the United States owed much to the appointment of Bora Milutinovic as national team coach.

1992 Olympics in Barcelona. Under new eligibility regulations, the tournament was limited to players—both amateurs and pros—under the age of 23.

The saddest story of the year was the fate of the Argentine superstar Diego Maradona. After testing positive for cocaine following an Italian league game, Maradona fled back to Buenos Aires, declaring that he was finished with soccer. A few days later he was slapped with a 15-month suspension. Less than a month later, Maradona was arrested for cocaine possession and agreed to enter a drug rehabilitation program. His suspension from Italian soccer was turned into a worldwide ban.

**South America.** The Copa America—the South American championship for national teams—was won by Argentina under its new coach Alfio Basile. The reigning champion, Brazil, finished an unimpressive second. Raul Amarilla, goal-scoring midfielder for Olimpia of Paraguay, was voted the 1990 South American Player of the Year.

**Europe.** Elimination games for the European Championship, to be played in Sweden in

The American Professional Soccer League shrank to only eight clubs with the collapse of the Salt Lake Sting halfway through the 1991 season. The San Francisco Bay Blackhawks took the APSL title. The San Diego Sockers beat the Cleveland Crunch to take their fourth straight championship in the (indoor) Major Soccer League, which shrank to seven teams for 1991-1992 with the folding of the Kansas City Comets.

In U.S. college soccer, the University of Virginia took the men's 1991 NCAA Division I final title with a penalty kick win over Santa Clara University. North Carolina-Chapel Hill made it six in a row by taking the women's NCAA Division I title. P.G.

### SWIMMING

According to a statement by a group of former East German coaches in December 1991, East Germany's domination of women's swimming since 1973 was achieved through the systematic use of anabolic steroids. In 1991 the combined German men's and women's team achieved less than the East Germans alone had done, and the United States dominated the sport, winning 24 of the 32 gold medals at the Pan American Games in Havana and 25 of 34 at the Pan Pacific meet in Alberta, Canada. At the latter games, Australian Kieren Perkins won the three longest freestyle races for men, breaking a world record in the 1,500-meter.

At the quadrennial World Championships, held January 7-13 in Perth, Australia, the leading medal winners were the United States with 23 and Germany with 20. Six world records were broken in men's events (none in women's), by Tamas Darnyi of Hungary in both individual medleys, Norbert Rozsa of Hungary in the 100-m breaststroke, Mike Barrowman of Potomac, Md., in the 200-m breaststroke, Melvin Stewart of Fort Mill, S.C., in the 200-m butterfly, and Jörg Hoffmann of Germany in the 1,500-m freestyle. In August, Rozsa and Barrowman bettered their records.

Among the leading women, Hayley Lewis of Australia took one gold and two silver; she lost the women's 400-meter individual medley to Lin Li of China by a hundredth of a second. Janet Evans of Placentia, Calif., won three medals, including gold in the women's 400-meter and 800-meter freestyles. Nicole Haislett of St. Petersburg, Fla., won three gold medals, two in relays. Krisztina Egerszegi of Hungary won both women's backstroke titles.
**European Championships.** In the biennial European Championships in Athens (August 17-25), the Soviet Union won 6 of the 16 races for men. In the 16 women's races, the Soviet Union, Hungary, and Denmark won 3 each. Egerszegi won three titles—two with world backstroke records—for 100 m. Egerszegi's records were the only ones all year in the 17 events for women. Martin Zubero of Spain won both backstroke titles for men.

At the U.S. Open swimming championships, held in Minneapolis from November 29 to December 1, Glen Housman of Australia set a U.S. Open record in the 1,500-meter freestyle. Australians won 14 golds all told; the United States won 15.          F.L.

## TENNIS

While the youngest pros continued to startle with performances beyond their years, the year's highlight was supplied by Jimmy Connors, at 39 the game's oldest player. He defied all odds with a series of comebacks against men half his age to reach the U.S. Open semifinals for the 14th time.

**Men's Tour.** Germany's Boris Becker reached the No. 1 spot after beating Ivan Lendl at the Australian Open, but his stay lasted only one month; Stefan Edberg took over until midsummer knee tendinitis affected his play. By the end of the year the serve-and-volley Swede had recovered, capturing his first U.S. Open and solidifying his top spot. He and resurgent Frenchman Guy Forget each won six titles, the most among the men.

Five-time Wimbledon champ Bjorn Borg attempted a comeback in Monte Carlo, but the

*At 39, Jimmy Connors appeared to have discovered the fountain of youth; he whipped players half his age and exhilarated the crowd as he advanced to the semifinals of the U.S. Open for the 14th time in his long career.*

The winner in the men's singles at Wimbledon was the unheralded German player Michael Stich, winner of only one previous professional tournament, who beat Stefan Edberg and then upset his countryman Boris Becker in the final.

media frenzy far surpassed the caliber of his play as he lost in the first round. The true Cinderella story among the men, perhaps, was the rise of the feisty Floridian Jim Courier, whose gritty style reminded many of his hero, Connors. Courier's ferocious forehand brought him three titles and No. 2 ranking. Possibly, however, the Cinderella title belonged to German Michael Stich, who came out of nowhere to beat Edberg and Becker back-to-back for the Wimbledon crown.

The withdrawal of Lendl from the French Open because of a hand injury opened the way for American bashers Courier and Andre Agassi, and for the original boomer, Becker, who played his way into the semis with an impressive quarterfinal dismissal of 1989 champ Michael Chang. Courier fought past Edberg and Stich to gain the final against Agassi, whom he came from behind to defeat.

The 1990 U.S. Open champ, Pete Sampras, defeated Courier in the final ATP Tour World Championship in Frankfurt, Germany, confirming his selection as Courier's replacement on the Davis Cup team. He ended the year with four titles.

**Women's Tour.** Monica Seles (*see profile in* PEOPLE IN THE NEWS) knocked Steffi Graf from the top rung of the women's game in March, and then dominated the second half of the year, reaching a remarkable 16 out of 16 finals. Seles won ten titles—among them the Australian, French, and U.S. Opens—but garnered the most headlines with her mysterious eleventh-hour withdrawal from Wimbledon, which brought her a hefty fine.

Graf ended a long drought without a Grand Slam title by winning her third Wimbledon championship in a thrilling three-set final over Gabriela Sabatini. Martina Navratilova, after undergoing surgery on both knees in late 1990, returned to the tour in February and went on to win four titles.

America's new sweetheart, Jennifer Capriati, started the year in a sophomore slump, but at Wimbledon she upset nine-time champ Navratilova en route to the semifinals. In late summer the 15-year-old became the youngest pro to win back-to-back events, with titles at San Diego—where she upset Seles in a furious three-set match—and Toronto (over the injured Sabatini).

**Wimbledon.** Edberg and Becker failed to meet in the Wimbledon final, for the first time in three years, as the wiry Stich upset Edberg in the semi. Stich seemed certain to fall to three-time champion Becker in the final, but he proved to be a nerveless competitor, knocking Becker off in straight sets. Steffi Graf reclaimed her Wimbledon crown in a tightly fought battle with Sabatini. Capriati pulled the upset of the event by defeating Navratilova in the quarters, 6-4, 7-5.

**U.S. Open.** Jimmy Connors gave new meaning to the word comeback, returning from two sets and three-love down to Patrick McEnroe in the opening round of the U.S. Open. Subsequently, defying age and physical condition, he went the distance against Aaron Krickstein, for a five-set win. In the semis Connors finally fell to Courier, who was then badly beaten by Edberg in the finals. On the women's side, Seles survived a scare in the semis against Capriati, and went on to win her first U.S. crown, 7-6, 6-1, over Navratilova.

**Davis Cup.** Aided especially by their No. 1 player Guy Forget, France won the Davis Cup after a 59-year drought, defeating the defending champion U.S. team, 3-1, in the final in Lyon, France, at the end of November.

D.K.D.

### TRACK AND FIELD

The 1991 track and field season was spectacular. In the world outdoor championships, held August 23 through September 1 in Tokyo, Mike Powell, a 27-year-old American, broke Bob Beamon's hallowed world record by clearing 29 feet, 4½ inches in the men's long jump, snapping Carl Lewis's record of 65 consecutive victories in that event. Earlier in the year, in the USA/Mobil championships, the 30-year-old Lewis lost his world record for the 100-meter dash to teammate Leroy Burrell, but he regained it in the world championships, edging out Burrell in the final to win in a record 9.86 seconds.

Sergei Bubka, the Ukrainian champion with textbook technique, broke the world pole vault record four times indoors and four times outdoors while becoming the first person to clear 20 feet. His world records total of 28 was bettered only by the late Paavo Nurmi of Finland.

In the 24 men's events of the world championships, the United States won 9 gold medals, 4 silver, and 7 bronze. Next were the Soviet Union (3-4-3), Kenya (4-3-0), Great Britain (1-0-4), and the united German team (1-0-3). In the 19 women's events, the leaders were the Soviet Union (6-5-7), Germany (4-4-4), the United States (1-4-1), and China (2-1-1).

U.S. men's sprinters won four gold medals—in the 100-meter dash (Lewis), the 200 (Michael Johnson), the 400 (Antonio Pettigrew), and the 400-m relay. U.S. jumpers won the men's long jump (Powell), the women's long jump (Jackie Joyner-Kersee with 24 feet, ¼ inch), the men's high jump (Charles Austin with 7 feet, 9¾ inches), and the men's triple jump (Kenny Harrison with 58 feet, 4 inches). In the five men's races from 800 to 10,000 m, Kenyans triumphed, with four gold and three silver medals. Billy Konchellah finished first in the 800, Moses Kiptanui first in the 3,000-m steeplechase, Yobes Ondieki first in the 5,000, and Moses Tanui first in the 10,000. Huang Zhihong of China won the women's shot put with 68 feet, 4¼ inches. Algerians won the 1,500-m titles—Noureddine Morceli among the men and Hassiba Boulmerka among the women. Katrin Krabbe of Germany won the women's 100 and 200 m.

*Mike Powell broke what was probably the most awesome record in sports when he topped Bob Beamon's 23-year-old long jump record with a leap of 29 feet, 4½ inches at the world outdoor championships in Tokyo.*

At the world indoor championships held on March 8-10 in Seville, Spain, the medal leaders were the Soviet Union with 18 (8 gold, 6 silver, and 4 bronze), Germany with 9, and the United States with 7.

Wanda Panfil of Poland won the women's marathon world championship and the Boston Marathon. Hiromi Taniguchi of Japan was a surprise winner of the men's championship; Kenya's Ibrahim Hussein was the men's winner in Boston. In New York, Scotland's Liz McColgan breezed to an easy victory; on the men's side, Mexican athletes, led by winner Salvador García, finished first, second, and fifth. F.L.

### YACHTING

Paul Cayard sailed the Italian yacht *Il Moro de Venezia* to a decisive victory over New Zealand's *NZL-12* in the final race of the International America's Cup World Championships off San Diego in May, making Italy's Campagnia Della Vela syndicate the early favorite to win the America's Cup in 1992.

France's 31-year-old Christophe Auguin, sailing the high-tech, 60-foot cutter *Groupe Sceta*, won the single-handed, round-the-world 1990-1991 BOC Challenge in 120 days, 22 hours, 36 minutes, 35 seconds (nearly 14 days faster than the previous record). Another French team earned a surprise victory in the biennial Admiral's Cup series early in August in European waters.

Alex Smigelski won the U.S. senior sailing championship for the Mallory Cup, in a series sailed from the Cleveland Yachting Club. Betsy Alison captured the Adams Cup for the U.S. women's sailing championship, in a series sailed from the Corinthian Yacht Club on San Francisco Bay. Brigham North took the U.S. single-handed championship for the O'Day Trophy, in a series sailed at Lake Geneva, Wis. Dennis Conner won the Etchells 22 world championship on San Francisco Bay, and former Rolex Yachtsman of the Year Larry Klein won the Soling World Championship at Rochester, N.Y. D.M.P.

*The Italian yacht* Il Moro de Venezia *won the International America's Cup World Championships in May, becoming the early favorite to win the America's Cup in 1992.*

**SRI LANKA.** During 1991 fighting continued between Sri Lankan government forces and Tamil rebels based in the north and east of the nation. The government carried out extensive bombing strikes aimed at the rebel Liberation Tigers of Tamil Eelam (LTTE), but inaccuracy led to an extremely high civilian death toll.

On the ground, military death squads were active primarily in the Eastern Province, where the government was able to maintain control over the principal towns. The LTTE responded with attacks on villages near the border between the Northern and Eastern provinces, which usually resulted in wholesale massacres of civilians, generally members of the majority Sinhalese ethnic group.

On March 2 a bomb set off in Colombo, the capital city, killed Minister of National Security Ranjan Wijeratne and 31 others. On June 21, 23 people died in a bombing at the military's command headquarters in Colombo. A month earlier, a woman identified as an LTTE suicide bomber activated an explosive device as she presented a bouquet of flowers to former Indian Prime Minister Rajiv Gandhi at an election rally in the southern Indian state of Tamil Nadu. The assassination led to the arrest of thousands of LTTE sympathizers in India.

In the Tamil heartland of the Northern Province, government control was limited to a handful of military bases located at strategic sites, and the LTTE initiated major attacks against several of them. On March 19 an unsuccessful attack on camps in the Mannar district resulted in the deaths of nearly 400 LTTE fighters.

The largest battle of the war began on July 10, when the LTTE launched a massive assault against the government fort at Elephant Pass on the Jaffna Peninsula. The 800 soldiers guarding the causeway from the mainland were besieged by an LTTE force of several thousand. On July 14 a relief force of 8,000 government troops made an amphibious landing, then spent nearly three weeks fighting its way to relieve the beleaguered soldiers. In the end the army was able to hold the fort, but nearly 200 soldiers died, along with an estimated 1,500 to 2,000 rebels.

In late August a group of dissidents within President Ranasinghe Premadasa's United National Party submitted an impeachment petition to the speaker of the Parliament. The petition charged Premadasa with various offenses, including abuse of power in allowing the army's death squads to kill thousands of young people. Later, many petition signers withdrew their support of the document, claiming that their names had been placed on it under false pretenses, and the speaker refused to accept the impeachment resolution. The dissidents were ultimately expelled from the ruling party, thus losing their seats in Parliament.

*See* STATISTICS OF THE WORLD. R.C.O.

**STAMPS, POSTAGE.** Increases in U.S. postal rates went into effect on February 3, 1991, requiring more than the usual number of new stamps. Coinciding as it did with Postal Service efforts to procure more stamps from private printers, rather than from the U.S. Treasury Department's Bureau of Engraving and Printing, this event resulted in a series of embarrassments.

**Problems and Controversies.** Among other problems that arose, the first printing of the 29-cent William Saroyan commemorative, a joint issue with the Soviet Union, had to be destroyed because the stamps could not be properly perforated. On some 29-cent wood duck stamps, ink flaked off when soaked in water. The marginal inscription on sheets of the 52-cent Hubert H. Humphrey stamp gave incorrect dates for his years as U.S. vice president. Meanwhile, the 29-cent Black Heritage stamp honoring Jan E. Matzeliger, inventor of the shoe-lasting machine, offended many blacks by the use of his first name in a marginal inscription, instead of a surname. The Postal Service also came under fire because the 35-cent Dennis Chavez stamp, honoring the U.S. senator from New Mexico who died in 1962, had been contracted to a printer in Canada, the first time U.S. stamps had ever been printed in a foreign country.

**Other U.S. Issues.** The year began with nondenominated F flower stamps for the rate increase and a plastic F stamp for automatic teller machines, plus a nondenominated stamp designated to add 4 cents to the 25-cent stamps then in circulation, to meet the new 29-cent letter rate. Flower stamps were issued later in the year with a 29-cent denomination.

The 50th anniversary of World War II was commemorated on a souvenir sheet featuring ten stamps and a world map depicting events of 1940 and 1941. Another stamp honored those who served in Operation Desert Shield and Operation Desert Storm, the campaigns to evict Iraq from Kuwait. Ten different stamps saluted the Olympic Games, and the annual America stamp commemorated the arrival of the first Americans, who crossed the Bering Strait land bridge from Asia at least 13,000 years ago. Stamps issued in booklet form included a five-stamp set of famous comedians drawn by caricaturist Al Hirschfeld and a ten-stamp set celebrating U.S. space exploration missions. New postal cards depicted Niagara Falls, a Yankee Clipper ship, and Carnegie Hall and commemorated the bicentennial of the ratification of the Bill of Rights.

**Around the World.** In late 1990 and in 1991, Latvia, Lithuania, and Estonia issued their first stamps. Stamps from Yugoslavia's breakaway republics of Croatia and Slovenia also appeared, but it was unclear whether they had been sanctioned by governing authorities. Denmark signaled the end of the cold war by revealing that in 1963 it had secretly prepared and distributed emergency stamps, and kept them ready to retain normal postal service in Denmark in the event of war. One million of the stamps were placed on sale to collectors on Stamp Day, March 14, 1991.

*Opposite page: some of the more noteworthy stamps issued in 1991. Top left: portion of a souvenir sheet depicting war-related events around the world 50 years earlier. First row (at right): the Marshall Islands recalls the German invasion of the Soviet Union in World War II. Second row: a Micronesia stamp on the theme of world peace. Third row: U.S. tribute to troops serving in the Persian Gulf conflict; a Danish stamp, unveiled after the cold war, meant for use in past decades in case of war emergency. Fourth row: fishing flies from a U.S. booklet; depiction of Sweden's Drottningholm Palace; the People's Republic of China observes the 30th anniversary of ratification of the Antarctic Treaty. Bottom left: commemorative for American inventor Jan Matzeliger, with controversial marginal inscription using his first name. Fifth row (at right): a Sierra Leone stamp features a native African butterfly; the United Nations salutes children's rights. Bottom row: wrongly captioned Hubert Humphrey commemorative; Dennis Chavez stamp, a U.S. issue that was printed in Canada; stamp issued by independent Lithuania.*

Despite a continuing slump in the stamp market, a world record price for a philatelic item was set at a March 23 auction in Lugano, Switzerland. The British Penny Black—the first postage stamp—postmarked May 2, 1840 (its first known use), on a "turned" (reused) Mulready stamped envelope, was sold for approximately $2.4 million to a Japanese businessman.                                                     K.L.

**STATE GOVERNMENT REVIEW.** The bottom dropped out of the economy for more than 30 U.S. states in 1991, leaving them facing wide deficits in the spring. The rising public discontent with government, heightened by well-publicized scandals, was reflected in election results in many states.

**Finance.** New or higher personal and corporate income taxes passed in some 35 states were expected to yield an estimated $10 billion in revenues, with another $5 billion coming from expanded sales and use taxes. Connecticut adopted a personal income tax, pushed through by new Governor Lowell Weicker, who had vetoed legislative attempts to expand the sales tax to remedy the state's estimated $2.3 billion shortfall. The income tax provoked widespread and heated opposition, and in a special legislative session late in the year lawmakers voted to repeal it. They were, however, unable to overcome Weicker's quick veto.

Connecticut was among a handful of states that could not pass a budget in time to begin its fiscal year. Not until mid-July did California settle on spending cuts and tax increases to tackle its massive $14 billion budget shortfall. Pennsylvania also missed its budget deadline, before hammering out a plan for some $3 billion in new taxes and budget cuts, including layoffs of state workers. State workers took the brunt of many states' budget woes. A few state governments briefly shut down to save money, while roughly half the states took such steps as leaving positions vacant and furloughing or laying off workers.

**Public Discontent.** The popularity of New Jersey Governor Jim Florio (D) continued to plunge, the year after he pushed through some $2.8 billion in higher taxes to pay for a new school finance plan and close a budget deficit. While Florio was not on the ballot, all 120

After Governor Lowell P. Weicker of Connecticut succeeded in implementing a state income tax, a crowd of more than 40,000 demonstrators gathered in Hartford, the capital, and angrily demanded its repeal. The turnout marked one of the largest protests in the state's history.

state legislative seats were up for election in November, and voters gave the Republicans control of both houses.

In Maryland, Governor William Donald Schaefer (D) faced protests by angry state employees who had lost their jobs and by others who saw their government programs cut. Reductions in welfare aid, programs for the arts, and higher education budgets resulted in marches on statehouses elsewhere. Meanwhile, California Governor Pete Wilson (R) touched off protests by gay rights activists when he vetoed a bill to outlaw job discrimination against homosexuals.

A clear sign of citizen discontent was the growing movement to restrict the number of years officials can serve. A ballot measure was initiated by California citizens in November 1990 to limit the terms of state officeholders. When it was upheld by the California Supreme Court in October, legislators appealed. A measure on the November 1991 ballot in Washington state would have applied to members of Congress as well, but it was rejected by voters.

Seven sitting legislators were indicted in Arizona in February in a local police sting involving the buying of votes for legalized casino gambling legislation. Six of the seven eventually resigned, and the seventh was expelled. In South Carolina, an FBI investigation resulted in indictments of nearly 30 legislators, other officials, and lobbyists on vote-selling or drug charges; almost all were convicted or pleaded guilty. Meanwhile, in Alaska, Governor Walter J. Hickel, who faced a recall campaign, was charged by an independent counsel with violating the state's ethics law.

**New Governors.** In Arizona, Republican Fife Symington settled the undecided November 1990 gubernatorial election by winning a runoff on February 26. In Vermont, Democratic Lieutenant Governor Howard Dean became governor following the death of GOP Governor Richard Snelling on August 14. The elections on November 5 saw Mississippi's incumbent Democratic governor, Ray Mabus, unseated by political neophyte Kirk Fordice (R), while Kentucky voters chose Lieutenant Governor Brereton C. Jones (D) for the statehouse. In a mid-November runoff, a controversial gubernatorial race in Louisiana was decided by the victory of former Governor Edwin Edwards, a Democrat, over Republican State Representative David Duke, a former neo-Nazi and grand wizard of the Ku Klux Klan.

**Abortion.** Demonstrations at three Wichita, Kan., abortion clinics, mounted in the summer by the anti-abortion group Operation Rescue, highlighted the bitter conflict in states across the nation between "pro-life" and "pro-choice" forces. In legislative action, Utah passed a tough abortion law banning the procedure except in cases of rape, incest, immediate danger to the woman, or a threat of serious congenital defects. The Louisiana legislature overrode a gubernatorial veto of its strict abortion law, but the measure was then struck down as unconstitutional by a federal district court judge; the state appealed the decision. In Mississippi the legislature overrode Governor Mabus's veto of a bill requiring a 24-hour waiting period before a woman could obtain an abortion. In Pennsylvania such a waiting period was upheld in a federal appeals court ruling, though a provision requiring spousal notification was struck down. Meanwhile, crackdowns on abortion were vetoed by governors in Idaho and North Dakota, and Washington State voters narrowly approved a ballot measure designed to keep abortion legal if the U.S. Supreme Court should overturn its 1973 ruling in *Roe* v. *Wade*.

**Health.** For reasons of economy, Massachusetts postponed implementation of a universal healthcare plan scheduled to take effect in January 1992. Meanwhile, Medicaid, which is jointly financed by the federal government and the states, was a source of concern for many states. Oregon agreed on a plan to set priorities for spending its Medicaid funds. Under the plan, which required a federal waiver of the standard priorities, basic healthcare would be guaranteed to all the state's poor citizens, but the state would withhold coverage for procedures ranked lowest on its priority list.

Many states were angry over a proposal by the Bush administration to end federal pay-

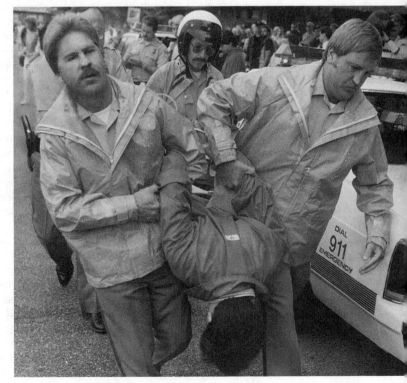

Police haul a demonstrator away from a Wichita, Kan., abortion clinic in August. Over 2,000 protesters were arrested as the anti-abortion group Operation Rescue tried to block access to three Wichita abortion clinics as part of what it called its "Summer of Mercy" campaign.

ments of some $3 billion to $5 billion for the coverage. The revision in federal rules, handed down in September, was aimed at forcing states to supply their share of Medicaid funding via broad-based taxes. In November the White House and governors agreed on a compromise, which was largely implemented in legislation passed by Congress soon thereafter. The new measure limited, but did not bar, states' use of taxes on hospitals and other healthcare providers to raise their share of Medicaid funds.

**Education.** Texas finally passed a school finance plan that met a state court mandate to equalize school spending between rich and poor districts by May 1990; court challenges were filed against the plan. Oklahoma voters approved higher taxes to pay for improved teachers' salaries and smaller classes. The Illinois General Assembly rescued a plan to reform Chicago schools through local school councils in place of entrenched bureaucracies. To meet a court's objections to the plan, Illinois allowed all community residents, not just parents, to vote for the six parents and two community representatives on each council.

Tennessee joined the long list of states having to come to grips with school equity suits, when a chancery court held the state's school funding system unconstitutional. The Tennessee legislature failed to finalize action on education and tax reform proposed by Governor Ned McWherter (D) and even reduced school funding to curb the state budget.        E.S.K.

**STOCK MARKETS.** Despite concerns about slow economic growth, a majority of the world's stock markets chalked up healthy gains during 1991.

**United States.** After a 1990 year-end rally that lasted into early 1991, the Dow Jones industrial average plunged 39 points to close at 2,470 on January 9, as U.S.-Iraqi talks aimed at averting war collapsed. But stock prices exploded after the first bombshells hit Baghdad. On January 17, the Dow advanced almost 115 points, or 4.6 percent, with investors convinced that the allies would win an easy victory in the Persian Gulf War. Oil prices dropped, easing inflationary pressures and thereby allowing long-term interest rates to fall. The Federal Reserve also cut its discount

rate on February 1. On February 15 the Standard & Poor's 500-stock index, a broader measure of blue-chip stocks, reached its first new high for the year.

The gains after February were generally less impressive. From March through September the Dow worked its way higher, but fluctuated narrowly between 2,855 and 3,055. The recession was hard on corporate profits, which kept stocks from making further gains. On the other hand, the easing of interest rates put a floor under stock prices.

The closing months of 1991 showed a more complex picture. From mid-October to mid-November the Dow rose 698 points. But the gains were viewed as fragile because of the continued weak economy, and on November 15 the Dow fell 120.31 points for its greatest one-day loss in two years. The loss was prompted in part by a proposed cap on credit-card interest rates. Although the market steadied itself somewhat, it was weakened by consumer pessimism and hit 2,863, its lowest point since summer, on December 10. Ten days later, however, the Fed cut its discount rate to 3.5 percent—the lowest since 1964—spurring a strong end-of-the-year surge.

The Dow ended 1991 at 3,168.83, a gain of 20 percent for the year, which also saw the S&P 500 climb 26 percent. Small stocks performed brilliantly; the Nasdaq Composite, a key index of over-the-counter stocks, gained nearly 57 percent in 1991, making it the best year in the index's history.

As investors showed robust appetites for stocks, corporations and investment bankers rushed to sell equity to the public. Companies that had "gone private" reemerged as public companies with new stock issues, and many new enterpreneurial outfits went public by selling shares.

Merger-making was generally subdued. The biggest corporate linkups were financed through stock swaps, not cash or junk bonds. Among the year's big mergers was American Telephone & Telegraph's acquisition of the computer maker NCR Corporation.

**Around the World.** High interest rates prevented the Japanese stock market from making major gains in 1991. By mid-October the Nikkei was near 24,000—about the point at which it had started the year. After dropping further, the market showed signs of recovery near year's end.

Battlefield successes and lower interest rates helped the British market surge in the early part of the year and grind out smaller gains later on. The British Financial Times-Stock Exchange 100 index climbed 16.3 percent for the year. The Bundesbank, Germany's central bank, kept interest rates high to dampen inflation and attract the massive amounts of capital needed to rebuild East Germany. As a result, German stock market gains were modest—about 13 percent for 1991.

Markets in Argentina, Brazil, Chile, and Mexico all showed strong gains.            J.M.L.

**SUDAN.** In 1991 famine continued to convulse the Sudan. The International Committee of the Red Cross estimated that one-third of Sudan's people were threatened with starvation, and the United Nations claimed that 1.2 million tons of food would be needed from foreign donors. During January and February, Sudan's Islamic government, in an attempt to starve the separatist Sudanese People's Liberation Army (SPLA) into submission, continued to block food deliveries to rebel-held areas in the south. Meanwhile, as part of its effort to defeat the SPLA, the government bombed civilian targets in the southern Sudan.

Despite proclamations of self-sufficiency, the developing famine forced the government in March to allow relief supplies to enter both the northern and southern sectors of the country. A month later, the United States lifted an embargo, paving the way for more than 1 million tons of food rations to be transported into Sudan.

Sudan supported Iraq in the Persian Gulf War. As a result, Saudi Arabia cut off all oil supplies to Sudan, and banks in Saudi Arabia and Kuwait (after its liberation) severed financial support for Sudan's Muslim Brotherhood, the fundamentalist organization that dominates the Sudanese government. Soon after the war began, the U.S. embassy in Sudan was evacuated, and the British government warned all its citizens to leave the country. As the year ended, Sudan was taking an increasing role in the expansion of Islamic fundamentalism in the Middle East.

Hundreds of thousands of Sudanese refugees who had fled to Ethiopia to escape the civil war poured back into the Sudan throughout the spring, amid fierce fighting that climaxed with the overthrow of the Ethiopian government in May. At the same time, some 200,000 Ethiopian refugees fled into the Sudan. In the midst of the refugee crisis, floods caused by torrential rains left thousands homeless in the southeastern region of the country. Sudan was allocated a portion of the $22 million authorized by the United States to meet the needs of more than 2 million refugees throughout the Horn of Africa.

See STATISTICS OF THE WORLD.            P.J.S.

**SUPREME COURT OF THE UNITED STATES.** See UNITED STATES OF AMERICA: *Supreme Court.*

**SURINAME.** See STATISTICS OF THE WORLD. See also CARIBBEAN BASIN.

**SWAZILAND.** See STATISTICS OF THE WORLD.

**SWEDEN.** In 1991, Sweden faced its severest economic recession since World War II—one apparent reason why the governing Social Democrats lost power after September parliamentary elections.

**Troubled Economy.** For a long time, cooperation between government, labor, and industry in Sweden had been able to temper the ups and downs of the business cycle. With the advent of the 1990s, however, the country was experiencing high inflation, increased unemployment, and decreased international competitiveness. By tightly controlling the money supply, the government was able to cut inflation sharply. Unemployment, however, presented a more intractable problem. Because unemployment for a long time had averaged less than 2 percent, the increase to over 3 percent in 1991—though still untroublesome by international standards—was traumatic for Sweden. Influenced by its new economic problems, Sweden had decided to seek membership in the European Community (EC) and submitted its application for entrance in July.

**Elections and the New Parliament.** Through earlier negotiation with the other parties, the Social Democrats succeeded in defusing as campaign issues the topics of tax reform, an interparty energy agreement, and application for membership in the EC. The economic situ-

Carl Bildt, head of the Moderate Party and known for his fondness for commuting by bicycle, became Sweden's new prime minister when, after September elections, he put together a coalition that toppled the long-dominant Social Democrats. Here he is seen pedaling away from the polling place after casting his vote.

ation remained a major issue, along with such topics as use of national pension funds and spending on education.

In the September 15 elections, the Social Democrats received the support of only 38 percent of the voters, down from 43 percent in 1988, and so qualified for only 138 seats in the Riksdag (Parliament), as against 156 in 1988. The Moderate Party drew increased voter support; it attracted 22 percent of the vote and received 80 seats. Its two main partners, the Liberal Party (9 percent and 33 seats) and the Center (formerly Agrarian) Party (8.5 percent and 31 seats), lost some popularity but combined with the Moderates to form a government. Also included in the government was a fourth party, the Christian Democrats, who had won 7 percent of the vote to qualify for Parliament for the first time, with 26 seats.

The four governing parties combined had only 170 seats, more than the Social Democrats and Left Party (154), but not enough for a clear majority in the 349-seat Riksdag, which meant they would likely need some support from the New Democracy Party. That party,

formed early in the year by an industrialist and an amusement park owner, was described by some as a right-wing "party of discontent." Its platform emphasized cutting government spending and the bureaucracy, tightening immigration policy, liberalizing drinking laws, and making politics "more fun." It drew considerable support from male voters and received 7 percent of the vote and 25 parliamentary seats.

When Moderate Party leader Carl Bildt became prime minister, his presentation of the new government's policy emphasized four major tasks: entering the EC, overcoming economic stagnation, developing more freedom of choice in social welfare programs, and creating a cleaner environment.

See STATISTICS OF THE WORLD.          R.S.

**SWITZERLAND.** During 1991 the Swiss Confederation celebrated its 700th anniversary. The entire federal council, the national executive body, participated in ceremonies in Bellinzona, Ticino, opening the celebration early in the year. A three-day extravaganza in Zurich in early July culminated in a huge fireworks display, and on July 31 and August 1, the national day, in the city of Schwyz, the official federal celebrations included a banquet hosted by the president of the confederation, Flavio Cotti.

To protest sex discrimination, the Swiss Trade Union Federation organized a national strike of women that drew an estimated 500,000 participants. In other developments, the federal government established a grievance procedure for pay discrimination charges that put the burden of proof on the employer. Parliament made marital rape a criminal offense. The federal tribunal ruled against Appenzell Inner Rhodes in its effort to remain the last canton to exclude women from its legislature. And in Berne, the city council ruled that neither sex could form more than 60 percent of its membership.

In early June voters approved a law permitting conscientious objectors to substitute work for military service.

In the parliamentary elections of October 20, the four parties forming the government coalition maintained their large majority. Big gainers were three right-wing protest groups, the Auto Party, the Swiss Democrats, and the Lega dei Ticinesi; these all opposed a government effort to reduce smog by imposing speed limits of 100 kilometers (60 miles) per hour for cars and 70 kilometers (45 miles) per hour for trucks. The right-wing parties also had campaigned for restrictions on the growing influx of foreigners.

See STATISTICS OF THE WORLD.        C.S.

**SYRIA.** In the aftermath of the Persian Gulf War, Syria, during 1991, took part in the Middle East peace negotiations and helped the Lebanese government consolidate its control over most of Lebanon.

**Persian Gulf War.** Syria participated in the U.S.-led coalition to drive Iraq from Kuwait. However, President Hafez al-Assad was unwilling to use his forces in the invasion of Iraq, agreeing only to deploy them in the defense of Saudi Arabia. Even this degree of support was unpopular within Syria. On January 12, Assad publicly appealed to "brother" Saddam Hussein to withdraw Iraqi forces from Kuwait; Saddam Hussein rejected the appeal and urged Syrians to overthrow Assad.

When Iraq attacked Israel with Scud missiles on January 18, Syria said it would not desert the alliance even if Israel counterattacked. This posture paved the way for improved relations with the United States and moderate Arab states. On March 6, Syria, Egypt, and the six states of the Gulf Cooperation Council (Saudi Arabia, Bahrain, Oman, Kuwait, Qatar, and

*In Appenzell Inner Rhodes, the last Swiss canton to deny women the vote, women were for the first time allowed to take part in the annual open-air assembly, or* Landsgemeinde, *seen here; in this assembly, voters signify their choices on issues before them by raising their hands.*

A treaty of "brotherhood, cooperation, and coordination" was signed by Syrian President Hafez al-Assad (right) and Lebanese President Elias Hrawi in Damascus in May. While the accord strengthened Hrawi's hand as he sought to bring lasting peace to Lebanon, long wracked by civil war, some observers feared that it confirmed Syria's de facto annexation of the country.

the United Arab Emirates) agreed in principle that Syria and Egypt would form the nucleus of an Arab peacekeeping force in the Arabian Peninsula.

**Middle East Peace Process.** Following the expulsion of Iraq from Kuwait, the United States actively engaged Syria in the Arab-Israeli peace process. Syria initially stated that it would attend an international conference only if the United Nations played a central role, but it eventually agreed to attend a conference sponsored by the United States and Soviet Union and, with other Arab states, to take a "unified Arab stand throughout all phases of the conference." At the peace conference's opening ceremonies in Madrid, Farouk al-Sharaa, Syria's foreign minister, delivered an uncompromising speech, demanding that "every inch" of Arab land occupied by Israel be returned to its "legitimate owners." Syria and Israel then held one session of direct, bilateral talks in Madrid on November 3; the bilateral talks reconvened in December in Washington, D.C., and recessed after ten days, with no discernible progress having been made.

**Lebanon.** Syria's role in the Gulf War earned it a freer hand in Lebanon, where it consoli-

dated its influence. President Assad and President Elias Hrawi of Lebanon signed a far-reaching cooperation agreement on May 22, to coordinate their defense, internal security, economic policy, and foreign affairs. A second accord, signed on September 1, authorized the parties to suppress any activities within their respective borders that would threaten the security of the other country. It also allowed each nation's security forces to arrest "criminals" in the other country.

Syria also used its military power to back the Hrawi government's efforts to pacify Lebanon. In February, Lebanese Army units pressed south to Tyre, deploying in areas that had been controlled by the Palestine Liberation Organization (PLO) and two Shiite militias. When President Hrawi ordered all militias to surrender their weapons to the Lebanese Army, Syria supported the call but later permitted the Iranian-backed Hezbollah militia and the Iranian Revolutionary Guards to keep their weapons. In July the Lebanese government took control of the Sidon area, a major PLO stronghold. Israel maintained its presence in southern Lebanon, and Syria vowed not to pull out until Israel did.

As the dominant military power in Lebanon, Syria played an important role in the release of Western hostages during the year, a factor in improving relations with the United States.

**Relations With the PLO.** In November the Syrian government agreed to let the Palestine Liberation Organization reopen its offices in Damascus, ending eight years of conflict between the two parties.

**Domestic Affairs.** As a reward for its support for Saudi Arabia and Kuwait in the Persian Gulf War, Syria received some $2 billion in Arab aid. The temporary increase in oil prices during the Gulf crisis and a substantial boost in Syria's oil output also helped the economy. A new investment law was passed in May to promote the private sector and encourage foreign investment. Controls over foreign currency exchange procedures were relaxed, and sweeping tax reforms were enacted.

In an uncontested election in December, President Assad was reelected to a fourth seven-year term.

*See* STATISTICS OF THE WORLD. A.D.

# T

**TAIWAN.** In April 1991, President Lee Teng-hui declared an end to the Period of Mobilization begun in 1949 as a response to the Communist takeover of China. The National Assembly rescinded the Temporary Provisions that had granted emergency presidential powers for 40 years, during a special April session. However, amid outbreaks of pandemonium (fisticuffs included) in the National Assembly, members of the opposition Democratic Progressive Party charged that the Nationalists' package of new constitutional amendments did not go far enough. They walked out and organized a 15-hour protest march through Taipei, returning only after the Nationalists gave assurances on moves to limit presidential control.

In May the Legislative Yuan repealed a controversial 1949 antisedition law that had been used to quash political opposition. In Decem-

*In Taiwan's National Assembly the anger of opposition delegates frustrated by the slow pace of reform sporadically escalated into violence. Here, members restrain a colleague who is trying to strike the assembly's speaker.*

ber, Taiwan held its first full election in over four decades. Voters elected 327 new members to the National Assembly as replacements for the "life seats" that had been allocated for mainland constituencies in 1949. The Nationalists won 71 percent of the vote and 254 seats in the legislature. Only about 22 percent of those elected in December were originally from the mainland.

Early in the year, the Nationalist Party's Central Standing Committee endorsed a national reunification program in an attempt to clarify Taiwan's policy toward China. The Beijing government lauded the decision but condemned Taipei's call for recognition as an independent government and rejected a demand that it reform its Communist system as a precondition for any dialogue on reunification.

In April, President Lee acknowledged the existence of a Communist government in China, in effect ending Taiwan's formal state of war against the Beijing government. Taiwan also sent a 14-member delegation from the government-linked Strait Exchange Foundation to meet with officials in Beijing, and China ended its loudspeaker war aimed at the Taiwan-controlled islands of Quemoy and Matsu. Taiwan later ended its policy of rewarding defectors from the mainland. Meanwhile, Taipei drew criticism for increasing its indirect trade and investment in China despite Beijing's human rights record.

See STATISTICS OF THE WORLD.          J.F.C.

**TANZANIA.** Tanzania in 1991 saw heightened debate over the system of one-party rule. While the ruling party, Chama Cha Mapinduzi (CCM), was regarded as having more legitimacy in the public eye than most other ruling parties in Africa, it faced daring opposition, particularly from lawyers and other professionals. In February the party's National Executive Committee, despite vigorous opposition by old guard socialists, permitted party members to engage in commercial activities. In May the committee decided that CCM labor and cooperative organizations should become fully independent.

A presidential commission, composed mostly of CCM members, began to take public testimony on political reform at the end of April. However, only a CCM congress could

make changes in the constitution. In February multiparty advocates formed a "steering committee," which later called on President Ali Hassan Mwinyi to replace the government with a transitional one aimed at creating a multiparty democracy.

Because of a sharply reduced grain harvest caused by a severe dry season and transport difficulties, a slightly lower growth rate was expected in 1991. In June the government was forced to import grain from Uganda. The country's severe trade deficit continued. At the multinational interagency Consultative Group meeting held in Paris under sponsorship of the International Monetary Fund and the World Bank in June, donor agencies pledged $980 million for Tanzania.

The minimum wage was raised 40 percent on July 1, still far below the cost of living for unskilled workers. In June prices of nine consumer goods, including beer, were decontrolled. A new banking act enabled private banks to compete with the state, beginning in 1993. Parliament also approved a Cooperative Societies Act, reducing the power of the Tanzanian government to intervene in the affairs of cooperatives.

In early January and again in late June, lack of rain in some parts of the country, and flooding in others, led to severe food shortages for large numbers of Tanzanians. Cholera spread to new areas of the country, demonstrating how drastically the economic crisis had reversed the impressive strides Tanzania had made in healthcare in the past 25 years. Approximately 400,000 people were estimated to be carrying the HIV virus, with 2,000 AIDS deaths recorded since 1983.

See STATISTICS OF THE WORLD.          N.K.

**TECHNOLOGY.** See COMPUTERS; ELECTRONICS; LIFE SCIENCES; SPACE EXPLORATION.

**TELEVISION AND RADIO BROADCASTING.** See BROADCASTING.

**TENNESSEE.** See STATISTICS OF THE WORLD.

**TEXAS.** See STATISTICS OF THE WORLD.

**THAILAND.** Prime Minister Chatichai Choonhavan was arrested on February 23, 1991, by the air force chief, General Kaset Rojananil, and a small group of soldiers. Supreme Army Commander General Sunthorn Kongsompong then appeared on television, flanked by the military chiefs, to declare martial law. The constitution was abolished, Parliament dissolved, the cabinet dismissed, and press censorship imposed.

The stated purpose of the bloodless coup was to end corruption in the Chatichai administration; other possible reasons included the recent appointment of the coup leaders' rival to a top post and the military's anger at the erosion of its traditional strength.

On March 2 a leading businessman and ex-career diplomat, Anand Panyarachun, was appointed prime minister, and he announced a cabinet composed largely of respected technocrats and businessmen. This helped to restore confidence, especially among foreign investors. A new Legislative Assembly was appointed on March 15, with more than half of the members being retired or active military officers. Martial law was lifted on May 3.

Thailand was active in regional diplomacy, working with China, Vietnam, and its partners in the Association of Southeast Asian Nations to promote Cambodian peace negotiations (a peace treaty was signed on October 23). Thai business and government representatives negotiated mineral and logging rights in Laos and mineral, logging, and extended fishing rights in Cambodia and Vietnam.

The Persian Gulf War, a sluggish world economy, and government-imposed austerity slowed the Thai economy; gross domestic product was expected to grow 8 percent, with inflation held at around 6 percent. Thailand's industrial diversification continued, extending into chemicals, machine tools, spare parts, and many other industries.

The nation's industrial growth remained concentrated in and around Bangkok, with severe strains on natural resources. A growing trade deficit, a languishing rural sector, a congested infrastructure, and a shortage of skilled labor also were major constraints.

In 1991 the United States officially cited Thailand for its failure to protect intellectual property rights. Also, the United States and European nations agreed to end all trade in Thai wildlife and wildlife products, because of Thailand's failure to restrict trafficking in endangered species.

See STATISTICS OF THE WORLD.     G.H.

**THEATER.** In the United States as in Canada and Great Britain, the theater likes to think of itself as a fabulous invalid, perpetually on its deathbed but perpetually arising anew to display its vigor and relevance. With this attitude the American stage community managed to maintain a plucky good cheer throughout 1991, despite financial and creative setbacks.

**Broadway.** The season that ended at midyear had the fewest new productions in history, 28, and attendance declined. Ticket sales totaled $267 million, down (despite inflation) from $283 million the season before but still the second-highest tally ever. About a third of the revenue, however, was owing to the ongoing popularity of three long-running British musical imports: Cats, The Phantom of the Opera, and Les Misérables.

The three hits were joined late in the season by a fourth British import, Miss Saigon, which played to sold-out houses and gave promise of similar staying power. The thrilling and distressing narrative tells of a young Vietnamese woman in the final days of the U.S. presence in Saigon. Forced into prostitution after her family dies in the war, she meets a U.S. soldier who plans to take her back with him, but by mischance she is left behind when the U.S. forces pull out. She is pregnant by her lost lover and endures terrible struggles to help their son.

Among American musicals, the best effort was The Secret Garden, adapted from a beloved 1911 novel for children by Frances Hodgson Burnett about an orphan girl sent back "home" to an unfamiliar England after her unloving parents die in a cholera epidemic in India. She meets a sickly boy cousin and a secretive hunchback uncle; in trying to lift her own sad spirits, she saves them too.

The patriotic favorite was the flashy but shallow The Will Rogers Follies, staged by master director-choreographer Tommy Tune. Part biography of the Oklahoma rope twirler who became the most popular entertainer of the 1930s and part loving recreation of the kind of gaudy revue that Broadway staged in that era, its features included flag waving, a precision kick line, bare breasts and bottoms, a dog act, a lit-up rainbow-colored staircase, opulent dresses, and sweeping fantasy sets.

The Secret Garden, *based on the beloved children's novel, was one of the more successful attempts by American creators of musicals to counter the onslaught of the British megamusicals that have dominated Broadway in recent years. It starred (left to right) Daisy Eagan, Rebecca Luker, and Howard McGillin.*

A third big American musical, *Nick and Nora*, was derived from the popular 1930s *Thin Man* movies. Its adaptors to the stage had award-winning credits, and it was cast with three Tony winners and designed by two more. But audiences disliked both the show's poorly executed murder mystery and writer-director Arthur Laurents's conception of the title characters as a mismatched couple whose marriage was on the rocks. The show quickly flopped.

On a more successful note, Neil Simon (*see profile in* PEOPLE IN THE NEWS) had a hit with his play *Lost in Yonkers*, the story of two boys just entering adolescence who, during a family financial crisis, are sent to live with their fierce grandmother and mentally retarded aunt. *Lost in Yonkers* garnered the Tony for best play, as well as Tonys for Irene Worth as the grandmother, Kevin Spacey as a tough uncle, and Mercedes Ruehl as the mentally shortchanged aunt. Meanwhile, Simon also achieved his dream of winning the Pulitzer Prize for drama.

Also very highly esteemed was Brian Friel's *Dancing at Lughnasa*, an import from Dublin's Abbey Theater via London, where it had won the 1991 Laurence Olivier Award for best play. Peopled by poor and isolated characters, the richly original play had many themes: the close bonds that make family life both possible and unendurable, the persistence of pagan impulses in a Christian world, and the way in which dull days become sweet Eden in memory. Another London prizewinner, *Our Country's Good* by U.S. expatriate Timberlake Wertenbaker, told of the first staging of a play in white Australia during its days as a penal colony. Polemical, preachy, and performed without subtlety, the show managed only a very short run, but it won the New York Drama Critics Circle prize as best foreign play.

*Mule Bone*, a 1930 collaboration between black poet Langston Hughes and short-story write Zora Neale Hurston that had never been produced, proved slight but full of charm and was enlivened in performance with twangy Taj Mahal songs. Paul Rudnick's *I Hate Hamlet* had an amusing premise: A television actor playing Hamlet in Central Park leases an apartment once occupied by the most renowned American interpreter of the role, John Barrymore, and Barrymore's ghost comes back to tutor (and bully) him. However, the show was sunk by the author's inability to sustain the plot and humor and by two disastrous strokes of casting. Evan Handler was cranky, charmless, and inert as the TV actor. As the ghost, Nicol

Williamson seemed more out of control than the legendarily rowdy Barrymore.

**Off Broadway.** Producers of Off Broadway shows shied away from truly challenging texts, but they did offer some splendid and serious entertainment. The best new work by an American writer was *From the Mississippi Delta*, an autobiography by Endesha Ida Mae Holland, who rose from dire poverty and adolescent prostitution to become a university professor. Also much admired were Terrence McNally's *Lips Together, Teeth Apart*, which centered on the enormous social gulf between straights and homosexuals; A. R. Gurney's *The Old Boy*, also about the misunderstandings between straights and gays; cartoonist Linda Barry's *The Good Times Are Killing Me*, a story of a black-white girlhood friendship in the 1960s disrupted by society's racial battles; Tom Dulack's *Breaking Legs*, a broad and bellicose farce about Mafia men investing in a college professor's play; *Beggars in the House of Plenty*, an autobiographical recollection of the unhappy Bronx boyhood of John Patrick Shanley; and *Night Dance*, the briefly seen middle play of a lovely coming-of-age trilogy by novelist Reynolds Price.

The best import, from Edmonton, Alberta, by way of Chicago, was *Unidentified Human Remains and the True Nature of Love*, an MTV-style drama about loveless, aimless, and sexually reckless young people in an era of serial killers and AIDS. Also notable were *Remembrance*, an Irish tale of a doomed Catholic-Protestant romance between elderly people, starring Malachy McCourt and Aideen O'Kelly in superb performances, and *A Room of One's Own*, a two-part monologue derived from Virginia Woolf's landmark feminist essay that brought numerous honors for British star Eileen Atkins.

**Regional Theater.** The biggest trend in regional theater was coproduction, the practice of sharing costs of a large cast or elaborate set among two or more companies, each of whom then offers the show in its schedule. The 1991 Tony Award for a regional company went, aptly, to the Yale Repertory Theater, whose departing artistic director Lloyd Richards pioneered coproduction with the plays of August Wilson, including *Two Trains Running*, which started at Yale in 1990 and moved on to theaters in Boston, Seattle, San Diego, Washington, and Los Angeles on its way to a scheduled

### "Miss Saigon"

A seasoned performer who has been working before audiences since she was five, Lea Salonga, 20, was located by British producer Cameron Mackintosh a few years ago in the Philippines during his global talent search to fill the title role in *Miss Saigon*. He made a good choice. The musical, a story of star-crossed lovers in the final days of the American presence in South Vietnam, opened to rave reviews in London in 1989. Critics particularly admired Salonga's delicate grace, intense acting, and dynamic singing voice, and she won Britain's Laurence Olivier award as best actress in a musical.

A dispute between Mackintosh and the U.S. performers' union nearly caused cancellation of the Broadway production, but when it finally opened in New York in April 1991, audiences again cheered, as did the critics. Ticket sales were booming, and at the Tony ceremonies Salonga won another best actress in a musical award for her show-stopping performance.

*Lea Salonga*

1992 Broadway debut. Harvard's American Repertory Theater and Houston's Alley Theater divided the burden of mounting Robert Wilson's *When We Dead Awaken*. Hartford Stage Company, San Diego's Old Globe Theater, and Boston's Huntington Theater shared costs of A. R. Gurney's *The Snow Ball*. Perhaps the most innovative play was Lee Blessing's *Fortinbras*, which opened the new stage at the La Jolla Playhouse in California. A stew of ideas, about everything from Shakespeare's role in literature to the nature of the afterlife, it was at its sharpest in probing mediagenic politicians.

**Awards and Honors.** The virtual sweep of the Tony Awards by *Lost in Yonkers* was interrupted only by a best actor nod to Nigel Hawthorne for the British play *Shadowlands*, and a directing award to Jerry Zaks for his staging of John Guare's *Six Degrees of Separation*, which also won the New York Drama Critics Circle award for best play. Among musicals, the top Tony went to *The Will Rogers Follies* in what was widely interpreted as a backlash vote against *Miss Saigon* producer Cameron Mackintosh. He drew resentment both for his personal wealth and because he clashed with the performers' union, Actors Equity, over his insistence on retaining *Miss Saigon*'s London leads for the Broadway production. Ironically, the performers Mackintosh wanted, Jonathan Pryce and Lea Salonga, were named best actor and best actress in a musical, and the veteran dancer Hinton Battle added a Tony as best supporting actor for his *Miss Saigon* role. *Will Rogers* took Tony honors for Tommy Tune's direction and choreography, for the score, and for lights and costumes. *The Secret Garden* took the supporting actress award for Daisy

*From the Mississippi Delta, written by Endesha Ida Mae Holland, was hailed by critics as one of the best new plays on the Off Broadway scene; below, cast members Cheryl Lynn Bruce, Sybil Walker, and Jacqueline Williams.*

With the outbreak of the Persian Gulf War, worry about possible terrorist attacks on airliners caused air travel to drop off dramatically and induced airports to step up security.

Eagan, a tiny 11-year-old (in what was actually the leading role), along with awards for Marsha Norman's book and producer Heidi Landesman's set. A crisp *Fiddler on the Roof* was named best revival.

**Deaths.** New York City theater suffered a heavy blow with the death on October 31 of Joseph Papp at age 70. A populist showman and shameless self-promoter, he built his Public Theater into a venue where new playwrights blossomed, and brought classic plays to new audiences with his New York Shakespeare Festival. Another major loss was actress Colleen Dewhurst, who died on August 22 at 67. W.A.H.

**TOGO.** See STATISTICS OF THE WORLD.

**TONGA.** See STATISTICS OF THE WORLD. See also PACIFIC ISLANDS.

**TRANSPORTATION.** See AVIATION; TRAVEL AND TOURISM.

**TRAVEL AND TOURISM.** Domestic and international travel by Americans was dealt a double blow in 1991 by the recession and the Persian Gulf War. In January and February travel came to a near standstill, and it never regained the momentum of 1990.

**Effects of the Gulf War.** The Gulf War, fought from January 17 to February 28, with rumblings going back as far as August 1990, aroused fears of terrorism. In mid-January telephones in travel agencies rang constantly as clients called to cancel plans, especially those involving international air travel. Airports introduced stepped-up security measures, including detailed inspection of luggage and tighter identification procedures, but remained virtually empty during the war. Newspaper travel sections that had touted the charms of Malaysia, Australia, and Hong Kong—not to mention Paris and Rome—were suddenly extolling the virtues of biking on Cape Cod, strolling in Key West, hiking in Colorado.

The Gulf War greatly curtailed Americans' traditional winter migration to the Caribbean. The most popular destinations—like the Bahamas, Bermuda, Puerto Rico, St. Maarten, Jamaica, and Barbados—were hardest hit, with more than a 10 percent drop in tourism from 1990. Club Med properties in Egypt, Tunisia, and Turkey were closed temporarily during the war, and because few Americans would go near the Mediterranean even after the fighting ended, cruise ships relocated from there to the Caribbean, Alaska, and Canada.

Travel to Europe never fully recovered after the war. Great Britain saw tourism drop by an estimated 15 percent for the year. The previous year, 1990, had been the country's second busiest tourism year ever.

**Effects of the Recession.** The recession forced Americans to budget their vacations carefully. They stayed closer to home, took shorter trips, visited relatives and friends instead of staying in hotels, and searched out bargains. People accustomed to staying at topflight hotels continued to do so, but smaller hotels lost business and began discounting prices. Train travel for business and leisure was down, following the record set in 1990; air travel was also down. Airlines tried to lure travel-shy Americans back with prices so low people could hardly afford to stay home: New York to Florida or the Caribbean for $258 round-trip; New York to Paris or London for $350 round-trip.

The eastern seaboard was particularly hard hit. Colonial Williamsburg in Virginia, which draws almost half its visitors from the Northeast and the Mid-Atlantic states, saw a significant decline in tourism. In Orlando, Walt Disney World suffered, although its 20th anniversary, a 15-month celebration that began in October 1991, was expected to attract more visitors in 1992.

**Popular Destinations.** Even in tough times special events lure travelers. The 50th anniversary of Mount Rushmore in South Dakota and the International Gathering of the Clans in Nova Scotia both drew large crowds. Another special event, the 75th anniversary of the San Diego Zoo, attracted many visitors. In general, the West did relatively well; the Grand Canyon, Arizona's top tourist attraction, saw a 10 percent increase in tourism.

Americans visited Washington, D.C., as much as in 1990; the U.S. capital remains a bargain in tough economic times because nearly all its attractions are free. Travelers also ventured north and south of the U.S. border. Canada particularly benefited from the increased number of cruise ships that called there in the spring and summer. Mexico was still a destination where the dollar carried some clout.

Although the rapid pace of change and the lower prices in Eastern European countries piqued travelers' desire to visit them, war and recession, coupled with a still-fledgling tourism infrastructure in the countries themselves, curtailed travel to this part of the world.

As the year drew to a close, few people made advance travel bookings, although Europe tempted with the winter and summer Olympics, Expo 92, and the opening of Euro Disney.                                    A.G.

**TRINIDAD AND TOBAGO.** See STATISTICS OF THE WORLD. See also CARIBBEAN BASIN.

**TUNISIA.** The Persian Gulf War dominated attention in the the early part of 1991 and had a continuing impact on domestic politics. When UN-backed coalition forces began their air campaign against Iraq in January, President Zine-al-Abidine Ben Ali called for Iraqi withdrawal from Kuwait. However, he also proclaimed solidarity with the Iraqi people (as distinguished from the regime of Saddam Hussein), condemned the bombings, and joined with six other Arab states in the United Nations in an effort to end the coalition forces' assault. These positions caused a deterioration in Tunisia's relations with Arab states participating in the coalition, notably Syria, Egypt, and Morocco, as well as with France and the United States.

On the domestic scene, the government found itself under heavy pressure to embrace a position sympathetic to Iraq. Many Tunisians regarded Saddam Hussein favorably for his ability to strike directly at Israel through Scud missile attacks. The coalition forces' bombing elicited waves of revulsion, and large street protests became commonplace. Many demonstrations had official government sanction.

On February 17 the ruling party's headquarters in Tunis were attacked by some 30 masked men, allegedly Islamic extremists. Two security guards were doused with gasoline and set on fire. The incident prompted an immediate reshuffling of the cabinet to strengthen internal security. The government accused the illegal Islamic fundamentalist al-Nahda ("renaissance") Party of having perpetrated the attack. Despite denials by Nahda officials, public opinion shifted against the party. Security forces arrested Nahda members and destroyed Nahda's control of a major university student organization (the Tunisian General Union of Students).

Following the war, Ben Ali gave opposition parties more access to state-owned media resources, but at the same time tried to deliver a deathblow to the Nahda Party through a campaign called Operation Eradication. That campaign triggered severe criticism from Amnesty International and other human rights organizations, which held Tunisian authorities responsible for the death and torture of several political prisoners.

The war damaged the economy, as tourists stayed away. Kuwaiti aid and investment were withheld, and trade with Iraq, Tunisia's largest Arab trading partner, was blocked. After the war, relations with anti-Iraqi Arab states remained tense. Relations with the United States and European countries improved, resulting in new promises of economic aid.

*See* STATISTICS OF THE WORLD. K.J.B.

**TURKEY.** In 1991, Turkey elected a new Parliament dominated by the True Path Party and also faced challenges in the wake of the Persian Gulf War and the cold war.

**Elections.** In June, after winning control of the ruling Motherland Party (MP) at the party's national convention, liberal politician Mesut Yilmaz became prime minister, replaced the religious conservatives in the cabinet with pro-Western liberals, and set early elections for October 20. However, his party fell to second place in the October elections, with 24 percent of the vote and only 115 parliamentary seats, 117 fewer than in the old Parliament. Yilmaz resigned, and Suleyman Demirel again became prime minister, as his moderately conservative, generally pro-Western True Path Party won 27 percent of the vote and 178 seats (a gain of 119) in the 450-seat unicameral Parliament. The Social Democratic Populist Party, which placed third in the October election, agreed to a coalition with Demirel's True Path Party.

**Gulf War.** By shutting off Iraq's oil pipeline through Turkey and by allowing U.S. forces to use Turkish air bases for attacks on Iraqi targets, Turkey played an important role in the Persian Gulf campaign, reaffirming its strategic position in the volatile Middle East and strengthening its ties to the West.

*Plainclothes policemen and soldiers attacked Kurdish demonstrators during a rally in the southeastern Turkish city of Silopi in October. Kurdish separatism remained a thorny problem in Turkey as rebels heightened the level of confrontation and the government stepped up land and air strikes against guerrilla bases.*

Events after the war, however, tarnished Turkey's image. In April over a half-million Iraqi Kurds fleeing Iraqi President Saddam Hussein's vengeance massed along the Turkish-Iraqi border. Fearing the creation of a long-term Kurdish refugee burden, the Turkish government closed the border and restricted the refugees to inhospitable and barely accessible highlands. With little food and no shelter or medical supplies, hundreds of refugees died every day. Under Western pressure, Ankara finally changed its policy, announcing that the refugees would be relocated to camps on hospitable terrain in Turkey and Iraq. Soon the United States, Britain, and France flew in military units and stocks of supplies. They established a security zone for the Kurds in northern Iraq, to which most of the Kurdish refugees returned.

During the Gulf crisis increased oil prices, the loss of exports to Iraq and Kuwait, and the loss of revenue from the Iraqi oil pipeline through Turkey all had negative effects. These were partly offset, however, by foreign aid, especially from Saudi Arabia and Kuwait.

In the summer and fall Turkish military efforts to subdue the insurgent forces of the separatist Kurdish Workers Party (PPK) intensified, with extensive land and air strikes on the rebel bases in northern Iraq. Ankara claimed Saddam Hussein was arming the PPK in retaliation for Turkey's role in the Gulf War. The PPK was thought to be behind the December 25 fire-bombing of an Istanbul department store that killed 11 people.

**International Developments.** President Turgut Ozal visited Washington, D.C., in March and then hosted U.S. President George Bush's visit to Turkey in July. Ozal also visited Russia, Ukraine, Azerbaijan, and Kazakhstan for high-level talks and signed a 20-year treaty of friendship with the Soviet Union. Agreements were also reached with Iran, whose president visited Turkey in April.

*See* STATISTICS OF THE WORLD. P.J.M.

**TUVALU.** *See* STATISTICS OF THE WORLD.

# U

**UGANDA.** In 1991, President Yoweri Museveni's government faced political unrest, as well as border conflicts.

Debate over a proposed new constitution grew heated as opposition parties barred from political activity in 1986 argued for a multiparty system, which Museveni opposed. However, in November, Museveni agreed that the opposition could take part in elections to occur by 1995. A draft constitution was to be completed by June 1992.

Following attacks in northern Uganda in February and March by the Uganda People's Democratic Christian Army, the Ugandan Army launched a major campaign that lasted four months. Thousands of civilians were arrested, including a cabinet minister and two members of Parliament. These and 15 other northern politicians were put on trial in early May. Major rebel leaders surrendered in July and August.

Relations with Rwanda were acrimonious, in the wake of an invasion of Rwanda by Ugandan-based Rwandan rebels in late 1990. Each government claimed its villages had been shelled from across the border. In November 1991, a Ugandan district capital near the border was hit by Rwandan artillery, and ten people were killed. While Museveni repeatedly denied that his government was supplying the Rwandan rebels, Uganda's new ambassador to Rwanda admitted that individuals in Uganda might have aided them.

Border clashes with Kenya and Sudan also occurred. On one occasion, in September, Sudanese Air Force MIGs bombed a northern Ugandan village, killing two people.

Over 1.5 million people, 9 percent of the population, were estimated to be infected with the virus that causes AIDS. By June, 25,000 cases had been reported.

*See* STATISTICS OF THE WORLD. N.K.

# UNION OF SOVIET SOCIALIST REPUBLICS.

The Soviet Union came to an end in 1991. The collapse of the ruling Communist Party, the disintegration of the Soviet Union, and the downfall of its president, Mikhail Gorbachev— along with the rise of Boris Yeltsin, president of the Russian republic—were precipitated by a failed attempt by Communist hard-liners to oust Gorbachev from power in August.

The short-lived coup accelerated trends that had been evident earlier. Reform efforts aimed at introducing elements of a free-market economy had made limited, halting progress under Gorbachev. As central authority dissipated in the latter part of the year, a free-market infrastructure was still in large part lacking, and the economic plight worsened. Long food lines became more common than ever, and the value of the ruble plummeted. By year's end Russia, followed by most of the 14 other republics that had previously made up the Soviet Union, was preparing to undergo a shock therapy program involving rapid economic liberalization.

Meanwhile, even place names associated with the Soviet era were often changed. Most strikingly, Leningrad readopted its old tsarist name of St. Petersburg. Some republics rejected the Russianized versions of their names that the Soviet government had imposed upon them.

**Prelude to the Coup.** The main actors in the August coup were the two presidents—Yeltsin and Gorbachev—and the two opposing political camps: the Communist hard-liners and the democratic reformers.

As president of the Soviet Union, Gorbachev (*see profile in* PEOPLE IN THE NEWS) had struggled to find ways to push through radical political and economic reforms while keeping the country together. But by assuming a mediating, centrist role, he succeeded only in alienating both radical reformers on the left and anxious conservatives on the right, while stoking the rising nationalist passions that threatened to tear the nation apart. From about November 1990 to April 1991, Gorbachev seemed to have thrown in his lot with right-of-center

*The breakup of the Soviet Union saw 11 of its 15 republics form a loosely knit Commonwealth of Independent States; a few altered their names (below, old name is given in italics).*

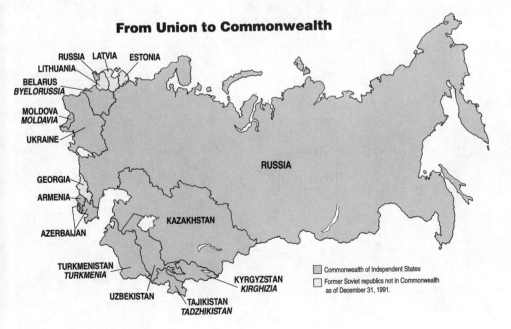

**From Union to Commonwealth**

RUSSIA LATVIA ESTONIA
LITHUANIA
BELARUS
*BYELORUSSIA*
MOLDOVA
*MOLDAVIA*
UKRAINE
GEORGIA
ARMENIA
AZERBAIJAN
KAZAKHSTAN
RUSSIA
TURKMENISTAN
*TURKMENIA*
KYRGYZSTAN
*KIRGHIZIA*
UZBEKISTAN
TAJIKISTAN
*TADZHIKISTAN*

☐ Commonwealth of Independent States
☐ Former Soviet republics not in Commonwealth as of December 31, 1991.

forces, giving several hard-liners government posts and equivocating on responsibility for such actions as the January 1991 storming of a Lithuanian television tower by Soviet troops that left more than a dozen people dead. In April, however, Gorbachev moved to make peace with Yeltsin and enter into a power-sharing agreement with leaders of nine of the republics. This led to a series of meetings in which officials drafted a new treaty of national union, scheduled to be signed on August 20. The treaty, however, was not signed.

Boris Yeltsin (see profile in PEOPLE IN THE NEWS) followed a different road. In mid-1990, not long after the Russian republic's legislature had chosen him as its leader, he resigned from the Communist Party, thereby acquiring a power base independent of it. Then, when Gorbachev scheduled a national referendum in March 1991 on whether the Soviet Union should be preserved, Yeltsin tacked onto the Russian ballot a proposal that the republic's president be directly elected. It was approved

by a large majority, and he emerged from the subsequent presidential balloting on June 12 with more than 60 percent of the vote and the distinction of being the first popularly elected national leader in Russian history. He was also a leader in promoting democratic reform.

Of the eight members of the junta set up during the hard-liners' coup, three were directors of the security services (Defense Minister Dmitri Yazov, Minister of the Interior Boris Pugo, and KGB Chairman Vladimir Kryuchkov), and two were high-ranking government officials (Prime Minister Valentin Pavlov and Vice President Gennady Yanayev). In the months preceding the coup attempt, the coup leaders expressed with surprising openness their view that the Soviet Union was facing a life-and-death crisis, with its political and economic system being sabotaged by outside forces, domestic criminals, and extremists.

Before their August grab for power, the hard-liners had sought to salvage what remained of the Soviet empire. Soviet security forces were

With their economies in shambles, the various republics of what was formerly the Soviet Union badly needed emergency food and medical aid from the West. Below, a load of humanitarian supplies bound for the Russian city of Rostov.

implicated in the raid on the Lithuanian television tower and in subsequent attempts to overthrow Lithuania's nationalist government. In June, Pavlov (with the backing of Kryuchkov, Pugo, and Yazov) asked the Soviet Parliament, the Supreme Soviet, to grant him extended powers to deal with the dire situation in the country. Gorbachev persuaded the lawmakers to reject this proposal but did not publicly question the loyalty of his subordinates. The hard-liners knew that the union treaty to be signed in August would strengthen the republics at the expense of the Soviet central government. They also knew that the Communist Party itself was in danger of losing its predominance. In what some hard-liners feared was a precursor of things to come, Yeltsin, in mid-July, banned the party from its traditional niche in the workplace and in Army and police units in the Russian republic.

Prominent leaders of the democratic reform movement predicted the coup. Foreign Minister Eduard Shevardnadze quit his post in December 1990, warning of a possible attempt by reactionaries to reinstitute repressive policies. In July he joined with Aleksandr Yakovlev (an architect of the *perestroika* program) and several other reform leaders to create a political opposition group called the Democratic Reform Movement. Shortly thereafter, he abandoned the Communist Party. Yakovlev renounced Communism on August 16 and warned of an imminent coup.

**Failed Coup.** After placing Gorbachev under house arrest at his vacation residence in the Crimea, the coup leaders announced on August 19 the formation of a junta called the State Committee for the State of Emergency and tried to convince the world that Gorbachev's health did not permit him to continue as president. Tanks rolled into Moscow, and all but a few newspapers were closed down.

What followed was Boris Yeltsin's finest hour. Climbing on top of a tank in front of the White House (the nickname for the building that houses the government of the Russian republic), he condemned the coup as illegal, insisted that Gorbachev be returned to office, and called on local officials not to obey the junta's orders.

Despite attempts by the coup leaders to control the press, Yeltsin's defiance became widely known. Barricades were formed around the White House, and in a clash with tanks not far away three young men were killed. The coup leaders had to either arrest Yeltsin or back down. They failed to act, and just days after it began, the coup collapsed ingloriously on August 21.

When Gorbachev returned to Moscow the next day, he refused to condemn the Communist Party, asserting it could still be a vehicle of unity and reform once it was purged of reactionaries. His advisers soon persuaded him otherwise, however. On August 24, Gorbachev quit as party chief and called for the dissolution of central party organs, an act which essentially marked the end of the party's dominant role.

**Separate Republics.** After the coup the very existence of the Soviet Union in any form was in question. The once all-powerful principles of centralized planning and state ownership were crumbling as the republics looked to exert their sovereignty.

*Baltic Republics.* Estonia, Latvia, and Lithuania, which were annexed by the Soviet Union in 1940, had long maintained their right to independence. Lithuania had declared itself independent in March 1990; the August coup spurred Estonia and Latvia to follow suit. The Soviet Union recognized the independence of the Baltic states on September 6.

*Moldova.* Moldova (formerly Moldavia) declared independence on August 29. Leaders of Moldova's ethnic minorities, especially the Gagauz (a Turkish people) and Russian-speakers living near the Ukrainian border, opposed the move, fearing that Moldova's ethnic Romanian majority would ultimately opt for unification with Romania, and declared the formation of their own small Soviet-affiliated republics.

*Georgia.* Georgia proclaimed its independence in April, and nationalist leader Zviad Gamsakhurdia, head of the Georgian legislature since November 1990, was elected president in May. Gamsakhurdia's paranoia (he insisted that his political enemies were plotting to kill him), his suppression of ethnic minorities, and the jailing of opposition leaders brought Georgia to the brink of civil war after

*Meeting in early December, Russian President Boris Yeltsin (seated second from right), Ukrainian President Leonid Kravchuk (second from left), and Stanislav Shushkevich, chairman of the Supreme Soviet of Belarus (third from left), created a commonwealth among the three republics. By year's end, eight other republics had joined the Commonwealth of Independent States; members committed themselves to democracy and free-market reforms.*

the August coup. The president responded by declaring a state of emergency in late September. Sporadic conflicts intensified in late December when Gamsakhurdia's supporters fired on rebels near the Georgian Parliament building in Tbilisi and the rebels responded by hammering the building with artillery, rockets, and automatic weapons. The year ended with Gamsakhurdia and hundreds of armed supporters under siege in the building.

*Armenia and Azerbaijan.* The conflict between Armenia and Azerbaijan over the secession efforts of Nagorno-Karabakh, an "autonomous" Armenian enclave inside Azerbaijan, moved into its fourth year. In the spring the situation deteriorated further when troops under the control of the central government reportedly began helping Azerbaijan evict Armenians from villages bordering the Nagorno-Karabakh region. Peace negotiations headed by Yeltsin and Kazakhstan President Nursultan Nazarbayev yielded a fragile accord in which Armenia renounced its claim to Nagorno-Karabakh and Azerbaijan prom-

ised to respect self-rule in the enclave. Ethnic violence continued, however, and in November, Azerbaijan canceled the autonomous status of Nagorno-Karabakh. At the end of the year, the peacekeeping forces of the former Soviet regime were pulled out by the Russian government.

*Central Asian Republics.* Kazakhstan, Kyrgyzstan (formerly Kirghizia), Tajikistan, Turkmenistan, and Uzbekistan, the least industrialized republics of the Soviet Union, were least affected by Gorbachev's economic and political reforms. Kyrgyzstan President Askar Akayev and Kazakhstan President Nazarbayev strongly supported reform goals, but the leaders of Uzbekistan favored the strong-arm tactics of the old-style Kremlin. Evidence that an Islamic revival had taken hold in the region sparked fears that the Central Asian republics would seek to strengthen their ties with Iran and other Islamic nations.

*Belarus.* The reputation of Belarus (formerly Byelorussia) as "the last bulwark of Bolshevism in East Europe" was shaken in April by widespread protest strikes in which workers demanded higher pay and a multiparty government. Communists in the republic's Parliament reacted to Gorbachev's abandonment of the party on August 24 by uniting with nationalists to declare independence from the Soviet Union the next day. The republic's Communist president, who had voiced support for the coup, resigned.

*Ukraine.* The Ukrainian legislature had passed a declaration of sovereignty in July 1990. After the coup the legislature approved a declaration of independence, and Ukrainian President Leonid Kravchuk resigned from the Communist Party.

Ukraine, the second most populous Soviet republic (after Russia), remained cautious about joining in postcoup pacts with other Soviet republics, and Ukrainian officials at first refused to sign an economic union treaty drawn up in October for the 12 remaining Soviet republics. They finally bowed to Western pressure and endorsed the treaty on November 4. In a December 1 referendum Ukrainian voters opted by a margin of 9 to 1 to declare full independence. (In balloting for president, Kravchuk took 60 percent of the vote.)

*Russia.* After the coup, Russian leaders seemed more interested in replacing the central government than in preserving it. Yeltsin obtained authorization from the Russian Parliament to cut off Russian financing to about 80 percent of central government ministries, to remove most price controls in Russia by the end of 1991 (he later extended the deadline to early January 1992), to privatize many Russian state farms and industries, and to close unprofitable factories. Acknowledging that this radical program would cause prices and unemployment rates to soar, Yeltsin promised concrete results by the fall of 1992 and named himself prime minister so that he could bear the brunt of the expected popular discontent.

Yeltsin issued decrees in mid-November that gave the Russian government control over the oil, gold, diamonds, and other natural resources on Russian territory and opened the door for Russian companies to engage directly in foreign trade. Yeltsin was also a key figure in late November talks between representatives of eight Soviet republics and of the Group of Seven industrial democracies, who agreed to defer payments on foreign debt accumulated by the Soviet Union. And on November 30, the Russian government agreed to assume financing of the Soviet payroll.

**A New Commonwealth.** The August coup, which was an effort to preserve a strong centralized union, had the opposite effect. The central legislature, the Congress of People's Deputies, dissolved itself in September and established a new executive body, the Council of State, which was little more than a negotiating arena for the republics. Gorbachev was repeatedly rebuffed in his efforts to form a loose Union of Sovereign States—a configuration that offered the republics far more autonomy than they would have gotten from the planned union treaty that had led to the coup.

On December 8 the leaders of Russia, Ukraine, and Belarus, meeting at Brest in Belarus, proclaimed that the Soviet Union had ceased to exist and announced the formation of the Commonwealth of Independent States, with its seat at Minsk, capital of Belarus. The agreement called for borders to remain open and unchanged, for the ruble to remain the currency of common commerce, and for the states to cooperate economically and militarily and to respect each other's sovereignty. People would be citizens of their own state; there would be no Commonwealth citizenship.

By mid-December the five Central Asian republics, as well as Azerbaijan, Armenia, and Moldova, had signed on, leaving Georgia the sole holdout. The leaders of the 11 participating republics met in the Kazakh capital of Alma-Ata on December 21 and signed an agreement formally linking their republics in the Commonwealth of Independent States. The Commonwealth was to be headed by councils of the chiefs of state and government of the 11 members. The 11 vowed to work toward free-market prosperity and full democracy and agreed that Russia would take over the Soviet seat on the United Nations Security Council. With no union left for him to govern, Gorbachev resigned on December 25. On December 26 the Supreme Soviet voted to disband and recognize the new Commonwealth. The United States and other nations recognized the independence of the 12 former So-

On December 25, Soviet President Mikhail Gorbachev, acknowledging the breakup of the Soviet Union, went on television (above) to announce that he was resigning his post. Gorbachev transferred to Russian federation President Boris Yeltsin the suitcase containing the controls that could launch the nuclear arsenal of the former union. At right, the secrets of the suitcase are explained to Yeltsin (far right) by a military specialist.

viet republics and began the process of establishing diplomatic relations with them (most nations had already recognized Estonia, Latvia, and Lithuania).

Near the end of December, leaders of the Commonwealth members met in Minsk and decided that each republic could form its own army, with nuclear weapons to be placed under a single joint command. Custody of the briefcase with nuclear launch codes passed from Gorbachev to Yeltsin. But the ultimate disposition of the Soviet military remained a highly controversial issue.

**Foreign Policy.** Despite his shifts during the year in domestic policy, in foreign policy Gorbachev had consistently pushed for "new thinking," a doctrine that stressed integration into the world community. Moscow acquiesced in the U.S.-led action to reverse Iraq's occupation of Kuwait and cosponsored (with Washington) the Middle East peace conference that convened in Madrid on October 30.

Immediately after the August coup, Foreign Minister Aleksandr Bessmertnykh, who had assumed a neutral posture during the putsch, was replaced by Boris Pankin, one of the few diplomats who had publicly repudiated the junta. Under Pankin the Soviet government stopped supplying arms to the Afghan government, started a military withdrawal from Cuba, and showed a new willingness to negotiate with Japan over the disputed Kuril Islands, which the Soviet Union had seized from Japan at the end of World War II. The Soviet Union also resumed diplomatic relations with Israel in October, ending a rift that began with the 1967 Arab-Israeli war.

With the breakup of the Soviet Union, the central foreign policy concern for the new independent states was the search for help from abroad in easing shortages of food and other essentials, in preventing economic collapse, and in smoothing the transition to market economies. Foreign countries sent shipments of food, medical supplies, and other aid, but the dismal state of what remained of the Soviet distribution system hampered delivery.

*See* STATISTICS OF THE WORLD.          L.T.L.

**UNITED ARAB EMIRATES.** *See* STATISTICS OF THE WORLD. *See also* ARABIAN PENINSULA.

**UNITED NATIONS.** The end of the cold war helped make possible the reversal of Iraq's conquest of Kuwait in an operation that involved unprecedented cooperation among the five permanent members of the United Nations Security Council and received the support of most other UN members. Negotiating peace terms and monitoring cease-fires in the Persian Gulf and around the world put an unprecedented strain on the secretariat in 1991.

**New Leadership.** In November the Security Council unanimously endorsed Egyptian Deputy Prime Minister Boutros Ghali to succeed Secretary-General Javier Pérez de Cuéllar, who stepped down from the top UN post on December 31, 1991, after serving two five-year terms. Ghali was the first Arab and first African to become secretary-general.

**New Members.** The decision by the Soviet Union and China not to block a South Korean seat in the UN opened the way for both North and South Korea to be admitted when the 46th General Assembly convened in September. Also admitted were Estonia, Latvia, and Lithuania (newly freed from Soviet control), along with the Marshall Islands and the Federated States of Micronesia, formerly U.S. trustee-

ships, bringing total membership to 166. The dissolution of the Soviet Union late in the year saw its Security Council seat transferred to the Russian Federation.

**War in the Middle East.** The UN Security Council had authorized UN member states to use "all necessary means" to force Iraqi troops out of Kuwait if they did not withdraw voluntarily by January 15, 1991. After Secretary-General Pérez de Cuéllar made a final, fruitless attempt to negotiate withdrawal, a U.S.-led coalition began an air bombardment of Iraq on January 17. The coalition launched a ground assault on February 24, and Kuwait City was soon liberated. Combat operations were suspended on February 28 (Gulf time), after Iraq announced it would accept all Security Council resolutions concerning Kuwait.

The Security Council's resolution of March 2 made Iraq liable for losses and damage to Kuwait and other states and required Iraq to give the location of land and sea mines and to free all prisoners of war. A subsequent resolution required that Iraq dismantle all of its weapons of mass destruction and missiles with a range of more than 90 miles and turn over to the International Atomic Energy Agency (IAEA) its weapons-grade nuclear materials. These measures would be financed by a fund drawn from a percentage of Iraq's oil revenues. The Security Council also voted to establish a demilitarized zone along the Iraq-Kuwait border to be monitored by a 1,440-member international peacekeeping force. A formal cease-fire went into effect on April 11, after which Iraq submitted what it said was an inventory of its nuclear, chemical, and biological weapons sites.

At the same time, in response to Iraq's crushing of the postwar rebellion of the Kurds, the Security Council passed a resolution demanding an end to the oppression of Kurds and access for international humanitarian organizations. On April 18, under UN auspices, Iraq signed an agreement that called for a "safe zone" for Kurdish refugees north of the 36th parallel. At first coalition troops policed this zone, but a lightly armed UN force soon replaced them. A modest international force remained just inside the Turkish border to offer the Kurds protection if needed. In the south,

**A Man for All Seasons**
The man selected in November to succeed Javier Pérez de Cuéllar on January 1, 1992, as secretary-general of the United Nations was, in some ways, not a logical choice. At 69, he was, some thought, too old for the job. Many Africans would have preferred a black, and some observers wondered if, as an Egyptian, he would be impartial with respect to Arab-Israeli issues. But Boutros Boutros-Ghali (Boutros is the Arabic equivalent of "Peter") had many qualifications for the post. Fluent in French and English, as well as Arabic, and known as an able negotiator, he served for 14 years as Egypt's minister of state for foreign affairs. He helped negotiate the 1979 Egyptian-Israeli peace treaty and helped win the 1990 release of anti-apartheid leader Nelson Mandela from a South African jail.

As secretary-general Ghali planned, among other things, to streamline the UN bureaucracy.

*Boutros Ghali*

protection of Shiites who had unsuccessfully rebelled against Saddam Hussein was left to the United Nations Commission on Human Rights and the International Committee of the Red Cross.

The effects of economic sanctions and the bombardment on the health of Iraq's civilian population was a continuing UN concern. A Security Council team surveying civilian damage in March reported "near apocalyptic" conditions. By August, famine threatened. A resolution passed by the Security Council in September permitted Iraq to sell $1.6 billion worth of oil over a six-month period to pay for food, medicine, and similar goods, provided that 30 percent of the money be set aside to compensate victims of the invasion of Kuwait and pay other expenses connected with Iraqi aggression. Iraq refused to accept the offer.

Earlier, in June, the inspectors for the special Security Council commission charged with weapons destruction had been barred from inspecting a convoy of trucks believed to hold nuclear bomb-making equipment. The Security Council responded by demanding "unequivocal assurances" that the cease-fire terms would be met. Facing the possibility of an air strike, Saddam Hussein backed down, but the Council's July 25 deadline for the destruction of Iraq's chemical and biological weapons and nuclear weapons installations passed with UN experts still not satisfied with the extent of Iraq's compliance.

On September 23, Iraq detained 44 UN inspectors who had uncovered secret Iraqi plans for nuclear weapons. The inspection team was released after complying with an agreement to give Iraq a list of the seized documents. The commission then established that Iraq had a highly sophisticated nuclear-weapons research program. On October 23 the Security Council approved a plan for destroying the plants and equipment associated with Iraq's nuclear program.

**Israel and the Arab Nations.** In January the Security Council unanimously condemned Israel's treatment of Palestinians in the occupied territories. A similar resolution was passed in May. Later in the year, however, the UN General Assembly, in a major action of great symbolic import, overturned a controversial 1975 resolution characterizing Zionism as "a form of racism and racial discrimination." The statement was repealed by a lopsided vote of 111-25, with 13 abstentions; 17 other nations did not vote.

**Hostage Drama.** On August 8 the Islamic Holy War group in Lebanon called on the UN secretary-general to negotiate for the release of Western hostages and of some 400 Israeli-held Arab prisoners. Hostages John McCarthy (a Briton) and Edward A. Tracy (an American) were freed in August, but negotiations bogged down when Israel pressed for information on its servicemen held in Lebanon. On September 11, the day after the secretary-general went to Iran to discuss hostages, Israel released 51 prisoners. British hostage Jack Mann was freed two weeks later. Then Israel, having received information on two missing soldiers and the body of a third, released 15 Arab detainees on October 21, and American hostage Jesse Turner was freed the same day. Anglican envoy Terry Waite and American educator Thomas Sutherland were freed on November 18; soon afterward, the United States repaid the Iranians $278 million for undelivered arms Iran had purchased from the United States before the fall of the shah. A final UN-brokered agreement that included a promise to release Arab prisoners in Israel, southern Lebanon, and Europe and a pledge by the United States and Germany not to retaliate against the Muslim fundamentalist kidnappers led to the release of Americans Joseph Cicippio, Alann Steen, and Terry Anderson at 24-hour intervals beginning December 2.

**Cambodia.** A Security Council plan to end the 13-year civil war in Cambodia called for the Phnom Penh government and three rebel groups to disarm and permit UN-monitored free elections by 1993. The factions agreed in late June to honor an indefinite truce, to stop receiving foreign arms, and to set up a Supreme National Council led by Prince Norodom Sihanouk and composed of repre-

*The first members of the United Nations peacekeeping force in Cambodia, a group of Australian soldiers armed with pistols and knives, arrived in the capital city of Phnom Penh in November. They were slated to be joined by troops from 22 other countries, as part of a UN effort to monitor a cease-fire and implement a peace plan in the war-torn country.*

sentatives of the four factions. After further hurdles were cleared, a formal peace accord was signed in Paris on October 23, and an advance 268-member UN peacekeeping mission arrived soon afterward. Sporadic rioting delayed the next meeting of the four factions until December 30, when they agreed to appeal to the UN to accelerate its timetable for sending a much larger peacekeeping force.

**Latin America.** Intensive negotiations under UN auspices between El Salvador's government and the rebel Farabundo Martí National Liberation Front (FMLN) led to apparent results. Municipal and legislative elections, monitored by the UN, went forward smoothly in March; three months later, the Security Council sent a UN observer commission to monitor human rights violations and compliance with any cease-fire agreement. A deadlock that developed when the rebels insisted that FMLN members be incorporated into the armed forces was broken in September by Pérez de Cuéllar, who helped forge an agreement for the guerrillas to serve on a civilian-controlled national police force. As the year ended, Pérez de Cuéllar, in the last official act of his tenure, persuaded both sides to formally accept a cease-fire to take effect on February 1, 1992.

The UN Observer Group for the Verification of Elections in Haiti completed its mission in February with the inauguration of President Jean-Bertrand Aristide. After Aristide was ousted on September 30 in a military-led coup, the UN General Assembly adopted a resolution calling for his restoration.

**Africa.** The secretary-general's recommendations for conducting a referendum enabling the people of Western Sahara to choose independence or to remain part of Morocco were approved unanimously by the Security Council in April. A small force of UN troops was deployed in late spring, and a truce between the government and the rebels was declared on September 6. The referendum was initially scheduled to follow 20 weeks later.

One day prior to the signing of a peace treaty on May 31 between the Angolan government and Unita rebels, the Security Council voted unanimously to expand to 350 the UN Angola Verification Mission to monitor the cease-fire

in that country. Elections were scheduled for the fall of 1992.

The South African government and the UN Office of the High Commissioner for Refugees agreed in August on an amnesty for political exiles and their UN-assisted return. This marked the first UN presence in South Africa since the country's membership in the General Assembly was suspended in the early 1960s. The General Assembly unanimously recommended in mid-December that all nations begin renewing sports, cultural, scientific, and academic ties with South Africa. No suggestion was made, however, to lift financial and trade sanctions.

**Yugoslavia.** UN efforts to halt the civil war in Yugoslavia between Serbian-led forces and the secessionist republic of Croatia showed some promise in late November when a peace accord put together by UN special envoy Cyrus Vance was signed in Geneva. But the cease-fire did not hold, although at the end of the year Vance was able to secure a formal agreement from Serbian and Yugoslav officials to a plan providing for the dispatch of a UN peacekeeping force and the withdrawal of troops from Croatia. The Croatian president had previously accepted a draft of the plan.

**Arms Control.** In early December the General Assembly voted to set up a register of international arms sales. The register—the first of its kind—was aimed at identifying potential trouble spots.

**Funding and Reorganization.** With some nine UN peacekeeping operations in place in late 1991, Pérez de Cuéllar moved to request new contributions from UN members and to ask governments, private corporations, and wealthy individuals to set up a $1 billion fund to help finance the organization's endeavors. The UN stood on the brink of insolvency because several members—principally the United States—had not paid their dues fully and on time.

In December an agreement was reached to appoint a coordinator to combine the often overlapping activities of the UN's various relief agencies. The accord also broadened the UN's right to bring aid to people without a specific invitation from a country's government.

I.C.B.

# United States
# of America

**After leading a successful effort to drive Iraq from Kuwait in the Persian Gulf War, the United States during 1991 confronted the disintegration of the Soviet Union, while seeking to cope with a slumping economy at home.**

### THE PRESIDENCY

President George Bush was preoccupied during the year by dramatic events abroad, including the first major U.S. military conflict since the Vietnam War and crisis in the Soviet Union, and he generally won praise for his handling of foreign policy. But by late in the year, with Americans increasingly concerned about a slumping economy, the perception that he had little to offer on the home front had begun to take a political toll.

**Persian Gulf War.** President Bush began 1991 determined to bring to a resolution the confrontation with Iraq. On January 8 he asked Congress to approve a resolution authorizing the use of "all necessary means" to oust Iraqi forces from Kuwait if Iraq did not withdraw voluntarily by the January 15 deadline set

by the United Nations. On January 12 the Senate voted, 52-47, and the House voted, 250-183, to give Bush the authorization he wanted. Three days later, he signed a national security directive to begin a massive air assault early on January 17 (Gulf time).

By early February, when allied bombs had inflicted devastating damage but failed to dislodge the Iraqis, the president began preparing public opinion for the inevitability of a ground war. Given the possibility that any diplomatic settlement would allow Iraqi President Saddam Hussein to claim at least a moral victory, the White House brushed off a Soviet peace effort and on February 22 demanded that Iraq begin a withdrawal by the next day. When that failed to happen, Bush ordered the ground as-

*Confronted with a stubborn recession, President George Bush tried to encourage consumer spending as one way out, but many questioned whether he was doing enough, and some analysts, as seen here, saw the tough economic times as a serious threat to his re-election prospects.*

*In a year of foreign policy triumphs, President Bush journeyed to Moscow in July, where he and then Soviet President Mikhail Gorbachev signed a treaty designed to sharply reduce stockpiles of long-range nuclear arms. The pens they used and then exchanged were made of metal from destroyed nuclear missiles.*

sault. On February 27, only 100 hours after the operation began, he announced in an Oval Office address that Kuwait had been liberated and called a halt to the ground war.

Politically, this represented the high point in Bush's handling of the Gulf crisis; polls showed his job approval rating hovering at a record 90 percent. But in part because of Bush's decision not to prolong the ground offensive by attacking fleeing troops, Saddam Hussein was able to salvage enough of his forces and equipment to put down revolts by Iraq's Kurdish minority in the north and Shiite Muslim minority in the south. The dangers posed by Saddam Hussein's remaining in power were underlined when UN inspectors discovered that the Iraqis had apparently been concealing the remains of an ambitious nuclear weapons program.

**Soviet Relations and Arms Control.** Bush's personal rapport with Soviet President Mikhail

Gorbachev paid dividends throughout the first part of the year, particularly during the Persian Gulf crisis. Bush and Gorbachev also overcame disagreements that had been holding up treaties for reducing conventional military forces in Europe and long-range strategic nuclear weapons. At the end of July, Bush made his first trip to the Soviet Union as president and signed the strategic arms reduction treaty with Gorbachev. Bush also said he would send Congress a trade agreement giving the Soviets most-favored-nation status. He met privately with Russian President Boris Yeltsin, who on an earlier trip to the United States had been given short shrift at the White House.

The failure of the hard-line Communist coup in August accelerated the radical changes that were sweeping the Soviet Union and prompted President Bush to undertake changes in U.S. policy. In late September he announced deep unilateral cuts in U.S. nuclear weapon stockpiles, among other moves, and urged new negotiations to eliminate all intercontinental missiles with multiple warheads. Gorbachev soon announced comparable initiatives.

The continuing disintegration of the Soviet state in the wake of the coup, however, made U.S. policies focused on Gorbachev and his government increasingly untenable. When citizens of Ukraine voted in favor of independence in a December 1 referendum, the administration welcomed the outcome and indicated full diplomatic recognition would eventually follow, but asked for assurances about what Ukraine intended to do with nuclear weapons on its soil. A week later, when the leaders of Russia, Ukraine, and Belarus (Byelorussia) declared that the Soviet Union "had ceased to exist" and that they had formed a Commonwealth of Independent States, Bush again reacted cautiously.

In a speech on December 12, Secretary of State James Baker outlined overall U.S. policy in the Soviet crisis, which involved providing food and medical aid but little in the way of direct financial guarantees. By the time Baker left on a trip to Moscow on December 15, the Gorbachev government was almost defunct, and Baker devoted most of his efforts to obtaining the pledges of Yeltsin and the leaders of other republics with strategic nuclear weapons on their soil to abide by the arms control agreements Gorbachev had made. When Gorbachev finally resigned on December 25, signaling the formal demise of the Soviet Union, Bush made a televised speech praising him and announcing U.S. recognition of several of the newly independent republics.

**Israel and the Arabs.** U.S. relations with Israel reached a high point during the Gulf War, when Israel heeded Bush's pleas not to strike back at Iraq for numerous Scud missile attacks. Later in the year, Bush angered Israel and American Jewish groups when he persuaded Congress to delay consideration of a request by Israel for $10 billion in loan guarantees, intended to help cope with the influx of Jewish immigrants from the Soviet Union. The administration feared that seeming to foster the settlement program would set back the delicate negotiations over a peace conference. Despite the strains in U.S.-Israeli relations, Israeli and Arab representatives met in Madrid in October, and again in Washington in December, to hold direct face-to-face peace talks.

**Congress and Politics.** In a March 6 address to Congress on the Gulf War, the president tried to seize the initiative on domestic issues by challenging his Capitol Hill critics to quickly pass administration-backed legislation on transportation and crime. But Democrats had their own competing versions of both proposals. A transportation bill did clear Congress just before adjournment in late November, but in the face of a threatened veto of revised anticrime legislation, lawmakers left town without taking final action on that measure. A package of education reforms also got tangled in partisan politics. Nevertheless, Bush dominated the Democrats through his use of the veto. In November he ran his unbroken string of vetoes to 24 when the House sustained his veto of a bill that would have overturned an administration ban on abortion counseling in family planning clinics receiving federal funds.

## Cabinet of the United States

**Vice President**  Dan Quayle

**Secretary of State**  James A. Baker III
**Secretary of the Treasury**  Nicholas P. Brady
**Secretary of Defense**  Richard B. Cheney
**Attorney General**  William P. Barr
**Secretary of the Interior**  Manuel Lujan, Jr.
**Secretary of Agriculture**  Edward R. Madigan
**Secretary of Commerce**  Robert A. Mosbacher
**Secretary of Labor**  Lynn Martin
**Secretary of Health and Human Services**  Dr. Louis W. Sullivan
**Secretary of Housing and Urban Development**  Jack F. Kemp
**Secretary of Transportation**  Samuel K. Skinner (until December 16)
**Secretary of Energy**  James D. Watkins
**Secretary of Education**  Lamar Alexander
**Secretary of Veterans Affairs**  Edward J. Derwinski

**Director, Office of Management and Budget**  Richard G. Darman
**Counselor to the President**  John Sununu
**Chief of Staff**  Samuel K. Skinner (from December 16)
**Special Trade Representative**  Carla A. Hills

None of Bush's domestic efforts seemed to be invested with the same zeal as his foreign policy, and this discrepancy began to take its toll in the fall. In a Washington *Post* poll, 70 percent of those surveyed felt Bush "spends too much time on foreign problems and not enough on problems in this country."

As he publicly downplayed the seriousness of the economy's slump, his own advisers were split on how to counteract it. Some urged tax cuts and other measures; others believed the economy would recover by itself. Moreover, Bush felt that the huge federal budget deficit precluded stimulating the economy through new government spending programs.

Bush's postponement of a trip to Australia and Asia and his decision to compromise on a new civil rights bill and an extension of unem-ployment benefits that had been pushed by the Democrats were seen as concessions to mounting political pressures—and therefore signs of weakness. He even had to share the blame for a 120-point drop in the stock market in November after he suggested that the economy might get a boost if banks lowered interest rates on credit card balances.

In December expectations that the administration's "wait and see" approach to the economy would end rose when the president's contentious chief of staff, John Sununu, resigned. Sununu was replaced with Transportation Secretary Samuel K. Skinner, who convinced Bush that action on the economy was required to stop his political slide. At year's end, Bush was contemplating a variety of measures to be proposed in January 1992.

*President Bush, flanked by aides Brent Scowcroft (left) and John Sununu, is visited in the hospital by two of his grandchildren, Sam and Ellie LeBlond. Bush was hospitalized briefly in May after he complained of fatigue and shortness of breath while jogging; the problem—a thyroid condition—was treated, and he soon was able to resume a full schedule, jogging included.*

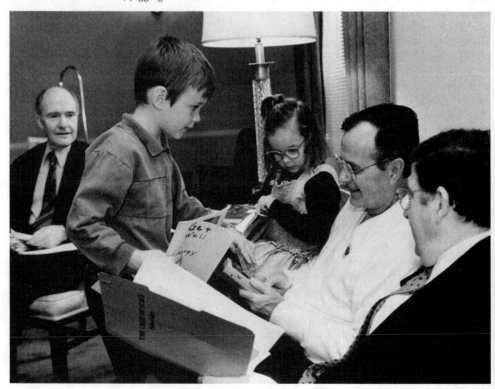

**Nominations and Confirmations.** The president waged major battles to put black conservative Clarence Thomas on the Supreme Court and to install Robert Gates, his deputy national security adviser, as director of the Central Intelligence Agency.

Bush chose Thomas, 43, a federal appeals court judge, to take the seat being vacated by the Court's first black justice, Thurgood Marshall. In selecting him, the president could take credit for putting a black on the Court at a time when he was under fire for his civil rights policies; at the same time, Thomas appeared likely to bolster the Court's conservative majority. After extended televised hearings into a last-minute charge that he had sexually harassed a woman who had worked for him years earlier, Thomas was narrowly confirmed by the Senate, 52-48, on October 15.

Gates had been President Ronald Reagan's choice to head the CIA in 1987 but had been forced to withdraw because of questions on how much he knew about the Iran/contra affair during his tenure as deputy director of the agency. During hearings into his 1991 nomination, Gates defused Iran/contra questions by admitting "misjudgments" and also withstood a controversy over whether he had slanted intelligence reports for political reasons. The Senate confirmed him on November 5 by a 64-31 vote.

Bush also won Senate confirmation of three new cabinet secretaries: Lamar Alexander, who succeeded Lauro Cavazos at Education; Lynn Martin, who followed Elizabeth Dole at Labor; and William Barr, who took over as attorney general from Richard Thornburgh. The president announced that he would nominate Barbara H. Franklin, a corporate director and Republican activist, to succeed Commerce Secretary Robert Mosbacher, who was to leave the cabinet in early 1992 to head Bush's reelection campaign.

**Bush's Health.** Bush gave the nation a brief scare when he was hospitalized on May 4 after complaining of shortness of breath and fatigue while jogging at Camp David. Doctors found him to be suffering from an irregular heartbeat, caused by an overactive thyroid gland that in turn resulted from Graves' disease. In an apparent coincidence, the same disease afflicted his wife, Barbara. Bush received treatment to destroy the thyroid and was apparently fully recovered by August.

The political fallout from the health issue mostly affected Vice President Dan Quayle, since it renewed concern about his qualifications and the apparent lack of public confidence in him. Bush characteristically defended his vice president.                B.D.

## POLITICAL PARTIES

In the afterglow of the Persian Gulf War early in 1991, as President George Bush's approval rating soared past 90 percent, Republicans looked toward 1992 with anticipation, considering Bush's reelection a near certainty. By the end of 1991, however, the ailing U.S. economy—and the perception that the president was more interested in foreign travel than domestic issues—made Bush seem vulnerable.

**Fall Elections.** In the biggest election upset of 1991, Harris Wofford (D, Pa.), who had never before run for elective office, defeated former U.S. Attorney General Richard Thornburgh (R), 55 to 45 percent, in a U.S. Senate race. Not only had Thornburgh enjoyed Bush's all-out support, but the issues on which Wofford capitalized—middle-class dissatisfaction with the economy and the rising cost of health insurance—highlighted the president's potential vulnerabilities.

In the highly publicized campaign for the Louisiana governorship, Bush's candidate, incumbent Governor Charles E. ("Buddy") Roemer III, was eliminated in the first round of balloting. This left former Governor Edwin W. Edwards (D), twice tried but never convicted on federal corruption charges, and David Duke (R), a former grand wizard of the Ku Klux Klan. Disavowed by the White House and the national party, Duke lost the November 16 runoff to Edwards by a wide margin.

However, not all the election news was bleak for the GOP. For example, New Jersey's legislative elections saw a backlash against Governor James J. Florio (D), who had rammed through a $2.8 billion tax increase in 1990, and Kirk Fordice became Mississippi's first Republican governor since Reconstruction. (See also ELECTIONS IN THE UNITED STATES.)

**Looking to 1992.** In January the White House named Agriculture Secretary Clayton Yeutter to

*Satirists had a grand time poking fun at Mario Cuomo, who spent months waffling on whether or not to enter the race for the Democratic presidential nomination. Late in the year, the New York governor said he would not run.*

DANA SUMMERS © WASHINGTON POST WRITERS GROUP. REPRINTED WITH PERMISSION.

head the Republican National Committee. Meanwhile, as the year drew on, the president's reelection effort appeared to be lagging, reportedly because of controversy over the role to be played by abrasive White House Chief of Staff John H. Sununu. When Sununu resigned under pressure on December 3, Bush replaced him with Transportation Secretary Samuel K. Skinner, a moderate with a more ingratiating management style. Bush then appointed other moderates to key positions on his campaign team. Late in the year, right-wing commentator Patrick J. Buchanan announced he would run against Bush in the New Hampshire primary, a move that could draw away conservative support.

The Democrats had troubles of their own. Some prominent prospects declined to run, and the only declared candidate for months was former Senator Paul Tsongas, whose home state (Massachusetts) and ethnic heritage (Greek) reminded many Democrats of their ill-starred 1988 standard-bearer, Michael Dukakis. By November, however, Tsongas had been joined by other hopefuls—Arkansas Governor Bill Clinton, Virginia Governor L. Douglas Wilder, former California Governor Edmund Brown, Jr., and Senators Tom Harkin (Iowa) and Robert Kerrey (Neb.). These candidates, who appeared on December 15 in the first of several televised "debates," were all underfunded—in part because contributors were waiting to see whether New York's

chronically indecisive governor, Mario M. Cuomo, was in or out of the race. Cuomo finally bowed out in December, citing New York's continuing budget crisis, and Clinton was left as the apparent early front-runner.

G.M.H.

## CONGRESS

The year began with dramatic and dignified debates in both houses of Congress on a resolution—which was adopted—authorizing President George Bush to send U.S. troops into combat to liberate Kuwait from the forces of Iraqi President Saddam Hussein. But by autumn, the public's opinion of Congress had plummeted, after news of House members bouncing checks at their exclusive bank and controversy over the Senate's handling of sexual harassment charges against Supreme Court nominee Clarence Thomas.

The slow-moving 102nd Congress reacted to events rather than charting its own course, remained stymied by the threat of presidential vetoes, and left much of its most important work for the next session. Congress did manage to pass—much of it in the final chaotic hours—some major legislation, including, among other measures, a highway and mass transit bill, an extension of unemployment benefits, banking legislation (see BANKING AND FINANCE), a civil rights bill (see CIVIL LIBERTIES AND CIVIL RIGHTS), and aid to help dismantle the nuclear arsenal of the former Soviet Union (see MILITARY AND NAVAL AFFAIRS).

Among the legislative casualties were an attempt to repeal a ban on abortion counseling at family planning clinics receiving federal funds, a campaign finance bill, and an anticrime bill that included a five-day waiting period for those purchasing handguns (see also CRIME AND LAW ENFORCEMENT). On other issues, time simply ran out before Congress adjourned in late November.

**Inside Congress.** In September a report by the Government Accounting Office revealed that House members had written 8,331 bad checks on accounts at their exclusive bank during the 12-month period ending June 30, 1991. The bad checks were covered with money from other members' accounts, and the check bouncers were not charged penalties or interest. Then came reports of House members failing to pick up the tabs at House restaurants, where the government-subsidized prices are already extremely low. The House leadership later closed the bank and stopped members from running up tabs at the restaurants.

On August 2, senators voted to give themselves a 23 percent raise, bringing their salaries to the House level of $125,100. (At the same time, the Senate barred members from accepting outside speaking fees, a practice already banned by the House and in the rest of the federal government.)

The impression that members of Congress were becoming a privileged class fueled calls to limit the terms national and state lawmakers could serve. Term-limit bills were introduced in most states, but the movement lost some momentum on Election Day, November 5, when voters in the state of Washington defeated a sweeping term-limitation measure that would have ended the career of House Speaker Thomas Foley, among others.

Meanwhile, the Senate Ethics Committee chastised five senators (the so-called Keating Five) who had intervened in 1987 with federal regulators on behalf of Charles Keating, Jr., head of the failed Lincoln Savings and Loan Association—and a contributor of $1.5 million to the senators' political campaigns and causes. The committee, which had conducted a 22-month investigation, reserved the harshest discipline for Senator Alan Cranston (D, Calif.); he was strongly reprimanded before the full Senate in November for having intervened on Keating's behalf while soliciting $1 million in contributions to his campaign and voter registration groups from Keating's company. In February the committee had chastised John McCain (R., Ariz.), John Glenn (D., Ohio), Donald W. Riegle, Jr. (D., Mich.), and Dennis DeConcini (D., Ariz.) for poor judgment. Riegle and DeConcini were also cited for the appearance of impropriety.

**Economic Issues.** The five-year budget agreement put together by Congress and the White House in 1990 showed signs of unraveling under the strain of a recalcitrant recession and the collapse of the Soviet Union. Under attack were provisions that set up separate spending limits for defense and for domestic programs and that barred shifting money from one category to another. Some lawmakers argued that money should be transferred from defense to

---

### Fortune in a Frame

It's the dream of everyone who's ever poked around a flea market, secondhand store, or garage sale—to discover that something picked up for a mere pittance is actually a treasure.

In the summer of 1989, that's what happened in a flea market in Adamstown, Pa. A browser came across a painting, and although the dull, torn picture itself wasn't much, the ornate frame was interesting. The price: four bucks.

At first, the buyer was disappointed to find that the frame was unusable. Hidden in the backing, however, was a folded-up piece of paper which turned out to be a perfectly preserved copy of the first printing of the U.S. Declaration of Independence. Only 24 such copies are known to exist, few in such superb condition.

Experts at the New York office of Sotheby's, the prestigious auction house, estimated the document might bring as much as a million dollars, but on June 13, 1991, it was sold to an Atlanta arts investment firm for $2,420,000—"far and away the highest price for historical Americana ever," according to David Redden, the auctioneer. The lucky discoverer has chosen to remain anonymous.

# MEMBERSHIP OF THE 102nd CONGRESS IN 1991

|  | Term |
| Senators | Expires |

**ALABAMA**
Howell T. Heflin (D) . . . . . . . . . . 1997
Richard C. Shelby (D) . . . . . . . . 1993
**ALASKA**
Ted Stevens (R) . . . . . . . . . . . . . 1997
Frank H. Murkowski (R) . . . . . . . 1993
**ARIZONA**
Dennis DeConcini (D) . . . . . . . . 1995
John McCain (R). . . . . . . . . . . . . 1993
**ARKANSAS**
Dale Bumpers (D). . . . . . . . . . . . 1993
David Pryor (D). . . . . . . . . . . . . . 1997
**CALIFORNIA**
Alan Cranston (D). . . . . . . . . . . . 1993
John Seymour (R)[1]. . . . . . . . . . 1995
**COLORADO**
Timothy E. Wirth (D) . . . . . . . . . 1993
Hank Brown (R) . . . . . . . . . . . . . 1997
**CONNECTICUT**
Christopher J. Dodd (D) . . . . . . . 1993
Joseph I. Lieberman (D) . . . . . . . 1995
**DELAWARE**
William V. Roth, Jr. (R) . . . . . . . . 1995
Joseph R. Biden, Jr. (D) . . . . . . . 1997
**FLORIDA**
Bob Graham (D). . . . . . . . . . . . . 1993
Connie Mack (R). . . . . . . . . . . . . 1995
**GEORGIA**
Sam Nunn (D). . . . . . . . . . . . . . . 1997
Wyche Fowler, Jr. (D) . . . . . . . . . 1993
**HAWAII**
Daniel K. Inouye (D) . . . . . . . . . 1993
Daniel K. Akaka (D). . . . . . . . . . 1997
**IDAHO**
Steven D. Symms (R) . . . . . . . . 1993
Larry Craig (R) . . . . . . . . . . . . . . 1997
**ILLINOIS**
Alan J. Dixon (D) . . . . . . . . . . . . 1993
Paul Simon (D) . . . . . . . . . . . . . . 1997
**INDIANA**
Richard G. Lugar (R). . . . . . . . . . 1995
Dan Coats (R). . . . . . . . . . . . . . . 1997
**IOWA**
Charles E. Grassley (R) . . . . . . . 1993
Tom Harkin (D) . . . . . . . . . . . . . . 1997
**KANSAS**
Robert Dole (R). . . . . . . . . . . . . . 1993
Nancy Landon Kassebaum (R) . . 1997
**KENTUCKY**
Wendell H. Ford (D). . . . . . . . . . . 1993
Mitch McConnell (R) . . . . . . . . . 1997
**LOUISIANA**
J. Bennett Johnston (D) . . . . . . . 1997
John B. Breaux (D) . . . . . . . . . . . 1993
**MAINE**
William S. Cohen (R). . . . . . . . . . 1997
George J. Mitchell (D) . . . . . . . . . 1995
**MARYLAND**
Paul S. Sarbanes (D). . . . . . . . . . 1995
Barbara A. Mikulski (D). . . . . . . . 1993
**MASSACHUSETTS**
Edward M. Kennedy (D) . . . . . . . 1995
John F. Kerry (D) . . . . . . . . . . . . 1997
**MICHIGAN**
Donald W. Riegle, Jr. (D) . . . . . . 1995
Carl Levin (D) . . . . . . . . . . . . . . . 1997
**MINNESOTA**
Dave Durenberger (R). . . . . . . . . 1995
Paul Wellstone (D) . . . . . . . . . . . 1997

**MISSISSIPPI**
Thad Cochran (R). . . . . . . . . . . . 1997
Trent Lott (R). . . . . . . . . . . . . . . . 1995
**MISSOURI**
John C. Danforth (R) . . . . . . . . . 1995
Christopher S. Bond (R) . . . . . . . 1993
**MONTANA**
Max Baucus (D) . . . . . . . . . . . . . 1997
Conrad Burns (R) . . . . . . . . . . . . 1995
**NEBRASKA**
J. James Exon (D). . . . . . . . . . . . 1997
Robert Kerrey (D) . . . . . . . . . . . . 1995
**NEVADA**
Harry Reid (D). . . . . . . . . . . . . . . 1993
Richard H. Bryan (D). . . . . . . . . . 1995
**NEW HAMPSHIRE**
Warren Rudman (R) . . . . . . . . . . 1993
Bob Smith (R) . . . . . . . . . . . . . . . 1997
**NEW JERSEY**
Bill Bradley (D) . . . . . . . . . . . . . . 1997
Frank R. Lautenberg (D). . . . . . . 1995
**NEW MEXICO**
Pete V. Domenici (R). . . . . . . . . . 1997
Jeff Bingaman (D) . . . . . . . . . . . . 1995
**NEW YORK**
Daniel Patrick Moynihan (D). . . . 1995
Alfonse M. D'Amato (R) . . . . . . . 1993
**NORTH CAROLINA**
Jesse Helms (R). . . . . . . . . . . . . 1997
Terry Sanford (D) . . . . . . . . . . . . 1993
**NORTH DAKOTA**
Quentin N. Burdick (D) . . . . . . . . 1995
Kent Conrad (D) . . . . . . . . . . . . . 1993
**OHIO**
John Glenn (D) . . . . . . . . . . . . . . 1993
Howard M. Metzenbaum (D) . . . 1995
**OKLAHOMA**
David Lyle Boren (D). . . . . . . . . . 1997
Don Nickles (R). . . . . . . . . . . . . . 1993
**OREGON**
Mark O. Hatfield (R). . . . . . . . . . . 1997
Bob Packwood (R). . . . . . . . . . . . 1993
**PENNSYLVANIA**
Arlen Specter (R) . . . . . . . . . . . . 1993
Harris Wofford (D)[2]. . . . . . . . . . 1995
**RHODE ISLAND**
Claiborne Pell (D). . . . . . . . . . . . 1997
John H. Chafee (R) . . . . . . . . . . 1995
**SOUTH CAROLINA**
Strom Thurmond (R) . . . . . . . . . 1997
Ernest F. Hollings (D) . . . . . . . . . 1993
**SOUTH DAKOTA**
Larry Pressler (R) . . . . . . . . . . . . 1997
Thomas A. Daschle (D). . . . . . . . 1993
**TENNESSEE**
Jim Sasser (D) . . . . . . . . . . . . . . 1995
Albert Gore, Jr. (D) . . . . . . . . . . 1997
**TEXAS**
Lloyd Bentsen (D). . . . . . . . . . . . 1995
Phil Gramm (R). . . . . . . . . . . . . . 1997
**UTAH**
Jake Garn (R) . . . . . . . . . . . . . . . 1993
Orrin G. Hatch (R) . . . . . . . . . . . 1995
**VERMONT**
Patrick J. Leahy (D) . . . . . . . . . . 1993
James M. Jeffords (R) . . . . . . . . 1995
**VIRGINIA**
John William Warner (R). . . . . . . 1997
Charles S. Robb (D) . . . . . . . . . 1995

**WASHINGTON**
Brock Adams (D) . . . . . . . . . . . . 1993
Slade Gorton (R) . . . . . . . . . . . . 1995
**WEST VIRGINIA**
Robert C. Byrd (D). . . . . . . . . . . . 1995
John D. Rockefeller IV (D) . . . . . 1997
**WISCONSIN**
Robert W. Kasten, Jr. (R) . . . . . . 1993
Herbert H. Kohl (D) . . . . . . . . . . 1995
**WYOMING**
Malcolm Wallop (R) . . . . . . . . . . 1995
Alan K. Simpson (R) . . . . . . . . . 1997

**Representatives**

**ALABAMA**
1. Sonny Callahan (R)
2. William L. Dickinson (R)
3. Glen Browder (D)
4. Tom Bevill (D)
5. Robert E. (Bud) Cramer, Jr. (D)
6. Ben Erdreich (D)
7. Claude Harris (D)
**ALASKA**
At large: Don Young (R)
**ARIZONA**
1. John J. Rhodes III (R)
2. Ed Pastor (D)[3]
3. Bob Stump (R)
4. Jon L. Kyl (R)
5. Jim Kolbe (R)
**ARKANSAS**
1. Bill Alexander (D)
2. Ray Thornton (D)
3. John Paul Hammerschmidt (R)
4. Beryl Anthony, Jr. (D)
**CALIFORNIA**
1. Frank D. Riggs (R)
2. Wally Herger (R)
3. Robert T. Matsui (D)
4. Vic Fazio (D)
5. Nancy Pelosi (D)
6. Barbara Boxer (D)
7. George Miller (D)
8. Ronald V. Dellums (D)
9. Fortney H. (Pete) Stark (D)
10. Don Edwards (D)
11. Tom Lantos (D)
12. Tom Campbell (R)
13. Norman Y. Mineta (D)
14. John T. Doolittle (R)
15. Gary Condit (D)
16. Leon E. Panetta (D)
17. Calvin M. Dooley (D)
18. Richard H. Lehman (D)
19. Robert J. Lagomarsino (R)
20. William M. Thomas (R)
21. Elton Gallegly (R)
22. Carlos J. Moorhead (R)
23. Anthony C. Beilenson (D)
24. Henry A. Waxman (D)
25. Edward R. Roybal (D)
26. Howard L. Berman (D)
27. Mel Levine (D)
28. Julian C. Dixon (D)
29. Maxine Waters (D)
30. Matthew G. Martinez (D)
31. Mervyn M. Dymally (D)
32. Glenn M. Anderson (D)
33. David Dreier (R)

34. Esteban Edward Torres (D)
35. Jerry Lewis (R)
36. George E. Brown, Jr. (D)
37. Alfred A. (Al) McCandless (R)
38. Robert K. Dornan (R)
39. William E. Dannemeyer (R)
40. C. Christopher Cox (R)
41. Bill Lowery (R)
42. Dana Rohrabacher (R)
43. Ron Packard (R)
44. Randy "Duke" Cunningham (R)
45. Duncan Hunter (R)

**COLORADO**
1. Patricia Schroeder (D)
2. David E. Skaggs (D)
3. Ben Nighthorse Campbell (D)
4. Wayne Allard (R)
5. Joel Hefley (R)
6. Dan Schaefer (R)

**CONNECTICUT**
1. Barbara B. Kennelly (D)
2. Samuel Gejdenson (D)
3. Rosa L. DeLauro (D)
4. Christopher Shays (R)
5. Gary A. Franks (R)
6. Nancy L. Johnson (R)

**DELAWARE**
At large: Thomas R. Carper (D)

**FLORIDA**
1. Earl Hutto (D)
2. Douglas (Pete) Peterson (D)
3. Charles E. Bennett (D)
4. Craig T. James (R)
5. Bill McCollum (R)
6. Cliff Stearns (R)
7. Sam Gibbons (D)
8. C. W. Bill Young (R)
9. Michael Bilirakis (R)
10. Andy Ireland (R)
11. Jim Bacchus (D)
12. Tom Lewis (R)
13. Porter J. Goss (R)
14. Harry A. Johnston II (D)
15. E. Clay Shaw, Jr. (R)
16. Lawrence J. Smith (D)
17. William Lehman (D)
18. Ileana Ros-Lehtinen (R)
19. Dante B. Fascell (D)

**GEORGIA**
1. Robert Lindsay Thomas (D)
2. Charles Hatcher (D)
3. Richard Ray (D)
4. Ben Jones (D)
5. John Lewis (D)
6. Newt Gingrich (R)
7. George (Buddy) Darden (D)
8. J. Roy Rowland (D)
9. Ed Jenkins (D)
10. Doug Barnard, Jr. (D)

**HAWAII**
1. Neil Abercrombie (D)
2. Patsy Mink (D)

**IDAHO**
1. Larry LaRocco (D)
2. Richard H. Stallings (D)

**ILLINOIS**
1. Charles A. Hayes (D)
2. Gus Savage (D)
3. Marty Russo (D)
4. George E. Sangmeister (D)
5. William O. Lipinski (D)
6. Henry J. Hyde (R)
7. Cardiss Collins (D)
8. Dan Rostenkowski (D)
9. Sidney R. Yates (D)
10. John Edward Porter (R)
11. Frank Annunzio (D)
12. Philip M. Crane (R)

13. Harris W. Fawell (R)
14. J. Dennis Hastert (R)
15. Thomas W. Ewing (R)[4]
16. John W. Cox, Jr. (D)
17. Lane Evans (D)
18. Robert H. Michel (R)
19. Terry L. Bruce (D)
20. Richard J. Durbin (D)
21. Jerry F. Costello (D)
22. Glenn Poshard (D)

**INDIANA**
1. Peter J. Visclosky (D)
2. Philip R. Sharp (D)
3. Tim Roemer (D)
4. Jill L. Long (D)
5. Jim Jontz (D)
6. Dan Burton (R)
7. John T. Myers (R)
8. Frank McCloskey (D)
9. Lee H. Hamilton (D)
10. Andrew Jacobs, Jr. (D)

**IOWA**
1. Jim Leach (R)
2. Jim Nussle (R)
3. David R. Nagle (D)
4. Neal Smith (D)
5. Jim Lightfoot (R)
6. Fred Grandy (R)

**KANSAS**
1. Pat Roberts (R)
2. Jim Slattery (D)
3. Jan Meyers (R)
4. Dan Glickman (D)
5. Dick Nichols (R)

**KENTUCKY**
1. Carroll Hubbard, Jr. (D)
2. William H. Natcher (D)
3. Romano L. Mazzoli (D)
4. Jim Bunning (R)
5. Harold Rogers (R)
6. Larry J. Hopkins (R)
7. Carl C. Perkins (D)

**LOUISIANA**
1. Bob Livingston (R)
2. William J. Jefferson (D)
3. W. J. (Billy) Tauzin (D)
4. Jim McCrery (R)
5. Jerry Huckaby (D)
6. Richard H. Baker (R)
7. James A. Hayes (D)
8. Clyde C. Holloway (R)

**MAINE**
1. Thomas H. Andrews (D)
2. Olympia J. Snowe (R)

**MARYLAND**
1. Wayne T. Gilchrest (R)
2. Helen Delich Bentley (R)
3. Benjamin L. Cardin (D)
4. C. Thomas McMillen (D)
5. Steny H. Hoyer (D)
6. Beverly B. Byron (D)
7. Kweisi Mfume (D)
8. Constance A. Morella (R)

**MASSACHUSETTS**
1. John W. Olver (D)[5]
2. Richard E. Neal (D)
3. Joseph D. Early (D)
4. Barney Frank (D)
5. Chester G. Atkins (D)
6. Nicholas Mavroules (D)
7. Edward J. Markey (D)
8. Joseph P. Kennedy II (D)
9. John Joseph Moakley (D)
10. Gerry E. Studds (D)
11. Brian J. Donnelly (D)

**MICHIGAN**
1. John Conyers, Jr. (D)
2. Carl D. Pursell (R)

3. Howard Wolpe (D)
4. Frederick S. Upton (R)
5. Paul B. Henry (R)
6. Bob Carr (D)
7. Dale E. Kildee (D)
8. Bob Traxler (D)
9. Guy Vander Jagt (R)
10. Dave Camp (R)
11. Robert W. Davis (R)
12. David E. Bonior (D)
13. Barbara-Rose Collins (D)
14. Dennis M. Hertel (D)
15. William D. Ford (D)
16. John D. Dingell (D)
17. Sander M. Levin (D)
18. William S. Broomfield (R)

**MINNESOTA**
1. Timothy J. Penny (D)
2. Vin Weber (R)
3. Jim Ramstad (R)
4. Bruce F. Vento (D)
5. Martin Olav Sabo (D)
6. Gerry Sikorski (D)
7. Collin C. Peterson (D)
8. James L. Oberstar (D)

**MISSISSIPPI**
1. Jamie L. Whitten (D)
2. Mike Espy (D)
3. G. V. (Sonny) Montgomery (D)
4. Mike Parker (D)
5. Gene Taylor (D)

**MISSOURI**
1. William (Bill) Clay (D)
2. Joan Kelly Horn (D)
3. Richard A. Gephardt (D)
4. Ike Skelton (D)
5. Alan Wheat (D)
6. E. Thomas Coleman (R)
7. Melton D. Hancock (R)
8. Bill Emerson (R)
9. Harold L. Volkmer (D)

**MONTANA**
1. Pat Williams (D)
2. Ron Marlenee (R)

**NEBRASKA**
1. Doug Bereuter (R)
2. Peter Hoagland (D)
3. Bill Barrett (R)

**NEVADA**
1. James H. Bilbray (D)
2. Barbara F. Vucanovich (R)

**NEW HAMPSHIRE**
1. William H. Zeliff, Jr. (R)
2. Dick Swett (D)

**NEW JERSEY**
1. Robert E. Andrews (D)[6]
2. William J. Hughes (D)
3. Frank Pallone, Jr. (D)
4. Christopher H. Smith (R)
5. Marge Roukema (R)
6. Bernard J. Dwyer (D)
7. Matthew J. Rinaldo (R)
8. Robert A. Roe (D)
9. Robert G. Torricelli (D)
10. Donald M. Payne (D)
11. Dean A. Gallo (R)
12. Dick Zimmer (R)
13. Jim Saxton (R)
14. Frank J. Guarini (D)

**NEW MEXICO**
1. Steven H. Schiff (R)
2. Joe Skeen (R)
3. Bill Richardson (D)

**NEW YORK**
1. George J. Hochbrueckner (D)
2. Thomas J. Downey (D)
3. Robert J. Mrazek (D)
4. Norman F. Lent (R)

5. Raymond J. McGrath (R)
6. Floyd H. Flake (D)
7. Gary L. Ackerman (D)
8. James H. Scheuer (D)
9. Thomas J. Manton (D)
10. Charles E. Schumer (D)
11. Edolphus Towns (D)
12. Major R. Owens (D)
13. Stephen J. Solarz (D)
14. Susan Molinari (R)
15. Bill Green (R)
16. Charles B. Rangel (D)
17. Ted Weiss (D)
18. José E. Serrano (D)
19. Eliot L. Engel (D)
20. Nita M. Lowey (D)
21. Hamilton Fish, Jr. (R)
22. Benjamin A. Gilman (R)
23. Michael R. McNulty (D)
24. Gerald B. H. Solomon (R)
25. Sherwood L. Boehlert (R)
26. David O'B. Martin (R)
27. James T. Walsh (R)
28. Matthew F. McHugh (D)
29. Frank Horton (R)
30. Louise McIntosh Slaughter (D)
31. L. William Paxon (R)
32. John J. LaFalce (D)
33. Henry J. Nowak (D)
34. Amory Houghton (R)

**NORTH CAROLINA**
1. Walter B. Jones (D)
2. Tim Valentine (D)
3. H. Martin Lancaster (D)
4. David E. Price (D)
5. Stephen L. Neal (D)
6. Howard Coble (R)
7. Charles Rose (D)
8. W. G. (Bill) Hefner (D)
9. J. Alex McMillan (R)
10. Cass Ballenger (R)
11. Charles H. Taylor (R)

**NORTH DAKOTA**
At large: Byron L. Dorgan (D)

**OHIO**
1. Charles J. Luken (D)
2. Willis D. Gradison, Jr. (R)
3. Tony P. Hall (D)
4. Michael G. Oxley (R)
5. Paul E. Gillmor (R)
6. Bob McEwen (R)
7. David L. Hobson (R)
8. John A. Boehner (R)
9. Marcy Kaptur (D)
10. Clarence E. Miller (R)
11. Dennis E. Eckart (D)
12. John R. Kasich (R)
13. Donald J. Pease (D)
14. Thomas C. Sawyer (D)
15. Chalmers P. Wylie (R)
16. Ralph S. Regula (R)
17. James A. Traficant, Jr. (D)
18. Douglas Applegate (D)
19. Edward F. Feighan (D)
20. Mary Rose Oakar (D)
21. Louis Stokes (D)

**OKLAHOMA**
1. James M. Inhofe (R)
2. Mike Synar (D)
3. Bill K. Brewster (D)
4. Dave McCurdy (D)

5. Mickey Edwards (R)
6. Glenn English (D)

**OREGON**
1. Les AuCoin (D)
2. Robert F. (Bob) Smith (R)
3. Ron Wyden (D)
4. Peter A. DeFazio (D)
5. Michael J. Kopetski (D)

**PENNSYLVANIA**
1. Thomas M. Foglietta (D)
2. Lucien Blackwell (D)[7]
3. Robert A. Borski (D)
4. Joe Kolter (D)
5. Richard T. Schulze (R)
6. Gus Yatron (D)
7. Curt Weldon (R)
8. Peter H. Kostmayer (D)
9. Bud Shuster (R)
10. Joseph M. McDade (R)
11. Paul E. Kanjorski (D)
12. John P. Murtha (D)
13. Lawrence Coughlin (R)
14. William J. Coyne (D)
15. Don Ritter (R)
16. Robert S. Walker (R)
17. George W. Gekas (R)
18. Rick Santorum (R)
19. William F. Goodling (R)
20. Joseph M. Gaydos (D)
21. Thomas J. Ridge (R)
22. Austin J. Murphy (D)
23. William F. Clinger, Jr. (R)

**RHODE ISLAND**
1. Ronald K. Machtley (R)
2. Jack Reed (D)

**SOUTH CAROLINA**
1. Arthur Ravenel, Jr. (R)
2. Floyd Spence (R)
3. Butler Derrick (D)
4. Elizabeth J. Patterson (D)
5. John M. Spratt, Jr. (D)
6. Robin Tallon (D)

**SOUTH DAKOTA**
At large: Tim Johnson (D)

**TENNESSEE**
1. James H. (Jimmy) Quillen (R)
2. John James Duncan, Jr. (R)
3. Marilyn Lloyd Bouquard (D)
4. Jim Cooper (D)
5. Bob Clement (D)
6. Bart Gordon (D)
7. Don Sundquist (R)
8. John S. Tanner (D)
9. Harold E. Ford (D)

**TEXAS**
1. Jim Chapman (D)
2. Charles Wilson (D)
3. Sam Johnson (R)[8]
4. Ralph M. Hall (D)
5. John Bryant (D)
6. Joe Barton (R)
7. Bill Archer (R)
8. Jack Fields (R)
9. Jack Brooks (D)
10. J. J. Pickle (D)
11. Chet Edwards (D)
12. Pete Geren (D)
13. Bill Sarpalius (D)
14. Greg H. Laughlin (D)
15. E. de la Garza (D)
16. Ronald D. Coleman (D)

17. Charles W. Stenholm (D)
18. Craig A. Washington (D)
19. Larry Combest (R)
20. Henry B. Gonzalez (D)
21. Lamar S. Smith (R)
22. Tom DeLay (R)
23. Albert G. Bustamante (D)
24. Martin Frost (D)
25. Michael A. Andrews (D)
26. Richard K. Armey (R)
27. Solomon P. Ortiz (D)

**UTAH**
1. James V. Hansen (R)
2. Wayne Owens (D)
3. Bill Orton (D)

**VERMONT**
At large: Bernard Sanders (ind.)

**VIRGINIA**
1. Herbert H. Bateman (R)
2. Owen B. Pickett (D)
3. Thomas J. Bliley, Jr. (R)
4. Norman Sisisky (D)
5. Lewis F. Payne, Jr. (D)
6. Jim Olin (D)
7. George F. Allen (R)[9]
8. James P. Moran (D)
9. Rick Boucher (D)
10. Frank R. Wolf (R)

**WASHINGTON**
1. John R. Miller (R)
2. Al Swift (D)
3. Jolene Unsoeld (D)
4. Sid Morrison (R)
5. Thomas S. Foley (D)
6. Norman D. Dicks (D)
7. Jim McDermott (D)
8. Rod Chandler (R)

**WEST VIRGINIA**
1. Alan B. Mollohan (D)
2. Harley O. Staggers, Jr. (D)
3. Robert E. Wise, Jr. (D)
4. Nick Joe Rahall II (D)

**WISCONSIN**
1. Les Aspin (D)
2. Scott L. Klug (R)
3. Steve Gunderson (R)
4. Gerald D. Kleczka (D)
5. Jim Moody (D)
6. Thomas E. Petri (R)
7. David R. Obey (D)
8. Toby Roth (R)
9. F. James Sensenbrenner, Jr. (R)

**WYOMING**
At large: Craig Thomas (R)

**PUERTO RICO**
Resident Commissioner:
Jaime B. Fuster (D)

**AMERICAN SAMOA**
Delegate: Eui F. H.
Faleomavaega (D)

**GUAM**
Delegate: Ben Garrido Blaz (R)

**VIRGIN ISLANDS**
Delegate: Ron de Lugo (D)

**WASHINGTON, D.C.**
Delegate: Eleanor Holmes
Norton (D)

---

[1]Appointed to fill vacancy due to resignation of Pete Wilson.  [2]Appointed to fill vacancy due to death of John Heinz; elected November 5 to serve remainder of term.  [3]Elected September 24 to fill vacancy due to resignation of Morris K. Udall.  [4]Elected July 2 to fill vacancy due to resignation of Edward R. Madigan.  [5]Elected June 4 to fill vacancy due to death of Silvio O. Conte.  [6]Elected November 6, 1990, to fill vacancy due to resignation of James J. Florio.  [7]Elected November 5 to fill vacancy due to resignation of William H. Gray III.  [8]Elected May 18 to fill vacancy due to resignation of Steve Bartlett.  [9]Elected November 5 to fill vacancy due to resignation of D. French Slaughter, Jr.

more pressing domestic needs, since the Soviet threat had receded. However, the agreement remained intact during 1991.

In the pell-mell race to adjournment, Congress and the White House suddenly decided something had to be done about the sagging economy. House Republicans threw together a package that included cutting the capital gains tax, and, a day before Congress was set to adjourn, President Bush supported the plan, which he had earlier rejected, calling on Congress to vote on it before Thanksgiving. The move left Democrats, who had earlier introduced tax cuts favoring the middle class, debating whether to come back in December to pass legislation. Ultimately, all action was left to 1992.

**Abortion.** In November, Congress failed to override Bush's veto of a bill that would have blocked the administration's regulations barring abortion counseling in family planning clinics receiving federal funds. Earlier in the year, the president vetoed the District of Columbia's annual spending bill because it would have allowed the city to use its own money to pay for abortions for low-income women. Abortion rights advocates also lost legislative battles to allow military personnel to obtain abortions at overseas military hospitals and permit Medicaid-funded abortions for rape and incest victims.

**Family Leave.** A requirement that businesses offer workers family and medical leave gained congressional if not presidential support. The Senate overwhelmingly approved such a measure in October, and the House passed an almost identical version of the bill the next month. But the vote in the House fell short of the two-thirds majority needed to override an almost certain presidential veto, and Congress put off finalizing the bill.

**Transportation.** Passage of a massive $151 billion highway and mass transit bill, hammered out shortly before Congress adjourned for the year, was one of Congress's major achievements. Lawmakers hoped the six-year authorization of funds for the nation's transportation system would help spur the economy with new jobs, as well as combat traffic congestion and encourage the use of mass transit. The measure focused more on maintaining and improving existing roads than on constructing new highways, and it increased funding for mass transit. By consolidating the number of federal transportation grant programs, it also gave states more flexibility in how the money is to be spent.

**Unemployment Benefits.** Congress and President Bush finally agreed in mid-November on a measure to provide additional unemployment benefits to an estimated 3 million unemployed workers who had exhausted the regular 26 weeks of assistance. The new measure pro-

*Senator Alan Cranston (D, Calif.) was reprimanded before the full Senate for having interceded with bank regulators on behalf of Charles Keating, a major figure in the savings and loan scandal. Speaking to reporters afterward, Cranston expressed "deep remorse" but also said he had been unjustly singled out for censure.*

vided up to 20 weeks of extended benefits, with the number of weeks depending on economic conditions in a worker's home state. The cost (slightly over $5 billion) was to be offset by speeding up some estimated tax collections and by extending a tax surcharge on employers and a provision allowing deductions from tax refunds of those owing overdue student loans.

**Medicaid.** In the final hours of the 1991 session, Congress passed legislation setting new rules for the financing of Medicaid, the healthcare program for the nation's poor. The measure, intended to stem escalating costs, will limit the amount states can collect from hospitals to pay for their share of Medicaid; since state funding is matched by Washington, federal outlays will be held down as well. The legislation also ended special payments to hospitals with very high proportions of low-income patients.

**Telemarketing.** In another action taken just before adjournment, Congress banned telephone solicitations made by computers and recorded messages unless a consumer consents to such calls.

**Gulf War Resolution.** On January 12, after three days of debate, both houses of Congress passed a resolution authorizing the president to use U.S. forces to oust Iraqi troops from Kuwait. The resolution was seen as an important assertion of Congress's role in determining when the United States should go to war. The vote was 52-47 in the Senate and 250-183 in the House (the closest votes to send U.S. forces into combat since the War of 1812). During the debates a number of members argued that economic sanctions against Iraq should have been given more time to work.

**Foreign Aid.** Responding to the collapse of Soviet Communism—and of the Soviet Union itself—Congress just before adjournment approved $500 million to help Washington's former cold war adversary. Most of the money was earmarked to help dismantle nuclear weapons. The remainder was to be used for humanitarian aid.

Concerns about economic problems at home and the threat of a presidential veto prompted the House to defeat a $25 billion foreign aid authorization bill for fiscal 1992. Al-

though the bill was rejected, it progressed farther than any such measure since 1985, the last time a foreign aid bill was enacted. Foreign aid funding for the first six months of fiscal 1992 was covered in a continuing resolution passed in October.

**Arms Control.** In November the Senate approved the 1990 Conventional Forces in Europe treaty, between NATO countries and the former members of the Warsaw Pact. The treaty mandates reductions in tanks, aircraft, and other nonnuclear weapons from the Atlantic Ocean to the Ural Mountains.

**Thomas Nomination.** In July, President Bush nominated Clarence Thomas to succeed retiring Supreme Court Justice Thurgood Marshall. After a round of hearings before the Senate Judiciary Committee Thomas seemed headed for easy confirmation, despite opposition from many senators who believed him too conservative. But a second set of hearings was called when allegations of sexual harassment against Thomas, made to the committee staff by law professor Anita Hill, were leaked to the media two days before the scheduled Senate confirmation vote. The Judiciary Committee drew criticism for having initially ignored Hill's charges and kept them secret from the full Senate, as well as for its handling of the new hearings, in which sordid details of the alleged incidents were fully explored.

At the new hearings both Thomas and Hill testified before the committee, as did character witnesses for each. Thomas categorically denied the charges and called the procedure "a high-tech lynching of an uppity black who in any way deigns to think for himself." Republicans on the committee attempted to portray Hill as a woman scorned or out of touch with reality. When the nomination came to a vote in the Senate on October 15, 11 Democrats, mainly Southerners, joined Republicans in confirming Thomas, 52-48—the closest vote in this century to approve a Supreme Court nomination. K.L.S.

## SUPREME COURT

In its 1990-1991 term the U.S. Supreme Court included four appointees of Ronald Reagan or George Bush, most named to replace liberal or moderate justices, and already seemed firmly in conservative control. That control was ap-

In a closely watched case, the Supreme Court ruled employers could not exclude women from certain jobs on the grounds of possible on-the-job risk to unborn children. Here, the successful plaintiffs, workers at Johnson Controls, the company involved in the case, celebrate their victory.

parently reinforced by the replacement for Justice Thurgood Marshall.

**Thomas Nomination.** In June, Marshall, the first black justice (and before that a leading civil rights lawyer), announced he was retiring. Aged 82 and in failing health, he followed the example set a year earlier when his longtime liberal ally, William J. Brennan, had stepped down.

As a successor to Marshall, Bush named black conservative Clarence Thomas, a 43-year-old federal appeals court judge (*see profile in* PEOPLE IN THE NEWS). The nominee seemed headed for certain Senate confirmation when, shortly before the Senate's scheduled vote, it was reported that a former employee, Anita Hill (*see profile in* PEOPLE IN THE NEWS), had accused him of sexual harassment. Revelation of the allegation, which had been made to the staff of the Senate Judiciary Committee, prompted three days of dramatic, nationally televised committee hearings on the charges. Hill, a law school professor, testified that when Thomas was her supervisor at two federal agencies in the early 1980s, he pressed her to go out with him and told her in graphic detail about pornographic movies and his own sexual prowess. Thomas denied all of the accusations and portrayed himself as a victim of character assassination and racist stereotyping. Character witnesses supported both Hill and Thomas in the ultimately inconclusive hearings. On October 15, in a 52-48 vote,

Thomas was confirmed by the Senate, and he joined the Court a week later.

**Shift to the Right.** Bush had previously named David H. Souter to the Court; Ronald Reagan had named Justices Sandra Day O'Connor, Antonin Scalia, and Anthony M. Kennedy and promoted William H. Rehnquist (put on the Court by President Richard Nixon) to chief justice. Marshall's resignation left Justice Byron R. White as the lone remaining appointee of a Democratic president (John Kennedy), and White more often than not sided with the conservative majority. Justices Harry A. Blackmun and John Paul Stevens, labeled as moderates earlier in their careers, were the most liberal voices left on the Court (they had been named by Presidents Nixon and Gerald Ford, respectively).

**Criminal Law.** Conservative dominance was nowhere more apparent than in cases involving the rights of criminal defendants. In one case that drew wide notice, *Payne* v. *Tennessee*, the Court overturned close 1987 and 1989 decisions and ruled, 6-3, that juries weighing the death penalty may be told of the victim's character and the effect his or her death had on surviving family members. And in *Harmelin* v. *Michigan* the Court voted, 5-4, to uphold a mandatory life prison sentence without parole for a first-time drug offender. The Court said the life term did not amount to cruel and unusual punishment, as forbidden by the Constitution's Eighth Amendment.

421

# UNITED STATES OF AMERICA

Among other cases, the Court found, 6-3, in *Florida* v. *Bostick*, that police without warrants or suspicion of criminal activity may board a bus and ask passengers to consent to have their luggage searched for drugs. In *California* v. *Hodari D.*, a 7-2 majority found that drugs or other material dropped by a fleeing suspect can be used as evidence whether or not police had reason to suspect the person had committed a crime when they began the chase.

In *McCleskey* v. *Zant*, the Court said state prisoners seeking federal court review of claims their constitutional rights were violated generally are entitled to only one round of hearings. In *Coleman* v. *Thompson*, the justices held that state prisoners who fail to comply with their state's procedural rules for criminal cases generally are barred from having their cases reviewed in federal court. Both were 6-3 decisions.

The justices, voting, 5-4, in *Arizona* v. *Fulminante*, said a coerced confession in a criminal case does not always mandate a new trial. The guilty verdict may stand if there is an adequate showing that the defendant would have been convicted even without the confession.

In *County of Riverside* v. *McLaughlin* the Court ruled, 5-4, that people arrested without a warrant may be incarcerated for up to 48 hours while awaiting a determination of whether the arrest was proper. And a 5-4 majority, in *Wilson* v. *Seiter*, held that inmates suing over inhumane prison conditions must prove prison officials were deliberately indifferent to them.

In a rare victory for criminal defendants (*Powers* v. *Ohio*), the Court, voting 7-2, said the rights of whites are violated if they are convicted by juries from which black potential jurors were excluded because of their race. And in *Minnick* v. *Mississippi*, the Court ruled, 6-2, that once an accused person has invoked the so-called Miranda right to a lawyer, police may not resume questioning outside the lawyer's presence.

**Desegregation and Civil Rights.** The Supreme Court found in *Board of Education of Oklahoma City Public Schools* v. *Dowell* that federal courts could terminate supervision of school districts desegregation plans if a district had acted in good faith to eliminate as much segregation as "practicable."

Blacks may not be excluded because of their

race from serving on juries in civil cases, the Court ruled, 6-3, in *Edmonson* v. *Leesville Concrete Company*. Meanwhile, in cases from Texas and Louisiana, the Court ruled that the Voting Rights Act of 1965 applies to elections for judges. The decisions are expected to benefit minority candidates for judgeships, particularly in the South.

In *International Union, UAW* v. *Johnson Controls*, the justices unanimously ruled that women of childbearing age may not be barred from hazardous jobs by employers who say they are trying to protect fetuses.

**Freedom of Speech and the Press.** In probably the most closely watched case of the 1990-1991 term, *Rust* v. *Sullivan*, the Court ruled that the federal government may prohibit family planning clinics receiving federal funds from discussing abortion with their clients. The 5-4 ruling upheld regulations adopted by the Reagan administration to replace long-standing rules requiring health counselors to inform pregnant women of all their options, including abortion. The justices found that even though women have a right to abortion, the government is not required to subsidize speech about the subject. The ruling touched off a congressional effort—ultimately unsuccessful—to overturn the Court's decision.

In a 5-4 decision in *Barnes* v. *Glen Theatre, Inc.*, the Court found that states may ban erotic nude dancing even though the activity is a form of expression that enjoys some constitutional protection.

The Court ruled, 7-2, in *Masson* v. *New Yorker Magazine* that fabricated quotes may be grounds for a libel suit by a public figure—but only if the individual doing the suing can show the quotes changed the meaning of what was actually said. The decision permitted Dr. Jeffrey Masson's libel case against writer Janet Malcolm to go to trial. In *Cohen* v. *Cowles Media Company*, a 5-4 decision by the Court said news organizations may be sued for breaking promises of confidentiality to news sources.

In December the Court struck down New York's "Son of Sam" law, requiring that a criminal's profits from a book, film, or other creative work recounting the criminal activity be placed in a state victim compensation fund. In a broad 8-0 ruling, the Court held that such a

*Confirmation hearings on Supreme Court nominee Clarence Thomas, shown testifying at left, turned into a lurid media event when he faced charges that he had sexually harassed former employee Anita Hill. Below, Senator Orrin Hatch (R, Utah) suggested that some of Hill's charges may have been fabricated and in his estimation seemed to have been inspired by the novel* The Exorcist. *Hill, like Thomas, marshaled an array of character witnesses (right, Hill's witnesses are sworn in).*

*After the Persian Gulf War, U.S. Secretary of State James Baker invested considerable time and prestige in putting together Arab-Israeli peace talks. He is seen above (at left) talking in Jerusalem to Palestinian representatives Faisal al-Husseini and Hanan Ashrawi; right, conferring with Arab representatives at a conference in Saudi Arabia, and far right, meeting with Israeli Prime Minister Yitzhak Shamir (center) and Foreign Minister David Levy.*

selective ban violated the First Amendment's free speech guarantees. The ruling called into question the constitutionality of more than 40 other state laws modeled on the New York law, passed in the 1970s to prevent "Son of Sam" serial murderer David Berkowitz from collecting huge sums for selling his story.

**Business and Finance.** The Court handed down a key ruling that rejected a broad constitutional attack on skyrocketing punitive damage awards. The 7-1 ruling in *Pacific Mutual Life Insurance Company* v. *Haslip* said such awards in personal injury lawsuits against businesses generally do not violate due process rights even when they are disproportionately larger than the awards for actual damages. The decision left juries with broad discretion and was a setback to the insurance industry and other businesses that said they are being denied fair treatment.                    J.Ru.

### FOREIGN RELATIONS

War against Iraq and the disintegration of the Soviet Union were the two focal points of U.S. foreign policy during 1991. The United States also organized a peace conference between Israel and its Arab adversaries.

**War in the Persian Gulf.** As the year began, five months of economic sanctions and diplomacy had failed to end Iraq's occupation of Kuwait. A U.S.-led international coalition was poised to use military force if the Iraqis did not withdraw by January 15, a deadline set in a United Nations Security Council resolution. At President George Bush's request, both the Senate and the House of Representatives on January 12 authorized "all necessary means" to dislodge the Iraqis if they failed to meet the UN deadline.

The deadline having passed, on January 17 (Kuwait time) the United States and its coalition partners unleashed an intense air attack concentrated on Baghdad and military units in and around Kuwait. When the air assault failed to force an Iraqi pullout, on February 24 the allies began a ground offensive that lasted exactly 100 hours, during which Iraqi forces retreated north, surrendered, or were killed. Kuwait was liberated on February 27. President Bush then made the subsequently controversial decision to end the fighting, leaving Iraqi President Saddam Hussein in power and a part of his fighting force and equipment intact.

To the disappointment of U.S. strategists, no coup materialized against Saddam Hussein, who used his remaining military power to crush rebellions by Shiite Muslims in southern Iraq and by Kurds in the north. The United States provided emergency food, medicine, clothing, and other supplies for the tens of thousands of Kurds who fled into Turkey to

escape Iraqi troops, and it set up militarily protected camps in northern Iraq for the refugees to initially return to. But it did not provide military support to the Kurdish rebels.

Meanwhile, inspection teams turned up evidence during the year that Iraq's nuclear weapons program was dangerously advanced and had suffered far less damage under the allied air attack than American intelligence had estimated. In Kuwait hundreds of oil well fires, deliberately ignited by the Iraqis, daily consumed millions of barrels of oil and polluted the environment before the last ones were extinguished by November.

**Other Middle East Developments.** The achievement of an Israeli-Palestinian settlement was undeniably essential for lasting peace in the Middle East. Accordingly, getting the parties to negotiate with each other became the primary American foreign policy objective for the region once the Gulf War was won. After eight trips to the Middle East, Secretary of State James Baker finally succeeded in bringing together representatives of Israel, the Palestinians, Lebanon, Syria, and Jordan at a conference in Madrid that opened at the end of October. A second round of discussions was held in Washington in December, with further talks slated for 1992.

Despite the success of Baker's peacemaking efforts, relations between the United States and Israel were rocky through most of 1991. The Israelis continued to build new Jewish settlements in the occupied territories, and the Bush administration continued to object to this "expansionism." In September, Bush asked Congress to delay for 120 days consideration of U.S. guarantees for $10 billion in loans to Israel to provide housing for Soviet Jewish émigrés; Congress acquiesced.

Also in September, in a speech to the UN General Assembly, Bush urged the delegates to repeal a 1985 resolution stating that "Zionism is a form of racism." After heavy lobbying by the United States, and with the support of the former Soviet bloc, in December the Assembly voted, 111-25, to do so.

The hostage crisis that had bedeviled U.S. foreign policy since 1985 came to a conclusion in 1991. The shadowy terrorist groups who had been holding American and other Western hostages in Lebanon released most of them one by one during the late summer and fall. The last American held, journalist Terry Anderson, was freed in December.

In November U.S. and Scottish authorities issued arrest warrants for two Libyan intelligence agents who were charged with placing the bomb that had exploded on Pan Am Flight 103 over Scotland in 1988, killing 270 people.

425

A Libyan judge announced that the two had been placed under house arrest, but U.S. and British officials demanded that they be handed over rather than tried in Libya.

**End of the Soviet Union.** Even more dramatic than events in the Middle East was the disintegration of the Soviet Union. Throughout 1991 this process piled surprise upon surprise, leaving even the most informed "experts" dizzy and U.S. policy in constant flux.

Early in the year hard-line Communists in Moscow appeared to be putting an end to the process of reform that had made President Mikhail Gorbachev such a heroic figure in American eyes. In December 1990, Soviet Foreign Minister Eduard Shevardnadze, who had been instrumental in ending the cold war, had resigned from the government and criticized Gorbachev for playing into the hands of the hard-liners. In January, after Soviet troops gunned down Lithuanian protesters, Moscow seemed on the verge of squashing the independence movements in the Baltic republics of Lithuania, Latvia, and Estonia.

Bush postponed a planned February summit meeting with Gorbachev in Moscow, but he refrained from heavy criticism in the hope that Soviet policy would shift back toward liberalization. By July the hope seemed justified. At the end of the month, Bush went to Moscow for the signing of a strategic arms reduction treaty (Start), which cut the number of long-range nuclear warheads allowed to each side by approximately one-third and provided for effective inspection to ensure compliance. As an indication of his support for Gorbachev, Bush recommended that Congress grant the Soviet Union most-favored-nation trade status and, in the Ukrainian capital of Kiev, supported the concept of a central Soviet government by warning against the hazards of "suicidal" nationalism.

In mid-August, however, a group of hard-liners attempted a coup. Boris Yeltsin, president of the Russian republic, rallied throngs of supporters in defense of reform, and after the coup collapsed he had clearly become the key political figure. As he moved to shift power from the Soviet to the Russian government, separatist movements in the other Soviet republics gained strength.

Official U.S. policy continued to support the idea of a single Soviet Union with Gorbachev as its leader. Washington belatedly acknowledged the independence of the Baltic republics in September but was reluctant to go further. In September, Bush sought simultaneously to bolster Gorbachev's prestige and to speed the process of nuclear disarmament by announcing deep unilateral cuts in U.S. nuclear arms and the end of the decades-old alert status for nuclear-armed strategic bombers. Gorbachev responded with a promise of comparable Soviet reductions.

This good news, however, did not help Gorbachev at home, where the economy continued its drastic collapse. On December 1, Ukrainians voted overwhelmingly for independence, and later in the month the leaders of all the former Soviet republics except Georgia and the Baltic states formed a Commonwealth of Independent States. The end of the Soviet Union was clearly at hand, and on December 25, Gorbachev formally resigned. The same day Bush announced that the United States would recognize the independence of Georgia and the Commonwealth members and would establish diplomatic relations with Armenia, Belarus (Byelorussia), Kazakhstan, Kyrgyzstan (Kirghizia), Russia, and Ukraine. Diplomatic ties with the remaining six republics were contingent on their meeting guidelines on democracy and human rights that had been set down earlier by Baker.

The United States, as Baker stated in a speech in early December, was ready to extend modest aid for food and medicine, but the enormity of the economic problems was beyond the capacity of American will or resources to solve, especially when the U.S. economy was itself in difficulty. Americans were also disturbed by uncertainty about how and by whom the thousands of nuclear warheads within the territory of the former Soviet Union would ultimately be controlled. Yeltsin took control of the Soviet nuclear-weapons launching codes from Gorbachev when the latter resigned, and on December 30 the members of the Commonwealth of Independent States announced that their nuclear weapons would remain under a joint command. In mid-December, Baker had visited the four republics with long-range nuclear weapons on their territory—Russia, Ukraine, Belarus, and Kazakhstan—and had obtained pledges from their leaders to honor the arms-reduction commitments made by Gorbachev.

**Asia.** The long U.S. military presence in the Philippines drew to an end in 1991. A volcano in June destroyed the usability of Clark Field, a huge air base, and the Philippine Senate also ordered the United States to withdraw from the Subic Bay Naval Station by the end of 1992.

Elsewhere in Asia, the United States announced plans to reduce its forces in South Korea and to remove all its nuclear weapons from that country. Relations between the United States and Vietnam improved, and preliminary conversations about the establishment of formal diplomatic ties were held.

Relations with Japan were strained by Bush's decision to postpone, for domestic political reasons, a planned November visit to Tokyo, and by the commemoration of the 50th anniversary of the Japanese attack on Pearl Harbor on December 7. Bush rescheduled the visit for early 1992. As for China, a trip by Baker to Beijing in November elicited only a few modest concessions on trade and human rights. Later that month U.S. Trade Representative Carla Hills announced that she would seek to restrict some Chinese imports in retaliation for China's failure to place effective restrictions on the piracy of American patents, copyrights, and trademarks.

**Other Regions.** South Africa continued to dismantle the legal structure of apartheid, and in recognition Bush on July 10 issued an executive order terminating U.S. economic sanctions against that country. In the western hemisphere, the Bush administration encouraged a role for the UN in arranging a cease-fire and political accords between the Salvadoran government and leftist rebels. And through the Organization of American States, the United States participated in economic sanctions against the military regime that ousted President Jean-Bertrand Aristide of Haiti on September 30. When the distress in Haiti produced a flight of refugees in small, unseaworthy boats toward the United States, the initial American response was to keep them from

landing and to return them to Haiti. A series of federal court orders halted the repatriation program, but the fate of thousands of refugees was uncertain at year's end. G.S.

**UPPER VOLTA.** See STATISTICS OF THE WORLD: *Burkina Faso.*

**URUGUAY.** In 1991, President Luis Alberto Lacalle Herrera found himself unable to meet several important political objectives as Uruguay remained mired in a recession. On January 18, the seventh national strike in the ten months since Lacalle had assumed power took place, reflecting labor's resistance to privatization of state-owned industries and other sweeping economic reforms. In May former President Julio Sanguinetti, leader of the Foro Battlhista faction, withdrew his support for Lacalle's governing coalition, protesting Lacalle's proposals to sell off (totally or partially) the nation's telephone company and national airline, as well as to scrap state monopolies in the insurance, electricity, gas, and alcohol sectors. Lacalle toned down his privatization plans, and the two leaders reached a fragile accord to preserve the coalition.

In September, Tabaré Vázquez, the mayor of Montevideo and leader of the Frente Amplio coalition, faced off with the national government over the construction in Montevideo of a major power plant. Citing environmental concerns, Vázquez announced a moratorium on construction. Lacalle proposed talks between municipal and national government representatives on the future of the project.

On July 4, the Uruguayan Senate voted unanimously to ratify the Mercosur Treaty, paving the way for a Latin American common market. The treaty established a free-trade zone among Uruguay, Argentina, Brazil, and Paraguay, to be set up by 1995. Uruguay also signed treaties with the United States calling for greater cooperation on issues of international crime and drug running. One treaty restricted money-laundering operations in Uruguay, whose Swiss-style banking secrecy laws have long made it South America's only "offshore" banking center.

Uruguay became the first recipient of a new type of debt-reduction loan package offered by the World Bank and the Inter-American Development Bank. The arrangement involved the

Uruguayan government's buying back $628 million worth of loans from the creditors, paying 56 cents on each dollar owed. Of the nation's remaining $1 billion in debt, $447 million was rescheduled to be paid back over a longer period than originally stipulated, with the remaining $553 million being converted to interest-bearing bonds. Altogether, the package cut the nation's debt by $503 million. See STATISTICS OF THE WORLD.

J.F. & A.O'R.

**UTAH.** See STATISTICS OF THE WORLD.

# V

**VANUATU.** See STATISTICS OF THE WORLD. See also PACIFIC ISLANDS.

**VENEZUELA.** Economic conditions continued to improve in 1991 in Venezuela, while President Carlos Andrés Pérez remained the dominant figure in national politics.

In an important step, Pérez signed a decree setting aside more than 30,000 square miles of Amazon forest for Venezuela's 14,000 Yanomami Indians, who, with several thousand Yanomamis living in Brazil, represent perhaps the last major native Western Hemisphere culture largely untouched by modern civilization. In the new Upper Orinoco-Casiquiare Biosphere Reserve, all mining, farming, and colonization would be prohibited.

The economy benefited from a reduction in the foreign debt and increased investment from abroad. The Pérez government continued the progressive lowering of import tariffs and maintenance of a single floating exchange rate and moved ahead with plans for privatization. In August the state international airline, Viasa, was sold to a consortium headed by Spain's Iberia airline. In November the Caracas Telephone Company was sold to an international consortium. Two major banks were privatized during the year.

The economy owed much of its strength to higher oil prices. With President Pérez committed to an increase in production from 2 million to 3.5 million barrels per day by 1995, the cooperation of foreign companies received high priority. As Latin America's senior democratic leader, Pérez joined with the Colombian and Mexican presidents to constitute an informal Big Three. They agreed to a free-trade zone and moved toward liberalization of trilateral trade by the close of 1993. Venezuela was also active in other free-trade negotiations. See STATISTICS OF THE WORLD.

J.D.M.

**VERMONT.** See STATISTICS OF THE WORLD.

**VICE PRESIDENT OF THE UNITED STATES.** See PEOPLE IN THE NEWS: Dan Quayle.

**VIETNAM.** In both the political and diplomatic arenas, 1991 was a year of advancing change for Vietnam. There were many new faces among the 1,176 delegates at the Seventh Party Congress in June, where Premier Do Muoi, 74, was named general secretary, replacing the ailing Nguyen Van Linh, who resigned. Also replaced were Foreign Minister Nguyen Co Thach, a critic of China, Interior Minister Mai Chi Tho, and President Vo Chi Cong. Newcomers reduced the average age of the ruling body from 71 to 60. At a meeting of the National Assembly in July, Vo Van Kiet, 69, was elected premier, replacing Do Muoi.

The government continued efforts to stimulate private enterprise while maintaining firm political control. Restrictions on the press were tightened. In April, Nguyen Dan Que, a physician who attempted to form a human rights movement, was convicted of treason and sentenced to 20 years in prison.

Vietnam moved on a number of fronts to improve relations with other countries. A key event came in October with the signing of a Cambodian peace accord negotiated with Vietnamese help. Meanwhile, a U.S. liaison office was established in Hanoi to help in accounting for Americans listed as prisoners of war (POWs) or missing in action (MIA) in the Vietnam War. Late in the year, senior U.S. and Vietnamese officials held the first in a series of talks on normalizing relations.

*Full diplomatic relations were restored between longtime foes Vietnam and China in November, as Vietnamese Prime Minister Vo Van Kiet (second from left) journeyed to Beijing and met with Chinese Prime Minister Li Peng (right).*

In October, Hanoi agreed to accept the forced return of tens of thousands of Vietnamese living in refugee camps in Hong Kong and elsewhere in Southeast Asia who were classified as illegal immigrants. Groups of refugees were repatriated in November and December. The Vietnamese also agreed to monitoring by UN observers to ensure that the returnees were not persecuted.

In November, Vietnamese Communist Party chief Do Muoi and Premier Vo Van Kiet met with top Chinese leaders in Beijing. The high-level talks marked a normalization of bilateral relations after more than a decade of mutual hostility.

Vietnam remained one of the poorest countries in Asia. A virtual cessation in Soviet eco-nomic and military aid had greatly exacerbated Vietnam's economic difficulties. Meanwhile, the U.S. trade embargo and American opposition to loans from international financial agencies limited new investment. The return of Vietnamese troops from Cambodia and a 50 percent reduction in the military added 500,000 job seekers to civilian labor force.

Still, economic momentum picked up, especially in the expanding free market sector, and inflation, which had been running around 400 percent in recent years, slowed to below 100 percent.

*See* STATISTICS OF THE WORLD.     G.B.H.

**VIRGINIA.** *See* STATISTICS OF THE WORLD.

**VIRGIN ISLANDS.** *See* STATISTICS OF THE WORLD.

**WOMEN.** The abortion issue continued to be a focus of attention in 1991, with a U.S. Supreme Court decision and some new state laws provoking controversy. When President George Bush's nominee to the Supreme Court was accused of sexual harassment, the topic of sexual harassment became an object of increased attention.

**Abortion.** In a highly controversial decision, the U.S. Supreme Court voted in May to uphold a federal rule that prohibited employees in family planning clinics assisted by federal funds from providing information or counseling about abortion. Opponents of the decision vehemently criticized it as a violation of free speech, and Congress passed legislation to remove the restriction, but could not override a veto by Bush.

In October a U.S. court of appeals overturned a federal district court's finding that the three central provisions of a 1989 Pennsylvania abortion law, requiring parental consent for minors, pre-abortion counseling, and a 24-hour waiting period, were unconstitutional. The American Civil Liberties Union, and Planned Parenthood petitioned the Supreme Court to review the decision.

In August a U.S. district court declared Louisiana's stringent anti-abortion law unconstitutional, a decision that was appealed. The law prohibited abortion except to save the mother's life and in cases of rape where the crime is reported within seven days and the victim is examined to determine whether she was pregnant beforehand. Under the law, any abortion

had to be performed within 13 weeks of conception, and doctors violating the law were subject to imprisonment and heavy fines.

In January, Utah enacted a strict abortion law limiting abortion to cases of rape or incest, pregnancies seriously endangering a woman, or instances where the fetus suffers from defects incompatible with survival. A somewhat similar measure in North Dakota was vetoed by the governor. The Mississippi legislature enacted a law requiring a woman seeking an abortion to be informed of the procedure's medical risks and then wait 24 hours before it could be performed.

Meanwhile, Maryland enacted one of the most liberal abortion laws in the nation, allowing unrestricted abortions up until fetal viability. An abortion rights measure in the state of Washington, meant to nullify the effect of any Supreme Court reversal of *Roe* v. *Wade*, squeezed by in November, and in Corpus Christi, Texas, citizens rejected a proposed amendment to the city charter declaring that "human life begins at conception and continues until natural death."

The most visible fight over abortion took place in Wichita, Kan., during the summer, when some 2,500 protestors were arrested for trying to shut down three abortion clinics.

**Sexual Harassment.** A storm erupted in the fall when President Bush's Supreme Court nominee, Judge Clarence Thomas, was accused of sexual harassment by former employee Anita Hill, a University of Oklahoma law professor. Thomas was eventually confirmed by the Senate, and national polls showed that more women actually believed Judge Thomas than his accuser. Still, other women felt betrayed. Relationships, private and professional, between men and women became subject to increased scrutiny.

Meanwhile, an independent fact-finding panel investigating complaints by women members of the Texas A&M University Corps of Cadets confirmed in November that female cadets there were subject to pervasive harassment and discrimination. Women cited verbal abuse, social ostracism, and threats of physical assault and rape. Corps Commandant Major General Thomas G. Darling promised measures to deal with the problem.

*Fed up with what she called a long-standing pattern of unwelcome sexual advances and demeaning comments, Frances Conley, M.D., resigned her professorship at Stanford Medical School. She later agreed to return, but her outspokenness drew considerable attention in a year when sexual harassment was much in the news.*

Citing "pervasive sexism," neurosurgeon Frances Conley resigned from Stanford University Medical School in May. She rejoined the faculty in September after she said she could see that Stanford was taking steps to remedy the problem.

**Discrimination Cases.** In one of the largest such awards ever, a Los Angeles jury in October ordered Texaco to pay $5.3 million in compensatory damages and $15 million in punitive damages to Janella Sue Martin, a credit manager passed over for promotion in what the jury agreed was sex discrimination. Texaco announced it would appeal. Earlier in the year, Continental Airlines retracted a rule requiring female employees to wear makeup, after an employee, fired for refusing to wear it, filed a sex discrimination complaint against the airline.

In January the all-male Tiger Inn, a Princeton University eating club, was required by the New Jersey Supreme Court to admit women when accepting new members. In October it was Yale's turn, as more tradition-bound alumni failed to prevent the university's Skull and Bones society from voting to admit women for the first time in its 159-year history.

**Women in the Headlines.** Khaleda Zia, widow of General Ziaur Rahman, became prime minister of Bangladesh in February. A leader of the conservative Bangladesh National Party, Zia promised to develop capitalism in her impoverished country. In May, Socialist Edith Cresson was appointed by President François Mitterrand as the first female premier of France. As premier she had to cope with soaring unemployment.

In the United States, the U.S. Naval Academy appointed Juliane Gallina, 20, as its first female brigade commander. Susan O'Malley, 29, was named president of the Washington Bullets basketball team. Patricia Ireland, named the new president of the National Organization for Women, acknowledged being involved in an ongoing relationship with another woman.

See also CIVIL LIBERTIES AND CIVIL RIGHTS; UNITED STATES: Supreme Court.            J.L.D.

**WYOMING.** See STATISTICS OF THE WORLD.

# Y

**YEMEN.** See STATISTICS OF THE WORLD. See also ARABIAN PENINSULA.

**YUGOSLAVIA.** Limited violence in Slovenia following declarations of independence by Croatia and Slovenia—two of Yugoslavia's six constituent republics—escalated into civil war by late summer 1991. The fighting was the heaviest in central Europe since World War II, claiming thousands of lives in Croatia and producing hundreds of thousands of Croatian and Serbian refugees.

With Communists ousted from power in much of the country, there were two competing visions of the future Yugoslavia: one a loose confederation of sovereign states, the other (insisted on by the republic of Serbia) a strong, centralized federation. Meanwhile, within each republic (and in the formally autonomous Serbian provinces of Voivodina and Kosovo) a political struggle continued between militant nationalists and dogmatic former Communists.

**Moving Toward Crisis.** By 1991 federal Prime Minister Ante Markovic's rigorous 1990 economic reform program had been, as a Western diplomat put it, "ripped to shreds." The federal government was increasingly unable to collect taxes from republics. Separatist forces were also strengthened by the federal government's inability to promulgate a new constitution and to agree on procedures for a promised federal election, as well as by manipulation of ethnic passions by both Serbian President Slobodan Milosevic and Croatian President Franjo Tudjman. Nationalist fever in Croatia and Tudjman's anti-Serbian rhetoric elicited protests from Croatia's sizable Serb minority. And in Serbia on March 9, students and opposition parties staged a massive demonstration in Belgrade against Milosevic's eco-

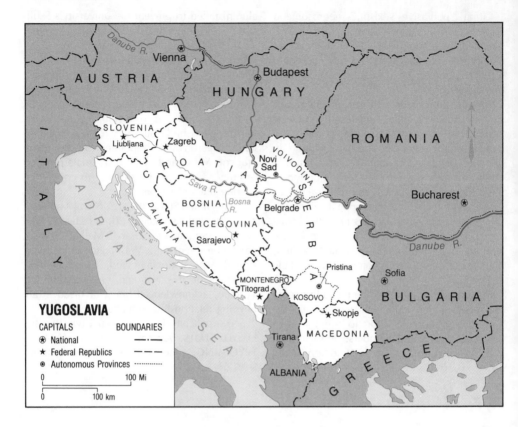

YUGOSLAVIA

CAPITALS      BOUNDARIES
⊛ National      —·—
★ Federal Republics      — — —
◉ Autonomous Provinces    ············

0           100 Mi
0         100 km

nomic mismanagement and confrontational style. Tensions escalated in May when Serbia and Montenegro temporarily prevented Croatian representative Stjepan Mesic from taking his turn as head of the Yugoslav collective state presidency. The long-expected rupture came on June 25 when Croatia and Slovenia declared independence.

**War Begins.** Slovene leaders participated in peace negotiations but set up their own border posts, reneging on an agreement to allow a joint Slovenian-federal customs presence on Slovenia's borders while talks continued. The shooting started June 27 when federal troops sent into Slovenia to escort federal customs officers back to their posts exchanged fire with Slovene militia.

The European Community used threats and promises to broker a cease-fire and a cooling-off period, and Slovenia and Croatia put their declarations of independence on hold for a three-month period of negotiation. Federal

troops apparently stopped firing during the cease-fire, while Slovenes kept shooting. But by midsummer moderate federal officers were either purged or silenced. The Army became more dominated by Serbs and sided more openly with Croatia's Serbian minority.

An EC peace conference in the Netherlands made little headway against escalating violence. In October, Slovenia and Croatia, declaring that the moratorium on independence was up, again asserted their sovereignty. Macedonia and Bosnia-Hercegovina joined the march toward independence. Later that month, the members of the presidency from Serbia, its ally Montenegro, and the provinces of Kosovo and Voivodina announced they were taking over the powers of the federal Parliament. This move was declared illegal by the representatives from Slovenia, Macedonia, and Bosnia-Hercegovina, as well as by Croatian Representative Mesic, the official head of the presidency, who stayed away from Bel-

*Civil war erupted in Yugoslavia, after Croatia and Slovenia, two of the country's constituent republics (see map, left), declared independence. The Croatian city of Vukovar underwent weeks of bombardment by the Yugoslav Army; above, bodies of the slain lie in the courtyard outside a hospital.*

grade out of fear for his life. By this time the Markovic government had lost so much of its authority that the prime minister was routinely excluded from EC cease-fire negotiations.

As the Croatian military position weakened in late September, the Tudjman government gambled that if Croatian forces could blockade or capture federal garrisons in Croatia, the Army's retaliatory violence might press Germany into following through on its threat to recognize Slovenia and Croatia. The Croatian blockade deprived Army garrisons of food, water, and electricity and changed the character of the civil war. Instead of a struggle between Serbian and Croatian forces to win territory and gain political advantages it became a war between Croatia and a professional Army. The military launched a relentless bombardment of the Croatian city of Dubrovnik. Meanwhile, in late November, Vukovar, in eastern Croatia, fell to Army forces after being reduced to rubble during an 86-day siege.

**An Elusive Peace.** With the federal Army and Serbian irregulars occupying about one-third of Croatia's territory, UN special envoy Cyrus Vance arrived in Belgrade on December 1 to shore up a 14th fragile cease-fire accord and arrange for a possible deployment of UN peacekeeping forces. On December 5, amid reports of renewed fighting, Mesic stepped down as head of Yugoslavia's collective presidency. A day earlier, Croatian officials had granted the republic's ethnic Serbs a measure of self-rule. Despite pressure from the EC, the UN, and the United States to refrain from unilaterally recognizing Slovenia and Croatia, Germany announced in mid-December that it would go ahead with recognition. Fighting intensified, but Vance managed to broker a New Year's Eve agreement that offered some hope of ending the civil war.

*See* STATISTICS OF THE WORLD. R.A.R.

**YUKON TERRITORY.** *See* STATISTICS OF THE WORLD.

# Z

**ZAIRE.** The year 1991 was marked by political turmoil as Zaire's new political parties fought President Mobutu Seso Seko's dogged determination to remain head of state. Following Mobutu's October 1990 announcement that there would be no limits on the number of parties allowed, more than 200 had come into being, many under the umbrella of an opposition coalition called the Sacred Union. Ultimately, Mobutu did agree to a power-sharing arrangement.

Mobutu in April had agreed to the holding of a national conference to discuss a new constitution and a timetable for elections. Later, however, the government declared that the conference's decisions would not be sovereign but would be subject to approval by the president, the legislature, and the people (via a referendum). The conference was suspended and reconvened a number of times during the year and had achieved little by year's end.

In September mutinous soldiers, unpaid for months, went on a rampage in Kinshasa. As the unrest spread to other parts of the country, over 100 people were killed, stores and private homes were looted, and France and Belgium sent in troops to rescue their nationals and other foreigners. Under intense international pressure, Mobutu then agreed to share power with the opposition and named Etienne Tshisekedi, once a determined adversary, as the country's prime minister.

Tshisekedi managed to put together Zaire's first opposition-led cabinet, but he failed to persuade Mobutu to relinquish control of the key ministries of defense and of mines. In October the president replaced Tshisekedi with Bernardin Mungul-Diaka, but Mungul-Diaka had little credibility and his appointment led to renewed violence. He was succeeded in late November by yet another erstwhile opposition stalwart, Nguza Karl-I-Bond. Meanwhile, Mobutu, whose seven-year presidential term ended on December 4, announced his intention to remain in office, as he said the constitution entitled him to do, until new elections were held.

Political turmoil was accompanied by economic devastation. Inflation had soared with the Persian Gulf War crisis; by mid-1991 it was running at 50 percent a month. Striking workers wreaked havoc in the copper and cobalt mines of Shaba Province; in many of the largest mines production virtually halted. In the summer the United States, citing Zaire's human rights abuses as well as its failure to service its debt, suspended economic assistance; the World Bank and the International Monetary Fund suspended loans.

A notable casualty of the turmoil was Project SIDA (from the French acronym for AIDS), a research project that had helped define the scope of the AIDS epidemic in the 1980s and whose continuing studies were providing valuable data about the spread, deterrence, and prevention of the disease. By late September, Project SIDA's foreign scientists had left Zaire; it was feared that if political instability continued, many vital studies would have to be abandoned.

In May the Supreme Court of Justice announced sentences for the defendants tried after the violence at Lubumbashi University in 1990, when government security forces responding to student violence against alleged police spies in their midst killed a number of students. The sentences ranged from life imprisonment for two defendants to 10-15 year prison terms for six others; five defendants were acquitted.

*See* Statistics of the World.            T.E.T.

**ZAMBIA.** In October 1991, Kenneth Kaunda, president of Zambia since its independence in 1964, was soundly defeated in a multiparty election, the first since 1972. The victor was Frederick Chiluba, a 48-year-old trade union leader and the candidate of the Movement for Multiparty Democracy (MMD), which captured 125 of the 150 seats in Parliament. International election observers, including former U.S. President Jimmy Carter, pronounced the election fair. Chiluba reportedly garnered 80 percent of the vote.

The former government, under intense pressure, had legalized alternative political parties in December 1990, although in an effort to prevent the MMD from capitalizing on its popularity among first-time voters, Kaunda forbade registration of any new voters. The Kaunda government had continued to limit permits for MMD rallies and hinder the party's access to the state-run media. His supporters violently broke up MMD rallies, and in March, Kaunda closed down the university.

Such repressive tactics did not help Kaunda's popularity. One of several new privately owned newspapers, the *Weekly Post*, launched in May, vigorously exposed government scandals. The MMD fought government repression in court and frequently won; as election day neared, it was able to campaign more freely. At an Africa Cup match in July, soccer fans enthusiastically hailed Chiluba and other opposition figures but stoned Kaunda's motorcade.

Before the election, evidence of economic discontent surfaced frequently. There were over 30 major strikes. Farmers refused to plant crops for which the government controlled prices and instead planted more lucrative crops with market-based prices. About a third of the annual maize harvest was smuggled to Malawi and Zaire, where higher prices prevailed. An added burden was a cholera outbreak that hit seven of the country's nine provinces in March and claimed more than 800 lives.

The new president named a diverse cabinet that included some former Kaunda associates and one white minister (Guy Scott, for agriculture). Chiluba faced an economy in shambles with a $7 billion debt and debt service charges equal to 150 percent of annual export earnings. In his campaign he promised to embrace the International Monetary Fund's structural adjustment program. He planned to sell off the copper mines and other state-owned corporations, end the state of emergency, place greater resources into agriculture, and end subsidies on most staples.

*See* STATISTICS OF THE WORLD. K.W.G.

**ZIMBABWE.** In 1991 the government of Zimbabwe launched a major program of economic reform, replacing socialism with a market-driven economy. At the same time the ruling party continued its suppression of rival political forces and its plans to redistribute farmland from white commercial farmers to landless black peasants.

Government leaders outlined plans to cut the civil service by 20 percent, end subsidies for many staple goods, and reduce subsidies to parastatal corporations. Foreign donors provisionally agreed to provide about $700 million in grants and loans to help implement the plan. Late in the year, however, donors were reported to be withholding funds until Zimbabwe signed a document detailing budget cuts.

Seemingly at odds with the movement toward a market economy was the proposed redistribution of land from many of the country's 4,000 mainly white commercial farmers to some 110,000 black peasant farmers. The largely white Commercial Farmers Union argued that the policy would create an exodus of skilled white farmers, thereby reducing Zimbabwe's ability to feed itself and its foreign exchange earnings from agriculture. Much depends on whether skilled or unskilled peasants are resettled. If the peasants are skilled, the falloff in productivity need not be so marked as it has been with those resettled over the last decade.

Under popular pressure the ruling party, Zanu-PF, in June deleted references to the ideologies of "Marxism-Leninism" and "scientific socialism" from its constitution. Still, the three opposition members in Parliament, who belonged to the Zimbabwe Unity Movement, were regularly harassed by the police. The media remained controlled by the government, the ruling party's bureaucrats were still on the state payroll, and the national university was coming under the direction of Zanu-PF. The opposition was also hampered by internal divisions; the founder and president of ZUM, Edgar Tekere, was "retired" by the group's executive council after he rejected the council's new constitution.

In May, Ethiopia's deposed President Mengistu Haile Mariam was given political refuge in Zimbabwe. The heads of state of the Commonwealth of Nations met in Harare in October, with Queen Elizabeth in attendance.

*See* STATISTICS OF THE WORLD. K.W.G.

# THE COUNTRIES OF THE WORLD

| Nation<br>Capital | Population | Area of<br>Country<br>(sq mi/<br>sq km) | Type of<br>Government | Heads of State and<br>Government | Currency:<br>Value of<br>U.S. Dollar<br>(July 1) | GNP<br>(millions)<br>GNP<br>Per Capita |
|---|---|---|---|---|---|---|
| AFGHANISTAN<br>Kabul | 16,600,000<br>3,000,000 | 251,826<br>652,229 | People's<br>republic | President: Najibullah<br>Prime Minister:<br>Fazi Haq Khaleqlar | Afghani<br>55.00 | $ 3,100<br>214 |
| ALBANIA<br>Tiranë | 3,300,000<br>239,000 | 11,100<br>28,748 | Republic | President:<br>Ramiz Alia<br>Prime Minister:<br>Ylli Bufi | Lek<br>6.2139 | 3,800<br>NA |
| ALGERIA<br>Algiers | 26,000,000<br>1,722,000 | 919,595<br>2,381,741 | Republic | President:<br>Chadli Benjedid<br>Premier:<br>Sid Ahmed Ghozali | Dinar<br>21.09[1] | 53,116<br>2,170 |
| ANGOLA<br>Luanda | 8,500,000<br>1,500,000 | 481,354<br>1,246,700 | People's<br>republic | President:<br>José Eduardo dos Santos<br>Prime Minister:<br>França Van Dunem | Kwanza<br>89.754 | 6,010<br>620 |
| ANTIGUA AND<br>BARBUDA<br>St. Johns | 85,000<br><br>30,000 | 171<br>443 | Parliamentary<br>state (C) | Governor-General:<br>Sir Wilfred E. Jacobs<br>Prime Minister:<br>Vere C. Bird, Sr. | East<br>Caribbean<br>dollar<br>2.70 | 302<br>3,880 |
| ARGENTINA<br>Buenos Aires | 32,700,000<br>2,900,000 | 1,068,302<br>2,766,889 | Federal<br>republic | President:<br>Carlos Saul Menem | Austral<br>9,992.5 | 68,780<br>2,160 |
| AUSTRALIA<br>Canberra | 17,100,000<br>285,000 | 2,967,909<br>7,686,848 | Federal<br>parliamentary<br>state (C) | Governor-General:<br>William George Hayden<br>Prime Minister:<br>Paul Keating | Dollar<br>1.3026 | 242,131<br>14,440 |
| AUSTRIA<br>Vienna | 7,700,000<br>1,518,000 | 32,374<br>83,849 | Federal<br>republic | President:<br>Kurt Waldheim<br>Chancellor:<br>Franz Vranitzky | Schilling<br>12.7275 | 131,899<br>17,360 |
| BAHAMAS<br>Nassau | 256,000<br>136,000 | 5,380<br>13,935 | Parliamentary<br>state (C) | Governor-General:<br>Henry Taylor<br>Prime Minister:<br>Lynden O. Pindling | Dollar<br>1.00 | 2,820<br>11,370 |
| BAHRAIN<br>Manama | 486,000<br>152,000 | 240<br>622 | Emirate | Emir:<br>Isa bin Sulman<br>al-Khalifa<br>Prime Minister:<br>Khalifa bin Sulman al-Khalifa | Dinar<br>0.3777 | 3,009<br>6,360 |
| BANGLADESH<br>Dacca (Dhaka) | 116,600,000<br>4,770,000 | 55,598<br>143,998 | Republic<br>(C) | President:<br>Abdur Rahman Biswas<br>Prime Minister:<br>Khalida Zia | Taka<br>36.51 | 19,913<br>180 |
| BARBADOS<br>Bridgetown | 260,000<br>7,500 | 166<br>431 | Parliamentary<br>state (C) | Governor-General:<br>Nita Barrow<br>Prime Minister:<br>Erskine Sandiford | Dollar<br>2.0113 | 1,622<br>6,370 |
| BELGIUM<br>Brussels | 9,900,000<br>970,500 | 11,781<br>30,513 | Constitutional<br>monarchy | King:<br>Baudouin<br>Prime Minister:<br>Wilfried Martens | Franc<br>37.215 | 162,026<br>16,390 |

The section on countries presents the latest information available. All monetary figures are expressed in United States dollars. The symbol (C) signifies that the country belongs to the Commonwealth of Nations. NA means that the data were not available. * indicates that the category does not apply to the country under discussion. Footnotes at the end of the section contain more specialized information.

| Imports Exports (millions) | Revenue Expenditure (millions) | Elementary Schools: Teachers Students | Secondary Schools: Teachers Students | Colleges and Universities: Teachers Students |
|---|---|---|---|---|
| $ 936 | $ NA | 16,414 | NA | 1,418 |
| 235 | NA | 611,106 | 107,000 | 17,509 |
| NA | 1,635.6 | 28,440 | 9,004 | 1,659 |
| NA | 1,627.1 | 550,656 | 194,124 | 25,201 |
| 7,342 | 16,800.0 | 139,917 | 84,676 | 12,204 |
| 7,679 | 17,200.0 | 3,911,388 | 1,850,756 | 154,700 |
| 451 | 1,600.0 | NA. | NA. | NA |
| 2,190 | 2,600.0 | NA | NA | NA |
| 225 | 80.4 | 446 | 319 | NA |
| 22 | 85.8 | 9,097 | 4,413 | 631 |
| 4,078 | 11,750.7 | 259,579 | 247,804 | 41,797 |
| 12,353 | 13,722.2 | 4,998,963 | 1,862,325 | 755,206 |
| 43,032 | 78,006.4 | 91,979 | 103,171 | 24,001 |
| 39,837 | 76,832.8 | 1,529,781 | 1,296,641 | 393,734 |
| 49,146 | 40,874.5 | 33,594 | 70,755 | 11,060 |
| 41,265 | 46,197.4 | 360,542 | 606,323 | 179,484 |
| 1,674 | 555.3 | 1,409 | 1,555 | 249 |
| 733 | 564.2 | 29,518 | 29,765 | 5,305 |
| 3,650 | 1,250.0 | 2,887 | 2,270 | 430 |
| 3,719 | 1,570.0 | 60,605 | 40,540 | 5,556 |
| 3,650 | 1,427.7 | 186,872 | 124,760 | 2,811 |
| 1,671 | 1,333.0 | 11,285,445 | 3,340,120 | 48,275 |
| 700 | 381.5 | NA. | NA. | NA |
| 209 | 395.3 | 28,235 | 21,501 | 6,691 |
| 119,702[2] | 40,960.0 | 71,064 | 114,628 | 5,349 |
| 117,703[2] | 50,392.5 | 728,718 | 805,647 | 103,505 |

| Nation Capital | Population | Area of Country (sq mi/ sq km) | Type of Government | Heads of State and Government | Currency: Value of U.S. Dollar (July 1) | GNP (millions) GNP Per Capita |
|---|---|---|---|---|---|---|
| BELIZE .............. Belmopan | 193,000... 4,500 | 8,867..... 22,965 | Parliamentary state (C) | Governor-General:............... Minita Gordon Prime Minister: George Price | Dollar ........ 2.00 | $ 294 1,600 |
| BENIN ................ Porto-Novo | 4,800,000... 209,000 | 43,484..... 112,622 | Republic...... | President: ................ Nicéphore Soglo | CFA franc[3] 306.375 | 1,753 380 |
| BHUTAN .............. Thimbu | 1,400,000... 15,000 | 18,147..... 47,000 | Monarchy.... | King: .................. Jigme Singye Wangchuk | Ngultrum ..... 17.47 | 266 190 |
| BOLIVIA............... Sucre La Paz | 7,500,000... 96,000 1,050,000 | 424,165..... 1,098,581 | Republic...... | President: ................ Jaime Paz Zamora | Boliviano ..... 3.57 | 4,301 600 |
| BOTSWANA ........... Gaborone | 1,300,000... 112,000 | 231,805..... 600,372 | Republic...... (C) | President: ................ Quett K. J. Masire | Pula........... 2.0743 | 1,105 940 |
| BRAZIL ............... Brasilia | 153,300,000... 1,803,000 | 3,286,488..... 8,511,965 | Federal...... republic | President: ................ Fernando Collor de Mello | Cruzeiro...... 1034.30[1] | 375,146 2,550 |
| BRUNEI............... Bandar Seri Begawan | 267,000... 51,000 | 2,226..... 5,765 | Constitutional monarchy (C) | Sultan:................... Muda Hassanal Bolkiah | Dollar ........ 1.7645 | 3,290[4] NA |
| BULGARIA ............ Sofia | 9,000,000... 1,137,000 | 42,823..... 110,912 | Republic...... | President: ................ Zheliu Zhelev Prime Minister: Dimitur Popov | Lev .......... 28.25 | 20,860 2,320 |
| BURKINA FASO ....... Ouagadougou | 9,400,000... 442,000 | 105,869..... 274,200 | Republic..... | Head of State and Govt.: Blaise Compaoré | CFA franc[3] ... 306.375 | 2,716 310 |
| BURMA (MYANMAR).... Rangoon (Yangon) | 42,100,000... 2,500,000 | 261,218..... 676,552 | Socialist .... republic | Head of State and Govt.: Saw Maung | Kyat ......... 6.5613 | 16,540[4] NA |
| BURUNDI ............. Bujumbura | 5,800,000... 273,000 | 10,747..... 27,834 | Republic...... | President: ................ Pierre Buyoya Prime Minister: Adrien Sibomana | Franc ........ 179.0126 | 1,149 220 |
| CAMBODIA............ Phnom Penh | 7,100,000... 820,000 | 69,898..... 181,035 | Republic...... | Head of State: ................ Norodom Sihanouk Premier: Hun Sen | Riel ................. 750.00[1] | NA NA |
| CAMEROON........... Yaoundé | 11,400,000... 654,000 | 183,569..... 475,442 | Republic...... | President: ................ Paul Biya | CFA franc[3] ... 306.375 | 11,661 1,010 |
| CANADA .............. Ottawa | 26,990,000... 891,000 | 3,831,033..... 9,922,330 | Federal....... parliamentary state (C) | Governor-General:............. Ramon Hnatyshyn Prime Minister: Brian Mulroney | Dollar ........ 1.1423 | 500,337 19,020 |
| CAPE VERDE.......... Praia | 400,000... 57,700 | 1,557..... 4,033 | Republic..... | President: ................ Antonio Monteiro Premier: Carlos Viega | Escudo....... 78.12 | 281 760 |
| CENTRAL AFRICAN..... REPUBLIC Bangui | 3,000,000... 597,000 | 240,535..... 622,984 | Republic...... | President: ................ Gen. André Kolingba Premier: Edouard Franck | CFA franc[3] ... 306.375 | 1,144 390 |
| CHAD................. N'Djamena | 5,100,000... 600,000 | 495,755..... 1,284,000 | Republic...... | President: ................ Gen. Idriss Déby Premier: Jean Alingue Bawoyéu | CFA franc[3] ... 306.375 | 1,038 190 |
| CHILE ................ Santiago | 13,400,000... 4,385,000 | 292,258..... 756,945 | Republic...... | President: ................ Patricio Aylwin Azócar | Peso......... 308.48 | 22,910 1,770 |
| CHINA, PEOPLE'S ...... REPUBLIC OF Beijing | 1,151,300,000... 6,000,000 | 3,691,515..... 9,560,980 | People's.... republic | President: ................ Yang Shangkun Premier: Li Peng | Yuan........ 5.3556 | 393,006 360 |
| COLOMBIA............ Bogotá | 33,600,000... 4,802,000 | 439,737..... 1,138,914 | Republic...... | President: ................ César Gaviría Trujillo | Peso......... 628.13 | 38,607 1,190 |
| COMOROS............ Moroni | 500,000... 17,000 | 838..... 2,171 | Islamic .... republic | President: ................ Said Muhammad Djohar | CFA franc[3] ... 306.375 | 209 460 |

| Imports Exports (millions) | Revenue Expenditure (millions) | Elementary Schools: Teachers Students | Secondary Schools: Teachers Students | Colleges and Universities: Teachers Students |
|---|---|---|---|---|
| $ 214 | $ 66.1 | 1,611 | 599 | 37 |
| 131 | 65.6 | 40,729 | 7,560 | 1,170 |
| 349 | 156.3 | 13,821 | 3,657 | 1,110 |
| 114 | 265.7 | 482,451 | 102,171 | 10,112 |
| 94 | 57.37 | 1,513 | 695 | 206 |
| 33 | 105.59 | 55,340 | 3,456 | 2,341 |
| 716 | 463.6 | 48,133 | 9,789 | 4,924 |
| 927 | 480.7 | 1,299,664 | 218,268 | 95,052 |
| 1,873 | 163.0 | 8,104 | 2,573 | 193 |
| 1,285 | 174.0 | 261,352 | 44,306 | 2,062 |
| 22,459 | 19,918.0 | 1,119,907 | 229,183 | 125,483 |
| 31,390 | 19,122.0 | 26,821,134 | 3,339,930 | 1,503,560 |
| 708 | 1,327.3 | 2,225 | | 130 |
| 1,688 | 1,213.1 | 36,983 | | 747 |
| 14,881[5] | 21,201.0 | 64,470 | 27,613 | 17,759 |
| 16,014 | 23,722.7 | 1,076,947 | 392,407 | 132,020 |
| 489 | 504.0 | 5,780 | NA | 253 |
| 142 | 577.4 | 390,414 | 72,207 | 4,405 |
| 270 | 5,422.3 | 116,950 | 61,089 | 4,211 |
| 325 | 7,925.3 | 5,046,471 | 1,358,788 | 51,460 |
| 231 | 183.2 | 7,256 | 1,908 | 327 |
| 75 | 222.2 | 452,424 | 29,027 | 2,237 |
| NA | NA | 116,950 | NA | NA |
| NA | NA | 5,046,471 | NA | NA |
| 1,272[6] | 1,778.9 | 36,548 | 17,032 | 984 |
| 928[6] | 1,778.9 | 1,875,221 | 416,764 | 19,588 |
| 124,422 | 112,837.3 | 315,748 | NA | 36,300 |
| 131,665 | 139,442.4 | 2,319,300 | 2,249,305 | 805,551 |
| 112 | NA | 1,892 | 268 | 53 |
| 7 | NA | 62,727 | 6,413 | 211 |
| 150[6] | 166.7 | 4,226 | 1,052 | 330 |
| 134[6] | 368.0 | 297,457 | 45,340 | 2,563 |
| 419 | 68.4 | 4,779 | 966 | NA |
| 141 | 91.5 | 337,616 | 44,379 | 1,991 |
| 7,023 | 12,227.0 | 55,268 | 41,657 | NA |
| 8,579 | 11,416.0 | 1,987,758 | 695,863 | 156,755 |
| 52,275 | 62,160.5 | 5,501,300 | 3,387,700 | 393,185 |
| 60,920 | 65,042.3 | 125,357,800 | 52,460,600 | 2,065,923 |
| 5,590 | 5,900.0 | 135,924 | 107,084 | 37,557 |
| 6,766 | 4,386.0 | 4,002,543 | 2,136,239 | 331,150 |
| NA | 16.7 | 1,777 | NA | NA |
| 18 | 29.7 | 64,737 | 21,168 | NA |

| Nation Capital | Population | Area of Country (sq mi/ sq km) | Type of Government | Heads of State and Government | Currency: Value of U.S. Dollar (July 1) | GNP (millions) GNP Per Capita |
|---|---|---|---|---|---|---|
| CONGO Brazzaville | 2,300,000 1,000,000 | 132,047 342,000 | Republic | President: Denis Sassou-Nguesso Premier: Andre Milongo | CFA franc[3] 306.375 | $  2,045 930 |
| COSTA RICA San José | 3,100,000 890,000 | 19,575 50,700 | Republic | President: Rafael Calderón Fournier | Colón 123.50 | 4,898 1,790 |
| CUBA Havana | 10,700,000 2,014,800 | 44,218 114,524 | Socialist republic | President: Fidel Castro Ruíz | Peso 0.7965 | NA NA |
| CYPRUS Nicosia | 719,000 167,000 | 3,572 9,251 | Republic (C) | President:[7] George Vassiliou | Pound[8] 2.0374 | 4,892[8] 7,050 |
| CZECHOSLOVAKIA Prague | 15,700,000 1,212,000 | 49,370 127,869 | Federal republic | President: Vaclav Havel Premier: Marian Calfa | Koruna 31.03 | 123,100[4] NA |
| DENMARK Copenhagen | 5,100,000 1,337,000 | 16,629 43,069 | Constitutional monarchy | Queen: Margrethe II Prime Minister: Poul Schlüter | Krone 6.9825 | 105,263 20,510 |
| DJIBOUTI Djibouti | 484,000 301,000 | 8,495 22,000 | Republic | President: Hassan Gouled Aptidon Premier: Barkat Gourad Hamadou | Djibouti franc 177.72 | 400,000[4] NA |
| DOMINICA Roseau | 81,200 8,400 | 290 751 | Republic (C) | President: Clarence A. Seignoret Prime Minister: (Mary) Eugenia Charles | East Caribbean dollar 2.70 | 136 1,670 |
| DOMINICAN REPUBLIC Santo Domingo | 7,300,000 1,657,000 | 18,816 48,734 | Republic | President: Joaquín Balaguer | Peso 12.77 | 5,513 790 |
| ECUADOR Quito | 10,800,000 1,138,000 | 109,484 283,561 | Republic | President: Rodrígo Borja Cevallos | Sucre 860.50 | 10,774 1,040 |
| EGYPT Cairo | 54,500,000 8,179,000 | 386,660 1,001,450 | Republic | President: Hosni Mubarak Prime Minister: Atef Siedki | Pound 3.3377[1] | 32,501 630 |
| EL SALVADOR San Salvador | 5,400,000 1,400,000 | 8,124 21,041 | Republic | President: Alfredo Cristiani | Colón 8.03 | 5,356 1,040 |
| EQUATORIAL GUINEA Malabo | 400,000 15,000 | 10,831 28,051 | Republic | President: Teodoro Obiang Nguema Mbasogo | CFA franc[3] 306.375 | 149 430 |
| ESTONIA Tallinn | 1,588,000 482,000 | 17,400 45,100 | Republic | Prime Minister: Edgar Savisaar | NA | NA NA |
| ETHIOPIA Addis Ababa | 53,200,000 1,495,000 | 483,000 1,250,970 | Republic | Transitional President: Meles Zenawi Prime Minister: Tamrat Layne | Birr 2.07 | 5,953 120 |
| FIJI Suva | 727,000 72,000 | 7,056 18,274 | Republic | President: Penaia Ganilau Prime Minister: Kamisese Mara | Dollar 1.5049 | 1,218 1,640 |
| FINLAND Helsinki | 5,000,000 491,000 | 130,129 337,032 | Republic | President: Mauno Koivisto Prime Minister: Harri Holkeri | Markka 4.2845 | 109,705 22,060 |
| FRANCE Paris | 56,700,000 2,175,000 | 211,208 547,026 | Republic | President: François Mitterrand Premier: Edith Cresson | Franc 6.1275 | 1,000,866 17,830 |
| GABON Libreville | 1,200,000 350,000 | 103,347 267,667 | Republic | President: Omar Bongo Premier: Casimir Oye-Mba | CFA franc[3] 306.375 | 3,060 2,770 |

| Imports<br>Exports<br>(millions) | Revenue<br>Expenditure<br>(millions) | Elementary<br>Schools:<br>Teachers<br>Students | Secondary<br>Schools:<br>Teachers<br>Students | Colleges and<br>Universities:<br>Teachers<br>Students |
|---|---|---|---|---|
| $ 524[6] | $ 880.0 | 7,858 | 6,697 | 783 |
| 912 | 1,000.0 | 495,015 | 226,952 | 12,043 |
| 2,026 | 772.0 | 12,829 | 6,701 | 5,211 |
| 1,457 | 775.0 | 409,621 | 118,357 | 50,033 |
| 7,579 | 15,625.0 | 73,216 | 108,078 | 23,364 |
| 5,518 | 17,725.8 | 899,936 | 1,127,035 | 250,604 |
| 2,568[8] | 907.7[8] | 2,703[8] | 3,524[8] | 430[8] |
| 957 | 1,062.5 | 58,720 | 42,613 | 5,066 |
| 13,712 | 5,080.0 | 97,853 | 84,422 | 25,127 |
| 11,840 | 4,946.2 | 2,013,901 | 812,182 | 184,849 |
| 31,761 | 43,476.9 | 34,376 | NA | NA |
| 35,065 | 48,015.3 | 391,895 | 485,842 | 96,795 |
| 188 | 134.9 | 680 | 323 | 13 |
| 20 | 134.9 | 29,833 | 8,902 | 117 |
| 107 | 39.2 | 835 | NA | NA |
| 45 | 37.5 | 12,600 | 6,308 | NA |
| 2,280 | 785.3 | 31,213 | NA | NA |
| 928 | 839.7 | 1,271,120 | 463,511 | 88,000 |
| 1,862 | 1,400.0 | 58,326 | 53,568 | 12,874 |
| 2,714 | 1,400.0 | 1,822,252 | 771,928 | 239,227 |
| 9,216 | 15,255.5 | 235,586 | 230,089 | 31,809 |
| 2,585 | 16,494.2 | 7,034,617 | 4,130,812 | 770,221 |
| 1,152 | 526.2 | 23,476 | 3,600 | 3,821 |
| 497 | 661.3 | 1,029,341 | 101,400 | 61,323 |
| 50 | 22.8 | NA | NA | NA |
| 39 | 39.2 | NA | NA | NA |
| NA | NA | NA | NA | NA |
| NA | NA | NA | 260,100 | 24,270 |
| 1,081 | 1,381.1 | 65,993 | 21,983 | 1,366 |
| 298 | 1,800.4 | 2,855,846 | 882,243 | 23,837 |
| 743 | 257.2 | 4,322 | 2,838 | 224 |
| 534 | 355.5 | 131,201 | 46,457 | 2,247 |
| 27,001 | 35,604.4 | NA | NA | 7,650 |
| 26,571 | 34,839.4 | 388,756 | 401,992 | 103,895 |
| 234,426 | 256,275.5 | 198,922 | 414,268 | 45,222 |
| 216,580 | 210,420.5 | 4,176,391 | 5,390,489 | 1,045,949 |
| 732[6] | 1,360.0 | 4,229 | 2,271 | 364 |
| 1,288 | 1,960.0 | 195,049 | 48,274 | 2,741 |

| Nation<br>Capital | Population | Area of<br>Country<br>(sq mi/<br>sq km) | Type of<br>Government | Heads of State and<br>Government | Currency:<br>Value of<br>U.S. Dollar<br>(July 1) | GNP<br>(millions)<br>GNP<br>Per Capita |
|---|---|---|---|---|---|---|
| GAMBIA, THE | 900,000 | 4,361 | Republic | President: | Dalasi | $ 196 |
| Banjul | 44,000 | 11,295 | (C) | Sir Dawda K. Jawara | 8.777 | 230 |
| GERMANY, | 79,500,000 | 137,858 | Federal | President: | Mark | 1,272,959[9] |
| Berlin | 3,327,000 | 357,052 | republic | Richard von Weizsäcker | 1.8082 | 20,750[9] |
| Bonn | 277,000 | | | Chancellor:<br>Helmut Kohl | | |
| GHANA | 15,500,000 | 92,098 | Republic | Chairman, Provisional | Cedi | 5,503 |
| Accra | 2,000,000 | 238,533 | (C) | National Defense Council:<br>Jerry J. Rawlings | 367.00 | 380 |
| GREAT BRITAIN[10] | 57,500,000 | 94,227 | Limited | Queen: | Pound | 834,166 |
| London | 6,794,000 | 244,046 | monarchy (C) | Elizabeth II<br>Prime Minister:<br>John Major | 1.6254 | 14,570 |
| GREECE | 10,100,000 | 50,944 | Republic | President: | Drachma | 53,626 |
| Athens | 886,000 | 131,944 | | Constantine Karamanlis<br>Prime Minister:<br>Constantine Mitsotakis | 197.90 | 5,340 |
| GRENADA | 99,200 | 120 | Parliamentary | Governor-General: | East | 179 |
| St. George's | 10,000 | 311 | state (C) | Sir Paul Scoon<br>Prime Minister:<br>Nicholas Brathwaite | Caribbean<br>dollar<br>2.70 | 1,900 |
| GUATEMALA | 9,500,000 | 42,042 | Republic | President: | Quetzal | 8,205 |
| Guatemala City | 2,000,000 | 108,889 | | Jorge Serrano Elías | 4.93 | 920 |
| GUINEA | 7,500,000 | 94,926 | Republic | President: | Franc | 2,372 |
| Conakry | 705,000 | 245,857 | | Lansana Conté | 620.00 | 430 |
| GUINEA-BISSAU | 1,000,000 | 13,948 | Republic | President: | Peso | 173 |
| Bissau | 125,000 | 36,125 | | João Bernardo Vieira | 650.0 | 180 |
| GUYANA | 800,000 | 83,000 | Republic | President: | Dollar | 248 |
| Georgetown | 188,000 | 214,969 | (C) | Desmond Hoyte<br>Prime Minister:<br>Hamilton Green | 127.00 | 310 |
| HAITI | 6,300,000 | 10,714 | Republic | Provisional | Gourde | 2,556 |
| Port-au-Prince | 1,144,000 | 27,750 | | President:<br>Joseph Nerette | 5.00 | 400 |
| HONDURAS | 5,300,000 | 43,277 | Republic | President: | Lempira | 4,495 |
| Tegucigalpa | 679,000 | 112,088 | | Rafael Leonardo Callejas | 5.64 | 900 |
| HUNGARY | 10,400,000 | 35,919 | Republic | President: | Forint | 27,078 |
| Budapest | 2,016,000 | 93,030 | | Arpad Göncz<br>Prime Minister:<br>József Antall | 76.93[1] | 2,560 |
| ICELAND | 300,000 | 39,769 | Republic | President: | Króna | 5,351 |
| Reykjavik | 98,000 | 103,000 | | Vigdís Finnbogadottir<br>Prime Minister:<br>David Oddsson | 62.60 | 21,240 |
| INDIA | 859,200,000 | 1,269,346 | Federal | President: | Rupee | 287,383 |
| New Delhi | 273,000 | 3,287,590 | republic<br>(C) | Ramaswamy Venkataraman<br>Prime Minister:<br>P.V. Narasimha Rao | 21.11 | 350 |
| INDONESIA | 181,400,000 | 782,636 | Republic | President: | Rupiah | 87,936 |
| Jakarta (Djakarta) | 9,500,000 | 2,027,087 | | Suharto | 1,951.00 | 490 |
| IRAN | 58,600,000 | 636,296 | Islamic | President: | Rial | 318,400 |
| Tehran | 7,800,000 | 1,648,000 | republic | Hojatolislam Ali Akbar<br>Hashemi Rafsanjani | 69.7172<br>1,400.00 | 6,132 |
| IRAQ | 17,100,000 | 167,925 | Republic | President: | Dinar | 65,800 |
| Baghdad | 5,400,000 | 434,924 | | Saddam Hussein | 0.3109 | 3,742 |
| IRELAND,<br>REPUBLIC OF | 3,500,000 | 27,136<br>70,283 | Republic | President: | Pound | 30,054 |
| Dublin | 478,000 | | | Mary Robinson<br>Prime Minister:<br>Charles J. Haughey | 1.4803 | 8,500 |
| ISRAEL[12] | 4,900,000 | 7,992 | Republic | President: | New shekel | $ 44,131 |
| Jerusalem | 499,000 | 20,700 | | Chaim Herzog<br>Prime Minister:<br>Yitzhak Shamir | 2.3865 | 9,750 |

| Imports Exports (millions) | | Revenue Expenditure (millions) | | Elementary Schools: Teachers Students | Secondary Schools: Teachers Students | Colleges and Universities: Teachers Students |
|---|---|---|---|---|---|---|
| $ 127 | ..................... | $ 65.9 | .................... | 2,604 .............. | 658 ............ | NA |
| 40 | | 65.8 | | 73,673 | 15,978 | NA |
| 346,153 | ..................... | 223,400.0 | .................... | 188,509 .............. | 602,062 ............ | 181,901 |
| 410,104 | | 253,300.0 | | 3,233,342 | 7,637,430 | 1,620,890 |
| 907 | ..................... | 1,000.0 | .................... | 65,826 .............. | 53,514 ............ | 1,160 |
| 1,014 | | 900.0 | | 2,705,843 | 862,914 | 8,327 |
| 222,777 | ..................... | 368,153.1 | .................... | 215,000 .............. | NA ............ | 34,423 |
| 185,160 | | 381,643.9 | | 4,370,000 | 4,508,000 | 367,000 |
| 19,777 | ..................... | 22,900.0 | .................... | 37,497 .............. | 51,706 ............ | 7,435 |
| 8,105 | | 32,100.0 | | 865,660 | 835,845 | 117,193 |
| 89 | | 52.3 | | 806 .............. | NA ............ | NA |
| 32 | | 54.8 | | 20,976 | 6,437 | NA |
| 1,626 | | 280.0 | | 31,441 .............. | 16,332 ............ | NA |
| 1,211 | | 1,000.0 | | 1,097,851 | 241,053 | 51,860 |
| NA | ..................... | 543.5 | .................... | 7,849 .............. | 4,642 ............ | 805 |
| NA | | 543.5 | | 302,809 | 92,754 | 6,245 |
| NA | | 78.0 | | 3,065 .............. | 764 ............ | NA |
| NA | | 88.6 | | 75,892 | 6,450 | NA |
| NA | ..................... | NA | .................... | 3,948 .............. | 2,324 ............ | 371 |
| 249[11] | | 16,400.0 | | 112,581 | 76,546 | 2,245 |
| 270 | ..................... | 262.3 | .................... | 22,421 .............. | NA ............ | 479 |
| 132 | | 415.0 | | 780,660 | 143,758 | 4,471 |
| 1,028 | ..................... | 750.0 | .................... | 20,732 .............. | 6,945 ............ | 2,599 |
| 916 | | 1,100.0 | | 810,412 | 179,444 | 32,368 |
| 8,669 | ..................... | 11,352.2 | .................... | 90,620 .............. | 9,103 ............ | 12,168 |
| 9,597 | | 12,371.5 | | 1,242,672 | 108,440 | 65,337 |
| 1,680 | ..................... | 1,508.1 | .................... | NA .............. | NA ............ | NA |
| 1,592 | | 1,553.1 | | 25,420 | 28,586 | 5,006 |
| 23,642 | ..................... | 45,318.0 | .................... | 1,587,697 .............. | 2,265,202 ............ | 302,843 |
| 17,975 | | 49,769.8 | | 95,739,976 | 49,440,814 | 4,470,844 |
| 21,768 | ..................... | 37,870.0 | .................... | 1,278,889 .............. | 788,929 ............ | NA |
| 25,675 | | 51,406.0 | | 30,130,564 | 11,693,361 | 1,663,900 |
| 9,454 | ..................... | 1,470.0 | .................... | 316,989 .............. | 205,217 ............ | 14,380 |
| NA | | 1,750.0 | | 8,262,441 | 4,297,623 | 215,898 |
| 10,268 | ..................... | 56,400.0 | .................... | 130,777 .............. | 53,937 ............ | 11,072 |
| NA | | 77,400.0 | | 3,023,132 | 1,166,859 | 209,818 |
| 20,669 | ..................... | 13,174.0 | .................... | 15,880 .............. | 20,350 ............ | 2,787 |
| 23,743 | | 13,542.0 | | 423,402 | 319,122 | 40,682 |
| $ 16,508 | ..................... | $ 21,491.9 | .................... | 37,623 .............. | 41,636 ............ | NA |
| 11,704 | | 25,606 | | 705,756 | 279,130 | 65,080 |

443

| Nation Capital | Population | Area of Country (sq mi/ sq km) | Type of Government | Heads of State and Government | Currency: Value of U.S. Dollar (July 1) | GNP (millions) GNP Per Capita |
|---|---|---|---|---|---|---|
| ITALY Rome | 57,700,000 2,804,000 | 116,304 301,225 | Republic | President: Francesco Cossiga Prime Minister: Giulio Andreotti | Lira 1,346.00 | $ 871,955 15,150 |
| IVORY COAST (CÔTE D'IVOIRE) Abidjan | 12,500,000 1,850,000 | 124,503 322,462 | Republic | President: Félix Houphouët-Boigny | CFA franc[3] 306.375 | 9,305 790 |
| JAMAICA Kingston | 2,500,000 700,000 | 4,244 10,991 | Parliamentary state (C) | Governor-General: Howard Cooke Prime Minister: Michael Manley | Dollar 10.02 | 3,011 1,260 |
| JAPAN Tokyo | 123,800,000 11,640,000 | 145,824 377,682 | Constitutional monarchy | Emperor: Akihito Prime Minister: Kiichi Miyazawa | Yen 138.18 | 2,920,310 23,730 |
| JORDAN Amman | 3,400,000 1,160,000 | 35,468 91,862 | Constitutional monarchy | King: Hussein I Prime Minister: Taher al-Masri | Dinar 0.687 | 5,291[17] 1,730 |
| KENYA Nairobi | 25,200,000 1,800,000 | 224,961 582,646 | Republic (C) | President: Daniel arap Moi | Shilling 28.725 | 8,785 380 |
| KIRIBATI (GILBERT ISLANDS) Tarawa | 68,900 NA | 342 886 | Republic (C) | President: Teatao Teannaki | Dollar 1.3026 | 48 700 |
| KOREA, DEMOCRATIC PEOPLE'S REPUBLIC OF P'yongyang | 21,800,000 1,500,000 | 46,540 120,538 | People's republic | President: Kim Il Sung Premier: Yon Hyong Muk | Won 0.97 | 29,200 1,328 |
| KOREA, REPUBLIC OF Seoul | 43,200,000 10,103,000 | 38,025 98,484 | Republic | President: Roh Tae Woo Prime Minister: Ro Jai Bong | Won 724.60 | 186,467 4,400 |
| KUWAIT Kuwait City | 1,400,000 NA | 6,880 17,818 | Constitutional emirate | Emir: Jabir al-Ahmad al-Jabir al-Sabah Prime Minister: Saad al-Abdullah al-Salem al-Sabah | Dinar 0.2938 | 33,082 16,380 |
| LAOS Vientiane | 4,100,000 377,000 | 91,429 236,800 | People's republic | President: Kaysone Phomvihan Premier: Khamtay Siphandone | Kip 700.00 | 693 170 |
| LATVIA Riga | 2,692,000 915,000 | 24,600 63,700 | Republic | President: Anatolijs Gorbunovs Prime Minister: Ivars Godmanis | NA | NA NA |
| LEBANON Beirut | 3,400,000 1,500,000 | 4,015 10,400 | Republic | President: Elias Hrawi Prime Minister: Omar Karami | Pound 905.00 | NA NA |
| LESOTHO Maseru | 1,800,000 80,000 | 11,720 30,355 | Constitutional monarchy (C) | King: Letsie II Chairman, Military Council: Elias Ramaema | Maloti 2.8868 | 816 470 |
| LIBERIA Monrovia | 2,700,000 425,000 | 43,000 111,369 | Republic | Interim President: Amos Sawyer | Dollar 1.00 | NA NA |
| LIBYA Tripoli | 4,400,000 991,000 | 679,362 1,759,540 | Socialist republic | Leader: Muammar al-Qaddafi Prime Minister: Abu Said Omar Bourda | Dinar 0.2961 | 22,976 5,410 |
| LIECHTENSTEIN Vaduz | 30,000 4,900 | 62 161 | Constitutional monarchy | Sovereign: Prince Hans Adam Chief of Government: Hans Brunhart | Swiss franc 1.5585 | NA NA |

| Imports<br>Exports<br>(millions) | Revenue<br>Expenditure<br>(millions) | Elementary<br>Schools:<br>Teachers<br>Students | Secondary<br>Schools:<br>Teachers<br>Students | Colleges and<br>Universities:<br>Teachers<br>Students |
|---|---|---|---|---|
| $181,984<br>170,348 | $252,000.0<br>338,000.0 | 258,535<br>3,237,594 | 582,570<br>5,284,637 | 53,142<br>1,286,708 |
| 2,080<br>2,770 | 1,465.2<br>1,465.2 | NA<br>NA | NA<br>272,911 | NA<br>NA |
| 1,801<br>967 | 1,055.7<br>904.0 | 10,251<br>339,163 | 9,061<br>241,000 | 401<br>4,634 |
| 235,368<br>287,581 | 509,099.7<br>268,325.4 | 445,222<br>9,872,520 | 647,200<br>11,310,029 | 204,881<br>2,081,066 |
| 2,125<br>1,107 | 1,360.0<br>1,700.0 | 19,133<br>570,795 | 21,729<br>357,475 | 1,553<br>34,994 |
| 2,124<br>1,031 | 2,450.1<br>2,634.5 | 155,694<br>5,123,582 | 26,025<br>544,745 | NA<br>18,545 |
| NA<br>NA | 15.6<br>15.6 | 507<br>14,321 | 236<br>2,903 | NA<br>NA |
| 2,500<br>1,800 | 16,950.0<br>16,950.0 | 59,000<br>1,543,000 | 111,000<br>2,468,000 | 23,000<br>325,000 |
| 69,640<br>64,956 | 37,514.5<br>NA | 6,396<br>4,894,261 | 168,976<br>4,545,896 | 30,565<br>1,097,530 |
| 6,295<br>11,476 | NA<br>NA | 10,288<br>185,464 | 21,112<br>265,001 | 1,181<br>17,988 |
| 162<br>81 | NA<br>NA | 20,384<br>558,852 | 11,173<br>135,583 | 478<br>4,492 |
| NA<br>NA | NA<br>NA | NA<br>NA | NA<br>665,800 | NA<br>44,000 |
| 2,457<br>709 | 117.4<br>259.2 | NA<br>399,029 | NA<br>310,256 | NA<br>NA |
| NA<br>NA | 345.0<br>236.0 | NA<br>331,857 | 2,074<br>43,368 | 244<br>4,224 |
| 308<br>382 | 455.0<br>460.0 | NA<br>80,048 | NA<br>NA | 444<br>4,855 |
| 5,879<br>6,683 | NA<br>10,942.2 | 41,515<br>788,780 | 35,825<br>430,885 | NA<br>30,000 |
| NA<br>1,242 | 225.7<br>221.9 | 107<br>2,591 | 108<br>1,686 | NA<br>NA |

445

| Nation<br>Capital | Population | Area of<br>Country<br>(sq mi/<br>sq km) | Type of<br>Government | Heads of State and<br>Government | Currency:<br>Value of<br>U.S. Dollar<br>(July 1) | GNP<br>(millions)<br>GNP<br>Per Capita |
|---|---|---|---|---|---|---|
| LITHUANIA | 3,690,000 | 25,200 | Republic | President: | NA | NA |
| Vilnius | 582,000 | 65,200 | | Vytautas Landsbergis<br>Prime Minister:<br>Gediminas Vagnorius | | NA |
| LUXEMBOURG | 400,000 | 998 | Constitutional | Grand Duke: | Franc | 9,408 |
| Luxembourg | 74,000 | 2,586 | monarchy | Jean<br>Premier:<br>Jacques Santer | 37.215 | 24,860 |
| MADAGASCAR | 12,400,000 | 226,658 | Socialist | President: | Franc | 2,543 |
| Antananarivo | 802,000 | 587,041 | republic | Didier Ratsiraka<br>Prime Minister:<br>Guy Razahamasy | 1,370.2493 | 230 |
| MALAWI | 9,400,000 | 45,747 | Republic | President: | Kwacha | 1,475 |
| Lilongwe | 234,000 | 118,484 | (C) | Hastings Kamuzu Banda | 2.9675 | 180 |
| MALAYSIA | 18,300,000 | 127,317 | Federal | Supreme Head of State: | Ringgit | 37,005 |
| Kuala Lumpur | 920,000 | 329,749 | constitutional<br>monarchy<br>(C) | King Azlan Shah<br>Prime Minister:<br>Mahathir Mohamed | 2.783 | 2,130 |
| MALDIVES | 214,000 | 115 | Republic | President: | Rufiyaa | 87 |
| Male | 56,060 | 298 | | Maumoon Abdul Gayoom | 9.97 | 420 |
| MALI | 8,300,000 | 478,767 | Republic | President: | CFA franc[3] | 2,109 |
| Bamako | 500,000 | 1,240,000 | | Amadou Toumani Touré<br>Premier:<br>Zoumana Sacko | 306.375 | 260 |
| MALTA | 355,000 | 122 | Republic | President: | Lira | 2,041 |
| Valletta | 9,300 | 316 | (C) | Vincent Tabone<br>Prime Minister:<br>Eddie Fenech Adami | 2.9103 | 5,820 |
| MARSHALL ISLANDS | 43,380 | 70 | Republic | President: | U.S. dollar | NA |
| Majuro | NA | 181 | | Amata Kabua | 1.00 | NA |
| MAURITANIA | 2,100,000 | 397,955 | Islamic | President and Chairman, | Ouguiya | 953 |
| Nouakchott | 500,000 | 1,030,700 | republic | Military Committee for<br>National Salvation:<br>Maaouiya Ould<br>Sidi Ahmed Taya | 83.06 | 490 |
| MAURITIUS | 1,000,000 | 790 | Parliamentary | Governor-General: | Rupee | 2,068 |
| Port Louis | 139,000 | 2,045 | state (C) | Veersamy Ringadoo<br>Prime Minister:<br>Aneerood Jugnauth | 16.82 | 1,950 |
| MEXICO | 85,700,000 | 761,604 | Federal | President: | Peso | 170,053 |
| Mexico City | 8,237,000 | 1,972,547 | republic | Carlos-Salinas de Gortari | 3,075.80[1] | 1,990 |
| MICRONESIA | 100,000 | 271 | Republic | President: | U.S. dollar | NA |
| Palikir | NA | 702 | | John R. Haglelgam | 1.00 | NA |
| MONACO | 29,900 | 0.58 | Constitutional | Prince: | French franc | NA |
| | | 1.49 | monarchy | Rainier III<br>Minister of State:<br>Jean Ausseil | 6.1275 | NA |
| MONGOLIA | 2,200,000 | 604,250 | Republic | President: | Tugrik | 2,230[4] |
| Ulan Bator | 575,000 | 1,565,000 | | Punsalmaagiyn Ochirbat<br>Premier:<br>Dashiyn Byambasuren | 3.3555 | NA |
| MOROCCO | 26,200,000 | 172,414 | Constitutional | King: | Dirham | 22,069 |
| Rabat | 1,350,000 | 446,550 | monarchy | Hassan II<br>Prime Minister:<br>Azzedine Laraki | 9.0736 | 900 |
| MOZAMBIQUE | 16,100,000 | 309,496 | Republic | President: | Metical | 1,193 |
| Maputo | 1,007,000 | 801,590 | | Joaquim A. Chissano<br>Prime Minister:<br>Mário de Graça Machungo | 1,515.61 | 80 |
| NAMIBIA | 1,500,000 | 317,818 | Republic | President: | Rand | 1,165[4] |
| Windhoek | 115,000 | 823,147 | | Samuel Nujoma<br>Prime Minister:<br>Hage Geingob | 2.8868 | NA |

| Imports / Exports (millions) | Revenue / Expenditure (millions) | Elementary Schools: Teachers / Students | Secondary Schools: Teachers / Students | Colleges and Universities: Teachers / Students |
|---|---|---|---|---|
| NA | NA | NA | NA | NA |
| NA | NA | NA[16] | 569,400[16] | 70,100 |
| —[2] | 2,429.1 | 1,768 | 1,724 | NA |
| — | 2,360.4 | 21,959 | 22,496 | 997 |
| 386 | NA | 37,894 | 16,176 | 995 |
| 319 | 820.6 | 1,534,142 | 345,302 | 36,933 |
| 575 | 410.1 | 16,124 | 1,286 | 313 |
| 417 | 449.5 | 1,022,765 | 26,732 | 2,177 |
| 29,251 | 11,055.2 | 109,563 | 68,629 | 4,211 |
| 29,409 | 10,614.4 | 2,338,418 | 1,432,699 | 51,460 |
| 129 | 32.3 | 1,134 | 116 | NA |
| 52 | 53.3 | 53,412 | 1,313 | NA |
| 500 | 906.3 | 8,124 | | 715 |
| 271 | 929.9 | 307,587 | | 5,536 |
| 1,958 | 972.6 | 1,805 | 2,509 | 128 |
| 1,127 | 1,069.1 | 36,726 | 30,210 | 1,682 |
| NA | 69 | NA | NA | NA |
| NA | NA | NA | NA | NA |
| 639 | 279.3 | 3,166 | 1,915 | 252 |
| NA | 279.3 | 157,341 | 39,341 | 5,289 |
| 1,621 | 579.6 | 6,203 | 3,643 | 234 |
| 1,181 | 579.6 | 134,136 | 73,341 | 1,354 |
| 31,149 | 132,000.0 | 468,044 | 397,148 | 128,481 |
| 27,032 | 134,000.0 | 14,656,357 | 6,865,763 | 1,309,943 |
| NA | NA | NA | NA | NA |
| NA | NA | NA | NA | 838 |
| NA | 413.9 | NA | NA | NA |
| NA | 406.2 | 1,750 | 2,118 | NA |
| 799 | 180.1 | 5,045 | 12,321 | 1,488 |
| 640 | 215.9 | 155,740 | 267,805 | 17,358 |
| 6,800 | 7,271.0 | 84,411 | 76,634 | 5,922 |
| 4,265 | 7,871.7 | 2,110,719 | 1,366,324 | 169,223 |
| 715 | 293.0 | 20,756 | 4,645 | 368 |
| 103 | 348.0 | 1,260,482 | 155,353 | 2,335 |
| NA | 826.0 | NA | NA | NA |
| NA | 875.0 | 281,660 | 81,991 | NA |

# STATISTICS OF THE WORLD

| Nation<br>Capital | Population | Area of Country<br>(sq mi/<br>sq km) | Type of Government | Heads of State and Government | Currency:<br>Value of<br>U.S. Dollar<br>(July 1) | GNP<br>(millions)<br>GNP<br>Per Capita |
|---|---|---|---|---|---|---|
| **NAURU** . . . . . . . . . . . . . . .<br>Yaren | 9,100 . . . .<br>NA | 8. . . . .<br>21 | Republic. . . . .<br>(C) | President: . . . . . . . . . . . . . . . . .<br>Bernard Dowiyogu | Dollar . . . . . . . .<br>1.3026 | NA<br>NA |
| **NEPAL** . . . . . . . . . . . . . . .<br>Kathmandu | 19,600,000 . . . .<br>400,000 | 54,362. . . . .<br>140,797 | Constitutional<br>monarchy | King: Birendra . . . . . . . . . . . . . . . .<br>Bir Bikram Shah Deva<br>Prime Minister:<br>Girija Prasad Koirala | Rupee. . . . . . . .<br>42.691[1] | $  3,206<br>170 |
| **NETHERLANDS, THE**. . . .<br>Amsterdam<br>The Hague | 15,000,000 . . . .<br>695,000<br>684,000 | 16,133. . . . .<br>41,784 | Constitutional<br>monarchy | Queen: Beatrix. . . . . . . . . . . . . . . . .<br>Prime Minister:<br>Ruud Lubbers | Guilder . . . . . . .<br>2.0369 | 237,415<br>16,010 |
| **NEW ZEALAND** . . . . . . . .<br>Wellington | 3,500,000 . . . .<br>325,000 | 103,736. . . . .<br>268,676 | Parliamentary<br>state (C) | Governor-General:. . . . . . . . . . . . . .<br>Paul Reeves<br>Prime Minister:<br>Jim Bolger | Dollar . . . . . . . .<br>1.7342 | 39,437<br>11,800 |
| **NICARAGUA**. . . . . . . . . . .<br>Managua | 3,900,000 . . . .<br>1,300,000 | 50,193. . . . .<br>130,000 | Republic. . . . .<br> | President: . . . . . . . . . . . . . . . . .<br>Violeta Barrios<br>de Chamorro | Córdoba. . . . . .<br>5.00 | 2,600[4]<br>NA |
| **NIGER** . . . . . . . . . . . . . . .<br>Niamey | 8,000,000 . . . .<br>399,000 | 489,191. . . . .<br>1,267,000 | Republic. . . . .<br> | President: . . . . . . . . . . . . . . . . .<br>Ali Seybou<br>Prime Minister:<br>Mamane Oumarou | CFA franc[3] . . .<br>306.375 | 2,195<br>290 |
| **NIGERIA** . . . . . . . . . . . . .<br>Lagos | 122,500,000 . . . .<br>6,000,000 | 356,669. . . . .<br>923,768 | Federal. . . . . .<br>republic (C) | President: . . . . . . . . . . . . . . . . .<br>Ibrahim Babangida | Naira. . . . . . . . .<br>10.45 | 28,314<br>250 |
| **NORWAY**. . . . . . . . . . . . . .<br>Oslo | 4,300,000 . . . .<br>451,000 | 125,182. . . . .<br>324,219 | Constitutional<br>monarchy | King:. . . . . . . . . . . . . . . . . . . . . . .<br>Harald V<br>Prime Minister:<br>Gro Harlem Brundtland | Krone . . . . . . . .<br>7.0515 | 92,097<br>21,850 |
| **OMAN** . . . . . . . . . . . . . .<br>Muscat | 1,600,000 . . . .<br>445,000 | 82,030. . . . .<br>212,450 | Sultanate . . . .<br> | Sultan and Prime Minister: . . . . . . .<br>Qabus bin Sa'id | Rial . . . . . . . . . .<br>0.385 | 7,756<br>5,220 |
| **PAKISTAN**. . . . . . . . . . . .<br>Islamabad | 117,500,000 . . . .<br>408,000 | 310,404. . . . .<br>803,943 | Federal. . . . . .<br>republic | President: . . . . . . . . . . . . . . . . .<br>Ghulam Ishaq Khan<br>Prime Minister:<br>Mian Nawaz Sharif | Rupee. . . . . . . .<br>24.2757 | 40,134<br>370 |
| **PANAMA** . . . . . . . . . . . . . .<br>Panama City | 2,500,000 . . . .<br>578,000 | 29,762. . . . .<br>77,082 | Republic. . . . .<br> | President: . . . . . . . . . . . . . . . . .<br>Guillermo Endara | Balboa . . . . . . .<br>1.00 | 4,211<br>1,780 |
| **PAPUA NEW GUINEA** . . .<br>Port Moresby | 3,900,000 . . . .<br>152,000 | 178,260. . . . .<br>461,691 | Parliamentary<br>state (C) | Governor-General:. . . . . . . . . . . . . .<br>Serei Eri<br>Prime Minister:<br>Rabbie Namaliu | Kina . . . . . . . . .<br>0.9595 | 3,444<br>900 |
| **PARAGUAY**. . . . . . . . . . . . .<br>Asunción | 4,400,000 . . . .<br>729,000 | 157,048. . . . .<br>406,752 | Republic. . . . .<br> | President: . . . . . . . . . . . . . . . . .<br>Andrés Rodriguez | Guarani . . . . . .<br>1,324.00 | 4,299<br>1,030 |
| **PERU** . . . . . . . . . . . . . . . .<br>Lima | 22,000,000 . . . .<br>6,405,000 | 496,225. . . . .<br>1,285,216 | Republic. . . . .<br> | President: . . . . . . . . . . . . . . . . .<br>Alberto Fujimori<br>Prime Minister:<br>Carlos Torres y Torres<br>Lara | New sol . . . . . .<br>.839 | 23,009<br>1,090 |
| **PHILIPPINES** . . . . . . . . . .<br>Manila | 62,300,000 . . . .<br>1,728,400 | 115,830. . . . .<br>300,000 | Republic. . . . .<br> | President: . . . . . . . . . . . . . . . . .<br>Corazon C. Aquino | Peso . . . . . . . . .<br>25.87 | 42,754<br>700 |
| **POLAND** . . . . . . . . . . . . . .<br>Warsaw | 38,200,000 . . . .<br>1,680,000 | 120,725. . . . .<br>312,677 | Republic. . . . .<br> | President: . . . . . . . . . . . . . . . . .<br>Lech Walesa<br>Premier:<br>Jan Olszewski | Zloty . . . . . . . . .<br>11,458.00 | 66,974<br>1,760 |
| **PORTUGAL** . . . . . . . . . . .<br>Lisbon | 10,400,000 . . . .<br>831,000 | 35,553. . . . .<br>92,082 | Republic. . . . .<br> | President: . . . . . . . . . . . . . . . . .<br>Mário Soares<br>Prime Minister:<br>Aníbal Cavaço Silva | Escudo. . . . . . .<br>157.65 | 44,058<br>4,260 |
| **QATAR** . . . . . . . . . . . . . . .<br>Doha | 500,000 . . . .<br>217,300 | 4,250. . . . .<br>11,000 | Constitutional<br>emirate | Emir and . . . . . . . . . . . . . . . . . . . .<br>Prime Minister:<br>Sheikh Khalifa bin Hamad<br>al-Thani | Riyal . . . . . . . . .<br>3.64 | 6,650[4]<br>NA |
| **ROMANIA** . . . . . . . . . . . .<br>Bucharest | 23,400,000 . . . .<br>2,300,000 | 91,699. . . . .<br>237,500 | Republic. . . . .<br> | President: . . . . . . . . . . . . . . . . .<br>Ion Iliescu<br>Prime Minister:<br>Theodor Stolojan | Leu . . . . . . . . . .<br>189.00[1] | 117,700<br>5,107 |

| Imports Exports (millions) | Revenue Expenditure (millions) | Elementary Schools: Teachers Students | Secondary Schools: Teachers Students | Colleges and Universities: Teachers Students |
|---|---|---|---|---|
| $ NA | $ 45.4 | 71 | 40 | NA |
| NA | 54.7 | 1,451 | 482 | NA |
| $ 686 | $ 352.3 | 57,209 | 21,132 | NA |
| 210 | 644.2 | 2,108,739 | 612,943 | 82,969 |
| 126,098 | 67,509.3 | 84,006 | 98,002 | NA |
| 131,802 | 78,295.0 | 1,431,428 | 1,342,243 | 177,572 |
| 9,501 | 15,989.0 | 16,057 | NA. | 6,085 |
| 9,488 | 16,740.0 | 312,998 | 343,587 | 56,930 |
| NA | 900.0 | 18,137 | NA. | 1,678 |
| 236 | 1,400.0 | 583,725 | 177,202 | 23,873 |
| NA | 346.0 | 7,859 | 2,035 | NA |
| 243 | 346.0 | 324,760 | 58,489 | NA |
| 5,688 | 7,780.0 | 302,669 | 133,743 | NA |
| 13,670 | 7,134.0 | 12,225,337 | 2,934,469 | NA |
| 26,852 | 51,645.1 | 52,230 | NA. | 4,277 |
| 34,030 | 55,506.4 | 312,230 | 365,938 | 47,884 |
| 2,255 | 4,100.0 | 8,529 | 5,249 | 262 |
| 3,933 | 4,710.0 | 232,181 | 71,572 | 1,819 |
| 7,376 | 10,000.0 | 186,260 | 170,449 | 7,891 |
| 5,589 | 10,764.0 | 7,609,069 | 3,068,077 | 236,972 |
| 1,539 | 900.0 | 14,980 | 9,796 | 3,581 |
| 321 | 1,400.0 | 345,202 | 190,166 | 62,143 |
| 1,184 | 1,171.3 | 13,171 | 3,057 | 400 |
| 1,133 | 1,157.0 | 417,818 | 67,007 | 3,413 |
| 1,313 | 899.0 | 24,729 | NA. | NA |
| 959 | 899.0 | 627,190 | 152,727 | 27,586 |
| 3,230 | 3,134.9 | 106,600 | 68,541 | 23,480 |
| 3,277 | 4,210.0 | 3,711,592 | 1,427,261 | 409,654 |
| 13,041 | 7,113.8 | 302,195 | 111,734 | 52,482 |
| 8,068 | 11,084.7 | 9,972,571 | 3,737,104 | 1,115,832 |
| 9,781 | 20,920.3 | 325,789 | 161,868 | 59,006 |
| 14,322 | 23,406.8 | 5,087,005 | 1,751,111 | 397,949 |
| 25,263 | 24,407.2 | 75,456 | 48,352 | 9,555 |
| 16,417 | 29,164.8 | 1,234,293 | 572,697 | 96,427 |
| 1,326 | 2,320.0 | 3,980 | 3,105 | 501 |
| NA | 3,220.0 | 48,097 | 26,659 | 5,889 |
| 9,843 | 50,654.3 | 141,609 | 46,270 | 12,036 |
| 5,870 | 50,654.3 | 3,027,196 | 1,529,372 | 157,041 |

449

| Nation Capital | Population | Area of Country (sq mi/ sq km) | Type of Government | Heads of State and Government | Currency: Value of U.S. Dollar (July 1) | GNP (millions) GNP Per Capita |
|---|---|---|---|---|---|---|
| RWANDA............ Kigali | 7,500,000 157,000 | 10,169.... 26,338 | Republic...... | President:....................... Juvénal Habyarimana | Franc........$ 132.0039 | 2,157 310 |
| SAINT KITTS- .......... NEVIS Basseterre | 43,000 14,300 | 65.... 105 | Parliamentary state (C) | Governor-General:.............. Sir Clement Arrindell Prime Minister: Kennedy Simmonds | East Caribbean dollar 2.70 | 119 2,860 |
| SAINT LUCIA........... Castries | 147,000 53,000 | 238.... 616 | Parliamentary state (C) | Governor-General:............... Stanislaus James Prime Minister: John G. M. Compton | East Caribbean dollar 2.70 | 267 1,810 |
| SAINT VINCENT ........ AND THE GRENADINES Kingstown | 114,000 29,000 | 150.... 388 | Parliamentary state (C) | Acting Governor-General: ........ David Jack Prime Minister: James Mitchell | East Caribbean dollar 2.70 | 135 1,200 |
| SAN MARINO........... San Marino | 23,000 4,000 | 24.... 61 | Republic...... | Captains-Regents:.............. Adolmiro Bartolini Ottaviano Rossi | Italian lira..... 1,346.00 | NA NA |
| SÃO TOMÉ AND ........ PRÍNCIPE São Tomé | 116,000 35,000 | 372.... 964 | Republic...... | President: ...................... Miguel Trovoada Prime Minister: Daniel Lima dos Santos Daio | Dobra........ 240.00[1] | 43 360 |
| SAUDI ARABIA ......... Riyadh | 15,500,000 2,000,000 | 830,000..... 2,149,690 | Monarchy..... | King and Prime Minister: ........ Fahd ibn Abdul-Aziz | Riyal........ 3.7504 | 89,986 6,230 |
| SENEGAL .............. Dakar | 7,500,000 1,382,000 | 75,750.... 196,192 | Republic...... | President: ...................... Abdou Diouf Premier: Habib Thiam | CFA franc[3] ... 306.375 | 4,716 650 |
| SEYCHELLES........... Victoria | 67,000 23,000 | 108..... 280 | Republic...... (C) | President: ...................... France Albert René | Rupee........ 5.5788 | 285 4,170 |
| SIERRA LEONE........ Freetown | 4,300,000 470,000 | 27,699.... 71,740 | Republic...... (C) | President: ...................... Joseph Momoh | Leone........ 410.00[1] | 813 200 |
| SINGAPORE............ | 2,800,000 | 240.... 622 | Republic...... (C) | President: ...................... Wee Kim Wee Prime Minister: Goh Chok Tong | Dollar ........ 1.7645 | 28,058 10,450 |
| SOLOMON ISLANDS .... Honiara | 309,000 32,000 | 10,983..... 28,446 | Parliamentary state (C) | Governor-General:............... George Lepping Prime Minister: Solomon Mamalon | Dollar ........ 2.7012 | 181 570 |
| SOMALIA .............. Mogadishu | 7,700,000 1,300,000 | 246,200.... 637,658 | Republic...... | President: ...................... Ali Mahdi Mohammed | Shilling ....... 2,620.00 | 1,035 170 |
| SOUTH AFRICA,[13] ...... REPUBLIC OF Cape Town Pretoria | 31,100,000 777,000 443,000 | 471,445..... 1,221,037 | Republic...... | President: ...................... Frederik Willem de Klerk | Rand.......... 2.6582 | 86,029 2,460 |
| SPAIN ................. Madrid | 39,000,000 3,121,000 | 194,897.... 504,782 | Constitutional monarchy | King:............................ Juan Carlos I Prime Minister: Felipe González Márquez | Peseta ....... 113.40 | 358,352 9,150 |
| SRI LANKA............. Colombo | 17,400,000 609,000 | 25,332.... 65,610 | Republic..... (C) | President: ...................... Ranasinghe Premadasa Prime Minister: Dingiri Banda Wijetunga | Rupee........ 41.1688 | 7,268 430 |
| SUDAN ................ Khartoum | 25,900,000 505,000 | 967,500.... 2,505,813 | Republic...... | Head of State and Premier: ...... Omar Hassan Ahmed al-Bashir | Pound........ 15.00[1] | 10,094 420 |
| SURINAME............. Paramaribo | 417,000 192,000 | 63,037.... 163,265 | Republic...... | President: ...................... Ronald Venetiaan | Guilder ....... 1.785 | 1,314 3,020 |
| SWAZILAND........... Mbabane | 800,000 38,000 | 6,704.... 17,363 | Monarchy..... (C) | King:............................ Mswati III Prime Minister: Obed Dlamini | Lilangeni ..... 2.8868 | 683 900 |

| Imports Exports (millions) | Revenue Expenditure (millions) | Elementary Schools: Teachers Students | Secondary Schools: Teachers Students | Colleges and Universities: Teachers Students |
|---|---|---|---|---|
| $ 369 | $ 375.4 | 16,975 | 3,616 | 402 |
| 101 | 375.4 | 969,908 | 50,631 | 1,855 |
| 94 | 32.2 | 331 | 288 | 37 |
| 28 | 32.2 | 7,473 | 4,204 | 194 |
| 155 | 132.9 | 1,082 | 352 | 62 |
| 83[11] | 137.1 | 33,120 | 6,391 | 389 |
| 195 | 45.8 | 1,374 | 446 | 34 |
| NA | 45.8 | 25,702 | 7,237 | 795 |
| NA | 183.3 | 189 | 179 | NA |
| NA | 183.3 | 1,266 | 1,222 | NA |
| NA | 28.5 | 616 | 331 | NA |
| NA | 28.5 | 18,095 | 6,171 | NA |
| 21,153 | 31,500.0 | 90,535 | 45,798 | 10,384 |
| 27,741 | 38,100.0 | 1,460,283 | 654,202 | 119,428 |
| 1,024 | 2,156.8[15] | 12,843 | 4,515 | 770 |
| 606 | 2,156.8[15] | 658,102 | 146,310 | 14,833 |
| 186 | 737.2 | 781 | 329 | NA |
| 40 | 737.2 | 14,595 | 4,052 | 15,324 |
| 146 | 39.6 | 12,601 | 4,945 | 373 |
| 138 | 50.4 | 399,028 | 101,700 | 2,985 |
| 60,899 | 10,150.0 | 9,998 | 9,236 | NA |
| 52,752 | 9,320.0 | 257,833 | 199,076 | 50,627 |
| 114 | 52.0 | 1,849 | 276 | NA |
| 75 | 52.0 | 39,563 | 5,336 | NA |
| 132 | 18.2 | 10,338 | 2,786 | 817 |
| 104 | 23.3 | 196,496 | 45,686 | 15,672 |
| 17,477[14] | 21,047.2 | 265,575[16] | —[16] | 47,697 |
| 23,628 | 21,642.6 | 6,684,350[16] | —[16] | 438,254 |
| 87,696 | 122,700.0 | 131,389 | 229,145 | 51,453 |
| 55,642 | 127,300.0 | 3,246,655 | 4,798,337 | 951,419 |
| 2,685 | 1,791.6 | 143,452 | NA | 1,955 |
| 1,983 | 1,708.6 | 2,037,313 | NA | 26,241 |
| 1,060 | 1,307.7 | 50,389 | 23,035 | 1,635 |
| 509 | 2,170.4 | 1,766,738 | 556,587 | 33,934 |
| 195 | 171.2 | NA | 2,330 | 187 |
| 232 | 141.0 | 62,633 | 34,608 | 1,198. |
| 581 | 297.0 | 4,665 | NA | 115 |
| 443 | 298.0 | 152,895 | 33,670 | 1,289 |

| Nation Capital | Population | Area of Country (sq mi/ sq km) | Type of Government | Heads of State and Government | Currency: Value of U.S. Dollar (July 1) | GNP (millions) GNP Per Capita |
|---|---|---|---|---|---|---|
| SWEDEN Stockholm | 8,600,000 672,200 | 173,732 449,964 | Constitutional monarchy | King: Carl XVI Gustaf Prime Minister: Carl Bildt | Krona 6.5295 | 184,230 21,710 |
| SWITZERLAND Bern | 6,800,000 135,000 | 15,943 41,292 | Federal republic | President: Flavio Cotti | Franc 1.5585 | 197,984 30,270 |
| SYRIA Damascus | 12,800,000 1,258,000 | 71,500 185,180 | Socialist republic | President: Hafez al-Assad Prime Minister: Mahmoud Zubi | Pound 21.00 | 12,444 1,020 |
| TAIWAN (REPUBLIC OF CHINA) Taipei | 20,500,000 2,275,000 | 13,900 36,000 | Republic | President: Lee Teng-hui Premier: Hau Pei-tsun | New Taiwan dollar 27.17 | 148,820 NA |
| TANZANIA Dodoma | 26,900,000 24,500 | 364,900 945,087 | Republic (C) | President: Ali Hassan Mwinyi Prime Minister: Joseph S. Warioba | Shilling 230.40 | 3,079[18] 120 |
| THAILAND Bangkok | 58,000,000 6,312,000 | 198,456 514,000 | Constitutional monarchy | King: Bhumibol Adulyadej Prime Minister: Anand Panyarachun | Baht 25.73 | 64,437 1,170 |
| TOGO Lomé | 3,800,000 367,000 | 21,925 56,785 | Republic | President: Gnassingbé Eyadéma | CFA franc[3] 306.375 | 1,364 390 |
| TONGA Nukualofa | 95,200 29,000 | 270 699 | Constitutional monarchy | King: Taufa'ahau Tupou IV Prime Minister: Baron Vaea | Pa'anga 1.3026 | 89 910 |
| TRINIDAD AND TOBAGO Port of Spain | 1,300,000 51,000 | 1,981 5,130 | Republic (C) | President: Noor Hassanali Prime Minister: Arthur N. R. Robinson | Dollar 4.25 | 4,000 3,160 |
| TUNISIA Tunis | 8,400,000 597,000 | 63,170 163,610 | Republic | President: Zine al-Abidine Ben Ali Prime Minister: Hamed Karoui | Dinar 0.9853 | 10,089 1,260 |
| TURKEY Ankara | 58,500,000 3,236,000 | 301,382 780,576 | Republic | President: Turgut Ozal Prime Minister: Suleyman Demirel | Lira 4,393.81 | 74,731 1,360 |
| TUVALU (ELLICE ISLANDS) Funafuti | 9,000 2,800 | 10 26 | Parliamentary state (C) | Governor-General: Tupua Leupena Prime Minister: Bikenibeu Paeniu | Australian dollar 1.3026 | NA NA |
| UGANDA Kampala | 18,700,000 773,000 | 91,134 236,036 | Republic (C) | President: Yoweri Museveni Prime Minister: George C. Adyebo | Shilling 699.44 | 4,254 250 |
| UNION OF SOVIET SOCIALIST REPUBLICS[19] Moscow | 284,000,000 8,967,000 | 8,649,538 22,402,200 | Federal socialist state | President: Mikhail Gorbachev | Ruble 0.6044 | 2,105,880 NA |
| UNITED ARAB EMIRATES Abu Dhabi | 2,400,000 316,000 | 32,278 83,600 | Federal state | President: Sheikh Zayed bin Sultan al-Nahayan Prime Minister: Sheikh Rashid bin Said al-Maktoum | Dirham 3.671 | 28,449 18,430 |
| UNITED STATES OF AMERICA Washington, D.C. | 249,633,000 606,900 | 3,618,770 9,372,571 | Federal republic | President: George Bush Vice President: Dan Quayle | Dollar * | 5,237,707 21,100 |

| Imports<br>Exports<br>(millions) | Revenue<br>Expenditure<br>(millions) | Elementary<br>Schools:<br>Teachers<br>Students | Secondary<br>Schools:<br>Teachers<br>Students | Colleges and<br>Universities:<br>Teachers<br>Students |
|---|---|---|---|---|
| $ 54,435 | $ 76,200.4 | NA | NA | NA |
| 57,574 | 77,098.3 | 580,199 | 609,289 | 186,988 |
| 69,681 | 22,535.0 | NA | NA | NA |
| 63,784 | 23,372.0 | 383,042 | 377,008 | 80,628 |
| 2,084 | 6,147.3 | 85,598 | 61,241 | 4,605 |
| 2,986 | 9,449.9 | 2,304,544 | 933,661 | 138,743 |
| 52,507 | 54,036.0 | 80,849 | 81,986 | 25,581 |
| 66,195 | 63,332.0 | 2,384,801 | 1,767,835 | 535,064 |
| 800 | 986.0 | 95,503 | 6,678 | 1,087 |
| 276 | 1,013.0 | 3,159,726 | 113,546 | 4,395 |
| 33,379 | 18,400.0 | 349,210 | 123,152 | 14,666 |
| 23,068 | 18,400.0 | 6,518,540 | 2,071,107 | 150,355 |
| 487 | 301.9 | 10,217 | 4,374 | 299 |
| 242 | 301.9 | 527,853 | 115,390 | 6,972 |
| 62 | 33.0 | NA | 799 | 17 |
| 12 | 33.0 | 16,912 | 13,587 | 85 |
| 1,121 | 1,505.9 | 7,686 | NA | 286 |
| 1,718 | 1,788.2 | 182,764 | 97,444 | 4,252 |
| 5,542 | 4,421.7 | 44,208 | 29,762 | 3,901 |
| 3,526 | 4,915.7 | 1,333,490 | 530,004 | 54,466 |
| 15,763 | 14,960.4 | 220,943 | 144,543 | 26,854 |
| 11,627 | 14,960.4 | 6,880,304 | 3,288,309 | 352,979 |
| NA | 3.7 | 64 | NA | NA |
| NA | 3.0 | 1,364 | 293 | NA |
| 209 | 485.2 | 75,561 | 15,437 | 444 |
| NA | 749.2 | 2,632,764 | 260,069 | 5,533 |
| 114,567 | 715,107.3 | 2,906,000 | NA | 394,000 |
| 109,173 | 769,514.8 | 24,711,000 | 21,242,500 | 5,097,000 |
| 11,199 | 3,750.0 | 10,785 | 6,875 | 460 |
| NA | 4,470.0 | 197,869 | 85,586 | 7,428 |
| 516,987 | 1,054,260.1 | 1,280,808 | 912,453 | NA |
| 393,592 | 1,322,988.6 | 29,157,562 | 11,358,810 | 13,457,855 |

| Nation Capital | Population | Area of Country (sq mi/ sq km) | Type of Government | Heads of State and Government | Currency: Value of U.S. Dollar (July 1) | GNP (millions) GNP Per Capita |
|---|---|---|---|---|---|---|
| **URUGUAY**............. Montevideo | 3,100,000 1,309,000 | 68,037.... 176,215 | Republic...... | President: ........................ Luis Alberto Lacalle | New peso .... 1,975.00 | $ 8,069 2,620 |
| **VANUATU (NEW HEBRIDES)** Vila | 160,000 19,000 | 5,700..... 14,763 | Republic...... (C) | President: ........................ Fred Timakata Prime Minister: Donald Kalpokas | Vatu ......... 114.15 | 131 860 |
| **VENEZUELA**............ Caracas | 20,100,000 3,500,000 | 352,144.... 912,050 | Federal....... republic | President: ........................ Carlos Andrés Pérez | Bolivar ....... 55.59 | 47,164 2,450 |
| **VIETNAM**.............. Hanoi | 67,600,000 1,140,000 | 127,242.... 329,556 | Socialist ..... republic | President: ........................ Vo Chi Cong Premier: Vo Van Kiet | Dong.......... 8,250.00 | NA NA |
| **WESTERN SAMOA**...... Apia | 182,000 33,000 | 1,097..... 2,842 | Constitutional monarchy (C) | Head of State: ................. Malietoa Tanumafili II Prime Minister: Tofilau Eti Alesana | Talà.......... 2.3546 | 114 720 |
| **YEMEN** ................ Sana | 10,100,000 500,000 | 186,375..... 372,750 | Republic...... | President: ........................ Ali Abdullah Saleh Prime Minister: Haider Abu Bakr al-Attas | Rial........... 12.05 | 7,203 640 |
| **YUGOSLAVIA**[20] ........ Belgrade | 23,900,000 1,470,000 | 98,766..... 255,804 | Federal....... socialist republic | Acting Head:..................... of Presidency: Branko Kostic | Dinar......... 23.59 | 59,080 2,490 |
| **ZAIRE** ................ Kinshasa | 37,800,000 2,700,000 | 905,568..... 2,345,409 | Republic...... | President: ........................ Mobutu Sese Seko Prime Minister: Etienne Tshisekedi | Zaire ......... 3,695.00 | 8,841 260 |
| **ZAMBIA**............... Lusaka | 8,400,000 870,000 | 290,586..... 752,614 | Republic...... (C) | President: ........................ Frederick Chiluba | Kwacha ...... 65.8929 | 3,060 390 |
| **ZIMBABWE** ............ Harare | 10,000,000 681,000 | 150,804..... 390,580 | Republic...... (C) | President: ........................ Robert G. Mugabe | Dollar ........ 3.2175 | 6,076 640 |

[1] As of December 27, 1991.
[2] Data for Belgium and Luxembourg are combined in figures for Belgium, and exclude trade between the two countries.
[3] Communauté Financière Africaine franc.
[4] Gross Domestic Product.
[5] Imports F.O.B.
[6] Excludes trade within the Central African Customs Union (Cameroon, Central African Republic, Congo, Gabon).
[7] The president of the Turkish sector was Rauf Denktash; the prime minister was Dervish Eroglu.
[8] Information pertains to the Greek sector only.
[9] Figure is for Federal Republic of Germany, pre-unification.
[10] Entries include Northern Ireland.
[11] Includes re-exports.
[12] Entries exclude the West Bank and Gaza Strip.

| Imports / Exports (millions) | Revenue / Expenditure (millions) | Elementary Schools: Teachers / Students | Secondary Schools: Teachers / Students | Colleges and Universities: Teachers / Students |
|---|---|---|---|---|
| $ 1,318 | $ 295.4 | 15,188 | NA. | 6,141 |
| 1,693 | 313.7 | 351,984 | 243,135 | 62,461 |
| 68 | 36.5 | 1,036 | 133 | NA |
| 20 | 36.5 | 23,856 | 2,904 | NA |
| 7,383 | 8,500.0 | 112,157 | 61,671 | 23,951 |
| 17,498 | 7,800.0 | 2,880,333 | 1,058,058 | 347,618 |
| NA | 680.0 | 235,791 | 177,344 | NA |
| 1,000 | 1,340.0 | 8,125,836 | 4,022,858 | NA |
| 75 | 45.8 | 1,511 | 513 | NA |
| 9 | 36.8 | 31,412 | 20,168 | NA |
| NA | 2,940.0 | 27,732 | 7,197 | 470 |
| NA | 4,250.0 | 1,250,599 | 146,133 | 23,457 |
| 18,871 | 7,858.0 | 62,534 | 135,459 | 23,209 |
| 14,308 | 7,821.8 | 1,422,162 | 2,361,532 | 291,858 |
| 849 | 1,052.8 | 113,468 | 49,153 | 1,387 |
| 1,254 | 1,120.0 | 4,156,029 | 983,334 | 16,239 |
| 1,242 | 1,290.0 | 28,881 | NA. | 389 |
| 1,292 | 1,553.0 | 1,357,714 | 131,502 | 4,410 |
| NA | 2,600.0 | 57,762 | 19,507 | NA |
| 1,631[11] | 3,150.0 | 2,217,433 | 537,348 | 7,404 |

[13] Data generally exclude the homelands, which are nominally independent. The latest available population estimates for the homelands are: Bophuthatswana, 2,400,000; Ciskei, 1,000,000; Transkei, 4,400,000; Venda 700,000. Heads of state were: Bophuthatswana, Lucas Mangope; Ciskei, Oupa Gqozo; Transkei, Tutor Ndamse; Venda, Gabriel Ramushwana.
[14] Trade figures are for South African Customs Union (Botswana, Lesotho, Namibia, Swaziland); trade between these countries is excluded.
[15] Figures cover 15-month period.
[16] Combined figures for elementary and secondary education.
[17] Values are for East Bank only.
[18] Values are for mainland Tanzania only.
[19] The Soviet Union ceased to exist in late December 1991. A new Commonwealth of Independent States was formed by 11 of the Republics: Russia, Ukraine, Belarus (formerly Byelorussia), Moldava (formerly Moldavia), Azerbaijan, Armenia, Kazakhstan, Kyrgyzstan (formerly Kirghizia), Uzbekistan, Tajikistan, and Turkmenistan. Georgia did not join, and Estonia, Latvia, and Lithuania had been recognized as independent countries in September 1991.
[20] At year's end, the status of Yugoslavia's constituent republics was in transition; data are for the combined six republics.

# THE STATES AND OUTLYING AREAS OF THE UNITED STATES

| State<br>Capital | Population[1] | Area<br>(sq mi/<br>sq km) | Per<br>Capita<br>Personal<br>Income | Governor<br>Lieutenant-Governor | Revenue<br>Expenditure<br>(billions) |
|---|---|---|---|---|---|
| ALABAMA | 4,040,587 (3.8) | 51,718 | $14,826 | Guy Hunt (R) | $ 9.041 |
| Montgomery | 187,106 | 133,949 | | Jim Folsom, Jr. (D) | 8.108 |
| ALASKA | 550,043 (36.9) | 587,875 | 21,761 | Walter J. Hickel (I) | 5.500 |
| Juneau | 26,751 | 1,522,589 | | John B. Coghill (I) | 4.688 |
| ARIZONA | 3,665,228 (34.8) | 114,006 | 16,297 | Fife Symington (R) | 8.598 |
| Phoenix | 983,403 | 295,274 | | | 8.265 |
| ARKANSAS | 2,350,725 (2.8) | 53,182 | 14,218 | Bill Clinton (D) | 4.511 |
| Little Rock | 175,795 | 137,741 | | Jim Guy Tucker (D) | 4.223 |
| CALIFORNIA | 29,760,021 (25.7) | 158,647 | 20,795 | Pete Wilson (R) | 88.704 |
| Sacramento | 369,365 | 410,894 | | Leo McCarthy (D) | 78.867 |
| COLORADO | 3,294,394 (14.0) | 104,100 | 18,794 | Roy Romer (D) | 7.527 |
| Denver | 467,610 | 269,618 | | Mike Callihan (D) | 6.510 |
| CONNECTICUT | 3,287,116 (5.8) | 5,006 | 25,358 | Lowell P. Weicker (I) | 9.591 |
| Hartford | 139,739 | 12,965 | | Eunice S. Groark (I) | 8.880 |
| DELAWARE | 666,168 (12.1) | 2,026 | 20,039 | Michael N. Castle (R) | 2.316 |
| Dover | 27,630 | 5,247 | | Dale Edward Wolf (R) | 2.128 |
| DISTRICT OF | 606,900 (−4.9) | 68 | 24,181 | Mayor; Sharon Pratt Dixon (D) | 3.680 |
| COLUMBIA | | 176 | | | 3.798 |
| * | | | | | |
| FLORIDA | 12,937,926 (32.7) | 58,680 | 18,586 | Lawton Chiles (D) | 23.868 |
| Tallahassee | 124,773 | 151,980 | | Buddy Mackay (D) | 21.723 |
| GEORGIA | 6,478,216 (18.6) | 58,929 | 16,944 | Zell B. Miller (D) | 13.108 |
| Atlanta | 394,017 | 152,625 | | Pierre Howard (D) | 12.213 |
| HAWAII | 1,108,229 (14.9) | 6,459 | 20,234 | John Waihee (D) | 4.326 |
| Honolulu | 365,272 | 16,729 | | Ben Cayetano (D) | 3.832 |
| IDAHO | 1,006,749 (6.7) | 83,574 | 15,160 | Cecil D. Andrus (D) | 2.417 |
| Boise | 125,738 | 216,456 | | C. L. (Butch) Otter (R) | 2.047 |
| ILLINOIS | 11,430,602 (0.0) | 56,343 | 20,303 | Jim Edgar (R) | 24.313 |
| Springfield | 105,227 | 145,928 | | Bob Kustra (R) | 20.055 |
| INDIANA | 5,544,159 (1.0) | 36,185 | 16,864 | Evan Bayh (D) | 11.458 |
| Indianapolis | 741,952 | 93,719 | | Frank L. O'Bannon (D) | 10.410 |
| IOWA | 2,776,755 (−4.7) | 56,276 | 17,249 | Terry E. Branstad (R) | 6.728 |
| Des Moines | 193,187 | 145,754 | | Joy Corning (R) | 6.317 |
| KANSAS | 2,477,574 (4.8) | 82,282 | 17,986 | Joan Finney (D) | 5.136 |
| Topeka | 119,883 | 213,109 | | James Francisco (D) | 4.705 |
| KENTUCKY | 3,685,296 (0.7) | 40,411 | 14,929 | Brereton Jones (D) | 8.593 |
| Frankfort | 25,968 | 104,664 | | Paul Patton (D) | 7.772 |

456

The material in the following tables was the latest available. The symbol * indicates that the category is not applicable to the area mentioned or that the data were misleading for one reason or another. NA means that data were not available. The Office of Territorial Affairs was helpful in supplying some data for the table on Outlying Areas.

| Public Roads (miles) | Railways (miles) | Aircraft Departures | Daily News-papers | Public Elementary Schools (K-8): Teachers Students | Public Secondary Schools (9–12): Teachers Students | Colleges and Universities: Institutions Students |
|---|---|---|---|---|---|---|
| 90,672 | 3,229 | 39,359 | 29 | 22,211 525,730 | 17,717 197,613 | 87 208,562 |
| 13,485 | * | 81,516 | 8 | 3,723 81,698 | 2,021 27,582 | 8 28,627 |
| 51,612 | 1,520 | 169,231 | 21 | 23,458 451,311 | 8,676 156,304 | 37 252,614 |
| 77,085 | 2,483 | 15,386 | 32 | 13,204 311,060 | 12,242 123,900 | 37 88,572 |
| 163,574 | 6,202 | 760,258 | 157 | 151,019 3,470,574 | 56,259 1,301,404 | 310 1,744,879 |
| 77,680 | 3,280 | 190,475 | 30 | 16,157 407,525 | 15,797 155,230 | 54 201,114 |
| 19,991 | 285 | 31,006 | 24 | 18,310 338,378 | 12,490 123,182 | 48 169,438 |
| 5,444 | 226 | 32 | 2 | 2,935 70,699 | 3,033 27,109 | 10 40,562 |
| 1,102 | 38 | 168,451 | 4 | 3,270 60,662 | 2,534 20,639 | 17 79,800 |
| 108,085 | 2,662 | 249,133 | 53 | 45,710 1,303,439 | 40,003 468,910 | 95 573,712 |
| 109,601 | 4,274 | 292,558 | 37 | 41,319 828,426 | 20,168 298,109 | 95 239,208 |
| 4,099 | * | 164,502 | 6 | 4,692 123,496 | 3,130 45,997 | 14 54,186 |
| 62,435 | 2,126 | 35,053 | 12 | 5,678 156,602 | 4,938 58,330 | 11 48,969 |
| 135,944 | 7,319 | 393,996 | 82 | 60,439 1,280,021 | 28,973 517,334 | 166 709,937 |
| 91,908 | 4,082 | 66,124 | 78 | 26,440 671,036 | 23,423 283.129 | 78 275,921 |
| 112,541 | 3,354 | 25,243 | 38 | 17,303 338,422 | 12,058 140,064 | 58 169,901 |
| 133,578 | 6,935 | 14,916 | 47 | 14,345 313,588 | 11,392 117,276 | 54 158,497 |
| 69,668 | 2,447 | 32,417 | 25 | 24,051 451,858 | 11,680 178,830 | 59 166,014 |

| State<br>Capital | Population[1] | Area<br>(sq mi/<br>sq km) | Per<br>Capita<br>Personal<br>Income | Governor<br>Lieutenant-Governor | Revenue<br>Expenditure<br>(billions) |
|---|---|---|---|---|---|
| **LOUISIANA**..........<br>Baton Rouge | 4,219,973 (0.3)........<br>219,531 | 47,719......<br>123,592 | $14,391 .... | Charles E. Roemer III (R) ......<br>Paul J. Hardy (R) | $10.098<br>9.420 |
| **MAINE**..............<br>Augusta | 1,227,928 (9.2)........<br>21,325 | 33,128......<br>85,801 | 17,200 .... | John R. McKernan (R)..........<br>* | 3.246<br>3.044 |
| **MARYLAND** ........<br>Annapolis | 4,781,468 (13.4) ......<br>33,187 | 10,455......<br>27,078 | 21,864 .... | William Donald Schaefer (D).....<br>Melvin A. Steinberg (D) | 12.195<br>11.296 |
| **MASSACHUSETTS**...<br>Boston | 6,016,425 (4.9)........<br>574,283 | 8,262......<br>21,398 | 22,642 .... | William F. Weld (R)..............<br>Paul Cellucci (R) | 17.034<br>18.736 |
| **MICHIGAN** ..........<br>Lansing | 9,295,297 (0.4).......<br>127,321 | 58,513......<br>151,548 | 18,346 .... | John Engler (R)..............<br>Connie Binsfeld (R) | 23.405<br>23.098 |
| **MINNESOTA**........<br>St. Paul | 4,375,099 (7.3)........<br>272,235 | 84,397......<br>218,587 | 18,731 .... | Arne Carlson (R)..............<br>Joanell Drystad (R) | 13.162<br>11.355 |
| **MISSISSIPPI**........<br>Jackson | 2,573,216 (2.1)........<br>196,637 | 47,695......<br>123,529 | 12,735 .... | Ray Mabus (D) ................<br>Brad Dye (D) | 5.344<br>4.838 |
| **MISSOURI**..........<br>Jefferson City | 5,117,073 (4.1)........<br>35,481 | 69,709......<br>180,545 | 17,497 .... | John Ashcroft (R) ............<br>Mel Carnahan (D) | 9.343<br>8.326 |
| **MONTANA** ..........<br>Helena | 799,065 (1.6)........<br>24,569 | 147,046......<br>380,847 | 15,110 .... | Stan Stephens (R)..............<br>Allen Kolstad (R) | 2.225<br>2.007 |
| **NEBRASKA**..........<br>Lincoln | 1,578,385 (0.5)........<br>191,972 | 77,358......<br>200,356 | 17,221 .... | E. Benjamin Nelson (D)........<br>Maxine Morel (D) | 3.073<br>2.885 |
| **NEVADA** ............<br>Carson City | 1,201,833 (50.1)........<br>40,443 | 110,567......<br>286,367 | 19,416 .... | Bob Miller (D)................<br>Sue Wagner (R) | 3.266<br>2.929 |
| **NEW HAMPSHIRE** ...<br>Concord | 1,109,252 (20.5) ......<br>36,006 | 9,283......<br>24,043 | 20,789 .... | Judd Gregg (R) ...............<br>* | 1.922<br>1.972 |
| **NEW JERSEY** .......<br>Trenton | 7,730,188 (5.0)........<br>88,675 | 7,790......<br>20,176 | 24,986 .... | James Florio (D) ...............<br>* | 22.624<br>21.454 |
| **NEW MEXICO** ......<br>Santa Fe | 1,515,069 (16.3) ......<br>98,928 | 121,598......<br>314,937 | 14,288 .... | Bruce King (D)................<br>Casey Luna (D) | 4.731<br>4.172 |
| **NEW YORK** ........<br>Albany | 17,990,455 (2.5)........<br>292,594 | 49,112......<br>127,199 | 21,975 .... | Mario M. Cuomo (D)...........<br>Stan Lundine (D) | 64.253<br>59.139 |
| **NORTH CAROLINA**...<br>Raleigh | 6,628,637 (12.7) ......<br>207,951 | 52,672......<br>136,420 | 16,203 .... | James G. Martin (R)............<br>James R. Gardner (R) | 14.485<br>13.493 |
| **NORTH DAKOTA**.....<br>Bismarck | 638,800 (−2.1) ......<br>49,256 | 70,704......<br>183,122 | 15,255 .... | George Sinner (R)..............<br>Lloyd Omdahl (D) | 1.810<br>1.755 |
| **OHIO** ..............<br>Columbus | 10,847,115 (0.5)........<br>632,910 | 41,328......<br>107,039 | 19,473 .... | George Voinovich (R)...........<br>Mike DeWine (R) | 28.516<br>25.237 |
| **OKLAHOMA** ........<br>Oklahoma City | 3,145,585 (4.0)........<br>444,719 | 69,903......<br>181,048 | 15,444 .... | David Walters (D) ..............<br>Jack Mildren (D) | 7.201<br>6.515 |
| **OREGON**...........<br>Salem | 2,842,321 (7.9)........<br>107,786 | 97,052......<br>251,363 | 17,156 .... | Barbara Roberts (D)............<br>* | 7.001<br>6.352 |
| **PENNSYLVANIA**......<br>Harrisburg | 11,881,643 (0.1)........<br>52,376 | 45,309......<br>117,350 | 18,672 .... | Robert P. Casey (D)............<br>Mark Singel (D) | 27.223<br>24.231 |
| **RHODE ISLAND** .....<br>Providence | 1,003,464 (5.9)........<br>160,728 | 1,213......<br>3,142 | 18,841 .... | Bruce D. Sundlun (D) ..........<br>Roger N. Begin (D) | 3.034<br>3.014 |
| **SOUTH CAROLINA**...<br>Columbia | 3,486,703 (11.7) ......<br>98,052 | 31,117......<br>80,593 | 15,099 .... | Carroll A. Campbell, Jr. (R)......<br>Nick Theodore (D) | 8.750<br>7.910 |
| **SOUTH DAKOTA**.....<br>Pierre | 696,004 (0.8)........<br>12,906 | 77,121......<br>199,742 | 15,872 .... | George Mickelson (R)...........<br>Walter Dale Miller (R) | 1.494<br>1.344 |

| Public Roads (miles) | Railways (miles) | Aircraft Departures | Daily Newspapers | Public Elementary Schools (K-8): Teachers | Students | Public Secondary Schools (9–12): Teachers | Students | Colleges and Universities: Institutions | Students |
|---|---|---|---|---|---|---|---|---|---|
| 58,620 | 2,576 | 66,125 | 29 | NA. | 581,702 | NA. | 201,323 | 34 | 179,927 |
| 22,389 | * | 10,395 | 9 | 10,041 | 152,267 | 5,165 | 61,508 | 31 | 58,230 |
| 28,752 | 840 | 75,393 | 17 | 21,536 | 507,007 | 20,110 | 191,799 | 57 | 255,326 |
| 34,076 | 442 | 112,641 | 43 | 20,251 | 590,238 | 31,238 | 235,350 | 117 | 426,476 |
| 117,449 | 2,500 | 173,394 | 54 | 31,662 | 1,127,921 | 39,285 | 448,864 | 97 | 560,320 |
| 129,397 | 4,759 | 118,612 | 28 | 23,137 | 528,507 | 19,964 | 211,046 | 81 | 253,097 |
| 72,520 | 1,491 | 10,446 | 23 | 16,087 | 369,513 | 10,562 | 132,507 | 47 | 116,370 |
| 120,527 | 5,057 | 207,991 | 52 | 26,471 | 576,243 | 23,962 | 231,691 | 89 | 278,505 |
| 71,387 | 2,490 | 33,720 | 12 | 6,656 | 109,791 | 2,968 | 41,474 | 19 | 37,660 |
| 92,403 | 4,143 | 26,781 | 21 | 10,388 | 194,227 | 8,076 | 76,693 | 36 | 108,844 |
| 45,524 | 1,440 | 106,938 | 8 | 4,646 | 137,455 | 3,484 | 49,379 | 8 | 56,471 |
| 14,836 | * | 5,153 | 10 | 7,094 | 124,410 | 3,478 | 47,288 | 29 | 58,800 |
| 34,252 | 968 | 131,208 | 22 | 42,711 | 765,810 | 27,611 | 310,195 | 62 | 314,091 |
| 54,736 | 1,989 | 36,578 | 20 | 9,238 | 203,157 | 4,302 | 92,900 | 26 | 81,350 |
| 111,242 | 2,498 | 323,895 | 86 | 82,769 | 1,790,143 | 65,857 | 755,698 | 326 | 1,018,130 |
| 94,690 | 2,829 | 210,211 | 60 | 32,667 | 769,825 | 20,858 | 310,919 | 126 | 345,401 |
| 86,517 | 3,777 | 13,872 | 10 | 5,171 | 84,920 | 2,638 | 32,896 | 20 | 40,350 |
| 113,600 | 5,455 | 214,482 | 96 | 56,308 | 1,242,327 | 45,319 | 524,832 | 152 | 550,729 |
| 111,765 | 3,449 | 51,725 | 48 | 16,747 | 420,940 | 15,122 | 157,640 | 47 | 175,855 |
| 94,969 | 2,687 | 99,509 | 21 | 14,756 | 340,264 | 10,102 | 132,130 | 46 | 161,822 |
| 116,508 | 3,924 | 229,816 | 100 | 47,171 | 1,150,853 | 46,696 | 504,626 | 217 | 610,357 |
| 6,111 | * | 13,690 | 9 | 4,293 | 98,412 | 3,820 | 37,317 | 11 | 76,503 |
| 64,046 | 2,317 | 35,596 | 17 | 24,034 | 443,712 | 12,303 | 172,465 | 64 | 145,730 |
| 74,696 | 1,179 | 10,925 | 13 | 4,465 | 93,596 | 3,029 | 33,733 | 19 | 32,666 |

| State Capital | Population[1] | Area (sq mi/ sq km) | Per Capita Personal Income | Governor Lieutenant-Governor | Revenue Expenditure (billions) |
|---|---|---|---|---|---|
| TENNESSEE........ Nashville | 4,877,185 (6.2).... 510,784 | 42,146 109,158 | $15,798 ..... | Ned Ray McWherter (D) ........ John S. Wilder (D) | $ 9.110 8.403 |
| TEXAS.............. Austin | 16,986,510 (19.4) ...... 465,622 | 266,873 691,198 | 16,759 ..... | Ann W. Richards (D)............ Bob Bullock (D) | 30.975 26.127 |
| UTAH.............. Salt Lake City | 1,722,850 (17.9) ...... 159,936 | 84,904 219,900 | 14,083 ..... | Norman H. Bangerter (R)....... W. Val Oveson (R) | 4.302 3.857 |
| VERMONT.......... Montpelier | 562,758 (10.0) ...... 8,247 | 9,615 24,903 | 17,436 ..... | Howard Dean (D) .............. vacant | 1.592 1.565 |
| VIRGINIA........... Richmond | 6,187,358 (15.7) ...... | 40,598 105,148 | 19,746 ..... | L. Douglas Wilder (D)........... Donald Beyer (D) | 13.607 12.632 |
| WASHINGTON....... Olympia | 4,866,692 (17.8) ...... 33,840 | 68,127 176,448 | 18,858 ..... | Booth Gardner (D)............. Joel Pritchard (R) | 14.999 13.567 |
| WEST VIRGINIA ..... Charleston | 1,793,477 (−8.0)...... 57,287 | 24,231 62,758 | 13,747 ..... | W. Gaston Caperton (D) ........ * | 4.435 4.212 |
| WISCONSIN......... Madison | 4,891,769 (4.0)........ 191,262 | 56,144 145,412 | 17,503 ..... | Tommy Thompson (R) .......... Scott McCallum (R) | 13.388 11.416 |
| WYOMING .......... Cheyenne | 453,588 (−3.4)...... 50,008 | 97,818 253,347 | 16,398 ..... | Mike Sullivan (D).............. * | 1.900 1.641 |

# OUTLYING AREAS OF THE UNITED STATES

| Area Capital | Population[1] | Area (sq mi/ sq km) | Status | Governor Lieutenant-Governor | Revenue Expenditure (millions) | Roads (miles) |
|---|---|---|---|---|---|---|
| AMERICAN SAMOA ... Pago Pago | 46,800.... NA | 76 ....... 197 | Unincorporated... territory | Peter Tali Coleman ............. Galea'i Poumele | $ 128.1...... NA | 113 |
| GUAM .............. Agaña | 133,200.... NA | 212 ....... 549 | Unincorporated... territory | Joseph F. Ada ................. Frank F. Blas | NA...... NA | 419 |
| NORTHERN ........ MARIANA ISLANDS Saipan | 43,300.... 39,100 | 184 ....... 477 | Commonwealth... | Lorenzo I. ..................... De Leon Guerrero Benjamin M. Manglona | 144.7...... NA | NA |
| PALAU.............. Koror | 15,100.... 10,500 | 170 ....... 440 | Trust territory[2] | President: ..................... Ngiratkel Etpison | 41.1...... NA | NA |
| PUERTO RICO....... San Juan | 3,522,000.... 449,300 | 3,515 ....... 9,104 | Commonwealth... | Rafael Hernández Colón ........ * | 11,985.2...... 11,460.2 | 8,580 |
| VIRGIN ISLANDS .... Charlotte Amalie | 101,800.... NA | 136 ....... 352 | Unincorporated... territory | Alexander A. Farrelly ........... Derek M. Hodge | 389.5...... 443.1 | 660 |

1. Population figures for April 1, 1990, based on 1990 U.S. census. Figures in parentheses for states and the District of Columbia show percentage changes in population between 1980 and 1990 censuses.

| Public Roads (miles) | Railways (miles) | Aircraft Departures | Daily Newspapers | Public Elementary Schools (K-8): Teachers Students | Public Secondary Schools (9–12): Teachers Students | Colleges and Universities: Institutions Students |
|---|---|---|---|---|---|---|
| 84,639 | 2,208 | 178,741 | 29 | 26,979 819,660 | 15,845 229,539 | 86 218,866 |
| 305,951 | 12,117 | 588,499 | 107 | 106,196 3,328,514 | 93,201 885,269 | 174 877,859 |
| 43,244 | 1,419 | 76,385 | 8 | 9,277 437,446 | 6,258 114,557 | 14 114,815 |
| 14,121 | * | 7,081 | 9 | 3,175 94,779 | 3,194 25,676 | 22 35,948 |
| 67,700 | 3,260 | 59,572 | 31 | 36,420 985,346 | 25,191 273,049 | 78 344,284 |
| 81,299 | 3,467 | 182,035 | 27 | 21,101 810,232 | 15,391 224,414 | 55 255,760 |
| 34,592 | 2,974 | 11,213 | 26 | 10,289 327,540 | 7,741 100,289 | 28 82,455 |
| 109,876 | 2,078 | 62,685 | 39 | 29,069 782,905 | 17,870 233,762 | 61 290,672 |
| 39,213 | 1,795 | 11,223 | 12 | 2,405 97,172 | 3,421 27,042 | 9 29,159 |

| Aircraft Departures | Radio and Television Stations | Newspapers | Public Elementary and Secondary School Teachers | Public School Students: Elementary Secondary | Higher Education: Institutions Students |
|---|---|---|---|---|---|
| 399 | 3 | 2 | 659 | 9,309 2,949 | 1 1,011 |
| 5,931 | 8 | 2 | 1,622 | 19,291 7,202 | 4,350 |
| 3,821 | 4 | 3 | 358 | 4,626 1,475 | 1 419 |
| 656 | 2 | NA | NA | NA NA | 2 1,037 |
| 24,925 | 119 | 4 | 33,427 | 486,247 164,978 | 55 152,996 |
| 7,339 | 12 | 2 | 1,595 | 15,769 5,424 | 2 2,697 |

2. Palau is the only remaining district of the U.S. Trust Territory of the Pacific Islands; the other constituents became independent countries or U.S. Commonwealths.

# THE PROVINCES AND TERRITORIES OF CANADA

| Province Capital | Population | Area (sq mi/ sq km) | Per Capita Personal Income | Premier Lieutenant-Governor |
|---|---|---|---|---|
| **ALBERTA** | 2,472,500 | 246,422 | $21,972 | Donald Getty |
| Edmonton | 583,900 | 638,233 | | Helen Hunley |
| **BRITISH COLUMBIA** | 3,138,900 | 344,663 | 22,437 | William N. Vander Zalm |
| Victoria | 68,000 | 892,677 | | David C. Lam |
| **MANITOBA** | 1,090,700 | 211,469 | 19,258 | Gary Filmon |
| Winnipeg | 605,600 | 547,704 | | George Johnson |
| **NEW BRUNSWICK** | 724,300 | 27,633 | 17,060 | Frank McKenna |
| Fredericton | 44,400 | 71,569 | | Gilbert Finn |
| **NEWFOUNDLAND** | 573,000 | 143,488 | 15,846 | Clyde Kirby Wells |
| St. John's | 100,000 | 371,635 | | James A. McGrath |
| **NORTHWEST TERRITORIES** | 54,000 | 1,253,432 | 25,688 | Commissioner: |
| Yellowknife | 13,000 | 3,246,389 | | Dan Norris |
| **NOVA SCOTIA** | 892,000 | 20,402 | 18,151 | Roger S. Bacon |
| Halifax | 113,600 | 52,841 | | Lloyd Roseville Crouse |
| **ONTARIO** | 9,747,600 | 353,951 | 25,151 | Bob Rae |
| Toronto | 597,100 | 916,734 | | Lincoln Alexander |
| **PRINCE EDWARD ISLAND** | 130,400 | 2,185 | 16,316 | Joseph Ghiz |
| Charlottetown | 15,800 | 5,660 | | Robert Lloyd George MacPhail |
| **QUEBEC** | 6,770,800 | 524,252 | 20,567 | Robert Bourassa |
| Quebec | 164,600 | 1,357,812 | | Gilles Lamontagne |
| **SASKATCHEWAN** | 1,000,300 | 220,121 | 17,784 | Grant Devine |
| Regina | 175,100 | 570,113 | | Sylvia Fedoruk |
| **YUKON TERRITORY** | 26,000 | 205,345 | 25,747 | Commissioner: |
| Whitehorse | 20,700 | 531,844 | | Kenneth McKinnon |

1. Full-time only.

The material in this table has been prepared with the assistance of Statistics Canada. It should be noted that all dollar figures are in Canadian dollars.

| Revenue Expenditure (millions) | Motor Vehicle Registrations | Railways (miles) | Radio Stations Television Stations | Daily Newspapers | Elementary and Secondary Schools: Teachers Enrollment[1] | Postsecondary Education: Institutions Enrollment |
|---|---|---|---|---|---|---|
| $15,952.4 | 1,855,314 | 2,772 | 61 | 9 | 26,055. | 24 |
| 16,005.7 | | | 24 | | 492,910 | 73,755 |
| 18,029.6 | 2,556,539 | 3,937 | 105 | 19 | 29,620. | 25 |
| 18,099.7 | | | 24 | | 556,597 | 66,782 |
| 6,172.5 | 782,398. | 1,786 | 27 | 5 | 13,091. | 16 |
| 6,731.4 | | | 13 | | 219,245 | 23,349 |
| 4,094.4 | 446,896. | 683 | 29 | 4 | 7,866. | 13 |
| 4,235.1 | | | 6 | | 136,527 | 18,644 |
| 3,425.9 | 313,687. | 279 | 36 | 2 | 7,994. | 13 |
| 3,569.6 | | | 8 | | 130,503 | 15,124 |
| 1,166.5 | 18,287. | — | 14 | — | 824. | 1 |
| 1,153.9 | | | 4 | | 13,732 | 252 |
| 4,411.2 | 446,896. | 438 | 32 | 7 | 10,430. | 22 |
| 4,767.1 | | | 6 | | 169,630 | 28,345 |
| 47,758.3 | 6,290,424 | 8,399 | 196 | 48 | 116,383. | 53 |
| 56,495.4 | | | 75 | | 1,976,617 | 301,864 |
| 765.7 | 82,946. | — | 6 | 3 | 1,391. | 3 |
| 780.0 | | | 2 | | 28,804 | 3,283 |
| 38,596.8 | 4,027,408 | 2,916 | 158 | 12 | 63,938. | 98 |
| 42,643.2 | | | 62 | | 1,143,372 | 275,992 |
| 5,672.8 | 624,964. | 2,494 | 40 | 4 | 11,444. | 4 |
| 6,104.4 | | | 14 | | 212,676 | 24,153 |
| 354.4 | 31,442. | — | 8 | 1 | 319. | 1 |
| 341.8 | | | 2 | | 5,113 | 176 |

# KEY TO SIGNED ARTICLES

Here is a list of contributors to this Yearbook. The initials at the end of an article are those of the author or authors of that article.

**A.D.,** ALASDAIR DRYSDALE, PH.D.
Associate Professor, University of New Hampshire. Author, *The Middle East and North Africa: A Political Geography.*

**A.F.,** ANITA FINKEL, PH.D.
Editor and Publisher, *The New Dance Review.*

**A.G.,** ALICE GARRARD, B.A.
Free-lance Writer Specializing in Travel. Author, *Frommer's Guide to San Diego.*

**A.J.K.S.,** ALAN J. K. SANDERS
Lecturer in Mongolian Studies, University of London. Author, *Mongolia: Politics, Economy, and Society.*

**A.L.R.,** ARTHUR L. ROBINSON, PH.D.
Staff Scientist, Advanced Light Source, Lawrence Berkeley Laboratory.

**A.O'R.,** ANTHONY O'REGAN, B.A.,M.A.
Ph.D. Candidate, Political Science Department, University of California at Santa Barbara.

**A.P.,** AUDREY PAVIA, B.A.
Senior Editor, *Pure Bred Dogs/ American Kennel Club Gazette.*

**A.S.,** ANITA SILVEY, B.S., M.A.
Editor in Chief, *The Horn Book Magazine.*

**A.Sy.,** ANWAR SYED, B.A., M.A., PH.D.
Professor of Political Science, University of Massachusetts. Author, *The Discourse and Politics of Zulfikar Ali Bhutto.*

**B.A.A.,** BELINDA A. AQUINO, PH.D.
Director, Center for Philippine Studies, and Associate Professor, Political Science, University of Hawaii.

**B.B.R.,** BONNIE B. REECE, B.S., M.B.A., PH.D.
Associate Professor of Advertising, Michigan State University. Member, Editorial Review Board, *Journal of Public Policy and Marketing.*

**B.D.,** BRUCE DRAKE, B.A.
Senior Washington Editor, National Public Radio.

**B.D.J.,** BRIAN D. JOHNSON, B.A.
Senior Writer and Film Critic, *Maclean's* Magazine.

**B.K.,** BOB KLAPISCH, B.A.
Baseball Reporter, New York *Daily News.*

**B.V.,** BOB VERDI, A.B.
Columnist, Chicago *Tribune.*

**C.B.,** CRAIG BAXTER, B.S., M.A., PH.D.
Professor, Politics and History, Juniata College. President, American Institute of Bangladesh Studies.

**C.C.,** CHARLES COOPER, B.A., M.A.
Senior Editor, *Computer Shoppers* Magazine.

**C.Cu.,** CARLOS CUNHA, B.A., M.A., PH.D.
Guest Professor of Political Science, Sarah Lawrence College.

**C.H.,** CHARLES HAGEN, A.B., M.F.A.
Writer and Critic. Editor, *Aperture* Magazine.

**C.H.A.,** CALVIN H. ALLEN, JR., A.B., M.A., PH.D.
Consultant and Author.

**C.S.,** C. F. SCHUETZ, PH.D.
Assistant Professor of Political Science, Carleton University, Ottawa, Canada.

**C.S.J.W.,** CHARLES S. J. WHITE, B.A., M.A., PH.D.
Professor and Chairman, Department of Philosophy and Religion, American University.

**C.W.,** CHRIS WOOD
National Editor, *Maclean's* Magazine.

**D.A.,** DAVID ARTER, B.A., M.A., PH.D.
Professor of European Integration, Leeds Business School, Leeds, England. Author, *Politics and Policymaking in Finland.*

**D.D.B.,** DONALD D. BOHNING, B.A.
Latin American Editor, Miami *Herald.*

**D.F.A.,** DONALD F. ANTHROP, PH.D.
Professor of Environmental Studies, San Jose State University, Calif. Author, *Noise Pollution.*

**D.G.,** DAVID GIVENS
Director of Information, American Anthropological Association.

**D.J.P.,** DONALD J. PUCHALA, B.A., M.A., PH.D.
Charles L. Jacobson Professor of Public Affairs and Director, Institute of International Studies, University of South Carolina.

**D.K.D.,** DONNA K. DOHERTY, B.A.
Editor, *Tennis* Magazine.

**D.L.,** DANIEL LEWIS, M.A., PH.D.
Lecturer, California Polytechnic State University.

**D.M.P.,** DAVID M. PHILIPS, A.B.
Sports Writer, Providence *Journal.*

**D.N.,** DAVID NEWELL, B.A., M.A., PH.D.
Vice President, World Affairs Council of Philadelphia.

**D.N.C.,** DONALD N. CLARK, B.A., M.A., A.M., PH.D.
Professor of History, Trinity University, Texas. Editor, *Korea Briefing 1991.*

**D.P.W.,** DAVID P. WERLICH, B.A., M.A., PH.D.
Professor of History, Southern Illinois University. Author, *Peru: A Short History.*

**D.R.F.,** DAVID R. FRANCIS, B.A.
Editor, Economy Page, and Economic Columnist, *Christian Science Monitor.*

**D.V.,** DAVID VERSICAL, B.A., M.S.J.
National Editor, *Automotive News.*

**D.W.,** DENISE WILLIAMS, B.A., M.A.
Ph.D. Candidate in Sociology, University of California, Santa Barbara. Director, Isla Vista Mediation Program.

**E.C.R.,** EDWARD C. ROCHETTE
Retired Executive Director, American Numismatic Association. Numismatic Writer, Los Angeles *Times* Syndicate.

**E.G.,** EDUARDO GAMARRA, PH.D.
Associate Professor of Political Science, Florida International University. Author, *Revolution and Reaction: Bolivia 1964-1985.*

**E.J.F.,** ERIK J. FRIIS, B.S., M.A.
Editor and Publisher, *The Scandinavian-American Bulletin.* General Editor, *The Library of Nordic Literature.*

**E.J.P.,** ELIZABETH J. PENNISI, B.S., M.S.
Editor, Chemistry/Materials Science, *Science News.*

**E.P.,** ED PITONIAK, B.A.
Associate Publisher, *Ski* Magazine.

**E.S.,** EUGENE S. SCHWEIG III, B.S., M.S., PH.D.
Associate Research Professor, Center for Earthquake Research and Information, Memphis State University.

**E.S.E.,** ERIC S. EINHORN, B.A., M.A., PH.D.
Professor of Political Science, University of Massachusetts, Amherst. Coauthor, *Politics and Policy in Social Democratic Scandinavia.*

**E.S.K.,** ELAINE S. KNAPP, B.A.
Editor, *Council of State Governments.*

**F.B.C.,** FREDERICK B. CHARY, A.B., M.A., PH.D.
Professor of History, Indiana University Northwest.

**F.C.E.,** FREDERICK C. ENGLEMANN, A.B., A.M., M.A., PH.D.
Professor Emeritus of Political Science, University of Alberta.

**F.E.H.,** FREDERICK E. HOXIE, B.A., PH.D.
Director, D'Arcy McNickle Center of the History of the American Indian. Author, *The Crow Indians.*

**F.L.,** FRANK LITSKY, B.S.
Sports Writer, New York *Times.* Author, *Superstars; The Winter Olympics; The New York Times Official Sports Record Book.*

**G.B.H.,** GARY B. HANSEN, B.S., M.S., PH.D.
Professor of Economics, Utah State University. Director, Utah Center for Productivity and Quality of Working Life.

**G.D.S.,** GUSTAV D. SPOHN, B.A., M.A.
Associate Editor, Religious News Service.

**G.H.,** GEOFFREY HAINSWORTH, B.S., PH.D.
Professor of Economics, University of British Columbia.

**G.L.,** GEORGE LAMSON, B.A., M.A., PH.D.
Professor of Economics, Carleton College, Northfield, Minn.

**G.M.H.,** GEOFFREY M. HORN, A.B., M.A.
Free-lance Writer and Editor.

**G.S.,** GADDIS SMITH, B.A., M.A., PH.D.
Larned Professor of History, Yale University. Author, *Morality, Reason, and Power: American Diplomacy in the Carter Years.*

**H.C.H.,** HAROLD C. HINTON, PH.D.
Professor of Political Science and International Affairs, George Washington University. Editor, *The People's Republic of China, 1949-1979: A Documentary Survey.*

**H.H.,** HERBERT HOWE, B.S., M.A., PH.D.
Acting Chairman, African Studies Program, School of Foreign Service, and Research Professor of African Politics, Georgetown University.

**I.C.B.,** IRIRANGI COATES BLOOMFIELD, A.B., M.A., PH.D.
Lecturer and Writer. Former Member, New Zealand United Nations Delegation.

**I.K.,** INDULIS KEPARS, B.A.
Chief Librarian, Information Services, National Library of Australia.

**I.M.,** IVAN MAISEL, B.A.
Sports Writer, Dallas *Morning News.*

**J.A.K.,** JOSEPH A. KECHICHIAN, PH.D.
Consultant, the Rand Corporation, Santa Monica, Calif.

**J.A.P.,** JOHN ANTHONY PETROPULOS, PH.D.
Professor of History, Amherst College. Author, *Politics and Statecraft in the Kingdom of Greece.*

**J.B.,** JOHN BERSETH, B.A.
Free-lance Writer and Editor.

**J.C.,** JOE CARROLL, M.A.
Parliamentary Correspondent, *Irish TImes.* Author, *Ireland in the War Years 1939-45.*

**J.C.W.,** JAMES C. WEBSTER
Vice President-Communications, Sparks Companies, Inc.

**J.D.,** JOHN DAMIS, PH.D.
Professor of Political Science, Portland State University. Author, *Conflict in Northwest Africa: The Western Sahara Dispute.*

**J.D.M.,** JOHN D. MARTZ, A.B., A.M., PH.D.
Distinguished Professor of Political Science and Acting Head, Department of Political Science, Pennsylvania State University.

**J.F.,** JOHN FORAN, JR., A.B., M.A.
Assistant Professor, Department of Sociology, University of California, Santa Barbara.

**J.Fa.,** JAMES FANNING
Landscape Architect. Former Author, "Gardener's Notes," *House and Garden* Magazine.

**J.F.A.,** JOANN FAGOT AVIEL, M.A., M.A.L.D., PH.D.
Professor of International Relations, San Francisco State University. Author, *Resource Shortages and World Politics.*

**J.F.C.,** JOHN FRANKLIN COPPER, B.A., M.A., PH.D.
Stanley J. Buckman Professor of International Studies, Rhodes College, Memphis, Tenn.

**J.G.,** JOSEPH GUSTAITIS, PH.D.
Staff editor.

**J.G.D.,** JOHN G. DEEDY, A.B., M.A.
Former Managing Editor, *Commonweal* Magazine. Author, *Retrospect: The Origins of Catholic Beliefs and Practices.*

**J.G.K.,** JIDLAPH G. KAMOCHE, B.A., M.A., PH.D.
Associate Professor of History, University of Oklahoma.

**J.H.B.,** JAMES H. BUDD, B.A., M.S.
Free-lance Writer Based in Mexico. Correspondent, Murdoch Magazines and Gemini News Service.

**J.J.Z.,** JOSEPH J. ZASLOFF, A.B., M.A., PH.D.
Professor of Political Science, University of Pittsburgh. Specialist in Southeast Asian Affairs.

**J.L.D.,** JOAN L. DOWNS A.B.
Free-lance Writer and Editor.

**J.M.,** JOHN MUTTER, B.A.
Bookselling Editor, *Publishers Weekly.*

**J.M.L.,** JEFFREY M. LADERMAN, B.A., M.S.
Markets and Investments Editor, *Business Week.*

**J.R.,** JOHN RENNIE, B.S.
Science Writer. Member, Board of Editors, *Scientific American.*

**J.Ru.,** JIM RUBIN, B.A.
Supreme Court Correspondent, Associated Press.

**J.R.A.,** JAMES R. ASKER, B.A.
Space Technology Editor, *Aviation Week & Space Technology.*

**J.S.,** JOSEF SILVERSTEIN, B.A., PH.D.
Professor of Political Science, Rutgers University. Author, *Burmese Politics: The Dilemma of National Unity.*

**J.Su.,** JUDY SUND, B.A., M.A., PH.D.
Assistant Professor of Art History, Queens College, N.Y.

**J.T.S.,** JAMES T. SHERWIN, A.B., L.L.B.
Former New York State, Intercollegiate, and United States Speed Chess Champion and International Master.

**K.J.B.,** KIRK J. BEATTIE, A.B., M.A.
Assistant Professor of Political Science, Simmons College, Boston.

**K.L.,** KEN LAWRENCE
Columnist, *Linn's Stamp News.* Author, *Linn's Plate Number Coil Handbook.*

**K.L.S.,** KAREN L. SCRIVO, B.A., M.A.
Free-lance Writer. Former Capitol Hill Reporter, United Press International.

**K.M.,** KENT MULLINER, B.S., M.A.
Assistant to the Director, Ohio University Libraries.

**K.S.,** KAARE STROM, PH.D.
Associate Professor, University of Minnesota. Author, *Minority Government and Majority Rule*.

**K.T.,** KENNETH TERRY, B.A., M.A.
Senior News Editor, *Billboard*.

**K.W.G.,** KENNETH W. GRUNDY, A.B., M.A., PH.D.
Professor of Political Science, Case Western Reserve University, Cleveland, Ohio.

**L.C.H.,** LINDA C. HIGGINS, B.A.
Free-lance Health and Medical Writer. Columnist for *Hippocrates* Magazine.

**L.C.-K.,** LINDA CHION-KENNEY, B.A.
Free-lance Journalist and Consultant. Former Staff Writer, *Education Week*.

**L.E.,** LARRY EDSALL, B.S.
Deputy Managing Editor, News/Motorsports, *AutoWeek* Magazine.

**L.E.R.,** LEO E. ROSE, PH.D.
Retired Professor of Political Science, University of California at Berkeley. Editor, *Asian Survey*.

**L.G.,** LOIS GOTTESMAN, A.B., M.A.
Free-lance Writer. Former Research Analyst, American Jewish Committee.

**L.O.,** LORI OLIWENSTEIN, B.S.,M.A.
Researcher/Reporter, *Discover* Magazine.

**L.S.G.,** LOVETT S. GRAY, A.B.
Free-lance Writer and Consultant. Former Editor, National Council on Crime and Delinquency.

**L.T.L.,** LARS T. LIH, PH.D.
Associate Professor of Political Science, Wellesley College.

**M.B.,** MARY BIGGS, B.A., M.A., M.L.S., PH.D.
Director of Libraries, Mercy College, Westchester County and Bronx, N.Y.

**M.Br.,** MARTIN BROCHSTEIN, B.S.
Senior Editor, *Television Digest*. Former Editor, *Consumer Electronics Monthly*.

**M.C.E.,** MARSHALL C. EAKIN, B.A., M.A., PH.D.
Professor of History, Vanderbilt University.

**M.C.F.,** MAURA C. FLANNERY, B.S., M.S., PH.D.
Professor of Biology, St. Vincent's College, St. John's University, Jamaica, N.Y.

**M.C.W.,** MICHAEL C. WHITE, B.A.
Political Editor, *The Guardian* (London).

**M.D.,** MICHAEL DIRDA, A.B., M.A., PH.D.
Staff Writer and Editor, *The Washington Post Book World*.

**M.G.,** MICHAEL GAWENDA, B.E.
Journalist. Editor, *Time Australia* Magazine.

**M.Gr.,** MILTON GREENBERG, A.B., M.A., PH.D.
Provost, American University, Washington, D.C. Coauthor, *The American Political Dictionary*.

**M.G.G.,** M. GRANT GROSS, A.B., M.S., PH.D.
Director, Division of Ocean Sciences, National Science Foundation. Author, *Oceanography: A View of the Earth*.

**M.J.C.,** MARTIN J. COLLO, PH.D.
Assistant Professor of Government and Politics, Widener University. Associate Editor, *Journal of Third World Studies*.

**M.M.,** MATT MARSON, B.A.
Managing Editor, *Football News* and *Basketball Weekly*.

**M.M.D.,** MIRIAM M. DAVIDSON, B.A.
Free-lance Writer and Editor.

**M.P.,** MIKE PRICE
Contributor, *The Independent* and Associated Press (London).

**M.R.,** MARK ROSE, B.A., M.A.
Managing Editor, *Archaeology* Magazine. Doctoral Candidate in Classical Archaeology, Indiana University.

**M.S.,** MEIR SERFATY, B.A., M.A., PH.D.
Associate Professor of Political Science, Brandon University, Manitoba, Canada.

**M.W.,** MARGARET WILLY, F.R.S.L.
Lecturer, Centre for Continuing Education, University of Sussex (England). Poetry Collected in *The Invisible Sun; Every Star a Tongue*.

**N.C.P.,** NICHOLAS C. PANO, A.B., M.A.
Professor of History and Associate Dean, College of Arts and Sciences, Western Illinois University. Editor, *Journal of Developing Areas*.

**N.K.,** NELSON KASFIR, J.D., PH.D.
Professor of Government, Dartmouth College.

**N.K.B.,** NEIL K. BESNER, B.A., M.A., PH.D.
Associate Professor of English, University of Winnipeg. Author, *The Light of Imagination: Mavis Gallant's Fiction*.

**N.N.,** NANCY PEABODY NEWELL, A.B.
Research Associate, University of Nebraska. Coauthor, *The Struggle for Afghanistan*.

**N.W.H.,** NOEL W. HOLSTON, B.S., M.B.A.
Television Critic, Minneapolis-St. Paul *Star Tribune*. Coauthor, *Parents' Choice Guide to Children's Videos*.

**O.U.,** OTTO ULC, M.A., PH.D., J.D.
Professor of Political Science, State University of New York, Binghamton.

**P.G.,** PAUL GARDNER
Free-lance Writer. Author, *The Simplest Game; Nice Guys Finish Last*. Commentator, NBC Soccer Telecasts.

**P.G.K.,** PAUL G. KNIGHT, B.S., M.S.
Instructor in Meteorology, Pennsylvania State University. Senior Forecaster, New York *Times*.

**P.H.,** PIA HINCKLE, B.A.
Reporter, *Newsweek* Rome Bureau.

**P.J.M.,** PAUL J. MAGNARELLA, A.M., PH.D.
Professor of Anthropology, University of Florida. Author, *Tradition and Change in a Turkish Town; The Peasant Venture*.

**P.J.S.,** PETER SCHWAB, B.A., M.A., PH.D.
Professor of Political Science, State University of New York at Purchase. Author, *Ethiopia: Politics, Economics, and Society*.

**P.M.L.,** PETER LEWIS, B.A., M.A.
Assistant Professor, James Madison College, Michigan State University.

**P.McL.,** PATRICIA McLAUGHLIN, B.A.
Style Columnist, Philadelphia *Inquirer* Magazine.

**P.P.,** PETER PASTOR, B.A., M.A., PH.D.
Professor of History, Montclair State College, N.J. Editor, *Revolutions and Interventions in Hungary and Its Neighbor States, 1918-1919*.

**P.S.,** PETER SLATIN, B.A., M.A.
Associate Editor, *Architectural Record*.

**P.W.,** PETER WINN, A.B., PH.D.
Associate Professor of History, Tufts University. Senior Research Fellow, Institute on Latin American and Iberian Studies, Columbia University.

**R.A.M.,** ROBERT A. MORTIMER, A.B., M.A., PH.D.
Professor of Political Science, Haverford College. Author, *The Third World Coalition in International Politics.* Coauthor, *Politics and Society in Contemporary Africa.*

**R.A.R.,** ROBIN A. REMINGTON, A.B., M.A., PH.D.
Professor of Political Science, University of Missouri at Columbia.

**R.A.S.,** RONALD A. SCHORN, B.S., M.S., PH.D.
Planetary Astronomer and Technical Writer. Former Chief, Ground-Based Planetary Astronomy, NASA.

**R.C.,** RAY CONLOGUE, B.A., M.A.
Theater Critic, Toronto *Globe and Mail.*

**R.C.O.,** ROBERT C. OBERST, B.A., M.A., PH.D.
Associate Professor of Political Science, Nebraska Wesleyan University. Coauthor, *Government and Politics in South Asia.*

**R.E.B.,** ROGER E. BILSTEIN, B.A., M.A., PH.D.
Professor of History, University of Houston at Clear Lake. Author, *Orders of Magnitude: A History of the NACA and NASA.*

**R.E.K.,** ROGER E. KANET, PH.B., A.B., M.A., A.M., PH.D.
Professor of Political Science, University of Illinois at Urbana-Champaign. Co-Editor, *The Cold War as Cooperation.*

**R.J.W.,** RICHARD J. WILLEY, A.B., M.A., PH.D.
Professor of Political Science, Vassar College. Author, *Democracy in the West German Trade Unions.*

**R.O.F.,** ROBERT O. FREEDMAN, PH.D.
Dean and Professor of Political Science, School of Graduate Studies, Baltimore Hebrew College. Author, *Soviet Policy Toward Israel Under Gorbachev; Moscow and the Middle East.*

**R.S.,** ROBERT SAHR, B.A., M.DIV., PH.D.
Associate Professor of Political Science, Oregon State University. Author, *The Politics of Energy Policy Change in Sweden.*

**S.C.,** SEDGWICK CLARK, B.A.
Recordings Editor, *Musical America.* Former Editor, *Keynote* Magazine.

**S.E.,** SUSAN ELLIOTT, B.A.
Music Writer and Critic. Former Managing Editor, *High Fidelity* Magazine.

**S.L.,** STEPHEN LEVINE, B.A., M.A., PH.D.
Senior Lecturer, Department of Politics, Victoria University of Wellington (New Zealand).

**S.M.,** SIEGFRIED MANDEL, A.B., M.A., PH.D.
Professor Emeritus of English and Comparative Literature, University of Colorado at Boulder.

**S.M.G.,** SAM M. GOLDAPER
Sports Reporter, New York *Times.* New York Area Chairman, Professional Basketball Writers' Association.

**S.S.,** STEVENSON SWANSON, B.S.J., M.S.
Environment Writer, Chicago *Tribune.*

**T.D.,** THOMAS DeFRANK, B.A., M.A.
Deputy Bureau Chief and White House Correspondent, *Newsweek.*

**T.E.T.,** THOMAS E. TURNER, PH.D.
Professor of Political Science and Director of International Studies Program, Wheeling Jesuit College, W.Va.

**T.G.,** TROND GILBERG, M.A., PH.D.
Professor of Political Science and Director of the Slavic Center, Pennsylvania State University. Author, *Nationalism and Communism in Romania.*

**T.K.,** TOM KOPPEL, B.SC.
Free-lance Print and Broadcast Journalist in Tokyo.

**T.P.A.,** THOMAS P. ANDERSON, B.A., A.M., PH.D.
Chair, Department of History, Eastern Connecticut State University. Author, *Politics in Central America.*

**W.A.H.,** WILLIAM A. HENRY III, B.A.
Theater Critic and Senior Writer, *Time* Magazine. Pulitzer Prize Winner in Journalism, 1980.

**W.C.C.,** WILLIAM C. CROMWELL, B.A., M.A., PH.D.
Professor of International Relations, American University.

**W.D.,** WILLIAM DROZDIAK, B.S.
Paris Bureau Chief, Washington *Post.*

**W.F.R.,** WILLIAM F. ROYCE, B.S., PH.D.
Professor Emeritus, School of Fisheries, University of Washington.

**W.H.,** WALTER HAUSER, B.A., M.A., PH.D.
Associate Professor of History, University of Virginia. Author, *The Politics of Peasant Activism in 20th-Century India.*

**W.K.W.,** WILLIAM K. WEST, A.B., M.A., PH.D.
Free-lance Writer. Former Director of Publications, The Wharton School, University of Pennsylvania.

**W.L.,** WILLIAM LEGGETT, A.B.
Former Senior Writer, *Sports Illustrated.*

**W.M.,** WILLIAM MINTER, PH.D.
Scholar-in-Residence, American University. Author, *King Solomon's Mines Revisited: Western Interests and the Burdened History of Southern Africa.*

**W.W.,** WILLIAM WOLF, A.B.
Film Critic. Lecturer, New York University and St. John's University. Author, *Landmark Films: The Cinema and Our Century.*

# PICTURE CREDITS

468

# INDEX TO THE
# 1992 YEARBOOK
## EVENTS OF 1991

## INTRODUCTION

This Index is an alphabetical listing of persons, organizations, and events that are discussed in the 1992 Yearbook. Entries in **boldface** letters indicate subjects on which the Yearbook has an individual article. Entries in lightface type indicate individual references or sections within articles. In any entry, the letters a and b refer, respectively, to the left and right column of the page cited. If no letter follows a page number, the reference is to text that is printed in a different format. Usually only the first significant mention of a subject in a given article has been included in the Index.

In a main entry such as **Architecture,** 73a, the first number refers to the page on which the article begins. The succeeding page numbers refer to other text discussions in the volume. The first number in lightface entries, when these are not in numerical order, will similarly provide the most extensive information on the subject. Subtitles following major entries refer to further references on the main subject, as in **Australia,** 83a; agriculture, 65a. The discussion of foreign relations of the United States in the United States of America article may be augmented by reference to separate articles on the countries and international organizations concerned.

When an entry is designated by the abbreviation **illus.,** the reference is to a caption and picture on the page mentioned. When a text mention and an illustration of the same subject fall within the same article, usually only the text location is included in the Index.

### LIST OF ABBREVIATIONS USED IN THE INDEX

NATO  North Atlantic Treaty Organization
OPEC  Organization of Petroleum Exporting Countries
PLO  Palestine Liberation Organization
U.N.  United Nations
U.S.  United States
U.S.S.R.  Union of Soviet Socialist Republics

472

473

North Dakota, 328b, 383b, 430b, 458
Northern Ireland, 186a, 212a
Northern Mariana Islands, 460
Northwest Territories, 117a, 462
Norville, Deborah, 303a
**Norway,** 279a, 172b, 199b, 207b, 448
Nova Scotia, 144b, 396a, 462
Novello, Antonia, 59a
nuclear energy, 164b, 106a, 112b
nuclear weapons, 256a; Argentina, 76a; China, 124b; environment, 168b; France, 177b; Iran, 209a; Iraq, 211b, 425a; Japan, 220a; Korea, 223b; Pakistan, 297a; Persian Gulf War, 12; South Africa, 349b; U.N., 405b, 406b; U.S., 410b, 420a, 426b; U.S.S.R., 404a
Nunavut Territory, 117a
Nureyev, Rudolf, 142a
nutrition. *See* Diet and Nutrition


# O

**Obituaries,** 280a
obscenity and pornography, 128b, 267a, 322b
oceanography, 146b
O'Faolain, Sean, 291a
Ohio, 134b, 458
oil fires and spills, 165a, 56b, 144a, 146b, 162b, 225a, 346b, 425a
oil. *See* Petroleum
Oklahoma, 233a, 384a, 458
Okri, Ben, 247a
Olav V, King, 291b, 279a
Olbers paradox, 82b
Olympic Games, 129a, 351a
O'Malley, Susan, 362b, 431b
Oman, 70b, 12, 387b, 448
O'Neal, Tatum, 305b
Ontario, 117a, 462
opera, 270b, 273a
Operation Desert Shield and Desert Storm. *See* Persian Gulf War
Operation Rescue, 336b, 383a
Oregon, 74b, 145b, 383b, 458
Organization of African Unity, 61a, 279a
Organization of American States, 206a, 190a, 427a
Organization of Petroleum Exporting Countries (OPEC), 162b
Orion Pictures, 265a
Ortega, Daniel, 277b
Orthodox churches, 337a
O'Toole, Margot, 237
Ouko, Robert, 221b
Ozal, Turgut, 398b
ozone layer, 167a, 353b


# P

**Pacific Islands,** 295a
Pacific Ocean, 56a
Page, Ruth, 291b
**Pakistan,** 296a, 208a, 448; accidents, 55a; Afghanistan, 59b; Bangladesh, 95a; banking, 98a; China, 125a; climatology, 144a
Palau, 295b, 460

Palestine Liberation Organization (PLO), 230b, 389a
Palestinians, Belgium, 101b; Greece, 188b; Israel, 213a; Italy, 216b; Kuwait, 226a; Middle East peace, 67b, 206a, 213a, 221b; Norway, 279b; U.N., 406b
**Panama,** 297a, 137a, 448
Pan American Games, 364a
Pan American World Airways, 88a, 235a, 425b
Pankin, Boris, 404b
Panufnik, Andrzej, 272a
Papandreou, Andreas, 188a
Papp, Joseph, 292a, 395a
Papua New Guinea, 295a, 448
**Paraguay,** 298a, 76a, 106a, 448
Paris Club, 157a, 318b, 326b
Parks, Rosa, **illus.,** 102
Pendleton, Terry, 357b
Pennsylvania, 56a, 144b, 155b, 164b, 381b, 430a, 458
**People in the News,** 299a
Pepsi-Cola, 58b
Pérez, Carlos Andrés, 428a
Pérez de Cuéllar, Javier, 60b, 138b, 162a, 405a, 408a
Perry, Gaylord, 358b
**Persian Gulf War,** 8, 209a, 225a; Afghanistan, 60a; Arabian Peninsula, 70b; archaeology, 71b; Arnett, Peter, 306a; Australia, 84b; automobiles, 86a; aviation, 88a; Baker, James A. III, 306b; Belgium, 101b; blacks, 103a; Brazil, 105a; broadcasting, 109a; Canada, 114a; climatology, 143b; economy, 149a; energy, 162b; environment, 165a; European Community, 173a; France, 177b; Great Britain, 184a; India, 202b; Indonesia, 204b; Iran, 208b; Israel, 212b; Italy, 214b; Japan, 218b; Jordan, 220a; Kenya, 222a; Korea, 223b; Libya, 234b; Luxembourg, 252b; Morocco, 259a; Netherlands, 275a; New Zealand, 276b; Pacific Islands, 295a; Pakistan, 297a; photography, 323a; Poland, 327a; Portugal, 330a; Powell, Colin, 312a; religion, 338a, 343b; Saudi Arabia, 346a; Schwarzkopf, H. Norman, 314a; Spain, 354b; Sudan, 385a; Syria, 387a; travel, 395a; Turkey, 397b; U.N., 405b; U.S., 409a, 420a, 424a
**Peru,** 318a, 56a, 145b, 448
Pesci, Joe, 265a
petroleum, 162b; Algeria, 67b; Arabian Peninsula, 71a; archaeology, 72b; Brazil, 105a; Egypt, 156b; environment, 166b; European Community, 173a; Indonesia, 205a; Iraq, 211a; Kuwait, 226a; Libya, 234b; Mexico, 254a; Saudi Arabia, 347a; Turkey, 398a; U.N., 406a; Venezuela, 428a. *See also* Oil Fires and Spills
**Pets,** 134a, 240a, 319b
Pharaon, Gaith, 98b
**Philippines,** 321a, 208a, 302a, 448; accidents, 57a; climatology, 144b; Indonesia, 204b; military, 258a; U.S., 427a

Philip, Prince, 302b
Phillips, Julia, 330b
**Photography,** 322b, 198a
**Physics,** 324a, 92a
pigs, 238a
Pinochet, Augusto, 121b
Pittsburgh Penguins, 371a
plants, 238b
poetry, 243b, 245b, 246b
Poindexter, John M., 136a, 304b
Poitier, Sidney, 107a
**Poland,** 325b, 173a, 448; France, 178a; Germany, 182b; Hungary, 199a; motion pictures, 264a; religion, 340a, 342a
police brutality; Great Britain, 185b; Kuwait, 226a; U.S., 103a, 106b, 134b
political parties, U.S., 413b
political prisoners, Africa, 61b; China, 125b; Kuwait, 226a; Libya, 235a; Myanmar, 90b. *See also* Hostages
Pomus, Jerome "Doc," 269a, 292a
Popova, Liubov, 79b
popular music, 266a
**Population,** 327a; blacks, 103b; economy, 150a; Indians, American, 203b
pornography. *See* Obscenity and Pornography
Porter, Sylvia F., 292a
**Portugal,** 329b, 172a, 340a, 354b, 373b, 448
postal service, U.S., 229a, 379b
poverty, 150a
Powell, Colin L., 312a, 13, 24, 302a
Powell, Mike, 377a
Powers, Richard, 242a
POWs, 428b
pregnancy, 191b, 196a, 423a. *See also* Abortion; Contraceptives
Presbyterian Church, 336a
Presidency, U.S. *See* Bush, George
presidential campaign, U.S., 414a, 103b, 158a
press coverage of Gulf War, 23
Preston, Kelly, 305a
Prince Edward Island, 117b, 462; **illus.,** 218
prizes. *See* Awards and Prizes
Protestant churches, 336a, 337a
protests. *See* Civil Unrest and Violence
psychology. *See* Behavioral Sciences
puberty, 99a
Public Broadcasting Service (PBS), 108a
**Publishing,** 330b, 300b, 241a; advertising, 58a; awards, 92b; Persian Gulf War coverage, 23; photography, 323a, Supreme Court, 423b
**Puerto Rico,** 335a, 460
Pulitzer Prizes, 92a, 392a
Punjab, 203a, 344a


# Q

Qaddafi, Muammar al-, 234b
Qatar, 70b, 346a, 387b, 448
Quaid, Dennis, 305a
Quayle, Dan, 313a, 299b, 352b, 413b
Québec, 114b, 245b, 263b, 462

479